BED AND BREAKFAST
STOPS

Hotels, Guest Houses
Private Homes, for food and accommodation
throughout Britain. Includes Campus Holidays.

FHG

Other FHG Publications 1998

Recommended Short Break Holidays
Recommended Country Hotels of Britain
Recommended Wayside & Country Inns of Britain
Pets Welcome!
Bed and Breakfast in Britain
The Golf Guide: Where to Play/Where to Stay
Farm Holiday Guide England, Wales, Ireland & Channel Islands
Farm Holiday Guide Scotland
Self-Catering Holidays in Britain
Britain's Best Holidays
Guide to Caravan and Camping Holidays
Children Welcome! Family Holiday & Attractions Guide
Scottish Welcome

ISBN 1 85055 253 3 © FHG Publications Ltd. 1998
Cover picture: supplied by Images Colour Library.
Design by Cyan Creative Consultants, Glasgow.

Typeset by RD Composition Ltd., Glasgow.
Printed and bound by Benhams Ltd, Colchester.

Distribution – **Book Trade**: WLM, Downing Road, West Meadows Industrial Estate, Derby DE21 6HA.
(Tel: 01332 343332. Fax: 01332 340464; e-mail: John@wimsales.demon.co.uk).
News Trade: USM Distribution Ltd, 86 Newman Street, London W1P 3LD
(Tel: 0171-396 8000. Fax: 0171-396 8002).
E-mail:usm.co.uk

Published by FHG Publications Ltd.,
Abbey Mill Business Centre, Seedhill, Paisley PA1 1TJ (0141-887 0428. Fax: 0141-889 7204).
e-mail: 106111.3065@compuserve.com
———
US ISBN 1-55650-802-6
Distributed in the United States by
Hunter Publishing Inc., 130 Campus Drive,
Edison, N.J., 08818, USA

FOREWORD

BED AND BREAKFAST STOPS 1998

The popularity of Bed and Breakfast holidays has, in the past, been attributed mainly to value for money, accommodation of good quality and to friendly and personal service. For many years now, these are the qualities which the *FHG Bed and Breakfast Stops* has offered and encouraged. Our new edition for 1998 is no exception. Here is a larger range of choice than ever, with prices starting around £15 or £16 per person per night, and occasionally even lower. Our supplements showing details of accommodation especially for Non-Smokers, for the Disabled and for those on Special Diets are also growing and, of course, each listing also has a full entry in the appropriate county section.

Most of our entries are not, of course, hotels and although collectively they have excellent amenities, they cannot offer the range of service of larger, more commercial establishments. An exclusive visitors' lounge, evening meals, a choice of menu, a bar, a bedside telephone, 24 hour access . . . if you need this kind of facility, please be sure to enquire in advance.

It's easy to use *Bed and Breakfast Stops* and you may find the following suggestions helpful.

Enquiries and Bookings: The Contents page will lead you through the book in detail. Sections and counties are shown clearly at the top of each page. Make sure that you are using the section you want. Once you have seen what is suitable, contact the advertiser or advertisers by letter or telephone for further information or to make a booking. Give full details of dates, numbers etc. and any special requirements. If you write, enclose a stamped, addressed envelope for the reply. If booking by telephone, make sure that everything is confirmed in writing.

Complaints: FHG Publications Ltd. do not inspect or recommend accommodation. We accept our entries in good faith and we ask our advertisers to agree to adhere to our aims of clean and comfortable accommodation, wholesome and well-cooked food and courtesy and consideration towards guests. They are also subject to the Trades Description Act. Although we cannot accept responsibility for any of the services or accommodation advertised here, we do follow up complaints from our readers. Regretfully we cannot act as intermediaries but we invite you to let us know if you have problems or complaints. Please note, you should always try to speak to your host at the time about any complaints.

Holiday Insurance: Don't forget that as a guest or host you can insure against cancellation or other risks. There are many reputable brokers and companies who issue such policies. If you have trouble finding one let us know.

The FHG Diploma: If you have a particularly good holiday, let us know. You may help your host to win one of our annual FHG Diplomas for outstanding service and/or accommodation. The names of our 1997 Diploma winners are listed in this book and we will be happy to receive your recommendations for 1998.

It's not always necessary to book Bed and Breakfast in advance but in popular areas at holiday times it's obviously advisable, as it is in more remote parts. If you do book in advance and you change your plans, please tell your hosts that you've had to cancel. You may then be helping someone else who is looking for accommodation at short notice and your thoughtfulness will be appreciated in any case.

Please mention *BED AND BREAKFAST STOPS* when you are making enquiries or bookings and don't forget to use our Readers' Offer Voucher/Coupons if you're near any of the attractions which are kindly participating.

Anne Cuthbertson
Editor

CONTENTS

CONTENTS

SCOTLAND

WALES

REPUBLIC OF IRELAND

Special Welcome Supplements

Great Britain

Counties, unitary authorities and council areas

ORKNEY ISLANDS

SHETLAND ISLANDS

WESTERN ISLES

MORAY

HIGHLAND

CITY OF ABERDEEN

ABERDEENSHIRE

ANGUS

PERTH AND KINROSS

FIFE

ARGYLL AND BUTE

STIRLING

EAST LOTHIAN

NORTH AYRSHIRE

SOUTH LANARKSHIRE

SCOTTISH BORDERS

EAST AYRSHIRE

SOUTH AYRSHIRE

DUMFRIES AND GALLOWAY

NORTHUMBERLAND

TYNE & WEAR

ISLE OF MAN

CUMBRIA

DURHAM

NORTH YORKSHIRE

LANCASHIRE

YORK

EAST RIDING OF YORKSHIRE

WEST YORKSHIRE

ANGLESEY

NORTH WALES

MERSEYSIDE

GREATER MANCHESTER

SOUTH YORKSHIRE

ANGLESEY & GWYNEDD

CHESHIRE

DERBYSHIRE

NOTTS.

LINCOLNSHIRE

GWYNEDD

STAFFS.

CARDIGANSHIRE

POWYS

SHROPSHIRE

LEICESTER-SHIRE

NORFOLK

WEST MIDLANDS

HEREFORD AND WORCESTER

WARKS.

NORTHANTS.

CAMBRIDGE-SHIRE

SUFFOLK

PEMBROKESHIRE

CARMARTHEN-SHIRE

BEDS.

GLOUCESTER-SHIRE

OXFORD-SHIRE

BUCKS.

HERTS.

ESSEX

SOUTH WALES

BERKSHIRE

GREATER LONDON

CHANNEL ISLANDS

WILTSHIRE

SOMERSET

HAMPSHIRE

SURREY

KENT

WEST SUSSEX

EAST SUSSEX

DEVON

DORSET

ISLE OF WIGHT

CORNWALL

SCILLY ISLES

1. CITY OF DUNDEE
2. CLACKMANNANSHIRE
3. FALKIRK
4. EAST DUNBARTONSHIRE
5. WEST DUNBARTONSHIRE
6. INVERCLYDE
7. RENFREWSHIRE
8. CITY OF GLASGOW
9. NORTH LANARKSHIRE
10. WEST LOTHIAN
11. CITY OF EDINBURGH
12. MIDLOTHIAN
13. EAST RENFREWSHIRE
14. STOCKTON-ON-TEES
15. MIDDLESBROUGH
16. HARTLEPOOL
17. REDCAR & CLEVELAND
18. NORTH LINCOLNSHIRE
19. KINGSTON UPON HULL
20. NORTH EAST LINCOLNSHIRE

21. ABERCONWY & COLWYN
22. DENBIGHSHIRE
23. FLINTSHIRE
24. WREXHAM
25. SWANSEA
26. NEATH & PORT TALBOT
27. RHONDDA CYNON TAFF
28. MERTHYR TYDFIL
29. BLAENAU GWENT
30. TORFAEN
31. MONMOUTHSHIRE
32. BRIDGEND
33. VALE OF GLAMORGAN
34. CARDIFF
35. CAERPHILLY
36. NEWPORT
37. NORTH WEST SOMERSET
38. BRISTOL
39. SOUTH GLOUCESTERSHIRE
40. BATH & NORTH EAST SOMERSET
41. RUTLAND

Great Britain
Towns and Main Roads

Scale 1:5 750 000

| 0 | 50 | 100 | 150 km |

| 0 | 50 | 100 miles |

ORKNEY ISLANDS

Kirkwall

SHETLAND ISLANDS

Lerwick

OUTER HEBRIDES

Durness
Thurso
Wick

Stornoway

Ullapool

Tain
Dingwall
Nairn
Inverness
Elgin
Banff
Fraserburgh
Peterhead
Huntly
Grantown-on-Spey

Kyle of Lochalsh

Mallaig

Kingussie
Braemar
Ballater
ABERDEEN
Stonehaven

Spean Bridge
Fort William
Pitlochry
Montrose

Oban
Crianlarich
Blairgowrie
Forfar
Arbroath
Perth
Dundee
Crieff
St Andrews
Cupar
Stirling
Kirkcaldy
Lochgilphead
Falkirk
EDINBURGH
Greenock
GLASGOW
Motherwell
Berwick-upon-Tweed
Peebles
Kilmarnock
Galashiels
Ayr
Hawick
Jedburgh
Alnwick
Girvan
Moffat

Campbeltown

Dumfries

Stranraer
Castle Douglas
Carlisle
Newcastle upon Tyne
Sunderland
Durham
Penrith
Whitehaven
Keswick
Middlesbrough

ISLE OF MAN

Douglas

Kendal
Lancaster
Scarborough

York
Blackpool
Preston
LEEDS
BRADFORD
Huddersfield
KINGSTON UPON HULL
Bolton
MANCHESTER
Doncaster
LIVERPOOL
SHEFFIELD
Holyhead
Colwyn Bay
Buxton
Lincoln
Skegness
Caernarfon
Betws-y-coed
Chester
Boston
Pwllheli
STOKE-ON-TRENT
Cromer
Llangollen
Derby
NOTTINGHAM
King's Lynn
Norwich
Great Yarmouth
Dolgellau
Shrewsbury
LEICESTER
Peterborough
Lowestoft
Aberystwyth
WOLVERHAMPTON
Cambridge
Bury St Edmunds
BIRMINGHAM
COVENTRY
Northampton
Ipswich
Llandrindod Wells
Worcester
Stratford-upon-Avon
Banbury
Milton Keynes
Luton
Ross-on-Wye
Hereford
Colchester
Haverfordwest
Carmarthen
Merthyr Tydfil
Gloucester
Chelmsford
Pembroke
Newport
Oxford
Swansea
Swindon
Reading
Windsor
LONDON
Southend-on-Sea
CARDIFF
BRISTOL
Bath
Salisbury
Winchester
Crawley
Royal Tunbridge Wells
Canterbury
Dover
Barnstaple
Chichester
Brighton
Hastings
Taunton
Yeovil
Southampton
Bude
Exeter
Poole
Portsmouth
Lyme Regis
Bournemouth
Weymouth
Torquay

CHANNEL ISLANDS

St. Helier

Truro
Penzance
Plymouth

THE FHG DIPLOMA

HELP IMPROVE
BRITISH TOURIST STANDARDS

You are choosing holiday accommodation from our very popular FHG Publications. Whether it be a hotel, guest house, farmhouse or self-catering accommodation, we think you will find it hospitable, comfortable and clean, and your host and hostess friendly and helpful.

Why not write and tell us about it?

As a recognition of the generally well-run and excellent holiday accommodation reviewed in our publications, we at FHG Publications Ltd. present a diploma to proprietors who receive the highest recommendation from their guests who are also readers of our Guides. If you care to write to us praising the holiday you have booked through FHG Publications Ltd. – whether this be board, self-catering accommodation, a sporting or a caravan holiday, what you say will be evaluated and the proprietors who reach our final list will be contacted.

The winning proprietor will receive an attractive framed diploma to display on his premises as recognition of a high standard of comfort, amenity and hospitality. FHG Publications Ltd. offer this diploma as a contribution towards the improvement of standards in tourist accommodation in Britain. Help your excellent host or hostess to win it!

FHG DIPLOMA

We nominate ....

....

Because

Name ....

Address ....

.... Telephone No. ....

BOOKING

FOR THE
MUTUAL GUIDANCE OF
GUEST AND HOST

Every year literally thousands of holidays, short-breaks and overnight stops are arranged through our guides, the vast majority without any problems at all. In a handful of cases, however, difficulties do arise about bookings, which often could have been prevented from the outset.

It is important to remember that when accommodation has been booked, both parties — guests and hosts — have entered into a form of contract. We hope that the following points will provide helpful guidance.

GUESTS: When enquiring about accommodation, be as precise as possible. Give exact dates, numbers in your party and the ages of any children. State the number and type of rooms wanted and also what catering you require — bed and breakfast, full board, etc. Make sure that the position about evening meals is clear — and about pets, reductions for children or any other special points.

Read our reviews carefully to ensure that the proprietors you are going to contact can supply what you want. Ask for a letter confirming all arrangements, if possible.

If you have to cancel, do so as soon as possible. Proprietors do have the right to retain deposits and under certain circumstances to charge for cancelled holidays if adequate notice is not given and they cannot re-let the accommodation.

HOSTS: Give details about your facilities and about any special conditions. Explain your deposit system clearly and arrangements for cancellations, charges, etc, and whether or not your terms include VAT.

If for any reason you are unable to fulfill an agreed booking without adequate notice, you may be under an obligation to arrange alternative suitable accommodation or to make some form of compensation.

While every effort is made to ensure accuracy, we regret that FHG Publications cannot accept responsibility for errors, omissions or misrepresentation in our entries or any consequences thereof. Prices in particular should be checked because we go to press early. We will follow up complaints but cannot act as arbiters or agents for either party.

BED & BREAKFAST STOPS

1998

READERS' OFFER VOUCHERS

On the following pages you will find vouchers which offer free and/or reduced rate entry to a selection of Visitor Attractions in Britain.

Readers should simply cut out the coupons and present them if they are visiting any of the attractions concerned.

Please let us know if you have any difficulty.

11

READERS' OFFER 1998

VALID during 1998

Sacrewell Farm and Country Centre

Thornhaugh, Peterborough, Cambridgeshire PE8 6HJ Tel: (01780) 782254

GROUP RATE ADMISSION for all members of party

NOT TO BE USED IN CONJUNCTION WITH ANY OTHER OFFER

READERS' OFFER 1998

VALID during 1998

DAIRYLAND FARM WORLD

Summercourt, Near Newquay, Cornwall TR8 5AA Tel: 01872 510246

One child **FREE** when accompanied by adult paying full admission price

NOT TO BE USED IN CONJUNCTION WITH ANY OTHER OFFER

READERS' OFFER 1998

VALID Easter to October 1998

Tamar Valley Donkey Park

St Anns Chapel, Gunnislake, Cornwall PL18 9HW Tel: 01822 834072

10% OFF admission price for up to 6 people, free donkey ride for children included

NOT TO BE USED IN CONJUNCTION WITH ANY OTHER OFFER

READERS' OFFER 1998

VALID during 1998

COARSE FISHING AT CROSSFIELD

Crossfield, Staffield, Kirkoswald, Cumbria CA10 1EU Tel: 01768 898711

ADMIT two children for the price of one; three adults for the price of two
(Advance booking essential)

NOT TO BE USED IN CONJUNCTION WITH ANY OTHER OFFER

READERS' OFFER 1998

VALID March to September 1998

Lowther Leisure and Wildlife Park

Hackthorpe, Penrith, Cumbria CA10 2HG Tel: 01931 712523

£1.50 off standard admission price (per person) up to maximum of 5 persons

NOT TO BE USED IN CONJUNCTION WITH ANY OTHER OFFER

The fascinating story of farming and country life with working watermill, gardens, collections of bygones, farm and nature trails. Excellent for young children. Campers and Caravanners welcome.

DIRECTIONS: Junction A1/A47, 8 miles west of Peterborough.

OPEN: daily all year.

FHG PUBLICATIONS, ABBEY MILL BUSINESS CENTRE, PAISLEY PA1 1TJ

Britain's premier farm attraction - milking parlour, Heritage Centre, Farmpark and playground. Daily events include bottle feeding, "Pat-a-Pet" and rally karts.

DIRECTIONS: 4 miles from Newquay on the A3058 Newquay to St Austell road.

OPEN: from early April to end October 10.30am to 5pm. Also open from early December to Christmas Eve 11-4pm daily.

FHG PUBLICATIONS, ABBEY MILL BUSINESS CENTRE, PAISLEY PA1 1TJ

Donkey and donkey cart rides for children. Feed and cuddle tame lambs, goats, rabbits and donkeys. Playgrounds, cafe, gifts.

DIRECTIONS: just off A390 Tavistock to Callington road at village of St Anns Chapel

OPEN: Easter to end October 10am to 5pm

FHG PUBLICATIONS, ABBEY MILL BUSINESS CENTRE, PAISLEY PA1 1TJ

Relax, escape and enjoy a great day out - Carp, Rudd, Tench, Bream, Crucians, Ide, Roach

DIRECTIONS: from Kirkoswald follow signs for Staffield, turn right (signposted Dale/Blunderfield); Crossfield is 200m up narrow road via cattle grid.

OPEN: advance booking essential.
Please do not turn up without an appointment to view/fish.

FHG PUBLICATIONS, ABBEY MILL BUSINESS CENTRE, PAISLEY PA1 1TJ

Attractions, rides, adventure play areas, circus and wildlife, all set in undulating parkland amidst beautiful scenery, make Lowther the Lake District's premier all-day attraction.

DIRECTIONS: travelling North leave M6 at J39, follow brown signs; travelling South leave at J40, follow brown signs. A6 Shap Road, 6 miles south Penrith.

OPEN: March/April to September 10am to 5/6pm.

FHG PUBLICATIONS, ABBEY MILL BUSINESS CENTRE, PAISLEY PA1 1TJ

READERS' OFFER 1998
VALID until end March 1998

Tullie House Museum & Art Gallery
Castle Street, Carlisle CA3 8TP Tel: 01228 34781

One adult/child **FREE** with one adult paying full admission price

NOT TO BE USED IN CONJUNCTION WITH ANY OTHER OFFER

READERS' OFFER 1998
VALID to end October 1998

HEIGHTS OF ABRAHAM
Cable Car, Caverns and Country Park

Matlock Bath, Derbyshire DE4 3PD Telephone: 01629 582365

FREE child entry with one full paying adult

NOT TO BE USED IN CONJUNCTION WITH ANY OTHER OFFER

READERS' OFFER 1998
VALID during 1998

The Big Sheep
Bideford, Devon EX39 5AP   Telephone: 01237 472366

Admit one **FREE** with each paid admission

NOT TO BE USED IN CONJUNCTION WITH ANY OTHER OFFER

READERS' OFFER 1998
VALID during 1998

Plymouth Dome (and Smeaton's Tower)
The Hoe, Plymouth, Devon PL1 2NZ Tel: 01752 600608

One child **FREE** with one full-paying adult

NOT TO BE USED IN CONJUNCTION WITH ANY OTHER OFFER

READERS' OFFER 1998
VALID Easter to end Oct. 1998

Dorset Heavy Horse Centre
Edmondsham, Verwood, Dorset BH21 5RJ Telephone: 01202 824040

Admit one adult **FREE** when accompanied by one full-paying adult

NOT TO BE USED IN CONJUNCTION WITH ANY OTHER OFFER

Award-winning museum and art gallery. Journey back in time to the Roman occupation, Middle Ages, England's Civil War and the Land of the Reivers.

DIRECTIONS: from M6 Junctions 42, 43, 44, follow signs into Carlisle. Museum is opposite Carlisle Castle.

OPEN: daily except Christmas Day. Monday to Saturday 10am to 5pm, Sunday 12 noon to 5pm.

FHG PUBLICATIONS, ABBEY MILL BUSINESS CENTRE, PAISLEY PA1 1TJ

Cable car return journey plus two famous Show Caverns. Tree Tops Visitor Centre with restaurant, coffee and gift shops; nature trails and children's play areas.

DIRECTIONS: signposted from all nearby major trunk roads. On A6 at Matlock Bath.

OPEN: daily Easter to end October 10am to 5pm (later in High Season).

FHG PUBLICATIONS, ABBEY MILL BUSINESS CENTRE, PAISLEY PA1 1TJ

"England for Excellence" award-winning rural attraction combining traditional rural crafts with hilarious novelties such as sheep racing and duck trialling. "Devon Family Attraction of the Year" — *Good Guide to Britain 1997*.

DIRECTIONS: on A39 North Devon link road, 2 miles west of Bideford Bridge

OPEN: daily all year, 10am to 6pm

FHG PUBLICATIONS, ABBEY MILL BUSINESS CENTRE, PAISLEY PA1 1TJ

Award-winning centre sited on Plymouth's famous Hoe telling the story of the city, from the epic voyages of Drake, Cook and the Mayflower Pilgrims to the devastation of the Blitz. A must for all the family

DIRECTIONS: follow signs from Plymouth City Centre to the Hoe and seafront

OPEN: daily all year (Smeaton's Tower closed October to Easter)

FHG PUBLICATIONS, ABBEY MILL BUSINESS CENTRE, PAISLEY PA1 1TJ

Heavy horse and pony centre, also Icelandic riding stables. Cafe, gift shop. Facilities for disabled visitors.

DIRECTIONS: signposted from the centre of Verwood, which is on the B3081

OPEN: Easter to end October 10am to 5pm

FHG PUBLICATIONS, ABBEY MILL BUSINESS CENTRE, PAISLEY PA1 1TJ

FHG

READERS' OFFER 1998

VALID April to October 1998

Killhope Lead Mining Centre

Cowshill, Upper Weardale, Co. Durham DL13 1AR Tel: 01388 537505

Admit one child **FREE** with full-paying adult (not valid for Park Level Mine)

NOT TO BE USED IN CONJUNCTION WITH ANY OTHER OFFER

FHG

READERS' OFFER 1998

VALID during 1998

Cotswold Farm Park

Guiting Power, Near Stow-on-the-Wold, Gloucestershire GL54 5UG Tel: 01451 850307

Admit one child **FREE** with an adult paying full entrance fee

NOT TO BE USED IN CONJUNCTION WITH ANY OTHER OFFER

FHG

READERS' OFFER 1998

VALID during 1998

NATIONAL WATERWAYS MUSEUM

Llanthony Warehouse, Gloucester Docks, Gloucester GL1 2EH Tel: 01452 318054

20% off all museum tickets (Single or Family)

NOT TO BE USED IN CONJUNCTION WITH ANY OTHER OFFER

FHG

READERS' OFFER 1998

VALID during 1998

BEAULIEU

Near Brockenhurst, Hampshire SO42 7ZN Tel: 01590 612345

£2.00 off adult ticket when accompanied by adult paying full admission.
(Not valid on Bank Holidays or for special events; not valid in conjunction with Family Ticket)

NOT TO BE USED IN CONJUNCTION WITH ANY OTHER OFFER

FHG

READERS' OFFER 1998

VALID during 1998

Isle of Wight Rare Breeds and Waterfowl Park

St Lawrence, Ventnor, Isle of Wight PO38 1UW Tel: 01983 852582

Admit one child **FREE** with full-paying adult

NOT TO BE USED IN CONJUNCTION WITH ANY OTHER OFFER

Britain's best preserved lead mining site — and a great day out for all the family, with lots to see and do. Underground Experience — Park Level Mine now open.

DIRECTIONS: alongside A689, midway between Stanhope and Alston in the heart of the North Pennines.

OPEN: April 1st to October 31st 10.30am to 5pm daily

FHG PUBLICATIONS, ABBEY MILL BUSINESS CENTRE, PAISLEY PA1 1TJ

The home of rare breeds conservation, with over 50 breeding flocks and herds of rare farm animals. Adventure playground, pets' corners, picnic area, farm nature trail, Touch barn, Woodland Walk and viewing tower

DIRECTIONS: M5 Junction 9, off B4077 Stow-on-the-Wold road. 5 miles from Bourton-on-the-Water.

OPEN: daily 10.30am to 5pm April to September (to 6pm Sundays, Bank Holidays and daily in July and August).

FHG PUBLICATIONS, ABBEY MILL BUSINESS CENTRE, PAISLEY PA1 1TJ

---

3 floors of a Listed 7-storey Victorian warehouse telling 200 years of inland waterway history by means of video film, working exhibits with 2 quaysides of floating exhibits. Special school holiday activities.

DIRECTIONS: Junction 11 or 12 off M5 — follow brown signs for Historic Docks. Railway and bus station 10 minute walk. Free coach parking.

OPEN: Summer 10am to 6pm; Winter 10am to 5pm. Closed Christmas Day.

FHG PUBLICATIONS, ABBEY MILL BUSINESS CENTRE, PAISLEY PA1 1TJ

Beaulieu offers a fascinating day out for all the family. In the National Motor Museum there are over 250 vehicles from the earliest days of motoring; within Palace House many Montagu family treasures can be viewed. Plus a host of rides and drives to enjoy.

DIRECTIONS: off Junction 2 of M27, then follow brown tourist signs.

OPEN: daily 10am to 5pm (Easter to September to 6pm). Closed Christmas Day

FHG PUBLICATIONS, ABBEY MILL BUSINESS CENTRE, PAISLEY PA1 1TJ

One of the UK's largest collections of rare farm animals, plus deer, llamas, miniature horses, waterfowl, poultry, owls and otters in 30 beautiful coastal acres.

DIRECTIONS: on main south coast road A3055 between Ventnor and Niton.

OPEN: Easter to end October open daily 10am to 5.30pm; Winter open weekends only 10am to 4pm (weather permitting).

FHG PUBLICATIONS, ABBEY MILL BUSINESS CENTRE, PAISLEY PA1 1TJ

17

FHG **READERS' OFFER 1998** VALID during 1998

FLEET AIR ARM MUSEUM

RNAS Yeovilton, Ilchester, Somerset BA22 8HT Tel: 01935 840077

One child **FREE** with full paying adult (not valid Bank Holidays)

NOT TO BE USED IN CONJUNCTION WITH ANY OTHER OFFER

FHG **READERS' OFFER 1998** VALID until March 1999

Wookey Hole Caves and Papermill

Wookey Hole, Wells, Somerset BA5 1BB Telephone: 01749 672243

50p per person **OFF** full admission price (up to maximum 6 persons)

NOT TO BE USED IN CONJUNCTION WITH ANY OTHER OFFER

FHG **READERS' OFFER 1998** VALID during 1998

Pleasurewood Hills Family Theme Park

Corton, Lowestoft, Suffolk NR32 5DZ Tel: 01502 586000

£1.00 discount on full admission price for all visitors over 1 metre in height

NOT TO BE USED IN CONJUNCTION WITH ANY OTHER OFFER

FHG **READERS' OFFER 1998** VALID April to October 1998

American Adventure Golf

Fort Fun, Royal Parade, Eastbourne, East Sussex BN22 7LU Tel: 01323 642833

One **FREE** game of golf with every full-paying customer (value £2)

NOT TO BE USED IN CONJUNCTION WITH ANY OTHER OFFER

FHG **READERS' OFFER 1998** VALID during 1998

PARADISE FAMILY LEISURE PARK

Avis Road, Newhaven, East Sussex BN9 0DH Tel: 01273 512123

Admit one **FREE** adult or child with one adult paying full entrance price

NOT TO BE USED IN CONJUNCTION WITH ANY OTHER OFFER

Leading naval aviation museum with over 40 aircraft on display
— Concorde 002 and "Carrier". Based on an operational naval air station.

DIRECTIONS: just off A303/A37 on B3151 at Ilchester.
Yeovil rail station 10 miles.

OPEN: April to October 10am to 5.30pm; November to March 10am to 4.30pm

FHG PUBLICATIONS, ABBEY MILL BUSINESS CENTRE, PAISLEY PA1 1TJ

---

* Britain's most spectacular caves * Traditional paper-making *
* Penny Arcade * Magical Mirror Maze *

DIRECTIONS: from M5 Junction 22 follow brown-and-white signs via A38 and A371.
Wookey Hole is just 2 miles from Wells.

OPEN: Summer 9.30am to 5.30pm; Winter 10.30am to 4.30pm. Closed 17-25 Dec.
FHG PUBLICATIONS, ABBEY MILL BUSINESS CENTRE, PAISLEY PA1 1TJ

The Theme Park for all the family. East Anglia's Number One attraction boasts over
50 rides, shows and attractions set in over 70 acres of landscaped gardens.
This is your biggest day out ever — bet you can't do it all in a day!

DIRECTIONS: between Lowestoft and Great Yarmouth

OPEN: from 10am to 5/6pm depending on season

FHG PUBLICATIONS, ABBEY MILL BUSINESS CENTRE, PAISLEY PA1 1TJ

18-hole American Adventure Golf set in 1/3 acre landscaped surroundings.
Played on different levels including water features.

DIRECTIONS: on the seafront 1/4 mile east of Eastbourne Pier.

OPEN: April until end October 10am until dusk

FHG PUBLICATIONS, ABBEY MILL BUSINESS CENTRE, PAISLEY PA1 1TJ

A unique attraction for all ages, including Planet Earth and the Living Dinosaur Mueum,
Playland, Sussex in Miniature, Leisure Gardens, Botanic Garden and Garden Centre.

DIRECTIONS: signposted off A26 and A259

OPEN: all year, except Christmas Day and Boxing Day.

FHG PUBLICATIONS, ABBEY MILL BUSINESS CENTRE, PAISLEY PA1 1TJ

READERS' OFFER 1998   VALID during 1998

SNIBSTON DISCOVERY PARK

Ashby Road, Coalville, Leicestershire LE67 3LN Telephone: 01530 510851

Admit one child **FREE** with one full-paying adult

NOT TO BE USED IN CONJUNCTION WITH ANY OTHER OFFER

READERS' OFFER 1998   VALID during 1998 except Bank Holidays

Southport Zoo and Conservation Trust

Princes Park, Southport, Merseyside PR8 1RX Telephone: 01704 538102

Admit one child **FREE** with two full paying adults

NOT TO BE USED IN CONJUNCTION WITH ANY OTHER OFFER

READERS' OFFER 1998   VALID March to October 1998

Hexham Herbs

Chesters Walled Garden, Chollerford, Hexham, Northumberland NE46 4BQ Tel: 01434 681483

One adult **FREE** with paid adult entry

NOT TO BE USED IN CONJUNCTION WITH ANY OTHER OFFER

READERS' OFFER 1998   VALID during 1998 except Bank Holidays

Galleries of Justice

Shire Hall, High Pavement, Lace Market, Nottingham NG1 1HN Tel: 0115 952 0555

One **FREE** child admission with one full paying adult to Condemned! **or** Nicked!

NOT TO BE USED IN CONJUNCTION WITH ANY OTHER OFFER

READERS' OFFER 1998   VALID during 1998

White Post Modern Farm Centre

Farnsfield, Near Newark, Nottinghamshire NG22 8HL Tel: 01623 882977

TWO child admissions for the price of one

NOT TO BE USED IN CONJUNCTION WITH ANY OTHER OFFER

Award-winning science and industry museum. Fascinating colliery tours and "hands-on" displays including holograms, tornado and virtual reality.

DIRECTIONS: 10 minutes from Junction 22 M1 and Junction 13 M42/A42. Well signposted along the A50.

OPEN: April to Oct.10am to 6pm; Nov. to March 10am to 5pm. Closed 25/26 Dec.

FHG PUBLICATIONS, ABBEY MILL BUSINESS CENTRE, PAISLEY PA1 1TJ

Lions, snow leopards, chimpanzees, penguins, reptiles, aquarium and lots more, set amidst landscaped gardens.

DIRECTIONS: on the coast 16 miles north of Liverpool; follow the brown tourist signs.

OPEN: daily except Christmas Day. Summer 10am to 6pm; Winter 10am to 4pm.

FHG PUBLICATIONS, ABBEY MILL BUSINESS CENTRE, PAISLEY PA1 1TJ

Beautiful walled garden with nearly 900 types of herbs, woodland walk, nursery, shop. Guide dogs only.

DIRECTIONS: 6 miles north of Hexham, next to Chesters Roman Fort.

OPEN: daily March to October/November.

FHG PUBLICATIONS, ABBEY MILL BUSINESS CENTRE, PAISLEY PA1 1TJ

Condemned!— a major crime and punishment exhibition. Witness the splendour of the Victorian courtroom and interact with warders and prisoners of the old county gaol. Nicked! (opens April 1998) — an exciting and interactive exhibition focussed on the police.

DIRECTIONS: in City Centre, 5 minutes from Broadmarsh Shopping Centre.

OPEN: Tuesday to Sunday and Bank Holidays. Closed 24-26 December. April to August: 10am to 6pm, September to March: 10am to 5pm.

FHG PUBLICATIONS, ABBEY MILL BUSINESS CENTRE, PAISLEY PA1 1TJ

A modern working farm with over 3000 animals including ducklings, deer, bees, rheas, piglets, snails, lambs (all year). New pet centre.

DIRECTIONS:off the A614 at Farnsfield, 12 miles north of Nottingham. From M1 Junction 27 follow "Robin Hood" signs for 10 miles.

OPEN: daily all year round.

FHG PUBLICATIONS, ABBEY MILL BUSINESS CENTRE, PAISLEY PA1 1TJ

FHG

READERS' OFFER 1998

VALID during 1998

Wilderness Wood

Hadlow Down, Near Uckfield, East Sussex TN22 4HJ Tel: 01825 830509

One **FREE** entry with full-paying adult (only one voucher per group)

Not valid Bank Holidays or special events

NOT TO BE USED IN CONJUNCTION WITH ANY OTHER OFFER

FHG

READERS' OFFER 1998

VALID during 1998 excluding Bank Holidays

The New MetroLand

39 Garden Walk, MetroCentre, Gateshead, Tyne & Wear NE11 9XY Tel: 0191 493 2048

Two all-day unlimited ride passes for the price of one

(pass excludes Monty Zoomers Adventure Play Area and Whirling Waltzer)

NOT TO BE USED IN CONJUNCTION WITH ANY OTHER OFFER

FHG

READERS' OFFER 1998

VALID during 1998

HATTON COUNTRY WORLD

Dark Lane, Hatton, Near Warwick, Warwickshire CV35 8XA Tel: 01926 843411

Admit **TWO** for the price of one into Farm Park

(not valid weekends or Bank Holidays)

NOT TO BE USED IN CONJUNCTION WITH ANY OTHER OFFER

READERS' OFFER 1998

VALID during 1998

Embsay & Bolton Abbey Steam Railway

Embsay, Skipton, North Yorkshire BD23 6AX Tel: 01756 794727

One adult travels **FREE** when accompanied by a full fare paying adult

(does not include Special Event days)

NOT TO BE USED IN CONJUNCTION WITH ANY OTHER OFFER

READERS' OFFER 1998

VALID until 31/12/1998

Eureka! The Museum for Children

Discovery Road, Halifax, West Yorkshire HX1 2NE Tel: 01422 330069

One child **FREE** with two adults paying full price

VALID SATURDAYS AND SUNDAYS ONLY

NOT TO BE USED IN CONJUNCTION WITH ANY OTHER OFFER

See woodland with new eyes at this family-run working wood — fascinating and fun for all the family. Trails, adventure playground, exhibition, picnic areas, BBQs for hire, teas.

DIRECTIONS: on main A272 in Hadlow Down village, 5 miles north east of Uckfield

OPEN: daily all year

FHG PUBLICATIONS, ABBEY MILL BUSINESS CENTRE, PAISLEY PA1 1TJ

Europe's largest indoor funfair theme park. 12 major traditional rides including Roller Coaster, Ferris Wheel, Waveswinger, Swashbuckling Ship, Waltzer and Dodgems. Children's Adventure Play Area.

DIRECTIONS: signposted MetroCentre, Gateshead on A1/M north and southbound.

OPEN: daily except Christmas

FHG PUBLICATIONS, ABBEY MILL BUSINESS CENTRE, PAISLEY PA1 1TJ

England's largest craft village, factory shops, butcher's and farm shops, antiques centre; restaurant, cafe and bar (no entrance charge). Rare breeds farm, pets' corner, nature trail, guinea pig village, falconry and farming displays and soft play centre

DIRECTIONS: 3 miles north of Warwick, 5 miles south of Knowle, just off Junction 15 of M40 via A46 (Coventry), and off A4177

OPEN: daily 10am to 5.30pm

FHG PUBLICATIONS, ABBEY MILL BUSINESS CENTRE, PAISLEY PA1 1TJ

Steam trains operate over a 4½ mile line from Embsay Station to Bolton Abbey. Many family events including Thomas the Tank Engine take place during major Bank Holidays.

DIRECTIONS: Embsay Station signposted from the A59 Skipton by-pass; Bolton Abbey Station signposted from the A59 at Bolton Abbey.

OPEN: steam trains run every Sunday throughout the year and up to 5 days a week in summer. 11am to 4.15pm

FHG PUBLICATIONS, ABBEY MILL BUSINESS CENTRE, PAISLEY PA1 1TJ

Britain's first hands-on museum designed especially for children between 3 and 12 years, where hundreds of interactive exhibits let them make fascinating discoveries about themselves and the world around.

DIRECTIONS: next to Halifax railway Station 5 minutes from Junction 24 M62

OPEN: daily 10am to 5pm (closed 24-26 December)

FHG PUBLICATIONS, ABBEY MILL BUSINESS CENTRE, PAISLEY PA1 1TJ

FHG   **READERS' OFFER 1998**   VALID during 1998

Alice in Wonderland Centre

3/4 Trinity Square, Llandudno, Conwy, North Wales LL30 2PY Tel: 01492 860082

One child **FREE** with two paying adults

NOT TO BE USED IN CONJUNCTION WITH ANY OTHER OFFER

FHG   **READERS' OFFER 1998**   VALID during 1998

Llanberis Lake Railway

Llanberis, Gwynedd LL55 4TY Telephone: 01286 870549

One child travels **FREE** with two full fare-paying adults

NOT TO BE USED IN CONJUNCTION WITH ANY OTHER OFFER

FHG   **READERS' OFFER 1998**   VALID March to October 1998

PILI PALAS – BUTTERFLY PALACE

Menai Bridge, Isle of Anglesey LL59 5RP Tel: 01248 712474

One child **FREE** with two adults paying full entry price

NOT TO BE USED IN CONJUNCTION WITH ANY OTHER OFFER

FHG   **READERS' OFFER 1998**   VALID during 1998

CENTRE FOR ALTERNATIVE TECHNOLOGY

Machynlleth, Powys SY20 9AZ Telephone: 01654 702400

One child **FREE** when accompanied by paying adult (one per party only)

NOT TO BE USED IN CONJUNCTION WITH ANY OTHER OFFER

FHG   **READERS' OFFER 1998**   VALID July to Dec 1998

Techniquest

Stuart Street, Cardiff Bay, South Wales CF1 6BW Tel: 01222 475475

One child **FREE** with one or more full-paying adults

NOT TO BE USED IN CONJUNCTION WITH ANY OTHER OFFER

Walk through the Rabbit Hole to the colourful scenes of Lewis Carroll's classic story set in beautiful life-size displays. Recorded commentaries and transcripts available in several languages.

DIRECTIONS: situated just off the main street, 250 yards from coach and rail stations

OPEN: 10am to 5pm daily Easter to end October; closed Sundays November to Easter.

FHG PUBLICATIONS, ABBEY MILL BUSINESS CENTRE, PAISLEY PA1 1TJ

A 40-minute ride on a quaint historic steam train along the shore of Llyn Padarn. Spectacular views of the mountains of Snowdonia.

DIRECTIONS: just off the A4086 Caernarfon to Capel Curig road. Follow the "Padarn Country Park" signs.

OPEN: most days Easter to October. Free timetable available from Railway.

FHG PUBLICATIONS, ABBEY MILL BUSINESS CENTRE, PAISLEY PA1 1TJ

Visit Wales' top Butterfly House, with Bird House, Snake House, Ant Avenue, Creepy Crawly Cavern, shop, cafe, adventure playground, picnic area, nature trail etc.

DIRECTIONS: follow brown-and-white signs when crossing to Anglesey; one-and-a-half miles from the Bridge.

OPEN: March to end October 10am to 5pm daily; November/December 11am to 3pm.

FHG PUBLICATIONS, ABBEY MILL BUSINESS CENTRE, PAISLEY PA1 1TJ

Europe's leading Eco-Centre. Water-powered cliff railway, interactive renewable energy displays, beautiful organic gardens, animals; vegetarian restaurant.

DIRECTIONS: three miles north of Machynlleth on the A487 towards Dolgellau.

OPEN: from 10am every day all year except Christmas and mid-January (last entry 5pm). Cliff railway closed November to Easter.

FHG PUBLICATIONS, ABBEY MILL BUSINESS CENTRE, PAISLEY PA1 1TJ

UK's leading Science Discovery Centre with 160 interactive exhibits, Planetarium, Science Theatre and Discovery Room. Fun for all!

DIRECTIONS: A4232 from Juntion 33 of M4. Follow brown tourist signs to Cardiff Bay and Techiquest (10 minutes)

OPEN: weekdays 9.30am to 4.30pm; weekends and Bank Holidays 10.30am to 5pm

FHG PUBLICATIONS, ABBEY MILL BUSINESS CENTRE, PAISLEY PA1 1TJ

READERS' OFFER 1998
VALID during 1998

Inveraray Maritime Museum
Arctic Penguin, The Pier, Inveraray, Argyll PA32 8UY Tel: 01499 302213

One child **FREE** with each full-paying adult

NOT TO BE USED IN CONJUNCTION WITH ANY OTHER OFFER

READERS' OFFER 1998
VALID March to November 1998

HEADS OF AYR FARM PARK
Dunure Road, Ayr, Ayrshire KA7 4HR Tel: 01292 441210

One child **FREE** when accompanied by one full-paying adult

NOT TO BE USED IN CONJUNCTION WITH ANY OTHER OFFER

READERS' OFFER 1998
VALID April 1998 to April 1999

EDINBURGH CRYSTAL VISITOR CENTRE
Eastfield, Penicuik, Midlothian EH26 8HB Telephone: 01968 675128

OFFER: Two for the price of one (higher ticket price applies).

NOT TO BE USED IN CONJUNCTION WITH ANY OTHER OFFER

READERS' OFFER 1998
VALID during 1998

MYRETON MOTOR MUSEUM
Aberlady, East Lothian EH32 0PZ Telephone: 01875 870288

One child **FREE** with each paying adult

NOT TO BE USED IN CONJUNCTION WITH ANY OTHER OFFER

READERS' OFFER 1998
VALID during 1998

Highland Folk Museum
Am Fasgadh
Duke Street, Kingussie, Inverness-shire PH21 1JG Tel: 01540 661307

One **FREE** child with accompanying adult paying full admission price

NOT TO BE USED IN CONJUNCTION WITH ANY OTHER OFFER

A fascinating collection of Clyde maritime displays, memorabilia, stunning archive film and entertaining hands-on activities on board a unique three-masted schooner

DIRECTIONS: at Inveraray on the A83

OPEN: daily 10am to 6pm April to September, 10am to 5pm October to March

FHG PUBLICATIONS, ABBEY MILL BUSINESS CENTRE, PAISLEY PA1 1TJ

From buffalo and bunnies to wallabies and snakes - hundreds of exciting animals. Buggy and pony rides, giant slides, aerial runway, indoor play areas and Combine Castle, outdoor playpark and picnic areas. Snack bar and gift shop.

DIRECTIONS: 4 miles south of Ayr on A719

OPEN: all year 10am to 5pm

FHG PUBLICATIONS, ABBEY MILL BUSINESS CENTRE, PAISLEY PA1 1TJ

Visitor Centre with Exhibition Room, factory tours (children over 8 years only), Crystal Shop, gift shop, coffee shop. Facilities for disabled visitors.

DIRECTIONS: 10 miles south of Edinburgh on the A701 Peebles road; signposted a few miles from the city centre.

OPEN: Visitor Centre open daily; Factory Tours weekdays (9am-3.30pm) all year, plus weekends (11am-2.30pm) April to September.

FHG PUBLICATIONS, ABBEY MILL BUSINESS CENTRE, PAISLEY PA1 1TJ

Motor cars from 1896, motorcycles from 1902, commercial vehicles from 1919, cycles from 1880, British WWII military vehicles, ephemera, period advertising etc

DIRECTIONS: off the A198 near Aberlady. 2 miles from A1

OPEN: daily October to Easter 10am to 5pm; Easter to October 10am to 6pm. Closed Christmas Day and New Year's Day.

FHG PUBLICATIONS, ABBEY MILL BUSINESS CENTRE, PAISLEY PA1 1TJ

One of the oldest open air museums in Britain! A treasure trove of Highland life and culture.

DIRECTIONS: Easily reached via the A9, 68 miles north of Perth and 42 miles south of Inverness.

OPEN: March to October: open daily.

FHG PUBLICATIONS, ABBEY MILL BUSINESS CENTRE, PAISLEY PA1 1TJ

Beneath the heather and high in the glen, the secrets of the ancient Highlander live on. Experience for yourself the energy of the myths and legends which have so powerfully governed the people here for centuries past. Three fabulous indoor attractions, shop and restaurant.

DIRECTIONS: just off A82 opposite Ballachulish village, 15 mins south of Fort William

OPEN: daily mid-March to end October. Peak 10am to 6pm; off-peak 10am to 4pm

FHG PUBLICATIONS, ABBEY MILL BUSINESS CENTRE, PAISLEY PA1 1TJ

Multi-award winning centre, "Heather Story" exhibition, gift shop/boutique, over 300 varieties of heather, gardens, trail. Famous Clootie Dumpling Restaurant — "21 ways to have your dumpling"! Gallery, antiques, shop

DIRECTIONS: signposted on A95 between Aviemore and Grantown-on-Spey

OPEN: daily 9am to 6pm (10am to 6pm Sun). Please check opening times in winter

FHG PUBLICATIONS, ABBEY MILL BUSINESS CENTRE, PAISLEY PA1 1TJ

STB award-winning museum designed to stimulate interest and wonder in the fascinating subjects of gems, crystals and mineralogy. Exciting audio-visual display.

DIRECTIONS: 7 miles from Newton Stewart, 11 miles from Gatehouse of Fleet; just off A75 Carlisle to Stranraer road.

OPEN: Open daily Easter to 30th November; December, January and February weekends only.

FHG PUBLICATIONS, ABBEY MILL BUSINESS CENTRE, PAISLEY PA1 1TJ

200-year old conservation village with award-winning Visitor Centre, set in beautiful countryside

DIRECTIONS: one mile south of Lanark; well signposted from all major routes.

OPEN: daily all year round 11am to 5pm

FHG PUBLICATIONS, ABBEY MILL BUSINESS CENTRE, PAISLEY PA1 1TJ

Highland croft open to public for "hands-on" experience with over 35 different breeds of farm animals - "stroke the goats and scratch the pigs"

DIRECTIONS: on A835 15 miles north of Ullapool

OPEN: mid-May to third week in September 10am to 5pm

FHG PUBLICATIONS, ABBEY MILL BUSINESS CENTRE, PAISLEY PA1 1TJ

ENGLAND

LONDON

ELTHAM. Oakfield, 36 Southend Crescent, London SE9 2SB (Tel & Fax: 0181-859 8989; E-mail: oakfield@dircon.co.uk). You want that special place to stay in London? A real high quality guest house where comfort, style and elegance combine with an informal and relaxed atmosphere? That's Oakfield! Spacious en suite rooms some with four-poster or gothic style iron king size beds have comfortable sofas or chairs, tea/coffee making facilities, cable TV, with the option of luxury towelling robes. After breakfast relax in our guest lounge with a coffee and newspaper or guide book. Excellent transport connections will take you to central London and Kent. We are entirely non smoking. Let Oakfield make your stay in London special. Terms from £27.50 to £35 per person.

HAMPTON COURT. Bushy Park Lodge, Sandy Lane, Teddington TW11 0DR (0181-977 4924; Fax: 0181-943 1917). 🏵🏵 Situated overlooking Bushy Park, close to Kingston town centre and the bridge over the River Thames. Hampton Court can be reached with a direct walk of 20 minutes through the park. Hampton Wick railway station is a seven minute walk where central London can be reached via Waterloo in 30 minutes. Bushy Park Lodge is a purpose-built six double-bedroomed property. All bedrooms have bathrooms n-suite, remote control colour TV, tea/coffee making facilities, hair dryers and trouser presses. There are mini bars and direct dial telephones in all rooms. Car parking exists for 10 cars. Single accommodation is £48, double £59; prices include VAT and Continental breakfast.

HARROW. Mrs P. Giles, Oak Lodge, Brookshill, Harrow Weald, Middlesex HA3 6RY (0181-954 9257). If you are looking for Ghoulies and Ghosties I'm afraid you won't find them in this lovely 200 year old lodge, or in the large garden. But you will find a warm welcome and pleasant surroundings and a genuine piece of old England. Rooms have TV, tea/coffee facilities and central heating. Car ideal, we have car park, but we are also on bus route. A short drive to Harrow, Watford, Wembley, or train journey to London very easy; six miles M25, four miles M1. Single from £17.50, double from £35 including full English breakfast. Non smoking guests appreciated.

HARROW. Mrs M. Fitzgerald, 47 Hindes Road, Harrow HA1 1SQ (0181-861 1248). Private family guest house built at the turn of the century, offering very clean, comfortable accommodation. Situated within five minutes of Harrow town centre, Harrow bus and train stations. Wembley Stadium and Conference Centre six minutes away. Central London 17 minutes. 20 minutes M1, M25 and M40 motorways. Accommodation comprises single, double, twin and family rooms, all with central heating, washbasins, tea/coffee making facilities and colour television. Sorry, no pets. Terms £16 per person, per night.

KING'S CROSS. MacDonald and Devon Hotels, 43-46 Argyle Square, King's Cross, London WC1

(0171-837 3552). MacDonald and Devon Hotels are centrally located and well served by public transport. Short walk from St. Pancras and King's Cross Stations which also have the only direct Underground line to Heathrow Airport. We have 64 single, double and family rooms equipped with washbasin. All heated. Individual temperature controlled baths and showers, conveniently located throughout. English breakfast is served from 7.30am in a cheerful and friendly atmosphere. Earlier service can be arranged. Please write, or telephone, for our brochure and further information.

LONDON. Europa House Hotel, 151 Sussex Gardens, Hyde Park, London W2 (0171-723 7343; Fax: 0171-224 9331). Europa House is a small privately owned hotel which aims to give personalised service of the highest standard. Full central heating, all rooms en suite. Within easy reach of the West End. Situated close to Paddington Station. Double and twins. Singles. Family rooms available. Special rates for children under 10 years. Full English breakfast. Terms available on request.

LONDON. Mr Steven Poulacheris, Five Kings Guest House, 59 Anson Road, Tufnell Park, London N7 0AR (0171-607 6466/3996). A well-maintained friendly guest house offering personal attention. Quietly situated yet only 15 minutes from Central London tourist attractions and London Zoo. Central heating, washbasins and shaving points in all rooms. Lounge with colour TV; bathroom, showers, toilets on all floors. No parking restrictions in Anson Road. Bed and Breakfast from £20 to £28 single; from £32 to £36 double/twin. Children from £8 to £10. En-suite rooms £2 extra per person.

LONDON. Kirness House, 29 Belgrave Road, Victoria SW1V 1RB (0171-834 0030). A small friendly guest house, please try us. Situated close to Victoria Station. All European languages spoken. Satisfaction guaranteed. Six rooms available for Bed and Breakfast. Competitive rates: £25 single, £35 double.

LONDON. Rose Court Hotel, 1 Talbot Square, London W2 1TR (0171-723 5128; Fax: 0171-723 1855).  The Rose Court Hotel is located close to Hyde Park, Park Lane and the major shopping street of London, Oxford Street. Other famous attractions such as Madame Tussauds, Buckingham Palace, museums and theatres are within easy reach. Pleasantly situated in a quiet garden square the hotel is privately run and offers comfort, courteous service, friendliness and hospitality. The bedrooms have en suite facilities, satellite TV, telephone and fridge. Hairdryer and ironing facilities are also available. Single room £35 to £56, double/twin rooms £56 to £72, triple rooms £66 to £84, family rooms £80 to £94. Credit cards are accepted. Rates are inclusive of taxes and English breakfast.

LONDON. Jill and Eric Seal, "Lakeside", 51 Snaresbrook Road, London E11 1PQ (0181-989 6100). Visiting London? Be our guest. We are proud of being one of the few Bed and Breakfast establishments to be awarded AA QQQQQ Premier Selected Classification. Our bedrooms are beautifully decorated as is our elegant dining room and garden terrace. All bedrooms are en suite with tea/coffee making facilities, colour TV and hair dryers. We are in a unique position located directly opposite a lake yet just two minutes' walk from the Central Line tube station giving direct access to all the sights of London. The exit of the M11 motorway is nearby, making both Heathrow and Gatwick Airports within one hour's drive. Airport pickup can be arranged at competitive rates; we have free parking. Bed and Breakfast from £23 per person per night, minimum stay two nights.

LONDON (Borough of Sutton). Mrs J. Dixon, 17 Osmond Gardens, Wallington, London SM6 8SX (0181-647 1943). Comfortable family home in quiet road offers friendly welcome to guests. Double/family room (sleeps maximum four) with own colour TV, en suite shower/washbasin and tea/coffee making facilities; twin room also available. London approximately 30 minutes by train from local British Rail station within a few minutes' walk. Gatwick 45 minutes' drive and local bus to Hampton Court, Kingston, Croydon, Sutton, etc. Bed and full English Breakfast from £18. Reductions for children. Sorry, no singles accepted.

HUTTONS HOTEL

53-57 BELGRAVE ROAD, LONDON SW1
TEL: 0171-834 3726   FAX: 0171-834 3389

Welcome to Huttons Hotel. Within a few minutes' walk of Victoria railway and coach stations. British Airways bus stop opposite the hotel. All rooms have hot and cold water, shaving points, central heating, radio, colour TV and telephone. Advance bookings accepted by MasterCard, Visa and American Express. Enjoy your stay in Central London.

ROMANO'S HOTEL

Small, homely, very clean hotel, 5 minutes' walk from Victoria Coach, rail, underground and air terminals. Full central heating. All rooms with washbasins; one en suite double. Toilets and shower on each floor.

BED & BREAKFAST RATES VARY ACCORDING TO SEASON.

Places of interest nearby:
• Buckingham Palace,
St James Park – 10 minutes' walk.
• Big Ben/Westminster Abbey/
Parliament Square – 15 minutes'
walk. • Piccadilly Circus,
Theatreland – 30 minutes' walk.
• Other attractions within easy
reach by bus or Tube.

Singles from £18–£35 pp; Doubles from £14–£23 pp. Triples from £13–£20; Family rooms from £11–£19 pp.

31 Charlwood Street, Off Belgrave Road, Victoria, London SW1V 2DU
For reservations write/phone/fax: 0181 954 4352/0171 834 3542 Fax: 0171 834 2290
WELCOME   BENEVENUTI   BIENVENU   WILLKOMMEN

Hazelwood House

865 Finchley Road, Golders Green, London NW11 8LX
Telephone: 0181 458 8884

Enjoy luxury in a friendly atmosphere at our RAC and SRAC Listed establishment. Whether on holiday or on business, this hotel is famous for its 'home from home' atmosphere in London's exclusive district of Golders Green. Private forecourt parking for 5/6 cars. Children welcome. Animals accepted. Single room from £27.50 per night, double room from £38 per night, breakfast included.

King's Campus Vacation Bureau, Box No.98/2, King's College London, 127 Stamford Street, Waterloo, London SE1 9NQ
Tel: 0171 928 3777; Fax: 0171 928 5777

KING'S College
LONDON
Founded 1829

King's College offers affordable accommodation for families, individuals and groups in conveniently located Halls of Residence in central and inner London, some with car parking. Single and twin rooms all have washbasins and shared bathrooms, showers and toilets. Over 500 single rooms with ensuite showers in a new Hall in Waterloo, a short walk from the South Bank Arts Complex and the Eurostar Terminal. 1998 dates: 5th–26th April and 6th June to 22nd September, which includes the Wimbledon Tennis Championships. Bed & Breakfast from £17.50 nightly per person. Room only for £13.50 per person. Weekly rates available and special terms for registered students and groups. Further information and colour brochure on request.

LONDON. Gower Hotel, 129 Sussex Gardens, Hyde Park, London W2 2RX (0171-262 2262/3/4; Fax: 0171-262 2006). The Gower is a small family-run hotel, centrally located, within easy reach of Paddington Station. This is an excellent base for sightseeing and shopping; close to Hyde Park, Madame Tussaud's, Oxford Street, Marble Arch and many other attractions. The hotel is fully centrally heated, with all bedrooms having private shower and toilet, tea/coffee making facilities, radio, TV (with video and Satellite channels) and direct-dial telephone. Singles from £28 to £44, doubles/twins from £24 to £32, triple and family rooms from £20 to £26. Prices are per person. All prices are inclusive of a traditional English breakfast and VAT.

LONDON. Mrs A. Louis, 18 Silver Crescent, Chiswick, London W4 5SE (0181-994 6265). Stay at my Bed and Breakfast and experience the high quality and friendly service I offer in my well maintained Edwardian home which retains all its original features. Situated in a quiet tree-lined street two minutes from Gunnersbury underground station, M4 and A4. Five minutes Kew Gardens and River Thames. 15 minutes Heathrow Airport and 20 minutes to central London and Theatreland. Pubs and restaurants within walking distance. Central heating and colour TV in all rooms. Non-smokers preferred. Free street parking.

LONDON. Mrs Anne Scott, Holiday Hosts, 59 Cromwell Road, Wimbledon, London SW19 8LF (0181-540 7942; Fax: 0181-540 2827). Tourist Board Listed. We offer Bed and Breakfast accommodation in selected friendly private homes. Our homes are chosen for their comfort and location in good residential areas of South and West London. They are convenient for transport, restaurants, museums, art galleries, theatres, shopping; Wimbledon Tennis, Hampton Court, Kew Gardens and Public Records Office, Windsor Castle, Heathrow and Gatwick Airports, M3/M4, A3, River Thames boat trips and interesting riverside walks — an ideal and economical alternative for business people, tourists and students and an excellent base for touring Southern England. TV and tea/coffee facilities. Parking no problem. £13.50 to £35 each per night. Reservations by post or telephone/Fax. Brochure on request. Tourist Board Member.

LONDON. Mrs B. Merchant, 562 Caledonian Road, Holloway, London N7 9SD (0171-607 0930). Comfortable well furnished rooms in small private home, full central heating. Two double and one single rooms, all non-smoking. Extra single beds for double rooms available. Eight bus routes; one minute for Trafalgar Square, Westminster, St Paul's. Piccadilly Line underground few minutes' walk. Direct Piccadilly and Heathrow. One-and-a-half miles King's Cross, Euston and St. Pancras Main Line Stations. Four and a half miles Piccadilly, three miles London Zoo and Hampstead Heath. Central for all tourist attractions. Unrestricted street parking. Full English Breakfast. Terms: £17.50 per person per night. Children under 10 years £15.50 per night. Minimum stay two nights. SAE, please.

Key to Tourist Board Ratings

The Crown Scheme
(England, Scotland & Wales)

Covering hotels, motels, private hotels, guesthouses, inns, bed & breakfast, farmhouses. Every Crown classified place to stay is inspected annually. *The classification:* Listed then 1-5 Crown indicates the range of facilities and services. Higher quality standards are indicated by the terms APPROVED, COMMENDED, HIGHLY COMMENDED and DELUXE.

The Key Scheme
(also operates in Scotland using a Crown symbol)

Covering self-catering in cottages, bungalows, flats, houseboats, houses; chalets, etc. Every Key classified holiday home is inspected annually. *The classification:* 1-5 Key indicates the range of facilities and equipment. Higher quality standards are indicated by the terms APPROVED, COMMENDED, HIGHLY COMMENDED and DELUXE.

The Q Scheme
(England, Scotland & Wales)

Covering holiday, caravan, chalet and camping parks. Every Q rated park is inspected annually for its quality standards. The more √ in the Q – up to 5 – the higher the standard of what is provided.

BEDFORDSHIRE

PULLOXHILL. Phil and Judy Tookey, Pond Farm, 7 High Street, Pulloxhill MK45 5HA (01525

712316). ETB Listed. Pond Farm is situated opposite the village green in Pulloxhill. Three miles from the A6 and five miles from the M1 Junction 12. We are within easy reach of Woburn Abbey and Safari Park, Whipsnade Zoo, The Shuttleworth Collection of Historic Aircraft at Old Warden and 11 miles from Luton Airport. Flitwick mainline station is only three miles away and 45 minutes by train to London. Pond Farm, built in the 17th century, is mainly arable although we have horses grazing on the meadow land. We also have a resident Great Dane. All bedrooms have tea/coffee facilities, washbasins and colour TV as no guest lounge is available. One WC and washbasin, one shower room with toilet and washbasin, one bathroom. Price from £15. Evening Meals at local inn.

SANDY. Mrs Joan M. Strong, Orchard Cottage, 1 High Street, Wrestlingworth, Near Sandy SG19

2EW (01767 631355). ☙ *COMMENDED.* Orchard Cottage is a picturesque 16th century thatched cottage with modern extension, formerly the village bakery. Comfortable accommodation includes one family and one twin bedrooms (both with washbasin), one single room; bathroom, shower, two toilets; diningroom and TV lounge. Centrally heated and no smoking throughout. Large, secluded garden. Ample parking. Cottage is situated in a quiet, country location on the Bedford/Cambridgeshire border convenient for visiting the Shuttleworth Collection of Historic Aeroplanes, RSPB, Wimpole Hall, Cambridge and Duxford. A1 and M11 nearby — convenient for travelling to London. Bed and Breakfast from £18, reductions for children.

BERKSHIRE

ASCOT. Graham and Sue Chapman, Lyndrick Guest House, The Avenue, Ascot SL5 8LS (01344 883520; Fax: 01344 891243). Lyndrick is a five bedroom Victorian house in a tree lined avenue. All bedrooms have colour TV and tea/coffee making facilities, most are en suite. Breakfast is served in a pleasant conservatory. Windsor 4 miles, Ascot Racecourse and Mill Ride Golf Club are two minutes and Wentworth and Sunningdale Golf Clubs are within 10 minutes. London/Waterloo 40 minutes by train; Heathrow Airport 25 minutes, easy access to M4, M3, M25 and A30. Open all year.

HENLEY-ON-THAMES near. Mrs H. Carver, Windy Brow, 204 Victoria Road, Wargrave RG10 8AJ

(0118 9403336). Tourist Board Listed *HIGHLY COMMENDED.* Detached Victorian family house in one third of an acre of garden. Ideal for touring the Thames valley, Windsor and Oxford; 30 minutes from Heathrow; 40 minutes from London by fast bus/train. Wargrave is a picturesque Thames-side village with excellent pubs. Accommodation consists of twin, family and single rooms all with colour TV; one double/twin (en-suite) on the ground floor available. Separate shower room and bathroom. Plenty of off-road parking. Coffee/tea facilities in rooms and hair dryer. Please phone for more details.

BERKSHIRE – OUTSTANDING NATURAL BEAUTY!

The North Wessex Downs, designated an 'Area of Natural Beauty' takes in much of Berkshire and the River Thames, the northern boundary of the county, is also a great attraction. Other places of interest include The Courage Shire Horse Centre, The Goning Gap, The Museum of English Rural Life at Reading and Windsor and Windsor Great Park.

NEWBURY. Mrs Kathleen Jones, Hillside Farm, Ashford Hill Road, Headley, Thatcham RG19 8AJ

(01635 268301). Large renovated Victorian farmhouse with garden in rural setting. A warm welcome in comfortable homely accommodation for tourists and businessmen alike; children and pets welcome. All rooms have colour TV, tea/coffee making facilities and central heating. Village pub serving food within walking distance. Bed and Breakfast from £17.50 each double, children half price sharing family room, cot free; £20 single; en suite also available. Directions: south of Newbury on A34, take A339 towards Basingstoke, in Headley take Ashford Hill Road, Hillside Farm is half a mile down on right.

READING, Three Mile Cross. Mrs M.S. Erdwin, Orchard House, Church Lane, Three Mile Cross, Reading RG7 1HD (01189 884457). Orchard House is well situated close to M4 Motorway, Heathrow 30 minutes away, Gatwick 45 minutes; Oxford 30 miles and London 35 miles (just 29 minutes by train); five minutes from Arborfield Garrison. Wealth of holiday interest to suit all tastes in the area. Ideal halt for that long journey to Cornwall or Wales. Accommodation all year round in this modern, large, homely house close to the Chilterns and Berkshire Downs. Children welcome. Babysitting can be arranged; high chair available. Evening drink; English or Continental Breakfast; Evening Meal/Light Supper available; Packed Lunches on request. Pets permitted at extra charge. Close to Thames, Kennet and Avon Canal/River for coarse fishing. Also close to Digital and Racal training centres. Tourist Board registered. Terms from £17.50 for Bed and Breakfast. Taxi service at moderate rates. SAE, please.

WINDSOR. Netherton Hotel, 96 St. Leonards Road, Windsor SL4 3DA (01753 855508). This recently

refurbished hotel offers a comfortable and friendly atmosphere. All rooms are en suite, with colour TV and tea/coffee making facilities. Also available are hairdryers and ironing facilities. There is a TV lounge for guests' use. Full English breakfast. We have a private car park and are only five minutes' walk from the town centre, train station, Castle, gardens, etc.

WINDSOR. Karen Jackson, Suffolk Lodge, 4 Bolton Avenue, Windsor SL4 3JB (01753 864186; Fax: 01753 862640). ♥♥ A large detached Victorian house situated in a quiet tree-lined avenue with private parking. Near castle, river, both railway stations and Legoland. Run by a family and highly recommended world-wide. All rooms have private facilities, direct dial telephone, colour TV, clock radio, coffee/tea facilities, shaver point, trouser press and hair dryer; also ironing facilities. Price includes full English breakfast. Heathrow 10 miles, Central London 25 miles, M4 two miles.

BUCKINGHAMSHIRE

HIGH WYCOMBE. Mrs Jane Vaughan, White House, North Road, Widmer End, High Wycombe

HP15 6ND (01494 712221). Built as three adjoining brick and flint cottages in the early 1700s, the White House was later extended and provides a restful, self contained suite to which many of our guests return time and time again. Fully modernised, it contains three rooms — a large restful bedroom, separate bathroom and toilet which remain apart from the rest of the house. The bedroom looks out onto the large garden and paddocks where ponies and sheep often graze during the year. A traditional or Continental breakfast is served. Accommodation consists of en suite twin room and en suite family room, (sleeps four). Bed and Breakfast from £17. Open all year.

CAMBRIDGESHIRE

CAMBRIDGE. Alan and Tracy Kilker, Six Steps Guest House, 93 Tenison Road, Cambridge CB1 2DJ (01223 353968; Fax: 01223 576702).

This family-run Victorian house is situated half a mile from the city centre and two minutes' walk from the railway station. All bedrooms have colour TV, telephone, beverage making facilities, heating, double glazing and shower, the majority have private toilet. A traditional English breakfast is served, vegetarian and special diets catered for. We can offer you morning newspapers, fax facilities, a baby listening service and ample car parking. Open all year round. All major credit cards accepted.

CAMBRIDGE. Mrs S. Barlow, Model Farm, Little Gransden, Sandy, Bedfordshire SG19 3EA (01767 677361).

A warm welcome awaits visitors to this traditional 1870s farmhouse situated on a working family farm. The farmhouse, providing comfortable and quiet accommodation with lovely views, is set in open countryside between the villages of Little Gransden and Longstowe. Guests are welcome to walk around the farm and garden. Model Farm is an ideal base for visiting Cambridge, Ely, Duxford Imperial War Museum, Shuttleworth (vintage aircraft and cars), Wimpole Hall and Farm (National Trust) and the RSPB at Sandy. M11, A1, A14 are all within 20 minutes' drive.

CAMBRIDGE. Mrs M.R. Jewitt, Blakemere, Old Mill Close, Barrington, Cambridge CB2 5SD (01223 871006).

A warm welcome awaits you in our comfortable family house quietly situated in a picturesque village with 22 acres of village green surrounded by thatched cottages. Barrington, easily located just off the A10 between Cambridge and Royston and four miles from M11, is ideal for Cambridge, Duxford War Museum, Wimpole Hall and many other places of interest. Good train service for London sightseeing. One twin room and two single rooms, all with colour TV, central heating and tea/coffee making facilities. Bed and Breakfast from £18. No smoking in bedrooms. No evening meal. Open all year, except Christmas period. Tourist Board registered.

CAMBRIDGE. Paul and Alison Tweddell, Dykelands Guest House, 157 Mowbray Road, Cambridge CB1 4SP (01223 244300; Fax: 01223 566746). 🏵 🏵

COMMENDED. Enjoy your visit to Cambridge by staying at our lovely detached guesthouse. Ideally located for city centre and for touring the secrets of the Cambridgeshire countryside. Easy access from M11 Junction 11, but only one and a half miles from the city centre, on a direct bus route. Near Addenbrookes Hospital. All bedrooms have colour TV, clock radio, tea/coffee making facilities; heating and double glazing; most with private shower or en-suite facilities; ground floor rooms available. Garden with children's play area for guests' use. Bed and full English Breakfast from £20singles, £34 doubles. Ample car parking. Access and Visa welcome. AA QQ. Open all year. Brochure on request.

Terms quoted in this publication may be subject to increase if rises in costs necessitate

CAMBRIDGE. Mrs Jean Wright, White Horse Cottage, 28 West Street, Comberton, Cambridge CB3

7DS (01223 262914). A 17th century cottage with all modern conveniences situated in a charming village four miles south west of Cambridge. Junction 12 off M11 — A603 from Cambridge, or A428 turn off at Hardwick Turning. Accommodation includes one double room, twin and family rooms. Own sitting room with colour TV; tea/coffee making facilities. Full central heating; parking. Excellent touring centre for many interesting places including Cambridge colleges, Wimpole Hall, Anglesey Abbey, Ely Cathedral, Imperial War Museum at Duxford and many more. Bed and Breakfast from £18 per person. Children welcome.

CAMBRIDGE. Cristina's Guest House, 47 St. Andrews Road, Cambridge CB4 1DH (01223 365855/

327700; Fax: 01223 365855). ❦❦ *COMMENDED.* Guests are assured of a warm welcome here, quietly located in the beautiful city of Cambridge, only 15 minutes' walk from the City Centre and colleges. All rooms have colour TV and tea/coffee making equipment, some rooms have private shower and toilet. Centrally heated with comfortable TV lounge. Private car park, locked at night. AA QQQ, RAC Acclaimed.

CAMBRIDGE (Caxton). Mr and Mrs Salt, The Old Vicarage, Gransden Road, Cambridge CB3 8PL (01954 719585). Beautiful old Vicrage in an acre of gardens, very quiet and peaceful approximately eight miles from centre of Cambridge, St. Neots, Royston, Huntingdon, St. Ives, Duxford. Large spacious theme room bedrooms and central heating throughout. Bed and Breakfast from £40 double. Please write or telephone for further information.

CAMBRIDGE near. Vicki Hatley, Manor Farm, Landbeach, Cambridge CB4 4ED (01223 860165).

Five miles from Cambridge and 10 miles from Ely. Vicki welcomes you to her carefully modernised Grade II Listed farmhouse, which is located next to the church in this attractive village. All rooms are either en suite or have private bathroom and are individually decorated. TV, clock radios and tea/coffee making facilties are provided in double, twin or family rooms. There is ample parking and guests are welcome to enjoy the secluded walled gardens. Bed and Breakfast from £19 per person double, and £25 single.

ELY. Mrs V. Beckum, Quarterway House, Ely Road, Little Thetford, Ely CB6 3HP (01353 648964).

Just two miles south of Ely, Quarterway House is ideally situated as a base for touring Cambridgeshire and East Anglia or walking the adjoining Fen River Way. Combining modern conveniences with traditional home comfort, all bedrooms have private/en suite bathrooms, individually controlled central heating, colour TV, radio alarm, tea/coffee making facilities, hair dryer and lovely views over the surrounding open countryside. Enjoy a warm welcome, relaxed friendly atmosphere, garden, conservatory and log fires in winter. A wide choice of breakfast is served in the farmhouse kitchen, with homemade preserves and eggs from our own free-range hens. Packed lunches, special diets and early breakfasts cheerfully catered for. Children over seven years welcome. Ample private parking. No smoking. Bed and Breakfast from £17.50.

ELY. Jenny Farndale, Cathedral House, 17 St. Mary's Street, Ely CB7 4ER (01353 662124).

Cathedral House is situated in the centre of Ely and within the shadow of its famous cathedral known as "The Ship of the Fens". Close by is Cromwell's House incorporating the TIC, the museum, shops, tea rooms and restaurants. A Grade II Listed house, it retains many original features and has a delightful walled garden. One twin, one double and one family bedrooms, all overlook the garden and are comfortably furnished with tea/coffee facilities and TV, are centrally heated and have en suite bathrooms. In cold months there is a log fire in the dining room. An ideal base for touring East Anglia, within easy reach of Cambridge, Welney and Wicken Fen wildlife reserves, Newmarket, Bury St. Edmunds and several National Trust properties. Open all year except Christmas and New Year. Off road parking. Prices from £20. Reductions for Short Breaks and weekly bookings. No smoking.

HEMINGFORD GREY. Maureen and Tony Webster, The Willow Guest House, 45 High Street, Hemingford Grey, St. Ives (Cambs.) PE18 9BJ (01480 494748).

Large private house in the centre of this picturesque village. 100 yards from a much photographed section of the Great Ouse River, and oldest (1150) inhabited house in England. One mile from 15th century bridge west of St. Ives, 15 minutes' drive from Cambridge City Centre. Family rooms, twin rooms, doubles and singles. All bedrooms are en suite and have colour TV, tea/coffee making facilities, hairdryers, clock radios, central heating. Private parking. Guest phone. Bed and Breakfast from £19 including VAT (full English Breakfast). Sorry no pets or smoking. Ideally situated for north/south and east/west travel being only one mile from A14 dual carriageway connecting M1-A1 and M11.

Bed & Breakfast at No. 19 West Street,
Kings Cliffe, Nr Stanford, Peterborough PE8 6XB
Telephone 01780 470365

A beautifully restored 500 year old listed stone house, reputedly one of King John's Hunting Lodges, situated in the heart of the stone village of Kings Cliffe on the edge of Rockingham Forest. Both the double and twin rooms have their own private bathrooms, and there is colour TV and a welcome tray in each. In the summer breakfast can be served on the terrace overlooking a beautiful walled garden. Off street parking is behind secure gates. Within 10 miles there are seven stately homes including Burghley House – famous for the Horse Trials, Rutland Water, and the beautiful old towns of Stamford and Oundle. Imaginative evening meals are available on request and prices range from £10 to £18. Open all year. Non smokers are much appreciated. *Bed and breakfast from £20 per person.*

MELBOURN. Peter and Monica Williams, Goldington Guest House, 1 New Road, Melbourn SG8 6BX (01763 260555; E-mail: peterw@dial.pipex.com). An attractive Victorian House with comfortably appointed family, twin, double and single rooms with TV and tea/coffee making facilities. Most bedrooms are equipped with fridges, microwave ovens and toasters. There is a private car park. We have been established for 27 years. Melbourn makes an ideal centre for visiting the historic city of Cambridge, just 10 miles away. From Royston Railway Station you can be in the heart of London within 45 minutes. Compare our tariff with London prices!! £18 per person per night. Children under five years free, six to 16 years sharing with two full paying guests £9.

CAMBRIDGESHIRE – FENLANDS AND CHALK HILLS!
Never is it easier to relax than when you are in Cambridgeshire. The flat fens in the north and gentle chalk hills in the south combine to create a unique ambience. Cambridge, a beautiful university town, is the final contribution to this county's perfection. Make sure you visit the twin villages of Hemingford Grey and Hemingford Abbots, Grafham Water, the Ouse Wash Reserves and Wicken Fen.

MILTON. Mrs V. Logan, Ambassador Lodge, 37 High Street, Milton, Cambridge CB4 6DF (01223

860168). Georgian House situated in village two miles from city centre; regular bus service close by. Easy access to A14, M11, A11, A1(M). Country park and River Cam within walking distance. Also close to renowned Cambridge Science Park and Regional College. En suite rooms available. TV and tea-making facilities in all rooms. Limited use of outdoor swimming pool. Off road enclosed parking. Please write or telephone for further details.

OVER. David and Julia Warren, Charter Cottage, Horse Ware, Over CB4 5NX (01954 230056; Fax:

01954 231062). A warm welcome and a friendly atmosphere await you in our peaceful cottage accommodation in an interesting corner of the village. Open all year, we offer two ground floor, centrally heated bedrooms, one twin bedded and one double, both with hot and cold water, tea/coffee making facilities and TV. Fully equipped bathroom also adjacent. Full English breakfast. Ample off-road parking, pleasant country garden with patio. Easy reach of Cambridge, Ely and St. Ives. Bed and Breakfast £17 single, £30 double. Directions: A14 Cambridge to Huntingdon, follow signs to Over, then first left immediately after Over Church.

ST. NEOTS. Mrs Eileen Raggatt, The Ferns, Berkley Street, Eynesbury, St. Neots PE19 2NE (01480

213884). An 18th century house (private family home) in large garden situated on Eynesbury Green. Two rooms available with double bed plus single bed, one with private bathroom, the other with washbasin. Central heating. Charges from £17 per person for Bed and Breakfast, reduced rates for children under 10. St. Neots is a market town on the River Ouse just off the A1; one and a half hours north of London, 16 miles west of Cambridge.

WISBECH. Jayne Best, Four Winds, Mill Lane, Newton, Wisbech PE13 5HZ (01945 870479; Fax:

01945 870274). Charming country house situated in the midst of the Fens countryside, although only four miles from Wisbech and close to King's Lynn, Norfolk coast (28 miles). Ideally situated for touring, fishing and cycling. Accommodation comprises one double en suite with shower, one twin en suite with bath, two singles with washbasins and one main bathroom with Airspa. Private parking. Terms from £17.

WYTON. Robin and Marion Seaman, The Elms, Banks End, Wyton, Huntingdon PE17 2AA (01480 453523). Rambling Edwardian house close to picturesque village of Houghton and Wyton, off the A1123 two miles between historic market towns of Huntingdon and St. Ives; five minutes from A1 and A14; M11 15 minutes. One double en suite room, one twin en suite room, and two single rooms with washbasins and private bathroom. All have tea/coffee making facilities and colour TV. Guests' sittingroom. Central heating. Bed and Breakfast from £19 per person. Non smoking. No pets. Friendly personal service and a warm welcome assured.

CHESHIRE

ALTRINCHAM. Dr Yau, Oasis Hotel, 46/48 Barrington Road, Altrincham WA14 1HN (0161-928 4523; Fax: 0161-928 1099). The Oasis Hotel is situated within walking distance of Altrincham Town Centre with Metrolink direct to Manchester City Centre and a short distance from Manchester International Airport with easy access from M6, M56, M63. All bedrooms include colour TV, coffee making facilities and have en suite shower rooms. Terms: Single room £30 per night; Double/Twin £45 per night; Family room (two beds) £50 per night; Family room (three beds) £55 per night. Prices include full English breakfast. Weekend £10 reduction.

BALTERLEY (near Crewe). Mrs Joanne Hollins, Balterley Green Farm, Deans Lane, Balterley, Near Crewe CW2 5QJ (01270 820214). 🐾 👑 *COMMENDED.* **Working farm, join in.** Jo and Pete Hollins offer guests a friendly welcome to their home on a 145-acre dairy farm in quiet and peaceful surroundings. Green Farm is situated on the Cheshire/Staffordshire border and is within easy reach of Junction 16 on the M6. An excellent stop-over place for travellers journeying between north and south of the country. We also offer a pets' corner and pony rides for young children. One family room en suite, one single and one twin-bedded room on ground floor suitable for disabled guests. Tea making facilities and TV in all rooms. Children welcome — cot provided. This area offers many attractions; we are within easy reach of historic Chester, Alton Towers and the famous Potteries of Staffordshire. Open all year. Bed and Breakfast from £16 per person.

CHESTER. Nigel and Clare Hill, Cotton Farmhouse, Cotton Edmunds, Chester CH3 7PT (Tel & Fax: 01244 336699). Our large farmhouse is only four miles from Chester yet set in beautiful open countryside, off the beaten track, providing a peaceful and memorable stay. The house has recently undergone extensive, sympathetic, internal renovation and offers three spacious bedrooms all with en suite bathrooms, central heating, tea/coffee making, radio alarm clock and colour TV. Walk the walls of Chester and learn about the city's Roman history. Visit the 900 year old cathedral or just relax in our lovely countryside. Bed and Breakfast from £23. Non-smoking accommodation.

CHESTER. Mr D.R. Bawn, The Gables Guest House, 5 Vicarage Road, Hoole, Chester CH2 3HZ (01244 323969). 🐾 Guests are welcomed to this pleasant Victorian family house situated in a quiet residential area just off the main bus route. Near park and tennis courts. Makes an ideal base for touring with easy access to all major roads. AA and RAC Listed, the guest house offers accommodation in family, double and twin bedrooms; hot and cold, central heating throughout, remote control colour TV and tea-making facilities; bathroom, shower room facilities. Television lounge. Open from January to December. Open parking. Bed and Breakfast from £16 per person; weekly terms available. Reductions for children.

CHESTER. Mrs Helen Mitchell, Mitchell's of Chester, Green Gables, 28 Hough Green, Chester CH4

8JQ (Tel & Fax: 01244 679004). 🌹🌹 *HIGHLY COMMENDED.* Relax in this tastefully restored Victorian residence set in campact landscaped gardens and secluded forecourt. The tall well appointed corniced rooms are complemented by a sweeping staircase and antique furniture. This small family run guest house has all en suite rooms with hospitality tray, alarm clock, hair dryer and many other comforts. It is within walking distance of the ancient Roman walled city with its wealth of historic buildings and its famous race course. It is also the gateway to North Wales. Guests have the convenience of a pay phone, off street parking, local golf course and being on a main bus route. We are situated on the south side of Chester on the A5104. Bed and breakfast from £20 per person.

CHESTER CITY. Frank and Maureen Brady, Holly House, 41 Liverpool Road, Chester CH2 1AB

(01244 383484). Holly House is a Victorian townhouse on the A5116, offering a friendly welcome in quiet, elegant surroundings. Comfort and high standards are our priority. Only five minutes' walk from the famous Roman walls which encircle this historic city with its 11th century Cathedral, castle, museum of Roman artifacts, buildings of architectural interest, Amphitheatre, walks by the river, shopping in "The Rows". Spacious accommodation comprises double room with en suite bathroom, two doubles with private showers; two of the rooms are available as family rooms. TV, tea/coffee facilities, own keys. Parking. Bed and Breakfast from £16 to £19 or as family rooms at £11 per additional person supplement. Vegetarians catered for. Non-smoking. A warm welcome from Frank and Maureen Brady.

CHESTER near. Mrs Jennifer Legge, The Hermitage, Church Lane, Neston, South Wirral L64 9US (0151-336 5171). Spacious twin bedded room with adjacent private bathroom and separate toilet in Georgian house with large secluded garden and views to the River Dee and the Welsh hills. Additional accommodation in self-contained converted coach house in the garden (sleeps three/four). The house is in a very quiet location but close to the village centre and is convenient for Chester, Liverpool, North Wales, Ness Gardens and golf courses. Bed and Breakfast from £17.

CHURCH MINSHULL. Brian and Mary Charlesworth, Higher Elms Farm, Minshull Vernon, Crewe

CW1 4RG (01270 522252). 🌹🌹 EN SUITE AVAILABLE. A 400 year old farmhouse on working farm. Oak-beamed comfort in dining and sitting rooms, overlooking Shropshire Union Canal. No dinners served but four pubs within two miles. Interesting wildlife around. Convenient for M6 but tucked away in the countryside; from M6 Junction 18, off A530 towards Nantwich. Family room, double, twin and single rooms all have colour TV, washbasin and tea/coffee facilities. Well behaved pets welcome. Within 15 miles of Jodrell Bank, Oulton Park, Bridgemere Garden World, Stapeley Water Gardens, Nantwich and Chester. Bed and Breakfast from £18. Half price for children under 12 years.

DELAMERE near. Mr and Mrs J. Mulholland, Springfield Guest House, Chester Road, Oakmere,

Near Delamere CW8 2HB (01606 882538). 🌹🌹 *COMMENDED.* Built in 1863 on the edge of Delamere Forest in the Vale Royal District of Cheshire. On the main A556, a direct route to the M6 and Manchester Airport. Chester 10 miles, Northwich six miles. Local places of interest include stately homes and gardens, canal waterways, the Boat and Salt Museums, Sandstone Trail Walkway, Oulton Park Motor Racing Circuit and golf courses. Spacious grounds and car parking facilities. Please send for our brochure.

WHEN MAKING ENQUIRIES PLEASE MENTION
FARM HOLIDAY GUIDES

FRODSHAM. Mrs Susan Ward, Long Croft, Dark Lane, Kingsley WA6 8BW (01928 787193). In a delightful secluded country lane and standing in an acre of woodland, Long Croft offers a wealth of charm and character together with modern conveniences. Double and twin-bedded rooms, both with en suite facilities, TV and tea/coffee making facilities; guests' own sitting room with private dining room overlooking secluded patio. Plenty of good pubs in the area and reasonably priced restaurants in Frodsham, a pretty market town just two miles away. Within striking distance of Chester, Manchester, Liverpool and North Wales and on the doorstep of Oulton Park racing circuit and Delamere Forest. Children welcome. Home cooked traditional English breakfast with own free range eggs. Evening meals specially prepared as requested. From £18 per person; reductions for children.

HARTFORD. Dee and Edwin McDonnell, "The Stables", Beech Road, Hartford CW8 3AB (01606 783752). Conveniently situated for Chester, North Wales and Manchester "The Stables" is an attractive stable conversion standing in its own grounds with open aspect. The small market town of Northwich is within walking distance. Accommodation comprises one double and one twin-bedded room, both non-smoking and have en suite facilities and complimentary tea/coffee tray. A feature of the house is its vaulted lounge which is available for use by guests. Open all year round, the accommodation is centrally heated and has ample parking space. Bed and Breakfast from £20 per person; Evening Meal on request.

HYDE, near Manchester. Mrs Charlotte R. Walsh, Needhams Farm, Uplands Road, Werneth Low, Gee Cross, Near Hyde SK14 3AQ (0161-368 4610). ♥♥♥ *COMMENDED.* **Working farm.** A cosy 16th century farmhouse set in peaceful, picturesque surroundings by Werneth Low Country Park and the Etherow Valley, which lie between Glossop and Manchester. The farm is ideally situated for holidaymakers and businessmen, especially those who enjoy peace and quiet, walking and rambling, golfing and riding, as these activities are all close by. At Needhams Farm everyone, including children and pets, receives a warm welcome. Good wholesome meals available in the evenings. Residential licence and Fire Certificate held. Open all year. Bed and Breakfast from £18 single minimum to £32 double maximum; Evening Meal £7. AA Listed, RAC Acclaimed.

KINGSLEY. Mrs Susan Klin, Charnwood, Hollow Lane, Kingsley WA6 8EF (01928 787097). AA Recommended QQQ. Charnwood provides spacious accommodation, set in its own landscaped grounds in the delightful village of Kingsley. Close by are Oulton Park and Delamere Forest. Also ideally situated for historic Chester just 20 minutes away, Granada Studios at Manchester, and Albert Docks in Liverpool 30 minutes away by car. A wide range of luxury accommodation is available from £18 per person, including a private suite sleeping up to five people. Each room adjoins a private comfortable sittingroom with TV. All rooms have colour TV, tea/coffee making facilities and hair dryers. Fax and photocopying services are available. Full traditional English breakfast is served in a comfortable dining room overlooking the garden. Secure parking provided.

KNUTSFORD. Virginia Brown, Pickmere House, Park Lane, Pickmere, Knutsford WA16 0JX (Tel & Fax: 01565 733433; Mobile 0831 384460). ♥♥ AA QQQ, RAC Highly Acclaimed. A Listed Georgian farmhouse in rural hamlet close to Arley Hall and Tatton Park, two miles west of M6 Junction 19 on B5391 giving swift access to airport and all major north west towns and tourist attractions. Spacious en suite rooms with TV, tea/coffee trays and hairdryers, overlooking farmlands. Parking at rear. No smoking policy. Bed and Breakfast £19.50 to £29.50 single, £42 to £44 double/twin; Evening Meal/Dinner £9.50. Minibus groups by negotiation. AA Approved. Also Mews Cottage (two bedrooms, two bathrooms) available for self catering lets.

MACCLESFIELD. Ann and Owen Thomas, Moorhayes House Hotel, 27 Manchester Road, Tytherington, Macclesfield SK10 2JJ (Tel & Fax: 01625 433228). ✿ ✿ ✿ *COMMENDED.* We welcome you and your children to Moorhayes House Hotel, situated half a mile north of Macclesfield town centre on the A538 at Tytherington, 20 minutes east of Junction 17 on the M6. Standing well back from the road surrounded by a large, quiet, mature garden, our 1930's house has nine comfortably furnished bedrooms, some ground floor, many with en suite facilities and garden views. Hostess trays and colour TV are in all rooms. Ample parking in grounds. Dogs welcome by prior arrangement. Excellent reasonably priced restaurant and pubs provide good food and atmosphere nearby. Situated between Chester and Buxton on the edge of the Peak National Park and only 25 minutes from Manchester and the airport, we are ideally placed for exploring the city, historic houses and the beautiful countryside of Cheshire and Derbyshire. Bed and Breakfast from £19.50 to £36 per person per night; Evening Meal from £6.50 to £10.

SANDBACH. Mrs Helen Wood, Arclid Grange, Arclid Green, Sandbach CW11 0SZ (01270 764750; Fax: 01270 759255). Set in the lovely Cheshire countryside, yet within one mile of Junction 17 M6, Arclid Grange offers six attractive double/twin-bedded rooms. All rooms have en-suite bathrooms, colour TV, tea/coffee making facilities, direct dial telephones. Delicious home-cooked meals are served in the beamed diningroom. Cosy log fires in winter. Residential licence. Ample private car parking. Standing in its own mature gardens, this recently extended Cheshire farmhouse has all the charm and character of an old house, combined with comfortable, modern accommodation — rated Category 3 for disabled facilities. Bed and Breakfast from £25 per person, Dinner from £15.

FOR THE MUTUAL GUIDANCE
OF GUEST AND HOST

Every year literally thousands of holidays, short-breaks and overnight stops are arranged through our guides, the vast majority without any problems at all. In a handful of cases, however, difficulties do arise about bookings, which often could have been prevented from the outset.

It is important to remember that when accommodation has been booked, both parties — guests and hosts — have entered into a form of contract. We hope that the following points will provide helpful guidance.

GUESTS: When enquiring about accommodation, be as precise as possible. Give exact dates, numbers in your party and the ages of any children. State the number and type of rooms wanted and also what catering you require — bed and breakfast, full board, etc. Make sure that the position about evening meals is clear — and about pets, reductions for children or any other special points.

Read our reviews carefully to ensure that the proprietors you are going to contact can supply what you want. Ask for a letter confirming all arrangements, if possible.

If you have to cancel, do so as soon as possible. Proprietors do have the right to retain deposits and under certain circumstances to charge for cancelled holidays if adequate notice is not given and they cannot re-let the accommodation.

HOSTS: Give details about your facilities and about any special conditions. Explain your deposit system clearly and arrangements for cancellations, charges, etc, and whether or not your terms include VAT.

If for any reason you are unable to fulfil an agreed booking without adequate notice, you may be under an obligation to arrange alternative suitable accommodation or to make some form of compensation.

While every effort is made to ensure accuracy, we regret that FHG Publications cannot accept responsibility for errors, omissions or misrepresentation of our entries or any consequences thereof. Prices in particular should be checked because we go to press early. We will follow up complaints but cannot act as arbiters or agents for either party.

CORNWALL

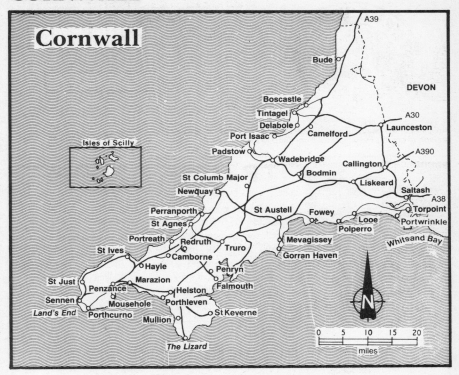

BODMIN. **Mrs Jenny Bass, Trehannick Farm, St. Teath, Bodmin PL30 3JW (01208 850312).**

Working farm. Mentioned in the Domesday Book in 1086, Trehannick is a family farm situated in the beautiful Allen Valley. Safe sandy beaches, coastal walks, golf, sailing and fishing are all within easy reach of this peaceful farmhouse. All rooms have beautiful south-facing views and the usual amenities (tea/coffee making facilities, etc). One double room is en suite. Non-smoking throughout. Ample parking. Sorry no pets. Please telephone for further details.

BODMIN. **Mrs S. Menhinick, Loskeyle Farm, St. Tudy, Bodmin PL30 3PW (01208 851005).** ♛

COMMENDED. Loskeyle is a working dairy farm in the Duchy of Cornwall where a warm welcome awaits you. Relax and enjoy the peace and tranquillity of farm life here where you can watch the milking, feed the hens, collect eggs or enjoy leisurely walks through open fields. Children especially welcome with reduced rates. Delicious farmhouse cooking using fresh local produce. Pretty bedrooms with tea/coffee facilities and vanity units. Ideal base for north/south coasts. Golf, Camel Trail nearby, also pony trekking over the moors only a stone's throw away. Bed and Breakfast from £15; Evening Meal £10.

BOSCASTLE. Mrs Cheryl Nicholls, Trerosewill Farm, Paradise, Boscastle PL35 0DL (01840 250545). Working farm. ♨♨♨ *HIGHLY COMMENDED.*

AA QQQQ Selected. Bed and Breakfast accommodation in modern farmhouse on working farm, only a short walk from the picturesque village of Boscastle. Rooms have spectacular coastal and rural views; all en suite, with tea making facilities. Colour TV and telephone available if required. Four-posters, mineral water and bath robes provided. Licensed. Centrally heated. Seasonal log fires. Large gardens. Traditional farmhouse fayre. Feed the calves. Superb coastal and countryside walks. Specially negotiated rates for nearby golf and pony trekking. One way walks arranged. Packed lunches available. Spring and Autumn breaks. Bed and Breakfast from £16. Strictly no smoking. FHG Diploma Award 1995.

TREHANE FARM

Trevalaga, Boscastle PL35 0EB   ♨♨ Commended

Welcome to Trehane, a dairy farm on the spectacular North Cornwall Heritage coast. Our farmhouse is set in a magnificent position overlooking the sea with superb coastal views. We offer a comfortable friendly atmosphere and wholesome nourishing food using fresh farm produce and home baked bread. Enjoy fine walks along the coast or inland on to Bodmin Moor. You can even learn to spin in this lovely place! We can accommodate six guests, children welcome – pets by arrangement. Bed and Breakfast from £17.

Proprietor: Mrs Sarah James – Telephone: 01840 250510

BOSCASTLE. Graham and Hazel Mee, Bottreaux House Hotel and Restaurant, Boscastle PL35 0BG (01840 250231; www.i.p.l.co.uk/bottreaux). ♨♨♨

HIGHLY COMMENDED. Boscastle is the Jewel of North Cornwall, a beautiful village stretching from the old harbour up the sides of the Jordan and Valency Valleys. The Bottreaux House Hotel which overlooks the village and surrounding hills is privately owned; seven en suite bedrooms, lounge, romantic candlelit restaurant. Car parking. When you stay with us you can be sure of a welcoming and relaxed atmosphere. Pets and children by arrangement. Free use of mountain bikes. Spring Specials from £14 to High Season from £20 per person for Bed and Breakfast. If you would like our free video of the hotel and surrounding area please telephone.

BOSCASTLE. Ruth and Michael Parsons, The Old Coach House, Tintagel Road, Boscastle PL35 0AS (01840 250 398; Fax: 01840 250 346). ♨♨ AA

and RAC Listed. Relax in a 300 year old former coach house now tastefully equipped to meet the needs of the late 1990's with all rooms en-suite, colour TVs, radios, tea/coffee makers and central heating. Accessible for disabled guests. Good cooking. This picturesque village is a haven for walkers with its dramatic coastal scenery, a photographer's dream, and an ideal base to tour both the north and south coasts. The area is famed for its sandy beaches and surfing whilst King Arthur's Tintagel is only three miles away. Come and enjoy a friendly holiday with people who care. Brochure on request. Bed and Breakfast from £18 to £20.

BOSCASTLE. Mr J. Perfili, Trefoil Farm, New Road, Boscastle PL35 0AD (01840 250606). Trefoil Farm is situated on the boundary of Boscastle, overlooking the harbour, valley and ocean. On the farm we breed and show pedigree Suffolk sheep. Large gardens to sit and relax in. Accommodation comprises family, double rooms, fully en suite, with colour TV and tea/coffee making facilities. Full central heating, TV, lounge, seasonal log fires. Full English breakfast. Evening meal optional, traditional farmhouse fare. There are superb coastal and countryside walks, and one way walks can be arranged. Leisure facilities, sandy beaches nearby. Spring and Autumn Breaks. No pets. No smoking in the house. Bed and Breakfast from £16.50 to £18.

Stamford Hill Hotel
"A Country House Hotel"

Set in five acres of gardens and woodland overlooking open countryside yet only a mile from the sandy beaches of Bude. Our spacious Georgian Manor House with 15 en-suite bedrooms with TV and tea/coffee making facilities, outdoor heated pool, tennis court, badminton court, games room and sauna is the ideal place for a relaxing holiday or short break. Daily Bed and Breakfast from £24.50; Three-day Break Dinner, Bed and Breakfast from £99. Pets welcome. ♥♥♥ Commended.

Contact: Ian and Joy McFeat, Stamford Hill Hotel, Stratton, Bude EX23 9AY Tel: (01288) 352709.

BUDE. Mrs Christine Nancekivell, Dolsdon Farm, Boyton, Launceston PL15 8NT (01288 341264).

Dolsdon was once a 17th century coaching inn, now modernised, situated on the Launceston to Bude road within easy reach of sandy beaches, surfing, Tamar Otter Park, leisure centre with heated swimming pool, golf courses, fishing, tennis and horse riding and is ideal for touring Cornwall and Devon. Guests are welcome to wander around the 260 acre working farm. All bedrooms have washbasins and tea making facilities (en suite family room available). Comfortably furnished lounge has colour TV. Plenty of good home cooking assured — full English breakfast. Parking. Bed and Breakfast from £15; reductions for children. Brochure available.

BUDE. Mrs Rosina Joyner, "Penrose", Dizzard, St. Gennys, Bude EX23 0NX (01840 230318).

Penrose is a delightful 17th century cottage with beamed ceilings and inglenook fireplaces. Tastefully modernised, yet retaining all its Olde Worlde charm. Set in one and a half acres of lawns and gardens within the National Trust area, close to the coastal path. It is ideal for those seeking peace and quiet. Nearby is the beautiful beach of Widemouth Bay. The views from the cottage are extensive. All bedrooms have washbasins, TV and tea/coffee making facilities; two rooms have double four-poster beds (one with shower). One bedroom with king-size bed with canopy, en suite and with sea views; ground floor en suite room suitable for disabled guests. Good English Breakfast, optional Evening Meal. Also available is a mobile home and cottage annexe for self catering; both sleep six from £150 low season to £375 high season. SAE, or phone, for booking form, brochure. Bed and Breakfast from £17.50 per night per person.

BUDE. Mrs Angela Mary Grills, Trelay, Marhamchurch, Bude EX23 0HP (01288 361218). Working

dairy farm for you to enjoy. Trelay has a large farmhouse and garden and is situated in the centre of a 360 acre dairy and arable farm where you may relax at your leisure. Although we are situated in the middle of the countryside, Widemouth Bay, a large surfing beach, is within approximately two miles and Bude is only three miles away. Our local village of Marhamchurch with its pub is only one mile. Market towns and Bodmin and Dartmoor are within easy reach. Two bedrooms, one en site, both with tea making facilities. A good farmhouse breakfast is served. Children welcome. Lounge with colour TV. Terms from £14 to £16.

FREE and REDUCED RATE Holiday Visits!
See our READERS' OFFER VOUCHER for details.

BUDE. Mr and Mrs M.J. Whattler, Marhayes Manor, Marhamchurch, Bude EX23 0HJ (Tel & Fax:

01288 341321; Mobile: 0831 742508). Grade II Listed farmhouse dating from Domesday. The existing building mainly circa 1640. It is set in 100 acres of the Cornish countryside yet only three miles from Widemouth Bay and National Trust coastline. We offer two bedrooms — one large double/family room, the other very large bed/sitting room with twin beds, bathroom, separate sittingroom/kitchen faclity. Tea/coffee provided. Colour TV, fridge/freezer, washing machine, iron and ironing board, food heating facilities, drying facilities all available. Central heating, wood burner. Private walled garden. Ample parking. Non-smoking. Bed and Breakfast from £15.

BUDE. Mrs S.A. Trewin, Lower Northcott Farm, Poughill, Bude EX23 7EL (01288 352350). ♥ ♥

COMMENDED. **Working farm.** Lower Northcott is built of stone in Georgian design and is situated one mile north of Bude. Set on the side of a secluded valley with outstanding views of the rugged Heritage coastline. All rooms are en suite and spacious with very comfortable furnishings. Tea/coffee facilities. Home cooking is our speciality. Children welcome. Open all year. Central heating. Bed and Breakfast from £17 per person.

BUDE. Michael and Pearl Hopper, West Nethercott Farm, Whitstone, Holsworthy (Devon) EX22

6LD (01288 341394). Working farm, join in. A warm welcome awaits you on this dairy and sheep farm. Watch the cows being milked, help with the animals. Free pony rides, scenic farm walks. Short distance from sandy beaches, surfing and the rugged North Cornwall coast. Ideal base for visiting any part of Devon or Cornwall. We are located in Cornwall though our postal address is Devon. The traditional farmhouse has washbasins and TV in bedrooms; diningroom and separate lounge with colour TV. Plenty of excellent home cooking. Access to the house at anytime. Bed and Breakfast from £13, four course Evening Meal available. Children under 12 years reduced rates. Weekly terms available.

CAMBORNE. Mrs Christine Peerless, Highdowns, Blackrock, Praze-an-Beeble, Camborne TR14

9PD (01209 831442). Highdowns is a comfortable, quiet and ideally situated base from which to explore the beautiful Cornish countryside and magnificent coastline. Set on a south-west facing hillside with extensive views towards St. Ives Bay. We offer traditional home-made and varied meals using fresh home grown and local produce whenever available with special and vegetarian diets catered for. All bedrooms en suite with tea/coffee making facilities. TV lounge. Easy parking. Fire Certificate. No smoking. Bed and Breakfast from £18 per night; Evening Meal £8.

CORNWALL – LAND'S END AND THE ISLES OF SCILLY

Britain's most westerly point, Land's End, is now under private ownership and offers multi-sensory exhibitions, craft workshops and play areas to the many thousands of visitors who are attracted by its unique, breathtaking views.

The 200-odd Isles of Scilly lie 22 miles south-west of Land's End (access by plane, ferry or helicopter). The temperate climate allows visitors to enjoy exotic flowers, palm trees and tropical gardens, and the islands are a bird-watcher's paradise (May and June are the best months).

FALMOUTH. Mrs D. Nethercot, "Telford", 47 Melvill Road, Falmouth TR11 4DG (01326 314581).

"Excellent accommodation, good food — see you again" — an actual quote from our Visitors' Book. Why don't YOU try our guest house this year for your annual holiday or out-of-season break? We really do try and make your holiday a happy one and many guests return annually. We are Cornwall Tourist Board registered and mentioned in Arthur Eperon's "Travellers' Britain". Singles, doubles and twin rooms are available, all with colour TV and complimentary tea-making facilities. En suite rooms. Private parking. Open March to mid-October. Tariff: Bed and Breakfast from £98 weekly.

FALMOUTH. Mrs Jean Eustice, Trevu House Hotel, 45 Melvill Road, Falmouth TR11 4DG (Tel & Fax: 01326 312852).

Trevu House is a small family-run hotel with a friendly home-from-home atmosphere, with special emphasis on comfort, cleanliness and personal service. The situation is ideal for a seaside holiday, being only about two minutes' walk from Gyllyngvase Beach and within easy reach of the town, harbour and local railway station. Spacious accommodation is tastefully furnished with bright modern decor. Large comfortable lounge and reading room. Bedrooms are en-suite and have modern divan beds, colour TVs, tea/coffee making facilities and central heating. We pride ourselves on our high standard of cuisine which is well presented and served at separate tables complemented, if required, by a variety of wines. Bed and Breakfast from £15.50. No single room supplement. Full Fire Certificate held. Car parking. Brochure available on request.

FALMOUTH. Celia and Ian Carruthers, Harbour House, 1 Harbour Terrace, Falmouth TR11 2AN (01326 311344).

AA Recommended (QQQ). Enjoy quality bed and breakfast accommodation, with some of the most fantastic harbour views in Cornwall. Clean, comfortable, tastefully decorated bedrooms with TVs and hot drink making facilities, half en suite. Delicious home cooking with a generous and varied menu. Close to idyllic walks, secluded coves, creekside pubs, watersports, ancient castles and country houses. Two minutes' walk into town. Private car parking. Drying and storage facilities for sailing, diving, walking gear, etc. Bed and Breakfast from a very reasonable £14.50. We welcome guests for short or long stays, almost all year. Please call for a brochure, directions or to check availability.

FOWEY. Bob and Jill Bullock, Trevanion Guest House, 70 Lostwithiel Street, Fowey PL23 1BQ (01726 832602). ETB Listed *COMMENDED*. AA QQQ. A warm and friendly welcome awaits you at this comfortable and spacious 16th century merchant's house. Situated in the historic estuary town of Fowey in the heart of Daphne Du Maurier country, it is an ideal base from which to walk the South West Coastal Path, visit the lost gardens of Heligan and local National Trust houses and gardens or explore the Cornish Riviera. En suite facilities available and all rooms are well furnished and have washbasins, colour TV and tea/coffee making facilities. Non-smoking. From £15 per person per night.

FOWEY. Mrs Moss, Trenant Guest House, Fowey PL23 1JU (01726 833477; Fax: 01726 832192).

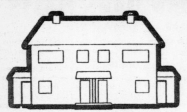

Trenant is a family-run guest house set well away from the road in a quiet valley. We are situated between Fowey and Par. The large extensive garden includes a kiddies' play area. Families are welcome, a cot and high chair available on request. All bedrooms have tea and coffee making facilities, razor points and washbasins. We have a comfortable lounge with colour TV and SKY. There are rural views from most of the rooms and ample parking space. Fowey, itself, is an enchanting town together with the superb estuary looking across to Bodinnick and Polruan.

FOWEY. David and Jenny Parnwell, Lanherriot Farm, Fowey PL23 1JT (Tel & Fax: 01726 832637; E-mail: Lanherriot@saqnet.co.uk).

Situated two miles from the harbour of Fowey, Lanherriot Farm is an ideal holiday base to explore Cornwall's beaches and tourist attractions. Set amidst rolling fields, the 10 acre site includes an outdoor heated swimming pool with patio, woodland, orchard and fields with two donkeys. The house offers a warm welcome with special attention to comfort and courtesy in two double and one twin room all with southerly aspect, TV, central heating and tea/coffee facilities. Two bathrooms and one shower. Full or Continental breakfast and three course evening meals available. Prices from £15 per person. Discounts available for Short Breaks and for children. Brochure on request.

HELSTON. Mr Joe Gormley, Alma House, Mullion, Helston TR12 7BZ (01326 240509).

A warm and friendly guest house with fully licensed restaurant offering Bed and Breakfast with Evening Meal available. Situated in the centre of Mullion with lovely sea views, car parking at the rear. Each room offers remote control TV and tea/coffee making facilities. Large lounge and well stocked bar. Rooms range from £18 to £20 (en suite). Reduced rates out of season. A warm welcome and comfortable stay assured.

HELSTON. Mrs J. Lugg, Tregaddra Farm, Cury Cross Lanes, Helston TR12 7BB (Tel & Fax: 01326 240235). ✿✿✿ *HIGHLY COMMENDED.* **Working farm.**

AA QQQQ Selected. Tregaddra is an early 18th century farmhouse set in half-an-acre of well-kept gardens. Ideally situated in the centre of The Lizard Peninsula with views of peaceful rolling countryside for a 15 mile radius. Pretty, large en suite bedrooms; inglenook fireplace in lounge, farmhouse Aga cooking and local produce used. Out of season breaks with candlelit dining room and open log fires for chilly evenings. Coastal walks, sailing, sandy beaches, horse riding, golf all nearby. Drying facilities for walking boots, etc. A warm welcome and family hospitality guaranteed. Send for colour brochure and local information.

HELSTON. Mrs P. Roberts, Hendra Farm, Wendron, Helston TR13 0NR (01326 340470). Hendra

Farm, just off the main Helston/Falmouth road, is an ideal centre for touring Cornwall; three miles to Helston, eight to both Redruth and Falmouth. Safe sandy beaches within easy reach — five miles to the sea. Beautiful views from the farmhouse of the 60 acre beef farm. Two double, one single, and one family bedrooms; bathroom and toilets; sitting room and two dining rooms. Cot, babysitting and reduced rates offered for children. No objection to pets. Car necessary, parking space. Enjoy good cooking with roast beef, pork, lamb, chicken, genuine Cornish pasties, fish and delicious sweets and cream. Open all year except Christmas. Evening Dinner, Bed and Breakfast from £110 per week which includes cooked breakfast, three course evening dinner, tea and home made cake before bed. Bed and Breakfast only from £12 per night also available.

HELSTON near. Mrs D.J. Hill, "Rocklands", The Lizard, Near Helston TR12 7NX (01326 290339).

"Rocklands" is situated overlooking part of Cornwall's superb coastline and enjoys uninterrupted sea views. The Lizard is well known for its lovely picturesque scenery, coastal walks and enchanting coves and beaches, as well as the famous Serpentine Stone which is quarried and sold locally. Open Easter to October. The Hill family have been catering for visitors on the Lizard since the 1850's. Three bedrooms with sea views, tea/coffee making facilities and electric heaters; sittingroom with TV and video; sun lounge; dining room with separate tables. Bed and Breakfast weekly terms from £126 per person. NO VAT. Children and well trained pets welcome.

LAUNCESTON. Maggie Fancourt, The Old Vicarage, Launceston PL15 8UQ (01566 781351). ETB

🌸🌸 *HIGHLY COMMENDED.* An elegant Grade II Listed Georgian Vicarage in an idyllic peaceful rural setting near the spectacular North Cornwall coast between Launceston and Boscastle. Ideally located as a touring base. Renowned for our hospitality and excellent food which, together with personal service and highest standards throughout, ensure your absolute comfort. A restful conservatory overlooks the garden. The en suite bedrooms are individually furnished and have fresh flowers, TV, tea/coffee, home made biscuits and other personal touches. Superb food, using produce from our own organic kitchen gardens. Delicious jams, marmalades, biscuits, cakes and even ice cream — all home made! Totally non-smoking. Bed and Breakfast from £21 to £24.

LAUNCESTON. Mary Rich, "Nathania", Altarnun, Launceston PL15 7SL (01566 86426). Christian couple offer Bed, Breakfast and Evening Meal accommodation on a small farm on Bodmin Moor within easy reach of coast, moors, towns, lakes and fishing. Visit King Arthur country — Tintagel, Dozmary Pool, famous Jamaica Inn, Wesley Cottage and cathedral of the moors. Double and twin rooms with en suite bathroom and tea making facilities. Conservatory and lounge for quiet relaxation. Prices from £10.50 per person per night. Please telephone, or write, for details — SAE, thank you.

LISKEARD. Mrs Stephanie Rowe, Tregondale Farm, Menheniot, Liskeard PL14 3RG (Tel & Fax:

01579 342407). 🌸🌸 *HIGHLY COMMENDED.* **Working farm, join in.** Feeling like a break near the coast? Come and relax, join our family with the peace of the countryside — breathtaking in Spring — on a 200 acre mixed farm, situated near Looe between A38 and A390. See pedigree South Devon cattle and sheep naturally reared, explore the new woodland farm trail amidst wildlife and flowers. This stylish characteristic farmhouse, which dates back to the Domesday Book, as featured in the Daily Telegraph, cream of Cornwall, provides exceptional comfort with en suite bedrooms all with colour TV, tea/coffee facilities, lounge dining room with log fires. A conservatory to enjoy each day's warmth capturing a beautiful view over the farm, set in an original walled garden including picnic table, tennis court and play area. Special activities can be arranged — golf, fishing, cycling and walking. Home produce a speciality, full English breakfast, four-course optional evening meal from £11. Bed and Breakfast from £20. AA QQQQ. Open all year. Self catering character cottage also available (♥♥♥ *HIGHLY COMMENDED*). A warm welcome awaits you to discover the beauty of Cornwall. Please phone for a brochure and discuss your requirements.

LISKEARD. Mrs E.R. Elford, Tresulgan Farm, Near Menheniot, Liskeard PL14 3PU (Tel & Fax: 01503 240268). 🌑 🌑 *HIGHLY COMMENDED.* **Working farm, join in.**

Tresulgan is a 115 acre arable dairy farm where picturesque views can be seen from the 17th century farmhouse, attractive garden and patio area. Delicious home cooked meals are served in our original oak-beamed dining room. Three en suite bedrooms are tastefully decorated to a high standard throughout, with colour TV and drinks facilities. Set in the countryside, yet within easy reach of the numerous attractions, sandy beaches and inviting coastline of this beautiful part of Cornwall. Always a warm welcome. SAE for brochure and terms please. FHB Member.

LOOE. John and Hazel Storer, Kantara Licensed Guesthouse, 7 Trelawney Terrace, West Looe PL13 2AG (01503 262093). 🌑 *COMMENDED.* AA QQ Recommended. Small but well appointed, licensed guesthouse situated near the centre of this picturesque resort and convenient for shops, restaurants, beach and watersports. The atmosphere is friendly and informal; guests have access to facilities at any reasonable time and 24 hour access to rooms. All bedrooms have washbasin, colour TV with satellite and video link, radio alarm, cordless kettle and beverages. A range of utilities is available on request; bar lounge with 28" colour TV. Kantara is very popular with anglers and we are happy to arrange trips for you on the best available boats. Cold storage is available for your catch. Bed and Breakfast from £13. Children and well behaved pets welcome. Frommers Recommended.

LOOE. Mrs D. Eastley, Bake Farm, Pelynt, Looe PL13 2QQ (Tel & Fax: 01503 220244). Working farm.

This is an old farmhouse, bearing the Trelawney Coat of Arms (1610), situated midway between Looe and Fowey. There are three double bedrooms all with washbasins, tea/coffee making facilities and night storage heaters; bathroom/toilet; shower room/toilet; sittingroom/diningroom. Children welcome at reduced rates. Sorry, no pets. Open from April to October. Plenty of fresh farm food, a lot of home produce including Cornish clotted cream and an abundance of roasts. A car is essential for touring the area, ample parking. There is much to see and do here — horse riding four miles, golf seven. The sea is only five miles away and there is shark fishing at Looe. Bed and Breakfast from £15; Evening Meal £9. Cleanliness guaranteed. Brochure available on request.

LOOE. Mrs Lynda Wills, Polgover Farm, Widegates, Looe PL13 1PY (01503 240248). Working farm.

Polgover Farm is situated in picturesque countryside, four miles from Looe on the B3252 and ideally situated to explore Cornwall and South Devon. Local attractions include horse riding, golf, fishing, water sports, Monkey Sanctuary and many beaches. There is always a warm welcome at Polgover's spacious 16th century Listed farmhouse, where you can have a peaceful and relaxing holiday. There are three tastefully decorated bedrooms, all with washbasins and tea/coffee facilities. Guests' bathroom. Lounge with colour TV incorporating breakfast room with separate tables. Sorry, no pets. Open Easter to October. Ample parking. Bed and Breakfast from £14. Weekly and child reductions. Brochure available.

LOOE. Mrs J.M. Gill, Cleese Farm, Nomansland, Looe PL13 1PB (01503 240224).

Cleese Farm is a family run dairy farm located just off the B3252 Plymouth to Looe Road. The twin towns of East and West Looe are one and a half miles away where there are sandy beaches and rock pools separated by the Looe River and the famous Banjo Pier. Our farmhouse is set in beautiful unspoilt countryside overlooking the sea and mini gorge of Morval. Ideal walking country. There are plenty of activities nearby including golf, horse riding and water sports. All rooms have sea or valley views some with washbasins, all have tea/coffee making facilties. Bathroom includes shower. Pets welcome. Ample parking. We are a genuine West Country family and offer you a warm welcome and friendly atmosphere. Bed and Breakfast from £14. 24 hour answermachine.

PLEASE ENCLOSE A STAMPED ADDRESSED ENVELOPE WITH ENQUIRIES

The Old Rectory Country House Hotel

St. Keyne, Near Liskeard
Cornwall PL14 4RL

Tel: 01579 342617
Fax: 01579 342293

♛♛♛
HIGHLY COMMENDED

Peacefully secluded in our own 3 acres of gardens, we are ideally situated for touring Cornwall and South-west Devon and its multitude of attractions. Enjoy the warm welcoming ambience of a family-run country house, we offer full English Breakfast and à la carte Dinners, comfortable, ensuite bedrooms (all with colour televisions & tea/coffee-making facilities). Bed and Breakfast from £27-£35 per person per night, Dinner from £16. Short Breaks (minimum 2 nights – October to March) from £38 p.p. per night Dinner, Bed and Breakfast. A comfortable lounge with open fires during cooler evenings and an "Honesty" Bar are also available for our guests' enjoyment.

NO SMOKING IN DINING ROOM · PETS WELCOME
AA★★ & ROSETTE · ETB HIGHLY COMMENDED

LOOE. Mrs Angela Eastley, Little Larnick Farm, Pelynt, Looe PL13 2NB (01503 262837). 🐾🐾 Get away from it all at Little Larnick, a dairy, beef and sheep farm in the beautiful Looe Valley, four miles from picturesque Looe and Polperro where we welcome guests from February to November. The character farmhouse offers twin, double and family rooms all with en suite facilities. The rooms are spacious and have comfy armchairs, colour TV, tea/coffee facilities, electric blankets and heating. The family room is in a downstairs annexe overlooking the garden. There is a sittingroom with colour TV and log fires on cold evenings and the beamed diningroom has separate tables. Bed and Breakfast from £18. No pets, no smoking.

LOOE. Mrs Jean Henly, Bucklawren Farm, St. Martin-by-Looe PL13 1NZ (01503 240738; Fax: 01503 240481). 🐾🐾🐾 *HIGHLY COMMENDED.* **Working farm.** Bucklawren is situated deep in unspoilt countryside, yet only one mile from the beach, two and a half miles from Looe, and one mile from the Woolly Monkey Sanctuary. It is mentioned in the Domesday Book but the Manor House is now replaced by a 19th century spacious farmhouse which has a large garden and beautiful sea views. We offer excellent accommodation with television lounge, family and ensuite rooms and farmhouse cooking in a friendly and relaxed atmosphere. There is ample parking. Open March to October. Reduced rates for children. Bed and Breakfast from £19 to £21; Evening Meal £10. Brochure on request. Member of Farm Holiday Bureau.

Terms quoted in this publication may be subject to increase if rises in costs necessitate

LOOE near. Jane and Barry Wynn, Harescombe Lodge, Watergate, Near Looe PL13 2NE (01503 263158).

Harescombe Lodge is a country guest house situated 'twixt Looe and Polperro in the secluded picturesque hamlet of Watergate. Once the shooting lodge of the Trelawne Estate, home of the Trelawney family. Beautiful river views and walks with interesting wildlife. Peaceful surroundings, idyllic location appealing to the discerning visitor to South East Cornwall. Ideal as a stopover or a base for a short break. All bedrooms comfortably furnished with en suite and tea/coffee making facilities. Ample off-road parking. Open all year for Bed and Breakfast; optional evening meal. Unsuitable for children under 12 years. Sorry no pets. AA QQQQ. Bed and Breakfast from £17.

MARAZION near. Jenny Birchall, Mount View House, Varfell, Ludgvan, Penzance TR20 8AW (01736 710179).

Mount View House is a Victorian former farmhouse standing in half an acre of gardens overlooking St. Michael's Mount. The house is furnished in traditional style and offers one room with sea views and another with rural views. Rooms have washbasins, central heating and tea/coffee making facilities. Guests' WC and shower room; sitting/dining room with open fire. Children welcome, cot available. Situated approximately three miles from Penzance and five miles from St. Ives. We are the ideal touring stopover. Our close proximity to the heliport (one mile) makes us an ideal stopover en route to the Scilly Isles. Bed and Breakfast from £15 per person per night. Self catering accommodation also available, please telephone for details.

MEVAGISSEY. Harbour Lights Hotel, Polkirt Hill, Mevagissey PL26 6UR (01726 843249).

This family-run freehouse/Hotel is situated on one of the finest cliff top positions in Cornwall, overlooking Mevagissey harbour and St. Austell Bay. All the public rooms and most of the bedrooms enjoy ever changing sea views. En suite rooms are available with TVs and tea/coffee making facilities. Bed and Breakfast from £19 per person per night. Enjoy a meal in the newly opened restaurant which is only a stone's throw from the water, or watch the fishing boats come in whilst having a drink in the bar. We have our own large car park. Ring or write for brochure.

MEVAGISSEY. Mrs Barbara Howson, Trevellion, Polstreath Hill, Mevagissey PL26 6TH (01726 844158).

This bustling fishing village is an ideal setting from which to explore Cornwall. Our family home offers two double and one single bedroom with washbasins, tea/coffee facilities. Guest bathroom, luxurious lounge, lovely garden. Bed and full English Breakfast £18 per person per night single room, £30 per night double room. Sorry, no smoking.

MEVAGISSEY. Mrs Dawn Rundle, Lancallan Farm, Mevagissey, St. Austell PL26 6EW (01726 842284).

Lancallan is a large 17th century farmhouse on a working 200 acre dairy and beef farm in beautiful rural setting, one mile from Mevagissey and surrounded by lovely coastal walks and sandy beaches. We are well situated for day trips throughout Cornwall. Enjoy a traditional farmhouse breakfast in a warm and friendly atmosphere. Accommodation comprises one family room, one double room, bathroom; lounge with colour TV and tea-making facilities. Terms available on request, reductions for children. SAE please.

MEVAGISSEY. Mrs Anne Hennah, Treleaven Farm, Mevagissey PL26 6RZ (01726 842413).

Working farm. Treleaven Farm is situated in quiet, pleasant surroundings overlooking the village and the sea. The 200 acre mixed farm is well placed for visitors to enjoy the many attractions of Mevagissey with its quaint narrow streets and lovely shops. Fishing and boat trips are available and very popular. The house offers a warm and friendly welcome with the emphasis on comfort, cleanliness and good food using local produce. A licensed bar and solar heated swimming pool add to your holiday enjoyment, together with a games room and putting green. Tastefully furnished throughout, with central heating, there are five double bedrooms and one family bedroom, all en suite with tea/coffee making facilities and TV; bathroom, two toilets. Sittingroom and diningroom. Open February to November for Evening Dinner, Bed and Breakfast from £28 or Bed and Breakfast from £19. Sorry, no pets. SAE, please, for particulars or telephone.

AA ★★   ETB ♛♛♛

Tregurrian Hotel

Watergate Bay, near Newquay, Cornwall TR8 4AB
Telephone: (01637) 860280

★ 27 rooms with radio/listening, tea-makers, heaters, most ensuite, TV in all rooms ★ Car park ★ Heated pool and sun patio, games room, solarium, sauna, jacuzzi ★ Parties and coaches by arrangement ★ Spring and Autumn Breaks ★ Family run: children welcome at reduced rates (some free offers) ★ Licensed bar ★ Central for touring all of Cornwall ★ Open Easter to November ★ Dinner, bed and breakfast £156 to £230 inclusive of VAT

Brochure from resident proprietors Marian and Derrick Molloy

NEWQUAY. Mr and Mrs John and Vera Connolly, "Stanford", 91a Henver Road, Newquay TR7 3DJ (01637 875474).

Luxury Guest Bungalow, open March to end October, ideally situated for all beaches, with lovely sea view and near to town. Five bedrooms (double and family), some with sea views; all with heating, hot and cold water, razor points, vanitory units, divan beds, modern furniture; some with showers and TV. Bathroom, two toilets. Attractive lounge; delightful diningroom; all home-made cooking at its best. Children welcome. Sorry, no pets. Car not essential, but plenty of parking space; buses stop by door. Fire Certificate. Everything for your comfort provided for a happy and restful holiday — evening snacks and morning tea on request at moderate charges. Bed, Breakfast and four-course Evening Dinner with tea or coffee from £115 per week. Reduced rates for Senior Citizens early and late season. Stamp, please, for brochure or telephone for a quick booking.

NEWQUAY. Mike and Doris Mortimer, Pensalda, 98 Henver Road, Newquay TR7 3BL (01637 874601). Tourist Board Listed.

Take a break in the "heart of Cornwall". An ideal location from which to explore and enjoy the finest coastline and beaches in Europe. A warm and friendly welcome awaits you at our family-run guest house, situated on the main A3058 approximately half a mile from the town and close to beaches and amenities. Accommodation available in one twin, one single, four double and two family bedrooms including two chalets situated in pleasant and peaceful garden surroundings. En suite rooms available. All have colour TV, tea making facilities. We have an excellent reputation for serving good freshly prepared food with choice of menu. Hot and cold snacks and packed lunches available on request. Licensed bar. Central heating. Parking on premises. Fire Certificate. Bed and Breakfast from £13; Bed, Breakfast and Evening Dinner from £17 per day. Special weekly terms, Bargain Breaks and reduced rates for Senior Citizens early and late season available. Brochure on request or phone for details.

NEWQUAY. Porth Enodoc Hotel, 4 Esplanade Road, Pentire, Newquay TR7 1PY (01637 872372).

♛ ♛ ♛ Standing in its own grounds overlooking Fistral Beach and Newquay Golf Course this delightful hotel offers a warm friendly welcome. Family owned and managed. Delicious home cooking. There are 15 well appointed bedrooms, most with sea views, all with en suite facilities, colour TV, radio/intercom/child listening, tea/coffee making facilities and central heating. There is a comfortable bar and the lounge and dining room have panoramic views over the Bay. Parking space for all within the hotel grounds. Bed and Breakfast from £15 daily. Dinner, Bed and Breakfast from £119 to £189 per week including VAT. Special terms for Short Breaks available throughout the year. AA QQQQ, RAC Highly Acclaimed. Self catering cottage also available.

OTTERHAM STATION. John and Angie Lapham, Sea View Farm, Otterham Station, Camelford PL32 9SW (01840 261355). Built at the turn of the century and set in 10 acres on the A39, Sea View Farm is ideally situated for coastal walks on the beautiful rugged north coast, or sandy beaches of the south for swimming/surfing; Bodmin Moor five minutes' drive away — visit the famous Jamaica Inn. All rooms have washbasins, tea/coffee facilities and central heating; dining room/lounge with colour TV. Children and dogs welcome. Own key. Private parking. Pretty garden; see our horses and foals. Good wholesome home cooking. Bed and Breakfast from £13 to £15; Evening Meal £8. Snacks available, lunch boxes on request. Open all year.

THE WHITE HERON

This well established, friendly, family-run hotel offers colour co-ordinated bedrooms, all with tea/coffee making facilities, TV, en-suite available. Cosy TV lounge. Come and go as you please. Ample car parking. Close to many North Cornwall attractions and surrounded by excellent surfing beaches (Polzeath 500 yards, Daymer Bay 700 yards). Courses galore for golfers, and walkers will enjoy the National Trust Coastal Path. Our popular licensed restaurant offers delicious homemade meals, reasonably priced. Bed and English Breakfast from £13.50.
For details on bargain breaks and June specials call

Paul and Margaret Mark, The White Heron, Old Polzeath PL27 6TJ. Telephone: (01208) 863623 ♛ ♛

PADSTOW. Mrs A. Woosnam-Mills, Mother Ivey Cottage, Trevose Head, Padstow PL28 8SL (Tel & Fax: 01841 520329). Mother Ivey Cottage is an old traditionally built Cornish house, furnished with antiques and having stunning sea views. The area is renowned for swimming, fishing and surfing. There is also a Championship Golf Course nearby. Bedrooms have en suite bathrooms and twin beds. There is a TV and sitting room for guests' use and evening meals are available with notice. There is easy access for many National Trust properties, historic fishing villages and the working harbour at Padstow. Car essential, ample parking. Bed and Breakfast from £20.

PADSTOW. The Old Mill Country House, Little Petherick, Padstow PL27 7QT (01841 540388).

👑👑 *COMMENDED.* AA QQQ Recommended, RAC Acclaimed. This is a 16th century Grade II Listed corn mill complete with waterwheel. Set in its own streamside gardens at the head of Little Petherick Creek just two miles from Padstow and in a designated area of outstanding natural beauty. The Old Mill is furnished throughout with antiques and collections of genuine artifacts to complement the exposed beams, original fireplaces and slate floors. This ensures that the Old Mill's original character and charm is retained. We regret the minimum age for children is 14 years. Licensed. En suite. Bed and Breakfast from £26.

BOSAVERN HOUSE 👑👑

Modernised 17th century country house in two acres of garden, one mile from the coast, four miles from sandy beach, Penzance six miles, near Land's End. Convenient for airport. An ideal walking and touring centre. The house is well appointed, double glazed and several rooms have their own showers and toilets. Home cooking, log fires and friendly personal service ensure your comfort. Open all year, except Christmas. Bed and Breakfast from £16.50. Write or phone for brochure.

Maria & Colin Lilley, Bosavern House, St. Just-in-Penwith, Penzance, Cornwall TR19 7RD – Telephone 01736 788301

PENZANCE. Rosemary and Bill Wooldridge, Camilla House Hotel, Regent Terrace, Penzance TR18 4DW (Tel & Fax: 01736 363771).

RAC Acclaimed, AA QQQ. We would like to welcome you to this lovely Listed building (with own car park) in a quiet terrace close to the harbour and town centre and within easy reach of the bus and rail stations. Penzance is an ideal base from which you can explore West Cornwall any time of year. Single, double, twin and triple rooms available (many with en suite facilities). Front facing rooms have delightful sea views. A warm welcome and an excellent breakfast, plus central heating for your out of season visit, we hope will make this one of your favourite places. Bed and Breakfast £17 to £25 per person per night.

PENZANCE. Mrs Monica Olds, Mulfra Farm, Newmill, Penzance TR20 8XP (01736 363940).

Superb accommodation on this hill farm high on the edge of the Penwith Moors. The 17th century stone built beamed farmhouse has far reaching views, is attractively decorated and furnished and offers two double en suite bedrooms with tea/coffee trays, TV, shaver points and heated towel rails. The comfortable lounge has an inglenook fireplace and Cornish stone oven. Dining room has separate tables; sun lounge. Car essential, ample parking. Warm friendly atmosphere, good food. Beautiful walking country. Ideal centre for exploring West Cornwall. We have our own Iron Age village as well as cows, calves and horses. Bed, Breakfast and Evening Meal £130 per week. Bed and Breakfast £16 per night. Further details with pleasure.

PENZANCE. Mr & Mrs G.W. Buswell, Penalva Private Hotel, Alexandra Road, Penzance TR18 4LZ (01736 369060). 👑👑👑 *APPROVED.* AA QQQ. The hotel is TOTALLY NON-SMOKING, offering full central heating, fresh immaculate interior, en suite facilities, excellent food and a real welcome with courteous service. Penalva is a well positioned imposing late Victorian hotel set in a wide tree-lined boulevard with ample parking, close to promenade and shops. Perfect centre for enjoying the wealth of beautiful sandy coves, historical remains and magnificent walks. Large guest lounge and separate dining room. Colour TV and tea/coffee making facilities in bedrooms. Open all year. Special diets by prior arrangement. Sorry, no pets. Bed and Breakfast from £11 to £18. Weekly reductions for children 6 to 12 half price if sharing family rooms. Highly recommended. SAE, please, for brochure.

PENZANCE. Mr and Mrs R.B. Hilder, Carnson House, East Terrace, Penzance TR18 2TD (01736 365589).

A friendly welcome awaits you in our centrally situated, licensed Private Hotel. We specially cater for rail and coach travellers being only yards from the station. A high standard of comfort is maintained together with a reputation for excellent food. We have a comfortable lounge, attractive dining room with separate dining tables, and eight bedrooms, all with heating, tea-makers and colour TV and some with en suite facilities. Penzance is a lively and interesting town with plenty of shops, gardens and promenade, and is the natural centre for exploring the Land's End Peninsula with its beaches, cliffs, coves and villages. We arrange many local excursions, including some to the Isles of Scilly as well as coach tours and car hire. RAC Listed. Bed and Breakfast from £16 daily.

PENZANCE. John and Andrea Leggatt, "Cornerways", 5 Leskinnick Street, Penzance TR18 2HA (01736 364645).

A small, friendly guest house conveniently situated close to coach/rail stations and car parks. All rooms offer good, clean basic amenities, washbasins, tea/coffee facilities, colour TV; en suite also available. Cornerways provides good home cooked meals, and vegetarians can be catered for; packed lunches are available if required, since Penzance is ideally situated for trips to Isles of Scilly or just touring West Cornwall. Bed and Breakfast from £15 per person per night, £17.50 per person en suite. Evening Meal £6.50 per person. 10% discount for week's stay.

PENZANCE near. Mrs Eileen Lawry, "Llawnroc", Truthwall Villa, Botallack, St. Just, Penzance TR19 7QL (01736 788814).

Enjoy a friendly welcome in a small guest house situated on the beautiful north coast, just five miles from Land's End, 10 miles from St. Ives, seven miles from Penzance. Ideal for walking, horse riding, golf and lovely sandy beaches. Family, twin and double rooms available, good home cooking. Non smoking accommodation available. Bed and Breakfast £14; optional Evening Meal £7. Weekly rate £93. Children under 12 years half price. Parking space.

PERRANPORTH. Chy an Kerensa, Cliff Road, Perranporth TR6 0DR (01872 572470). ETB

COMMENDED. Licensed Guest House situated on the Coastal Footpath directly overlooking three miles of golden sands, rugged coastline, dunes and heathland. Only 200 metres from beach and village centre with restaurants, shops and pubs to suit all tastes and ages. Golf, horse riding, tennis and bowls, surfboard and wetsuit hire nearby. Our comfortable bedrooms, some en suite, have colour TV, central heating and tea/coffee making facilities. Many have panoramic sea views, as do our lounge and dining room. Bed and Breakfast from £16 to £23 per person. Weekly rates and other reductions. A warm welcome from Wendy and Will all year. Brochure available.

CORNISH CUISINE!

The traditional Cornish Pasty was originally the tin-miners' portable lunch — shaped like a torpedo to fit in his pocket! The filling is usually mutton mixed with potatoes and swedes, and is enclosed in pastry pinched high along its entire length. Another Cornish speciality is Stargazey Pie, where pilchards are arranged in a dish like the spokes of a wheel, the pastry cover being cut to allow the eyes to gaze out. And to finish off — a clotted cream tea with scones and strawberry jam!

POLPERRO. Christine Kay, Penryn House Hotel, Polperro PL13 2RG (01503 272157; Fax: 01503 273055). ♛ ♛ ♛ Set in its own grounds, Penryn House is a country house style property in the heart of Cornwall's most photographed and painted fishing village. Offering delightfully appointed en suite bedrooms with colour TV, telephone, courtesey tray, central heating and a comfortable lounge with log fires on cooler evenings. Enjoy the warmth and ambience of our candlelit restaurant where our speciality chef offers a wide selection of freshly prepared dishes with local produce in season and fresh local fish. Nearby attractions include many National Trust properties, peaceful gardens and a lovely variety of walks for serious and casual walkers. MURDER MYSTERY WEEKENDS March and October. Dinner, Bed and Breakfast from £33 to £41; Bed and Breakfast from £20 to £28. Bargain Breaks available.

POLZEATH. Mrs P. White, Seaways, Polzeath PL27 6SU (0120886 2382). Seaways is a small family guest house, 250 yards from safe, sandy beach. Surfing, riding, sailing, tennis, squash, golf all nearby. All bedrooms with en suite or private bathrooms, comprising one family, two double, two twin and a single room. Sittingroom; diningroom. Children welcome (reduced price for under 10's). Cot, high chair available. Comfortable family holiday assured with plenty of good home cooking. Lovely cliff walks nearby. Padstow a short distance by ferry. Other places of interest include Tintagel, Boscastle and Port Isaac. SAE, please. Open all year round. Bed and Breakfast from £16.50; Evening Meal £8.

PORT ISAAC. David and Dorothy Crawford, Long Cross Hotel and Victorian Gardens, Trelights, Near Port Isaac PL29 3TF (01208 880243). One of Cornwall's most unusual hotels, situated as it is in magnificent and very popular public gardens and with its own Tavern attached. The Hotel boasts one of Cornwall's finest tea/Beer Gardens, where Cornish cream teas are served daily. Children love the Maze, the Adventure Play Area and the Pets' Corner with pygmy goats to feed. Hotel rooms are spacious, en suite, with colour TV, etc. An excellent base for walking, beach or touring. Food is served in the Tavern both lunchtime and evening, and also in the Restaurant at night. Special three day Breaks at £48 per person for Bed and Breakfast, September to June. Full details on request.

ROSELAND PENINSULA. Mrs Shirley E. Pascoe, Court Farm, Philleigh, Truro TR2 5NB (01872 580313). Working farm, join in. Situated in the heart of the Roseland Peninsula at Philleigh, with its lovely Norman church and 17th century Roseland Inn, this spacious and attractive old farmhouse set in over an acre of garden offers Bed and Breakfast accommodation. There are double, single and family bedrooms with washbasins and tea making facilities; bathroom, separate toilet; large comfortable lounge with colour TV. Enjoy a full English breakfast in the traditional farmhouse kitchen. Children welcome, cot, high chair, babysitting available. Sorry, no pets indoors. Car essential — ample parking. The family livestock and arable farm includes 50 acres of woodlands which border the beautiful Fal Estuary providing superb walking, picnic areas and bird watching opportunities, while the nearest beaches are just over two miles away. Please write or telephone for brochure and terms.

ST. AGNES. Ted and Jeanie Ellis, Cleaderscroft Hotel, 16 British Road, St. Agnes TR5 0TZ (01872

552349). This small, detached, family-run Victorian hotel stands in the heart of the picturesque village of St. Agnes, convenient for many outstanding country and coastal walks. Set in mature gardens and having a separate children's play area we can offer peace and relaxation after the beach, which is approximately half a mile away. Accommodation is provided in generous sized rooms, mostly en suite with colour TV, and there is also a self contained flat; public rooms comprise lounge, bar, dining rooms and games room. Non-smoking and smoking areas. Private parking. Bed and Breakfast from £20 with discounts for children sharing. Evening set menu. Self Catering annexe also available.

ST. AGNES. Dorothy Gill-Carey, Penkerris, Penwinnick Road, St. Agnes TR5 0PA (01872 552262).

PENKERRIS

An enchanting Edwardian licensed residence in garden with large lawn in unspoilt Cornish village. AA, RAC and Les Routiers Recommended. Penkerris has fields on one side yet there are pubs, shops, etc only 150 yards away on the other side. Attractive dining room, lounge with colour TV, video, piano and log fires in winter. Bedrooms with washbasins, TV, kettles, shaver points, radios; en suite if required. There is a shower room as well as bathrooms. Delicious meals, traditional roasts, fresh vegetables and home made fruit tarts. Beaches, swimming, surfing, gliding and magnificent cliff walks nearby. Children welcome; dogs by arrangement. From £15 per night Bed and Breakfast and from £22.50 with Dinner. Open all year.

ST. AUSTELL. Mr and Mrs Berryman, Polgreen Farm, London Apprentice, St. Austell PL26 7AP

(01726 75151). Polgreen is a family run dairy farm nestling in the Pentewan Valley in an Area of Outstanding Natural Beauty. One mile from the coast and four miles from the picturesque fishing village of Mevagissey. A perfect location for a relaxing holiday in the glorious Cornish countryside. Centrally situated, Polgreen is ideally placed for touring all of Cornwall's many attractions. Pentewan Valley Leisure Trail adjoining, Lost Gardens of Heligan three miles. Bed and Breakfast accommodation includes en suite rooms, colour TV in bedrooms, tea/coffee facilities. Guests' lounge. Children welcome. Terms from £15 per night; £98 per week.

ST. IVES. Mrs C. Verney, Chy Lelan, Bunkers Hill, St. Ives TR26 1LJ (01736 797560). Chy Lelan is a

quaint 17th century Cottage Guest House. Two fishermen's cottages have been restored yet still retain the original charm of the popular fishing quarter of St. Ives. We are in a pretty cobbled street literally 50 metres from the harbour, shops and car park and only 100 metres away from Porthmeor surfing beach and Tate Gallery. All bedrooms have colour TV, tea-making facilities, fitted carpets, washbasins, shaver points; access at all times, en suite available. Open all year. Children are very welcome at reduced rates. Tariff from £15. Brochure on request.

CORNWALL

There's much more to Cornwall than just sand and sea. Take time to explore the traces of the past at Chysauster Ancient Village, near Penzance, a collection of huge stone houses dating from prehistoric times, and Pendennis Castle, Falmouth, built by Henry VIII to guard against invasion. The legend of King Arthur lives on at Tintagel Castle and at Dozmary Pool, Bodmin Moor, reputed to be where he threw back the sword, Excalibur.

ST. IVES. Sue & John Wilson, Tregeraint House, Zennor, St. Ives TR26 3DB (Tel & Fax: 01736

797061). Traditional cottage in an acre of gardens overlooking the Atlantic coastline in one of the most beautiful parts of Cornwall. The house has been lovingly restored, providing a base from which to explore this fascinating area. Each bedroom (one twin, one double, one family) is comfortably furnished with a plumbed-in traditional pine washstand and central heating. Vegetarian and other diets can be catered for and there are nearby pubs where reasonable meals can be had while St. Ives and Penzance offer excellent eating, artistic and other facilities. Open all year except at Christmas. £17 per person (£2 single supplement).

ST. IVES. Miss B. Delbridge, Bella Vista Guest House, St. Ives Road, Carbis Bay, St. Ives TR26 2SF

(01736 796063). ♛ First class accommodation, highly recommended, satisfaction guaranteed. Extensive views of sea and coastline. Washbasins in all rooms. Colour TV. Central heating. Own key to rooms. Free parking on premises. Personal supervision. Fresh farm produce. Radio intercom and baby listening service in all rooms. Fire Certificate held. Bed and Breakfast from £15. Open all year. Non-smokers welcome. SAE for brochure.

ST. IVES. Mrs N.I. Mann, Trewey Farm, Zennor, St. Ives TR26 3DA (01736 796936). Working farm.
On the main St. Ives to Land's End road, this attractive granite-built farmhouse stands among gorse and heather-clad hills, half-a-mile from the sea and five miles from St. Ives. The mixed farm covers 300 acres, with Guernsey cattle and fine views of the sea; lovely cliff and hill walks. Guests will be warmly welcomed and find a friendly atmosphere. Five double, one single and three family bedrooms (all with washbasins); bathroom, toilets; sittingroom, dining room. Cot, high chair and babysitting available. Pets allowed. Car essential, parking. Open all year. Electric heating. Bed and Breakfast only. SAE for terms, please.

TINTAGEL. Cate West, Chilcotts, Bossiney, Tintagel PL34 0AY (Tel & Fax: 01840 770324). Without

stepping onto a road, slip through the side gate of this 16th Century listed cottage into a landscape owned by the National Trust and designated as an Area of Outstanding Natural Beauty. Closest cottage to nearby Bossiney beach for rock pools, surfing, safe swimming and caves to explore. Walk the airy cliff path north to nearby Rocky Valley or on to picturesque Boscastle Harbour. Southwards takes you to the ruins of King Arthur's Castle and onwards to busy Trebarwith Strand. Notice you have not stepped onto a road yet? Detached traditional country cottage ideal for a small number of guests. Home cooking, warm informal atmosphere, large bright double/family bedrooms with beamed ceilings and olde worlde feel. All rooms have TV, tea/coffee makers. Self catering annexe available. May I send you a brochure? Bed and Breakfast from £15. Directions: Bossiney adjoins Tintagel on the B3263 (coast road), Chilcotts adjoins large lay-by with telephone box.

PUBLISHER'S NOTE

TREGONY. Mrs Sandra R. Collins, Tregonan, Tregony, Truro TR2 5SN (01872 530249). ☕

COMMENDED. **Working farm.** Discover Tregonan, tucked away down a half mile private lane. This comfortable, spacious farmhouse is set in a secluded garden amidst our 300 acre sheep and arable farm. On the threshold of the renowned Roseland Peninsula, six miles west of Mevagissey. St. Austell 7 miles, Truro 12 miles and St. Mawes and Fowey 14 miles. Car essential, ample parking. Bedrooms with washbasin, radio and beverage making facilities. TV lounge. Limited to six guests. Regret no pets. Bed and full English Breakfast from £15.50. A good selection of gardens, beaches and eating places in the locality. OS Ref: SW 955 452.

TRURO. Mrs J.C. Gartner, Laniley House, Near Trispen, Truro TR4 9AU (01872 75201). Laniley

House, a Gentleman's Residence built in 1830, stands in two acres of gardens amidst beautiful, unspoilt countryside, yet only three miles from the Cathedral City of Truro. Ideally situated for discovering Cornwall and close to major towns, beaches and National Trust properties, Laniley offers unequalled privacy and peace. Our aim is to make you feel at home, giving each person individual attention; only six guests at any one time. Accommodation consists of three large double bedrooms, two with washbasins, one with en-suite bathroom; separate breakfast room; lounge with colour TV. All rooms with TV, radio and Teasmaid. Regret, unable to accommodate children under 13 years, also no pets. Bed and Breakfast from £17 per person. SAE, please. Highly recommended accommodation.

TRURO. Marcorrie Hotel, 20 Falmouth Road, Truro TR1 2HX (01872 277374; Fax: 01872 241666). ☕ ☕ ☕ *APPROVED.* Victorian town house in conservation area, five minutes' walk from the city centre and cathedral. Centrally situated for visiting country houses, gardens and coastal resorts. All rooms are en suite and have central heating, colour TV, telephone, tea-making facilities. Ample parking. Credit Cards: Visa, Access, Amex. Open all year. Bed and Breakfast from £21 per person per night.

HELP IMPROVE BRITISH TOURIST STANDARDS

You are choosing holiday accommodation from our very popular FHG Publications. Whether it be a hotel, guest house, farmhouse or self-catering accommodation, we think you will find it hospitable, comfortable and clean, and your host and hostess friendly and helpful. Why not write and tell us about it?

As a recognition of the generally well-run and excellent holiday accommodation reviewed in our publications, we at FHG Publications Ltd. present a diploma to proprietors who receive the highest recommendation from their guests who are also readers of our Guides. If you care to write to us praising the holiday you have booked through FHG Publications Ltd. – whether this be board, self-catering accommodation, a sporting or a caravan holiday, what you say will be evaluated and the proprietors who reach our final list will be contacted.

The winning proprietor will receive an attractive framed diploma to display on his premises as recognition of a high standard of comfort, amenity and hospitality. FHG Publications Ltd. offer this diploma as a contribution towards the improvement of standards in tourist accommodation in Britain. Help your excellent host or hostess to win it!

- -

FHG DIPLOMA

We nominate ....

....

Because

Name ....

Address ....

.... Telephone No. ....

TRURO. Mrs M.A. Hutchings, Lands Vue Country House, Three Burrows, Truro TR4 8JA (01872 560242). You will find a warm welcome at our peaceful country home, set in two acres of garden where you may relax or enjoy a game of croquet. There are three lovely bedrooms all with en suite facilities, TV and tea making facilities. There is a cosy lounge with log fire and the large dining room where we serve a delicious farmhouse breakfast has superb views over the Cornish countryside. Being very central for all Cornwall's famous gardens and coastline, Lands Vue is an ideal base highly recommended by many of our guests who return year after year. AA QQQQ Selected.

TRURO. Mrs Diane Dymond, Great Hewas Farm, Grampound Road, Truro TR2 4EP (Tel & Fax: 01726 882218; mobile 0860 117572). ETB ❦ ❦ Great Hewas is ideally situated in central Cornwall, just two miles from the main A30. This spacious centrally heated farm guesthouse has extensive views from all bedrooms and is ideal for touring or relaxing. Personal attention and good home cooking assured. Double, twin, single and family rooms, three en suite, all with TV and tea/coffee facilities. Public WC. Comfortable lounge, dining room with separate tables. Fire Certificate/Food and Hygiene Certificate. Traditional breakfast or fresh fruit and yoghurt. Bed and Breakfast £16.50 to £18 nightly. Three course Evening Dinner £7 to £8. Family room and weekly terms available on request. Open Easter to October. Car essential. From A30 take exit to Grampound Road. Please telephone for brochure, without obligation.

TRURO. Mrs Maltwood, Old Inn Cottage, Mingoose, Mount Hawke, Truro TR4 8BX (01209 890545). 16th/17th century cottage in pretty hamlet near St. Agnes. A short walk leads through lovely National Trust valley to Chapelporth beach. Old Inn Cottage has two bedrooms, each with four-poster bed, one twin-bedded room and one single room; bathroom, toilet; large cosy sitting room with colour TV, books and open granite fireplace; oak beamed dining room. Self catering facilities available on request. Off road parking. Regret no smokers or pets. Bed and Breakfast from £15 per person.

TRURO. Mrs Shirley Wakeling, Rock Cottage, Blackwater, Truro TR4 8EU (01872 560252). ❦ ❦ ❦ HIGHLY COMMENDED. 18th century beamed cottage, formerly the village schoolmaster's home. A haven for non-smokers. Two double and one twin en suite rooms with beverage facilities, toiletries, clock/radio, colour TV, hairdryer and shaver point. Centrally heated. Attractive guest sittingroom with colour TV. Cosy dining room with antique Cornish range. Separate tables. Optional dinner by prior arrangement, from à la carte menu. Private parking. Village location three miles from sea and six miles from Truro. We cannot accommodate children or pets. Open all year. Bed and Breakfast from £22. AA QQQQ Selected. RAC Acclaimed. Telephone for brochure and menu.

Rock Cottage

CORNWALL – SOMETHING FOR EVERYONE!

Sea, sand, cliffs and quite often the sun, but that's not all you will find in this interesting county. Cornwall has many fascinating places to visit, such as the Charlestown Shipwreck Centre, the Tropical Bird Gardens at Padstow, Cornwall Aeronautical Park near Helston, Botallack Tin Mine, The Cornish Seal Sanctuary, Perranporth and of course, St. Michael's Mount.

TRURO. Mrs Margaret Retallack, Treberrick Farm, Tregony, Truro TR2 5SP (01872 530247).

Working farm. Treberrick is a 250 acre working farm situated on the edge of the Roseland Peninsula and two miles from unspoilt beaches at Carhays and Portholland and six miles from Mevagissey. Most parts of Cornwall reached by car within one hour. Guests are welcome to walk around the farm. Spacious house, bedrooms have washbasins and tea making facilities. Dining room with separate tables, lounge with TV always available. Guests can expect traditional home cooked food using own produce where possible. Maximum number of guests six. Sorry no smoking. Bed and Breakfast from £15; Evening Meal available. Near Heligon Manor Gardens — Restoration Project. Please telephone or write for brochure.

TRURO. Andrew and Catherine Webb, Tregony House, 15 Fore Street, Tregony, Truro TR2 5RN

(01872 530671). Grade II Listed building on main street of Tregony, nine miles Truro, many beaches close by. Ideally situated for exploring all of Cornwall. Accommodation comprises front — double with en suite facilities, twin and single room sharing bathroom, back — double with en suite facilities and twin with private bathroom, both overlooking garden. All have tea/coffee making facilities. Guests' sitting room with colour TV and open fire. Breakfast and dinner served in low beamed 18th century dining room. Private or off-road parking available. Access and Visa cards accepted. Children over seven years welcome. Terms from £18.75 Bed and Breakfast, £11 for four-course Dinner. Brochure available.

TRURO/ST. MAWES. Mrs Ann Palmer, Trenestrall Farm, Ruan High Lanes, Truro TR2 5LX (01872

TRENESTRALL FARM

501259). Working farm, join in. A family run farm offers accommodation in 200-year-old stone built barn. Centrally situated in the beautiful and peaceful Roseland Peninsula close to St. Mawes. Accommodation comprises one double and one twin-bedded rooms with washbasin and one further twin room, all with tea making facilities; bathrooms and shower rooms for guests' use only; sittingroom with TV. Children welcome. A friendly personal service assured. Pets welcome by arrangement. Bed and Breakfast from £14 per person per night.

WADEBRIDGE near. Mr W. R. Veall, Roskarnon House Hotel, Rock, Near Wadebridge PL27 6LD (01208 862785 or 862329). 🌸 🌸 🌸 The golden sands of Rock and the Camel Estuary offer a glorious holiday to the visitor to Roskarnon House Hotel, an ideal place in which to enjoy to the full the delights of a visit to Cornwall. Under the personal supervision of the Resident Hosts, the highest standard of comfort is offered. Ten double bedrooms, two single bedrooms and four family rooms, some with private bath; all have spring interior mattresses, razor points, bed lights; most have sea views, colour TV and tea/coffee making facilities. Ample conveniences. Well-appointed lounge and diningroom overlook lawns and beach. Open March to October, the house is suitable for the disabled. Car essential; parking for 12 cars. Sorry, no pets. Bed and Breakfast from £19.50; Evening Meal from £12.50. Reduced rates for children sharing parents' room. AA QQ, RAC Two Stars. Also self-catering cottage fully equipped for four persons.

CUMBRIA — including "The Lakes"

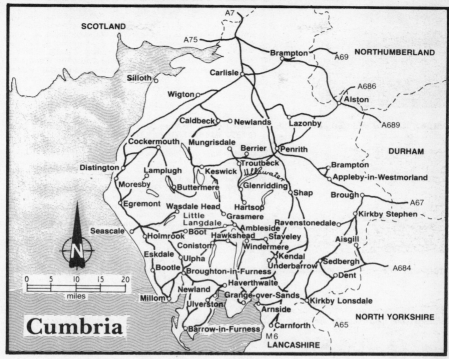

Cumbria

ALSTON. Clare and Mike Le Marie, Brownside House, Leadgate, Alston CA9 3EL (01434 382169; Fax: 01434 382100). Alston, England's highest market town, is in the heart of the unspoilt North Pennines, an ideal centre for walking, cycling, birdwatching and exploring old lead mines. Easy reach for Lake District, Hadrian's Wall, Northumberland. A warm welcome awaits you at Brownside House, dating back to 1849, set in open country with superb views. One family, one twin-bedded, both with washbasin, one single all with tea/coffee facilities. Shared bathroom with bath and shower. Residents lounge with log fire, TV. Full central heating. Children and pets welcome (babysitting available). Bed and Breakfast £15; Evening Meal £6. Weekly and Short Break terms available.

AMBLESIDE. Peter and Anne Hart, Bracken Fell, Outgate, Ambleside LA22 0NH (015394 36289). ❦❦ COMMENDED. Bracken Fell is situated in beautiful open countryside between Ambleside and Hawkshead in the picturesque hamlet of Outgate. Ideally positioned for exploring the Lake District and within easy reach of Coniston, Windermere, Ambleside, Grasmere and Keswick. All major outdoor activities are catered for nearby including wind surfing, sailing, fishing, pony trekking, etc. All six bedrooms have private facilities, complimentary tea/coffee making and outstanding views. There is central heating throughout, a comfortable lounge and dining room, together with ample private parking and two acres of gardens. Fire Certificate. Open all year. Bed and Breakfast from £20. Non-smoking. Self catering accommodation also available. Write or phone for brochure and tariff.

Bracken Fell

PLEASE SEND A STAMPED ADDRESSED ENVELOPE WITH ENQUIRIES

FERNDALE HOTEL
Lake Road, Ambleside LA22 0DB

This friendly, family-run hotel at the heart of the popular Lakeland village of Ambleside is renowned for exceptional value for money accommodation. Our guests are assured of a warm welcome and excellent service throughout their stay. The nine comfortable, en suite rooms have colour television and tea/coffee facilities. Private car park, residential licence, magnificent views onto Loughrigg, Wansfell and the Horseshoe Range. Within easy walking distance of the lake, boat trips and some of the most beautiful scenery in Britain. Open all year. Bed and Breakfast from £17.50 to £22.00.

Telephone: 015394 32207 👑👑

AMBLESIDE. Mrs Sheila Briggs, High Wray Farm, High Wray, Ambleside LA22 0JE (015394 32280). ETB Listed *COMMENDED.* Charming 17th century olde worlde farmhouse once owned by Beatrix Potter. Original oak beams, cosy lounge with log burning fire. Pretty colour co-ordinated bedrooms, one with en suite facilities. Heating and tea/coffee trays are in all rooms. Situated in a quiet unspoilt location, panoramic views and lake shore walks close by. A warm welcome awaits all who visit us where comfort, cleanliness and personal attention are assured. Follow the B5286 from Ambleside toward Hawkshead, turn left for Wray. Follow road to High Wray, the farm is on the right. Families welcome. Terms from £15.50. FHG Diploma Winner.

AMBLESIDE. Colin and Rosemary Haskell, Borwick Lodge, Outgate, Hawkshead, Ambleside LA22 0PU (015394 36332). 👑👑 *HIGHLY COMMENDED.* A leafy driveway entices you to the most enchantingly situated house in the Lake District, a very special 17th century country lodge with magnificent panoramic lake and mountain views, quietly secluded in beautiful gardens. Ideally placed in the heart of the Lakes and close to Hawkshead village with its good choice of restaurants and inns. Beautiful en suite bedrooms with colour TV and tea/coffee facilities, including "Special Occasions" and "Romantic Breaks", two king-size four-poster rooms. Colin and Rosemary welcome you to their "haven of peace and tranquillity" in this most beautiful corner of England. Ample parking. NON SMOKING THROUGHOUT. Bed and Breakfast from £18. May we send our brochure?

AMBLESIDE. Liz, May and Craig, Wanslea Guest House, Lake Road, Ambleside LA22 0DB (015394 33884). 👑👑👑 *COMMENDED.* Wanslea is a spacious family-run Victorian non-smoking guest house with fine views, situated just a stroll from the village and Lake shore with walks beginning at the door. We offer a friendly welcome and comfortable rooms, all of which have colour TV and tea/coffee tray; most rooms are en suite. A good breakfast will start your day before enjoying a fell walk or maybe a more leisurely stroll by the lake. Relax in our licensed residents' lounge with a real fire on winter evenings. Children are welcome and pets accepted by arrangement. Bed and Breakfast from £17.50 per person. Evening Meal also available. Autumn, Winter, Spring Breaks at reduced rates. Brochure on request.

AMBLESIDE. Mrs E. Peers, Fisherbeck Farmhouse, Old Lake Road, Ambleside LA22 ODH (015394 32523). 👑👑 This charming 16th century farmhouse is situated in a quiet side lane at the foot of Wansfell to the south of the village. Not a working farm. Warm, comfortable rooms with washbasins. Single, double, twin and family rooms. Lounge with television. Separate morning/breakfast room. Tea/coffee making facilities. Adequate parking on own ground, road and free car park. Car not essential as village is only five minutes' level walk away. Only one minute's walk to the bus stop. Bed and Breakfast from £14 to £18. SAE for terms and more details.

AMBLESIDE. Helen and Chris Green, Lyndhurst Hotel, Wansfell Road, Ambleside LA22 0EG

(015394 32421). 👑👑 *COMMENDED.* RAC Acclaimed, AA Listed. Attractive Victorian Lakeland stone family-run small hotel with private car park, quietly situated in its own garden. Lovely bedrooms, all en suite and with colour TV, tea/coffee tray. Four poster bedroom for that special occasion. Scrumptious food, friendly service. Full central heating for all-year comfort. Cosy bar. Winter and Summer Breaks. A delightful base from which to explore the Lakes either by car or as a walker. Bed and Breakfast from £17.50. Phone or write for colour brochure, please.

AMBLESIDE. Bob and Anne Jeffrey, The Anchorage, Rydal Road, Ambleside LA22 9AY (015394

32046). 👑👑 *COMMENDED.* RAC Acclaimed. Situated two minutes' walk from the centre of Ambleside, with its many shops, restuarants and inns, this modern guest house has a private car park, comfortable lounge, tastefully furnished bedrooms with colour TV, tea/coffee making facilities and central heating. Each bedroom has pleasant views over parkland or surrounding fells. En suite rooms available. Choice of English, Vegetarian or Continental breakfast. Ideal base for walkers or those wishing to tour the Lake District. Non-smoking. Sorry, no pets. Open February to November. Weekly rates/mid-week breaks available at various times. Bed and Breakfast from £18 to £24.

AMBLESIDE. Mrs Margaret Rigg, The Dower House, Wray Castle, Ambleside LA22 0JA (015394

The Dower House, Wray Castle, Ambleside

33211). 👑 *COMMENDED.* Lovely old house, quiet and peaceful, stands on an elevation overlooking Lake Windermere, with one of the most beautiful views in all Lakeland. Its setting within the 100-acre Wray Castle estate (National Trust), with direct access to the Lake, makes it an ideal base for walking and touring. Hawkshead and Ambleside are about ten minutes' drive and have numerous old inns and restaurants. Ample car parking; prefer dogs to sleep in the car. Children over five years welcome, reduced rates if under 12 years. Bed and Breakfast from £22; optional Evening Meal from £11. Open all year round.

AMBLESIDE. Mr D. Sowerbutts, 2 Swiss Villas, Vicarage Road, Ambleside LA22 9AE (015394 32691). A small Victorian terrace house set just off the main road in the centre of Ambleside, near the church, in a slightly elevated position overlooking Wansfell. There is immediate access to the cinema and shops and the wide variety of restaurants and cafes in the town. There are three double bedrooms (one with twin beds) recently refurbished in the traditional style. Each room has central heating, tea making facilities and colour TV. A full English Breakfast or vegetarian meal available. We are open all year round and you are sure of a friendly welcome and good home cooking. Bed and Breakfast from £18 per person.

OUT AND ABOUT IN CUMBRIA

Take a trip back in time on a narrow-gauge railway: The Lakeside and Haverthwaite runs through the beautiful Leven Valley, Ravenglass and Eskdale travels 7 miles from the coast up into the fells, and the South Tynedale Railway offers a journey through a beautiful North Pennine Valley.

The perfect way to appreciate the magnificent Lakeland scenery is on a leisurely Lake cruiser — Ullswater, Coniston, Derwentwater all have scheduled services daily in season.

AMBLESIDE. Jim and Joyce Ormesher, Rothay House, Rothay Road, Ambleside LA22 0EE (015394 32434). Rothay House is an attractive detached guest house set in pleasant gardens with views of the surrounding fells. There is ample space for parking in the grounds. All bedrooms are en suite, comfortable and well furnished with colour TV and tea/coffee trays. Our visitors are assured of warm and friendly service in pleasant surroundings. Children welcome. We are within easy walking distance of Ambleside village centre which has a variety of interesting shops and commendable restaurants, and makes an ideal base for walking, touring or enjoying sailing, watersports and angling on Lake Windermere. Bed and Breakfast from £18 to £22. We are open all year round and offer special rates for out-of-season breaks.

AMBLESIDE. Mrs Elizabeth Culbert, Kingswood, Old Lake Road, Ambleside LA22 0AE (015394 34081). ☙ *COMMENDED.* Kingswood is ideally situated near the town centre, yet off the main road. Ample car parking. Well-equipped and comfortable bedrooms with hot and cold water, and tea/coffee making facilities. Colour TV. Central heating. Single, double, twin and family rooms. Pets welcome. Open most of the year, with special bargain breaks off season. No smoking. Write or phone for rates and details.

AMBLESIDE. Maureen Rushby, Fern Cottage, 6 Waterhead Terrace, Ambleside LA22 0HA (015394 33007). Homely Lakeland stone terraced house situated on the edge of Ambleside only two minutes' walk from the head of Lake Windermere and the Steamer Piers and one mile from the village. Ideal base for touring the Lakes. Kendal approximately 12 miles, Bowness-on-Windermere five miles, Hawkshead and Grasmere about 20 minutes' drive away. The accommodation comprises two double rooms and one twin room, all with tea/coffee making facilities and vanity units; shared bathroom, lounge/diner with TV. Brochure available.

APPLEBY. The Gate Hotel, Bongate, Appleby CA16 6LH (017683 52688). An attractive family-run business on the outskirts of Appleby in easy reach of the town centre with its shops, castle and swimming pool and approximately one mile from the golf course. It is tastefully decorated with panelling from the steam ship The Berengaria. A traditional log fire enhances the warm and friendly service offered all year round. Our rooms are en suite and well furnished with colour TV and tea/coffee trays. There is ample parking, a pleasant enclosed garden and play area. Pets welcome by arrangement. Specialising in Thai food we also offer conventional English food. Licensed. Bed and Breakfast from £17.50 to £27.50 per person; Evening Meal from £4.95 to £10.95.

APPLEBY. Mrs K.M. Coward, Limnerslease, Bongate, Appleby CA16 6UE (017683 51578). Limnerslease is a family run Guest House five minutes' walk from the town centre. A good half-way stopping place on the way to Scotland. There is a good golf course and an indoor heated swimming pool. Many lovely walks are all part of the charm of Appleby. Two double and one twin bedrooms, all with washbasin, colour TV, tea/coffee making facilities at no extra charge; bathroom, toilet; diningroom. Open January to November with gas heating. Ample parking. Bed and Breakfast from £15.

APPLEBY-IN-WESTMORLAND. Mrs Edith Stockdale, Croft House, Bolton, Appleby-in-Westmorland CA16 6AW (017683 61264).

Croft House is situated in Bolton, an unspoilt village of sandstone houses and an inn on the banks of the River Eden. Three miles north of Appleby off A66. This is an excellent base for exploring Eden Valley, Lakes, Dales and Border Country or as a midway break from Scotland. This historic town of Appleby welcomes visitors to its ancient castles and churches and to the country's oldest Gypsy Fair, which is held annually in June. Local attractions include pony trekking, golf, fishing and swimming. The comfortable farmhouse offers traditional farmhouse breakfast, and guest accommodation comprises sittingroom with colour TV, diningroom, one twin and two double bedrooms with washbasins. Separate bathroom and shower. Children welcome at reduced rates, cot and babysitting available. Pets welcome by arrangement. Open all year (except Christmas). Rates from £15.

BOOTLE. Jennifer and Rodney Light, The Stables, Bootle, Near Millom LA19 5TJ (01229 718644).

Set on the western edge of the Lake Disrict National Park within two miles of the sea, we offer comfortable accommodation in a pleasing modern stable conversion set in gardens with two rivers, in a tranquil setting off the beaten tourist track but within an hours' drive of most of the Lake Districts major attractions. We have two lovely bedrooms, a twin and a double/family room which has a full en suite bathroom and guests TV lounge and dining room. Bed and Breakfast with optional Evening Meal (normally all ingredients are fresh, some from our own gardens) from £15 per person.

AA ★
RAC ★

THE CHANNINGS

VISA
ACCESS

Bare Promenade, Morecambe
Telephone: 01542 417925

The Channings is situated on the promenade with superb views across the bay to Lakeland hills. A short walk to Happy Mount Park and Morcambe Golf Club. Ideal base for touring holidays – with Lake Winderemere a 40 minute drive – Yorkshire Dales and Blackpool 60 minutes. Fully licensed, all en suite rooms and furnished to a high standard. Highly recommended with competitive rates. Single, double, twin and family rooms available.

Group and coach party rates on request. Dinner, bed and breakfast from £140 per week. Please send a stamp for brochure.

BOWNESS-ON-WINDERMERE. Philip and Betty Kilduff, Storrs Gate House, Longtail Hill, Bowness-on-Windermere LA23 3JD (015394 43272).

Storrs Gate is a small country guest house offering olde worlde charm, set in attractive gardens with ample parking. A leisurely 15 minute stroll takes you into Bowness centre. Situated on the A592 at the junction with the B5284 opposite the Marina and Lake close by the Hawkshead Ferry. We offer accommodation daily or lower rates for four days or more. En suite rooms if desired. There is central heating, TV and tea/coffee making facilities in all rooms. Dining room and a separate lounge for guests. Children welcome. Please write or telephone for our brochure and tariff.

WHEN MAKING ENQUIRIES PLEASE MENTION
THIS *FHG* PUBLICATION

Terms quoted in this publication may be subject to increase if rises in costs necessitate

BRAMPTON. Mrs Ann Thompson, Low Rigg Farm, Walton, Brampton CA8 2DX (016977 3233).

Tourist Board Listed COMMENDED. We are a family-run dairy farm in beautiful Hadrian's Wall country, three miles Brampton, nine miles Carlisle. Conveniently situated for the Scottish Borders, Northumberland and the Lake District. The farmhouse is comfortably furnished with guests' own lounge, dining room. The bedrooms have king size-beds, tea/coffee facilities and clock radios. Free range eggs, homemade bread rolls and preserves are served for breakfast. Evening meals are available by arrangement. There is a large garden and ample parking space. Guests are welcome to view the farm activities including milking. Bed and Breakfast from £16; Evening Meals from £10. Reductions for children and more than one night's stay.

CALDBECK. Mrs M. Monkhouse, Denton House Guest House, Caldbeck CA7 8JC (016974 78415)

and Norman Cragg Farm Bed & Breakfast, Caldbeck CA7 8HX (017684 84376). Denton House is a large 17th century house with a new extension, modernised to 20th century standards but still retaining character. We are an ideal base when travelling to or from Scotland, walking the Northern Fells or touring the Lakes. Norman Cragg Farmhouse also has lots of character. Log fires welcome everyone in both places. Marvellous views from rooms. Denton House has en suite facilities. We offer all home cooking. Children and pets welcome. Ample parking. Bed and Breakfast; Evening Meal optional. SAE for brochure.

CALDBECK. Mr and Mrs A. Savage, Swaledale Watch, Whelpo, Caldbeck CA7 8HQ (016974

78409). ✿✿ *HIGHLY COMMENDED.* Ours is a mixed farm of 300 acres situated in beautiful countryside within the Lake District National Park. Easy reach of Scottish Borders, Roman Wall, Eden Valley. Primarily a sheep farm (everyone loves lambing time). Visitors are welcome to see farm animals and activities. Many interesting walks nearby or roam the peaceful fells where John Peel hunted. Enjoyed by many Cumbrian Way walkers. Very comfortable accommodation with excellent home cooking. All rooms have private facilities. Central heating. Tea making facilities. Bed and Breakfast from £17 to £20; Evening Meal £10.50. AA QQQQ Selected.

CARLISLE. Eric and Daphne Houghton, Corner House, Carlisle CA1 2AW (Tel & Fax: 01228

41942). AA QQQ Recommended. Situated on the corner of Warwick Road and Petteril Street, one mile from M6 Junction 43, five minutes' walk from Carlisle city centre. Eric and Daphne offer a very homely run guest house. All rooms are en suite and fully centrally heated, and all have satellite TV, hair dryer, welcome tray and radio alarm. Choice of double, single, twin and family accommodation available. A substantial English breakfast is included, vegetarian and special diets catered for whenever possible. If arriving by coach or train a courtesy car will be provided upon request. Prices from £16 per person.

CARLISLE. Ronnie and Jackie Fisher, Cornerways Guest House, 107 Warwick Road, Carlisle CA1

1EA (01228 21733). Ronnie and Jackie welcome you to their family-run Guest House. A Grade II Listed building situated in the heart of historic Carlisle just two minutes' walk from city centre with castle, cathedral, bus and railway stations. An ideal base for visiting the Lake District, Hadrians Wall and Gretna Green. Colour TV, welcome tray, shaver points and central heating in all rooms; en suite rooms available. Payphone and off-street parking. Reasonable rates from £13 per person with reductions for children. Home cooked meals available by arrangement. To reach us by car turn off M6 at Junction 43.

CARLISLE. Mrs G. Elwen, New Pallyards, Hethersgill, Carlisle CA6 6HZ (01228 577308). ♥ ♥ ♥

COMMENDED. GOLD AWARD WINNER. Working farm, join in. AA, HWFH, FHB. Relax and see beautiful North Cumbria and the Borders. A warm welcome awaits you on our 65-acre livestock farm tucked away in the Cumbrian countryside, yet easily accessible from M6 Junction 44. In addition to the surrounding attractions there is plenty to enjoy including hill walking, peaceful forests and sea trout/salmon fishing or just nestle down and relax with nature. Two double en-suite, two family en-suite and one twin/single bedrooms, all with tea/coffee making equipment. Menu choice. Filmed for BBC TV. Best Breakfast in Britain Competition Winner. Bed and Breakfast from £20 to £21; Dinner £13. Dinner, Bed and Breakfast £160 to £170 per week. Self-catering cottages also available.

CARLISLE. Mrs C.M. Murray, Parkland Guest House, 136 Petteril Street, Carlisle CA1 2AW (01228 48331). ♥ ♥ ♥ COMMENDED. AA QQQ. A warm welcome

awaits you at Parklands, just off M6 (Junction 43). Ideal for an overnight stop en route to Scotland and Ireland. Also an ideal base to tour Scotland and the Lake District with a short drive to Hadrian's Wall. In walking distance of Carlisle town centre, the Lanes Shopping, the Cathedral and Castle. Also award-winning golf course close by. All rooms en suite and tastefully decorated with colour TV and welcome tray. Relax in our lounge bar with a quiet drink after a tiring day (satellite TV). Meals available. Ground floor rooms and family rooms, doubles, twins. Open all year round. Private parking. Prices from £17.50 per person. Colour brochure available.

CARLISLE. Mrs Jennifer Bainbridge, Beech House, Whitrigg, Kirkbride, Carlisle CA5 5AA (016973 51249). Beech House is situated on the Solway Firth and

overlooks the Lake District Hills from the front and the Scottish Hills from the rear. This is an ideal place for a quiet holiday and a birdwatcher's paradise. Guests are assured of a friendly welcome at the house which is surrounded by lawns and flower gardens. Excellent home cooking using fresh garden produce and Solway-caught salmon. Two family and one single rooms; two bathrooms, two toilets; lounge and diningroom. Children welcome and cot and babysitting available. Open all year except Christmas for Evening Dinner, Bed and Breakfast from £20 or Bed and Breakfast from £14. Welcome cup of tea at bedtime (inclusive). Reductions for children. Car essential — parking.

CARLISLE. James and Elaine Knox, The Steadings, Townhead, Houghton, Carlisle CA6 4JB (01228 23019). We offer you a warm welcome to our new self-contained barn conversion adjoining our Grade II Listed Georgian house circa 1700. Exposed beams, tastefully decorated. Eight rooms, six en suite, two standard, all are centrally heated, double glazed and with colour TV and tea/coffee making facilities. Private parking. Excellent breakfasts. Tearoom on site. Situated minutes from M6 Junction 44; rural location yet only three miles from Carlisle City Centre. Extremely easy to find. Ideal location for visiting historic Carlisle, Lake District, Roman Wall, Scottish Borders. To find us leave Junction 44, take A689 Hexham Road for three-quarters of a mile, first on right. Bed and Breakfast £16 to £17.50 double/twin, £18 to £20 single.

CARLISLE. Mrs L. Young, 7 Hether Drive, Lowry Hill, Carlisle CA3 0ED (01228 27242). ♛ Detached bungalow in quiet location with easy access English Lake District and Scottish Border country (M6 Junction 44). One room specially adapted for disabled guests — ramped access, wheel-in shower, six grab rails, adjustable toilet seat, all light switches and sockets at wheelchair height. Also family room, sleeps five, cot available, French window into garden play area. Both rooms have TV and tea making facilities. Central heating throughout. Tariff: 18 twin or double room, half price for children sharing with adults. 20 for single occupancy. AA QQ Recommended.

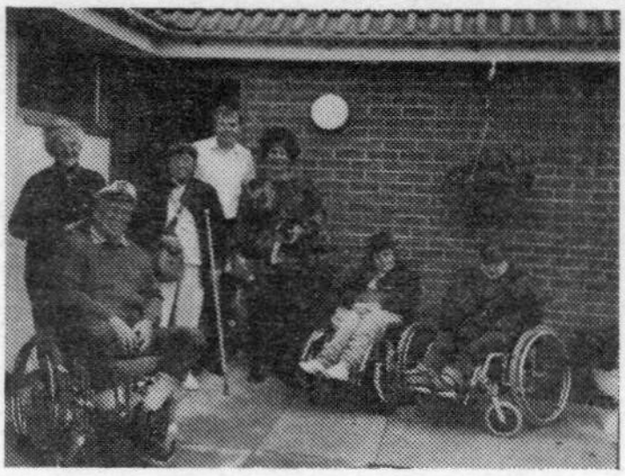

CARLISLE. Mike and Wendy Pattinson, Fern Lee Guest House, 9 St. Aidan's Road, Carlisle CA1 1LT (01228 511930). ♛♛♛ *COMMENDED.* A warm welcome awaits you in our attractive Edwardian townhouse. Tastefully decorated spacious, comfortable rooms are all en suite and have satellite TV, welcome tray, radio/alarm, towels, toiletries, constant hot water and are thoroughly recommended by guests. This family-run guest house has built its reputation on cleanliness and high standards of decoration- you won't be disappointed! At Fern Lee we don't believe in short measures so our hearty breakfast should set any visitor ready for the day to view our fine city. We are just 10 minutes' walk from both rail and bus stations and the city centre. Private parking.

CHAPEL STILE. Mrs Jackie Rowand, Baysbrown Farm, Chapel Stile, Great Langdale, Ambleside LA22 9JZ (015394 37300). Working farm, join in. Baysbrown Farm is set at the beginning of the Langdale Valley. It has Herdwick sheep and beef cows, with 835 acres of land. It is a good "stopping off" place for Cumbrian Way walkers and within easy reach of Ambleside (five miles), Windermere (nine miles), Coniston (six miles) and Hawkshead (nine miles). Enjoy a relaxing evening in front of an open log fire after a home cooked meal. Accommodation comprises one family, one twin room, one double room, all with tea/coffee making facilities. Reductions for children, cot provided. Non-smoking accommodation available. Pets welcome. Open February to October. Bed and Breakfast from £18; Evening Meal £9. ELDHCA Award.

COCKERMOUTH. Mrs Dorothy E. Richardson, Pardshaw Hall, Cockermouth CA13 0SP (01900 822607). Old farmhouse in a small, quiet village three and a half miles from Cockermouth with views to the Fells. Children most welcome — cot, high chair and babysitting available, and a large garden to play in. Pardshaw Hall is ideally situated for touring the Lakes; children delight in the miniature railway at Ravenglass and there are some lovely walks. Accommodation is in one double, one single and one family or twin room, most with washbasins. Good home cooking with fresh produce. Log fires. Open all year. Sorry, no pets in house. Car essential, parking. Bed and Breakfast from £14; Evening Meal optional. Reduced rates for children.

COCKERMOUTH. Mrs M.E. Chester, Birk Bank Farm, Brandlingill, Cockermouth CA13 0RB (01900 822326). Treat yourself to the peace and quiet of Cockermouth, Wordsworth's birthplace, and also the hustle and bustle of all that the Lakes can offer in the busy towns, by staying on our working farm in our friendly farmhouse accommodation. Three well appointed rooms (bath and shower room alongside), with electric blankets to keep you cosy after a pleasant day either golfing, fishing, climbing, trekking or just shopping. Guests can relax in our TV lounge. Children over five years welcome, reduced rates. Dinner using our own fruit and vegetables available on request. Bedtime drink and biscuits included in our reasonable rates. Rates on request, weekly rates available. Car essential with ample parking. Sorry, no pets. Open March-October.

COCKERMOUTH. The Rook Guesthouse, 9 Castlegate, Cockermouth CA13 9EU (01900 828496). Interesting 17th century town house, adjacent to historic castle, we offer comfortable accommodation with full English, vegetarian and Continental breakfast served in rooms which are equipped with washbasin, colour TV, tea/coffee facilities and central heating. En suite and standard rooms available. Cockermouth is an unspoilt market town located at the North Western edge of the Lake District within easy reach of the Lakes, Cumbrian Coast and Border country. We are ideally situated as a base for walkers, cyclists and holiday-makers. Bed and Breakfast from £15 per person sharing room, single occupancy £20. Open all year.

COCKERMOUTH. Mr and Mrs J.F. Graham, Rose Cottage Guest House, Lorton Road, Cockermouth CA13 9DX (01900 822189). 👑👑 *COMMENDED.* A well

established 10 bedroomed guest house in residential area of Cockermouth, just 10 minutes' walk from the interesting town centre. An excellent base for touring, within easy reach of Coast, Lakes and Fells. Private parking for 10/12 cars. Some of the comfortable bedrooms have en suite facilities, all have colour TV, tea/coffee making and full central heating. No smoking areas within the guest house. Open all year except Christmas and New Year. Pets accepted by arrangement; children welcome. Bed and full English Breakfast from £16.50 to £22. Write for brochure.

CONISTON. Mrs Diana Munton, Piper Croft, Haws Bank, Coniston LA21 8AR (015394 41778). Small friendly Bed and Breakfast, "home from home", warm welcome assured. Ideally situated for walking and touring South Lakeland. Coniston Water Yachting Club and Cumbrian Way five minutes' walk. Two double rooms, one twin with washbasins and central heating. Lounge with TV. Private parking. No smoking. Double £32 per night. Open all year.

CONISTON. Mr and Mrs R. Newport, Brigg House, Torver, Coniston LA21 8AY (015394 41592).

👑👑 *HIGHLY COMMENDED.* Explore the Lake District from our tranquil early 19th century house set in its own wooded grounds at the foot of Coniston Old Man. All our comfortable rooms have en suite facilities, colour TV, radio, tea/coffee. Excellent views over fields and hills. Varied breakfast menu catering for the traditional or the more adventurous! Guests' lounge. Private parking. Splendid walks start from our door and there are opportunities for riding, sailing, birdwatching, etc nearby or simply relax and enjoy the scenery. Two pubs within five minutes' walk serve good food. Bed and Breakfast from £20 to £21 per person. Pets welcome. No smoking.

DENT (Yorkshire Dales/Cumbria). Mrs Mary Ferguson, Scow Cottage, Cowgill, Near Dent, Sedbergh LA10 5RN (015396 25445). Scow was built

approximately 1750, situated at the head of Dentdale surrounded by hills and trees and alongside the River Dee; fishing permits can be obtained locally. Ideal for touring the Lake District and the Yorkshire Dales, near to the village of Dent famous for the "terrible Knitters of Dent", Adam Sedgwick, and narrow cobbled streets. Guests are accommodated in large beautifully decorated and comfortably furnished rooms with washbasins and central heating; bathroom and separate toilet; lounge. Lovely landscaped gardens in which to relax and enjoy Dentdale's peace and quiet. Bed and Breakfast £16; Evening Meal £10. Further details on request.

GRANGE-OVER-SANDS. Corner Beech, Kents Bank Road, Grange-over-Sands LA11 7DP (015395 33088). 🐾 🐾 *COMMENDED.* John and Linda Bradshaw

offer a home from home in their spacious Victorian house. Good generous home cooking, stylish comfort and personal attention. Most rooms en suite, all with tea/coffee facilities, thermostatically controlled heating and colour TV. Overlooking Morecambe Bay, close to Promenade. Grange is a quiet genteel haven, an ideal walking and touring location for South Lakeland. Bed and Breakfast from £16 per person, weekly from £110; Dinner, Bed and Breakfast from £23 per person, weekly from £158. Reduced rates for children. Phone or write for brochure.

GRASMERE. Dunmail House, Keswick Road, Grasmere LA22 9RE (015394 35256). 🐾 🐾 *COMMENDED.* A traditional Lakeland stone house on the edge of the

village and set in spacious gardens with outstanding views. Ideally located for all the activities for which this area of Lakeland is noted. Personally run by Trevor and Lesley Bulcock who aim to provide a friendly family atmosphere. Guest lounge with TV. All rooms have tea/coffee facilities, central heating, double glazing and beautiful views. Some en suite. Non smoking. Ample parking. No pets. Easily accessible by public transport. Bed and Breakfast from £18.50 per person per night. Weekly rates and special winter breaks available.

Dunmail House

HAWKSHEAD. Peter and Anne Hart, Bracken Fell, Outgate, Ambleside LA22 0NH (015394 36289). 🐾 🐾 *COMMENDED.* Bracken Fell is situated in beautiful

open countryside between Ambleside and Hawkshead, in the picturesque hamlet of Outgate. Ideally positioned for exploring the Lake District and within easy reach of Coniston, Windermere, Ambleside, Grasmere and Keswick. All major outdoor activities are catered for nearby including wind surfing, sailing, fishing, pony trekking, etc. All six bedrooms have private facilities, complimentary tea/coffee making and outstanding views. There is central heating throughout, a comfortable lounge and dining room, together with ample private parking and two acres of gardens. Fire Certificate. Open all year. Bed and Breakfast from £20. Non-smoking. Self catering accommodation also available. Write or phone for brochure and tariff.

Bracken Fell

HAWKSHEAD near. Paul and Fran Townsend, Pepper House, Satterthwaite LA12 8LS (Tel & Fax: 01229 860206). 🐾 🐾 *COMMENDED.* A warm welcome

awaits in 16th century former farmhouse with elevated position in tranquil valley on edge of Grizedale Forest, four miles from Hawkshead. Red and roe dee and other wildlife abound. Trout fishing nearby. Excellent, peaceful base for exploring the Lakes, close to Beatrix Potter's farm and Ruskin's Brantwood. Miles of forest trails for walking and cycling. Sympathetically updated, all bedrooms have en suite facilities. Two comfortable lounges, one with TV. Central heating, log fires; dining room and terraces with wonderful views. Licensed bar, generous home cooking. No pets. Bed and Breakfast from £22.50; with Dinner from £32.

KENDAL. Mrs Judith Keep, West Mount, 39 Milnthorpe Road, Kendal LA9 5QG (01539 724621).

Friendly, non-smoking, centrally heated Victorian guest house on southern outskirts of Kendal. Easy access Junction 36, M6. One double, one family room both en suite and have colour TV, clock radio alarms, hair dryers. Private parking. Open all year. Terms from £16 to £18 per person per night.

KENDAL. Glynis Byrne, Marwin House, Duke Street, Holme, Near Carnforth LA6 1PY (01524 781144). Tourist Board Listed *COMMENDED.* Marwin

House is a delightful country cottage situated in the small unspoilt village of Holme, gateway to the Lake District and Yorkshire Dales, yet only five minutes from M6 Junction 36. We are an ideal base for walking. Bedrooms are comfortable and tastefully decorated with colour TV, tea/coffee making facilities and central heating. Private lounge with colour TV/video. Children are most welcome. Off road parking. Breakfast a speciality served in a warm friendly atmosphere. Bed and Breakfast from £15 to £17. Open all year.

KENDAL. Mrs Val Sunter, Higher House Farm, Oxenholme Lane, Natland, Kendal LA9 7QH (015395 61177; Fax: 015315 61520). 👑👑👑 *HIGHLY*

COMMENDED. In a peaceful village south of Kendal, this 17th century beamed farmhouse offers comfortable accommodation wth delicious breakfast. Two double and one twin, each with private bathroom. Four-poster bed. TV, hair dryer and coffee/tea making facilities in all bedrooms. Residents' lounge with colour TV. Central heating throughout. Pay phone in hall. Overlooking the Lakeland Fells, lakes and Yorkshire Dales, convenient for the M6 and Oxenholme station. Historic visits nearby. Bed and Breakfast from £18 to £25. Pets welcome. No smoking. AA QQQQ Selected. Self catering accommodation also available.

KENDAL. Sundial House, 51 Milnthorpe Road, Kendal LA9 5QG (01539 724468). 👑 *APPROVED.* Sundial House is on the A6, a quarter of a mile from Kendal town centre, directly opposite the College. Known as "The Gateway to the Lakes" Kendal is a charming and historic market town and is the perfect base for a visit to the Lake District. Whatever your pastime — walking, golfing, fishing or sightseeing — Kendal has it all. We offer you a homely and warm welcome here at Sundial House; Bed and Breakfast from £16. The cosy bedrooms all have tea/coffee making facilities and colour TV; en suite available. There is a reading lounge and ample parking. Follow the Kendal signs from Junction 36 M6.

KENDAL. Mrs A. Taylor, Russell Farm, Burton-in-Kendal, Carnforth, Lancs. LA6 1NN (01524 781334; Fax: 01524 782511).

Why not spend a few days at Russell Farm? The proprietors pride themselves on trying to give guests an enjoyable holiday with good food, friendly atmosphere, relaxing surroundings away from the hustle and bustle. The 150-acre dairy farm is set in a quiet hamlet one mile from the village of Burton-in-Kendal, and five miles from the old market town of Kirkby Lonsdale. An ideal centre for touring Lakes and Yorkshire Dales, or going to the coast. Ideal stopover for people travelling south or to Scotland, only five minutes from M6 Motorway. One double, one single and one family bedrooms; bathroom, toilet; sittingroom and diningroom. Children welcome; cot, high chair and baby-sitting offered. Pets accepted, if well-behaved. Open from March to November for Evening Dinner, Bed and Breakfast or Bed and Breakfast. Reductions for children. Car essential, parking. Send large SAE, please, for terms and brochure.

KENDAL. The Jolly Anglers, Burneside, Kendal LA9 6QS (01539 732552). Cumbria Tourist Board Listed.

Situated in the village of Burneside, a mile north of the market town of Kendal and within six miles of Lake Windermere. This old traditional Lakeland inn offers Bed and Breakfast accommodation in Taylors Cottages (attached to the inn and once the village smithy) and Strickland Ketel Guest House situated in a quieter position at the rear. Some rooms have en suite facilities, all have colour TV and tea/coffee making facilities. Guests are offered good home cooking in the ground floor rooms of Taylors Cottages. Real ale is served in the bars, which have low beamed ceiling and log fires. Moderate rates with special bargain breaks. Children and pets welcome. Bed and Breakfast from £14 per person. Free fishing is available, and there is an 18 hole golf course close by. RAC Listed.

KENDAL. Mrs D.M. Swindlehurst, Tranthwaite Hall, Underbarrow, Near Kendal LA8 8HG (015395 68285). Working farm.

Commended and AA Selected for excellent standards of Comfort and Quality. Tranthwaite Hall is said to date back to 1186, a charming olde world farmhouse with beautiful oak beams, doors and rare black iron fire range. This working dairy/sheep farm has an idyllic setting half a mile up an unspoilt country lane where deer can be seen, herons fish in the stream and there are lots of wild flowers. This is a very peaceful and quiet retreat yet only minutes from all Lakes and local attractions. Attractive bedrooms, all en suite with tea/coffee making facilities, hair dryer and radio. Full central heating. Lounge with colour TV. Full English breakfast is served with eggs from our farm, plus home made jam and marmalade. We like guests to enjoy our home and garden as much as we do. Walking, pony trekking and many good country pubs and inns nearby. Bed and Breakfast from £18 to £20.

KENDAL. Mrs S. Beaty, Garnett House Farm, Burneside, Kendal LA9 5SF (01539 724542). 👑👑 COMMENDED. **Working farm.**

This is an AA/RAC Acclaimed 15th century farmhouse on large dairy/sheep farm, situated a half mile from the A591 Kendal/Windermere road. Accommodation comprises double, twin and family rooms (some en suite), all with washbasins, colour TV, clock/radio and tea making facilities. Lovely oak panelling, beams, door and spice cupboard. Full English breakfast and five course dinners served at separate tables; all prepared in the farmhouse kitchen including homemade soups, lamb and beef from the farm and delicious sweets. Children welcome at reduced rates if sharing with two adults. Good private parking. Near village and public transport. Special offer November to mid-March — three nights Bed and Breakfast £45, en suite £50. AA QQQ.

KENDAL near. Mrs Olive M. Knowles, Cragg Farm, New Hutton, Near Kendal LA8 0BA (01539 721760). Working farm. Tourist Board Listed COMMENDED. Cragg Farm is a delightful 17th century oak beamed farmhouse which retains its character yet has all the modern comforts. This 280 acre working dairy/sheep farm is set in peaceful countryside and ideally positioned for exploring the Lake District and Yorkshire Dales. Located four miles from Kendal on A684 road and three miles M6 Junction 37. This makes an ideal stopover between England and Scotland. We have one double, one family and one single bedrooms, all with tea/coffee facilities; bathroom with shower and toilet; lounge/dining room with colour TV. Full central heating. Full English breakfast served. Families are welcome, reduced rates for children. Weekly terms and Short Breaks available. Open March to November for Bed and Breakfast from £15.50 per person. Self catering caravan also available; weekly terms.

TARN HOWS

3–5 Eskin Street, Keswick CA12 4DH Cumbria
Telephone (017687) 73217
ETB ♛♛ Commended   RAC Acclaimed

Pleasantly situated in a quiet location only a few minutes walk from the town centre and all amenities. We have established a reputation for warm hospitality and a genuine concern for the success and comfort of your stay in Keswick. Freshly prepared food is served in our spacious licenced dining room. Most rooms en-suite with colour TV etc. Comfortable residents lounge, car park, secure cycle store and drying facilities for outdoor clothes. We are a No Smoking establishment. Bed and Breakfast from £17. Dinner £9.50.

KESWICK. Ken and Heather Armstrong, Kiln Hill Barn, Bassenthwaite, Keswick CA12 4RG (017687 76454). Kiln Hill Farm is set in open countryside with beautiful views. It offers single, twin and family bedrooms. TV. Lounge with a log fire for cooler evenings and central heating throughout. Coffee and tea making facilities in each room. En suite available. Evening meals and packed lunches on request. Meals served in the Barn Dining Room adjacent to the farmhouse. Terms and further details available on request.

KESWICK. Lindisfarne Guest House, 21 Church Street, Keswick CA12 4DX (017687 73218). A cosy, friendly guest house with home cooking and hearty breakfasts. Situated within a residential area close to the town centre of Keswick and within easy walking distance of Lake Derwentwater and Fitz Park. We have some en suite rooms and all bedrooms have colour TV, tea/coffee facilities, central heating and washbasin. Bed and Breakfast from £16.50; Evening Meal optional. Chris and Alison Burns look forward to welcoming you.

KESWICK. Bowfell, Chestnut Hill, Keswick CA12 4LR (017687 74859). Tourist Board Listed COMMENDED. Bowfell is a Victorian house on the edge of Keswick, but within walking distance of town. We are a small, warm and comfortable guest house. Private off road parking. Small patio barbecue area for guests enjoyment. All bedrooms have central heating, tea/coffee/hot chocolate facilities, colour TV and open views of the surrounding fells. Muddy boots and mountain bikes welcome; cycle storage and drying room provided. We are open all year with out of season bargain breaks. Bed and Breakfast from £13.50 per person per night; three-course evening meals (pre-booked) £7.50. Vegetarians catered for.

KESWICK. Mrs Marion Robinson, "Thelmlea" Country Guest House, Braithwaite, Keswick CA12 5TD (017687 78305). 🏵🏵🏵 Friendly family-run guest house set in one and three-quarter acres of grounds commanding superb views in Lakeland village two miles from Keswick. Boating, fishing, bowling, tennis, golf and horse riding available nearby. Central heating throughout. All bedrooms have full facilities including tea/coffee, colour TV and radio alarms. Packed lunches available. Access to rooms at all times including guests' lounge. A hair dryer, iron/ironing board and drying facilities are provided for use by guests. Children and pets welcome. Car park and garden area for guests' use. Reductions for weekly bookings. Brochure on request.

KESWICK. Lyndhurst Guest House, 22 Southerby Street, Keswick CA12 4EF (017687 72303). Well established Bed and Breakfast for non-smokers, two minutes' walk from town centre and ideally situated for local walks. All rooms are fully en suite and have colour TV, central heating and tea/coffe making facilities. Family, twin and double rooms available. Children and groups welcome; child discount applies. Cyclists welcome and cycle storage available. Packed lunches available. Bed and full English Breakfast £18.50 per person. We hold full Fire Certificate and are currently awaiting ETB classification.

KESWICK. Helen Taylor, The Bridgedale Cottage Guest House, 101-3 Main Street, Keswick CA12 5BE (017687 73914). Being situated right in the centre of Keswick, Bridgedale has offered comfortable and "value for money" accommodation since the days of Victorian charabancs. We are close to the bus station, Lake Derwentwater and the Tourist Information Office at The Moot Hall. Our decor is unique and unpretentious offering quality accommodation at a reasonable price. Relaxed lounge and licensed premises. Cobbled rear yard with sun chairs, surrounded by colourful bedding plants and honeysuckle (Winner of Keswick in Bloom Special Award 1997). Free-range eggs. Private parking. Please send for further information and our tariff. Room only rates available.

The Bridgedale Cottage Guest House

KESWICK. Grasslees B&B, Rickerby Lane, Portinscale, Keswick CA12 5RH (Tel & Fax: 017687 71313). Small country house of spacious and generous proportions situated in the quiet village of Portinscale approximately one mile from Keswick. Furnished and equipped to provide the luxury of hotel amenities in a comfortable and relaxed atmosphere of a luxurious Bed and Breakfast. Local village inn, two minutes' walk, is an ideal venue for locals and visitors alike serving light snacks and hearty meals both lunchtime and evening. The owners pride themselves on providing personal service whilst retaining guests' privacy and freedom. Private parking. Pets welcome by prior arrangement. Bed and Breakfast from £20. AA QQQ Listed, Guestaccom Member. Please telephone, or fax, for our colour brochure.

KESWICK. Heather and Lawrence Ashworth, Winchester Guest House, 58 Blencathra Street, Keswick CA12 4HT (017687 73664). Tourist Board

Listed. An attractive corner Victorian town house situated in a quiet part of Keswick just five minutes' walk from the town centre and parks. We have fell views from most of our spacious rooms. Enjoy a full English breakfast with beautiful view of Skiddaw. We have en suite and standard bedrooms, all are centrally heated and have colour TV, washbasin and tea/coffee making facilities. Open all year and our prices are from £16. Reduced rates for children sharing with parents. We are a non-smoking house.

KESWICK. Bay Tree, Wordsworth Street, Keswick CA12 4HU (017687 73313). ♛♛ Small,

family-run, licensed, non-smoking Guest House situated just three minutes' walk from the town centre on the Penrith road. Most rooms have lovely views over River Greta and Fitz Park to the mountains. All rooms have washbasins, central heating, double glazing, colour TV, tea/coffee making facilities; some rooms en suite. Home cooking, residents' lounge. Fire Certificate. Own key. Excellent location for touring Lake District and, for those who enjoy walking, we are near many of the well-known mountains. Lake, museums, leisure pool, etc only a short distance away. Bed and Breakfast from £16; Evening Meal; packed lunches by arrangement.

KESWICK. The Swan Hotel & Country Inn, Thornthwaite, Keswick CA12 5SQ (017687 78256). A

family-run 17th century former coaching inn set in idyllic surroundings twixt lake and mountains. For a true sense of beauty, history and relaxation, cossetted by polite friendly staff catering for your every need. Enjoy an open fire, lake walks, imaginative home-cooking and real ales. Bed and Breakfast from £25 per person per night; Dinner, Bed and Breakfast from £42 per night. Three nights Dinner, Bed and Breakfast from £118 per person per night. Children and pets welcome. Open all year. Excellent restaurant and bar food. Winter Breaks November to March from £16 per person per night. Please call Colin or Joy Harrison for a brochure.

KESWICK. Mrs Jane Vickers, Langdale, 14 Leonard Street, Keswick CA12 4EL (017687 73977). Victorian town house, quietly situated, yet close to town, park, lake and fells. Comfort and cleanliness our top priority. All rooms are tastefully decorated and centrally heated with colour TV, and tea making facilities; en suite facilities available. We also have a comfortable residents' lounge with colour TV and video. Enjoy a good home cooked English breakfast or our very popular extensive continental style breakfast. We have a non-smoking policy throughout the house. Bed and Breakfast from £15.50 per person.

KESWICK. J.W. and S. Miller, Acorn House Hotel, Ambleside Road, Keswick CA12 4DL (017687 72553; Fax: 017687 75332). ♛♛ *HIGHLY COMMEN-DED.*

Georgian house situated in gardens with private car parks yet only a few minutes from town centre, ideal for touring the Lake District. Traditional furniture enhances the character of each of the 10 spacious bedrooms complemented by the co-ordinated decor. All have ensuite bath/shower rooms, colour TV and tea/coffee making facilities; four poster beds also available. The generous full English breakfast will set you up for the day whether walking, climbing or sightseeing, and after the day's exertions you can relax in the large comfortable, elegant lounge. The Hotel is open most of the year and you can be sure of a warm welcome. Bed and Breakfast from £25 per person. Reduced rates for children. Directions, from M6 take A66 to Keswick. AA Listed, RAC Highly Acclaimed.

KESWICK. Ian and Janice Picken, Lynwood House Licensed Guest House, 35 Helvellyn Street, Keswick CA12 4EP (017687 72398). ♛ *COMMENDED.*

Fantastic scenery, fabulous fell walking; five minutes from town centre, 10 minutes to Lake Derwentwater. Free from smoke. Full Fire Certificate. Full breakfast menu. Finest cuisine — optional four-course evening meal. Facilities for tea/coffee making, heating; TV; washbasins and shaver points. Furnished distinctively. Friendly welcome. In short . . . absolutely fabulous!! Bed and Breakfast from £15 per person per night.

KESWICK. Mrs Sharon Helling, Beckside Guest House, 5 Wordsworth Street, Keswick CA12 4HU (017687 73093). ♛ *COMMENDED.* Beckside is a small, very comfortable guest house for non-smokers. We are situated close to the town centre and are convenient for the shops, Fitz Park, pool, lake, walking and touring. Our bedrooms are tastefully decorated and furnished; all have en suite facilities, colour TV, hospitality tray and central heating. We offer full English breakfast (or vegetarian alternative). Packed lunches are also available by arrangement. Bed and Breakfast £18.50 per person per night. AA QQQ, RAC Highly Acclaimed.

KESWICK. Mrs Elizabeth Scott, Woodside, Penrith Road, Keswick CA12 4LJ (017687 73522).

Situated on the outskirts of Keswick, "Woodside" is an ideal centre for sightseeing in the picturesque Lake District. This is a family-run bed and breakfast establishment offering the very highest of standards. Bedrooms with en suite, TV, tea making facilities and central heating. Large car park and lovely gardens. Many local attractions and country walks. Open all year round. Full English Breakfast. Bed and Breakfast from £17. Reduced rates in winter.

KESWICK. Gladys and David Birtwistle, Kalgurli Guest House, 33 Helvellyn Street, Keswick CA12 4EP (017687 72935). ♛♛ *COMMENDED.* Be assured of a warm and friendly welcome at this comfortable non-smoking four bedroomed guest house. Excellent grilled breakfast, served between 8am and 9am. Menu choice. Vegetarians catered for. Packed lunches available. Kalgurli is an ideal location for touring and walking, plenty of on-street parking. Rooms accessible all day. Own key. Accommodation comprises one large en suite family room/twin, one en suite double room and two standard rooms, all with colour TV and tea/coffee making facilities. Standard rooms £15.50; en suite £17 to £18.

KESWICK. Alan and Jean Redfern, Heatherlea, 26 Blencathra Street, Keswick CA12 4HP (017687 72430). This charming and friendly guest house is personally run by the owners. A full and varied breakfast menu is served (8am to 9am) in our delightful dining room with its views of the Skiddaw Fells. The house is centrally heated and each room offers every comfort, with en suite facilities, remote control colour TV, electric blankets, heated towel rail, hair dryer, clock radio and tea/coffee facilities. Heatherlea is close to the town centre and an ideal place from which to tour and walk this wonderful part of the Lake District. Residential licence. Non-smokers only. Bed and Breakfast £18 to £19. AA QQQ.

KESWICK. David and Valerie Fisher, Howe Keld Lakeland Hotel, 5-7 The Heads, Keswick CA12 5ES (Tel & Fax: 017687 72417). 🦢🦢 *COMMENDED.*

Delightful Lakeland hotel situated in one of the most beautiful and convenient locations in Keswick. Personally run by resident owners, offering well appointed en suite bedrooms with colour TV. Licensed bar and separate lounge. Home cooked meals, vegetarian food is a speciality and there is an exceptional choice for breakfast. Children and pets welcome. Bed and Breakfast from £20. RAC Acclaimed, AA QQQ. Please ring for brochure.

KESWICK. Mr A. and Mrs P.H. Smith, Goodwin House, 29 Southey Street, Keswick CA12 4EE (017687 74634). 🦢🦢

Goodwin House is an attractive Victorian centrally heated residence, quietly situated close to town centre and Derwentwater Lake. All bedrooms are comfortable, tastefully decorated and have en suite facilities, colour TV and tea/coffee trays. Our visitors are assured of warm and friendly service in pleasant surroundings. Excellent and plentiful breakfasts. Bed and Breakfast from £18. Weekly terms by arrangement. No children or dogs. Open all year. Non smokers only. AA QQQQ Recommended.

KESWICK. Mr & Mrs J.M. Pepper, Beckstones Farm, Thornthwaite, Keswick CA12 5SQ (017687 78510). 🦢🦢 *COMMENDED.*

Beckstones Farm
Thornthwaite, Keswick, Cumbria.

Keswick three-and-a-half miles, near the head of Bassenthwaite Lake. Beckstones is a homely and comfortable converted Georgian farmhouse built in 1726. Set in peaceful surroundings and enjoying superb views of Skiddaw and Helvellyn ranges, yet an excellent touring centre for the motorist. Run as a smallholding; all modern amenities along with traditional comfort in our cosy oak-beamed diningroom and in the TV lounge; all bedrooms are centrally heated with full en suite facilities and tea/coffee making. Ample private parking. Dogs welcome by arrangement. Bed and Breakfast from £21.

KESWICK. Mr and Mrs J. McMullan, Jenkin Hill Cottage, Thornthwaite, Keswick CA12 5SG (017687 78443). 🦢🦢 *HIGHLY COMMENDED.*

Situated in a quiet village, nestled between Bassenthwaite Lake and Thornthwaite Forest, some four miles from Keswick; within 20 minutes of M6 Junction 40 this is an ideal base for a Lakeland holiday or stopover when travelling north or south. There are award-winning gardens on all sides of the cottage giving all the bedrooms a garden view. Each room is tastefully decorated and furnished with matching en suite bath and shower rooms. Tea/coffee making facilities, colour TV, central heating available in all rooms. Full four-course English breakfast offered and diets will be catered for whenever possible. Highly recommended bar meals available at local Hotel. We have a non-smoking policy throughout the premises. Private parking with security lighting. Terms from £20 to £23 per person. Open all year except Christmas.

CUMBRIA – LAKELAND SPLENDOUR!

The Lake District has for long been a popular tourist destination; however, the Fells and Pennine areas are also worth exploring. The many attractions of Cumbria include the Ennerdale Forest, St. Bees Head, Langdale Pikes, Bowness-on-Solway, the market town of Alston, Lanercost Priory, Scafell Pike – England's highest mountain – and the Wordsworth country around Ambleside, Grasmere and Cockermouth.

KESWICK. I. and M. Atkinson, "Dancing Beck", Underskiddaw, Keswick CA12 4PY (017687

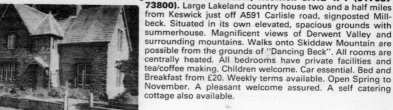

73800). Large Lakeland country house two and a half miles from Keswick just off A591 Carlisle road, signposted Millbeck. Situated in its own elevated, spacious grounds with summerhouse. Magnificent views of Derwent Valley and surrounding mountains. Walks onto Skiddaw Mountain are possible from the grounds of "Dancing Beck". All rooms are centrally heated. All bedrooms have private facilities and tea/coffee making. Children welcome. Car essential. Bed and Breakfast from £20. Weekly terms available. Open Spring to November. A pleasant welcome assured. A self catering cottage also available.

KESWICK. Annie Scally and Ian Townsend, Latrigg House, St. Herbert Street, Keswick CA12 4DF

(017687 73068). 🛏️🛏️ An attractive Victorian house in a quiet area, only a few minutes' walk from the town centre and Lake, providing an excellent base for visiting the Lake District. We promise a very warm welcome, good food, comfort and hospitality (vegetarian and vegan meals provided if required). We offer a no-smoking environment for the well being and comfort of guests, comfortable rooms (some with en suite facilities), all with colour TVs and tea/coffee facilities and heating. Comfortable residents lounge with TV. Bed and Breakfast from £14 to £18.50 (evening meals available). Children under 12 special rate if sharing adult room. Sorry no pets.

KESWICK. David and Margaret Raine, Clarence House, 14 Eskin Street, Keswick CA12 4DQ

(017687 73186). 🛏️🛏️ *COMMENDED.* A lovely Victorian house ideally situated for the Lake, parks and market square. Bedrooms are decorated to a high standard, have full en suite facilities, colour TVs, hospitality trays and central heating. A four-poster room and ground floor room are available. A warm welcome and hearty breakfast await you. Bed and Breakfast from £19 per person. Non smoking. Brochure sent with pleasure on request.

KESWICK. Barry and Cathy Colam, Cumbria Hotel, Ambleside Road, Keswick CA12 4DR (Tel &

Fax: 017687 73171). An attractive Victorian family house but with all the modern comforts which guests expect. Central but quiet the Cumbria is close to town, parks, lake and fells. From the dining room look out over St. John's Church and the Newlands Fell; where better to enjoy a freshly cooked breakfast. In the lounge dip into guide books to help plan your holiday; or relax with a drink by the fire or on the patio – depending on season. Individuals, families, groups and dogs welcome. We have a car park, bike storage and a drying room. Bed and Breakfast from £18 per person per night. Evening meals and packed lunches by arrangement.

KESWICK (Lake District). Tony and Ann Atkin, Glencoe Guest House, 21 Helvellyn Street, Keswick CA12 4EN (017687 71016). Cycling, walking or touring, a warm welcome is guaranteed. Our renovated Victorian Guest House is conveniently situated only five minutes' stroll from centre of Keswick and all amenities. Glencoe offers spacious en suite and standard rooms, all decorated and furnished to a high standard, each with their own colour TV and hospitality tray. Double, twin and single rooms available. This is a totally non-smoking guest house with full central heating and Fire Certificate. Local knowledge and maps are available to those wishing to explore the Northern Lakes and Fells. Cycle storage also available. Bed and Breakfast from £16 per person.

KESWICK near. Mrs Val Bradley, North Mount, North Row, Bassenthwaite, Near Keswick CA12 4RJ (017687 76044). Picturesque small village near north end of Bassenthwaite Lake, in an area with a large variety of activities, lovely walks, fishing and horse riding all nearby. North Mount is delightfully situated in the Lake District National Park enjoying spectacular views over the village and Skiddaw. There is a 15th century inn serving excellent food within 100 yards. Val Bradley offers a warm welcome to all who visit; single, double, family or twin rooms have tea/coffee making facilities and colour TV. Tea, coffee and biscuits supplied. Guests' own bathroom. Available all year. Private parking. From £16 per person per night. Optional Evening Meals. Special children's rates.

KESWICK near. Maureen and Roy Butcher, Thornthwaite Hall, Thornthwaite Village, Near Keswick CA12 5SA (Tel & Fax: 017687 78424). ♥♥♥ *APPROVED*. Thornthwaite Hall is a traditional 17th century farmhouse, modernised and converted to make very comfortable country house accommodation. All rooms are en suite with TV, tea/coffee making facilities. We offer an extensive menu providing a variety of good home cooking with a residential licence. Thornthwaite is a peaceful hamlet close to Keswick and ideally located for walking or touring the northern lakes, fells and forest. Dogs and children are welcome. Open all year except Christmas. Bed and Breakfast £22 to £25; Dinner, Bed and Breakfast from £32.50. Weekly terms from £205. Major credit cards accepted.

KESWICK/BORROWDALE. Mrs S.A. Roscamp, Stable Rigg, Grange-in-Borrowdale, Keswick CA12 5UQ (017687 77605). Stable Rigg is situated in the village of Grange in the Borrowdale Valley which is renowned for splendid scenery, Derwentwater, a wealth of walks and places of interest and four miles from Keswick town. Comfortable accommodation offered in this small cottage converted from a stable, is one double and one single room with tea/coffee tray, private facilities. Sitting room with TV for guests' use. An open log fire burns early/late season. Easy off road parking. Choice of good eating places nearby for evening meal. Open Easter to end October, then by request. Bed and full Breakfast from £17.

KESWICK/BORROWDALE. Mrs S. Bland, Thorneythwaite Farm, Borrowdale, Keswick CA12 5XQ (017687 77237). Thoneythwaite Farm has a beautiful, peaceful position in the Borrowdale Valley standing half a mile off the road. The 220 acre sheep farm is seven miles from Keswick and half a mile from Seatoller. The 18th century farmhouse has great character inside and out, several rooms having oak beams and panelling and being furnished to suit. Two double and one family bedrooms, all with tea/coffee making facilities; sitting room with open or electric fire; dining room; bathroom and toilet. Cot, high chair and reduced rates for children. Sorry no pets. Open from April to November, mid-week bookings accepted. A perfect base for a honeymoon or for those who enjoy fell walking. Bed and Breakfast from £16.

KIRKBY LONSDALE near. Pat Nicholson, Green Lane End Farm, Lupton, Kirkby Lonsdale, Carnforth LA6 2PP (015395 67236). Working farm.

Three miles from M6 Junction 36. Excellent stopover when travelling to and from Scotland. 17th century farmhouse with oak beams and fine old staircase in quiet unspoilt area of South Lakeland. Ideally situated for touring Lakes and Dales. Tea/coffee making facilities. Pets by arrangement. Terms from £15. Directions: From M6 take A65 to Kirkby Lonsdale, first right after Plough Inn, follow Farm B&B signs. From Kirkby Lonsdale, fourth left after Kirkby Motors follow signs.

KIRKBY LONSDALE. Mrs Pauline Bainbridge, Tossbeck Farm, Middleton, Kirkby Lonsdale, via Carnforth, Lancs. LA6 2LZ (015242 76214). Tossbeck

Farm is a 110 acre dairy and sheep farm situated in the beautiful unspoilt countryside of the Lune Valley midway between the market towns of Kirkby Lonsdale and Sedbergh. The farmhouse is a 16th century listed building featuring oak panelling. Ideally situated for visiting both the Lake District and the Yorkshire Dales; the biggest Show Cave in England is only eight miles away. One family room and one double room, both spacious with washbasins and tea/coffee making facilities. Lounge with TV, dining room, visitors' bathroom and central heating. Bed and full English Breakfast from £12.50. No smoking please.

KIRKBY STEPHEN. Mrs Sylvia Capstick, Duckintree House, Kaber, Kirkby Stephen CA17 4ER (017683 71073). Duckintree is a working family farm set in

the quiet Eden Valley countryside just off the A685 Kirkby Stephen to Brough road. Easy access to the Lakes and Yorkshire Dales or ideal for breaking your journey from the south of England/Midlands to Scotland. Car essential, ample parking. The rooms comprise family, double and twin (cot available) with tea/coffee making facilities. Lounge/dining room with colour TV. All rooms overlook a large garden and countryside. Bed and Breakfast from £16. Reductions for children under 12 years. Pets welcome by arrangement. Evening meal can be provided. Open from March to October. Write or phone for details.

LEVENS/KENDAL. Mrs A.H. Parsons, Olde Peat Cotes, Sampool Lane, Levens, Kendal LA8 8EH (015395 60096). Tourist Board Listed. Handy distance to seaside, Lakes or Scotland. Modern, comfortable bungalow with every facility. Sleeps four in two double bedrooms, one with twin beds. Children welcome at reduced rates. Situated in peaceful surroundings with lovely views. Farm adjacent. Fishing permits available on River Kent. Parking space. All local pubs do excellent bar snacks. Bed and Breakfast from £10.

LOWICK (near Coniston). Garth Row, Lowick Green, Ulverston LA12 8EB (01229 885633). Tourist

Board Listed *COMMENDED.* Traditional, beamed cottage only three miles from Coniston Water in this beautiful and little-known corner of the National Park. The house stands alone amidst farmland and common with lovely valley and mountain views. We offer quality accommodation with two attractive rooms for guests. Our super family room with its gallery (children love it!) can also serve as a double or twin. Comfortable lounge with books, TV and a real fire on cold nights. Good food, tea/coffee in rooms, dogs welcome, wonderful walking, drying room, no smoking. Super quiet holiday spot or overnight stay. Bed and Breakfast from £15. Brochure.

MILNTHORPE. Mrs Carey, Homestead, Ackenthwaite, Milnthorpe LA7 7DH (015395 63708).

Small, friendly, non-smoking guest house situated in South Lakeland. Approximately 10 minutes by car from Kendal and conveniently positioned between the Lakes, Dales and Lancashire Border making an ideal base for walking and touring; we are close enough to the A6 and M6 motorway to be convenient for your overnight stop to and from Scotland. The small but busy market town of Milnthorpe is within strolling distance and the Nature Reserves at Leighton Moss and Silverdale are close by. En suite double, family, twin or standard single/twin rooms available. Bed and Breakfast from £16.50. Evening Meals by arrangement.

NEWBIGGIN ON LUNE. Mrs B.M. Boustead, Tranna Hill, Newbiggin-on-Lune, Near Kirkby Stephen

CA17 4NY (015396 23227). Tranna Hill offers a relaxing and friendly atmosphere in a non-smoking environment. Five miles from M6 (Junction 38), beautifully situated on fringe of Newbiggin-on-Lune village, ideal base for country lovers and walkers with nature reserve and Sunbiggin Tarn nearby. Well placed for touring the Lake District, Yorkshire, Durham Dales and for breaking your journey. Relax in guests' lounge with TV and then have a good night's sleep in en suite rooms with tea making facilities, central heating and beautiful views, followed by a delicious breakfast. RIPHH Certificate. Bed and Breakfast from £17.

NEWBY BRIDGE near. Hazel and David Brown, Cobblestones, Causeway End, Haverthwaite,

Ulverston LA12 8JW (015395 31391). AA QQQQ Selected. Enjoy peace and tranquillity within a 16th century former farmhouse offering old world charm with a wealth of original features. Panoramic views over meadow, forest and moorland to Coniston Fells. Situated between Windermere Lake and Coniston Water, Grizedale Forest and Hawkshead village, the home of Beatrix Potter, are a short drive away — an ideal base for exploring the whole Lake District. Benefitting from a residential licence, optional three-course home cooked dinner is available. Two double and one twin/double bedrooms are all en suite. Easy access from A590, 20 minutes from M6 Junction 36. No smoking, ample parking, cycle hire, walkers welcome. Bed and Breakfast from £20. Terms for longer stays.

NEWLANDS. Mrs M.A. Relph, Littletown Farm, Newlands, Keswick CA12 5TU (017687 78353).

Working farm. Littletown has all the facilities of a small hotel and most bedrooms are en suite. Situated in a peaceful part of the beautiful Newlands Valley, with surrounding hills providing excellent walking and climbing. Market towns of Keswick and Cockermouth, Lakes Derwentwater and Bassenthwaite all within easy distance. Farmhouse, though fully modernised, still retains a traditional character with comfortable lounge, dining room and cosy licensed bar. All bedrooms have tea-making facilities, heating and washbasins. Traditional four-course dinner (roast beef, lamb, etc) served six nights a week; full English breakfast every morning. Littletown Farm is featured in Beatrix Potter's "Mrs Tiggy Winkle". Ample parking. Dinner, Bed and Breakfast from £36 to £40 per person; Bed and Breakfast from £24 to £29 per person. SAE please.

Littletown farm

PENRITH. Mrs Jean Raynor, Blue Swallow Guest House, 11 Victoria Road, Penrith CA11 8HR (01768 866335). ☙☙ *COMMENDED.* A comfortable Victorian house set in the attractive market town of Penrith, ideally situated to explore the delightful Eden Valley, the wonderful scenery of the Lake District and the Yorkshire Dales National Park. For the golfing enthusiast Penrith boasts an 18 hole course and there are several more within easy driving distance. Resident proprietors Jean and Mel Raynor look forward to welcoming you whether you are on holiday, just breaking a long journey or in the area for business — you'll be made to feel at home. All rooms have colour TV, tea trays and central heating. Full and varied English breakfast served. Bed and Breakfast from £15 to £19 per person.

BANNERDALE VIEW

Mungrisdale, Near Penrith, Cumbria CA11 0XR

Tel: 017687 79691   Mike & Penny Sutton

If you love the Lakes, but prefer to avoid the crowds, welcome to our centrally-heated 17th century Lakeland cottage. Surrounded on three sides by Fells and with a river running through the 2 acres of garden, a more peaceful and idyllic location would be hard to imagine. Though we have a double and a twin-bedded room, each with beverage making facilities, we only accept one booking at a time, for up to 4 people, so that the adjoining bathroom is for the exclusive use of that booking. There is also a toilet and wash basin on the ground floor, as well as a guests' lounge with colour TV. As retired hoteliers, we are renowned for good food and breakfasts to satisfy the heartiest appetites, although we provide a Continental Breakfast if you insist! Mountain or low level walks can be made from the Cottage and any part of the Lakes can easily be explored in the day by car. Well-behaved dogs are welcomed. We are a non-smoking establishment. Rates from £18. Dinner (pre-booking essential) £13.50. Brochure.

PENRITH. Jean and Ron Forrester, "Lonnin End", Pallet Hill, Penrith CA11 0BY (017684 83453). Pallet Hill is a quiet hamlet on the B5288 Penrith to Greystoke road. Two miles approximately M6 Junction 40. Ideal for exploring the beauty of the Lake District/Eden Valley/Scottish Borders. One double, one family room, both with central heating, colour TV and tea/coffee facilities including biscuits. No smoking. No pets. A friendly welcome with that personal touch, a substantial English breakfast; vegetarians catered for. Jean and Ron do their best to make all guests feel at home, in pleasant surroundings. Bed and Breakfast £15.

PENRITH. Mrs Eileen Lamond, Prospect House, Piper Lane, Kirkby Thore, Penrith CA10 1UP (017683 61672). Prospect House is situated in a quiet location on the edge of Kirkby Thore village in an elevated position with beautiful views of the Lake District hills to the west and the Pennines to the East. We are situated in the Eden Valley, nine miles south of Penrith and four miles north of Appleby on the A66. Ideal for walking and touring with easy access to Lakes, Yorkshire Dales and Scottish Borders. A special welcome awaits you in our Victorian farmhouse, with comfortable and friendly accommodation and a hearty English breakfast to start the day.

PENRITH. Mrs C. Tully, Brandelhow Guest House, 1 Portland Place, Penrith CA11 7QN (01768 864470). ☙ *COMMENDED.* A warm welcome assured at this AA QQQ guest house offering a high standard of comfort and cleanliness. Five spacious, tastefully decorated bedrooms, all with hot and cold water, central heating, double glazing, colour TV and tea/coffee making facilities. Twin, double and family rooms available, including one excellent family room for five. Ideally situated, close to M6, A6 and A66, for touring the Lake District, Scottish Borders, Hadrian's Wall and for overnight stops en route to and from Scotland. Local amenities include Lowther Fun Park, golf, sailing and pony trekking. Bed and Breakfast from £15 double, £18 single inclusive. Weekly terms available.

PENRITH. Mrs Brenda Preston, Pallet Hill Farm, Penrith CA11 0BY (017684 83247). Pallet Hill Farm

is pleasantly situated two miles from Penrith on the Penrith-Greystoke-Keswick road (B5288). It is four miles from Ullswater and has easy access to the Lake District, Scottish Borders and Yorkshire Dales. There are several sports facilities in the area — golf club, swimming pool, pony trekking; places to visit such as Lowther Leisure Park and the Miniature Railway at Ravenglass. Good farmhouse food and hospitality with personal attention. Double, single, family rooms; dining/sitting room. Children welcome, cot, high chair. Sorry no pets. Car essential, parking. Open Easter to November. Bed and Breakfast from £10.50 (reduced weekly rates). Reduced rates for children.

PENRITH. Norcroft Guest House, Graham Street, Penrith CA11 9LQ (Tel & Fax: 01768 862365).

👑👑👑 *COMMENDED*. Spacious Victorian house in a quiet area. Large and comfortable ensuite bedrooms with colour TV and beverage making facilities. We have two family suites, with main bedroom and separate connecting children's bedrooms. We have a very pleasant dining room. Residential licence. Private car park. Penrith is an ideal centre for touring the Lake District, the Eden Valley, Hadrian's Wall and the Borders. It is an ideal stopover for travellers going north to Scotland or south to holiday in England or the Continent. Bed and Breakfast from £16, Dinner from £10.50. A warm welcome awaits you. Children welcome. Directions: Leave M6 at Junction 40 into one way system, left at town hall opposite R.C. Church.

PENRITH. Angela and Ivor Davies, Woodland House Hotel, Wordsworth Street, Penrith CA11 7QY

(01768 864177; Fax: 01768 890152; E-mail: idaviesa@cix.compulink.co.uk). 👑👑 *COMMENDED*. Small, friendly and elegant licensed private hotel situated at the foot of Beacon Hill, and only five minutes' walk from the centre of the town. Large car park. All rooms are en suite and have tea/coffee making facilities and colour TV. We serve delicious food using the best fresh local produce and, with notice, will gladly meet any special dietary requirements. Whether on business or pleasure an ideal base for exploring Lakes, Borders, Pennines, Eden Valley or stopover to/from Scotland. Library of maps and books for walkers, nature lovers and sightseers. Open all year. Sorry, no pets. The Hotel is NO SMOKING throughout. Bed and Breakfast from £28; Dinner from £9.50. AA QQQ, RAC Acclaimed. Brochure.

PENRITH. Mrs C. Blundell, Albany House, 5 Portland Place, Penrith CA11 7QN (01768 863072).

ETB *COMMENDED*. AA QQQ. Close to town centre, Albany House is a large mid-Victorian terraced house. A high standard of cleanliness, comfort and personal friendly attention is assured at all times. Five spacious nicely decorated bedrooms (one double, three triple, all with washbasins; one family en suite). All have central heating, colour/satellite TV and tea/coffee making facilities. Situated close to M6, A6 and A66, ideal base for touring Lake District, Eden Valley, Hadrian's Wall, Scottish Borders and an excellent stopover between England and Scotland. Within easy reach are Lowther Leisure Park, sailing, wind surfing, fell walking, pony trekking, golf and swimming. Bed and Breakfast from £16.

PENRITH. Mrs Ann Toppin, Gale Hall, Melmerby, Penrith CA10 1HN (01768 881254). Working farm. Mrs Ann Toppin welcomes guests to her home on a working beef/sheep farm 10 miles east of Penrith and the M6, a mile and a half from the peaceful village of Melmerby. Beautiful setting at the foot of the Pennines and with extensive views of the Lakeland Fells. Ideal for walking, convenient for the Lake District. Single, double, twin or family rooms available; cot and babysitting. Residents' lounge. Pets welcome by arrangement. Bed and Breakfast from £15; reductions for children under 12 years. Special diets catered for. Full English or Vegetarian Breakfast served. Excellent bar meals available locally.

PENRITH. Tim and Jane Metcalfe, Home Farm, Edenhall, Penrith CA11 8SS (01768 881203).

Working farm. A warm welcome awaits you at Home Farm, situated on the outskirts of the peaceful village of Edenhall three miles east of Penrith. We are ideally situated for seeing the Eden Valley, North Pennines, Hadrian's Wall and are conveniently located for the Lake District or en route to/from Scotland. Full English Breakfast, evening meals obtainable locally. Accommodation comprises double, family or twin rooms. Reduced rates for children. Bed and Breakfast from £17 per person.

PENRITH. Mrs Jean Ashburner, Lattendales Farm, Berrier Road, Greystoke, Penrith CA11 0UE (017684 83474). Working farm, join in. Comfortable 17th century farmhouse in quiet attractive village five miles from Penrith. Ideal for touring the Northern Lakes. Accommodation comprises one twin room and two double rooms; lounge with colour TV. Children and pets welcome; reductions for children. Non-smoking. Bed and Breakfast from £15 to £16 per person. Directions, follow B5288 from Penrith, in Greystoke take Berrier Road and Lattendales Farm is first B&B on left.

SEDBERGH. Mike and Liz Clark, Farfield Country Guest House, Garsdale Road, Sedbergh LA10 5JN (015396 20537). The warmest of welcomes await you in our Victorian former Millowners country house set in large grounds full of mature trees with fabulous views of the Howgill Fells. Ideally situated for visiting both the Lake District and Yorkshire Dales. We have two guest lounges, one with open fire, seven bedrooms most with en suites, all with tea/coffee facilities and central heating throughout. Evening dinner also available where everything is home made. So come and stay with us and really enjoy great hospitality, superb food in a lovely home — guests are continually saying this to us. Non smoking. Bed and Breakfast from £20; packed lunches available.

SHAP. Mr and Mrs D. L. and M. Brunskill, Brookfield, Shap, Penrith CA10 3PZ (01931 716397). AA Listed. Fire Certificate granted. Situated one mile from M6 Motorway (turn off at Shap interchange No. 39), first accommodation off motorway. Excellent position for touring Lakeland, or overnight accommodation for travelling north or south. Central heating throughout, renowned for good food, comfort and personal attention. All bedrooms are well appointed and have colour TV and tea/coffee making facilities; en suite available. Diningroom where delicious home cooking is a speciality. Well-stocked bar. Residents' lounge. Sorry, no pets. Open from February to December. Terms sent on request. Car essential — ample parking.

TEBAY. Carmel House Guest House, Mount Pleasant, Tebay CA10 3TH (015396 24651). ♛ ♛ Ideally situated between the beautiful Lune and Eden Valleys, quarter of a mile from M6 Junction 38. Ideal stopover or base for touring — midway between Lakes and Yorkshire Dales — or fishing the River Lune and walking the lovely surrounding countryside. Three double, one twin and two singles, all en suite with colour TV, central heating and tea/coffee facilities. Full Fire Certificate. Private parking. Bed and Breakfast from £16.50. AA QQQ, RAC Acclaimed.

FREE and REDUCED RATE Holiday Visits!
See our READERS' OFFER VOUCHER for details.

TROUTBECK. Gwen and Peter Parfitt, Hill Crest, Troutbeck, Penrith CA11 0SH (017684 83935).

Gwen and Peter assure you of a warm and friendly welcome at Hill Crest, their unique Lakeland home which offers two en suite double/family rooms, one twin room. Home cooking, choice of menu including vegetarian; non smoking lounge/dining room, early morning tea, bedtime drinks; packed lunches. Panoramic mountain views. Aira Force waterfalls, Ullswater 10 minutes, Keswick 15 minutes, a good base for walking, boating, touring, Lakes, Hadrian's Wall and the Borders. Books, maps and hints from Gwen on what to see. Walkers, children and dogs welcome. Bed and Breakfast £14 per person twin room, £16 per person en suite rooms. Children half price sharing. Dinner from £5 (optional). Weekly rates. 10 minutes Junction 40 M6. At Hill Crest we aim to create a relaxed and informal atmosphere where guests are treated as part of the family. Highly recommended by previous guests.

ULLSWATER. Mrs S. Hunter, Grove Foot Farm, Watermillock, Penrith CA11 0NA (017684 86416).

Working farm. Grove Foot is a 90 acre dairy farm just off the A66 and two miles from Lake Ullswater. The house, built around 1650, has oak beams and open fires and sleeps six guests. Close by are historic houses and gardens, fishing, swimming pools, golf and pony trekking. Open March to October. Children welcome. Sorry, no pets. Bed and Breakfast from £14.

WINDERMERE. Mr and Mrs R. Tyson, Holly-Wood Guest House, Holly Road, Windermere LA23 2AF

(015394 42219). Comfortable accommodation in elegant stone-built Lakeland guest house. Situated in quiet position away from the main road but within easy walking distance of buses, trains and local amenities. An ideal central base for touring the Lake District. Also within easy reach of Morecambe Bay and the Dales. Single, double, twin and family rooms are available (some en-suite). Central heating, tea/coffee makers, colour TV. Reductions for children and long stays. Low Season Mini Breaks. Open March to November. Bed and Breakfast from £14 per person. RAC Acclaimed. Sorry no pets. SAE please for brochure and tariff.

FOR THE MUTUAL GUIDANCE OF GUEST AND HOST

Every year literally thousands of holidays, short-breaks and overnight stops are arranged through our guides, the vast majority without any problems at all. In a handful of cases, however, difficulties do arise about bookings, which often could have been prevented from the outset.

It is important to remember that when accommodation has been booked, both parties — guests and hosts — have entered into a form of contract. We hope that the following points will provide helpful guidance.

GUESTS: When enquiring about accommodation, be as precise as possible. Give exact dates, numbers in your party and the ages of any children. State the number and type of rooms wanted and also what catering you require — bed and breakfast, full board, etc. Make sure that the position about evening meals is clear — and about pets, reductions for children or any other special points.

Read our reviews carefully to ensure that the proprietors you are going to contact can supply what you want. Ask for a letter confirming all arrangements, if possible.

If you have to cancel, do so as soon as possible. Proprietors do have the right to retain deposits and under certain circumstances to charge for cancelled holidays if adequate notice is not given and they cannot re-let the accommodation.

HOSTS: Give details about your facilities and about any special conditions. Explain your deposit system clearly and arrangements for cancellations, charges, etc. and whether or not your terms include VAT.

If for any reason you are unable to fulfil an agreed booking without adequate notice, you may be under an obligation to arrange alternative suitable accommodation or to make some form of compensation.

While every effort is made to ensure accuracy, we regret that FHG Publications cannot accept responsibility for errors, omissions or misrepresentation in our entries or any consequences thereof. Prices in particular should be checked because we go to press early. We will follow up complaints but cannot act as arbiters or agents for either party.

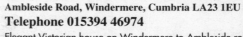

WINDERMERE. Mrs P. Wood, The Haven Guest House, Birch Street, Windermere LA23 1EG (015394 44017). The Haven is a comfortable Victorian Guest House conveniently located in the attractive lakeside village of Windermere, a short walk from the railway station, restaurants, shops and all local amenities. Sports such as walking, mountaineering, pony trekking and water ski-ing can be enjoyed in the area. All rooms have TV and tea/coffee making facilities. Open all year. Bed and Breakfast from £15. Vegetarians catered for. Reductions for children. No smoking. Parking. Brochure on request. AA QQ.

WINDERMERE. The Beaumont Hotel, Holly Road, Windermere LA23 2AF (Tel & Fax: 015394 47075; e-mail: the beaumonthotel@btinternet.com). An elegant Victorian Villa occupying an enviable position for all the amenities of Windermere/Bowness and an ideal base from which to explore Lakeland. The highest standards prevail and the lovely en suite bedrooms (three superb four-poster rooms) are immaculate, offering all modern comforts — quality beds, colour TVs, hairdryers and welcome trays. Freshly cooked hearty breakfasts are served in the delightful dining room and the charming sitting room is a restful place to relax with a book. Excellent private car park. Children over 10 years. Non smoking. Tariff: Low Season £23 to £36; High Season £25 to £38. All prices are per person per night and include full English breakfast. Please phone or write for full colour brochure.

WINDERMERE. Diane and David Weatherley, Crookleigh Guesthouse, 15 Woodland Road, Windermere LA23 2AE (Tel & Fax: 015394 48480; Mobile: 0410 538061). A comfortable high quality Victorian home, tastefully furnished and close to the village and station. Our four-course breakfast consists of fruit juices, cereals/fresh fruit, full English/vegetarian or our Special Healthy alternative. Combined with freshly brewed coffee, speciality teas, home baked rolls, free-range eggs, local produce, it makes our breakfasts both memorable and long lasting! All rooms are individually decorated, have colour TV, generous hospitality trays and represent Excellent Value for Money. Family, double and twin rooms available. Pets welcome by arrangement. Seasonal and party reductions available on request. Prices from £15 to £22.50 per person per night.

WINDERMERE. John and Liz Christopherson, Villa Lodge, Cross Street, Windermere LA23 1AE (Tel & Fax: 015394 43318). ❦❦ *COMMENDED.* Friendliness and cleanliness guaranteed. Extremely comfortable accommodation in peaceful area overlooking Windermere village, yet two minutes from station. All six bedrooms are tastefully decorated, mostly en-suite (some four-posters), with colour TV, tea/coffee making facilities and full central heating. Most have magnificent views of the Lake and mountains. Access to rooms at all times. Superb English Breakfast served in our delightful dining room. Vegetarian and special diets catered for. Open all year. Special offers November-March. Safe, private parking for six cars. An excellent base for exploring the whole of the Lake District. Bed and Breakfast from £18. AA QQQ. Ring John and Liz Christopherson for details.

Terms quoted in this publication may be subject to increase if rises in costs necessitate

WINDERMERE. Mrs R. Phelps, Winbrook House, 30 Ellerthwaite Road, Windermere LA23 2AH

(015394 44932). ❦❦ *COMMENDED.* A friendly welcome awaits you at Winbrook House which is convenient for village and lake. Ideal touring centre. We offer personal service, together with excellent English cooking, under the personal supervision of the proprietors. All rooms are decorated to a high standard; residents' lounge with colour TV; full central heating. All bedrooms have private showers/baths, colour TV, tea/coffee making facilities, and most have private toilets. Access to rooms at all times. Private parking. Full Fire Certificate. AA Listed, RAC Acclaimed. Open all year. Bed and Breakfast from £16 to £22.

WINDERMERE. Gill and Barry Pearson, Broadlands Guest House, 19 Broad Street, Windermere LA23 2AB (Tel & Fax: 015394 46532). ❦❦ *COMMENDED.* AA QQQ Recommended. A warm welcome awaits you at Broadlands overlooking Ellerthwaite Gardens in the centre of Windermere. It is close to all amenities and is an ideal base for the Lake District, being only 300 yards from train/coach station and convenient for the Lakes, walks, tours, etc. Car not essential but plenty of public parking is available. Double, twin and family rooms, all en suite with colour TV, central heating and tea/coffee making facilities. Substantial full English breakfast or vegetarian breakfast provided. Bed and Breakfast from £16 to £21. Reductions for children. Open all year. All major credit cards accepted.

WINDERMERE. Sue and Dick Clothier, Ivy Bank, Holly Road, Windermere LA23 2AF (015394 42601).

 COMMENDED. An elegant stone built Victorian non-smoking home in a quiet central location, Ivy Bank is attractively and comfortably furnished throughout. All bedrooms are en suite and have color TV, tea/coffee making facilities and central heating. The atmosphere is relaxed and informal and in the residents lounge there is a good selection of books, guides and childrens toys/games. Within 30 minutes walk from Ivy Bank are several excellent view points. A substantial choice of breakfast is included in the price which ranges from £15 to £22 dependant upon season and duration of stay. Private car park and storage for bikes available.

WINDERMERE. Mick and Angela Brown, Haisthorpe Guest House, Holly Road, Windermere LA23 2AF (Tel & Fax: 015394 43445; E-mail: haisthorpe @aol.com.).

AA QQQQ Selected and RAC Highly Acclaimed family-run guest house concentrating on high standards of accommodation and service at reasonable prices. We are situated in a quiet central area of Windermere and convenient for the local train/coach station (free collection by arrangement). All rooms have colour TV with satellite channel, hospitality tray and hair dryer. Five rooms have en suite bathrooms and one has private bathroom. No smoking in bedrooms. Private off-street parking. Credit cards accepted. Bed and Breakfast from £14 to £18 low season, £16 to £21 high season, reductions for long stays.

WINDERMERE. College House, College Road, Windermere LA23 1BU (015394 45767).

 COMMENDED. A non-smoking, spacious Victorian family home offering a warm and friendly welcome, in a quiet area close to village centre and railway station. Some rooms have superb mountain views, all are either en suite or have private bathroom, colour TV, tea/coffee making facilities and full central heating. We have plenty of interesting local guides, maps, books, pictures and fresh flowers plus a small private garden with furniture for guests' use. We can pre-arrange local minibus tours, hire of mountain bikes or horse riding facilities. Bed and Breakfast from £17 to £25. Vegetarians welcome. Private car spaces and garage for bikes.

WINDERMERE. St. John's Lodge, Lake Road, Windermere LA23 2EQ (015394 43078).

 COMMENDED. A private hotel situated midway between Windermere and the Lake, close to all amenities. AA, RAC Highly Acclaimed. All 14 bedrooms have en suite facilities and are comfortably furnished with colour TV and tea/coffee making facilities. Centrally heated throughout. There is a comfortable lounge for residents, and a friendly bar, where you may take an aperitif before enjoying a four course dinner which has been personally prepared by the chef/proprietor. Bed and Breakfast from £18.50 to £26; Evening Meal £12.50. Bargain Breaks available.

CUMBRIA – THE GREAT OUTDOORS

Lakes, rivers, mountains and moors (and a mild climate) make Cumbria a paradise for the outdoor enthusiast — with something to suit every age group and every level of ability. Practically every kind of watersport can be enjoyed — if you haven't tried water ski-ing, canoeing, windsurfing or yachting, then now's your chance! Climbing, abseiling, walking, cycling, mountain biking, pony trekking, fishing, orienteering . . . the list is endless!

WINDERMERE. Mrs B.J. Butterworth, Orrest Head House, Windermere LA23 1JG (015394 44315).

This beautiful house is part 17th century, located in three acres of lush garden and woodland. Nestling above Windermere village it enjoys superb views of the Lake and mountains. From February to December guests are assured of comfortable Bed and Breakfast accommodation in five en suite rooms, three double and two twin, all non-smoking with central heating and tea-making facilities. Separate dining room. Private parking for up to 10 cars. The ideal choice for a really relaxing holiday. Terms from £20 Bed and Breakfast.

WINDERMERE. Brian and Margaret Fear, Cambridge House, 9 Oak Street, Windermere LA23 1EN (015394 43846). ETB Listed *COMMENDED.*

Cambridge House is a traditional, family run Lakeland guesthouse situated in the middle of Windermere village convenient for all amenities including buses and trains. It is also central for all South Lakes beauty spots. One hour to Keswick and the Northern Lakes and only 20 minutes from M6 Junction 36. Double, twin and family rooms are available; all are modern and comfortable and include en suite facilities, colour TV and tea/coffee making. A full English, Continental or vegetarian breakfast is provided. Centrally heated throughout. Bed and Breakfast from £15. Open all year.

WINDERMERE. Roger Wallis and James Peters, Holly Park House, 1 Park Road, Windermere LA23 2AW (015394 42107). 🐦🐦🐦 *COMMENDED.*

An elegant stone-built house which has retained all its Victorian character but offers every comfort and is furnished to a high standard. All the spacious bedrooms have a private bathroom or shower room, colour TV and tea/coffee making facilities. Licensed bar. Holly Park House is situated in a quiet district but is convenient for shops, train, bus and tour services and restaurants. A warm welcome is assured from the resident proprietors. Bed and Breakfast from £18. Credit cards welcomed. AA QQQQ, RAC Highly Acclaimed.

WINDERMERE. Mr and Mrs J.N. Fowles, Rockside Guest House, Ambleside Road, Windermere LA23 1AQ (015394 45343). 🐦🐦 A Lakeland Guest House, full of character, Rockside is RAC Acclaimed. Centrally situated two minutes from the railway station, shops and restaurants of Windermere. Parking for 12 cars. All bedrooms have washbasins, central heating, colour TV, clock, radio and telephone. Most rooms en suite with tea/coffee making facilities. A choice of Breakfast is served from 8.30am to 9.15am. Open all year for singles, twins, doubles and families to enjoy "the most beautiful corner of England". Car routes and walks arranged if required. Bed and Breakfast from £14.50 to £22.50. Reductions for children. Visa, Mastercard, Switch, etc accepted.

DERBYSHIRE

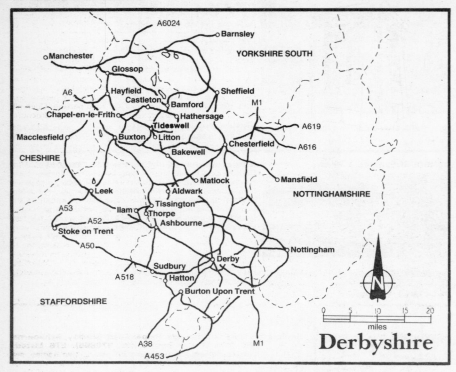

Derbyshire

ALKMONTON, near Ashbourne. Mr and Mrs A. and D. Harris, Dairy House Farm, Alkmonton, Longford, Ashbourne, Derby DE6 3DG (Tel & Fax: 01335 330359). ❀ ❀ ❀ *COMMENDED.* Working farm. This is a working farm with accommodation for guests in two double, one twin bedroom and one single bedroom en-suite, one double and two single bedrooms standard. Tea making facilities. Two lounges, diningroom and colour TV. Open all year with central heating and log fires in inglenook fireplace. Warm welcome and hospitality guaranteed in a comfortable, homely atmosphere with good food and residential licence. No children under 12 years. Sorry, no pets. Non-smokers only. Car essential, parking. AA listed. Bed and Breakfast from £17, en suite from £20; Evening Meal from £14.

AMBERGATE. Mrs Carol Oulton, Lawn Farm, Whitewells Lane, off Holly Lane, Ambergate DE56 2DN (01773 852352). ❀ Working farm, join in. Enjoy comfortable bed and breakfast accommodation on a working beef and sheep farm, one mile from the A6 at Ambergate. Ambergate has many woodland walks and a picturesque canal which leads to nearby Cromford, home of the Arkwright Mill. Matlock Bath is 10 miles away and offers many attractions including the Cable Cars. Within easy travelling distance of Haddon Hall, Chatsworth House and Gardens, the Peak District National Park and the National Tramway Museum at Crich. Accommodation comprises double en suite room and family room with handbasin. Terms on request from £15 per night. Children welcome at reduced rates. Pets welcome by arrangement. Non-smokers preferred.

ASHBOURNE. Paula and Alan Coker Mayes, The Coach House, The Firs, Ashbourne DE6 1HF (01335 300145; Fax: 01335 300958). ETB Listed *DE LUXE.*

A private house, formerly a Victorian Coach House, now offering its guests luxurious accommodation and warm hospitality in a quiet location near Ashbourne town centre. We have three ground floor double rooms ranging from small and cosy to sumptuously panelled with en suite and a handcrafted four-poster bed. All the usual facilities are offered. Rooms include TV, tea and coffee tray, central heating and a few little extras to make your stay memorable. Breakfast is cooked individually to order from our menu and evening meals and packed lunches are available by arrangement. Bed and Breakfast from £18 to £25 per person per night, discounts for longer stays. Off road parking. Open all year. Children and pets welcome. Non-smoking. Brochure available.

ASHBOURNE. Mrs E.J. Harrison, Little Park Farm, Mappleton, Ashbourne DE6 2BR (01335 350 341). 👑 *COMMENDED.* **Working farm.**

This 125 acre dairy farm is situated in the peaceful Dove Valley, ideally placed for the Derbyshire Dales, National Trust properties and Alton Towers. Nearby cycle hire, five minutes' ride from Ashbourne, and in walking distance of the village local, where bar meals are served. Plenty of wildlife and beautiful walks, ideal place for unwinding. The oak beamed listed farmhouse is over 300 years old and is tastefully furnished with lounge (colour TV), diningroom (separate tables, tea making facilities); two double and one twin-bedded rooms with wash-basins; bathroom and toilet. Sorry no pets. Open March to end of October. Bed and Breakfast from £15. Non smoking establishment.

ASHBOURNE. Mrs Paula Catlin, Jinglers Inn/The Fox & Hounds, Belper Road, Bradley, Ashbourne DE6 3EN (Tel & Fax: 01335 370855). ETB Listed.

Character Country Inn famous for having two names, set adjacent to 18 acres. Pub food is served together with Real Ale and the menu ranges from filled cobs to steaks. Pool/family room, public/lounge bar, pool and darts. Six letting bedrooms for Bed and Breakfast; some en suite, all have separate entrances and tea/coffee making facilities. Children and pets are most welcome. Bed and Breakfast from £20 per person. Conveniently placed for Derbyshire Dales, Alton Towers, Chatsworth House, Dovedale, American Adventure and several golf courses. Carsington Water is only two miles where sailing, wind surfing, cycle hire and fishing are available. Clay pigeon shooting. Everybody welcome. Licensed site for 34 caravans with hook-ups and hard standings.

ASHBOURNE. Mrs A.M. Whittle, Stone Cottage, Green Lane, Clifton, Ashbourne DE6 2BL (01335 343377). 👑 *COMMENDED.* A charming cottage in the quiet village of Clifton, one mile from Georgian market town of Ashbourne. Ideal for visiting Chatsworth House, Haddon Hall, Dovedale, Carsington Waters and the theme park of Alton Towers. Each bedroom is furnished to a high standard with all rooms en suite and having TV and coffee making facilities. Large garden to relax in. A warm welcome is assured and a hearty breakfast in our delightful cottage. Nearby good country pubs serving evening meals. Please write or telephone for further details. AA QQQ Recommended.

The Dog & Partridge Country Inn

Mary and Martin Stelfox welcome you to a family run 17th century inn and motel, set amidst five acres. Close to Alton Towers, Dovedale and Ashbourne. We specialise in family breaks, and special diets and vegetarians are catered for. All bedrooms are ensuite, with colour TV, direct dial telephone, tea making facilities and baby listening service. Ideally situated for touring the Stoke Potteries, Derbyshire Dales and Staffordshire moorlands. Restaurant is open all day, non residents welcome. Open Christmas and New Year.

The Dog and Partridge Country Inn, Swinscoe, Ashbourne, Derbyshire DE6 2HS
Telephone: 01335 343183   Fax: 01335 342742

ASHBOURNE. Alan and Liz Kingston, Old Boothby Farm, The Green, Ashbourne DE6 1EE (01335 342044). The converted Hayloft and Stables of our 17th century farmhouse are an idyllic location for your stay in the "Gateway to the Peak District". Just a five minute level walk to the centre of Ashbourne with its historic pubs and wide variety of restaurants. Handy for visiting Alton Towers, Dovedale, Buxton, Matlock and numerous stately homes. Excellent walking country. The Hayloft with its verandah, exposed beams, log fire, fully equipped kitchen, lounge with colour TV, two double bedrooms and one twin bunk bedroom is ideal for party or family bookings; cot and high chair available. The Stables studio flat with en suite facilities, king-size bed, colour TV and kitchen is the perfect setting for that romantic break away from it all. Bed and full English, or alternative, Breakfast from £17.50 per person per night. Also let as self catering accommodation from £15 per person per night low season.

ASHBOURNE. Mrs Catherine Brandrick, Sidesmill Farm, Snelston, Ashbourne DE6 2GQ (01335 342710). Tourist Board Listed *COMMENDED.* Peaceful dairy farm located on the banks of the River Dove. A rippling mill stream flows quietly past the 18th century stone-built farmhouse. Delicious English breakfast and the warmest of welcomes are guaranteed. Comfortable accommodation; guests' own lounge, diningroom; bathroom; TV in lounge. Ideal base for touring: within easy reach of Dovedale, Alton Towers, stately homes and many other places of interest. Open Easter-October. Car necessary, parking available. Bed and Breakfast from £15 per person. A non-smoking establishment.

ASHBOURNE near. Mrs Heathcote, Yerley Farm, Oakeover, Near Ashbourne DE6 2BR (01335 350244). Working farm. Working farm set in 180 acres of beautiful countryside situated two miles north of Ashbourne. Ideal for walking in the Dales and visiting historic houses. Five miles from Alton Towers and within easy reach of the American Adventure Park. Lounge tastefully decorated. Cosy dining room with good wholesome cooking. One twin, two double rooms with washbasins. Central heating, log fires, colour TV. Bed and Breakfast from £15. Reductions for children. Non-smoking establishment.

Terms quoted in this publication may be subject to increase if rises in costs necessitate

ASHBOURNE near. Tony and Linda Stoddart, Cornpark Cottage, Upper Mayfield, Near Ashbourne

DE6 2HR (Tel & Fax: 01335 345041). If you want tea and coffee making facilities, stale biscuits, UHT milk and TV in your bedrooms, we don't have them. We will however make you endless coffee or tea in your own lounge, with log fire, TV and video. If you want a shower cubicle in the bedroom masquerading as en suite we don't have it. We have got a bathroom with hot and cold water and a toilet (and we can pronounce en suite). We have got en suite tennis court and multi gym, off road parking, duvets, pillows and beds. We are 10 minutes from Alton Towers or Dovedale, we are friendly, witty and our breakfasts are cooked on the same day. All for £16 (children £11). Self catering also available. Phone, fax or write for a brochure. Open March to November.

ASHBOURNE near. Mrs Carole Eastwood, The Old Kennels, Birdsgrove Lane, Mayfield, Near Ashbourne DE6 2BP (01335 344418). Tourist Board

Listed *COMMENDED*. Set away from the road in a quiet and peaceful location with lovely views, the Old Kennels is only two miles from Ashbourne and its many surrounding attractions (Alton Towers eight miles). The accommodation comprises guests' dining room with colour TV, guests' bathroom with shower, and two roomy bedrooms, one with a double bed and one with a double and two single beds. Each bedroom has a colour TV and tea/coffee making facilities. Ample parking. Bed and Breakfast from £16. Open March to October. Further details on request.

ASHBOURNE near. Mrs Dot Barker, Waterkeepers Cottage, Mappleton, Near Ashbourne DE6 2AB

(01335 350444). Tourist Board Listed. Set in the Dove Valley on the edge of the Peak District. this 19th century cottage consists of two double rooms with washbasin and one single room; sitting room/dining room. Tea making facilities, central heating and open fires on cooler days. The large attractive garden, edged by fields and hills is a paradise for pets who are welcome in this family atmosphere. The Dove meanders by forming the boundary between Staffordshire and Derbyshire, approximately 20 miles from Buxton, Bakewell and Matlock while just eight miles away is the popular Alton Towers. Bed and Breakfast £16.50. Reductions for children and stays of three nights or more.

ASHOVER. The Red Lion Inn, Butts Road, Ashover, Chesterfield S45 0EW (01246 590271). A

picturesque Tudor Inn, in the very historic, pretty village of Ashover. Recently refurbished, with an extensive menu of home cooked foods. Activities nearby include fishing, shooting (clays), riding and country walks. Bed and Breakfast from £30 double, £45 en suite; Evening Meals available. Please write or telephone for further details.

DERBYSHIRE

The major portion of the Peak District, England's first National Park, lies within the county, high wind-swept heather moors and gritstone outcrops providing a vivid contrast to the softer rural landscapes of the south. Derbyshire's rich industrial heritage can be traced at Arkwright's Mill, Cromford; National Tramway Museum, Crich; Peak District Mining Museum, Matlock Bath; Royal Crown Derby Works, Derby, plus a host of other fascinating exhibitions and museums.

BAKEWELL. Pamela Stanley, Ferndale Mews, Buxton Road, Bakewell DE45 1DA (01629 814339).

A beautifully restored stone cottage with cosy beamed rooms. Ferndale Mews is tucked away in an exclusive courtyard just three minutes from the centre of the delightful market town of Bakewell. Close to all of the Peak Park's many attractions. Private parking. Individual attention and a warm welcome assured. Pets welcome. Bed and Breakfast from £18 to £24.50. AA QQ.

BAKEWELL. Mrs Julia Finney, Mandale House, Haddon Grove, Bakewell DE45 1JF (01629 812416). 🏵🏵 Relax in the warm and friendly atmosphere of our peaceful farmhouse situated on the edge of Lathkill Dale, now a nature reserve managed by English Nature. Our rooms have en suite facilities, colour TV and tea making equipment, and two are on the ground floor making them suitable for disabled visitors. A varied breakfast menu is offered and packed lunches are available. Excellent local inns and restaurants a short drive away. Bed and Breakfast from £19 to £22. 10% reductions for weekly bookings. Three night Bargain Breaks available in March, April and October. No smoking in the house. Telephone for brochure.

BAKEWELL. Mrs Jenny Spafford, Barleycorn Croft, Sheldon, Near Bakewell DE45 1QS (01629 813636). A well converted small attached barn with private bathroom and TV lounge. Accommodates two, three or four people in a twin and/or double room with washbasins, shaver points, thermostatically controlled heaters and tea/coffee making facilities, creating a pleasant private apartment. Also provided: full English or vegetarian breakfast, ironing facilities, hairdryer; independent access with own key and private parking. Sheldon is a unique, unspoilt farming village with no through traffic, only three miles from Bakewell and ideal for visiting Chatsworth House, Haddon Hall, Matlock, Buxton and all parts of the Peak District. Open all year. Non-Smokers only please. Bed and Breakfast from £15 to £17.50. AA QQ Recommended.

BAKEWELL. Gayle and Hugh Tyler, Sheldon House, Chapel Street, Monyash, Near Bakewell DE45 1JJ (01629 813067). 🏵🏵 *HIGHLY COMMENDED.* An 18th century listed building in the picturesque village of Monyash (five miles from Bakewell), in the heart of the Peak National Park. Recently renovated to a high standard, we offer comfortable accommodation and a friendly atmosphere. Three doubles with en suite facilities (two with colour TV), guests' sittingroom. All rooms have central heating and tea/coffee making facilities. Ideal base for visits to Chatsworth House, Haddon Hall, Hardwick Hall and excellent for cycling and walking. Open all year round except Christmas. No smoking. Bed and Breakfast from £19.50.

BAKEWELL. Mrs Sheila Gilbert, Castle Cliffe Private Hotel, Monsal Head, Bakewell DE45 1NL (01629 640258). 🏵🏵 *COMMENDED.* Monsal Head is a popular beauty spot in the heart of the Derbyshire Dales. There are superb views from all the bedrooms in Castle Cliffe Hotel, some overlooking Monsal Dale and the famous viaduct. It is an ideal centre for visiting the dales, caverns and historic houses. Most of the hotel's three double, two family and four twin rooms have en suite shower/WC, all have tea making facilities. Centrally heated plus open fires in the lounge and bar. Food is home cooked with the emphasis on British dishes from old traditional recipes. Children welcome. Sorry, no pets. Christmas and New Year and Special mini Breaks available. Licensed. Bed and Breakfast from £25 to £27.50. AA Listed QQQ, Les Routiers.

BAKEWELL near. Mr and Mrs Clarke, Upperdale House, Monsal Dale, Buxton SK17 8SZ (01629 640536). Tourist Board Listed. Idyllic riverside guesthouse enjoying a unique setting in the prettiest of Derbyshire Dales. Accommodation includes two double and two twin-bedded rooms, all en suite (one with private bathroom), with colour TV, tea/coffee facilities, full central heating and river views. Splendid local walks, numerous outdoor activities including trout fishing available. Closed Christmas and New Year. No pets. Sorry no smoking in the bedrooms. Monsal Dale signposted from A6 near Bakewell. Bed and Breakfast from £22 per person. Special off-peak Breaks available. Vegetarians/medical diets catered for.

BAMFORD. Pioneer House, Station Road, Bamford S33 0BN (01433 650638). ✿ ✿ *COMMENDED.* AA QQQ. A warm welcome awaits you in our friendly and comfortable Edwardian home in the Hope Valley area of the Peak District. All our bedrooms have en suite/private facilities, colour TV, hair dryer, beverage tray, etc. Hearty breakfasts, including vegetarian are provided with packed lunches on request. We are open all year and have central heating and drying facilities. Off-road parking and secure cycle facilities, if required. Bamford is a tranquil village set in spectacular scenery, ideal for walking, sightseeing and just relaxing. We are a non-smoking establishment. Please telephone for further details.

BELPER. Mrs C. Emery, The Hollins, 45 Belper Lane, Belper DE56 2UQ (01773 823955). Small family-run guest house in semi-rural location uniquely situated for both Peak District (Ashbourne/Matlock 10 miles) and Amber Valley areas and also Alton Towers and American Adventure Theme Parks. Comfortable rooms with colour TV, washbasin and hostess trays (private bath optional). Prices include excellent full English breakfast with local free-range produce. Non-smoking establishment. Prices per person per night £16 to £22. AA Recommended.

BUXTON. Buxton View, 74 Corbar Road, Buxton SK17 6RJ (01298 79222). ✿ ✿ ✿ *COMMENDED.* A friendly welcome awaits you at this stone built guesthouse with its pleasing garden and splendid views over Buxton and the surrounding hills. Only a short walk from this spa town's Georgian centre, the Peak National Park surrounds you with its glorious scenery and a host of varied attractions. Comfortable en suite rooms are provided with every thoughtful touch and a spacious guest lounge is stocked with maps and guide books. Delicious English breakfasts are served in the conservatory and you will be warmed by the interest we take in our guests; you will leave wishing you had stayed longer! Bed and Breakfast from £18 per person per night; Evening Meals available. Children and pets welcome. AA QQQ Recommended.

BUXTON. Mrs Ann Oliver, "Westlands", Bishop's Lane, St. John's Road, Buxton SK17 6UN (01298 23242). ETB Listed *COMMENDED.* Close to Staffordshire and Cheshire borders, this well established Bed and Breakfast is for non-smokers. Situated on country lane one mile from town centre and Opera House, Westlands offers three rooms with central heating, washbasins, TV and drinks making facilities. Full English Breakfast provided. Ample off-road parking available. Very convenient for Chatsworth House, the Potteries, etc. An excellent centre for walking in the Peak District. Golf facilities available locally. Rates from £15 per person for Bed and Breakfast. Weekly reductions. Special diets catered for by arrangement.

THE CHARLES COTTON HOTEL

The Charles Cotton is a small, comfortable hotel with 3 Crowns. The hotel lies in the heart of the Derbyshire Dales, pleasantly situated in the village square of Hartington, with nearby shops catering for all needs. It is renowned throughout the area for its hospitality and good home cooking. Pets and children welcome, and special diets catered for. The Charles Cotton makes the perfect centre to relax and enjoy the area, whether walking, cycling, pony trekking, brass rubbing or even hang gliding. Open Christmas and New Year.
**Hartington, near Buxton, Derbyshire SK17 0AL
Tel: 01298 84229; Fax: 01335 42742**

Key to Tourist Board Ratings

The Crown Scheme
(England, Scotland & Wales)

Covering hotels, motels, private hotels, guesthouses, inns, bed & breakfast, farmhouses. Every Crown classified place to stay is inspected annually. *The classification:* Listed then 1-5 Crown indicates the range of facilities and services. Higher quality standards are indicated by the terms APPROVED, COMMENDED, HIGHLY COMMENDED and DELUXE.

The Key Scheme
(also operates in Scotland using a Crown symbol)

Covering self-catering in cottages, bungalows, flats, houseboats, houses, chalets, etc. Every Key classified holiday home is inspected annually. *The classification:* 1-5 Key indicates the range of facilities and equipment. Higher quality standards are indicated by the terms APPROVED, COMMENDED, HIGHLY COMMENDED and DELUXE.

The Q Scheme
(England, Scotland & Wales)

Covering holiday, caravan, chalet and camping parks. Every Q rated park is inspected annually for its quality standards. The more √ in the Q – up to 5 – the higher the standard of what is provided.

BUXTON. Mrs S. Fosker, Brunswick House, 31 St. Johns Road, Buxton SK17 6XG (01298 71727).
We are situated two minutes from the Opera House and Pavilion Gardens. An ideal base for visiting the Peak District with its beautiful walks and charming villages. All rooms have TV and tea/coffee facilities. Parking available in the grounds. Children and pets welcome. Self catering cottage alos available. A warm welcome awaits you. Bed and Breakfast from £18 to £20 per person per night.

BUXTON. Maria and Roger Hyde, Braemar, 10 Compton Road, Buxton SK17 9DN (01298 78050).

Guests are warmly welcomed all the year round into the friendly atmosphere of Braemar, situated in a quiet residential part of this spa town. Within five minutes' walk of all the town's many and varied attractions i.e., Pavilion Gardens, Opera House, swimming pool; golf courses, horse riding, walking, fishing, etc are all within easy reach in this area renowned for its scenic beauty. Many of the Peak District's famous beauty spots including Chatsworth, Haddon Hall, Bakewell, Matlock, Dovedale and Castleton are nearby. Accommodation comprises comfortable double and twin bedded rooms fully en suite with colour TV and hospitality trays, etc. Full English Breakfast served and diets catered for. Non-smokers preferred. Terms £18.95 inclusive for Bed and Breakfast. Weekly terms available.

CASTLETON. Mrs B. Johnson, Myrtle Cottage, Market Place, Castleton, Near Sheffield S30 2WQ (01433 620787). Myrtle Cottage is pleasantly situated near the village green in the picturesque village of Castleton, famous for its castle and caverns. It is an ideal base for walking, caving, hang-gliding or touring the Peak District and Derbyshire Dales. Buxton, Bakewell, Chatsworth House and the plague village of Eyam are within 20 minutes' drive. The guest accommodation comprises family, twin and double bedrooms all with private shower/toilet, colour TV and tea/coffee making facilities; sittingroom with TV and diningroom. One en suite ground floor room suitable for disabled guests. Central heating. Fire Certificate held. Parking. Regret no pets. Open all year (except Christmas) for Bed and Breakfast only.

CASTLETON. D. Broome and L. Garside, Kelseys Swiss House Hotel and Restaurant, How Lane, Castleton, Hope Valley S33 8WJ (01433 621098).

♥♥♥ COMMENDED. Situated in a historic village in the heart of the Peak District. Ideal centre for all beauty spots (Chatsworth House, Dovedale, Derwent Dams, Monsal Dale, Buxton, Bakewell, Tissington Trail, local caverns and castles, Matlock and many others). Stay with us in our family-run licensed restaurant and guest house with clean, comfortable accommodation. All rooms en-suite with colour TVs and tea-making facilities. You will be assured of excellent and interesting food — all diets catered for — with friendly service and hopefully good weather! Bed and Breakfast from £22.50; Evening Meal optional. Fire Certificate held. Private parking. Access to rooms all day. Please telephone or SAE for brochure.

CHAPEL-EN-LE-FRITH. Mrs Maureen Howarth, The Forge, Top o' th' Plane, Ashbourne Lane, Chapel-en-le-Frith SK23 9UG (01298 815172). The

Forge is on the south edge of town, half a mile from A6 old road. Above the residential area overlooking the moors, this unique Listed building (c. 1797) is in a peaceful garden setting. Ideal for walking and touring the Dales and Peak National Park and visiting stately homes and many places of interest including Stockport and Manchester. The accommodation comprises three double, one twin-bedded room; bathroom includes shower and WC, plus separate WC; breakfast/sitting room with TV. Central heating. Parking. Open all year. Directions: from Buxton on approaching bypass take slip road for Chapel-en-le-Frith, take third turning on left into Ashbourne Lane. After white cottage at bottom of hill take third driveway on left, signposted Top o' th' Plane. Forward through courtyard. Bed and Breakfast from £15.

DERBY. Mr and Mrs J. Richardson, Rangemoor Park Hotel, 67 Macklin Street, Derby DE1 1LF (01332 347252; Fax: 01332 369319). 🐾 Long estab-

lished family-run Hotel. Privately owned and run by the present owners since the late 70s. The hotel is modern with traditional standards offering outstanding hospitality and comfort. All 24 bedrooms have colour TV and tea/coffee making with 13 also having en suite facilities, direct-dial telephone and hair dryer. Ideally situated just a few minutes' walk from the centre of Derby. For your convenience there is ample free car parking, own front door key and night porter. Whether for business or holiday the proprietors pride themselves on personal and attentive service.

DERBY. Mrs Catherine Dicken, Bonehill Farm, Etwall Road, Mickleover DE3 5DN (01332 513553).

This 120 acre mixed farm with Georgian farmhouse is set in peaceful rural surroundings, yet offers all the convenience of being only three miles west of Derby, on the A516 between Mickleover and Etwall. Within 10 miles there is a choice of historic houses to visit; Calke Abbey, Kedleston Hall, Sudbury Hall. Peak District 20 miles, Alton Towers 20 miles. Accommodation in three bedrooms (one twin, one double, one family room with en suite facilities), all with tea/coffee making facilities. Cot and high chair provided. Open all year. Bed and Breakfast from £16. Tennis, croquet available. A warm and friendly welcome awaits you.

EDALE. Sue and Tony Favell, Skinners' Hall, Edale S30 2ZE (01433 670281; Fax: 01433 670481).

Attractive 18th century home standing in a delightful country garden with grounds bordering the River Noe, small lake, ducks and fish! The spacious bedrooms enjoy spectacular views and offer en suite bathrooms, colour TV and tea/coffee making facilities, hair dryers, etc. Edale, one of the most beautiful valleys in Britain, lies at the foot of the Pennine Way and is an ideal base for other beauty spots and places of interest in the Peak National Park. Local activities include walking, golf, pony trekking, hang gliding, potholing, tennis, rock climbing, cross-country ski-ing and fishing on the famous Ladybower Reservoir. Bed and Breakfast £22.50 per person per day; £125 per week. Please send for our brochure.

DERBYSHIRE – PEAK DISTRICT AND DALES!

The undulating dales set against the gritstone edges of the Pennine moors give Derbyshire its scenic wealth. In the tourists' itinerary should be the prehistoric monument at Arbor Low, the canal port of Shardlow, the country parks at Elvaston and Shipley, the limestone caves at Creswell Crags and Castleton and the market towns of Ashbourne and Bakewell. For walkers this area provides many excellent opportunities.

HARTINGTON. The Manifold Inn, Hulme End, Hartington SK17 0EX (01298 84537). 🌺🌺🌺 The

Manifold Inn is a 200 year old coaching inn now owned by Frank and Bridgette Lipp. It offers warm hospitality and good "pub food" at sensible prices. This lovely mellow stone inn nestles on the banks of the River Manifold opposite the old toll house that once served the turnpike and river ford. All guests' accommodation is in the converted old stone blacksmith's shop in the secluded rear courtyard of the inn. The bedrooms have en suite shower, colour TV, tea/coffee facilities and telephones. Bed and Breakfast £21 to £29. Brochure available.

HATHERSAGE. Mrs M.K. Venning, 'The Old Vicarage', Church Bank, Hathersage, Hope Valley S32 1AB (01433 651099). 🌺🌺 *COMMENDED.* The Old Vicar-

age, dating back to 1700, is situated on a hill, five minutes' walk from the village, with glorious views of the Hope Valley. Charlotte Bronte stayed here in 1845 and based her novel 'Jane Eyre' on the village and vicarage. Little John's Grave is in the local churchyard and Robin Hood's Cave nearby. Hathersage is a delightful village and conveniently situated for Chatsworth House and Adventure Playground, the Derwent Valley Reservoir, the Pennine Way, Castleton caves and castle. There is trout fishing on the reservoir and excellent walking all around. Superb bird-watching. Bed and Breakfast from £20 to £27.50, reductions for children.

HATHERSAGE. Mrs Jean Wilcockson, Hillfoot Farm, Castleton Road, Hathersage, Hope Valley S32 1EG (01433 651673). Tourist Board Listed *COMMEN-*

DED. Welcome Host. Newly built accommodation onto existing farmhouse offering comfortable, well appointed, en suite rooms. All with central heating, colour TV, tea/coffee making, hair dryer and comfortable easy chairs. We have a large car park and public telephone for guests' use. Excellent home cooked food including vegetarian meals. Bed and Breakfast from £18 to £20 per person. We are situated in the heart of the Peak District, ideal for walking or visiting Chatsworth House, Bakewell, Castleton, Edale and many more places of interest. Current Fire Certificate held. Open all year. Non-smokers.

HILLFOOT FARM

ILAM. Mrs M. Richardson, Throwley Hall Farm, Ilam, Ashbourne DE6 2BB (01538 308202 or 308243). 🌺🌺 *COMMENDED.* Situated on a working beef

and sheep farm in quiet countryside near the Manifold Valley, on the public road from Ilam to Calton. Within easy reach of Dovedale and Alton Towers, also stately homes. Accommodation comprises two double and two twin rooms, two rooms en suite, all with washbasins and TVs. Dining/sitting room with colour TV. Full central heating, also open fire. Tea/coffee making facilities. Bed and Breakfast from £18. Reduced rates for children, cot and high chair available.

MATLOCK. Mrs Lynda Buxton, Winstaff Guest House, Derwent Avenue, Matlock DE4 3LX (01629 582593). 🌺🌺 *APPROVED.* Winstaff is a large late Victorian semi, standing in a quiet cul-de-sac with the garden going down to the River Derwent. Fishing can be enjoyed in this quiet conservation area and on the opposite side of the river there is a park. At the same time Winstaff is only five minutes' walk from the town centre and bus and train stations. Accommodation comprises five double rooms, three with washbasins and two en suite; one en suite family room which sleeps four, and one twin room with washbasin. All are centrally heated and have colour TV and tea/coffee making facilities. Parking available. Open all year. Bed and Breakfast from £18 per person.

WHEN MAKING ENQUIRIES PLEASE MENTION
FARM HOLIDAY GUIDES

MATLOCK. Mrs Barbara Martin, Tuckers Guest House, 48 Dale Road, Matlock DE4 3NB (01629

583018). A large Victorian home where you can feel most relaxed. Spacious, well equipped rooms. Pets most welcome. Close to rail and bus stations. You can be assured of a jolly good English or Vegetarian breakfast and your hosts will make every effort to help you discover the wonderful Peak District. Marvel at the glorious rugged scenery, enjoy splendid walks, visit the famous stately homes of Chatsworth, Haddon and Hardwick; ride on trams, steam trains, cable cars and carriages; visit caves, mills and mines; canoe, cycle, climb, sail, swim (or just relax!). Something for everyone. Bed and Breakfast from £17.

MATLOCK. Mrs S. Elliott, "Glendon", Knowleston Place, Matlock DE4 3BU (01629 584732). 🐦

Warm hospitality and comfortable accommodation in this Grade II Listed building. Conveniently situated by the Hall Leys Park and River Derwent, it is only a short level walk to Matlock town centre. Large private car park. Rooms are centrally heated and have washbasins, colour TV and tea/coffee making facilities. En suite available. No smoking in the dining room. An ideal base for exploring the beautiful Peak District of Derbyshire, with easy access to many places of interest including Chatsworth House, Haddon Hall, National Tramway Museum and Heights of Abraham cable car. Bed and Breakfast from £17.50 per person.

MATLOCK BATH. Mrs P. Clayton, Woodlands View, 226 Dale Road, Matlock Bath DE4 3RT (01629 55762). 🐦 Ideal for tourists and only three minutes from the railway station. Close to shops and restaurants and beautiful scenery around. Two double, one family and one twin-bedded rooms; two bathrooms and three toilets. Open from January to December with Bed and Breakfast from £12.50 per person per night. Children half price. Tea making facilities in all rooms. Central heating. Children are welcome and pets permitted. Only one minute to the new tourist attraction "The Heights of Abraham Cable Car". Telephone for further details.

MATLOCK near. Simon and Gilly Groom, Littlemoor Wood Farm, Littlemoor Lane, Riber, Near

Matlock DE4 5JS (Tel & Fax: 01629 534302). A private lane leads to this peaceful and informal traditional Derbyshire stone farmhouse. Set among 20 acres of meadows and enjoying wonderful open views, our working smallholding is the perfect place to unwind. Roooms are attractive and comfortable with TV and tea/coffee tray. Meals are thoughtfully prepared and our own free range bacon, sausages and home produce is used wherever possible. Many stately homes including Chatsworth House and other popular places of interest are nearby. Bakewell, Ashbourne and M1 are all within 20 minutes' drive. Bed and Breakfast from £18 per person. Open all year except Christmas and New Year.

MATLOCK near. Ray and Pauline Sanders, Sycamore Guest House, Town Head, Bonsall, Near Matlock DE4 2AR (01629 823903). 🐦🐦 A lovely 18th century family guest house in the village of Bonsall, nestling high on Masson Hill on the edge of the Peak District National Park. Easy access to Matlock Bath (for cable cars), Chatsworth House, Haddon Hall, Dovedale, Alton Towers and Carsington Water. Five very comfortable en suite rooms equipped with tea/coffee makers, colour TV, hair dryers and alarm clocks. Guest lounge. Full central heating. Residential licence. Own off street car park. AA QQQ Recommended. Bed and Breakfast from £21; Evening Meal from £13. Open all year with special breaks from November to March. Ring or write for details.

MONYASH/BAKEWELL. Mr G. Mycock, Cheney Lodge, Rowson House Farm, Monyash, Bakewell DE45 1JH (01629 815336/813521; Fax: 01629 815336). At almost 1000ft the village sits at the head of the beautiful Lathkill Dale, a National Nature Reserve and is surrounded by the beautiful scenery of the White Peak. Rooms (single, double and twin) have tea/coffee, TV, radio and en suite facilities. Aga cooked breakfasts. They look out over unspoilt countryside to the Peak District and moors. The lodge is situated on 180 acres of quiet farmland looking to the moors. Children and pets welcome by arrangement. Bed and Breakfast from £14 to £25. Clean, quiet and comfortable accommodation awaits you.

PEAK FOREST. Mrs T.H. Warburton, Pedlicote Farm, Peak Forest, Near Buxton SK17 8EG (01298 22241). Situated within a few miles of Chatsworth, Haddon Hall, Bakewell, and Castleton's famous Blue John Caverns, Pedlicote Farm is a charming 17th century farmhouse conversion with oak beams, an open log fire and relaxed atmosphere. Standing in its own gardens and grounds of two acres within the Peak National Park, it offers glorious views of the surrounding hills. This is magnificent walking country and the farm itself sits 1100 feet above sea level. Accommodation comprises three simply but pleasantly furnished twin-bedded or double-bedded rooms with TV in each. Terms: Bed and Breakfast from £15 per person; Bed, Breakfast and Evening Meal from £22 per person.

TIDESWELL. Pat and David Harris, Laurel House, The Green, Litton, Tideswell, Near Buxton SK17 8QP (01298 871971). *COMMENDED.* A warm welcome awaits you in this elegant Victorian House overlooking the green in the pretty village of Litton. There are many lovely dales and rivers virtually on the doorstep, yet Tideswell is only one mile away. We are ideally situated for discovering all Derbyshire has to offer. One double with en suite facilities and a twin with washbasin and private use of bathroom and toilet; tea/coffee making facilities in both rooms. A lounge with colour TV is available. Bed and Breakfast from £16. Non-smoking establishment. Directions: Off A623 at Tideswell. We look forward to seeing you.

TIDESWELL. Mr D.C. Pinnegar, "Poppies", Bank Square, Tideswell, Buxton SK17 8LA (01298 871083). Tourist Board Listed. "Poppies" is situated in the centre of an attractive Derbyshire village in the Peak District. Ideal walking country and within easy reach of Castleton, Bakewell, Matlock and Buxton. Accommodation comprises one family room and twin room with washbasins, one double room en suite, all with TV and tea/coffee making facilities. Bathroom and two toilets. Restaurant with interesting menu which always includes good selection of vegetarian dishes. Children welcome. Bed and Breakfast from £15; Evening Meal from £10.

PUBLISHER'S NOTE

While every effort is made to ensure accuracy, we regret that FHG Publications cannot accept responsibility for errors, omissions or misrepresentation in our entries or any consequences thereof. Prices in particular should be checked because we go to press early. We will follow up complaints but cannot act as arbiters or agents for either party.

DEVON

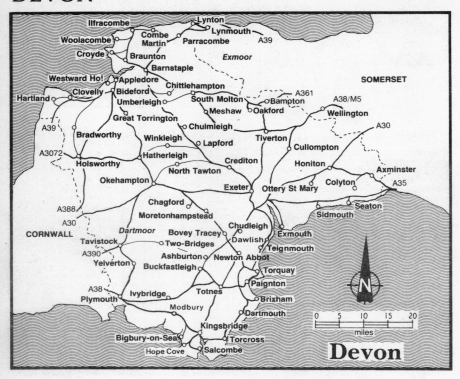

ASHBURTON. Margaret Phipps, New Cott Farm, Poundsgate, Ashburton, Newton Abbot TQ13 7PD (Tel & Fax: 01364 631421). ♛♛ *COMMENDED.*

Disabled Accessible Category 3. A friendly welcome, beautiful views, pleasing accommodation await you at New Cott in the Dartmoor National Park. Enjoy the freedom, peace and quiet of open moorland and the Dart Valley. Farm trail, birds and animals on the farm. Riding, golf, leisure centre locally. Bedrooms en suite, tea/coffee/chocolate, central heating. Ideal for less able guests, special diets catered for — lots of lovely homemade food. Bed and Breakfast from £18; Evening Dinner £10.50. Weekly reductions, short breaks welcome. Open all year. AA QQQQ.

ASHBURTON. Chris and Annie Moore, Gages Mill, Buckfastleigh Road, Ashburton TQ13 7JW (Tel & Fax: 01364 652391). ♛♛♛ *COMMENDED.* Relax in the

warm and friendly atmosphere of our lovely 14th century former wool mill, set in an acre of gardens on the edge of Dartmoor National Park. Eight delightful en suite bedrooms, one on the ground floor, all with tea-making facilities, central heating, hair dryers, radio and alarm clocks. We have a large comfortable lounge with corner bar and granite archways leading to the dining room, and a cosy sittingroom with colour TV. Home cooking of a very high standard. Licensed. Ample car parking. Being one mile from the centre of Ashburton, this is an ideal base for touring South Devon or visiting Exeter, Plymouth, Dartmouth, the many National Trust properties and other places of interest. Children over five years welcome. Sorry no pets. Bed, Breakfast and Evening Meal or Bed and Breakfast only. AA QQQQ Selected, RAC Acclaimed.

ASHBURTON (Dartmoor). Mrs Anne Torr, Middle Leat, Holne, Near Ashburton TQ13 7SJ (01364

631413). Middle Leat, set in three acres, offers very comfortable accommodation with wonderful views, in the picturesque village of Holne, three and a half miles west of Ashburton in the Dartmoor National Park. We have one large ground floor bedroom with a double bed, bunk beds and a single bed, private bathroom and full facilities; available as a double or family room. Full English Breakfast. Vegetarians welcome. Large garden, free range rare breed chickens and ducks, pets, ponies and foals. Visitors are welcome to join in, feeding chicks and ducklings, collecting eggs, etc. A warm welcome and relaxed friendly atmosphere assured in very peaceful surroundings. Sorry, no smoking in the house. Bed and Breakfast from £17. Reductions for children. SAE for details or telephone for brochure.

AXMINSTER. Ms C.M. Putt, Highridge Guest House, Lyme Road, Axminster EX13 5BQ (01297 34037). Let me make you feel at home, pamper you with good food and make you comfortable in pretty, clean rooms, all with vanity units, colour TV and tea/coffee facilities. Take tea in our beautiful gardens with ponds and ornamental ducks. Nearby there are six lovely beaches and several golf courses and a wild life park are easily accessible. We can provide maps and details of no less than 15 fishing venues, encompassing sea fishing, fly fishing, coarse fishing. Enjoy a day on Dartmoor or a trip to Exeter, Taunton or Yeovil for shopping, or walk the Coastal Path from Lyme Regis to Seaton. End your day with a well cooked three-course meal for only £6.50. Bed and Breakfast £14.50. Reduced rates for under 10 year olds. Pets welcome.

BAMPTON. Mr and Mrs P.R. Rostron, The Old Rectory, Oakford, Tiverton EX16 9EW (01398

351486). ✿ ✿ A beautiful, historic, former rectory in the tranquil Domesday village of Oakford. Set in the outstanding beautiful Exe Valley with Exmoor nearby, it is a perfect location for a peaceful stay, with easy access to a range of pursuits from salmon and trout fishing to deer watching. We have our own four acre vineyard with red and white varieties, and offer an en suite double room with full English breakfast from £18.50 per person or twin with shared bathroom for £15. Three course evening meal £9. Central heating, colour TV, tea/coffee facilities, special diets by request. Nonsmoking. German, Spanish and French spoken.

BARNSTAPLE. Mr and Mrs D. Woodman, The Old Rectory, Challacombe, Barnstaple EX31 4TS

(01598 763342). Within the Exmoor National Park, easily accessible on a good road, The Old Rectory is tucked away peacefully on the edge of Challacombe. A glance at the map of North Devon will show how excellently the house is placed, either for touring the spectacular coastline or for walking on Exmoor. Superbly furnished bedrooms, with tea/coffee making equipment, washbasins and heating. Ample bathroom, toilet, shower facilities. Comfortable diningroom, lounge with colour TV. Bed and Breakfast from £17 per night, from £105 per week. No VAT charge. Further particulars on request.

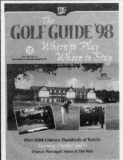

BARNSTAPLE. Mrs B. Isaac, Alscott Barton, Alverdiscott, Near Barnstaple EX31 3PT (01271 858336). Our family-run traditional Devonshire farmhouse offers a delightful holiday base within easy reach of coast and moors. Situated in tiny rural village commanding panoramic views, there are acres of farmland to enjoy incorporating three private lakes for trout and coarse fishing, recreation barn, landscaped gardens and ample parking. Charming accommodation with visitors' lounge, dining room, family and double bedrooms with washbasins, also single and twin rooms. Bathroom and shower room facilities. Cots, high chairs provided. Pony available. Pets welcome out of season at our discretion. Bed and Breakfast from £15.50 per day, from £130 weekly; Bed, Breakfast and Evening Meal from £21.50 per day. Reductions for children. Brochure available.

BARNSTAPLE. Mrs Sheelagh Darling, Lee House, Marwood, Barnstaple EX31 4DZ (01271 74345).

Stone-built Elizabethan Manor House dating back to 1256, standing in its own secluded gardens and grounds with magnificent views over rolling Devon countryside. James II ceilings, an Adam fireplace, antiques and the work of resident artist add interest. Easy access to coast and moor. Family-run, friendly and relaxing atmosphere. Walking distance to local pub with excellent food. Open April to October. One double, one twin room and one four-poster room, all en suite with colour TV and tea/coffee making facilities. Bed and Breakfast from £19.

BARNSTAPLE. Mrs V.M. Chugg, "Valley View", Guineaford, Marwood, Barnstaple EX31 4EA (01271 43458). Working farm.

"Valley View" is a bungalow set in 320 acres of farmland which visitors are free to enjoy. It is near Marwood Hill Gardens and Arlington Court, properties renowned for their beauty, and which are open from March to December. Situated three and a half miles from Barnstaple, the Market Town. Accommodation comprises two bedrooms each containing a double and single bed. Dining/sittingroom with colour TV and video. Bathroom/toilet. Good English Breakfast. Bed and Breakfast from £13. Evening Meal supplied if required from £6. Children are welcomed, half price for those under 12 years. Babysitting free of charge. Pets by arrangement. Car essential — parking. Open all year.

BARNSTAPLE near. Mrs J. Ley, West Barton, Alverdiscott, Near Barnstaple EX31 3PT (01271 858230). Working farm.

Our family run working farm of 250 acres situated in a small rural village between Barnstaple and Torrington on the B3232. Ideal base for your holiday within easy reach of Exmoor or visiting our rugged coastline of many sandy beaches. Also Dartington Glass, RHS Rosemoor Gardens, Clovelly and many other beauty spots. West Barton farmhouse is situated beside the B3232 with panoramic views of the beautiful North Devon countryside. Children welcome with reductions. Comfortable accommodation family room, twin beds, single and double rooms available. Visitors' own lounge with colour TV. Dining room. Good farmhouse cooking including a variety of our own produce when available. Basic Food Hygiene Certificate. Regret no pets. Bed and Breakfast from £15; Evening Meal optional. Weekly terms on request.

BEER. Nikki and Richard Oswald, Bay View Guest House, Fore Street, Beer EX12 3EE (01297 20489).

Beer is a charming uncommercialised fishing village on the East Devon Heritage Coast, ideally situated for walking, fishing or simply relaxing on the beach. Bay View is beautifully placed right on the sea front with stunning views of the headland and sea. There are three en suite bedrooms and six bedrooms with shared bathrooms. All are centrally heated and have colour TV, tea/coffee facilities and attractive furnishings. Bed and Breakfast from £15. For evening meals Beer has a good selection of reasonably priced restaurants. Open March to November. We look forward to welcoming you to Bay View and Beer. AA QQQ.

PLEASE SEND A STAMPED ADDRESSED ENVELOPE WITH ENQUIRIES

BIDEFORD. Sunset Hotel, Landcross, Bideford EX39 5JA (01237 472962). ❦ ❦ ❦ COMMENDED.

SOMEWHERE SPECIAL in North Devon. Small country hotel in quiet peaceful location, overlooking spectacular scenery in an area of outstanding natural beauty, one and a half miles from Bideford town. Beautifully decorated and spotlessly clean. Highly recommended quality accommodation. All en suite with colour TV, tea/coffee facilities. Superb cooking, everything homemade wth all fresh produce. Vegetarians and special needs catered for. Excellent reputation. Book with confidence in a NON SMOKING ESTABLISHMENT. Licensed. Private parking. AA QQQ. Bed and Breakfast £23 to £25; Bed, Breakfast and Evening Meal £33.50 to £35.50 daily, £222.50 to £225 weekly. Mr and Mrs C.M. Lamb, resident proprietors since 1971.

BIDEFORD. Mrs C. Colwill, Welsford Farm, Hartland EX39 6EQ (01237 441296). Working farm, join in.

Relax, enjoy the peaceful countryside yet be within easy reach of towns, interesting places and picturesque beaches with miles of scenic cliff walks. This 360 acre dairy farm is situated two miles from Hartland Village; four miles from cobblestoned Clovelly and the rugged Hartland coastline. Comfortably furnished farmhouse with colour TV lounge and washbasins in bedrooms. Children welcome at reduced rates. Wander around the farm and "pets' corner". Babysitting always available. Good country food using home grown produce. Car essential. Bed and Breakfast £15 per night, Evening Meal £8. Bed, Breakfast and four-course Evening Meal from £140 weekly. Warm welcome. Regret no pets. Open April to October.

BRAUNTON. Christine and Roy Gardner, Hillside Gardens, Heddon Mill, Knowle, Near Braunton EX33 2NG (01271 815721).

Hillside Gardens, in six acres of gardens and grounds, is ideally situated for exploring the beautiful coastline and countryside of North Devon and Exmoor. Nearby are the gardens of Marwood Hill and Rosemoor and Braunton Burrows Nature Reserve. Ideal location for surfing, riding, golf, bird watching and walking. Barnstaple market town is seven miles away. Comfortable accommodation consists of two double rooms (one en suite) and one single. Tea/coffee making facilities. Guests' lounge with TV. Bed and Breakfast from £14.50. Evening Meals by arrangement using fresh garden produce. Ample space for parking.

BRAUNTON. Mrs Roselyn Bradford, "St. Merryn", Higher Park Road, Braunton EX33 2LG (01271 813805).

Set in beautiful, sheltered garden of approximately one acre, with many peaceful sun traps to sit and relax. Ros extends a warm welcome to her guests. Rooms (£18-£19 per person) include single, double and family rooms, all with central heating, colour TV and tea/coffee facilities. All rooms either en suite or with private bathrooms. Dinner (£10) may be served indoors or out. Guests may bring own wine. Guest lounge with books, games, colour TV/ video, patio door access to garden. Swimming pool, fish ponds, hens, thatched summerhouse, barbecue facilities plus excellent parking. Please send for brochure.

DEVON – LAND OF DOONE AND DRAKE

Exmoor is the setting of R.D. Blackmore's "Lorna Doone", and visitors today can still soak in the romantic atmosphere of Doone Valley where the outlaws lived, and Oare Church, near Lynmouth, the scene of Lorna's wedding. Devon's most famous son is undoubtedly Sir Francis Drake, born at Crowndale, near Tavistock. It was to Plymouth he returned after sailing round the world in 1580 and on Plymouth Hoe he reputedly finished his game of bowls before tackling the Spanish Armada in 1588.

BRIXHAM. Angela and Peter Ellis, "Westbury", 51 New Road, Brixham TQ5 8NL (01803 851684).

Brixham, a quaint harbour town with winding streets and steps leading to steep terraced slopes, an ideal base for exploring the beautiful Devon countryside. Westbury is a short level walk from the harbour (approximately 5-10 minutes) and has six bedrooms, most en suite. All bedrooms have washbasins, colour TV and tea making facilities. Private parking is to the front, but a car is not essential as there are frequent buses, also boats to Paignton, Torquay and Dartmouth. Courtesy car from stations provided. Children over seven years welcome. Pets by arrangement. Bed and Breakfast from £16 per person.

BRIXHAM. Graham and Yvonne Glass, Raddicombe Lodge, 102 Kingswear Road, Brixham TQ5 0EX (01803 882125). The Lodge lies midway between the

picturesque coastal harbour towns of Brixham and Dartmouth, overlooking sea and country, with National Trust land between us and the sea. The Lodge is reached by a short drive off the B3205, in a quarter acre garden with the charm and character of pitched ceilings, lattice windows and cosy open log fires for the winter months. Scrumptious traditional English breakfast with locally baked crusty bread of Continental Breakfast with batons and croissants; light/vegetarian breakfast also available. Colour TV and tea/coffee making facilities in all bedrooms. Come and go as you please, make the Lodge your home from home. Smoking restricted to the lounge area only. Ample parking. Open all year. Children welcome. Sorry no pets. Offering room and breakfast only from £17.40 to £19.10 per night each. En suite rooms £3.20 per night extra. Popular carvery restaurant just 400 yards away. MasterCard/Access/Visa/Diners Club cards accepted.

BUCKFASTLEIGH. Mrs Rosie Palmer, Wellpark Farm, Dean Prior, Buckfastleigh TQ11 0LY (01364 643775). ETB Listed *HIGHLY COMMENDED.* Set on the

edge of Dartmoor near Buckfast Abbey. A warm and friendly welcome is extended to all our guests. Very comfortable rooms available with colour TV, tea/coffee facilities and clock radio. Relaxing lounge with log fire and colour TV. Delicious farmhouse breakfasts are served. Enclosed garden with slide and swings. Excellent local 11th century inn is well worth a visit. Bed and Breakfast from £ to £18. Reductions for children and weekly bookings.

WELLPARK FARM

BUCKFASTLEIGH. Suzanne Lewis and Graham Rice, Kilbury Manor Farm, Colston Road, Buckfastleigh TQ11 0LN (01364 644079; Fax: 01364 644059).

This 18th century farmhouse is in a peaceful setting in the Dart Valley, an ideal base for touring Dartmoor and the South Hams Peninsula. Good walking, fishing and golf nearby and many interests for children including wildlife parks, animal sanctuaries, steam trains and good beaches. Bedrooms are attractive and comfortable with TV, tea/coffee facilities; en suite available and a separate bath/shower room. English and Continental breakfast, picnic lunches are provided. Suzanne delights in preparing delicious home cooked food including vegetarian using mostly our own garden produce. Our hospitality will make your stay enjoyable and memorable. Pay phone. Brochure on request. Price from £17.50 per night.

BUCKLAND MONACHORUM. Annabel and John Foulston, Store Cottage B&B, The Village, Buckland Monachorum PL20 7NA (01822 853117).

♛♛ *HIGHLY COMMENDED.* Buckland Monachorum lies in unspoilt countryside on the western edge of Dartmoor. National Trust houses, lovely gardens, the market town of Tavistock and the City of Plymouth are not far away. Store Cottage is a Listed house with a south-facing terrace in the centre of the village. An inn, noted for its food, is nearby. We have two well equipped and comfortable en suite rooms, a double and a twin. We offer comfort and tranquillity and a choice of breakfasts using local produce where possible. Children over 12 years welcome. Dogs by arrangement. Bed and Breakfast £20 per person all inclusive.

CHAGFORD. Mrs Elizabeth Law, Lawn House, Mill Street, Chagford TQ13 8AW (01647 433329).

Lawn House

On the edge of Dartmoor within the National Park, Chagford is a beautiful unspoilt former stannary town dating back to the Middle Ages. In the centre of Chagford stands Lawn House, a small but elegant 18th century listed thatched house providing an ideal base for walking expeditions onto the moor. Lawn House offers friendly, comfortable, en suite Bed and Breakfast accommodation in spacious rooms with tea/coffee making facilities; TV lounge. Open all year round. Prices are from £18 per person. Discounts are available for stays of five nights and over; reductions for children. Packed lunches available.

CHAGFORD. Jeanette and Graham Smitheram, Throwleigh Manor, Throwleigh, Near Chagford, Okehampton EX20 2JF (01647 231630).

♛♛ *COMMENDED.* Escape to the peace and tranquillity of a bygone age in idyllic surroundings. This beautiful country house is situated in a 12 acre parkland setting within the Dartmoor National Park. All rooms are individually furnished and decorated to a high standard with private bath/shower, beverage facilities, colour TV, radio, etc and there is a wealth of oak panelling and ornate plaster ceilings. We are renowned for our excellent breakfasts. Guest can use the heated swimming pool, games room, play croquet or take the woodland walk to our private lake and picnic with the ducks! Ideally situated to explore West Country, both coasts 25 miles. Rates from £19 per person.

CHUDLEIGH. Jill Shears, Glen Cottage, Rock Road, Chudleigh TQ13 0JJ (01626 852209). 17th

century thatched cottage idyllically set in secluded garden, with stream surrounded by woods. Adjoining a beauty spot with rocks, caves and waterfall. A haven for wildlife and birds; Kingfishers and Buzzards are a common sight. Outdoor swiming pool. Central for touring the moors or sea. Bed and Breakfast from £15. Tea/coffee all rooms.

CLOVELLY. Mrs Joanne Wade, Holloford Farm, Higher Clovelly, Bideford EX39 5SD (01237 441275). ETB Listed *HIGHLY COMMENDED.* We invite you

to stay on our 300 acre dairy farm, the farmhouse dates back to 16th century, with oak beams, open fireplace and pretty bedrooms, all set in peaceful, unspoilt surroundings. Two bedrooms, one twin and one double with single bed. Both have washbasins and drinks trays. Lovely bathroom, sitting room and dining room all beautifully decorated and for guests sole use. Outside enjoy our sheltered garden or take a quiet walk. Come to Holloford to sample a real Devonshire Farmhouse Breakfast and very warm welcome. Two miles from Clovelly and coast. Children welcome. Bed and Breakfast from £18.

CLOVELLY. Mrs J. Johns, Dyke Green Farm, Clovelly, Near Bideford EX39 5RU (01237 431699 or

431279). ETB 👜 COMMENDED. Situated on the edge of the ancient Iron Age fortress at the entrance of famous Clovelly. The tastefully converted barn offers beautiful accommodation furbished to a high standard throughout. Three bedrooms (two en suite and one with private WC and washbasin), all have colour TV and tea/coffee making facilities. Ideal base for Devon and Cornwall especially lovely Dartmoor and Exmoor. Close to Coastal Path on South West Way. Amenities close by include golf, tennis, fishing, swimming; perfect for walks and sandy beaches. This lovely home offers you first class Bed and Breakfast from £17 with a warm friendly welcome all year. All rooms non-smoking. Special rates for children. Please apply for full details.

CLOVELLY. Mrs P.M. Vanstone, The Old Smithy, Slerra Hill, Clovelly, Bideford EX39 5ST (01237

431202). The Old Smithy is a 16th century cottage and converted forge, situated one mile from the sea and the unspoilt picturesque village of Clovelly. Open all year. Three family or double rooms, all with colour TV and tea/coffee making facilities. Children welcome. Dogs allowed (except in the dining room). Large car park. This is an excellent base for touring Exmoor, Dartmoor and Cornwall. Also beautiful coastal walks on the South West Way. Bed and Breakfast from £15 standard, £18 en suite. Reductions for children in family room.

CLOVELLY near. Mrs Caroline May, Lower Waytown, Horns Cross, Bideford EX39 5DN (01237

451787). This delightful, unique Roundhouse offers excellent accommodation in beautiful surroundings. Extensive grounds with ornamental waterfowl and black swans on the stream-fed ponds create the perfect ambience in which to relax and unwind. Situated five miles from Clovelly and with the coastal footpath nearby, Lower Waytown makes an ideal centre for walking, touring and beaches. Tastefully furnished accommodation comprises three en-suite bedrooms; two double (one on ground floor), and one round twin-bedded room, all with tea/coffee making facilities, hair dryers and colour TV. Spacious dining room, round sitting room with beams and inglenook. Central heating. Private parking. Children over 12 years welcome. Sorry no smoking. Bed and Breakfast from £22.50. AA QQQQQ Premier Selected. Also thatched self catering cottages available.

COLYTON. Mrs Norma Rich, Sunnyacre, Northleigh, Colyton EX13 6DA (01404 871422). Need a

quiet and peaceful break? A warm welcome, with a relaxing atmosphere, is what we aim to provide at Sunnyacre which is on a working farm situated centrally between Honiton and Exeter (A30) and Lyme Regis to Exeter (A3052) in a beautiful valley with glorious views. This very scenic area provides plenty of attractions including golf courses, country parks, lovely quaint villages and coves. Accommodation comprises one family, one double and one twin bedrooms with washbasins. Children welcome at reduced rates; cot and high chair available. Bed and Breakfast from £12 per person per night. Traditional home cooked evening meals available using fresh and home-grown produce.

CREDITON. Sandra Turner, Creedy Manor, Long Barn Farm, Crediton EX17 4AB (01363 772684).

We would like to warmly welcome you to our spacious Victorian manor farmhouse amid our mixed working farm. Our centrally heated home is tastefully decorated, comfortable, with en suite or private facilities, colour TV and beverages. Choose one of the excellent eating places or eat a take-away in. Sip hot chocolate by the log fire in winter or have summer breakfast outside. Bicycle, boot or car, various places of interest and most sporting activities locally with on-site quality coarse fishing at Creedy Lakes. Bed and Breakfast from £14. Reductions for children, weekly stays and parties. New self-catering accommodation also available.

CREDITON. Mrs Janet Bradford, Oaklands, Black Dog, Crediton EX17 4QJ (01884 860645). Janet and Ivor warmly welcome you to enjoy a realxing stay, long or short, in peaceful surroundings with lovely views and countryside walks. Large comfortable bedrooms with en suite, tea/coffee facilities, colour TV and central heating. Large guest lounge with Sky TV and open fire in winter. Large garden with surrounding 20 acres of farmland where guests are free to wander. Walking distance of the 17th century Black Dog Inn pub/restaurant. Oaklands is situated between Dartmoor and Exmoor, ideal for touring all parts of Devon. Bed and Breakfast from £15. Reductions for children. Open all year.

CREDITON. Mr and Mrs R. Barrie-Smith, Great Leigh Farm, Crediton EX17 3QQ (01647 24297). Delightfully set in the mid-Devon hills between Cheriton Bishop and Crediton, two miles off the A30, Great Leigh Farm is ideally situated for a quiet holiday or for touring Devon and Cornwall. Guests are free to wander over the farmland and may also join in farm activities. The outstandingly comfortable accommodation, comprising one family, one double and two single rooms, is fully centrally heated, and two rooms have bathroom en suite. Children welcome at half price, babysitting available. Bed and Breakfast £15; Bed, Breakfast and Evening Dinner £21. Children half price.

West Winds Guest House

Small guest house located picturesquely by the water's edge overlooking Croyde Bay beach adjacent to Baggy Point National Trust coastal path. Private steps onto the beach. En suite rooms available, all with TV, radio, tea/coffee making facilities; some rooms have sea view. Dogs welcomed. Ample car parking. Residential bar and separate sun lounge overlooking sea. Fire certificate. Situated in an ideal position for surfing, touring Exmoor National Park and surrounding countryside with Saunton Golf Club only two miles away. Comfortable and relaxing atmosphere. Open all year. Bed and Breakfast from £23 per person. Write for brochure or telephone.

♔♔♔ Commended   AA QQQ Recommended.

Chris and Roslyn Gedling, West Winds Guest House, Moor Lane, Croyde Bay, Devon EX33 1PA.

Tel & Fax 01271 890489   Mobile 0831 211247

CULLOMPTON. Mrs B. Hill, Sunnyside Farm, Butterleigh, Near Cullompton, Tiverton EX15 1PP (01884 855322). Working farm. Here at Sunnyside Farm everything is done to give guests a happy holiday. Conveniently situated three and a half miles from the M5 Junction 28, it makes an ideal overnight stop and is three miles from the lovely village of Bickleigh, a great tourist attraction with a craft centre, etc. There is a spacious garden for children to play on the lawn. Trout fishing nearby and many places of interest. Comfortable accommodation has three rooms en suite, family and double/twin rooms with tea/coffee making facilities; bathroom, two toilets. Sittingroom has log fire and colour TV; dining room with separate tables; sun lounge with panoramic views. Cot, high chair, babysitting and reduced rates for children. Pets allowed. Car essential, parking. Open all year except Christmas. Traditional farmhouse food and plenty of it! Evening Meal, Bed and Breakfast from £24 daily, £150 weekly; Bed and Breakfast from £16. Short Breaks catered for. Fire Certificate. Essential Food Hygiene Certificate held.

Sunnyside Farm
Butterleigh, Devon

Terms quoted in this publication may be subject to increase if rises in costs necessitate

CULLOMPTON. Mrs Sylvia Baker, Wishay Farm, Trinity, Cullompton EX15 1PE (01884 33223).

👑👑 *COMMENDED.* **Working farm.** Wishay Farm is a 200 acre working farm with a recently modernised Grade II Listed farmhouse with some interesting features. It is situated in a quiet and peaceful area with scenic views, yet is central for touring the many attractions Devon has to offer. Comfortable and spacious accommodation in family room with en suite bathroom, double room with washbasin and private bathroom, both with colour TV, fridge, tea/coffee making facilities. Central heating, log fire when cold. Children welcome, cot and high chair available. Bed and Breakfast from £16. Reduced rates for children.

DARTMOUTH. Jill and Michael Fell, Victoria Cote, 105 Victoria Road, Dartmouth TQ6 9DY (01803 832997).

Victoria Cote is a comfortable Victorian house set in a lovely garden, within easy walking distance of the town centre. Bedrooms are spacious and attractively decorated, all with tea/coffee making facilities and colour TV. Accommodation comprises three double rooms with bath or shower rooms en suite. There is private parking for several cars — a must in this town! Open all year. Prices from £20 per person per night for Bed and Breakfast. Dinners are available, if booked. Children and dogs are also welcome.

DAWLISH. Dave and Pat Badcock, West Hatch Hotel, 34 West Cliff, Dawlish (Tel & Fax: 01626 864211).

👑👑 *HIGHLY COMMENDED.* AA QQQQ Selected, RAC Highly Acclaimed. West Hatch is your guarantee of a warm welcome and a relaxed stay in our small friendly, quality Hotel. A detached house of character with stained glass windows, antiques and oak panelled staircase. We are centrally situated overlooking the sea. All bedrooms are colour co-ordinated, very well equipped, en suite and are on the ground or first floor. Luxurious four poster bedroom. Bar and separate lounge, invigorating spa bath and private car park. Choose from our extensive English or Continental menu. Bed and Breakfast from £21 per person per night. Major credit cards accepted.

EXETER. Mr Derek Sercombe, "Rhona" Guest House, 15 Blackall Road, Exeter EX4 4HE (01392 77791).

A small family guest house situated within seven minutes' walk from the centre of historic Exeter, making an ideal base for touring the National Parks of Dartmoor and Exmoor. Luxury en suite accommodation. Colour TV, also tea/coffee making facilities in all rooms. Golf and riding parties catered for. Open all year. Private car park. Single rooms from £11; twin/family rooms from £21 with full English Breakfast. Dinner available on request.

EXETER. Mrs Dudley, Culm Vale Guest House, Stoke Canon, Exeter EX5 4EG (01392 841615).

A fine old country house of great charm and character, giving the best of both worlds as we are only three miles to the north of the Cathedral city of Exeter, with its antique shops, yet situated in the heart of Devon's beautiful countryside on the edge of the pretty village of Stoke Canon. An ideal touring centre. Our spacious comfortable Bed and Breakfast accommodation includes full English breakfast, there is a lounge with a colour TV, tea/coffee facilities, washbasin and razor point in all rooms, some with bathrooms en suite. Full central heating. Our lovely gardens boast a beautiful swimming pool and there is ample free parking. Bed and Breakfast £18.50 per person per night. Credit cards accepted.

EXETER. Janet Bragg, Marianne Pool Farm, Clyst St. George, Exeter EX3 0NZ (01392 874939). Tourist Board Listed. Situated in peaceful rural location

two miles from M5 Junction 30, and midway between the seaside town of Exmouth and the historic city of Exeter. This thatched Devon Longhouse offers an en suite family/double room, a twin-bedded room and a single room with shared bathroom, all rooms have tea/coffee making facilities. There is a comfortable lounge with colour TV and a dining room in which a full English Breakfast is served. Large lawned garden, ideal for children. Car essential. Open March to November. Bed and Breakfast from £17 to £20 per person.

EXETER. Mrs L.A. Branfield, Willhayes Farm, Longdown, Exeter EX6 7BN (01392 832636). ☙☙

COMMENDED. Standing some 700 feet high at the edge of Exeter Forest, the house has extensive views over the Teign Valley and Dartmoor. An ideal touring centre with the moors, coast, golfing and fishing facilities within easy reach. Accommodation comprises three double rooms each with en suite facilities. All rooms enjoy valley and moor views. Tea/coffee making facilities are provided. Strictly non-smoking. Terms: January to June and September to December (except Christmas) £16.50 per person per night Bed and Breakfast; July and August £20 per person per night Bed and Breakfast. Brochure available.

EXETER. Mrs Gillian Howard, Ebford Court, Ebford, Exeter EX3 0RA (01392 875353; Fax: 01392 876776). 15th century thatched farmhouse set in quiet

surroundings yet only five minutes from Junction 30, M5. The house stands in pleasant gardens and is one mile from the attractive Exe Estuary. The coast and moors are a short drive away and it is an ideal centre for touring and birdwatching. The two double bedrooms have washbasins and tea/coffee facilities; sitting/dining room with colour TV. Non smoking accommodation. Open all year. Ample parking. Bed and Breakfast from £15 per night; £90 weekly.

EXETER. Mrs Sally Glanvill, Rydon Farm, Woodbury, Exeter EX5 1LB (Tel & Fax: 01395 232341). ☙☙ *HIGHLY COMMENDED.* Come, relax and enjoy yourself

in our lovely 16th century Devon Longhouse. We offer a warm and friendly family welcome at this peaceful dairy farm. Ideally situated for exploring the coast, moors and the historic city of Exeter. Only 10 minutes' drive from the coast. Inglenook fireplace and oak beams. All bedrooms have private or en suite bathrooms, central heating, hair dryers and tea/coffee making facilities; one room with romantic four-poster. A traditional farmhouse breakfast is served with our own free range eggs and there are several excellent pubs and restaurants close by. Pets by arrangement. Open all year. Bed and Breakfast from £20 to £25. AA QQQQ Selected.

EXETER near. The Royal Oak Inn, Dunsford, Near Exeter EX6 7DA (01647 252256). ETB Listed *APPROVED.* Traditional Victorian country pub offering relaxation with six Real Ales, home-made food and the friendliest landlord you could find. Accommodation comprises eight bedrooms, five en suite. Bed and Breakfast from £20.

EXETER near. Mrs Christine Granger, Lyndale, London Road, Rockbeare, Near Exeter EX5 2PH

(01404 822304). A personal friendly welcome awaits you in this convenient but rural setting. Ideally situated for coast, moors or city; midway between Honiton and Exeter on A30 (next to Flowerland), four miles from M5 Junction 30. All bedrooms with washbasins, shaver points, tea/coffee making facilities. Non-smoking accommodation available. TV lounge. Large garden (barbecue available for guests' use). Traditional English breakfast using eggs from our own free range hens. Ample parking. Central heating. Open all year. Bed and Breakfast from £15.50 to £16.50.

EXMOUTH. New Moorings Guest House, 1 Morton Road, Exmouth EX8 1AZ (01395 223073). A

friendly "home from home" welcome by proprietors Irene and Ian Keith always awaits you at New Moorings. Conveniently situated on level ground close to the sea front, town centre, bus and train stations, we offer truly personal attention and all you need for a memorable holiday. All bedrooms en suite with tea/coffee facilities and TV. Excellent cuisine. Full central heating. Video link-up. All day access. Children welcome. Access and Visa registered. Price from £14 per night; Evening Meal £6. Mid-week bookings. Please contact Irene for further information.

HATHERLEIGH. Gill and Tony Gordon, Aish Villa, Petrockstowe, Okehampton EX20 3HL (01837 810581; E-mail: 113061.1334@compuserve.com). Aish Villa is a comfortable bungalow set in the peaceful village of Petrockstowe amongst the rolling Devon hills. We are two miles off the A386, surrounded by superb views. We have one double and one twin room, each with colour TV and tea/coffee tray, with guests' bathroom. Ideally situated for walking, cycling, touring on the Tarka Trail, South West Coast Path, Dartmoor, Exmoor and the coast. Local pub within walking distance offers excellent meals. Guests welcome all year. Rates from £15 per person. Reduction for children. Regret no pets or smoking. Ample car parking/cycle storage.

HOLSWORTHY. Mrs L.A. Cole, The Barton, Pancrasweek, Holsworthy EX22 7JT (01288 381315).

👑👑 COMMENDED. **Working farm, join in.** A peaceful holiday awaits you on our 200 acre working dairy farm on the Devon/Cornwall border, six miles from Cornish coast with quaint fishing villages, beautiful beaches and famous Clovelly. Fishing, sailing, sailboarding at Tamar Lakes, also close to leisure pool and sports centre. Historic Dartmoor and Bodmin Moor within easy reach. The 16th century farmhouse has three bedrooms for guests — two double rooms and one twin, all en suite with tea making facilities. Games room, lounge with TV, separate dining room. Traditional farmhouse cooking with home grown produce when available. Open Easter to end September. Bed and Breakfast from £16; Evening Meal £8. Brochure on request.

HONITON. Pamela and Derek Boyland, Barn Park Farm, Stockland Hill, Near Stockland, Honiton EX14 9JA (01404 861297). 👑 COMMENDED. **Working farm, join in.** Working dairy farm situated off a good secondary road one and a half miles south of the A30/A303 Junction, in peaceful countryside, ideal for bird watching and rambling. Within easy reach of many beauty spots, coast 12 miles. Traditional English breakfast (collect your own eggs from our free range hens), home grown produce used. Barn Park is a house brimming with character and has a home-from-home atmosphere. Accommodation comprises a twin or double room, family room on request. Open all year except Christmas Day. Bed and Breakfast £16; Evening Meal, if required, from £9. No smoking in the house please. West Country Tourist Board Member.

HONITON. Mrs June Ann Tucker, Yard Farm, Upottery, Honiton EX14 9QP (01404 861680).

A most attractively situated working farm. The house is very old traditional Devon farmhouse located just three miles east of Honiton and enjoying a superb outlook across the Otter Valley. Enjoy a stroll down by the River Otter which runs through the farmland. Try a spot of trout fishing. Children will love to make friends with Honey, our pony. Lovely seaside resorts 12 miles, swimming pool three miles. Traditional English breakfast, colour TV, washbasin, heating, tea/coffee facilities in all rooms. Bed and Breakfast £15; Dinner (if requested) £10. Reductions for children.

HONITON. Mrs K. Manley, Birds Farm, Awliscombe, Near Honiton EX14 0PU (01404 841620).
Comfortable 16th century beamed farmhouse situated in a peaceful hamlet. Within easy reach of Exmoor and Dartmoor; gliding club two miles; convenient for Crealy Country Adventure Park near Exeter. Honiton is known for its lacemaking. Accommodation is in two double, one family and one single bedrooms; bathroom with shower and WC, also separate shower; lounge with colour TV; dining room. Cot available. Lawned garden. Full English breakfast. Village inn two miles for evening meals. Sorry no pets. Car parking. No smoking. Bed and Breakfast from £14 to £15 per person.

ILFRACOMBE. Sunnymeade Country House Hotel, Dean Cross, West Down, Ilfracombe EX34 8NT (01271 863668). COMMENDED. AA QQQ. A

charming country house hotel in its own large gardens set in the rolling Devonshire countryside. Every effort is made to ensure that guests feel welcome and relaxed from the moment they arrive, a feeling which is enhanced by the standard of food and accommodation. Most of the 10 pretty bedrooms are en suite and all have tea making facilities, phone, radio, alarm and colour TV; some of the rooms are on the ground floor. Fresh local ingredients are used in the traditional English cooking which has a regional flavour. There is always a vegetarian choice and any special diets can be accommodated. Clothes drying facilities for walkers and garage for cycles. Sunnymeade is close to Woolacombe, Exmoor and Ilfracombe. Bed and Breakfast from £21.50 en suite daily; Dinner, Bed and Breakfast from £189 en suite weekly.

ILFRACOMBE. St. Brannocks House Hotel, St. Brannocks Road, Ilfracombe EX34 8EQ (01271 863873).

A detached Victorian hotel set in its own grounds and close to the beautiful Bicclescombe Park, Cairn Nature Reserve, town centre and seafront. The cosy well stocked bar is an ideal place to relax and socialise, while the dining room offers generous portions of good home cooked food and a selection of table wines. Choice of attractive, en suite bedrooms, with tea/coffee making facilities and TV. Large car park. An ideal base for a perfect holiday, special break or business trip. Open all year. Children and pets welcome. Bed and Breakfast from £19.50; Evening Meal from £8.75. RAC Acclaimed, Les Routiers.

IVYBRIDGE near. Mrs Susan Winzer, "The Bungalow", Higher Coarsewell Farm, Ugborough, Near Ivybridge PL21 0HP (01548 821560). Working farm.

Higher Coarsewell Farm is a traditional family-run dairy farm situated in the heart of the peaceful South Hams countryside, near Dartmoor and local unspoilt sandy beaches. It is a very spacious bungalow with beautiful garden and meadow views. One double room with bathroom en suite and one en suite family room. Guest lounge/dining room. Good home cooked food, full English breakfast served. Children welcome — cot, high chair and babysitting available. Bed and Breakfast from £14 daily; optional Evening Meal extra. Open all year. A379 turnoff from the main A38 Exeter to Plymouth road.

WHEN MAKING ENQUIRIES PLEASE MENTION
FARM HOLIDAY GUIDES

KINGSBRIDGE. Mrs Angela Foale, Higher Kellaton Farm, Kellaton, Kingsbridge TQ7 2ES (Tel & Fax: 01548 511514). 🏵🏵 COMMENDED. Working farm.

Smell the fresh sea air, delicious aga-cooked breakfast in the comfort of this lovely old farmhouse. Nestled in a valley our farm with friendly animals welcomes you. Spacious, well-furnished rooms, en suite, colour TV, tea/coffee making facilities, own lounge, central heating and log fires. Flexible meal times. Attractive walled garden. Safe car parking. Situated between Kingsbridge and Dartmouth. Visit Salcombe by ferry, one and a half miles the lost village of Hallsands and Lanacombe Beach. Beautiful, peaceful, unspoilt coastline with many sandy beaches, paths, wild flowers and wildlife. Ramblers haven. Good pubs and wet-weather family attractions. Open Easter to October. Non-smoking. Bed and Breakfast from £16.50.

KINGSBRIDGE. Centry Farm, Kingsbridge TQ7 2HF (01548 852037). Working farm. Centry is

located in a peaceful, secluded valley just a mile from Kingsbridge — the centre of the South Hams. Lovely views over garden to fields beyond. The area is well known for its scenery, beaches, cliff and moorland walks and many places of interest — a very good base for touring. Centry offers comfort and cleanliness in double/family and double/twin rooms. Both bedrooms are en suite with tea/coffee trays, hairdryer, radio/alarm clock, electric blanket. Lounge with colour TV and separate dining room where your delicious farmhouse breakfast will be served. Fridge for guests use. Gardens, patio and ample car and boat parking. Regret no smoking in farmhouse. Terms from £17.50 per person per night. Brochure available.

KINGSBRIDGE. Mrs M. Darke, Coleridge Farm, Chillington, Kingsbridge TQ7 2JG (01548 580274).

Coleridge Farm is a 600 acre working farm situated half a mile from Chillington village, midway between Kingsbridge and Dartmouth. Many safe and beautiful beaches are within easy reach, the nearest being Slapton Sands and Slapton Ley just two miles away. Plymouth, Torquay and the Dartmoor National Park are only an hour's drive. Visitors are assured of comfortable accommodation in a choice of one double and one twin-bedded rooms; private shower; toilet; shaver points and tea/coffee making facilities. Spacious lounge with TV. A variety of eating establishments in the locality will ensure a good value Evening Meal. Children welcome. Terms on request.

KINGSBRIDGE. Yvonne Helps, Hillside, Ashford, Kingsbridge TQ7 4NB (01548 550752). Character

house set in acre of orchard garden surrounded by lovely countryside, in quiet hamlet just off the A379 Plymouth to Kingsbridge road. Superb beaches and sandy coves nearby. Dartmoor 20 minutes' drive. Very comfortable accommodation with washbasins, shaver points, tea/coffee making facilities in all bedrooms. Two bathrooms. Colour TV in lounge. Diningroom with separate tables. Car parking. Visitors find a friendly, relaxed atmosphere with own keys. Full central heating. No dogs in the house please. Bed and Full English Breakfast from £15. Evening Meal optional. Open all year. Booking any day of the week. Write or phone for brochure.

FUN FOR ALL THE FAMILY IN DEVON

Arlington Court, near Barnstaple; Bygones Victoria Street, Torquay; Clovelly Village, near Bideford; Dartington Crystal, Great Torrington; Dartmoor Wildlife Park, Sparkwell; English Riviera Leisure Centre, Torquay; Exeter Maritime Museum; Exmoor Bird Gardens, Bratton Fleming; Kents Cavern Show Caves, Torquay; Babbacombe Model Village, Torquay; National Shire Horse Centre, Yealmpton; Paignton Zoo and Botanical Gardens; Plymouth Dome; Plym Valley Railway Steam Centre, Plymouth; Woodland Leisure Park, Blackawton.

LYNMOUTH. Tricia and Alan Francis, Glenville House, 2 Tors Road, Lynmouth EX35 6ET (01598 752202). Charming licensed Victorian house in sunny position overlooking East Lyn River at the beginning of Watersmeet Valley. Picturesque village and tranquil harbour a short stroll away. Ideally situated for touring/walking this beautiful part of Exmoor with its breathtaking scenery and spectacular coastline. Some bedrooms have private facilities and all have tea/coffee making. Comfortable TV lounge and attractive dining room offering a four course breakfast. Our guests will be assured a warm welcome, good food and friendly hospitality for their stay. Non-smoking. Bed and Breakfast from £17.50 to £22 per person per night. Dinner (optional) £12 per person. Open March to November.

LYNMOUTH. Mrs J. Parker, Tregonwell Riverside Guest House, 1 Tors Road, Lynmouth, Exmoor National Park EX35 6ET (01598 753369). ⚅⚅ *COMMENDED.* AA QQQQ. Truly paradise, our outstandingly elegant Victorian riverside stone-built house is snuggled into the sunny side of tranquil Lynmouth's deep wooded valleys, alongside beaches, waterfalls, cascades, England's highest cliff tops, enchanting harbour, all steeped in history! A wonderful walking area, where Exmoor meets the sea. Exceptionally dramatic scenery around our Olde Worlde smugglers village. Wordsworth, Shelley and Coleridge all kept returning here. An all year resort, each season unveiling its own spectacle. Pretty bedrooms, luxury en suites with breathtaking views. Guests' drawing room with open log fires in cooler seasons. Garage, parking. Bed and Breakfast from £18.50. Come as a resident then return again as our friend!

LYNTON. Combe Park Hotel, Hillsford Bridges, Lynton EX35 6LE (01598 752356). Originally a 17th century Hunting Lodge, is a comfortable Hotel uniquely situated within National Trust parkland. Nine bedrooms with private bath/shower rooms. Licensed with well furnished lounges. Fresh seasonal produce used where possible. Dogs welcome. A haven for walking, riding and fishing. Open April to October. AA Rosette for Cuisine 75%.

LYNTON. Croft House Hotel, Lydiate Lane, Lynton EX35 6HE (01598 752391). ⚅⚅⚅ *COMMEN-DED.* A delightful period hotel in England's little Switzerland offering delightful rooms, en suite, some with four-poster beds. All rooms with TV and tea/coffee making facilities. Home cooked meals served by candlelight. Pets are welcome. Fully licensed with bar. Special Winter Breaks. Pretty walled garden in which to relax and enjoy your evening drink. Please ring for brochure.

LYNTON. Mrs V.A. Ashby, Rodwell, 21 Lee Road, Lynton EX35 6BP (01598 753324). ⚅⚅ *COMMENDED.* Rodwell is a small, friendly guest house situated in the most level part of Lynton facing south with lovely views of the surrounding hills and close to all amenities. Many beautiful walks start at our door and the famous Valley of Rocks and the unique cliff railway to Lynmouth are a short walk away. Comfortable lounge with colour TV, double and twin bedrooms, all en suite, all with colour TV and tea/coffee making facilities. Parking. Bed and Breakfast from £16. Directions: opposite Cottage Hospital on the main road through Lynton.

LYNTON. Pat and Terry Emerson, Fernleigh, Park Street, Lynton EX35 6BY (01598 753575). ♛♛

HIGHLY COMMENDED. A warm welcome awaits you in purpose-built guesthouse standing on a quiet side street within walking distance of restaurants, pubs, shops and the harbour. We provide luxury accommodation in pretty and spacious en suite bedrooms at a standard of cleanliness we would expect ourselves. Both breakfast and evening meals are served at separate tables in the dining room which overlooks the garden. Vegetarians can be catered for. Unlicensed, but guests are welcome to bring their own wine. Totally non-smoking. Private car park. Please write or telephone for further information.

THE TURRETT

33 Lee Road, Lynton, Devon EX35 6BS   ♛♛ COMMENDED

Delightful, family-run Victorian hotel situated in the centre of this picturesque village, ideal for exploring Exmoor and its magnificent coastline.

All of our rooms have colour TV and beverage making facilities; most are en suite. Superb home cooking; vegetarians catered for. Licensed. Open all year.

Bed and Breakfast from £15–£22.
Reductions for Short Breaks and weekly bookings.
TELEPHONE FOR FREE BROCHURE **01598 753284**

LYNTON. Christine Hawkes, "The Fernery", Lydiate Lane, Lynton EX35 6AJ (01598 752440). ETB

Listed *APPROVED.* This picturesque village has beautiful Exmoor views, coastal walks and spectacular scenery. In this lovely old house, steeped in history, the warmest welcome and total comfort awaits you. Two pretty double bedrooms, plus one with twin beds, have new washbasins, colour TVs, clock radios, hairdryers and beverage facilities. A beautiful shower room and bathroom, both with toilets; separate cloakroom. A cosy lounge, satellite TV, log fires and central heating. In the sunflower parlour choose a wonderful freshly cooked breakfast from a delicious menu — and enjoy being spoilt. Bed and Breakfast from £18. Open all year.

LYNTON. Mrs R. Pile, Coombe Farm, Countisbury, Lynton EX35 6NF (01598 741236). ♛♛

Working farm. Coombe Farm, set amid 370 acres of beautiful hill farming country, dates back to the 17th century. Ideal holiday base from which to visit lovely Doone Valley and Exmoor countryside. Two double rooms with en-suite shower rooms; one twin and two family rooms with washbasins, and all with hot drinks facilities. Bathroom, shower, two toilets; lounge; diningroom. Central heating. Children welcome, cot, high chair and occasional babysitting. Dogs by arrangement. Car essential, parking space. Guests enjoy watching farm animals, including Exmoor Horn sheep and horses. Pony trekking, tennis, fishing, golf nearby. Open March to end October. Fire Certificate held. Excellent country fare served. Bed and Breakfast from £18 to £22 per night. Reductions for children 11 years and under sharing family room. Stamp, please, for brochure. Residential licence. No smoking.

PLEASE SEND A STAMPED ADDRESSED ENVELOPE WITH ENQUIRIES

LYNTON. Pine Lodge, Lynway, Lynton EX35 6AX (01598 753230). Situated on the outskirts of Lynton

but only a short walk from the village. Pine Lodge overlooks the West Lyn Valley and the wooded slopes of Summerhouse Hill with a large private garden and ample parking. Bright comfortable rooms (most en suite) with TV and tea/coffee making facilities. Bed and Breakfast from £15 per night. Dinner optional. Non smoking.

LYNTON. Don and Jenny Bowman, Gable Lodge, Lee Road, Lynton EX35 6BS (Tel & Fax: 01598

752367). We are sure that you will enjoy your stay at our Victorian Grade II Listed building in England's "Little Switzerland". Gable Lodge is situated in a level part of Lynton, with views over Countisbury Hill, the East Lyn Valley and Exmoor National Park. All our rooms have radio, TV, beverage trays and central heating. At Gable Lodge we offer a friendly and homely atmosphere with a good hearty breakfast to set you up for the day. An ideal spot for a relaxing holiday. Private car park and garden. Pets welcome. Non-smoking. Bed and Breakfast from £17. Please ring for brochure.

LYNTON. Woodlands, Lynbridge Road, Lynton EX35 6AX (01598 752324). ♥♥♥ *COMMENDED.*

Peacefully located yet only a few minutes' walk from the centre of Lynton, Woodlands overlooks Summerhouse Hill and the unspoilt wooded valley of the West Lyn River. There is a choice of single, double and twin rooms, all with colour TV, radio and tea/coffee making facilities. Most rooms are very spacious, fully en suite and have glorious views across the valley. Delicious home cooking using fresh produce. Choice of menu including vegetarian option. Private parking, licensed, cosy lounge, log fire and central heating. Non-smoking. Ideal base for exploring Exmoor and the stunning coastal scenery. Bed and Breakfast £18 to £22; Evening Meals £12.

LYNTON. South View Guest House, 23 Lee Road, Lynton EX35 6BP (01598 752289). ETB ♥♥

COMMENDED. South View is a small friendly guest house in the heart of the picturesque Exmoor village of Lynton. Open all year, our aim is to provide a comfortable base from which to explore this beautiful coastal region. We have five rooms, all fully en suite with colour TV, tea/coffee making facilities, hair dryer, alarm clock and individually controlled heating. We serve a full breakfast with a choice of menu. Our comfortable guests' lounge is always open. Private parking is available at the rear. Overnight guests welcome. Bed and Breakfast from £15 to £20 per person per night.

LYNTON. Ben and Jane Bennett, Victoria Lodge, Lee Road, Lynton EX35 6BS (Tel & Fax: 01598 753203; Freephone 0500 303026). ❦❦❦ *HIGHLY*

COMMENDED. AA QQQQQ Premier Selected, RAC Winner of the Best Small Hotel in South West England. An award-winning hotel that retains the charater of the Victorian age, with original fireplaces, brass beds and hundreds of prints and maps, whilst being completely modernised and luxuriously decorated throughout. All nine bedrooms are en suite. Dinner is a creative blend of English and Continental cuisine. Let us share our love and knowledge of Exmoor National Park with you, with its huge variety of stunning scenery. Explore our rugged heritage coastline and the sweeping moorland, relax in our secluded terraced gardens or wander around our village, known as "Little Switzerland". Licensed. Private car park. Bed and Breakfast £22 to £32 per person; Dinner £16. Children welcome. No pets and totally non smoking. Please telephone or send for a brochure.

LYNTON near. Christine and Ian Corderoy, Moorlands, Woody Bay, Parracombe EX31 4RA (01598 763224). ❦ *COMMENDED.* Moorlands (formerly Woody

Bay Station Hotel) is a family run establishment, in a most beautiful part of North Devon, surrounded by Exmoor countryside within two miles of the spectacular coastline. The Bed and Breakfast accommodation is comfortable and quiet, suitable for two persons or a family of four. En suite with shower, colour TV and tea/coffee making facilities. Moorlands has a private residents' bar with bar meals available, private outdoor swimming pool all set in six acres of gardens. Open Easter to end October. £17.50 per person per night. Reductions for family of four.

NEWTON FERRERS. Slade Barn and Netton Farm Holiday Cottages, Noss Mayo, Near Plymouth PL8 1HA (Tel & Fax: 01752 872235). Tourist Board

Listed *COMMENDED.* Coastal South Devon beside the beautiful Yealm estuary. Sandy Cherrington assures you of a warm welcome to Slade Barn. Only three bedrooms — one twin, one double and one with shower en suite. All rooms have central heating, TV/radio and hairdryers. Tea/coffee on request. Full English breakfast naturally! Lovely indoor pool, games room, tennis court and private gardens. Easy access to fabulous National Trust cliff walks; nearby sandy beaches, golf, fishing, riding. Ideal base for day trips to Cornwall or the Moors. Plenty of parking. Non smoking. Open all year. Bed and Breakfast from £19 to £22; Evening Meal on request. SPECIAL INTEREST: professional Reflexology/Aromatherapy Massage by appointment.

NEWTON FERRERS, near PLYMOUTH. Pat and John Urry, "Barnicott", Parsonage Road, Newton Ferrers, River Yealm, Plymouth PL8 1AS (01752 872843). 16th century thatched cottage situated in an area of outstanding natural beauty on a river valley. Facilities nearby for sailing, rowing, fishing, south Devon Heritage coastal path walks, short drives to beaches, Dartmoor National Park and historic Plymouth departure point of the Pilgrim Fathers. Accommodation comprises two double, one twin bedrooms, all with shaving points, heating, colour TV, washbasin, hospitality tray and rural views. Guests' bathroom. Full English breakfast or menu to suit. Three local inns and a Bistro serving Evening Meals all within walking distance. Private parking. Bed and Breakfast from £17 single; £28 double.

NORTH TAWTON. Nick and Amanda Waldron, Kayden House Hotel, High Street, North Tawton EX20 2HF (01837 82242). ❦❦❦ *APPROVED.* Family-run

hotel in mid Devon. All rooms en suite with TV and tea making facilities. Our à la carte restaurant has an extensive menu and a comprehensive wine list, and is open from Monday to Saturday. Our traditional Sunday lunch proves very popular and is good value. We have a full bar menu, and family celebrations are catered for. Bed and Breakfast from £23.50 single, £35 double/twin. Open all year.

OKEHAMPTON. Mrs E.G. Arney, The Old Rectory, Bratton Clovelly, Okehampton EX20 4LA (01837 871382). An ideal centre for a visit to Devon and Cornwall. With two acres of lawns, gardens and a paddock the Old Rectory is a beautifully quiet spot to spend a relaxing holiday. Thoroughly modernised property, so the visitor can be assured of comfortable accommodation and good food. Sandy beaches, beautiful countryside, rugged Dartmoor, a lake with prime fishing and water sports, all within a car journey. Three large double rooms, all with washbasins, one with shower. A warm welcome, friendly atmosphere and personal attention encourages visitors to return again and again. Pets welcome. Bed and Breakfast from £16; Evening Meal available.

HIGHER CADHAM FARM

139 acre beef and sheep farm just off the A3072, five miles from Dartmoor. 16th century farmhouse with barn conversions offering a total of nine rooms – five en suite, the rest have washbasins, shaver points, etc., with bathroom and toilets close by. Two of the four lounges are non-smoking as is the dining room, though smokers are welcome in other rooms. The accommodation is of the highest standard with plenty of hearty Devonshire food, a residential licence and a warm welcome. Babies and dogs are accepted by arrangement only but older children are very welcome. We have farm walks, ducks on the ponds and other animals to amuse all the family. Walkers on the Tarka Trail are fully catered for with drying room, packed lunches, etc. AA QQQQ Selected and DATI Warmest Welcome Award 1992 has helped make Higher Cadham Farm the 'place to stay' when in West Devon. Bed and Breakfast from £17; Dinner £8. Weekly from £158; supplement for en suite rooms. Member of Farm Holiday Bureau.

Mrs Jenny King, Higher Cadham Farm, Jacobstowe, Okehampton, Devon EX20 3RB
Telephone 01837 851647 – ❦❦❦ COMMENDED

ETB
❦❦❦

FLUXTON FARM HOTEL

AA
LISTED

OTTERY ST. MARY, DEVON EX11 1RJ
Telephone: 01404 812818

Cat Lovers' paradise at our charming 16th century farmhouse set in beautiful Otter Valley with two acre gardens including stream, trout pond and garden railway. Only four miles from beach at Sidmouth. Beamed candle-lit room; two lounges with colour TV, one non-smoking. Log fires, central heating. Teasmaids in all rooms, which are ensuite with colour TV. Good home cooking our speciality, using all local fresh produce, superbly cooked. Children and dogs welcome; dogs free of charge. Lovely touring and walking country. Peace and quiet. All mod cons.

Parking. Licensed. Open Christmas.
Terms: Bed & Breakfast £23.00 per person per day.
Dinner, Bed & Breakfast £30.00 per person per day.
Proprietors: Mr & Mrs E. A. Forth.

OTTERY ST MARY. Mrs Susan Hansford, Pitt Farm, Fairmile, Ottery St. Mary EX11 1NL (01404 812439). ❦❦ *COMMENDED.* Bed and Breakfast at this most attractive thatched farmhouse, with 190 acres, situated in peaceful village of Fairmile, quarter of a mile off the A30 on the B3176. Enjoying picturesque views of the surrounding countryside it is an ideal base for touring moors, East Devon, South Devon, Exeter. Double, twin and family rooms, some en suite; three bathrooms; lounge with colour TV; dining room. Regret no pets. Car essential — ample parking. Fire Certificate held. Bed and Breakfast from £17. SAE, or phone for terms; prompt reply.

PAIGNTON (Torbay). Mrs Mandy Tooze, Elberry Farm, Broadsands, Paignton TQ4 6HJ (01803 842939). Working farm. Elberry Farm is a working farm uniquely situated close to Broadsands Beach, Elberry Cove and a pitch and putt golf course. Close to many of Torbay's tourist attractions. Warm welcome and good hearty meals (using local and home grown produce) are guaranteed. The comfortable rooms (three family and one twin) all have tea/coffee making facilities. Baby listening, cot and high chair available. Pets by arrangement. Restricted smoking. Open January to November. Bed and Breakfast from £13 per person; Evening Meals £6. Reductions for children.

AMBER HOUSE HOTEL
6 Roundham Road, Paignton, South Devon TQ4 6EZ
Telephone 01803 558372

Family-run licensed hotel. Colour TVs and tea/coffee making facilities in all rooms. En-suite facilities and ground floor rooms.
Private telephones and clock radios in most rooms. Good food, highly recommended. Large car park. Whirlpool spa bath.
Spacious suntrap garden and patio. Park close by for doggy walks.
A warm welcome assured to pets and their families.

**Write or telephone now for further details to:
Mr and Mrs R.P. Neads, Resident Proprietors.**

PAIGNTON. Freda Dwane and Steve Bamford, Clifton Hotel, 9/10 Kernou Road, Paignton TQ4 6BA (01803 556545). Ideally located, friendly, relaxed, licensed small non-smoking hotel with excellent food, open Easter to November plus Christmas Breaks. A short level walk to sea, theatre, shops, rail and coach stations. Perfect spot for leaving the car and relaxing by exploring on foot or using the plentiful public transport. All bedrooms have TV and tea/coffee making facilities and are double glazed and centrally heated with radiator thermostats. All bedrooms are en suite or have private shower/bathroom. Bed and Breakfast from £16. Spring and Autumn breaks in en suite rooms (minimum two nights) £46 per night two persons Dinner, Bed and Breakfast.

PLYMOUTH. Mayflower Guest House, 209 Citadel Road East, The Hoe, Plymouth PL1 2JF (Tel: 01752 202727; Fax: 01752 667496; e-mail: mayflowergh@compuserve.co Web: http://www.swis. net/mayflower). ETB Listed *COMMENDED.* West Country Tourist Board Member. Family-run guest house, opposite Hoe Park, close to shops, marinas, restaurants, bus station. Most rooms en suite, colour TV, tea/coffee making facilities. Non-smoking room available. Central heating. All major credit cards accepted. Directions — leave expressway (A38) follow city centre signs, bear left at Hoe, seafront sign, 100 metres by third traffic lights, by sign turn left for Hoe, seafront, turn into Hoegate Street, top of road, turn right, we are in the middle cul-de-sac opposite Hoe Park.

FREE and REDUCED RATE Holiday Visits!
See our READERS' OFFER VOUCHER for details.

ALLINGTON HOUSE

Situated in secluded square between the city shopping centre and Hoe Promenade. An elegant Victorian town house which offers clean, comfortable accommodation. All bedrooms have colour TV, washbasin, central heating and beverage facilities. En suite rooms are available. Within close reach are railway and bus stations and the ferry port. The Pavilion, Theatre Royal, cinemas, Hoe seafront, Citadel and historic Barbican are within easy walking distance. A full English breakfast is included unless otherwise requested (vegetarians catered for). 15% discount on bookings of three days or more, two adults sharing. Bed and Breakast from £16 per person. Brittany Ferries Recommended.

6 St. James Place East, The Hoe, Plymouth PL1 3AS   Tel: 01752 221435

PLYMOUTH. The Lamplighter Hotel, 103 Citadel Road, The Hoe, Plymouth PL1 2RN (01752

663855). ₩₩ *COMMENDED*. AA QQQ. Lamplighter Hotel is a family-run business situated on Plymouth Hoe, close to the sea front, historic Barbican, Theatre Royal, Plymouth Pavilions and city centre. Only minutes from the railway and coach stations and 850 yards from the ferry terminal. HMS Raleigh is only three miles on a bus route. All rooms are of the highest standard with seven rooms fully en suite and two with private facilities. Full English breakfast, tea/coffee and biscuits are provided; colour TV, Sky, video. Separate lounge. Car park. Reductions for children. Pets by prior arrangement. Please telephone, or write, for further details.

PLYMOUTH. The Teviot Guest House, 20 North Road East, Plymouth PL4 6AS (01752 262656;

Fax: 01752 251660). ETB Listed *HIGHLY COMMENDED.* Guest House centrally located in Plymouth offering a full range of rooms from single to family. En suite and rooms with showers available. All rooms have international direct dial telephone, remote control colour TV, alarm clock/radios, hair dryers and toiletries and complimentary beverage tray. No smoking policy. Full central heating, full Fire Certificate. Easy overnight parking. Most major credit/charge cards accepted. Please send for further details and terms.

Beautiful 16th Century Coaching House with log fires and brasses. Jan and John Moore will give you the warmest of welcomes and help you plan your days if you wish. Set in an area of outstanding natural beauty. Central for sea or country. Footpaths lead through woodland. Cliff walks. Wonderful wildlife. Honiton's antique shops and lace, historic Exeter, all at hand. Sidmouth is just 10 minutes away. All bedrooms are centrally heated and have tea/coffee making facilities. Traditional jazz every Saturday night in the function room, so if you want a quiet drink in the lounge bar you're not disturbed. Real ales served. Bed and Breakfast from £14. ☻☻

THREE HORSESHOES INN

On the main A3052 between Sidmouth and Seaton

Branscombe, Seaton, Devon EX12 3BR
Telephone: 01297 680251

Bovett's Farm

Bovett's nestles amid the rolling hills of the truly breathtaking Roncombe Valley. There are many excellent walks nearby. Within easy reach of Exeter and East Devon's Heritage Coast. Guests have use of the garden and are free to come and go as they please. The comfortable lounge has a wood-burning stove, colour TV and a selection of books and games. A full English Breakfast is served in the lovely dining room. We offer a choice of three attractively furnished double/twin bedrooms all with ensuite shower room and shaver point. Bedrooms are heated and have tea/coffee making facilities. Friendly personal service. Ample parking. No smoking. *Call Bridget and Brian Hopkinson for further details.*
Bovett's Farm, Roncombe Lane, Sidbury, Sidmouth, Devon EX10 0QN Telephone: (01395) 597456

Berwick House

Salcombe Road, Sidmouth, Devon EX10 8PX Tel: 01395 513621

Attractive 19th century house situated close to the River Sid and National Trust Byes and within easy level walking distance of the sea and town centre. The locality is part of the Heritage Coast, offering ideal walking, and is also well placed for visiting many other attractions. We have two twin/family rooms, two double, one self-contained and two twin rooms. All rooms en suite with TV and tea/coffee-making facilities. Comfortable lounge. Car park. Sorry, no pets or smoking. Optional Evening Meal March-October. Terms from £17pp for Bed and Breakfast.
Further details from:
Rosemary Tingley and Tony Silversides
Members of Sidmouth & District Hotels & Caterers' Association
WCTB ☻☻ COMMENDED

SIDMOUTH. Mrs B.I. Tucker, Goosemoor Farm, Newton Poppleford, Sidmouth EX10 0BL (01395 568279).

Goosemoor Farmhouse is an old Devon Long House with a bread oven in the dining room. The 25-acre mixed farm is on the Exeter — Lyme Regis bus route, about four miles from the sea, and has streams running through its meadows. There are many delightful walks in country lanes, or over Woodberry and Alsbeare Commons. Guests may wander freely on the farmland. Coarse fishing available also. There are four double and one family rooms, all with wash-basins; two bathrooms, three toilets; sitting room; dining room. Open all year with log fires. Central heating throughout. Car not essential, but there is parking. No children under eight years. Bed and Breakfast from £15. Cream teas also available.

SIDMOUTH. Mrs Betty S. Sage, Pinn Barton, Peak Hill, Sidmouth EX10 0NN (01395 514004; Fax: 01395 514004). ✹✹ *COMMENDED.*

A 330-acre farm peacefully set just off the coastal road, two miles from Sidmouth and close to the village of Otterton. Safe beaches and lovely cliff walks. Pinn Barton has been highly recommended, and offers a warm welcome in comfortable surroundings with good farmhouse breakfast. All bedrooms have bathrooms en suite; colour TV; central heating; free hot drinks facilities; electric blankets. Children very welcome. Reductions for children sharing parents' room. Open all year. Bed and Breakfast including bedtime drink from £19. Own keys provided for access at all times.

TAVISTOCK. Mrs Rose Bacon, "April Cottage", Mount Tavy Road, Tavistock PL19 9JB (01822 613280). ✹✹ *HIGHLY COMMENDED.*

Recommended by "Which?" Good Bed and Breakfast Guide. Lovely Victorian cottage in a unique setting on the banks of the River Tavy with flower gardens and patios overlooking the River as it tumbles along towards the Tamar Valley. We are situated within two minutes' level walk of the centre of town. Local facilities include golf, fishing, tennis, swimming, canoe or cycle hire. Dartmoor on our doorstep offers walking, climbing or horse riding in an area of outstanding beauty, a natural habitat for wildlife. "April Cottage" offers extremely comfortable accommodation with attention to detail ensuring a very pleasant stay. En-suite facilities. Colour TV, radio, tea/coffee, also comfortable TV lounge with seasonal log fire overlooking the river. The house has central heating and double glazing. Parking. Bed and Breakfast from £14 nightly.

TAVISTOCK near. Ed and Merl Stevens, The Old Coach House Hotel, Ottery, Near Tavistock PL19 8NS (01822 617515). ✹✹✹

A lovely small country Hotel on edge of tiny hamlet of Ottery, close to historic Tavistock and beautiful Dartmoor. Ideal base for visiting any part of Devon or Cornwall. Peaceful setting amid rolling farmland adjacent to Tamar Valley, designated an area of outstanding beauty. Superb walking country, fishing and many National Trust houses and gardens nearby. Two golf courses within three miles and St. Mellion International Golf Club 20 minutes, or just relax in our tranquil walled garden. All rooms en suite and have colour TV, tea/coffee making facilities, telephone and clock/radios. Bargain Breaks from £62 to £90 for three nights Dinner, Bed and Breakfast. AA QQQQ.

RUSTIC DEVON

Inland from the coastal resorts lies the heart of Devon and the 365 square miles of Dartmoor National Park. Take time to explore the spectacular tors, hills and lakes, and watch out for the famous wild ponies. Picturesque rural villages reflect the unhurried pace of Devon life and there are traces everywhere of the Moor's rich heritage, dating back to the Bronze Age. In the north is Exmoor, one of Britain's smallest National Parks, ideal for rambling, pony trekking and bird watching.

TEIGN VALLEY. S. and G. Harrison-Crawford, Silver Birches, Teign Valley, Trusham, Newton Abbot TQ13 0NJ (01626 852172). A warm welcome awaits you at Silver Birches, a comfortable bungalow at the edge of Dartmoor. A secluded, relaxing spot with two acre garden running down to river. Only two miles from A38 on B3193. Exeter 14 miles, sea 12 miles. Car advisable. Ample parking. Excellent pubs and restaurants nearby. Good centre for fishing, birdwatching, forest walks, golf, riding; 70 yards salmon/trout fishing free to residents. Centrally heated guest accommodation with separate entrance. Two double-bedded rooms, one twin-bedded room, all with own bath/shower, toilet. Guest lounge with colour TV. Diningroom, sun lounge overlooking river. Sorry, no children under eight. Terms include tea on arrival. Bed and full English Breakfast from £23 nightly, £154 weekly. Evening Meal optional. Open all year. Self catering caravans also available.

TIVERTON. Mrs Ruth Hill-King, Little Holwell, Collipriest, Tiverton EX16 4PT (01884 257590). Little Holwell is an old Devon longhouse believed to date from the 13th century, set amidst rolling hills in the Exe Valley, just one and a half miles south of Tiverton. We offer a warm welcome with ample home cooking. Three guest rooms, two rooms with en suite facilities, all with washbasin, tea/coffee making facilities, radio and hairdryer. The house is centrally heated, with log fires in winter, and is open all year except Christmas; we are also a NON-SMOKING house. Essential Food Hygiene Certificate held. There are pleasant views from the garden over the surrounding countryside, and some interesting walks. We are in a quiet location, yet within 15 minutes you can be on the M5 motorway. There are many places to explore, and the coasts and moors are both within easy driving distance. We also have National Trust houses not far away, a museum, and plenty of other interesting things to find and do. Directions: from M5 take A361 towards Tiverton, take left junction at B3391, proceed to fourth roundabout, take left exit, follow round left, and proceed for one and a half miles, last property along lane on right. Bed and Breakfast from £16 per person per night; Bed, Breakfast and Evening Meal £24.50 per person per night.

TIVERTON. Colin and Christine Cook, Higher Western Restaurant, Oakford, Tiverton EX16 9JE (01398 341210). Licensed small country restaurant with en suite accommodation set in three-quarters of an acre. On the B3227 Taunton/Barnstaple Holiday Route, one-and-a-half miles west of Oakford, in an area of outstanding natural beauty. A relaxing base for touring Exmoor and the North Devon coast. Excellent food, cooked to order, specialising in imaginative menus using local and own produce, complemented by a carefully chosen wine list. We offer quality accommodation to those seeking peace and quiet. One twin-bedded and two double rooms, all en suite. Children welcome. Car essential: ample parking. Open all year round. Terms: Bed and Breakfast from £15 per night; three-course Luncheon £6.25. Caravan also available.

BRADDON HALL HOTEL

70 Braddons Hill Road East, Torquay TQ1 1HF
Telephone/Fax: 01803 293908
Proprietors: Peter and Carol White

This delightful personally run hotel is situated in a peaceful yet convenient position, only a few minutes from the harbour, shopping centre, beaches and entertainments.

★ All rooms are en suite, individual in character and tastefully decorated

★ All have remote control colour TVs and tea/coffee making facilities

★ Romantic four-poster bed available for that special occasion

★ Ground floor bedroom

★ Full central heating for those early and late breaks

★ Parking

★ Bed and Breakfast per person from £16 low season to £20 high season

Please write or telephone for our brochure and book with confidence

TORQUAY. Mike and Silvia Young, Chelston Banks Hotel, Old Mill Road, Torquay TQ2 6HW (01803 607129). A small family-run hotel set in peaceful surroundings yet within easy reach of the beach, railway station and the Riviera Centre. The picturesque village of Cockington is also nearby. All rooms are en suite and have complimentary tea/coffee facilities and central heating; own keys with access to rooms at all times; comfortable lounge with colour TV and a selection of video films for your entertainment. Enjoy a drink in our attractive Harbourside Inn where you can enjoy the company in a friendly holiday atmosphere (pool table). Home cooking and a good choice of menu is offered. Parking. Open all year. Special Christmas and New Year programme. Visitors' comments include ''Our best holiday ever'' — Mrs Rachel Gorman and family. Please write, or telephone, for our colour brochure.

Silverlands Hotel

27 Newton Road, Torquay, Devon TQ2 5DB
Telephone: 01803 292013

Situated on a main route to town and beach (approx. $\frac{1}{2}$ mile). Superb family run guest house. Twelve superior rooms furnished and decorated to a high standard, mostly ensuite. Relaxed and homely atmosphere. Satellite TV, hot and cold wash facilities, tea and coffee making, full central heating available in all rooms. Ample car parking. Full English Breakfast. Open all year. From £14 to £20 per person.

ETB COMMENDED   RAC Listed   AA QQQ

AA QQQ # GROSVENOR HOUSE HOTEL ETB 🌸🌸🌸

Falkland Rd Torquay TQ2 5JP

Licensed Hotel run by friendly Christian family in quiet central position 400 m from seafront. Good sized rooms all with en suite, tea-making and CTV. Excellent home cooked food with choice of menu at Breakfast and Dinner. Car parking at front of Hotel, 600 m from rail station B&B from only £113 per week with reductions for children sharing. Open all year including full Christmas programme.

Brochure from Nigel & Angela Pearce 01803 294110

TORQUAY. Clevedon Hotel, Meadfoot Sea Road, Torquay TQ1 2LQ (01803 294260). 🌸🌸🌸 AA QQQ, RAC Acclaimed. Small licensed family run hotel ideally situated in beautiful wooded suburb, 300 yards from beach, half a mile from harbour and town centre. Business and holiday guests alike enjoy our peaceful location, delicious food and genuine home from home atmosphere. All 12 bedrooms are comfortably furnished with private facilities en-suite, colour TV and tea/coffee making. Ground floor and family rooms available. Dogs accepted by arrangement (small charge of £1 per night). Ample parking. Open all year including Christmas. Bed and Breakfast from £21. Evening Meal optional.

HEATHCLIFF HOTEL

16 Newton Road, Torquay, Devon TQ2 5BZ

Telephone: 01803 211580

This former vicarage is now a superbly appointed hotel equipped for today yet retaining its Victorian charm. All the bedrooms have full ensuite facilities, colour TV and drink making facilities. The elegant licensed bar boasts an extensive menu and unlike many hotels, the car park has sufficient space to accommodate all vehicles to eliminate roadside parking. Torquay's main beach, High Street shops, entertainment and restaurants are all nearby and with full English breakfast included, it is easy to see why guests return time after time.

Tariff for B&B ranges between £15 and £21.50 pp. Family rooms from £42 per night. So, be it main holiday, touring or business, make the Heathcliff your 1st choice.

VISITORS	BOOK
Rick & Elaine	Best in Devon
Mr & Mrs T	Excellent !
The S Family	1st Class
Mac & June	Fantastic Hosts

TORQUAY. West Winds, Teignmouth Road, Maidencombe, Torquay TQ1 4TH (01803 314386).

Dennis and Wyvene Maisey welcome you to their family home; relaxed atmosphere, comfortably furnished, centrally heated. Attractive TV lounge, large conservatory overlooking gardens and fields. Some rooms with sea views and en-suite facilities. Tea/coffee making facilities and colour TV in all rooms. Full English Breakfast. Own key, ample parking. Bed and Breakfast from £15.50 per person. Reduced rates for weekly bookings and for children. Local beach is nearby with safe bathing from a sheltered cove and there is a Thatched Tavern within walking distance for a variety of meals and bar snacks.

TORQUAY near. Mrs Jacky Kirkham, Walmer Towers, Moles Lane, South Whilborough, Kingkers-well, Newton Abbot TQ12 5LS (01803 872105; Fax: 01803 875477).

Jackie and Bill Kirkham offer a warm and friendly welcome at Walmer Towers. Once a farmhouse, it is situated in seven acres of peaceful countryside with pano-ramic views towards Dartmoor. Ideal base for visiting coast, country, historic towns and castles. Many amenities nearby including golf, horse riding and water sports. We have two large and comfortable en suite double/family rooms which are centrally heated, have tea/coffee making facilities and colour TV. Breakfast includes free range eggs, home baked bread and home made preserves. Bed and Breakfast from £18 to £21. Special rates for family rooms and off season breaks.

FREE and REDUCED RATE Holiday Visits!
See our READERS' OFFER VOUCHER for details.

TOTNES. Mrs Jeannie Allnutt, The Old Forge at Totnes, Seymour Place, Totnes TQ9 5AY (01803 862174). 👒👒 *HIGHLY COMMENDED.* A charming 600-year-old stone building, delightfully converted from blacksmith and wheelwright workshops and coach houses. Traditional working forge, complete with blacksmith's prison cell.

We have our own bit of "rural England" close to the town centre. Very close to the River Dart steamer quay, shops and station (also steam train rides). Ideally situated for touring most of Devon — including Dartmoor and Torbay coasts. A day trip from Exeter, Plymouth and Cornwall. May to September — Elizabethan costume worn Tuesdays. Double, twin and family rooms with all en suite. Ground floor rooms suitable for most disabled guests. All rooms have colour TV, telephones, beverage trays (fresh milk), colour co-ordinated Continental bedding, central heating. Licensed lounge and patio. No smoking indoors. New conservatory style leisure

As seen on BBC TV's Holiday Programme

lounge with whirlpool spa. Parking, walled gardens. Excellent choice of breakfast menu including vegetarian and special diets. Children welcome but sorry, no pets. Bed and Breakfast from £25 per person (en suite). Cottage suite for two to four persons also available, suitable for disabled visitors. AA Selected (QQQQ) Award.

TOTNES near. Mrs Miller, Buckyette Farm, Littlehempston, Near Totnes TQ9 6ND (01803 762638). 👒👒 Grassland farm in attractive countryside.

From Totnes take A381 towards Newton Abbot, follow signpost to Littlehempston, turn right at phone box, farm third to left. Accommodation comprises six bedrooms — one twin with bath/shower, one double with bath and toilet and four family rooms, three with bath and toilet, one with shower and toilet. All rooms have tea/coffee facilities. Central heating. Children are welcome, babysitting available. Open March to October. Table licence. Bed and Breakfast from £18 to £22. Weekly and child rates available. Fire Certificate held. RAC Listed.

UMBERLEIGH. Mrs Pauline Warne, Emmett Farm, Umberleigh EX37 9AG (01769 540243). Emmett

is a full working farm set in quiet countryside. You will be most welcome to browse around the farm at your own leisure. The traditional farmhouse has a beamed dining room, comfortablelounge with open log fire and colour TV. The relaxing bedrooms are equipped with tea/coffee facilities and radio/clock/alarm. Fresh home grown produce is used (whenever possible) in the farmhouse cooking, with our farm-fresh eggs for breakfast and a different four-course meal each evening if required. We are situated approximately seven miles from Barnstaple, South Molton and Torrington. There are many local places of interest to visit with the sandy beaches of the North Devon coastline within easy reach, as is scenic Exmoor with its panoramic views. Bed and Breakfast from £16; Evening Meal £8.50. Ample car parking. Sorry, no pets.

UMBERLEIGH. Tony and Myra Pring, The Gables, On-the-Bridge, Umberleigh EX37 9AB (01769 560461). 👒👒 We offer friendly personal service here at

The Gables, which is situated facing the River Taw, famous for its salmon fishing and "Tarka the Otter". You will find us ideally placed for the beautiful Exmoor National Parks, Dartington Glass, Lynton and Lynmouth and the sandy beaches of Woolacombe. The Barnstaple to Exeter railway line is within easy access for those who do not wish to drive. The accommodation is in three en-suite rooms, one twin, one double and one single, all with central heating and tea/coffee facilities. There is a quiet lounge and a TV lounge. Maps with three circular walks available from tea rooms. Private parking. Sorry, no children under the age of 14. Open all year. Bed and Breakfast from £16.50 to £21.50.

If you've found
FARM HOLIDAY GUIDES
of service please tell your friends

WINKLEIGH. Mr and Mrs Davidson, Pixton Cottage, Iddesleigh, Winkleigh EX19 8BR (01837

811003 or 811007; Fax: 01837 811055). A warm and comfortable welcome awaits you at this traditional thatched Devon cob farmhouse with its oak beams and creaky floors. Set amidst the tranquillity of the rolling Devonshire Dales, convenient for Dartmoor, Exmoor and the spectacular North Devon cliffs and beaches. Dogs welcome. Good fishing on the Taw/Torridge. Well positioned for the Tarka Trail. Excellent local pubs for local real ales and good value food. Pixton is ideal at any time of the year for visitors wishing to slow down and re-charge their batteries! Bed and Breakfast from £15 per person.

WOODBURY, near Budleigh Salterton. David and Belinda Price, Greenacre, Couches Lane, Woodbury, Near Budleigh Salterton EX5 1HL (01395 233574). Secluded guest house surrounded by countryside and stream, only four miles from the sea and five miles from the Cathedral city of Exeter. The village centre is only a few minutes' walk away, boasting a Bistro (specialising in fish dishes), two pubs, a post office and two antique shops. An old fashioned welcome awaits you in this friendly family home. The comfortable bedrooms — two on the ground floor — all have either en suite or private facilities, colour TV and beverage tray. Well behaved pets and children are welcome. Plenty of car parking. Bed and Breakfast from £16 per person. Brochure available.

WOOLACOMBE. Mrs C. Robbins, Springside, Mullacott Road, Woolacombe EX34 7HF (01271 870452). Springside is a seven-bedroomed detached country residence standing in two and a half acres just off the B3343 road on the outskirts of Woolacombe, three miles from Ilfracombe. All bedrooms have en suite facilities, colour TV and tea/coffee making facilities. Own keys to bedrooms. Separate tables in large dining room. Residential licence. Central heating. Ample free off road car parking. Food is of the highest quality and is always highly recommended. Sorry, no pets. Bed and Breakfast available March to October. Also individual self-catering accommodation with all amenities for two people. Telephone for details.

YETTINGTON. Brenda and Colin Goode, Lufflands, Yettington, Budleigh Salterton EX9 7BP (01395 568422). Lufflands offers Bed and Breakfast in a comfortable 200 year old farmhouse. The accommodation includes a double room en suite, family room and single room, all non-smoking. Ample off road parking and a large garden. Lufflands is situated in a small hamlet surrounded by open farmland approximately three miles from the coast at Budleigh Salterton, five miles from Exmouth and nine miles from Exeter. Dartmoor and Exmoor National Parks are within easy driving distance. Bird watching nearby on the common, Otter Valley and Rive Exe. A warm welcome awaits you all year. Bed and Breakfast from £17.50.

DORSET

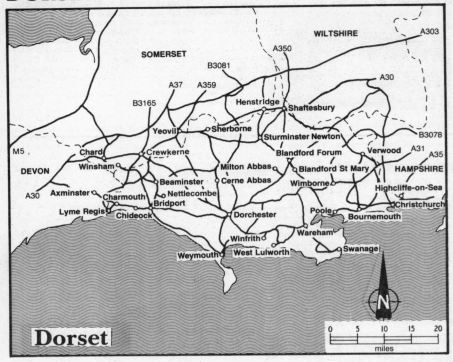

Dorset

ASHMORE/SHAFTESBURY. Mr and Mrs Millard, Glebe Cottage Farm, Ashmore, Shaftesbury SP5 5AE (01747 811974; Fax: 01747 811104). Situated on the Wessex Downs between Shaftesbury and Blandford lies Dorset's highest village. Picturesque Ashmore with its ancient dewpond is an ideal base for access to the Cranborne Chase and the Blackmore Vale with superb walking and panoramic views. The farmhouse set in an old courtyard next to the duck pond in the centre of this tiny village offers one double and one twin-bedded room, both en suite with TV and tea/coffee facilities. Full English or continental breakfast. Terms £20 per person.

BLANDFORD. The Anvil Hotel and Restaurant, Pimperne, Blandford DT11 8UQ (01258 453431/ 480182). ♛♛♛ *COMMENDED.*

A long, low thatched building set in a tiny village deep in the Dorset countryside two miles from Blandford — what could be more English? And that is what visitors to the Anvil will find — a typical old English hostelry offering good, old-fashioned English hospitality. A full à la carte mouthwatering menu with delicious desserts available in the charming beamed and flagged restaurant with log fire, and a wide selection of bar meals in the attractive, fully licensed bar. All bedrooms have private facilities. Ample parking. Pets welcome. Good Food Pub Guide, Les Routiers. £120 for two persons for two nights Bed and Breakfast or from £75 per night double room and from £47.50 per night single room. Dogs £2.50 per night.

BLANDFORD. Mr and Mrs D.A. Selby, "Simplers Joy", Tarrant Keynston, Blandford DT3 9EJ (01258 453686).

"Simplers Joy" is a tastefully renovated cob thatched 17th century Listed cottage overlooking the Tarrant Valley. Ideally situated for visiting Poole and Bournemouth and the National Trust's Kingston Lacy House, and the surrounding lovely Dorset countryside. Accommodation comprises ground floor twin room and first floor double room, each with its own luxury en suite bathroom. Each room has colour TV and tea/coffee-making facilities. Guests' sun lounge. Access at all times. Central heating. Easy parking. Full English Breakfast served. Terms £16 per person, per night. Brochure on request.

BOURNEMOUTH. Freshfields Hotel, 55 Christchurch Road, Bournemouth BH1 3PA (01202 394023).

Small licensed hotel, just a short walk to sandy beach through Boscombe Chine. Close to town and all Bournemouth's attractions, shops and theatres. Golf, tennis, putting and bowling are all nearby. All rooms have colour TV and tea/coffee, most are en suite. Access at all times with own keys. Front car park. BARGAIN BREAKS SEPTEMBER TO JUNE. Bed and Breakfast from £14. Reductions for Senior Citizens.

BOURNEMOUTH. Cherry View Hotel, 66 Alum Chine Road, Bournemouth BH4 8DZ (01202 760910).

RAC Acclaimed, AA Listed Quality Award. Family-run hotel ideally situated between shops and beaches. 11 en suite rooms with TV, radio, tea-making facilities and central heating. Non-smoking rooms available. Excellent food, choice of menu. Residents' bar. Private parking. Bed and Breakfast from £19 to £21 daily; weekly terms from £120 to £140 (based on two sharing). Room only and optional evening meal available. Two to Five Day Bargain Breaks available early/late season. Special tariff on request. Christmas and New Year programme. Open all year. Colour brochure available.

BOURNEMOUTH. Mayfield Private Hotel, 46 Frances Road, Bournemouth BH1 3SA (01202 551839).

Sandra and Mike Barling welcome you to this AA and ETB Two Crowns Commended and regularly inspected Hotel offering a high standard of catering and comfort. It overlooks gardens, bowls, putting and tennis; sea, shops, shows, rail and coach stations are a short walk away. Residential licence. Colour TV and tea making facilities in all rooms; some rooms have shower and toilet en suite. Other amenities include full central heating, own keys, evening refreshments, parking. Bed and Breakfast from £13 to £16 daily; Bed, full English Breakfast and four course Dinner with tea/coffee from £110 to £130 weekly. Bargain Breaks October/April; mid-week bookings early/late season; special package for Senior Citizens during May.

BOURNEMOUTH. Kath and Dennis Mackie, St. Antoine, 2 Guildhill Road, Southbourne, Bournemouth BH6 3EY (01202 433043). Friendly family Guest House four minutes from Blue Flag beach and close to river walks, boating, tennis, bowls and golf. We have two family en suite rooms, two double, two twin and one single, all with washbasins, power points and tea/coffee facilities. Off street parking for five cars. We are on the bus route for Christchurch and Bournemouth centres. Vegetarians, vegans welcome with option of evening meal on request. Bed and Breakfast from £18 per person; Half Board from £25. Half price for children under 12 years. Member of Hotel and Guest House Association.

BOURNEMOUTH. Seacrest Lodge, 63 Alum Chine Road, Bournemouth BH4 8DU (01202 767438).

A warm welcome awaits you whether you are here on business or for leisure. We are ideally situated at the head of beautiful Alum Chine, leading to miles of golden beaches. Also close to shops, restaurants and entertainments and within easy reach of the New Forest, Poole Harbour and many other attractions. Bed and Breakfast £16 to £18. Good accommodation en suite, tea/coffee making facilities, colour TV all rooms. Full English breakfast. Ample car parking. Large garden for guests' use.

BOURNEMOUTH. Gervis Court Hotel, 38 Gervis Road, East Cliff, Bournemouth BH1 3DH (01202 556871).

Alan and Jackie Edwards welcome you to a friendly and relaxing stay whether for business or pleasure. Our Victorian detached hotel of character is set in its own attractive gardens and has ample parking space. Non-smoking accommodation available. A few minutes' walk to the beautiful clean sandy beach, shops, theatres, B.I.C and other attractions. Bed and Breakfast from £18 to £25. Please ask about our Special Activity Breaks.

BOURNEMOUTH. David and Barbara Fowler, Sea Breeze Hotel, 32 St. Catherines Road, Southbourne, Bournemouth BH6 4AB (01202 433888). A small, peaceful hotel in a delightful location opposite beach where dogs are allowed at all times of year. Close to Hengistbury Head; New Forest 10 minutes' drive. Superb sea views. Family atmosphere. Full central heating. All rooms en suite; with TV and tea making facilities. Residential licence. Children from five to 16 sharing with parents half price. Parking. Open all year excluding Christmas. Bed and Breakfast from £18; Evening Meal £9.50.

Key to
Tourist Board Ratings

The Crown Scheme
(England, Scotland & Wales)

Covering hotels, motels, private hotels, guesthouses, inns, bed & breakfast, farmhouses. Every Crown classified place to stay is inspected annually. *The classification:* Listed then 1-5 Crown indicates the range of facilities and services. Higher quality standards are indicated by the terms APPROVED, COMMENDED, HIGHLY COMMENDED and DELUXE.

The Key Scheme
(also operates in Scotland using a Crown symbol)

Covering self-catering in cottages, bungalows, flats, houseboats, houses, chalets, etc. Every Key classified holiday home is inspected annually. *The classification:* 1-5 Key indicates the range of facilities and equipment. Higher quality standards are indicated by the terms APPROVED, COMMENDED, HIGHLY COMMENDED and DELUXE.

The Q Scheme
(England, Scotland & Wales)

Covering holiday, caravan, chalet and camping parks. Every Q rated park is inspected annually for its quality standards. The more √ in the Q – up to 5 – the higher the standard of what is provided.

BOURNEMOUTH. Joan and John Adams, Valberg Hotel, 1A Wollstonecraft Road, Boscombe, Bournemouth BH5 1JQ (01202 394644).

🥢🥢 Small modern hotel in superb position near Boscombe pier, two minutes' walk to cliff top. Five minutes to shopping centre. All bedrooms have shower and toilet en suite, central heating, tea/coffee making facilities and colour TV. Lounge with colour TV; diningroom with separate tables, overlooking a lovely garden. Licensed bar. Car parking. Access to hotel at all times, own key. Bed and Breakfast from £15 to £20 daily inclusive; £90 to £120 weekly. Dinner optional at £7. Please write or phone for brochure. AA QQQ, RAC Listed.

BOURNEMOUTH. Tony and Veronica Bulpitt, Sun Haven Hotel, 39 Southern Road, Southbourne, Bournemouth BH6 3SS (01202 427560).

The Sun Haven Hotel is in a superb position being only 150 yards from the cliff top, near the cliff lift and zig-zag path to the beach yet only a few minutes' walk to Southbourne shopping area, with its variety of cafes and restaurants. Bournemouth centre is a short drive away. All day access. All bedrooms have colour TV, shaver point, power point, washbasin and central heating. Tea making facilities. En suite available. Forecourt parking. Bed and Breakfast from £15 per night.

BOURNEMOUTH. Mr and Mrs B.T. Gwynne, Laguna Hotel, Suffolk Road South, Bournemouth BH2 6AZ (01202 767022).

A family-run hotel set in two acres of land a few minutes' walk to Bournemouth town centre. Large free car park. All bedrooms are en suite and have TV and tea making facilities. Lift; licensed cocktail bar. Come and enjoy our heated indoor swimming pool, spa bath, sauna, solarium; games room; children's play area; sun patios. Entertainment every evening (seasonal). Terms from £16 per night. Discounts for weekly stays. Send for full colour brochure. Self-catering holiday apartments also available in same complex.

BOURNEMOUTH. Sandy Beach Hotel, Southbourne Overcliff Drive, Southbourne, Bournemouth BH6 3QB (Tel/Fax: 01202 424385).

🥢🥢🥢 *COMMENDED.* Family run hotel with panoramic sea view over Bournemouth Bay. Easy access to safe, sandy, award-winning beach. Close to shops and buses. Near Bournemouth. Ideal base for touring New Forest and Dorset. All rooms en suite. Colour TV, tea/coffee facilities. Pleasant dining room with separate tables. Licensed bar. Scrumptious home cooking complements high standards of cleanliness and comfort. TV lounge. Central heating. Large car park. Access to hotel at all times. For brochure please write or phone resident proprietors Bryan and Caroline Channing, Adrian and Alison Homa. Bed and Breakfast from £15 per night. Evening Meal optional. Special weekly rates. Christmas programme.

DORSET – RURAL SPLENDOUR!

Absorbing old towns like Dorchester and Shaftesbury, surrounded by panoramic vales, undulating chalklands and peaceful villages contribute to Dorset's great appeal. Included in any tourist's itinerary should be, Abbotsbury Village and Swannery, Ackling Dyke Roman road, Brownsea Island, Lulworth Cove and, of course, the many locations that constitute Hardy's Dorset.

BOURNEMOUTH. Mrs Broom, Bournecliffe House, 31 Grand Avenue, Southbourne, Bournemouth

BH6 3SY (01202 426455). Enjoy a happy holiday in our small family guest house pleasantly situated in a quiet tree-lined avenue, just a few minutes' walk to the cliff top with easy access to beach via slope or cable car. Shops, cafes, restaurants and pubs close by. Tea/coffee, colour TV and showers in all rooms. Central heating. Forecourt parking. Access at all times. Babysitting and children's suppers available. Bed and Breakfast from £14 per day; £91 per week. The Guest House also runs a clinic offering treatments with Herbal Medicine and Aromatherapy by qualified therapists at special rates for guests. Please telephone for further details.

BRIDPORT. Ann and Dan Walker MHCIMA, Britmead House Hotel, West Bay Road, Bridport DT6

4EG (01308 422941; Fax: 01308 422516). 🌼🌼🌼 *HIGHLY COMMENDED.* AA QQQQ Selected, RAC Acclaimed. Guestaccom Good Room Award 1997. Delightful freshly cooked food, personal service and putting guests' comfort first means visitors return time after time. Situated between Bridport, West Bay Harbour with its beaches/golf course/walks, Chesil Beach and The Dorset Coastal Path. Full en suite rooms (one ground floor) all with colour TV, tea making facilities, hair dryers and mini bar. South-facing lounge and dining room overlooking the garden. Optional table d'hôte dinner menu, incorporating local fish and other produce. Licensed. Full central heating. Private parking. Dogs by arrangement. Children welcome. Break rates all year. Discount for two or more rooms for three or more nights. Open all year. Bed and Breakfast from £20 to £29.

BRIDPORT. Mrs D.P. Read, The Old Station, Powerstock, Bridport DT6 3ST (01308 485301).

Ex-GWR station set in two-and-a-half acres in an area of outstanding natural beauty which is especially pretty in the spring. The house dates from 1857 and the interior has been completely modernised. Our pipe-smoking ghost (no appearances, just the scent of his pipe and downstairs only!) was featured in the press and on TV. We ask guests to restrict their smoking to downstairs. All rooms have free hot drinks making facilities and tea, coffee, etc are provided free. Daytime access. Generous Breakfast. Evening Meals available locally. Tennis court, fun nine-hole golf. Very peaceful and relaxing. Two double, one single bedrooms, all with washbasins; bathroom, three toilets; sittingroom; diningroom. Central heating. Children welcome, cot, high chair and babysitting. Sorry no pets. Car essential, parking. Bed and Breakfast only from £14, reduced rates for children under 10 years.

CERNE ABBAS. Mrs V.I. Willis, "Lampert's Cottage," Sydling St. Nicholas, Cerne Abbas DT2 9NU

(01300 341659; Fax: 01300 341699). Bed and Breakfast in unique 16th century thatched cottage in unspoilt village. The cottage has fields around and is bounded, front and back, by chalk streams. Accommodation consists of three prettily furnished double bedrooms with dormer windows, set under the eaves, and breakfast is served in the diningroom which has an enormous inglenook fireplace and original beams. The village, situated in countryside made famous by Thomas Hardy in his novels, is an excellent touring centre and beaches are 30 minutes' drive away. West Dorset is ideal walking country with footpaths over chalk hills and through hidden valleys, perfect for those wishing peace and quiet. Open all year. Terms on request.

PUBLISHER'S NOTE

CHARMOUTH. Ann and Andy Gorfin, Kingfishers, Newlands Bridge, Charmouth DT6 6QZ (01297 560232). Come to Kingfishers and relax on your large sunny balcony overlooking the river and garden. Set in beautiful surroundings on the banks of the River Char Kingfishers offers a secluded setting yet only a short stroll to the beach and village amenities. Ann and Andy can assure you of a warm welcome, great food and a friendly atmosphere. From £17 per night we offer a full selection of breakfasts including vegetarian. All rooms are en suite or with private bathroom, balcony, drink making facilities, colour TV and central heating. Free access and ample parking. Children and pets welcome.

CHIDEOCK. Trevor and Jenny Yerworth, Chimneys Guest House, Main Street, Chideock, Bridport DT6 6JH (01297 489368). Comfortable 17th century thatched cottage in historic village just one mile from the sea. Much of the surrounding coastline and hills are owned by the National Trust and offer spectacular walking. Five bedrooms, including one with four-poster bed. Most rooms en suite with own TV. Tea/coffee making facilities. Chimneys has a large lounge with a beamed ceiling, log fires in winter and a TV available for guests' use. Easy walking distance of village pubs and shops. Bed and Breakfast from £17 per person. Sorry no pets. Children over five welcome. Non-smoking.

COMPTON ABBAS. Tim and Lucy Kerridge, The Old Forge, Compton Abbas, Shaftesbury SP7 0NQ (Tel & Fax: 01747 811881). ♛♛ *HIGHLY COMMENDED.* *Charming 18th century converted wheelwrights with magnificent views to National Trust downland. Ideal for relaxing, walking, wildlife, etc. Choose either Bed and Breakfast in pretty en suite bedrooms (one family, one double and one single), Victorian iron beds and antique furniture, all with colour TV and tea/coffee trays or self-catering (sleeping two adults, two children) in fully restored wheelwrights cottage. A traditional farmhouse breakfast is served using local organic produce. Guests have their own private sitting/dining room, garden and two acres of meadow to explore. Traditional log burning stove during colder months, we offer a warm welcome all year round. Bed and Breakfast from £20.*

THE OLD FORGE

DORCHESTER. Mrs Roffey, Coneygar, Turners Puddle, Dorchester DT2 7JA (01929 471375).

Beautiful small country house in six acres of land, lovely garden and setting. Seven miles from coast and in Thomas Hardy country. The accommodation is very comfortable and comprises two double/twin-bedded rooms, with private bathrooms, tea-making facilities and central heating; TV in one room. Children welcome; regret, no pets. Terms from £18 to £20 per person per night. All guests are made to feel at home.

DORCHESTER. The Poachers Inn, Piddletrenthide, Dorchester DT2 7QX (01300 348358). ♛♛♛

COMMENDED. AA QQQ. Country Inn set in the heart of the lovely Piddle Valley, within easy reach of all Dorset's attractions. All rooms are en suite and have colour TV, tea/coffee making facilities and telephone. Swimming pool and riverside garden. Half Board guests choose from our a2 la carte menu at no extra cost. Bed and Breakfast from £23 to £25 per person; Dinner, Bed and Breakfast from £33 to £35 per person. 10% discount for seven nights or more. Special offer Short Breaks 1st November to 31st March: two nights Dinner, Bed and Breakfast £66 per person, third night FREE. Send for brochure.

DORCHESTER. Mrs Marian Tomblin, Lower Lewell Farmhouse, West Stafford, Dorchester DT2 8AP (01305 267169). ♛

This old, historic house, originally a farmhouse, is situated in the Frome Valley, four miles east of Dorchester in the heart of Hardy country. It is two miles from his birthplace and is reputed to be the Talbothays Dairy in his famous novel "Tess of the d'Urbervilles". Situated as it is in quiet countryside yet so near the county town, it makes an ideal base from which to explore Dorset. There are one family bedroom and two double bedrooms, all with washbasins and tea/coffee making facilities. Visitors' lounge with colour TV. Car essential, ample parking. Terms from £18. Open January to December.

DORCHESTER near. Mr Howell, Appletrees, 23 Affpuddle, Dorchester DT2 7HH (01929 471300).
1960's character home on site of 16th century cottage with splendid views across farmland of rolling Dorset hills. Within easy direct reach of six towns, all of historic or Hardy interest. Thoroughly peaceful. Stop-over for Devon/Cornwall (A35 2km). Cyclists and walkers especially welcome. Transport services provided at minimum charge (BR main line 4km). Accommodation comprises one double, two single and one twin bedrooms all with TV and tea making facilities. Use of kitchen if required. Children welcome. Bed and Breakfast from £12.50 to £16; Evening Meal from £2.50 to £10.

DORCHESTER. Michael and Jane Deller, **Churchview Guest House, Winterbourne Abbas, Near Dorchester DT2 9LS (01305 889296).** ♛♛♛

COMMENDED. Our 300-year-old AA QQQ Guest House is set in a small village five miles west of Dorchester in an area of outstanding natural beauty. Noted for warm, friendly hospitality and delicious home cooked food, it makes an ideal base for exploring Hardy country. Churchview is a non-smoking establishment offering two comfortable lounges, attractive oak-beamed dining room and bar. Our character rooms have hospitality trays, colour TV and central heating; most en suite. Your hosts will give every assistance with local information to ensure a memorable stay. Pets welcome. Parking. Bed, Breakfast and four-course Evening Meal £32 to £39; Bed and Breakfast from £19.50 to £26.50.

DORCHESTER. Mrs Martine Tree, The Old Rectory, Winterbourne Steepleton, Dorchester DT2 9LG (01305 889468; Fax: 01305 889737). ♛♛ *HIGHLY*

COMMENDED. Built in 1850 on one acre of land situated in a quiet hamlet. The grounds have croquet lawns, putting green, children's swing. The outstanding natural surroundings offer country walks giving superb views of the valley. The five guest rooms are all individually furnished to a high standard, each with en suite or private facilities and containing a welcome basket filled with those little items you may have forgotten. Breakfast is a delight, enjoyed in The Garden Room with views of the beautiful little courtyard and a musical backdrop of a waterfall and taped birdsong. Private dining facilities are available on request for special occasions dinners. Our chef is highly qualified in Cordon Blue cuisine. Alternatively local pubs and a large selection of restaurants both in Dorchester (six miles) and Weymouth (eight miles) are available. Many activities for all can be enjoyed in Thomas Hardy country. French spoken. Open all year except Christmas. Bed and Breakfast from £19 per person. Brochure available.

LILLINGTON. Mrs M.E.G. Messenger, Ash House, Lillington, Sherborne DT9 6QX (01935 812490). Ash House is spacious, surrounded by farmland, with delightful views all round. Although so rural and peaceful it is only three miles south of the picturesque town of Sherborne, with its Abbey and other historic buildings. Easy access to Dorchester in one direction and Yeovil in the other. One double or family room (extra bed available) with washbasin, and one twin room. Two toilets, bathroom, shower room. Ample parking. Lounge, conservatory, TV, garden. Full English Breakfast and a friendly welcome. Pets by arrangement. Bed and Breakfast £14. Rates reduced for children. South from Sherborne — A352 Dorchester Road.

LULWORTH COVE. Val and Barry Burrill, Graybank Guest House, Main Road, West Lulworth BH20 5RL (01929 400256). ETB Listed *COMMENDED.* Victorian

guest house built of Purbech Stone and located in beautiful, quiet country just five minutes stroll from Lulworth Cove and the South West Coastal Path. Full breakfast menu. Parking. Bed and Breakfast from £16. Telephone Val or Barry for a FREE brochure.

LULWORTH COVE. Jenny and John Aldridge, The Orchard, West Road, West Lulworth, Near Wareham BH20 5RY (01929 400592). Comfortable home

in central yet quiet off-road position in old vicarage orchard. Accommodation comprises double room, twin room, and room with double and single beds. One room has large balcony. Ample parking in spacious walled garden. Mature fruit trees, lawns, barbecue and garden furniture for guests' use. Full English, vegetarian or vegan breakfasts. Home produced eggs, vegetables, etc. Central for South Dorset, Swanage, Poole, Weymouth, Dorchester; 10 minutes' walk to Lulworth Cove. Near coast path for other beaches, Durdle Door and Fossil Forest. Bed and Breakfast from £13 per person per night. Enquire for children's rates and low season discounts. Open all year.

LULWORTH COVE. Mrs Jan Ravensdale, Elads-Nevar, West Road, West Lulworth, Near Wareham BH20 5RZ (01929 400467). The house is set in the beautiful village of West Lulworth, half a mile from Lulworth Cove. The rooms are large enough for a family and all have tea/coffee making facilities and colour TV. West Lulworth is central for many towns and beaches; Weymouth 14, Swanage 18, Poole 23 miles, and there are many places of interest to visit. Reduced rates for Senior Citizens out of season and children sharing with adults; also weekly bookings. Open all year. Central heating. Bed and Breakfast from £14. Vegetarians and vegans catered for.

LYME REGIS. Andrew and Katie Bryceson, Amherst Lodge Farm, Uplyme, Near Lyme Regis DT7 3XH (01297 442773). 🦢 🦢 🦢 *COMMENDED.* Amherst lies in an idyllic secluded valley on the Dorset/Devon border. You could be miles from anywhere yet Lyme Regis and the seaside are just a nine minute drive away. Nestling in 140 acres of its own gardens, grounds, woodlands and lakes, Amherst is a very special place to stay. The extensive grounds include a magnificent two acre banked garden and offer walks, rare wildlife and good lake fishing. Inside you are greeted by an oak panelled lounge with an enormous stone fireplace. Upstairs the bedrooms are clean, spacious, en suite with comfortable beds and good facilities. A gem.

LYME REGIS. Mrs C.S. Ansell, Providence House, Lyme Road, Uplyme, Lyme Regis DT7 3TH (01297 445704). Set in the lovely village of Uplyme, one mile from Lyme Regis, our small Regency guest house has been beautifully renovated — we even have a Minstrels' Gallery! A warm welcome is extended to you from your hosts Clem and Jean Ansell. The meals are special, the beds very comfortable and as some guests recently said, "It's like being at home without the washing up". We have a small cat but your dog is welcome. There are always fresh flower arrangements around and part of our garden is upstairs where you are very welcome to sit and enjoy the sun. This is wonderful walking country. Cricket is played regularly in the village, where there are also tennis courts. All rooms are freshly decorated and are either en suite or have private facilities. Bed and Breakfast from £15.50 to £16; four-course Dinner and coffee £8.

LYME REGIS. Sheila and David Taylor, Buckland Farm, Raymonds Hill, Near Axminster EX13 5SZ (01297 33222). Situated back off the A35 in quiet and unspoilt surroundings with gardens and grounds of five acres which are ideal for guests to relax or stroll in; about three miles from the lovely coastal resort of Lyme Regis and Charmouth. A warm welcome awaits you. Accommodation mainly on the ground floor. Two family bedrooms, one double en suite shower and one twin bedded room, all with TV, washbasin, tea/coffee making facilites. Bathroom, shower in bath, separate WC. Lounge with colour TV, video and log fire. Dining area with separate tables. A good full English breakfast served, a real home from home plus our very friendly dog. Friendly pub within two minutes walk for evening meals. Payphone. No smoking in bedrooms. Bed and Breakfast from £13. Send SAE for further details. Self catering caravan available.

LYME REGIS. Mrs M.J. Powell, Meadow View, Green Lane, Rousdon, Lyme Regis DT7 3XW (01297 443262). A warm welcome awaits you at this working family farm situated quarter of a mile off the A3052 road at Rousdon just three miles from Lyme Regis, four from Seaton. Ideal centre to explore the Devon and Dorset countryside, sand and shingle beaches, fossil hunting. One family/double bedroom with washbasin and one double bedroom, both with colour TV, tea/coffee making facilities, central heating. Two guest bathrooms, one with shower over bath. Lounge with colour TV. Access at all times. Full English breakfast served at separate tables. Bed and Breakfast from £14 to £16. Reductions for children sharing parents' room. Ample car parking.

Terms quoted in this publication may be subject to increase if rises in costs necessitate

LYME REGIS. Lydwell House, Lyme Road, Uplyme, Lyme Regis DT7 3TJ (01297 443522; Fax: 01297 445897). 👑👑 *COMMENDED.* Situated close to the famous fossil beach at Lyme Regis, Lydwell Guest House offers a high standard of Bed and Breakfast accommoodation at the most affordable prices. This is a picturesque Victorian house set in a superb garden which features its own folly and ponds. The atmosphere is both warm and friendly and the standard of food served is of the highest order. All of the letting rooms are comfortable, spacious and well equipped; en suite facilities are available. Children and pets welcome. Open all year. Bed and Breakfast from £16.50.

LYME REGIS. Jenny and Ivan Harding, Coverdale Guesthouse, Woodmead Road, Lyme Regis DT7 3AB (01297 442882). 👑👑 *COMMENDED.* AA QQQ Recommended. Spacious non-smoking guesthouse situated in a residential area of Lyme Regis a short walk from the sea, town, pubs and restaurants. Fine views over Woodland Trust's land to rear and sea to front. Comfortable, well furnished bedrooms (double, twin, triple and single) with colour TV, tea making and excellent en suite facilities. Attractive lounge/dining room overlooking patio and cottage garden. Access to house all day. Private parking. Ideal base for exploring countryside and unspoilt scenic coastline on foot or by car. Walkers welcome. South Coast Path/Wessex Ridgeway nearby. Fossil hunting and boat trips available. Bed and Breakfast £15 to £20. Brochure available.

MIDDLEMARSH. Terry and Thelma, White Horse Farm, Middlemarsh, Sherborne DT9 5QN (01963 210222). Comfortable country farmhouse within three acres of gardens, paddock and lake. Our excellent facilities include pine-furnished rooms with comfortable beds en suite or private bathroom, all with washbasin, colour TV and tea/coffee making equipment. Our breakfasts are renowned! Set in peaceful Hardy countryside near Cerne Abbas, the ancient abbey town of Sherborne and historic Dorchester. Easy travelling distance to lovely coastline including Lulworth Cove, Weymouth and Lyme Regis. Enjoy walking, fishing, horse riding, golf, etc. 100 yards local inn. Open all year except Christmas. Bed and Breakfast from £15 to £20 per person. Also four attractive self-catering cottages where pets are welcome and ideal for partially disabled guests. Brochure available.

MILTON ABBAS. Mrs Lucienne Sumner-Fergusson, Stocklands House, Hilton, Near Blandford DT11 0DE (01258 880580; Fax: 01258 881188). 👑👑 *HIGHLY COMMENDED.* Set in 12 acres enjoying stunning views over the surrounding valley and hills. Heated outdoor swimming pool, table tennis, badminton and clay shooting available. Relax in the drawing room with log fire, baby grand piano and board games. Bring your horse and enjoy excellent hacking or hunting. Your hostess is an accomplished cook and will tempt you with sumptuous breakfasts, candlelit dinners or a Dorset cream tea! Closed Christmas and New Year. Babies welcome. Accommodation comprises one double and one twin bedroom, both on ground floor, both en suite and one double room with private bathroom. Prices from £20 to £26.

POOLE. Eileen and Michael Standhaft, Rosemount, 167 Bournemouth Road, Lower Parkstone, Poole BH14 9HT (01202 732138). Run by the same owners for the past 21 years, your comfort is a priority. We are situated on the A35 halfway between Bournemouth and Poole town centres and near many beaches — Sandbanks and Branksome Chine to name but two. Convenient for ferry to Cherbourg. All bedrooms have colour TV, tea making facilities; two are en suite and one is on the ground floor and has en suite shower. Bed and Breakfast from £15 to £18 per person. Full English breakfast served. Brochure on request.

PORTLAND/WEYMOUTH. Alessandria Hotel & Italian Restaurant, Portland, Weymouth DT5 1HW (01305 822270/820108; Fax: 01305 820561). ♛ ♛ ♛ *APPROVED.* This once 18th century Inn is now a unique Hotel and Italian Restaurant situated in a quiet location. Comfortable accommodation with most rooms en suite and having colour TV, tea/coffee making faciltiies, soft towels and toiletries. Ground floor bedrooms level with lounge and restaurant. Excellent fresh food cooked to order by chef/proprietor Giovanni Bisogno (award winner). Children welcome. Bed and Breakfast from £22.50 per person; Evening Meal from £8. Warm and friendly hospitality await you. Les Routiers Award for Quality and Good Value.

SHERBORNE. Mrs Pauline Tizzard, Venn Farm, Milborne Port, Sherborne DT9 5RA (01963

250598). The perfect stop when travelling, easy to find on main A30 three miles east of historic castle and abbey town of Sherborne, 30 minute drive to coast. Our 200 acre working dairy farm is situated in beautiful wooded parkland within walking distance of local village inn. Attractively furnished accommodation includes one twin, one double and one family room, all with washbasins, colour TV, tea/coffee making facilities. Bathroom equipped with shower and separate WC. Full central heating plus guests' lounge with log fires. Children welcome. AA QQ Recommended. Bed and Breakfast from £15. Reductions for children. Open all year.

SHERBORNE. Mrs E. Kingman, Stowell Farm, Stowell, Near Sherborne DT9 4PE (01963 370200).

A former 15th century Manor House, now a farmhouse on a family-run dairy and beef farm, set in beautiful countryside. It is a good area for walking and cycling and has a riding stable close by. Five miles from the A303, two miles from the A30. A good area for touring Somerset and Dorset. You will receive a warm welcome and good breakfast. There are two rooms, one double and one twin, both with tea/coffee facilities; guest bathroom and lounge with colour TV and log fires. £15 per night, special weekly rates. Reductions for children under 12 years. Evening meals by arrangement. Open all year. Good local pubs close by.

SIXPENNY HANDLEY. Mrs Ann Inglis, Town Farm Bungalow, Sixpenny Handley, Near Salisbury SP5 5NT (Tel & Fax: 01725 552319). Tourist Board

Listed. AA QQ. Guests receive a warm welcome at this pretty property in a quiet location off the beaten track, yet within easy reach of the south coast and such tourist attractions as Stonehenge and Salisbury cathedral. Situated in Cranborne Chase, an area popular with walkers, there are magnificent country views across three counties. Bedrooms are clean and comfortable and in addition to the smart sitting room, opening onto the garden, there is a dining room where tea and coffee is available and hearty breakfasts served at one big table. Bed and Breakfast from £17.50 to £19.50. Children welcome. Pets by arrangement.

STURMINSTER NEWTON. Mrs J. Miller, Lower Fifehead Farm, Fifehead St. Quinton, Sturminster

Newton DT10 2AP (01258 817335). ♛ ♛ *COMMENDED.* Come and stay with us on our 400 acre dairy farm. Our lovely Listed 17th century farmhouse with interesting mullion windows is pictured and mentioned in Dorset Books. We have three bedrooms — one double en suite, one double and one twin, each with private bathroom, own sitting room, TV and large garden. Tea and coffee making. No evening meals but we can recommend the local places. We also have a self contained one bedroom flat with en suite bathroom, private sitting room as well as a self catering annexe sleeping four/five. Bed and Breakfast from £18 per person. Three-day breaks from £48 per person. Right in the heart of the Blackmore Vale and ''Hardy'' country; lovely walks, golfing, fishing and riding can be arranged.

PLEASE SEND A STAMPED ADDRESSED ENVELOPE WITH ENQUIRIES

TOLPUDDLE. Paul Wright, Tolpuddle Hall, Tolpuddle, Near Dorchester DT2 7EW (01305 848986).

An historic house in village centre in an area of outstanding natural beauty, not far from the coast. Convenient for Bournemouth, Poole, Dorchester, Weymouth, Isle of Purbeck and many small market towns and villages. Centre for local interests e.g., birdwatching, walking, local history, Thomas Hardy, the Tolpuddle Martyrs, etc. Two double, one twin, one family and two single bedrooms. Full English breakfast. Tea/coffee making, TV sitting room. Pets welcome except high season. From £15 per person. Weekly rate available. Open all year.

WAREHAM. Miss Sarah Lowman, Long Coppice, Bindon Lane, East Stoke, Wareham BH20 6AS (01929 463123).

Long Coppice is situated in a peaceful country lane one and a half miles from the A352 at Wool. We have eight acres of our own meadows, woodlands and gardens. The large bungalow provides separate guest accommodation, all rooms en suite, spacious and comfortably furnished, with TV and tea facilities. The family room has its own patio and enclosed garden, ideal for those with young children or dogs. Lulworth is four miles away and there are many good local pubs nearby. Family and twin rooms all non-smoking. Bed and English Breakfast from £19. Safe parking. Open all year except Christmas.

WAREHAM. Mr and Mrs Axford, Sunnyleigh, Hyde, Wareham BH20 7NT (01929 471822). Mary and Eric offer their guests a friendly welcome to their bungalow with a cup of tea. Situated in the quiet hamlet of Hyde, five miles west of Wareham, we are adjacent to East Dorset Golf Club; follow the sign from Wareham and we are the first bungalow past the golf club on the right. It is an ideal base for visiting Swanage, Poole and Bovington Tank Museum, with many interesting coastal walks, including Lulworth Cove. Accommodation consists of three double bedrooms (one with twin beds), all with tea/coffee facilities, central heating. Bathroom and separate shower room; two toilets. Visitors' lounge with colour TV and log fires in winter. Open all the year except Christmas. Car essential, ample parking. Bed and Breakfast from £15; Room only £10.

WEYMOUTH. Anne & John Hepburn, Hazeldene Guest House, 16 Abbotsbury Road, Weymouth DT4 0AE (01305 782579).

Small comfortable guest house catering for up to 20 people. Ideally situated just a short walk from the sandy beach, boating lake, heated indoor pool, bowling green and shops. All rooms have washbasin, razor point and tea/coffee making facilities. Separate TV lounge. Guests have access to rooms at all times. Private car park. Bed and Breakfast from £14 to £17 per person per night. Brochure available.

WEYMOUTH. Jane Boucher-Coxhill, Southbrook, Preston Road, Overcombe, Weymouth DT3 6PU

(01305 832208). 🌸🌸 Situated near to the sea at Overcombe Corner, at the end of the new Preston Beach Wall and Esplanade with the Lodmoor RSPB Bird Reserve and Country Park between Overcombe and Weymouth. The accommodation is comfortable and homely, with one ground floor en suite room adapted for those with mobility problems. All rooms have colour TV, tea making facilities and central heating. Lounge. Children welcome, dogs accepted. Full breakfast menu. Car park. Winter Breaks available. Whatever the time of year, whether for a few days or a week — a warm welcome awaits you at Southbrook. Brochure available.

WEYMOUTH. Mrs S. Lambert, The Wessex Guest House, 128 Dorchester Road, Weymouth DT4

7LG (01305 783406). Quality detached residence close to sea and shops. The accent here is on good food and good service. Ideally situated for Lulworth Cove, Corfe Castle and Abbotsbury Swannery. Safe bathing, fishing and riding. Three family rooms and two double, all with washbasins. Ground floor bedroom available. Free tea/coffee anytime. Children welcome. Enclosed garden, play room available. Access at all times. Open May to September for Bed and Breakfast only from £13. Secure parking in grounds. Reductions for children. In the know for local bird watching and rarities. Also self catering holiday flat to let.

WEYMOUTH. The Cumberland Hotel, 95 The Esplanade, Weymouth DT4 7BA (Tel & Fax: 01305 785644). 🌸🌸🌸 Small friendly hotel personally run by the resident proprietors for over 20 years. The Cumberland is centrally situated with superb views of the bay and close to the town centre, Pavilion theatre, bus/coach/rail stations; only a few minutes from the harbour and ferry. There are 12 en suite bedrooms, seven with sea views and all with colour TV, tea tray, radio and central heating. There is a lounge on the ground floor and we serve a full English breakfast to start the day and four-course dinners in our charming cool dining room. AA QQQQ Selected, members of the Weymouth Hotel and Catering Association. Please send for our colour brochure should you require further information.

WEYMOUTH. Firtrees Guest House, 27 Rodwell Avenue, Weymouth DT4 8SH (01305 772967).

Margarette and Gordon extend a warm welcome to Firtrees. All rooms en suite with tea/coffee making facilities and Sky TV. English or Continental breakfast optional. Private parking. Fir trees is located four minutes' walk from harbour and sailing centre, 10 minutes' walk to Weymouth's seafront. Bournemouth/Poole/Swanage 40 minutes' drive. West Bay/Lyme Regis 15-25 miles. The towns of Shaftesbury, Blandford and Yeovil are all within easy driving distance. Firtrees is an ideal base for your holiday. Terms from £18 to £22 per person per night.

WINTERBOURNE ZELSTON. Mrs Irene Kerley, Brook Farm, Winterborne Zelston, Blandford DT11 9EU (01929 459267).

A warm welcome awaits you at Brook Farm, a friendly working farm situated in a pretty, peaceful hamlet overlooking the River Winterborne, between Wimborne and Dorchester. Central for coast and exploring the beautiful Dorset countryside, New Forest, etc. Comfortable family and twin rooms with either en suite or private facilities, TV, easy chairs, beverage tray and central heating. Access to rooms at all times. No parking problems. Hearty breakfasts are served with own free range eggs and homemade marmalade! The local country inns provide excellent food. Open all year except Christmas. Terms from £16.50 per person per night with favourable rates for longer stays and children sharing.

DURHAM

Glendale ♕♕ HIGHLY COMMENDED

Bed and Breakfast in beautiful spacious house; three double rooms en suite, TV, tea-making etc. Separate dining and sitting rooms. No smoking, no children under 10 years and no pets. Personal attention. We are situated in superb open countryside close to the village of Cotherstone. Splendid all round views, superb gardens and bedding displays, very large water feature with specimen fish. Our area is famous for Hannah of Yorkshire, High Force, Bowes Museum and breathtaking scenery for walking. Durham and Beamish 45 minutes. £32 double room. A warm welcome awaits. Brochure on request.

Mrs M. Rabbitts, Glendale, Cotherstone, Barnard Castle DL12 9UH. Tel: 01833 650384.

DURHAM. Mrs Delia Slack, Ash House, 24 The Green, Cornforth DL17 9JH (01740 654654).

Ideally situated on a lovely rural conservation village green, in the heart of "the Land of the Prince Bishops". Adjacent A1(M) motorway, 10 minutes from historic Durham, 25 minutes to Beamish Museum, Metro Centre, Newcastle and Darlington. Ash House is a beautifully appointed Victorian home lovingly restored. The elegant rooms are spacious and comfortable, equipped with washbasins, colour TV, hospitality tray, shaver point, hairdryer, clock/radio alarm and all with open views; traditional four-poster bed available. Mature trees surround the property. Hearty breakfasts are provided. Private parking. Well placed between York and Edinburgh. Excellent value from £18; Single £22; four-poster £45.

DURHAM. Mrs J. Dartnall, Idsley House, 4 Green Lane, Spennymoor DL16 6HD (01388 814237). ♛♛ *HIGHLY COMMENDED.* A large Victorian detached house situated in a quiet residential area close to the A167/A688 junction just eight minutes from Durham City. Direct route to Beamish, Metro Centre and the Dales. All rooms are spacious and well furnished. Double, twin and family bedrooms are all en suite and have colour TV and welcome tray. Full English or vegetarian breakfast is served in a pleasant conservatory overlooking a mature garden. Large guest lounge to relax. Safe parking on premises. Prices for a twin or double room £40. Open all year except Christmas. AA QQQ. Visa, Mastercard, Switch, Delta cards all accepted.

SALTBURN-BY-SEA. Mrs Bull, Westerlands Guesthouse, 27 East Parade, Skelton, Saltburn-by-Sea (01287 650690). This guest house is situated alongside Cleveland Way. It is a quiet, modern detached house with beautiful views of sea and countryside. An ideal base for touring Yorkshire Moors and the East Coast resorts, and there is a golf course nearby. Plenty of parking space. Bed and Breakfast £14 with packed lunches and flasks prepared and snack meals on request; Evening Meals by arrangement. Special meals available. Northumberland Tourist Board registered. Reduced rates for children and small reduction for Senior Citizens. Pets welcome free. Private bathrooms and/or showers and Teasmaid in all bedrooms. Open March till end September.

SPENNYMOOR near. John and Jean Thompson, Highview Country House, Kirk Merrington, Near Spennymoor DL16 7JT (01388 811006). ♛ *COMMENDED.* Highview stands in one acre of open and rolling countryside. The accommodation comprises four ground floor spacious bedrooms, all en suite, centrally heated overlooking gardens. There are two doubles, one twin and one family room all have colour TV and hospitality tray. Log fires are a feature of our dining room where full English breakfast (grilled) with fresh fruit is available. We are very quiet and private and yet within three minutes' walking distance of the village with its amenities and 15 minutes from the historic city of Durham. Bed and Breakfast from £20 per person. Special rates for children. Open all year round. Please telephone for brochure.

STANLEY. Mrs P. Gibson, Bushblades Farm, Harperley, Stanley DH9 9UA (01207 232722). Tourist Board Listed *COMMENDED.* AA QQ. Ideal stop-over when travelling north or south. Only 10 minutes from A1M Chester-le-Street. Durham City 20 minutes, Beamish Museum two miles, Metro Centre 15 minutes, Hadrian's Wall and Northumberland coast under an hour. Comfortable Georgian farmhouse set in large garden. Twin ground floor en suite room plus two double first floor bedrooms. All rooms have tea/coffee making, colour TV and easy chairs. Ample parking. Children welcome over 12 years. Sorry, no pets. Bed and Breakfast from £16 to £18.50 per person per night, single £20 to £25. Self catering accommodation also available.

ESSEX

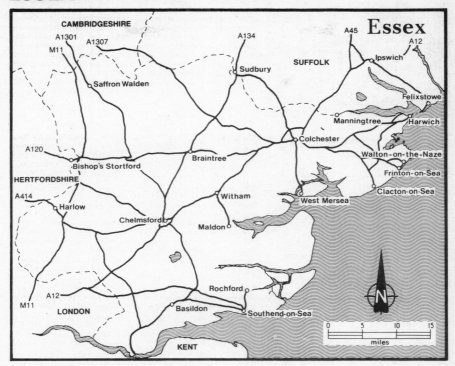

BRAINTREE. Mrs Delia Douse, Spicers Farm, Rotten End, Wethersfield, Braintree CM7 4AL (01371 851021). ♛♛ *HIGHLY COMMENDED.* **Working farm.** FHG Diploma Winner. Attractive farmhouse set in delightful peaceful position overlooking beautiful countryside. Comfortable centrally heated bedrooms all with en suite shower or bathrooms, colour TV, tea/coffee making facilities, clock radios and lovely views. Breakfast in our sunny conservatory overlooking the large garden and picturesque countryside. There is a separate lounge for guests. Excellent base for walking or touring and convenient for Stansted, M11, Harwich, Cambridge and Constable country. Plenty of parking. Bed and Breakfast double/twin £16 to £18 per person per night.

BRAINTREE near. Mrs J. Reddington, Park Farmhouse, Bradwell, Near Braintree CM7 8EP (01376 563584). ETB Listed *COMMENDED.* Listed 16th century timber-framed family home; superb views, large secluded garden with listed dovecote, tranquil countryside setting. Well placed for Stansted Airport, M11 and A12, picturesque places and historic houses Essex/Suffolk borders and Stour Valley. Double or twin-bedded rooms (one four-poster) with tea making facilities; guests' bathroom, ground floor family shower room. Continental/English breakfast. Ample parking. Children over 12 years welcome. Sorry no smoking or pets. Bed and Breakfast from £17.50 to £20 single, £34 to £36 double. Take A120; in Bradwell turn off beside "Swan" public house, drive for half a mile, Park Farmhouse on right hand side. AA QQQ.

CASTLE HEDINGHAM. Mrs Heather Hutchings, Fishers, Castle Hedingham, Near Halstead CO9 3EW (Tel & Fax: 01787 460382). Discover an unspoilt area on the north Essex/Suffolk border and stay in our Georgian Grade II Listed property situated in the main street of this picturesque medieval village with one of the best preserved Norman keeps in England and ideally situated for touring. Twin bedded room with own private adjoining bathroom overlooks a large well stocked garden offering a peaceful stay. TV and tea making facilities. Excellent restaurant and pubs in the village. Sorry no smoking or pets. Bed and Breakfast from £20 per person.

COLCHESTER. Mrs Wendy Anderson, The Old Manse, 15 Roman Road, Colchester CO1 1UR (01206 545154). Tourist Board Listed. This spacious Victorian family home is situated in a quiet square beside the Castle Park. Only three minutes' walk from bus/coach station or through the Park to town centre. We promise a warm welcome and a friendly, informal atmosphere. All rooms have central heating, TV and tea/coffee making facilities. Ground floor double room has private facilities; two twin-bedded rooms on first floor with two bathrooms. Full, varied English Breakfast. Bed and Breakfast from £26 single, £36 double. Only 30 minutes' drive from Harwich and Felixstowe. Within easy reach of Constable country and one hour's train journey from London. Sorry, no smoking.

COLCHESTER. Mrs S.P. Cox, The Maltings, Mersea Road, Abberton, Colchester CO5 7NR (01206 735780). ♛♛ Attractive period house dating back to 15th century set in walled garden with swimming pool. Owned and run by proprietor and family. Guests have their own lounge with log fire and colour TV. Open all year round, the house offers one double, one single, one family room; bathroom; diningroom. Central heating. Cot and babysitting. Ample parking provided, and bus stop outside. Four miles to sea at Mersea Island and boating facilities. Near Abberton Reservoir with its bird sanctuary and nature reserve. Bed and Breakfast from £18. Reduced rates for children.

KELVEDON. Mr and Mrs R. Bunting, Highfields Farm, Kelvedon CO5 9BJ (Tel & Fax: 01376 570334). ♛♛ *COMMENDED.* Highfields Farm is set in a quiet area on a 700 acre arable working farm. This makes a peaceful overnight stop on the way to Harwich or a base to visit historic Colchester and Constable country. Convenient for Harwich, Felixstowe and Stansted Airport. Easy access to A12 and main line trains to London. The accommodation comprises two twin rooms en suite and one twin room with private bathroom, all with TV and tea/coffee making facilities. Residents' lounge. Good English Breakfast is served in the oak beamed diningroom. Ample parking. Bed and Breakfast from £20 single, £36 to £38 twin.

GLOUCESTERSHIRE

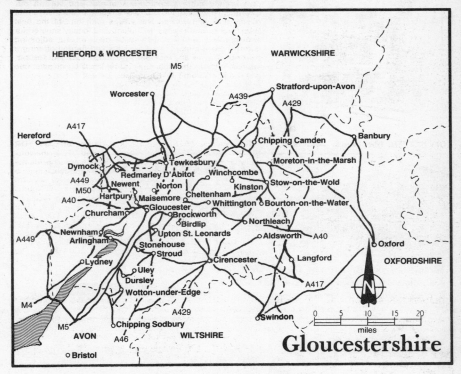

HEREFORD & WORCESTER

WARWICKSHIRE

M5

Worcester

A439

Stratford-upon-Avon

A429

A417

Hereford

Banbury

Chipping Camden

Dymock

Tewkesbury

Moreton-in-the-Marsh

Redmarley D'Abitot

Winchcombe

A449

Newent

Norton

Kinston

Stow-on-the-Wold

M50

Hartpury

Maisemore

Cheltenham

A40

Gloucester

Whittington

Bourton-on-the-Water

Churcham

Brockworth

Birdlip

Northleach

Newnham

Upton St. Leonards

Aldsworth

A40

A449

Arlingham

Stonehouse

Oxford

Lydney

Stroud

Cirencester

Langford

OXFORDSHIRE

Uley

Dursley

A417

M4

Wotton-under-Edge

N

A429

Swindon

0 5 10 15 20

M5

Chipping Sodbury

miles

AVON

A46

WILTSHIRE

Gloucestershire

Bristol

AMBERLEY, near Stroud. The Dial Cottage, Amberley, Near Stroud GL5 5AL (01453 872563; Fax: 01453 873057). ♥♥ *HIGHLY COMMENDED.* A warm welcome awaits you at our character filled Cotswold cottage. The Dial Cottage is situated within the "Royal Triangle" on 600 acres of a National Trust Common, Minchinhampton, with its picturesque views, ancient golf course and famous Five Valley Walks. Good pub food within walking distance. Well positioned to explore the Cotswolds, Sudeley and Berkeley Castles, Cirencester, Tetbury, Bath, world famous Westonbirt Arboretum and Slimbridge Wild Life Park. Golf, gliding, ballooning, horse riding; equestrian events at Gatcombe Park, Badminton and Cheltenham horse racing. The bedrooms with their antique beds retain their unique cottage atmosphere and all have en suite and modern facilities to add to your comfort. Licensed. Non-smoking. Children over 11 years. Sorry, no pets. Bed and Breakfast from £25 to £38.50 per person.

BATH near. Mrs Lynn Hooper, Greenway Farm, Bath Road, Wick, Near Bristol BS15 5RL (0117 9373201). Greenway is a small working beef farm with a large early Georgian house, just a few yards off the A420 leading to Lansdown, Bath and four miles from Exit 18 on the M4. We are overlooking/adjacent to Tracy Park Golf Course. All rooms have tea/coffee making facilities, colour TV, central heating; some en suite. We also have a spacious garden with Koi pond and are surrounded by beautiful country scenery. Bath four miles, Bristol six miles. Sorry, no pets. Terms from £19 per person.

BIRDLIP. Mrs P.M. Carter, Beechmount, Birdlip GL4 8JH (Tel & Fax: 01452 862262). ♥♥

COMMENDED. Good central base for touring Cotswolds, conveniently situated for many interesting places and picturesque views with lovely walks, Beechmount is in the centre of Birdlip village, convenient for post office/village shop. Front door key is provided so that guests may come and go freely. Bedrooms are equipped to a high standard, all having washbasins; some en-suite facilities; bathroom, separate shower, shaver point; toilet. Children welcome at reduced rates, cot, high chair provided. Pets allowed by arrangement. Parking space. Open January to December. Bed and Breakfast from £15 per person; Evening Meal by prior arrangement, using home produce when available. Choice of menu for breakfast. Small family-run guest house, Highly Recommended and with competitive rates.

BOURTON-ON-THE-WATER. Mr and Mrs Farley, Rooftrees, Rissington Road, Bourton-on-the-Water GL54 2EB (01451 821943; Fax: 01451 810614). ♥♥

HIGHLY COMMENDED. Warmth, comfort and hospitality are offered in the relaxed atmosphere of this detached Cotswold stone guest house, situated on the edge of the famous village of Bourton-on-the-Water which is eight minutes' level walking distance from the centre of the village. Bourton is central to all the main Cotswold attractions. Rooftrees offers four en suite bedrooms, all individually decorated, two on the ground floor. Two of the rooms have luxury four poster beds, TV and tea making facilities. A payphone is available. Optional traditional English home cooked dinners provided using fresh local produce. An enjoyable stay is assured here while visiting the Cotswolds. No smoking. Double rooms from £40 to £42; four poster rooms from £42.

BREDON'S NORTON. Michael and Pippa Cluer, Lampitt House, Lampitt Lane, Bredon's Norton, Tewkesbury GL20 7HB (01684 772295). ♥♥

COMMENDED. Lampitt House is situated in a large informal garden on the edge of a quiet village at the foot of Bredon Hill. Splendid views across to the Malverns. Ideal for visiting the Cotswolds, Stratford, Worcester, Cheltenham, Gloucester and the Forest of Dean. All rooms are furnished to a high standard and have private bathrooms, central heating, colour TV and tea/coffee making facilities. Ground floor room available. Children are welcome. Ample parking. No smoking. Open all year. Hill and riverside walks. Arrangements can be made for windsurfing and riding. Terms from £26 single room, £36 double room.

Terms quoted in this publication may be subject to increase if rises in costs necessitate

BRISTOL. Mrs Marilyn Collins, Box Hedge Farm, Coalpit Heath, Bristol BS17 2UW (01454 250786).

Box Hedge Farm is set in 200 acres of beautiful rural countryside on the edge of the Cotswolds. Local to M4/M5, central for Bristol and Bath and the many tourist attractions in this area. An ideal stopping point for the South West and Wales. We offer a warm, friendly atmosphere with traditional farmhouse cooking. The large spacious bedrooms (one single, one double and one family) have colour TV and tea/coffee making facilities. Adventure days or weekends can also be provided with Clay Pigeon Shooting, Quads and Pilots to name but three events. Bed and Breakfast from £17.50 single, from £30 double; Dinner from £7.50.

BRISTOL. Mrs Judi Hasell, Woodbarn Farm, Denny Lane, Chew Magna, Bristol BS18 8SZ (01275 332599). ♛♛ Woodbarn is a working mixed farm, five minutes from Chew Valley Lake. Chew Magna is a large village with pretty cottages, Georgian houses and is central for touring. There are two en suite bedrooms, one double and one family, both with tea trays. Guests' lounge and dining room. Cream teas Sunday June to September. Open March to December (closed Christmas). Children welcome. Bed and Breakfast from £18 to £22. Non smokers preferred. Brochure available.

CHELTENHAM. Mrs Sue Perkin, St. Michaels Guest House, 4 Montpellier Drive, Cheltenham GL50 1TX (Tel & Fax: 01242 513587). ♛♛ *COMMENDED.* AA QQQ. Elegant Edwardian guest house with parking in a quiet location five minutes' walk from the town centre, restaurants and theatres. Delightful non-smoking accommodation offering an excellent breakfast menu and a warm welcome. Most rooms are en suite. Close to all main routes and a convenient base for touring the Cotswolds. Bourton-on-the-Water, Bibury, The Wye Valley and Bath are all within easy reach. Easy to find — from the A40 Montpellier Terrace turn into Montpellier Parade this becomes Montpellier Drive at the right hand bend and we are the second property on the left. Visa, Access, Eurocard, Mastercard accepted.

CHELTENHAM. Chris and Liz Mallinson, Lonsdale House, Montpellier Drive, Cheltenham GL50 1TX (Tel & Fax: 01242 232379). ♛♛ *COMMENDED.* AA QQ. A Grade II Listed Regency town house offering a comfortable stay in the elegant Montpellier residential part of Cheltenham, yet less than 10 minutes easy walk into the lively town centre with its shops, theatre, cinema, pubs and restaurants. There is a choice of single, twin, double or family rooms, with some en suite. All rooms have colour TV and tea/coffee making facilities. Excellent touring base with easy access to the A46 for Stroud, Bath, Stratford; and the A40 for Oxford, The Cotswolds, Gloucester and Exit 11 on the M5. Bed and Breakfast from £19.

CHELTENHAM. Cressy Guest House, 44 St. Stephens Road, Cheltenham GL51 5AD (01242 525012). ♥ ♥ Comfortable Edwardian house offering accommodation in one double room with shower, two twin bedrooms, all with washbasins, colour TV and tea/coffee facilities. Bedrooms non-smopking. Other amenities include separate dining room and lounge. Friendly personal service. Ideal for touring the Cotswolds. Special diets catered for. Bed and Breakfast from £20 to £21. Reduced rates for children.

CHELTENHAM. Sid and Vera Smith, Lynden Lea, 6 Priory Terrace, Cheltenham GL52 6DS (01242 236776). Lynden Lea is a lovely family run Regency terraced house in the heart of Cheltenham — the home of Gold Cup Racing. The house has an old English garden with a hidden extra — a covered heated swimming pool for guests' use. The house is fully centrally heated and consists of one double, one twin and one family room, all en suite and having tea making facilities. There is also a private lounge with colour TV. We are within easy walking distance of the town centre and are only a short distance from many of the Cotswolds' attractions. Bed and Breakfast from £15 to £20 per night.

CHELTENHAM (Cotswolds). Mrs A. E. Hughes, Ham Hill Farm, Whittington, Cheltenham GL54 4EZ (01242 584415; Fax: 01242 222535). ♥ ♥ *HIGHLY COMMENDED.* This 160-acre farm has farmhouse, built in 1983 in true traditional style, with panoramic views. Two miles from the town of Cheltenham. Leisure activities nearby are horse riding, golf and walking the Cotswold Way. The tastefully decorated and comfortable en suite bedrooms all have colour TV, tea/coffee facilities. Two double, two twin, one family and one single. Two comfortable lounges, with maps and information about the area. Excellent farmhouse breakfast; non-smoking; open all year round. Bed and Breakfast from £20 to £23.50 per person. Colour brochure on request.

CHELTENHAM near. Mr and Mrs C. Rooke, Frogfurlong Cottage, Frogfurlong Lane, Down Hatherley, Near Cheltenham GL2 9QE (01452 730430). At Frogfurlong Cottage we offer exclusive accommodation for one couple; a truly "get away on your own" break. The 18th century cottage surrounded by fields is situated on the green belt area within the triangle formed by Cheltenham, Gloucester and Tewkesbury. The accommodation, which is totally non-smoking and self-contained, consists of a double bedroom with colour TV and teamaker, luxury en suite bathroom and jacuzzi; there is direct access to the 30' indoor heated swimming pool. Local attractions include the Cotswolds, Malverns, Forest of Dean, National Waterways Museum, National Falconry Centre, Three Choirs Vineyard, Slimbridge Wildfowl Trust, Nature in Art, Cheltenham Festivals. Sorry no pets. Bed and Breakfast from £18 per person per night; Evening Meals by arrangement.

CHELTENHAM. Mrs Lorna Seeley, Old Stables, 239A London Road, Cheltenham GL52 6YE (01242 583660). HETB Listed. Former coach house and stable, now a family home with stable block as Bed and Breakfast accommodation. One and a half miles east of town centre on A40. Easy car access and parking. Children and pets welcome. Non smoking. En suite facilities available. Bed and full Breakfast from £14 to £18. Reductions for children.

GLOUCESTERSHIRE – THE IDYLLIC COTSWOLDS COUNTY!

A combination of the Cotswolds and The Vale of Severn, Gloucestershire is a popular tourist destination. Visit Chipping Campden, Cirencester, The Cotswolds Farm Park, The Forest of Dean, Keynes Park and Tewkesbury and you will not be disappointed. If you are around at the right time, the Severn Bore can also be quite a spectacle.

CHELTENHAM. Mrs Helen Risborough, Wishmoor Guest House, 147 Hales Road, Cheltenham GL52 6TD (01242 238504; Fax: 01242 226090). ✿✿ *COMMENDED.*

At Wishmoor Guest House you will find a warm and friendly welcome from your hosts Helen and Robin Risborough whose aim is to provide a relaxed atmosphere so that you may enjoy your stay. Wishmoor is a late Victorian residence, carefully modernised to preserve its charm and character. Situated on the eastern side of Cheltenham at the foot of the Cotswold Hills it is an ideal base for touring the Cotswold Villages, Wye Valley, Malvern Hills and the Royal Forest of Dean. The scenic towns of Hereford, Stratford and Bath are conveniently situated for day visits. Single and double bedrooms available, some ensuite. All have colour TV and tea/coffee facilities. Full central heating; adequate hot water; quiet guest lounge. Non-smoking accommodation available. Off road parking. Fire Certificate. Bed and Breakfast from £19; Evening Meal from £12. Reductions for children. AA QQQ. Winner of Cheltenham Spa Award for Hygiene and Healthy Eating.

CHELTENHAM. Dove House, 128 Cheltenham Road, Bishops Cleeve, Cheltenham GL52 4LZ (Tel & Fax: 01242 679600).

Dove House is situated on the outskirts of Cheltenham, close to the Racecourse and is ideal as a base for touring/walking the Cotswolds, Forest of Dean, Tewkesbury, Evesham. Golf courses and private fishing lakes close by. All rooms are furnished to a high standard and have central heating, colour TV and tea/coffee making facilities. Ample parking and garden for guests use. Bed and Breakfast from £18 per person per night; en suite available. Open all year.

CHIPPING CAMPDEN. Mrs Gené Jeffrey, Brymbo, Honeybourne Lane, Mickleton, Chipping Campden GL55 6PU (01386 438890; Fax: 01386 438113). HETB Listed *COMMENDED.*

COTSWOLD COUNTRY BED AND BREAKFAST

A warm and spacious farm building conversion with large gardens in beautiful Cotswold countryside, ideal for walking and touring. Close to Stratford-upon-Avon, Broadway, Chipping Campden and with easy access to Oxford and Cheltenham. The comfortable bedrooms all have colour TV and tea/coffee making facilities; two rooms en suite. Ground floor bedrooms available. Sitting room with open log fire, breakfast room. Central heating. Parking. Maps, guides and sample menus from local hostelries for your information. FREE Four-Wheel Drive Tour of the area offered to three-night guests. Bed and Breakfast from £15. Home made preserves a speciality. Children and pets welcome. Brochure available.

CHIPPING CAMPDEN. Mrs C. Hutsby, Holly House, Ebrington, Chipping Campden GL55 6NL (01386 593213).

Holly House is set in the centre of the picturesque thatched Cotswold village of Ebrington. Ideally situated for touring the Cotswolds and Shakespeare's Stratford. Two miles from Hidcote Gardens and Chipping Campden, 10 miles from Stratford and 18 miles from Warwick. All rooms are beautifully appointed with en suite facilities, TV, radio, hair dryer and tea/coffee facilities. Ground floor rooms, laundry facility. Private parking. Garden. Village inn serves meals Monday to Saturday. Dinner by arrangement Sunday evenings at Holly House. Bed and Breakfast £18 to £20 per person. AA QQQQ Selected. Directions: from Chipping Campden take B4035 towards Shipston on Stour. Continue half a mile and turn left to Ebrington, we are in the centre of the village.

PLEASE SEND A STAMPED ADDRESSED ENVELOPE WITH ENQUIRIES

COLEFORD near. Lynda Steiner, The Old Vicarage, Christchurch, Near Coleford GL16 7NS (01594 835330). Offering more privacy and freedom than the usual Bed and Breakfast establishment this is a three bedroomed flat in a Grade II Listed former vicarage. Available for short breaks, long breaks or even overnight stops. In the kitchen you will find food for a delicious breakfast including home made bread and preserves and home produced eggs. The area is peaceful and has many spectacular views, wildlife abounds. The energetic can find a variety of activities including cycling, canoeing, climbing and horse riding. £38 per night for the whole flat (sleeps 5) including breakfast. Non-smokers only. No pets.

COTSWOLDS. Mrs Alison Coldrick, Hill Barn, Clapton Road, Bourton-on-the-Water GL54 2LF (01451 810472). In the midst of beautiful rolling pastures yet only five minutes' drive from the picturesque village of Bourton-on-the-Water, this 17th century converted barn offers high standard en suite accommodation, tea/coffee and TV in all rooms with a choice of breakfast from £17 per person. Beautiful views. Ample parking. Lovely walks directly from the property. Open all year. Sorry, no smoking or pets. Ideally situated for exploring the Cotswolds, Gloucestershire, Oxfordshire and Warwickshire.

DIDMARTON. Mrs M.T. Sayers, The Old Rectory, Didmarton GL9 1DS (01454 238233). ♥ ♥ *HIGHLY COMMENDED.* Small and comfortable, this former Rectory, with a pleasant walled garden, is set in an attractive little south Cotswold village on the A433. It has a very friendly informal atmosphere and is an ideal base for touring the Cotswolds, Severn Vale, North Wiltshire and Bath area, or as we are close to M4/5 is a convenient overnight stop. Westonbirt Arboretum is five minutes away and the antiques centre of Tetbury is less than 10. Three double/twin rooms with colour TV, hair dryer, en suite or private bathroom. Central heating. Guests' sitting room. Ample parking. Food available within walking distance. Terms: Double room from £38 to £40.

DURSLEY. Burrows Court, Nibley Green, North Nibley, Dursley GL11 6AZ (Tel & Fax: 01453 546230). ♥ ♥ *COMMENDED.* This 18th century mill is idyllically set in an acre of garden surrounded by open country with beautiful views of the Cotswolds. Decorated and furnished in the country style the house has six bedrooms, all with private bathroom, colour TV, beverage facilities and radio. Other facilities include two lounges, one with residents' bar; central heating. There is a good range of restaurants and pubs nearby. Children over five years welcome. Bed and Breakfast from £20 to £25 per person. Close to the M5 motorway, between Junctions 13 and 14. AA Listed, RAC Highly Acclaimed.

BURROWS COURT

RAC   AA

DURSLEY near. Bob & Linda Woodman and Neil Smith, Rose and Crown Inn, Nympsfield, Stonehouse GL10 3TU (Tel & Fax: 01453 860240). ♥ ♥ ♥ *COMMENDED.* Three-hundred-year-old Cotswold stone coaching inn situated in centre of quiet, friendly, unspoilt village, half a mile from Cotswold Way; with easy access to M5/M4. Ideal base for touring, walking, cycling and gliding in the Cotswolds. Accommodation includes centrally heated, spacious, en-suite family and double rooms. Evening meals are optional and can be selected from a comprehensive bar menu. Bed and Breakfast from £26 per night. AA, RAC, Relais Routiers Listed, Logis UK. Open all year. All credit/debit cards accepted.

FALFIELD. Mr and Mrs B.C. Burrell, Green Farm Guest House, Falfield, Gloucestershire GL12 8DL (01454 260319). ETB Listed. Delightful 16th century stone farmhouse, beautifully converted into a country guest house with style and traditional charm. Open all year. Bath, Cheltenham, Cardiff, Forest of Dean, Cheddar are all approximately 35 minutes away. Easy access M4 and M5 Junction 14, AZTEC Business Park 10 minutes. The ideal touring centre. Bed and Breakfast from £17. Excellent food always available from simple snacks to à la carte dinner. A warm welcome assured at Green Farm. Ample parking.

GLOUCESTER. Mrs S. Carter, Severn Bank, Minsterworth GL2 8JH (01452 750357). 👑👑 COMMENDED. Severn Bank is a fine country house standing in its own six-acre grounds on the bank of the River Severn, four miles west of Gloucester. Ideally situated for touring Cotswolds, Forest of Dean and Wye Valley, and at the recommended viewpoint for the Severn Bore tidal wave. Severn Bank has a friendly atmosphere and comfortable accommodation in spacious rooms with superb view over river and countryside. Full central heating, en-suite rooms, tea/coffee making facilities and colour TV. Completely non-smoking. Ample parking, with several excellent restaurants and pubs nearby. Terms: Bed and Continental Breakfast £18 to £22. Reduced rates for children.

GLOUCESTER. Penny and Peter Stevens, Edgewood House, Churcham, Gloucester GL2 8AA (01452 750232). 👑👑 HIGHLY COMMENDED. Family-run country guest house set in two acres of lovely gardens. Ideal for visiting Forest of Dean, Wye Valley, Cotswolds and Malverns. Close to RSPB Reserve and viewpoint for Severn Bore Tidal Wave. Spacious, centrally heated double, family and twin rooms tastefully furnished with comfortable beds. Most rooms are en suite and have tea/coffee making facilities. Spacious dining room and lounge with colour TV. Ample parking. Generous cooked breakfasts. Several excellent eating places nearby. Bed and Breakfast from £18 to £22.50. Children over eight years welcome with reductions if sharing with two adults. Sorry no smoking or pets. Open all year. Brochure available.

GLOUCESTER near. Mrs Judith Price, "Merrivale", Tewkesbury Road, Norton, Near Gloucester GL2 9LQ (01452 730412). 👑 COMMENDED. "Merrivale" is a bright and cheerful house and a warm welcome is given to all guests. The house is situated on the A38, three miles north of Gloucester. Ample garden for guests' use and plenty of parking space (car advisable). Tea and coffee making equipment and TV in all rooms, much enjoyed by the weary traveller. Ideal spot for those travelling from Scotland to South West resorts of England. For a longer stay there are many interesting places to visit: The Cotswolds, Forest of Dean, Herefordshire and Welsh Border, historic Tewkesbury and Severn and Avon Rivers. Packed lunches prepared. Bed and Breakfast from £16.50 to £18 per person. Reductions for children under 14. Fire Certificate held.

GLOUCESTER near. S.J. Barnfield, Kilmorie Guest House, Gloucester Road, Corse, Staunton, Near Gloucester GL19 3RQ (01452 840224). Kilmorie is Grade II Listed (c.1848) within conservation area in a lovely part of Gloucestershire. Deceptively spacious yet cosy, tastefully furnished all ground floor accommodation: double, twin, family or single bedrooms all with tea trays, colour TVs, radios, washbasin; some have private facilities. Very comfortable guests' lounge; traditional home cooking is served in the separate dining room overlooking large garden where there are seats to relax, watch our ducks and hens (who provide eggs for breakfast!!) or the wild birds and butterflies which we encourage to visit. Perhaps walk waymarked farmland footpaths which start here. Children may "help" with our sheep, poultry, child's pony, pygmy goats whose tiny pretty kids arrive in spring. Rural yet ideally situated to visit Cotswolds, Royal Forest of Dean, Wye Valley and Malvern Hills. Children over five years welcome. Three-course Evening Dinner, Bed and Breakfast from £21.50; Bed and full English Breakfast from £14. Ample parking.

LECHLADE near. Mrs Elizabeth Reay, Apple Tree House, Buscot, Near Faringdon SN7 8DA (01367 252592).

🐾🐾 17th century listed house situated in small interesting National Trust Village, two miles from Lechlade and four miles from Faringdon on the A417. River Thames five minutes' walk through village to Buscot lock and weirs. Ideal touring centre for the Cotswolds, Upper Thames, Oxford, etc. Good fishing, walking and cycling area. Access at all times to the three guest bedrooms, all of which have washbasins, razor points, tea/coffee facilities and central heating when necessary. En suite room available. Residents' TV lounge with log fire in winter. Bed and Breakfast from £18 per person per night. Choice of many restaurants, etc, within a five-mile radius of Buscot. I look forward to welcoming you to Apple Tree House.

MINCHINHAMPTON, near Stroud. Mrs Margaret Helm, Hunters Lodge, Dr Brown's Road, Minchinhampton Common, Near Stroud GL6 9BT (01453 883588; Fax: 01453 731449).

🐾🐾 *HIGHLY COMMENDED.* AA QQQQ Selected. Hunters Lodge is a beautiful stone built Cotswold country house set in a large secluded garden adjoining 600 acres of National Trust common land at Minchinhampton. Accommodation available — one double room en suite; one family and one twin-bedded rooms both with private bathrooms. All have tea/coffee making facilities, central heating and colour TV and are furnished and decorated to a high standard. Private lounge with TV and a delightful conservatory. Car essential, ample parking space. Ideal centre for touring the Cotswolds — Bath, Cheltenham, Cirencester, with many delightful pubs and hotels in the area for meals. You are sure of a warm welcome, comfort, and help in planning excursions to local places of interest. Bed and Breakfast from £20 per person. Non-smokers preferred. SAE please for details, or telephone.

NAILSWORTH. Mrs Lesley Williams-Allen, The Laurels at Inchbrook, Nailsworth GL5 5HA (Tel & Fax: 01453 834021).

A lovely rambling house, part cottage-style and part Georgian. The emphasis is on relaxation and friendly hospitality. All rooms are en suite and include family, twin and double rooms, each with colour TV and tea making facilities. We have a panelled study/reading room with piano, and a beamed lounge with snooker table and board games. In our licensed dining room we serve excellent breakfasts and home cooked dinners. The secluded garden backs onto fields and offers a swimming pool and the opportunity to observe wildlife. We are ideally situated for touring all parts of the Cotswolds and West Country, surrounded by a wealth of beautiful countryside and all kinds of activities. Children and pets welcome. Bed and Breakfast from £18 per person; Dinner by arrangement. Brochure on request. Self catering cottage also available.

NORTH WOODCHESTER. Mrs Carol Walsh, The Firs, Selsley Road, North Woodchester, Stroud GL5 5NQ (01453 873088; Fax: 01453 873053).

🐾🐾 *HIGHLY COMMENDED.* The Firs is located in the village where the famous Woodchester pavement is buried. A fine Georgian house, with many period features and a panoramic view over the Cotswold escarpment. In a quiet village location within walking distance of several excellent pubs and restaurants. Ideally situated for Woodchester Park and Mansion, the Cotswold Way, Bath, Cheltenham, Westonbirt Arboretum, Gatcombe, Badminton, Cirencester, Gloucester Docks and Bristol. All bedrooms are en suite, individually decorated, with colour TV and tea/coffee facilities. Laundry and cycle hire available. Children welcome. Sorry no pets. Bed and Breakfast from £20 per person. Open all year except Christmas.

NORTHLEACH. Theresa and Mike Eastman, Market House, The Square, Northleach GL54 3EJ (01451 860557).

A 400-year-old house of olde worlde charm, characterised by exposed beams, inglenook fireplace yet with modern facilities. Pretty bedrooms, one double en suite, one double/twin and two singles, each with wash-basin, central heating, tea/coffee making facilities and touring guides. Located in an unspoilt tiny town in the heart of the Cotswolds near the intersection of the A40 with A429, amidst a wide choice of inns and restaurants and surrounded by a variety of attractions and beautiful countryside. A delicious breakfast is cooked to order for your enjoyment, before you tour to nearby Bath, Stratford-upon-Avon or Oxford. Children over 12 years. No pets. No smoking. Packed lunches available. Bed and Breakfast from £18. "Which?" Recommended, AA QQQ Recommended.

PAINSWICK. Jan Haslam, Culvert Cottage, Kingsmill Lane, Painswick GL6 6RT (01452 812293).

COMMENDED. Once an old wheelwright's cottage, Culvert Cottage has been skilfully extended and is a homely guest house of unusual design. It is set in beautiful gardens of one and a half acres bordering a stream and opposite historic Kings Mill. The picturesque village of Painswick with its famous churchyard is an ideal centre for exploring the Cotswolds. Berkeley Castle, Slimbridge Wildfowl Trust, Gloucester and Cheltenham are nearby. The Cotswold Way footpath is within half a mile. Non smoking accommodation comprises one double and one twin bedroom, both en suite with colour TV and tea making facilities. Bed and Breakfast from £17.50. Reductions for children.

PAINSWICK. Jean Hernen, Brookhouse Mill Cottage, Tibbiwell Lane, Painswick GL6 6YA (Tel & Fax: 01452 812854).

Bed & Breakfast

Jean Hernen
Brookhouse Mill Cottage.

Brookhouse Mill Cottage is a beautiful 17th century cottage situated in Painswick — the "Queen of the Cotswolds" in an area of outstanding natural beauty. The cottage was once the village forge and has been lovingly restored by the proprietors, Brian and Jean Hernen, with exposed original beams and timbers, inglenook fireplace and cast iron range. It straddles a trout stream and the two-acre garden encompasses a lake and two waterfalls. Each bedroom has en suite facilities and is furnished to a very high standard in keeping with the cottage style. The beds are covered in hand-stitched patchwork quilts designed by Jean; some are for sale together with cot quilts and cushion covers. All this is topped by the use of the beautiful indoor swimming pool. Plenty of parking space and a totally "non smoking" house. Brochure.

RANDWICK. Mr and Mrs J.E. Taylor, Court Farm, Randwick, Stroud GL6 6HH (01453 764210; Fax: 01453 766428).

A 17th century beamed farmhouse on a small farm in the centre of hillside village of Randwick, cn the Cotswold Escarpment. Beautiful views over Stroud Valleys. Randwick is topped by a deciduous National Trust wood. Much of our food produced organically on seven acres of meadowland. A stream divides the sloping fields, haven for wildlife. Large garden for guests to enjoy, village pub food. Leisure centre one mile. Convenient overnight stop, good base. Tourist attractions nearby include Wildfowl Trust, Gloucester Waterways, Prinknash Abbey, Berkeley Castle. London two hours A419, M5 Junction 13 five miles. Bed and Breakfast from £15 to £17; Evening Meal can be provided. Children and pets welcome.

STONEHOUSE. Mrs D.A. Hodge, Merton Lodge, 8 Ebley Road, Stonehouse GL10 2LQ (01453 822018). ♛♛ A former gentleman's residence situated about three miles from Stroudwater interchange on the M5 (Junction 13), on A419 (keep going on old road) just outside Stonehouse towards Stroud. Opposite side to Kennedy's Garden Centre, 300 yards from the Cotswold Way. Full central heating and washbasins in all bedrooms; one en suite. Only cotton or linen sheets used. Two bathrooms with showers. Large sittingroom with panoramic views of Selsey Common. Well placed for Cotswold villages, Wildfowl Trust, Berkeley Castle, Westonbirt Arboretum, Bath/Bristol, Cheltenham and Gloucester ski slope and Forest of Dean. Satisfaction guaranteed. Excellent cuisine. Carvery/pub 200 yards away. Bed and Breakfast from £15 per person, en suite from £17 per person. Reductions for children. Friendly welcome. Sorry, no smoking or dogs.

STOW-ON-THE-WOLD. Mrs F.J. Adams, Aston House, Broadwell, Moreton-in-Marsh GL56 0TJ (01451 830475; e-mail: fja@netcomuk.co.uk). ETB Listed COMMENDED. Aston House is a chalet bungalow overlooking fields in the peaceful village of Broadwell, one and a half miles from Stow-on-the-Wold. It is centrally situated for all the Cotswold villages, while Blenheim Palace, Warwick Castle, Oxford, Stratford-upon-Avon, Cheltenham, Cirencester and Gloucester are within easy reach. Accommodation comprises a twin-bedded and a double/twin room, both en suite on the first floor and a double room with private bathroom on the ground floor. All rooms have tea/coffee making facilities, colour TV, radio and electric blankets. Bedtime drinks and biscuits are provided. Guests and children over 10 years are welcomed to our home February to November. No smoking. Car essential, parking. Pub within walking distance. Bed and good English Breakfast from £19 to to £21 per person daily; weekly from £135 per person.

STOW-ON-THE-WOLD. Mrs S. Davis, Fairview Farmhouse, Bledington Road, Stow-on-the-Wold, Cheltenham GL54 1AN (01451 830279). ♛♛ HIGHLY COMMENDED. You are assured of a warm welcome at Fairview Farmhouse situated one mile from Stow-on-the-Wold on a quiet B road with outstanding panoramic views of the surrounding Cotswold Hills. Ideal base for touring the pretty villages of Bourton-on-the-Water, The Slaughters, Broadway, Chipping Campden, also famous Stratford etc. The cosy bedrooms are furnished to a high standard with a king-size four-poster de luxe for that special occasion; all are en suite with colour TV and tea/coffee making equipment. Lounge and additional lounge area with books, maps, etc. Central heating. Ample parking. Open all year.

Fairview FARMHOUSE

FOR THE MUTUAL GUIDANCE OF GUEST AND HOST

Every year literally thousands of holidays, short-breaks and overnight stops are arranged through our guides, the vast majority without any problems at all. In a handful of cases, however, difficulties do arise about bookings, which often could have been prevented from the outset.

It is important to remember that when accommodation has been booked, both parties — guests and hosts — have entered into a form of contract. We hope that the following points will provide helpful guidance.

GUESTS: When enquiring about accommodation, be as precise as possible. Give exact dates, numbers in your party and the ages of any children. State the number and type of rooms wanted and also what catering you require — bed and breakfast, full board, etc. Make sure that the position about evening meals is clear — and about pets, reductions for children or any other special points.

Read our reviews carefully to ensure that the proprietors you are going to contact can supply what you want. Ask for a letter confirming all arrangements, if possible.

If you have to cancel, do so as soon as possible. Proprietors do have the right to retain deposits and under certain circumstances to charge for cancelled holidays if adequate notice is not given and they cannot re-let the accommodation.

HOSTS: Give details about your facilities and about any special conditions. Explain your deposit system clearly and arrangements for cancellations, charges, etc, and whether or not your terms include VAT.

If for any reason you are unable to fulfil an agreed booking without adequate notice, you may be under an obligation to arrange alternative suitable accommodation or to make some form of compensation.

While every effort is made to ensure accuracy, we regret that FHG Publications cannot accept responsibility for errors, omissions or misrepresentation in our entries or any consequences thereof. Prices in particular should be checked because we go to press early. We will follow up complaints but cannot act as arbiters or agents for either party.

STOW-ON-THE-WOLD. Graham and Helen Keyte, The Limes, Evesham Road, Stow-on-the-Wold GL54 1EN (01451 830034/831056). The centre of the Cotswolds. This is an RAC and AA Listed guest house. Large attractive garden with ornamental pond and waterfall overlooking fields. Only four minutes' walking distance to town centre. Central for places to visit like Stratford-upon-Avon, Burford, Cheltenham, Oxford, Broadway, Evesham, Chipping Campden, etc, all within 20 miles' radius. Good sized bedrooms; one four-poster, three rooms en-suite and one twin-bedded room, all with colour TV and tea/coffee making facilities; TV lounge; diningroom. Cot, high chair. Established for over 22 years, we have many guests returning each year, even from abroad, and are well recommended. Many guests book for one or two nights then stay for a week. Bed and Breakfast from £17 to £19.50. Central heating. Car park. Open all year except Christmas. Children and pets welcome.

STOW-ON-THE-WOLD. Robert and Dawn Smith, Corsham Field Farmhouse, Bledington Road, Stow-on-the-Wold GL54 1JH (01451 831750). 🐾🐾 Homely farmhouse with traditional features and breathtaking views, one mile from Stow-on-the-Wold. Ideally situated for exploring all the picturesque Cotswold villages such as Broadway, Bourton-on-the-Water, Upper and Lower Slaughter, Chipping Campden, Snowshill, etc. Also central point for places of interest such as Blenheim Palace, Cotswold Wildlife Park, Stratford and many stately homes and castles in the area. Twin, double and family rooms available, most with en suite facilities. Other rooms have washbasins, TV and tea/coffee making equipment. Pets and children welcome. AA Listed. Bed and full English Breakfast from £15 to £20 per person. Good pub food five minutes' walk away.

STROUD. Mrs E. Ewart-James, Home Farm, South Woodchester, Near Stroud GL5 5EL (01453

872470). Tourist Board Listed *APPROVED.* Home Farm is a Listed Cotswold stone former farmhouse with lovely views and central village location. A comfortable family home within walking distance of the pub, shop and church. Easy access to the Cotswold Way, Badminton and Gatcombe Horse Trials and within half an hour of Cheltenham Racecourse. One twin-bedded and one single room; private bathroom; small sitting room with colour TV available on request. Tea/coffee making facilities. Local attractions include Berkeley Castle, Woodchester Mansion, Slimbridge Wild Fowl Trust, Westonbirt Arboretum and Owlpen Manor. Children welcome. Pets by arrangement. Bed and Breakfast from £18 to £20 per person.

STROUD. Mrs Salt, Beechcroft, Brownshill, Stroud GL6 8AG (01453 883422). 🐾 *COMMENDED.* Our

Edwardian house is quietly situated in a beautiful rural area with open views, about four miles from Stroud. The house is set in an attractive garden with mature trees, shrubs and herbaceous borders. We are in the midst of good walking country, for which we can lend maps and guides. We provide a full cooked breakfast or fruit salad and rolls with homemade bread and preserves. We welcome the elderly and small children. We are within easy reach of Cheltenham, Gloucester, Cirencester and Bath, also Berkeley Castle, Slimbridge and the North Cotswolds. We are a non-smoking establishment. Evening meal by prior arrangement. Bed and Breakfast from £16 to £20.

STROUD near. Mrs Caroline Garrett, Lamfield, Rodborough Common, Stroud GL5 5DA (01453

873452). Delightful Cotswold stone house altered over the years from a row of cottages dating back to 1757. Situated 500ft above sea level bordering National Trust Common land two miles south east of Stroud between A46 and A419, we enjoy superb views across the valley. Lamfield offers one room with a double bed and one with twin beds. Both with washbasins. Shared bathroom. Sittingroom for guests (TV on request). Set in three-quarters of an acre of secluded garden. Ample off road parking. Excellent pubs locally for evening meals. Bed and Breakfast from £30 per room for two sharing. Come and share my home for a night or two.

TEWKESBURY. Mrs Lynn Bird, Green Gables, Ripple, Tewkesbury GL20 6EX (01684 592740).

Modern house set in beautiful quiet village of Ripple which is only three miles from Tewkesbury and Upton on Severn and one mile from Junction 1 of M50 and M5 in the heart of the Severn/Avon Valley with views of Malvern and Bredon Hills. Luxurious accommodation, all rooms en suite with tea maker and colour TV. Friendly comfortable lounge for evening relaxation. Children welcome. Sorry, no pets. Open all year. Car necessary, parking available. Bed and wonderful English Breakfast £17.50 single, £35 double/twin. Reductions for children.

TEWKESBURY. Caroline and Keith Page, Corner Cottage, Stow Road, Alderton, Tewkesbury GL20 8NH (01242 620630). 👑 👑 *COMMENDED.* Corner Cottage

was originally a pair of farm cottages now a family home standing in two acres. The rooms are decorated in cottage style and have views over surrounding countryside. Your hosts have extensive local knowledge and will help you plan your trips. The Cotswolds are nearby with the towns of Cheltenham, Broadway, Winchcombe and Stratford-upon-Avon within easy driving distance. The M5, Junction 9, is less than five miles away giving access to North and South. The house is easy to find with plenty of parking.

ULEY. Gerald and Norma Kent, Hill House, Crawley Hill, Uley, Near Dursley GL11 5BH (01453 860267). Cotswold stone house situated on top of a hill with

beautiful views of the surrounding countryside, near the very pretty village of Uley. Ideal spot for exploring the various walks in the area including the Cotswold Way and there are many places of interest within reasonable driving distance of Uley. Choice of bedrooms with or without en suite facilities, all with washbasins, central heating, shaver points, tea/coffee making facilities and TV. Your hosts' aim is to make your stay in the Cotswolds an enjoyable and memorable one, with comfort and hospitality of prime importance. Bed and Breakfast from £15 per person. Evening Meals are normally available if required. Please phone or write for brochure.

WINCHCOMBE near. Mr and Mrs Bloom, The Homestead, Smithy Lane, Greet, Near Winchcombe GL54 5BP (01242 603808). Tourist Board Listed. The

Homestead is a 16th century period country house, built in Cotswold stone and standing in one acre of lovely gardens, with commanding views of the Cotswold Hills. It is situated just one mile from the Anglo-Saxon village of Winchcombe and Sudeley Castle, and within easy reach of many Cotswold villages and Stratford-upon-Avon. There are several pubs and a restaurant nearby for evening meals. We have two double rooms, one with en-suite facilities, one family room ensuite and one twin room with washbasin. All rooms have exposed beams and lovely views. Tea making facilities in rooms. Bed and Breakfast from £17 to £20. Private parking for cars.

WOODCHESTER. Mrs Wendy Swait, Inschdene, Atcombe Road, South Woodchester, Stroud GL5 5EW (01453 873254). Inschdene is a comfortable family house with magnificent views across the valley, set in an acre of garden near the centre of a quiet village. A double room with private bathroom and a twin-bedded room are available, both being spacious with washbasin and tea/coffee making facilities. Colour TV available in the rooms. Woodchester is an attractive village with excellent local pubs renowned for their food, and all within easy walking distance. An ideal centre for the Cotswolds and close to Slimbridge, Berkeley Castle and Westonbirt Arboretum and more, including Badminton and Gatcombe Horse Trials. Guests are requested not to smoke in the house. Bed and Breakfast from £15 to £17.50.

WOTTON-UNDER-EDGE. Mrs Gloria Gomm, Beech Cottage, Southend, Wotton-under-Edge GL12 7PD (01453 545771). Spacious self-contained en suite accommodation in annexe of 18th century cottage. Our location reflects the peace, beauty and charm of the undiscovered southern Cotswolds and offers both comfort and friendly hospitality in two acres of private grounds with beautiful views of the Cotswold escarpment. Well placed for Wildfowl Trust, Berkeley Castle, Westonbirt Arboretum, Bath, Bristol, Cheltenham and Gloucester. Ideally placed for walking the Cotswold Way. Tea/coffee making facilities, colour TV. Private parking. Full English breakfast, vegetarian by arrangement. Well behaved pets welcome. Not suitable for disabled visitors. No smoking or children under 12 years. Bed and Breakfast £23.

WOTTON-UNDER-EDGE. Mrs K.P. Forster, Under-the-Hill House, Adey's Lane, Wotton-under-Edge GL12 7LY (01453 842557). Open Easter to October, Under-the-Hill is a fine Queen Anne Listed house on the edge of the ancient wool town of Wotton-under-Edge. We are bounded on the east by National Trust land which is let to the owners who run a breeding herd of Welsh Black cattle. The house is only a few minutes from the town centre and there are beautiful walks with views of the Severn Vale and River. Ideally situated for Bath, Berkeley Castle, Wildfowl Trust and the Cotswolds. The house is centrally heated and there are two guest bedrooms (one twin and one double) with wash-basins, colour TV and tea/coffee making facilities. Shared garden for guests' use. Bed and Breakfast from £17 per person per night for three or more nights, £19 per night for one or two nights. Sorry no pets, no children under 12 years and no smoking.

Key to Tourist Board Ratings

The Crown Scheme
(England, Scotland & Wales)

Covering hotels, motels, private hotels, guesthouses, inns, bed & breakfast, farmhouses. Every Crown classified place to stay is inspected annually. *The classification:* Listed then 1-5 Crown indicates the range of facilities and services. Higher quality standards are indicated by the terms APPROVED, COMMENDED, HIGHLY COMMENDED and DELUXE.

The Key Scheme
(also operates in Scotland using a Crown symbol)

Covering self-catering in cottages, bungalows, flats, houseboats, houses, chalets, etc. Every Key classified holiday home is inspected annually. *The classification:* 1-5 Key indicates the range of facilities and equipment. Higher quality standards are indicated by the terms APPROVED, COMMENDED, HIGHLY COMMENDED and DELUXE.

The Q Scheme
(England, Scotland & Wales)

Covering holiday, caravan, chalet and camping parks. Every Q rated park is inspected annually for its quality standards. The more √ in the Q – up to 5 – the higher the standard of what is provided.

HAMPSHIRE

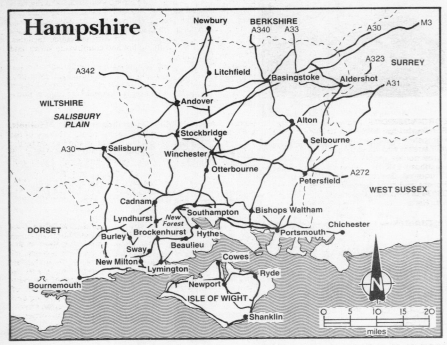

Hampshire

BEAULIEU near. Mick and Alexis McEvoy, Langley Village Restaurant, Lepe Road, Langley, Southampton SO45 1XR (01703 891667). A friendly family atmosphere will greet you in this large detached property on the edge of the beautiful New Forest. Ample off road parking. Each day begins with a hearty full English breakfast. Accommodation comprises one twin, one double and two single rooms, all tastefully decorated and having washbasins, central heating, colour TV and tea-making facilities. A restaurant is attached offering meals all day. Conveniently situated for golf, fishing, horse riding and walking. Close to Exbury Gardens, Lepe Country Park and Beaulieu Motor Museum. Open all year. Bed and Breakfast from £17. Special diets catered for by arrangement.

BURLEY (New Forest). Mrs Carole Hayles, Burbush Farm, Pound Lane, Burley, Near Ringwood BH24 4EF (Tel & Fax: 01425 403238). Burbush Farm is a secluded country house offering peace and tranquillity, nestling on 12 acres of scenic beauty, adjoining and having direct access onto the Forest. Warm welcoming atmosphere, comfortable rooms decorated to a high standard. Two rooms available one with en suite bathroom and one with private bathroom. Guest lounge with log fire. Stables, paddocks (own horses welcome). Enjoy walking, riding, cycling from our private gate onto the Forest, no roads to cross. Beaches, golf, sailing nearby. Ideal touring base. Terms from £22.

BURLEY. Mrs Gina Russell, Charlwood, Longmead Road, Burley BH24 4BY (01425 403242). Charlwood is situated on the edge of Burley, a picturesque little village in the midst of the New Forest. An ideal walking and touring base with Bournemouth and Southampton only 16 miles away and Isle of Wight ferry 12 miles. Riding and golf are nearby. The bedrooms, one double, one twin, have washbasins, colour TV and tea/coffee facilities. Central heating throughout. The friendly family home stands in its own attractive grounds on a no-through Forest road offering visitors a peaceful "away from it all" break. A full traditional English Breakfast is served. Pets welcome. No smoking. Open January to November. Bed and Breakfast from £17.50.

CADNAM (New Forest). Simon and Elaine Wright, Bushfriers, Winsor Road, Winsor, Near Cadnam,

Southampton SO40 2HF (01703 812552). Charming beamed cottage in peaceful farming village close to the New Forest and Test Valley. Central for Winchester, Salisbury and beaches. M27 two miles. Convenient for walking, riding, golfing and fishing. Accommodation comprises one triple/ twin room and one double room with tea/coffee facilities. Spacious TV lounge with log fire and countryside views, and a fragrant tranquil garden for guests' relaxation at the end of a perfect day, all reflecting the warm, friendly atmosphere. Highly-rated breakfast freshly prepared from local farm produce and home-made organic preserves. Terms from £16 per person per night. No smoking. Traditional 17th century pub a four minute walk away.

FORDINGBRIDGE (New Forest). Mrs S. Harte, Alderholt Mill, Sandleheath Road, Alderholt, Fordingbridge SP6 1PU (01425 653130). 🐾 *COMMENDED.* Alderholt Mill stands on a tributary of the Hampshire Avon, on the Hampshire/Dorset border. The Water Mill and house are on an island formed by the mill stream and race. Open to the public, with working machinery, dried flower emporium and craft shop. Three double rooms and one twin room, all en suite, £21 per person per night; one single room with washbasin £18 per person per night. Prices include Continental or English breakfast. Evening Meal available if required. Guests welcome to bring own wine. All rooms have colour TV, tea/coffee making facilities. Horses and dogs welcome. Rough fishing. Open all year. Car essential, parking. From M27 Cadnam take B3078 to Fordingbridge, continue to Sandleheath, left for Alderholt (half mile). Further details available from Mrs Harte.

FRITHAM (New Forest). John and Penny Hankinson, Fritham Farm, Fritham, Lyndhurst SO43 7HH

(Tel & Fax: 01703 812333). 🐾🐾 *COMMENDED.* AA QQQQ Selected. Lovely farmhouse on working farm in the heart of the New Forest. Dating from the 18th century, all bedrooms have en suite facilities and provision for tea/coffee making. There is a large comfortable lounge with TV and log fire. Fritham is in a particularly beautiful part of the New Forest, still largely undiscovered and with a wealth of wildlife. It is a wonderful base for walking, riding, cycling and touring. No smoking. Children 10 years and over welcome. Come and enjoy peace and quiet in this lovely corner of England. Bed and Breakfast £18 to £20.

HOOK. Mr Field, Oaklea Guest House, London Road, Hook, Near Basingstoke RG27 9LA (01256

762673). 🐾🐾 Oaklea is a fine Victorian house one mile from Junction 5 of M3. Ideally placed for the West Country with easy access to Southampton, Reading, London, Guildford also Heathrow and Gatwick Airports. Accommodation offered in single, double and family rooms, some en suite with TV. Guest lounge. Homely atmosphere. Bed and Breakfast from £25 to £44 including VAT. Licensed. AA Listed.

HYTHE, near Southampton. David and Marion Robinson, Four Seasons Hotel, Hamilton Road,

Hythe, Southampton SO45 3PD (01703 845151 or 846285). A warm welcome is extended to guests staying in this friendly, family run hotel. Situated on the edge of the New Forest it is ideal for touring. The picturesque market town of Hythe with its pubs and restaurants is one and a half miles distant. Here is an attractive Marina and a regular ferry service to Southampton and Isle of Wight. Golf, horse riding, wind surfing and other sports are available within five miles. Bedrooms have colour TVs and tea/coffee facilities; en suite facilities available. Highly praised for its standard of good home cooking, there is also a licensed bar, attractive garden and ample parking. Bed and Breakfast from £20; Evening Meal by arrangement.

WHEN MAKING ENQUIRIES PLEASE MENTION
FARM HOLIDAY GUIDES

LYMINGTON. Our Bench, Lodge Road, Lymington SO41 8HH (Tel & Fax: 01590 673141). ♥ ♥ ♥

COMMENDED. National Accessibility Scheme Category 3, Welcome Host, FHG Diploma Winner. A warm and friendly welcome awaits you in our large bungalow situated in a quiet area between the beautiful New Forest and the Coast. In the large garden stands a chalet which houses an indoor heated swimming/exercise pool, jacuzzi and sauna. We have double, twin and single rooms, all en suite and with colour TV. There is a separate lounge and a four-course breakfast is served in our dining room, where evening meals are also available if required. RAC Acclaimed, AA QQQQ Selected. For non-smokers only and sorry, no children. Tariff from £20 per person per night. Regional nominee England for Excellence 1997.

LYMINGTON. Mrs R. Sque, "Harts Lodge", 242 Everton Road, Everton, Lymington SO41 0HE (01590 645902).

Bungalow (non-smoking) set in three acres; large garden with wildlife pond and an abundance of bird life. Quiet location, convenient for A337, three miles west of Lymington. Friendly comfortable accommodation comprising three double bedrooms, two en suite, all with tea/coffee making facilities and colour TV. The sea and forest are five minutes away by car. Horse riding, golf, fishing and a real ale pub serving homemade meals are all nearby. Children and pets welcome. Bed and Breakfast from £18 per person per night.

LYMINGTON (New Forest). Jane and Mike Finch, "Dolphins", 6 Emsworth Road, Lymington SO41 9BL (01590 676108 or 679545; Fax: 01590 688275).

"Dolphins" is a very comfortable and homely Victorian cottage offering warm hospitality and the highest standard of accommodation. Single, twin, double and family rooms all have colour TV and tea/coffee making facilities; en suite available if required. Spacious and very comfortable sitting room with open log fire (in winter) and colour TV with satellite. Choice of breakfast; traditional home-cooked evening meals available. Very quiet position, centrally located, just five minutes' walk from railway/bus/coach stations and ferry. Beautiful Forest walks, excellent cycle rides in and around Lymington and the New Forest (maps provided, mountain bikes available). Leisure club facilities. Open all year. From £16 per person per night; Evening meals optional. Children half price. Access/Visa/Mastercard accepted. Please write or telephone for brochure.

LYNDHURST. Mrs E.M. Rowland, Forest Cottage, High Street, Lyndhurst SO43 7BH (01703 283461). ETB Listed *COMMENDED.* Charming 300 year old cottage.

Guests' sitting room with TV and a library of natural history, referece books, maps and local literature. Tea/coffee always available. Warm, pretty bedrooms: one double, one twin/double, one single. The garden contains an interesting collection of plants, some unusual. Lyndhurst is the centre of the New Forest, convenient for the many inland and coastal attractions and activities provided by the area. There is a wide choice of food in the village and nearby. Private parking. No smoking please. Bed and Breakfast from £18 per person per night.

Terms quoted in this publication may be subject to increase if rises in costs necessitate

NEW FOREST. Mrs Sandra Hocking, Southernwood, Plaitford Common, Salisbury Road, Near Romsey (01794 323255 or 322577). Modern country family home, surrounded by farmland, on the edge of the New Forest. Two double, one family and one twin bedrooms. Terms from £14. Full English breakfast. Cots and high chairs available for babies. Four miles from M27 off A36. Salisbury, Southampton 11 miles, Stonehenge 17 miles. Portsmouth half an hour. Winchester 14 miles, Romsey five miles. Within easy reach of Continental ferries. Large garden. Ample parking. Lounge area for guests. TV. Tea/coffee always available. Horse riding, golf, fishing, swimming, walking in New Forest 10 minutes. Local inns for good food. Open all year.

NEW FOREST. Mrs V. Burgess, Picket Hill, Canada Road, West Wellow SO51 6DD (01794 322550). A large country house in a quiet, secluded position with views over the New Forest. The house is set in six acres of gardens and paddocks with direct access onto the Forest for walking or riding. There is a good pub and restaurant within walking distance and Romsey, Salisbury, Southampton and Winchester are all an easy drive. Picket Hill is an ideal base for a New Forest holiday; all rooms have en suite facilities and prices are from £18 per person for Bed and Breakfast with special rates for families. Horses and dogs accepted by prior arrangement.

NEW FOREST. Mrs J. Pearce, "St. Ursula", 30 Hobart Road, New Milton BH25 6EG (01425 613515). ♛ ♛ ♛ Large detached family home offering every comfort in a friendly relaxed atmosphere. Off Old Milton Road, New Milton. Third right past traffic lights. Ideal base for visiting New Forest with its ponies and beautiful walks; Salisbury, Bournemouth easily accessible. Sea one mile. Leisure centre with swimming pool etc, town centre and mainline railway to London minutes away. Twin (en suite), double, family, single rooms, all with handbasins and tea-making facilities. High standards maintained throughout; excellent beds. Two bathrooms, one shower, four toilets. Downstairs twin bedroom suitable for disabled persons. Children and pets welcome. Cot etc available. Pretty garden with barbecue which guests are welcome to use. Lounge with colour TV. Two dining rooms. Smoke detectors installed. Full central heating. Open all year. Bed and Breakfast from £18. AA Recommended QQQ.

NEW FOREST (Brockenhurst). Mrs Pauline Harris, Little Heathers, 13 Whitemoor Road, Brockenhurst SO42 7QG (01590 623512). Little Heathers is on the edge of the village close to open forest where ponies, cattle and deer roam free. Wonderful countryside for walking, cycling (local hire available), riding (stables nearby), golf courses. Lymington Yacht Basin approximately six miles, Southampton and Bournemouth a short drive away. Family room en suite, double/twin bedroom with private shower/bathroom. TV and tea/coffee making facilities in bedrooms. Full English breakfast, special diets can be catered for. Ground floor bedrooms. No smoking. Bed and Breakfast from £19 per person, with reduced rates for three nights plus. Out of season Short Break Specials. Children accepted. Brochure available.

HAMPSHIRE – THE NEW FOREST

One of the most extensive tracts of oak woodland in England, interspersed with heathland and modern plantations of conifers, the New Forest was used by William the Conqueror as a hunting reserve. Today it is popular with walkers and riders, and is home to deer and half-wild ponies. To find out more, call in at the Visitor Centre at Lyndhurst and learn about traditional customs.

NEW FOREST (near Beaulieu). Mrs M. Stone, Heathlands, Lepe Road, Langley SO45 1YT (01703 892517). A Bed and Breakfast bungalow near Beaulieu, just two miles from Lepe Beach, an unspoilt natural beach and country park opposite Isle of Wight; ferries at Lymington (half an hour's drive). Centrally situated for touring the New Forest which is especially beautiful in autumn and spring with the new-born foals; three miles to Beaulieu and Exbury Azalea Gardens (Rothschild's collection), half an hour to Southampton and one hour to Bournemouth. The bungalow offers large breakfast in comfortable bedrooms for non-smoking couples. All rooms have washbasins, central heating, tea-making facilities and colour TV. There is a shower room and WC. Bed and Breakfast from £15 per person per night. Car parking. SAE, please.

PETERSFIELD. Mrs Mary Bray, Nursted Farm, Buriton, Petersfield GU31 5RW (01730 264278).

Working farm. This late 17th century farmhouse, with its large garden, is open to guests throughout most of the year. Located quarter of a mile west of the B2146 Petersfield to Chichester road, one and a half miles south of Petersfield, the house makes an ideal base for touring the scenic Hampshire and West Sussex countryside. Queen Elizabeth Country Park two miles adjoining picturesque village of Buriton at the western end of South Downs Way. Accommodation consists of three twin-bedded rooms (one with washbasin), two bathrooms/toilets; sitting room/breakfast room. Children welcome, cot provided. Sorry, no pets. Car essential, ample parking adjoining the house. Bed and Breakfast only from £16.50 per adult, reductions for children under 12 years. Open all year except Christmas, March and April.

PORTSMOUTH. Graham and Sandra Tubb, "Hamilton House", 95 Victoria Road North, Southsea, Portsmouth PO5 1PS (Tel & Fax: 01705 823502). 👑👑

COMMENDED. Delightful AA Recommended/RAC Acclaimed family-run Guesthouse centrally located five minutes by car from Continental and Isle of Wight ferry terminals, M27, stations, city centre, University and sea front, tourist attractions, heritage area and museums. Bright, modern rooms, all centrally heated with colour TVs and tea-making facilities; some en suites available. Ideal touring base for Southern England. Full English, vegetarian and Continental breakfasts served from 6am (for early travellers). Nightly/weekly stays welcome all year. Bed and Breakfast £17 to £19 per person per night standard; £20.50 to £22.50 per person per night en suite.

PORTSMOUTH/SOUTHSEA. Mr and Mrs Willett, Oakleigh Guest House, 48 Festing Grove, Southsea PO4 9QD (01705 812276). Southern Tourist

Board Listed COMMENDED. Small family run guest house two minutes from sea. Double, twin, family or single rooms, all with colour TV, washbasins, central heating and tea/coffee making facilities. En suite rooms available. Special rates for Senior Citizens and weekly bookings. Children welcome. Bed and Breakfast from £14; Evening Meal from £6 per head. Reductions for children. Open all year including Christmas and Easter. Close by — historic ships and Navy and Marine museums. Ferry port 10 minutes by car. Courtesy car service from local railway/bus stations.

RINGWOOD (New Forest). Mrs Yvonne Nixon, "The Nest", 10 Middle Lane, Ringwood BH24 1LE

(Tel & Fax: 01425 476724; Mobile 0589 854505). This lovely Victorian house is situated in a quiet residential lane within five minutes' walk of Ringwood town centre. The ancient riverside market town has many good restaurants and inns. Ample parking is provided. Beautifully decorated, very clean and well maintained. Breakfast times are flexible and the meal is served in the delightful sunny conservatory overlooking the gardens. Pretty colour-co-ordinated "Laura Ashley"-style bedrooms with pine furnishings, washbasins, colour TV and tea/coffee making facilities. Local activities include fishing, golf, riding, swimming, visiting historic houses and forest walks. This is an excellent base to explore the New Forest with Bournemouth, Poole, Salisbury, Southampton and Portsmouth nearby. AA QQQQ Selected. Highly recommended. Bed and Breakfast from £16. No smoking in the bedrooms.

RINGWOOD (New Forest). Picket Hill House, Picket Hill, Ringwood BH24 3HH (01425 476173; Fax: 01425 470022). ✿✿ *HIGHLY COMMENDED.*

Welcome Host. This attractive family home is a large country house standing in a lovely garden. The heathlands of the New Forest where the ponies and deer roam free can be accessed direct from the grounds. Spacious en suite accommodation. Tea/coffee facilities, wide choice of breakfasts. TV lounge. Pay phone. Splendid spot for walking, riding, bird watching and fishing. Ideal for touring New Forest, Dorset, Wiltshire. Only 20/30 minutes' drive to Bournemouth and Eastleigh Airports, and Poole for cross Channel ferries. Bed and Breakfast from £18 per person (twin/double room). A warm welcome awaits you. AA QQQQ.

SOUTHAMPTON. Mrs Pat Ward, Ashelee Lodge, 36 Atherley Road, Shirley, Southampton SO1 5DQ (01703 222095). Welcome extended to all our guests, including those from overseas, in friendly Bed and Breakfast accommodation with varied menus. Bright comfortable bedrooms, pleasant dining room and TV lounge. Nice garden with dip pool, weather permitting. Near town centre and an excellent touring base; ideal for visits to several places of historic interest — Romsey, Winchester, Stonehenge, Salisbury, New Forest and Portsmouth. Near Southampton Docks for liners, ferries, Sealink Stena; M27 and train station easily accessible. Terms from £16 per night. Brochures sent on receipt of enquiries.

SOUTHAMPTON. Rose and Dick Pell, Verulam House, 181 Wilton Road, Shirley, Southampton SO1 5HY (01703 773293 or 0378 563096). Tourist Board Listed. Rose and Dick warmly welcome guests to their comfortable, warm, roomy Edwardian establishment, in a nice residential area. Good cuisine. One double or family, one twin, one single bedrooms all with TV and tea/coffee making facilities; two bathrooms — plenty of hot water. Car parking space. Five minutes by car to historic Southampton city noted for its parks; railway station 10 minutes. Airport, Cross Channel ferries and Isle of Wight within easy reach and not far from M27, M3, Portsmouth, Winchester, Bournemouth, New Forest and coast. Bed and Breakfast from £18 per person; Evening Meal from £7 per person. Half Board per person from £25 daily, from £170 weekly. Non-smokers only.

STOCKBRIDGE. Mr and Mrs A.P. Hooper, Carbery Guest House, Stockbridge SO20 6EZ (01264 810771). ♛ ♛ ♛ *COMMENDED.* RAC Acclaimed. AA Listed. Ann and Philip Hooper welcome you to Carbery Guest House situated on the A30, just outside the village of Stockbridge, overlooking the famous trout fishing River Test. This fine old Georgian House has one acre of landscaped gardens, with swimming pool. Stonehenge and numerous places of interest nearby; sporting and recreational facilities close at hand. Accommodation includes double, twin, family and single rooms, available with private facilities. Centrally heated with colour TV, tea and coffee making equipment, hair dryers, radio alarms. Cots, high chairs. Car essential, parking. Open January to December for Evening Dinner, Bed and Breakfast or Bed and Breakfast only. Terms on application.

WINCHESTER. Mrs O. Fetherston-Dilke, 85 Christchurch Road, Winchester SO23 9QY (Tel & Fax: 01962 868661). ♛ ♛ *COMMENDED.* Comfortable centrally heated Victorian family house in St. Cross area of Winchester, near the water meadows and the beautiful Chapel and Almhouses of St. Cross, five minutes' drive from City Centre. Double and twin (en suite) from £44; or single rooms from £22 per person — all bedrooms with TV. Access to rooms at all times. Children welcome. Ideal centre for touring Hampshire, with Salisbury, Stonehenge, New Forest, Beaulieu and Portsmouth all under an hour's drive. Off-street parking. Public transport two minutes' walk. Open all year. Non-smoking.

WINCHESTER. Lang House, 27 Chilbolton Avenue, Winchester SO22 5HE (Tel & Fax: 01962 860620). Winchester is one of the most beautiful cities in Britain and somewhere that demands exploration. Good accommodation is a must, and that is to be found at Lang House. Built at the beginning of the 20th century it has all the graciousness of buildings of that time. You will be warm in winter and enjoy the cool airy rooms in summer. Ample parking in the grounds and the house overlooks the Royal Winchester Golf Course. All bedrooms are comfortable and well furnished with colour TV and tea/coffee facilities. You can be assured of a warm and friendly welcome and Winchester has a plethora of good eateries. Bed and Breakfast from £20 per person.

WINCHESTER. Mrs A. Farrell, The Farrells, 5 Ranelagh Road, Winchester SO23 9TA (01962 869555). ♛ ♛ *COMMENDED.* Number Five is a delightful Victorian house within 15 minutes' walk of Winchester Cathedral, City Centre, the unique water meadows, and the ancient Hospital of Cross. The New Forest, Salisbury, Stonehenge, and the South Downs are within easy reach. The area is also excellent for short local walks and excursions. Single, double, family rooms, most with washbasins, two rooms en suite. We offer central heating, tea-making facilities and a TV lounge. There is a bathroom, shower room and two toilets. A splendid English Breakfast is served. Bed and Breakfast from £18 to £21.

WINCHESTER. Mrs S. Buchanan, "Acacia", 44 Kilham Lane, Winchester SO22 5PT (01962 852259; 0585 462993 mobile). ☙☙ *HIGHLY COMMEN-DED.* First class Tourist Board inspected accommodation in a peaceful location on the edge of the countryside, yet only a five minute drive from Winchester city centre. Excellent and easy access to road and rail communications to many tourist areas, all within one hour including London (by rail), Portsmouth, the New Forest, Salisbury, Stonehenge, etc. The accommodation consists of one double and two twin bedrooms, all of which have en suite or private bathroom and tea/coffee making facilities. Charming sitting room with satellite TV. Excellent choice of breakfast. Non-smokers only. Off street parking. Leave Winchester by the Romsey road, Kilham Lane is right at the second set of traffic lights. "Acacia" is 200 metres on the right. Bed and Breakfast from £20 to £22 per person.

WINCHESTER. Richard and Susan Pell, "The Lilacs", 1 Harestock Close, off Andover Road North, Littleton, Winchester SO22 6NP (01962 884122). This attractive Georgian-style family home offers comfortable, clean and friendly accommodation, together with excellent home cooking. Situated on the outskirts of Winchester off the B3420, overlooking beautiful countryside, yet only one and a half miles from the city centre, which is convenient for all the attractions in the area. One twin-bedded room and one double/family room, both with tea/coffee making facilities, TV and central heating. Cot, high chair, babysitting available. Ironing facilities. Full English Breakfast is served. Pets by prior arrangement. Non-smokers please. Open all year. Bed and Breakfast from £16. Reductions for children and long stays. From Winchester, on Andover Road North, take left turn after Mountbatten Court, and before Harestock Road.

WOODLANDS, NEW FOREST. Mrs Rosemary Sawyer, Glen Rest, Bourne Road, Woodlands, Southampton SO40 7GR (01703 812156). A warm welcome awaits in this comfortable detached house situated in quiet village on the borders of the beautiful New Forest. Two letting rooms both have TV, tea/coffee facilities and central heating. Pleasant garden with ample off road parking. Good local pub food. Glen Rest is just five minutes from Junction 1 on M27, off A336, and offers an ideal base for exploring the forest and its attractions, with south coast beaches and cities all within easy reach. Bed and Breakfast from £16 per person per night. Children under 12 years £8. Single occupancy £20. Sorry no smoking.

FOR THE MUTUAL GUIDANCE OF GUEST AND HOST

Every year literally thousands of holidays, short-breaks and overnight stops are arranged through our guides, the vast majority without any problems at all. In a handful of cases, however, difficulties do arise about bookings, which often could have been prevented from the outset.

It is important to remember that when accommodation has been booked, both parties — guests and hosts — have entered into a form of contract. We hope that the following points will provide helpful guidance.

GUESTS: When enquiring about accommodation, be as precise as possible. Give exact dates, numbers in your party and the ages of any children. State the number and type of rooms wanted and also what catering you require — bed and breakfast, full board, etc. Make sure that the position about evening meals is clear — and about pets, reductions for children or any other special points.

Read our reviews carefully to ensure that the proprietors you are going to contact can supply what you want. Ask for a letter confirming all arrangements, if possible.

If you have to cancel, do so as soon as possible. Proprietors do have the right to retain deposits and under certain circumstances to charge for cancelled holidays if adequate notice is not given and they cannot re-let the accommodation.

HOSTS: Give details about your facilities and about any special conditions. Explain your deposit system clearly and arrangements for cancellations, charges, etc, and whether or not your terms include VAT.

If for any reason you are unable to fulfil an agreed booking without adequate notice, you may be under an obligation to arrange alternative suitable accommodation or to make some form of compensation.

While every effort is made to ensure accuracy, we regret that FHG Publications cannot accept responsibility for errors, omissions or misrepresentation in our entries or any consequences thereof. Prices in particular should be checked because we go to press early. We will follow up complaints but cannot act as arbiters or agents for either party.

HEREFORD & WORCESTER

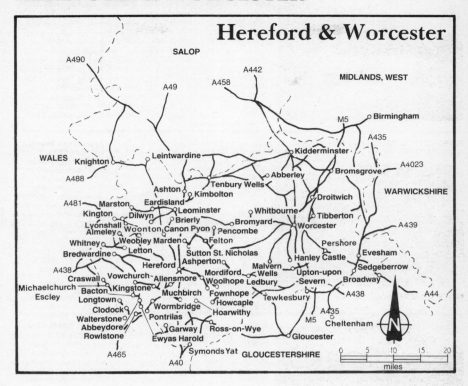

Hereford & Worcester

(Map showing towns and roads including: SALOP, MIDLANDS, WEST, WARWICKSHIRE, WALES, GLOUCESTERSHIRE, Birmingham, Kidderminster, Bromsgrove, Abberley, Droitwich, Tibberton, Worcester, Whitbourne, Pershore, Evesham, Sedgeberrow, Broadway, Cheltenham, Gloucester, Tewkesbury, Upton-upon-Severn, Malvern Wells, Hanley Castle, Ledbury, Ross-on-Wye, Symonds Yat, Hereford, Leominster, Tenbury Wells, Kimbolton, Knighton, Leintwardine, Ashton, Eardisland, Kington, Marston, Dilwyn, Brierly, Lyonshall, Almeley, Woonton, Canon Pyon, Pencombe, Bromyard, Whitney, Weobley, Marden, Felton, Bredwardine, Letton, Sutton St. Nicholas, Ashperton, Craswall, Vowchurch, Allensmore, Mordiford, Woolhope, Fownhope, Howcaple, Hoarwithy, Michaelchurch, Escley, Bacton, Kingstone, Muchbirch, Longtown, Clodock, Wormbridge, Walterstone, Pontrilas, Abbeydore, Garway, Rowlstone, Ewyas Harold; roads: A490, A49, A458, A442, A435, M5, A4023, A439, A44, A438, A488, A481, A465, A40, A435; scale 0–20 miles)*

BEWDLEY. Fleur Nightingale, Bank House, 14 Lower Park, Bewdley DY12 2DP (01299 402652).

Situated in the older part of the Georgian town of Bewdley, Bank House offers spacious bedrooms and a warm homely atmosphere from which to explore the delights of this unique area. Closely situated to the town centre with its fine architecture, antique shops, pubs and restaurants, leading on to Thomas Telford's bridge over the River Severn, through to the Severn Valley Railway. Almost adjoining Bank House is the Worcestershire Way giving easy access to a number of walks around the Wyre Forest. We are renowned for our generous breakfasts. Bed and Breakfast from £17 per person.

BROADWAY. Mrs Doreen Shaw, Milestone House Hotel, 122 High Street, Broadway WR12 7AJ (01386 853432).

Milestone House Hotel

Unspoilt 17th century Grade II Listed building in beautiful area. Conveniently situated on the High Street close to a variety of shops and restaurants. We have four bedrooms all en suite and with colour TV, tea/coffee tray, hair dryer, etc. Breakfast is served in delightful conservatory overlooking a pretty garden. Picnic hampers are available complete with wine. Guests can look forward to a friendly welcome and enjoyable stay at Milestone House which has a warm country house atmosphere. Ideally situated for touring the Cotswolds and Stratford-upon-Avon is only 15 miles away; Oxford, Blenheim Palace also within easy reach. Please write, or telephone, for our brochure.

BROADWAY. Mrs Jane Hill, Lower Field Farm, Willersey, Broadway WR11 5HF (01386 858273 or 0976 897525; Fax: 01386 854608).

Lower Field Farm offer genuine farmhouse comfort and hospitality in a late 17th century Cotswold stone and brick farmhouse looking out onto the Cotswold Hills. Delightful rooms, all en suite with tea/coffee making facilities and TV. This peaceful location provides an ideal base from which to explore the Cotswolds, Stratford-upon-Avon, Warwick Castle, Oxford, cheltenham and beyond. Evening meal by arrangement or wealth of good eating houses nearby. Open all year. Bed with full English Breakfast from £20 per person. Pets and children welcome.

BROMYARD. Mrs G. Williams, Littlebridge House, Norton, Bromyard HR7 4PN (Tel & Fax: 01885 482471).

Littlebridge stands in large gardens and open countryside with panoramic views to Bromyard Downs and the Malvern Hills. A Victorian gentleman's residence formerly built as the Estate Manager's home of the Saltmarshe Estate, Littlebridge has been decorated to high standards with period furniture and comfort in mind. Bedrooms have co-ordinated fabrics, en suite facilities, colour TV and hospitality trays; cots also available. Log fires burn in the lounge and dining room on cooler days, where hearty breakfasts and evening meals are served using local produce and some grown in our own walled garden. Positioned just three miles off the A44 Littlebridge is an ideal place to take a break or for touring the counties of Hereford and Worcester which contain many areas of outstanding natural beauty, are rich in black and white villages and towns, and civil war history is in abundance.

CLIFTON UPON TEME. David and Anne Blair-Gordon, The Threshing Barn, Harpley, Clifton upon Teme WR6 6HG (Tel & Fax: 01886 853578).

Luxury period barn offering olde world charm created by a wealth of oak beams and antique furniture. Peacefully yet conveniently situated in the beautiful Teme Valley on the Hereford/Worcestershire border between the pretty award-winning village of Clifton upon Teme and the glorious Malvern Hills. Discover an unspoilt area of hidden England full of interests and history yet only an hour's drive from Shakespeare country and the Cotswolds. Alternatively why not just relax and let the world go by. Delightful bedrooms all with private facilities, colour TV, tea/coffee. Try our special interest breaks or sporting packages. Bed and Breakfast from £19.50 per person with reductions for two or more nights. This is a no smoking establishment and is unsuitable for children.

CROWLE. Mrs Lucy Harris, Green Farm, Crowle Green, Worcester WR7 4AB (01905 381807). 🐝

COMMENDED. Green Farm is a peaceful and substantial oak-beamed Georgian farmhouse set in a large garden and 25 acres of farmland. Architecturally Grade II Listed. Accommodation consists of twin-bedded/double or single room with own basin, private bathroom, tea/coffee making facilities and central heating. Cosy lounge with wood burning stove and colour TV. Full English breakfast included in tariff. Evening meal available on request or our local country pub within easy walking distance offers good food. Open all year. Bed and Breakfast from £20. Just off M5 Junction 6, well situated for Worcester, Malverns, Stratford and Cotswolds.

Terms quoted in this publication may be subject to increase if rises in costs necessitate

DROITWICH. Mrs Tricia Havard, Phepson Farm, Himbleton, Droitwich WR9 7JZ (01905 391205).

👑👑 *HIGHLY COMMENDED.* **Working farm.** AA QQQQ. We offer a warm welcome and a comfortable and relaxed atmosphere in our 17th century farmhouse with oak beamed lounge and dining room. Situated on peaceful stock farm just outside the unspoilt village of Himbleton where visitors may see farm animals and walk on Wychavon Way. Full English breakfast. Double, twin and family rooms, all with en suite facilities, colour TV, radio alarms and tea/coffee making. Convenient for M5, M42 and central for touring the many places of interest in the Heart of England. Featured on "Wish You Were Here". Bed and Breakfast from £20. Self catering flat also available.

FELTON HOUSE
Felton, Near Hereford HR1 3PH
Telephone: (01432) 820366

Marjorie and Brian Roby offer guests, children and pets a very warm welcome to their home, a country house of immense character set in beautiful tranquil gardens in the heart of unspoilt rural England. Relax with refreshments in the library, drawing room, or garden room. Taste excellent evening meals at local inns. Sleep in an antique four-poster or brass bed and awake refreshed to enjoy, in a superb Victorian dining room, the breakfast you have selected from a wide choice of traditional and vegetarian dishes. Felton House is 8 miles from Hereford, Leominster and Bromyard off A417 between A49 and A465.

English Tourist Board
HIGHLY COMMENDED
👑👑

B&B £21 with ensuite or private bathroom.   AA **QQQQ** Selected.

GOLDEN VALLEY. Mrs Powell, The Old Vicarage, Vowchurch, Hereford HR2 0QD (Tel & Fax: 01981 550357). HETB 👑👑 *COMMENDED.* Warm hospitality guaranteed in this Victorian house of character, once the home of Lewis Carroll's brother. Ideal for walking/cycling through rich agricultural land, by historic churches and castles, near the Black Mountains (Welsh Border) and Offa's Dyke Path. Visit Hay-on-Wye, world famous town of books, or the Mappa Mundi; golf course five minutes away. Enjoy our attractively presented quality breakfasts after restful nights in individually decorated en suite rooms (single, double, family, twin) from £19 per person; refreshment trays, fresh fruit and flowers await you. Be greeted with a freshly baked scone and homemade preserves. Dinner from £11, including vegetarian and special diets, may be ordered in advance. Fresh local produce used.

GREAT MALVERN. Mrs F.W. Coates, Mill House, 16 Clarence Road, Great Malvern WR14 3EH (01684 562345). Originally a 13th century Water Mill at the foot of the beautiful Malvern Hills. Situated in tranquil grounds with croquet lawns and hill views. A few minutes' walk from the town centre or Great Malvern Station. Malvern is ideal for touring the Cotswolds, Severn and Wye Valleys and Welsh Marches. Comfortable accommodation with full central heating, washbasin and tea/coffee making facilities in all bedrooms (one double room with shower en suite). Guest bathroom, shower room, two separate WCs. Parking within grounds. NO SMOKING! Bed and English Breakfast from £18.

HEREFORD. Ashgrove House, Wellington Marsh, Hereford HR4 8DU (01432 830608). ♛♛ *HIGHLY COMMENDED.* Mike and Sandra Fletcher welcome you to luxurious accommodation with high standard furnishings and lovely gardens. Situated in a quiet rural location, overlooking cider apple orchards, three miles north of the historic Cathedral City of Hereford. Lovely walks nearby, golf and salmon fishing 10 minutes by car. Double, twin-bedded or single rooms, all en suite with TV and tea-making facilities. Good pub food in old inns nearby. Bed and full English Breakfast £18 to £22 per person.

Ashgrove

HEREFORD. Mrs R.T. Andrews, Webton Court Farmhouse, Kingstone, Hereford HR2 9NF (01981 250220). ♛♛ **Working farm.** Black and white Georgian farmhouse in the Wye Valley on a working farm. Situated midway between Hay-on-Wye, Ross-on-Wye just off the B4348, ideal for touring places of local interest. We offer a selection of bedrooms including en suite with TV, tea/coffee making facilities and washbasins. Large parties catered for. Rates £16 single, £15 per person double and £20 per person en suite; Evening Meal £8 per person by prior arrangement. Children welcome at reduced rates.

HEREFORD. Mr David Jones, Sink Green Farm, Rotherwas, Hereford HR2 6LE (01432 870223). ♛♛ **Working farm, join in.** Warm and friendly atmosphere awaits your arrival at this 16th century farmhouse, on the banks of the River Wye. Three miles south of the cathedral city of Hereford, with Ross-on-Wye, Leominster, Ledbury, Malvern and the Black Mountains within easy reach. All rooms en suite, tea/coffee making facilities and colour TV. One room with four-poster, family room by arrangement. Guests' own lounge. Pets by arrangement. Bed and Breakfast from £19 per person. AA QQQQ.

HEREFORD. Mrs Diana Sinclair, Holly House Farm, Allensmore, Hereford HR2 9BH (01432 277294; mobile 0589 830223). ♛♛ *COMMENDED.* Spacious luxury farmhouse and over 10 acres of land with horses, situated in beautiful and peaceful open countryside. Bedrooms en suite or with private bathroom, central heating, TV and tea/coffee making facilities. We are only five miles south west of Hereford city centre. Ideal base for Welsh Borders, market towns, Black Mountains, Brecon and Malvern Hills and the Wye Valley. We have a happy family atmosphere and pets are welcome. Brochure on request. From £18 per person per night and with your delicious English breakfast you will be fit for the whole day!

KIDDERMINSTER. Ms Nicola Deakin, The Granary Hotel, Heath Lane, Kidderminster DY10 4BS

(01562 777535; Fax: 01562 77722). ❤ ❤ ❤ *COMMEN-DED.* A friendly, independently owned small hotel with 18 modern en suite bedrooms. Visitors are assured of a warm welcome and comfortable stay, fantastic views of the Abberley Hills, pleasant gardens and plenty of car parking. Traditional Carvery Restaurant offers "olde worlde" charm with a mouthwatering sweet trolley. Bar food and room service also available. Golf and fishing available close by together with several places of historic interest — Hartlebury Castle, Harrington Hall. Dogs and children welcome. Easy access for disabled visitors — single storey building. Fully licensed. Terms available on request.

KIMBOLTON. Mrs Jean Franks, The Fieldhouse Farm, Kimbolton, Near Leominster HR6 0EP

(01568 614789). ❤ ❤ *COMMENDED.* **Working farm.** A warm friendly welcome awaits you on our working family farm three miles from the attractive market town of Leominster, and 11 miles from the historic town of Ludlow. We offer excellent accommodation in peaceful surroundings, with truly magnificent views. The comfortable and spacious bedrooms have tea-making facilities. Private bathroom available. There is an attractive guests' sitting/dining room with oak beams and inglenook fireplace. Home cooking is a speciality and delicious breakfasts are served by Mrs Franks, a former Home Economics teacher; Evening Meals on request. Personal attention and high standards are assured. Bed and Breakfast from £18 per person.

LEDBURY. Mrs Blandford, Underhill Farm, Putley, Ledbury HR8 2QR (01531 670695). ❤ ❤

COMMENDED. A warm homely welcome awaits you at Underhill Farm, a 16th century Listed farmhouse, with oak beams and hop kilns, surrounded by large mature gardens and 140 acres of arable land and orchards nestling at the foot of "The Woolhope Dome" a site of natural beauty, with breathtaking views of the Malvern Hills and the Cotswolds to the Black Mountains. Ideally situated for touring, walking, riding and relaxing. One large double bedroom en suite/shower room with tea/coffee facilities. Guests' own sitting room and dining room. Wholesome breakfasts with homemade preserves, free range eggs. Two award-winning inns nearby serving excellent evening meals. Bed and Breakfast from £18 per person per night.

LEDBURY. Mrs Jane West, Church Farm, Coddington, Ledbury HR8 1JJ (01531 640271). Tourist

Board Listed *COMMENDED.* **Working farm.** This accommodation is on a working farm with a Black and White 16th century Listed farmhouse, close to the Malvern Hills in quiet hamlet four and a half miles from Ledbury. It is ideal for touring. Warm hospitality assured in happy, relaxed atmosphere. There is accommodation in three double bedrooms, two with washbasins; bathroom, toilet; sittingroom; diningroom. Log fires, television. Open all year. Car essential, parking. Situated midway between Ross-on-Wye, Hereford, Gloucester and Worcester. Bed and Breakfast from £20. SAE, please, for full details. Also available, self catering cottage in immaculate condition (4 KEYS HIGHLY COMMENDED).

LEOMINSTER. Mrs J.S. Connop, Broome Farm, Pembridge, Leominster HR6 9JY (01544 388324). Working farm, join in. A comfortable 17th century farmhouse situated in beautiful rural Herefordshire midway between the picturesque Black and White villages of Pembridge and Eardisland, seven miles from the market town of Kington; Leominster six miles. An excellent stopping-off place on a journey to Wales or South Coast. Two double and two twin-bedded rooms; two bathrooms, toilet; sittingroom and diningroom. Cot, babysitting and reduced rates for children. Pets permitted but not encouraged. Car essential, ample parking. Open all year. Bed and Breakfast from £15 per night including bedtime drink.

MALVERN. Nick and Amanda Mobbs, Rock House, 144 West Malvern Road, Malvern WR14 4NJ (01684 574536). ♛♛ *APPROVED.* Attractive family-run Early Victorian Guest House situated high on hills in quiet peaceful atmosphere with superb views over 40 miles. Ideal for rambling on hills or open country. Eleven comfortable bedrooms, most overlooking our splendid view, en suite facilities available. TV lounge. Separate quiet room. Licensed bar enhancing the excellent cuisine. Groups welcome. Parking on premises. Bed and Breakfast from £19. Open all year; special Christmas package. Stamp only please for brochure. Also available pretty cottage for self catering holidays.

MALVERN. Barbara and Richard Rowan, The Red Gate, 32 Avenue Road, Great Malvern WR14 3BJ (Tel & Fax: 01684 565013). ♛♛♛ *HIGHLY COMMENDED.* Guestaccomm, RAC Highly Acclaimed, Which? Hotel Guide. Come, relax and be pampered in our centrally heated, beautifully restored Victorian hotel. Situated on a tree-lined road near to Great Malvern railway station, town centre and hills. Parking on the premises. Renowned for friendly informal atmosphere — "It's like coming home". Six individually decorated bedrooms with en suite facilities, all non-smoking with colour TV and tea/coffee facilities. We offer a breakfast menu to suit all tastes. Vegetarians welcome. Residential licence. Enjoy a good book from a wide selection in our attractive lounge. On better days relax on the verandah or sit in the south-walled garden and forget your cares. Bed and Breakfast from £25.

MALVERN near. Ann and Brian Porter, Croft Guest House, Bransford, Worcester WR6 5JD (01886 832227). ♛♛ AA QQ Listed. 16th-18th century part black and white cottage-style country house situated in the River Teme Valley, four miles from Worcester and Malvern. Croft House is central for visiting numerous attractions in Worcester, Hereford, Severn Valley and surrounding countryside. There is fishing close by and an 18-hole golf course opposite. Facilities include three en suite rooms (two double, one family) and two double rooms with washbasins, hospitality trays. Double glazing, central heating, residential licence and home cooked dinners. There is a TV lounge, sauna and large jacuzzi for guests' use. A cot and baby listening service are provided. Bed and Breakfast from £18 to £25. Festive Christmas and New Year Breaks available.

MALVERN WELLS. Mrs J.L. Morris, Brickbarns Farm, Hanley Road, Malvern Wells WR14 4HY (016845 61775). Working farm. Brickbarns, a 200 year old mixed farm, is situated two miles from Great Malvern at the foot of the Malvern Hills, 300 yards from the bus service and one and a half miles from the train. The house, which is 300 years old, commands excellent views of the Malvern Hills and guests are accommodated in one double, one single and one family bedrooms with washbasins; two bathrooms, shower room, two toilets; sitting room and dining room. children welcome and cot and babysitting offered. Central heating. Car essential, parking. Open Easter to October for Bed and Breakfast from £15 nightly per person. Reductions for children and Senior Citizens. Birmingham 40 miles, Hereford 20, Gloucester 17, Stratford 35 and the Wye Valley is just 30 miles.

HEREFORD & WORCESTERSHIRE – THE HEART OF ENGLAND!
A beautiful county which includes The Vale of Evesham and the rugged – if petite – Malvern Hills. It has been designated an "Area of Outstanding Beauty". Places of interest include The Avoncroft Museum of Buildings, Brockhampton, Ross-on-Wye, The Teme Valley and The Hereford & Worcester County Museum.

NEWNHAM BRIDGE. Mrs Gill Morgan, Deepcroft Farm House, Newnham Bridge, Tenbury Wells WR15 8JA (01584 781412). Set in the Teme Valley, off the A456, on the borders of Worcestershire, Herefordshire and Shropshire this secluded old farmhouse, with five acres of garden and orchard, offers easy access to the Severn Valley Railway, the historic towns of Ludlow and Worcester as well as to the Welsh Marches and the Shropshire Hills. Ideal for fishermen, cyclists and tourists the accommodation comprises two twin-bedded and one single room, all with hand basins, shaver points, and tea/coffee making facilities. A comfortable sitting room with colour TV is also available for guests. Bed and full English Breakfast £15.

OMBERSLEY. Mrs M. Peters, Tytchney, Boreley, Ombersley WR9 0HZ (01905 620185). 16th Century medieval Hall House cottage in peaceful country lane, two and a half miles from Ombersley. Ideal walking, touring Heart of England, fishing in River Severn and just half a mile to Ombersley Golf Course. Double, family and single rooms; cot available. Bed and Breakfast from £13.50.

PERSHORE. Jim and Margaret Coward, Oldbury House, George Lane, Wyre Piddle, Pershore WR10 2HX (Tel & Fax: 01386 553754; E-mail: james.coward@virgin.net). Warm, friendly welcome assured in a modern, centrally heated house situated on a quiet side road just off the A4538 in Wyre Piddle, two miles from Pershore. Meals available at nearby Anchor Inn. Guests facilities include lounge, garden, comfortably furnished bedrooms with colour TV, refreshment facilities, hair dryers and alarm cloack/radios. One bedroom has twin beds with adjacent private bathroom the other is a double with en suite bathroom. Ample, safe, off-road parking. Telephone, fax, e-mail, full computer facilities available on request. French is spoken. Bed and Breakfast from £19. No smoking please.

ROSS-ON-WYE. Geoffrey and Josephine Baker, Brookfield House, Ledbury Road, Ross-on-Wye HR9 7AT (01989 562188). 👑 👑 *APPROVED.* Large Queen Anne Georgian House close to town centre on M50 entrance into town. All rooms have TV, washbasin, central heating and tea/coffee facilities; some with bath/shower and WC. A good choice of breakfast (diets catered for). A large private car park. Ideal for overnight stop-offs. Bed and Breakfast from £18.50 per person. AA and RAC Listed, Travellers Britain Recommended.

ROSS-ON-WYE. Mrs Mary Savidge, Wharton Farm, Weston under Penyard, Ross-on-Wye HR9 5SX (01989 750255). 👑 *COMMENDED.* Situated on the edge of the Royal Forest of Dean and the Wye Valley,this is an arable farm. Part 17th and 18th century farmhouse. Four miles from Ross-on-Wye, just off the A40, 14 miles from Gloucester. Easily accessible from the M50/M5 motorway, also South Wales and the M4 motorway. Excellent accommodation comprises two double rooms — one en suite, one with private bathroom and shared separate toilet, one twin room with en suite shower room and shared separate toilet. All rooms have colour TV and tea/coffee making facilities. Children by arrangement. Bed and Breakfast from £19.

ROSS-ON-WYE. Mrs M.E. Drzymalska, Thatch Close, Llangrove, Ross-on-Wye HR9 6EL (01989 770300). 👑 👑 *COMMENDED.* **Working farm, join in.** Secluded Georgian farmhouse set in large colourful gardens in 13 acres of pasture situated in the beautiful Wye Valley between Ross and Monmouth. Thatch Close offers a comfortable, homely atmosphere where guests are welcome to help feed the sheep, cows, calves, or just relax and enjoy this traditionally run farm. Places of scenic beauty and historic attractions nearby include Forest of Dean, Black Mountains, Cathedral Cities, old castles and buildings. Guests have their own lounge and dining room with colour TV. Twin bedroom and one double room, both with bathrooms en suite, one double room with private bathroom; all bathrooms have showers. Central heating. Non-smokers please. Breakfast and optional evening meal are prepared using mainly home grown produce. Vegetarian and diabetic meals arranged. Bed and Breakfast from £15 to £19 with reductions for longer stays and reduced rates for children. SAE for further details.

ROSS-ON-WYE. The Skakes, Glewstone, Ross-on-Wye HR9 6AZ (01989 770456). 18th century

former farmhouse, set in an acre of pleasant gardens at the heart of the Wye Valley and Herefordshire's rolling unspoilt countryside. Close to Ross, Hereford, Monmouth and the Forest of Dean, with a wealth of places to visit and walk. Our bedrooms are mostly en suite and all contain colour TV, clock radios and beverage trays and downstairs are cosy lounges (with log fires when cold). We are well served for excellent local eating places on which we can advise you, and also local attractions. Children aged 10 years and over welcome and dogs by arrangement. Bed and Breakfast from £16.

ROSS-ON-WYE. Mrs H. Smith, Old Kilns, Howle Hill, Ross-on-Wye HR9 5SP (01989 562051). 🐾🐾
HIGHLY COMMENDED. A high quality bed and breakfast establishment in picturesque, quiet village location. Centrally heated, private parking. Easy walking distance to village inn where home-cooked meals are served. Some rooms with super king-size bed plus en suite shower, toilet; also brass king-size four-poster bed with private bathroom and jacuzzi. Colour TV and tea/coffee making facilities in bedrooms. Lounge with log fire. Full English breakfast. Central for touring Cotswolds, Malvern, Stratford-upon-Avon, Wye Valley and Royal Forest of Dean. Open all year. Bed and Breakfast from £10 per person. Children and pets welcome (high chair, cots and babysitting service provided). Please telephone for free brochure. Self catering cottages also available.

ROSS-ON-WYE. Jean and James Jones, The Arches Hotel, Walford Road, Ross-on-Wye HR9 5PT

(01989 563348). 🐾🐾🐾 Small family-run hotel set in half an acre of lawned garden, ideally situated only 10 minutes' walk from town centre. All rooms are furnished and decorated to a high standard, have views of the lawned garden, tea/coffee making facilities and colour TV; some rooms en suite. Also one ground floor en suite room available. Full central heating. There is a delightful Victorian-style conservatory to relax in and the garden to enjoy in the summer months. Licensed. Ample parking in grounds. A warm and friendly atmosphere with personal service. Bed and Breakfast £18, en suite rooms £22; Dinner by arrangement. Generous weekly reductions. AA Listed, RAC Acclaimed, Les Routiers Award. Please telephone or send SAE for colour brochure.

ROSS-ON-WYE near. Mrs L.M. Baker, Walnut Tree Cottage Hotel, Symonds Yat West, Near

Ross-on-Wye HR9 6BN (01600 890828). 🐾🐾🐾 We offer a high standard of accommodation in a friendly and relaxing atmosphere. Walnut Tree Cottage Hotel is set high on the River Wye and enjoys outstanding panoramic alpine-style views. There are excellent river and woodland walks. Above all the area offers the quiet timelessness of the English countryside at its finest and a true escape from the pressures and bustle of everyday life. All rooms are centrally heated; tea/coffee facilities; log fires in season. Bed and Breakfast from £24.50 per person in en suite room. Open 1st March to 31st October. Two night half board breaks (1st March to 3rd June) £72 per person excluding Public and Bank holidays.

WINFORTON. Mrs Jackie Kingdon, Winforton Court, Winforton HR3 6EA (01544 328498). A warm

welcome and country hospitality awaits you at historic 16th century Winforton Court, former home of Roger De Mortimer, Earl of March. Unwind and enjoy spacious and elegant surroundings in the beautiful Wye Valley. Set in old world gardens with rural views, Winforton Court offers delightfully furnished bedrooms all with private bathrooms, one with four-poster bed. Luxurious drwing room, library with wealth of local guide books, etc. Enjoy a hearty breakfast (vegetarian available) in historic former court room with its magnificent early 17th century oak staircase. The house abounds in oak beams, open fires, early stencilling, interesting collections of old china, samplers and antiques. Bed and Breakfast from £20 per person per night. 10% discount for five or more nights.

WORCESTER. "St. Helen's", Green Hill, London Road, Worcester WR5 2AA (01905 354035). A

particularly handsome Grade II Listed period residence with exceptional and spacious family accommodation. Set within partly walled gardens of approximately one third of an acre, close to town centre. Car parking. TV lounge. Tea facilities. Airport collection/return. Single £20, double £30, family room £40.

WORCESTER. Eddie and Sylvia Lewis, Heathside, Worcester Road, Fernhill Heath, Worcester WR3 7UA (Tel and Fax: 01905 458245). ♛ ♛ ♛ *COMMEN-*

DED. This Guest House offers accommodation in nine bedrooms, six with full en suite facilities, all with TV and tea/coffee making equipment. Situated two miles from Junction 6 of the M5, it is very near to pubs and a steak bar. Worcester itself offers a riverside racecourse, steamer trips on the River Severn, the Royal Worcester Porcelain Works and a museum. Within easy reach of Severn Valley Railway, Bewdley Safari Park, Black Country Museum, Dudley Zoo, Warwick Castle and the Royal Shakespeare Theatre. Bed and Breakfast from £21 single standard, £38 twin/double standard, en suite single £27, en suite twin £46. Reduced rates for children under 10. Open all year.

WORCESTER near. Miss Jo Morris, Knowle Farm, Suckley, Near Worcester WR6 5DJ (01886 884347). Part-timbered 17th-century farmhouse with 25

acres grassland, used mainly for horses. Adjacent to a small, quiet country inn, the house is in an elevated position with unrivalled views of the Malvern Hills and offers accommodation all year round. Large colourful garden. The quaint market towns of Bromyard, Ledbury and Hereford are nearby, and Knowle Farm is in the heart of a fruit-growing area where visitors enjoy the magnificent Spring blossoms. Superb walking country. Two double and two single bedrooms (one with washbasin); bathroom, two toilets; sitting-room with log fire, diningroom. Central heating keeps the house comfortable throughout the year. Car essential — parking. Traditional hearty English Breakfast. Fresh farm eggs. Bed and Breakfast from £15 (bedtime drink); no single supplement. This is a non-smoking establishment.

HERTFORDSHIRE

RICKMANSWORTH. Mrs Elizabeth Childerhouse, 6 Swallow Close, Nightingale Road, Rickmansworth WD3 2DZ (01923 720069). Tourist Board Listed. Large detached house situated in a quiet cul-de-sac with the centre of Rickmansworth only a short walk away. It is a small picturesque old town where there are many places to eat. We are five minutes' walk from the underground station, half an hour to central London. Full breakfast served with homemade bread and preserves. Vegetarians and Coeliacs catered for. Tea and coffee making facilities in rooms. Off street parking. Convenient for M25 and Watford. No pets. This is a non-smoking household. Bed and Breakfast from £19.

KENT

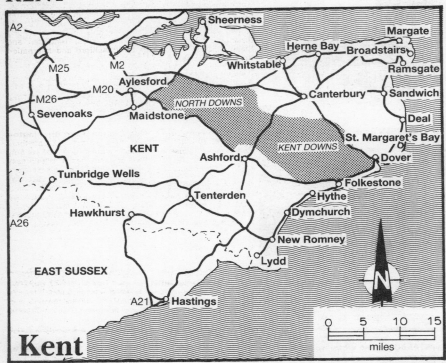

KENT

Kent

ALDINGTON. Ros and John Martin, Hogben Farm, Church Lane, Aldington, Ashford TN25 7EH (01233 720219). Tourist Board Listed. This farmhouse, dating from the 16th century, lies in a very quiet location down its own drive, set amongst extensive gardens and lawns. It is an ideal centre for visits to Canterbury, Rye, Tenterden, etc, and handy for the ferries, the Channel Tunnel and Eurostar Ashford International Station. Accommodation includes one double room and two twin rooms with en suite facilities. A sittingroom with inglenook fireplace and colour TV is available for guests. Conservatory for guests' use. Good home cooking for your Evening Meal by arrangement. Open all year. Bed and Breakfast from £19.50.

ASHFORD near. Pam and Arthur Mills, Cloverlea, Bethersden, Ashford TN26 3DU (01233 820353). A warm welcome awaits in spacious new country bungalow in lovely peaceful location with large garden surrounded by views of fields and woods. Patio area for breakfast (when fine). Ideal for Folkestone, Euro Tunnel (half hour), Ashford International Station (10 minutes), London (one hour), Leeds and Sissinghurst Castles and Gardens, Rye, Canterbury. Superb accommodation in two twin rooms, one en suite (family), one with private bathroom; both have colour TV, tea/coffee, biscuits. Full central heating. Excellent breakfast, home made bread everyday. Ample safe parking. Close to village pubs. Bed and Breakfast from £17.50 per person. No smoking.

BETHERSDEN. The Old Barn, Bridge Farm, Bethersden TN26 3LE (01233 820434; Fax: 01233 820547; E-mail: bed-breakfast@goodnight.org.). A warm welcome awaits you at our 18th century Listed Barn set in beautiful garden. De Luxe bedrooms, en suite or private bathroom, invigorating "Power Showers", colour TV, tea/coffee, radio alarm, etc. Good central base for visiting Sissinghurst, Leeds and Bodiam Castles, Tenterden and Steam Railway, Rye, Canterbury; Ashford and Internation Station 10 minutes, Euro Tunnel 20 minutes, Folkestone and Dover 30 minutes. Stay overnight before/after you Continental trip. Local station three miles, with London about an hour. Open all year. Bed and Breakfast from £19. Just Bed £15. Discounts for children and longer stays. Non-smoking. Ample off-road parking. Credit Cards accepted.

South East England Tourist Board
MEMBER

BIRCHINGTON near. Mrs Liz Goodwin, Woodchurch Farmhouse, Woodchurch, Near Birchington CT7 0HE (01843 832468). This attractive Elizabethan/Georgian farmhouse is situated in a quiet rural area yet only two miles from long stretches of sandy beach. Within easy reach of Canterbury, Sandwich, Rye, Chilham and the cross Channel ferries. There is ample parking, a car is essential. Very comfortable bedrooms with tea/coffee making facilities. Sitting room with TV. Bathroom and shower for guests' use only. Separate beamed dining room. A warm welcome and a comfortable stay assured at Woodchurch. Bed and Breakfast from £16. Please write or telephone for further details.

CANTERBURY. Raemore Guest House, 33 New Dover Road, Canterbury CT1 3AS (01227 769740; Fax: 01227 769432). SETB Listed *COMMENDED.* Family-run, ideally situated near to Canterbury city centre with private car parking facilities. Central location for touring East Kent. All rooms have TV and tea/coffee facilities. Family rooms from £12.50 per person, doubles from £18.50 per person, en suite rooms from £22.50 per person, single rooms from £20. All with full English breakfast.

CANTERBURY. The White House, 6 St. Peters Lane, Canterbury CT1 2BP (01227 761836). 🌑🌑🌑 A superb spacious Regency house in a quiet lane within the old city walls. All nine rooms are tastefully decorated and all are en suite with colour TV and tea/coffee making facilities. The famous Marlowe Theatre is close by as well as the Cathedral which is two minutes' walk away. A warm welcome awaits you at this lovely family-run house. Open all year. Bed and Breakfast from £45 to £65 for family room, £40 to £50 for double and £30 for single.

CANTERBURY. N.J. Ellen, Crockshard Farmhouse, Wingham, Canterbury CT3 1NY (01227 720464; Fax: 01227 721125). Exceptionally attractive farmhouse in beautiful gardens, pasture and woodlands on a 20 acre smallholding. Lots of different animals to see. Ideally situated for visiting any part of Kent — Canterbury 15 minutes, Dover 20 minutes, Folkestone 30 minutes. Accommodation comprises three family rooms one en suite and one double room en suite, all have tea/coffee making facilities, hair dryer and ironing facitiies. Separate guest lounge with log fire, TV and pianola. Children welcome, reduced rates if sharing with parents. Well behaved pets welcome. Prices from £17.50. Excellent eating establishments locally.

CANTERBURY. Maria and Alistair Wilson, Chaucer Lodge Guest House, 62 New Dover Road, Canterbury CT1 3DT (01227 459141). 👑👑 *HIGHLY COMMENDED.* A highly recommended friendly guest house which is elegantly decorated and immaculately clean. Fully double glazed and centrally heated. Secure parking. Seven bedrooms en suite, including family rooms, with colour TV, tea/coffee making facilities, radio/alarm and hair dryer. Open all year round. 10 minutes' walk to city centre, cathedral, bus and rail stations. Hospital and cricket ground only five minutes' walk. Ideal base for touring Kent and for trips to the Continent. Bed and Breakfast from £19 per person.

CANTERBURY. R. & D.J. Martin, The Tanner of Wingham, 44 High Street, Wingham, Canterbury CT3 1AB (01227 720532). Family run restaurant with bed and breakfast accommodation, situated in a building dating from 1440 in historic and picturesque village, midway between Canterbury and Sandwich. Ideal for touring East Kent and convenient for docks and Chunnel. Relax in a friendly atmosphere and enjoy optional evening meal from our monthly-changing menu — which includes the largest vegetarian and vegan options in East Kent. Rooms are individually decorated with antique beds and furniture — some rooms heavily beamed. Families welcome, cot available. The many local attractions include historic houses and gardens, wildlife and bird parks. Don't forget your day trip to the Continent! Bed and Breakfast from £12.25 to £20; Evening Meal £12.50.

CANTERBURY. Mrs A. Hunt, Bower Farmhouse, Stelling Minnis, Near Canterbury CT4 6BB (01227 709430). 👑👑 *HIGHLY COMMENDED.* Anne and Nick Hunt welcome you to Bower Farmhouse, a traditional 17th century Kentish farmhouse situated in the midst of Stelling Minnis, a medieval common of 125 acres of unspoilt trees, shrubs and open grassland; seven miles south of the cathedral city of Canterbury and nine miles from the coast; the countryside abounds in beauty spots and nature reserves. The house is heavily beamed and maintains its original charm. The accommodation comprises a double room and a twin-bedded room, each with private facilities. Full traditional English Breakfast is served with home-made bread, marmalade and fresh free-range eggs. Children welcome; pets by prior arrangement. Open all year (except Christmas). Car essential. Excellent pub food five minutes away. Bed and Breakfast from £19.50 per person.

CANTERBURY. Mrs Lewana Castle, Great Field Farm, Misling Lane, Stelling Minnis, Canterbury CT4 6DE (01227 709223). ETB Listed *HIGHLY COMMENDED.* In own pastures with friendly ponies, on a quiet country lane, adjacent B2068, comfortable farmhouse with Aga and full central heating. One double bedroom with own stairs, lounge, colour TV, kitchen and bathroom (also available for self catering); double bedroom, en suite bathroom; twin-bedded room with en suite bathroom and own lounge. Guests welcome in elegant lounge with colour TV, dining room and farmhouse kitchen. Babysitting, refreshments and laundry available. Local restaurants. Bed and farmhouse Breakfast from £18. Reductions for children. Pets by arrangement. Non-smoking establishment. SAE or telephone.

KENT – THE GARDEN OF ENGLAND!

The pleasant landscape of Kent, including The North Downs and The Weald, is the venue of many engaging places to visit. These include Chiddingstone, the half-timbered village, the sophisticated spa town of Tunbridge Wells and Swanton Mill. There are also day trips to the continent and for railway enthusiasts, The Sittingbourne & Kensley Light Railway, The Kent & East-Sussex Railway and the 'World's Smallest Public Railway' from Hythe to Dungeness.

CANTERBURY. Mrs Joy Wright, Milton House, 9 South Canterbury Road, Canterbury CT1 3LH (01227 765531). Family home built in 1906 situated in residential area just off the main road to Dover (15 miles). Established in 1967 and providing one double and one twin-bedded rooms with washbasins, TV and tea/coffee making facilities. One bathroom with shower, separate toilet. Central heating. Open all year. Full English Breakfast. Prices £15 to £18 per person. Easy walking distance for East Railway Station, Bus Station, Kent Cricket Ground, Cathedral etc. Ideal base for exploring Kent, visiting London, and passport day trips to the Continent. "Very comfortable and friendly" is a typical comment in our visitors' book.

CANTERBURY. Mr and Mrs R. Linch, Upper Ansdore, Duckpit Lane, Petham, Canterbury CT4 5QB

(01227 700672). ETB Listed. Beautiful secluded Listed Tudor farmhouse with various livestock, situated in an elevated position with far-reaching views of the wooded countryside of the North Downs. The property overlooks a Kent Trust Nature Reserve, is five miles south of the cathedral city of Canterbury and only 30 minutes' drive to the ports of Dover and Folkestone. The accommodation comprises one family, three double and one twin-bedded rooms. All have shower and WC en suite and tea-making facilities. Dining/sitting room, heavily beamed with large inglenook. Car essential. Bed and full English Breakfast from £20 per person. AA QQQ.

CANTERBURY. Mrs Prudence Latham, Tenterden House, The Street, Boughton, Faversham ME13

9BL (01227 751593). Enjoy Bed and Breakfast in the renovated gardener's cottage of this Tudor house. Close to Canterbury and the ferry ports, making an ideal base for day trips to France and for touring rural, historic and coastal Kent. Other amenities include golf (five minutes), walking and ornithology. Accommodation comprises two bedrooms (one double, one twin) with guests' own shower and toilet. Both rooms have washbasins and tea/coffee facilities. Full English breakfast is served in the main house. Open all year. Bed and Breakfast from £19. Excellent pub food within walking distance.

CANTERBURY. Mrs Joan Hill, Renville Oast, Bridge, Canterbury CT4 5AD (01227 830215). Renville

Oast is a 150 year old building previously used for drying hops for the brewery trade. It is situated in beautiful Kentish countryside only two miles from the cathedral city of Canterbury; 10 miles from the coast and one and a half hour's drive from London. Many interesting castles, historic houses, gardens and Howletts Wildlife Park within easy reach. All rooms are comfortably furnished, with tea making facilities. One family room en suite, one double en suite and one twin-bedded room with private bathroom. TV lounge for guests. Ample parking space. Friendly welcome. Excellent pub food nearby. Bed and Breakfast from £22 per person.

CANTERBURY near. Mrs J. Smith, 55 Guilton, Ash, Near Canterbury CT5 3HR (01304 812809). Situated in the village of Ash, three miles from Sandwich. A warm homely welcome awaits you. Ideal as an overnight stop for Dover or Ramsgate ferries and for touring East Kent. Manston Airport, Spitfire Museum, Nature Reserve, bird parks, vineyards, zoos, castles, windmills; hiking as well as seaside. Two double rooms — one en suite, one with toilet and washbasin, both with tea/coffee making facilities and TV. Full English breakfast; evening meal by arrangement. Log fire. Cottage garden. Open all year round except Christmas and Boxing Day. £29 double room including Breakfast.

DEAL. Mr and Mrs P.S.F. Jailler, "Blencathra Country Hotel", Kingsdown Hill, Kingsdown, Deal

CT14 8EA (01304 373725). ☙☙☙ Blencathra is a small private hotel situated in the picturesque unspoilt village of Kingsdown. With panoramic views over the Channel and countryside, it is an ideal centre for a touring, walking or golfing holiday (close to four golf courses). Kingsdown is only five miles from the ferries at Dover and early breakfasts are available. Blencathra is a family run hotel offering eight bedrooms, personal service and attention from the proprietors. The hotel is in a private road and a peaceful stay is guaranteed. Open all year. Evening snacks available by prior arrangement. AA and RAC Listed. Bed and Breakfast from £17 per person.

DOVER. "Dover's Restover" B&B, 69 Folkestone Road, Dover CT17 9RZ (01304 206031). ☙ COMMENDED. A warm, friendly welcome awaits you at our clean, highly recommended guesthouse. Situated opposite Dover Priory Railway Station and three minutes from Dover's ports (free buses runs from station to ports); Channel Tunnel 10 minutes' drive. Centrally situated for all amenities. Double, twin and family rooms, all with colour TV, tea/coffee facilities, washbasins, central heating and double glazing. Overnight stops our speciality. Hearty English breakfast served from 6.30am. Private parking available. Bed and Breakfast from £13 to £20 per person (room only rates available). Reductions for Senior Citizens and children. Smoking and non-smoking rooms available. Members of Dover Hotel and Guesthouse Group, AA QQ.

DOVER. Mr and Mrs Christo, Elmo Guest House, 120 Folkestone Road, Dover CT17 9SP (01304 206236). 🌣 Family-run guesthouse offering friendly personal service. Ideal for overnight stops and Short Breaks. Early breakfast catered for. Conveniently situated near town centre, stations, Hoverport and docks. 10 minutes' drive to Channel Tunnel. One single, one twin, two double and two family bedrooms, all with washbasin, shaver point, colour TV and tea/coffee making facilities. Private parking, lock-up garage. Bed and Breakfast from £12 to £18 per person. RAC Listed.

DYMCHURCH. Mrs Caroline Rasmussen, Wenvoe House, 88 Dymchurch Road, St. Mary's Bay, Romney Marsh TN29 0QR (01303 874426). Situated right on the sea front overlooking the English Channel, this family run guest house is ideal for a relaxing break. Half a mile from the smuggling village of Dymchurch on the Romney Marsh, the beach is one of the best in Kent. There is a golf course handy and the unique Romney, Hythe and Dymchurch 1/3 scale railway runs nearby. The ancient town of Rye is nearby as are the Channel Ports of Folkestone and Dover. Bed and Breakfast from £17.50. En suite chalets available from £20. Ideal for children. All bedrooms have tea/coffee facilities. TV in all rooms (satellite in family room).

EDENBRIDGE. Marjorie and Peter McEwan, "Four Oaks", Swan Lane, Edenbridge TN8 6BA (01732 863556; Fax: 01732 867022). ETB Listed. Welcome to our Bed and Breakfast establishment in homely and comfortable surroundings, half a mile from British Rail station and approximately 20 miles from Gatwick Airport Four miles to Hever Castle, Chartwell, Penshurst and Lingfield Park Racecourse. Convenient for M25. One double room en suite and two single rooms; all have tea/coffee making facilities and colour TV. Secure storage for bicycles, off road parking. No smoking.

Terms quoted in this publication may be subject to increase if rises in costs necessitate

FAVERSHAM. N.J. and C.I. Scutt, Leaveland Court, Leaveland, Faversham ME13 0NP (01233 740596). 🐦🐦 *HIGHLY COMMENDED.* Guests are warmly welcomed to our enchanting timbered 15th century farmhouse which nestles between Leaveland Church and woodlands in rural tranquillity. Offering high standards of accommodation whilst retaining their original character, all bedrooms are en suite with colour TV and hot drinks trays. Traditional breakfasts, cooked on the Aga, are available with a choice of alternatives. There is a large attractive garden with heated outdoor swimming pool for guests' use and ample car parking. Ideally situated for visiting Kent's historic cities, castles, houses and gardens with Canterbury only 20 minutes by car and also easy access to Channel ports, 30 minutes. Good walking country, being close to both the Pilgrims Way and the coast. Terms from £20 for Bed and Breakfast.

FOLKESTONE/ASHFORD. Duncan and Alison Taylor, Bolden's Wood, Fiddling Lane, Stowting, Near Ashford TN25 6AP (Tel & Fax: 01303 812011). Between Ashford/Folkestone. Friendly atmosphere on a working smallholding set in unspoilt countryside. Modern centrally heated accommodation built for traditional comforts. No smoking throughout. One double, one twin, two single rooms. Log burning stove in TV lounge. Full English breakfast. Evening meals by arrangement. Children love the old-fashioned farmyard, the free range chickens and friendly sheep and cattle. Our paddocks, ponds, stream and small wood invite relaxation. Nearby, our private secluded woodland and downland allow quiet visitors to observe bird life, rabbits, foxes, badgers and occasionally deer. To round off your stay you could even book a short sightseeing or fishing trip on our Folkestone fishing boat! Easy access to Channel Tunnel and Ferry Ports. Bed and Breakfast £17.50 per person.

GILLINGHAM. Mrs Y. Packham, 215 Bredhurst Road, Wigmore, Gillingham ME8 0QX (01634 363275). Friendly, comfortable Bed and Breakfast accommodation situated midway between Channel ports/Tunnel and London; close to M2 and M20. Hempstead Valley Shopping Centre and restaurants nearby; close to Rochester and Leeds Castles. Open all year. Full facilities. Quiet residential area with parking available. Reduced rates for children, cots available.

GILLINGHAM. Mrs B.L. Penn, 178 Bredhurst Road, Wigmore, Gillingham ME8 0QX (01634 233267). Wigmore is four minutes from M2 motorway via the A278. Midway between London and Channel Ports, close to the Weald of Kent, castles and countryside. Hempstead Valley Shopping Centre is also nearby. En-suite accommodation with own sittingrooms. Bed and Breakfast from £16 to £18. Reductions for children. Open all year.

HAWKHURST. Susan Woodard, Southgate, Little Fowlers, Rye Road, Hawkhurst TN18 5DA (01580 752526; Fax: 01580 752526). 🐦🐦 *COMMENDED.* AA QQQ Recommended. Stay in our Listed 300-year-old former Dower House on the Kent/Sussex borders. Historic Hawkhurst, once famous for smuggling, is near Sissinghurst, Rye, Bodiam, Batemans, Scotney, Tunbridge Wells, Battle, Hever and coast. Folkestone approximately half an hour's drive. En suite twin, double, triple Georgian bedrooms furnished with antiques, all with magnificent views, TV, tea/coffee facilities. Relax in our one acre gardens. Choice of breakfast in our flower-filled original Victorian conservatory. Guests' sitting room. Excellent village restaurant and inn a few minutes' walk. Helpful and friendly family. Non-smoking. Bed and Breakfast from £20.

HEADCORN. Mrs Dorothy Burbridge, Waterkant Guest House, Moat Road, Headcorn, Ashford TN27 9NT (01622 890154). SEETB Listed. Waterkant is a small guest house situated in the tranquil setting of olde worlde charm of Wealdon Village. A warm and friendly welcome is assured and the relaxed and informal atmosphere is complemented by fine cuisine, excellent service and comfortable surroundings. Bedrooms have private or en suite bathrooms, four-poster beds, tea/coffee making facilities, colour TV and are centrally heated and double glazed. Lounge with colour TV. The large secluded garden bounded by a stream provides a large pond, summerhouse for visitors' use and ample parking. Fast trains to London and a wealth of historic places to visit nearby. Open all year. Visitors return year after year. Bed and Breakfast from £17, with reduced rates for children and Senior Citizens.

MAIDSTONE. Mrs Merrilyn Boorman, The White Lodge, Loddington Lane, Linton, Maidstone ME17 4AG (01622 743129). Guests return again and again to this elegant house beautifully situated in parkland overlooking the Weald of Kent. Just 15 minutes from Leeds Castle, four miles from central Maidstone and within easy reach of Sissinghurst Castle and many other interesting places. The White Lodge is well established, with a friendly, relaxed atmosphere; guests are encouraged to enjoy the two and a half acre garden with its two ponds. Ample parking, quiet location. Terms from £22 per person per night with full English breakfast. En suite double/twin room . Now also available for marriage ceremonies. Directions: south on A229 left on to B2163, first right Loddington Lane, nearly to bottom of hill, on right.

MARGATE. Malvern Hotel, 29 Eastern Esplanade, Cliftonville, Margate CT9 2HL (01843 290192). Small seafront private hotel. Open all year. No VAT. All bedrooms with TV and tea/coffee making facilities — most have en suite shower and toilet. Bed and Breakfast (choice of menu). Double/twin £35 to £42 per night; family and single room prices on request. Within easy reach of Channel ports of Ramsgate, Dover, Folkestone and the Channel Tunnel "Le Shuttle" Terminal. Also ideal for visiting Canterbury (cathedral) and touring the area. Short Breaks, weekends, midweek and overnight stops. Local coach tours and daytrips to France and Belgium arranged. Access and Visa telephone bookings accepted. Send "stamp only" for details (mention Bed and Breakfast Stops when booking). Credit cards — Access/Visa/Amex/Diners.

RYARSH. James and Jean Edwards, Heavers, Chapel Street, Ryarsh, Near West Malling ME19 5JU (Tel & Fax: 01732 842074). Heavers is a traditional smallholding with sheep, geese, chickens and bees. This 17th century house with a clematis-covered porch is comfortable and compact with small rooms and low ceilings. One double and two twin bedrooms, all with washbasins. TV lounge. Children welcome, dogs by arrangement. Guests are treated as members of the family and invited to make themselves at home. Evening meals using home-grown produce are served by arrangement and vegetarians can be catered for. Honey from the owners' bees is for sale. Open all year except Christmas and New Year. Terms on request.

SANDWICH. Mrs Stobie, Ilex Cottage, Temple Way, Worth, Deal CT14 0DA (01304 617026). 🐾🐾

COMMENDED. This charming former coach house in large secluded grounds, surrounded by farmland, enjoys a peaceful yet convenient central position in picturesque Worth. Award winning pub nearby. An idyllic holiday base. Lovely walks from adjacent public footpath. Sandwich and Deal five minutes, Dover and Ramsgate 15 minutes, Canterbury 25 minutes. Non-smokers are welcomed to our lovely family home. The attractive, spacious bedrooms have en suite facilities, colour TV, free tea/coffee, hairdryers, etc. Enjoy the views while relaxing with hsopitality trays in the conservatory. Single, twin, double and ground floor accommodation. Ample parking. Pets welcome. Children half price. Bed and Breakfast from £18 to £20.

SITTINGBOURNE/LYNSTED. David and Peggy Bage, Forge Cottage, Lynsted, Sittingbourne ME9 0RH (01795 521213; http://www.s-h-systems.co.uk/hotels/forge.html). 17th century property in the pretty village of Lynsted on the North Downs, an ideal touring centre and within easy reach of the Isle of Thanet, seaside towns and the Weald of Kent. Many exposed timbers throughout and there is an inglenook fireplace in the visitors TV lounge. Accommodation comprises one twin-bedded room, one double and one family room and two bathrooms. For the comfort of our guests and the safety of the building a strict no smoking rule applies. Children over 10 years and pets welcome. Good English breakfast; other breakfasts, beverages, evening sandwiches and packed lunches available. Bed and Breakfast from £14.

Forge Cottage

SUTTON VALENCE. Mrs Stephanie Clout, Sparks Oast Farm, Forsham Lane, Sutton Valence, Maidstone ME17 3EW (01622 842213). Sparks Oast is a characteristic converted Kentish Oasthouse, on small sheep farm in quiet country lane overlooking the Weald of Kent. Ideally situated for visiting the many attractive castles, famous gardens such as Sissinghurst, Scotney Castle, etc and other places of interest in the Garden of England, or just rambling amid orchards and hop gardens. There is a wealth of excellent pubs offering good food. A warm welcome by the family including the animals, waterfowl, barn owls, etc. Bed and Breakfast from £18 per person. One double room, one twin and one en suite. TV. Guests' bathroom and beverage facilities. ALSO SELF CATERING SUITE from £175 weekly.

TONBRIDGE near. Mrs L. Tubbs, Dunsmore, Hadlow Park, Hadlow, Near Tonbridge TN11 0HX (01732 850611). Hadlow is a small village situated on the A26 between Tonbridge and Maidstone. The M25, M26 and M20 are just a few miles away, making Hadlow a convenient 'stop-over' point for Continental trips or a base for visiting the many places of interest that abound in Kent. The accommodation has its own entrance to a large ground floor twin bedded/sitting room, shower and WC. Additional children's beds available. Colour TV and tea-making facilities. Doors lead onto own patio with views of Downs. Easy parking. Bed and Breakfast from £20 per person per night. Very peaceful.

WHEN MAKING ENQUIRIES PLEASE MENTION
FARM HOLIDAY GUIDES

THE OLD PARSONAGE
Frant, Tunbridge Wells, Kent
Tel/Fax: 01892 750773

Quietly situated by the church in pretty Frant village, two miles south of Tunbridge Wells, this magnificent Georgian country house, built by the Marquess of Abergavenny in 1820, provides superior accommodation: luxurious en suite bedrooms, including two four-posters, antique-furnished reception rooms, plus a spacious conservatory and balustraded terrace overlooking the secluded walled garden. For evening meals, the two village pubs and restaurant are less than three minutes' walk away. Many historic houses and fine walks in the area.B&B from £30.00.

AA – Premier Selected QQQQQ   RAC Highly Acclaimed   ETB De Luxe
English Tourist Board Award Winner "Best B&B in S.E. England"
Gatwick 40 minutes, Heathrow 55 minutes, London 40 minutes by train

WALTHAM. Tracy Childs, Beech Bank, Duckpitt Lane, Waltham, Near Canterbury CT4 5QA (01227 700302). SEETB 👑👑 AA QQQ. 15th century Tudor style coach house situated on the valley downs. Surrounded by magnificent views with landscaped garden adjoining Nature Reserve. Oak king posts, minstrels' gallery and architectural features. Luxury bedrooms, three en suite, one of which has sunken bath. Four-poster room. Breakfast is served in Victorian conservatory. Children welcome. Open all year except Christmas. Bed and Breakfast from £30 to £45. Non-smoking.

WINGHAM. The Dog Inn, Canterbury Road, Wingham CT3 1AB (01227 720339). Colin and Vivienne McIntyre welcome you to their 13th century village inn situated in the old picturesque village of Wingham, five miles east of historic Canterbury on the A257. Sit and enjoy the fine ales, lagers and wines in our cosy, beamed pub with crackling log fire in winter or in our beer garden in summer. We serve food seven days a week in our restaurant, comprising separate smoking and non-smoking areas. Six en suite letting rooms provide quaint accommodation with TV and tea/coffee making facilities. Full English breakfast is served in our conservatory. We look forward to seeing you.

LANCASHIRE

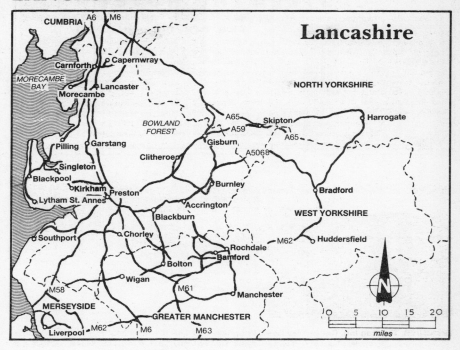

Lancashire

CUMBRIA A6 M6

Carnforth Capernwray

MORECAMBE BAY

Morecambe Lancaster

NORTH YORKSHIRE

BOWLAND FOREST A65 Skipton Harrogate

Pilling Garstang A59 Gisburn A65

Singleton Clitheroe A5068

Blackpool Kirkham Preston Burnley Bradford

Lytham St. Annes Accrington WEST YORKSHIRE

Blackburn

Southport Chorley Rochdale M62 Huddersfield

Bamford

Bolton

Wigan M61

M58 Manchester

MERSEYSIDE

Liverpool M62 M6 **GREATER MANCHESTER** M63

N

0 5 10 15 20

miles

BLACKBURN near. The Brown Leaves Country Hotel, Longsight Road, Copster Green, Near Blackburn BB1 9EU (01254 249523; Fax: 01254 245240). Conveniently situated on the A59 about half way between Preston and Clitheroe, five miles from Junction 31 on the M6. All rooms ground floor, have en suite facilities, TV, tea-making and hairdryer. Most credit cards are welcome.

BLACKPOOL. Mark and Claire Smith, The Old Coach House, 50 Dean Street, Blackpool FY4 1BP (01253 349195; Fax: 01253 344330). ♛ ♛ ♛ *HIGHLY COMMENDED.* An historic detached house surrounded by its own gardens in the heart of Blackpool. One minute from the sea and South Pier. Free car parking. All bedrooms are fully en suite with central heating, colour TV, telephone, trouser press, hair dryer, razor point, radio alarm and tea/coffee making facilities; four-poster beds available. Sun lounge. Open all year for Bed and Breakfast from £23.50. Licensed restaurant. Non-smoking dining room. Children welcome at reduced rates. Sorry, no pets. RAC Highly Acclaimed. AA QQQQ.

BLACKPOOL. Elsie and Ron Platt, Sunnyside and Holmesdale Guest House, 25-27 High Street, North Shore, Blackpool FY1 2BN (01253 23781). Two minutes from North Station, five minutes from Promenade, all shows and amenities. Colour TV lounge. Full central heating. No smoking. Late keys. Children welcome; high chairs and cots available. Reductions for children sharing. Senior Citizens' reductions May and June, always welcome. Handicapped guests welcome. Special diets catered for, good food and warm friendly atmosphere awaits you. Bed and Breakfast from £17; extra for optional Evening Meal. Morning tea available. Overnight guests welcome. Small parties catered for.

BLACKPOOL. Proprietress: Mrs Yvonne Anne Duckworth, "Kelvin Private Hotel", 98 Reads Avenue, Blackpool FY1 4JJ (01253 620293). Welcome to our comfortable small hotel. Centrally situated between sea and Stanley Park, Lake District, Scotland, North Wales and Yorkshire. TV lounge; plenty of good food. Bed and English Breakfast; Evening Dinner optional; light snacks. Tea/coffee facilities all bedrooms. Ground floor bedroom. Overnight, Short Break and period stays welcome. Open most of the year. Car park. Bed and Breakfast from £12 to £18 per person according to season. Reduced rates for children and Senior Citizens. Weekly rates competitive. Please do not hesitate to enquire. SAE for brochure.

BLACKPOOL near. Mrs Joan Colligan, High Moor Farm, Weeton, Kirkham PR4 3JJ (Tel & Fax: 01253 836273). 🐾🐾 High Moor Farm is situated six miles from Blackpool and is within easy reach of Lytham St. Annes, Lancaster, Morecambe, the Lake District and the Dales of Yorkshire. Local attractions include sea fishing, golfing, sand yachting, riding schools, Isle of Man ferry (July/August) Fleetwood. Guest accommodation comprises one double, one family, one twin-bedded and one single rooms; the double and family rooms have central heating, colour TV and tea-making facilities. Bed and Breakfast from £15 per person. Special family room (for four) at £35. Reductions for children under 12 years. Closed January until mid February. Travellers cheques accepted.

BURY. J.R. & B. Baxter, Loe Farm Country House, Redisher Lane, Hawkshaw, Bury BL8 4HX (01204 883668; Fax: 01204 888081). This 200-year-old farmhouse is situated off A676 approximately five miles east of Bolton and four miles north of Bury within four to five miles of M66, M62, M61. We have two double rooms both with en suite facilities, colour TV, radio alarm, tea/coffee making facilities and fridge freezers. The premises are centrally heated and double glazed. Both rooms have lovely views of the surrounding countryside which is renowned for its attractive walks and interesting history. Open all year round. Bed and Breakfast single from £25, double from £38.

CARNFORTH. Mrs Melanie Smith, Capernwray House, Capernwray, Via Carnforth LA6 1AE (Tel & Fax: 01524 732363). 🐾🐾 *COMMENDED.* Situated in the Lower Lunesdale Valley on the North Lancashire and Cumbria borders (M6 Junction 35, off B6254) where the peace and solitude of the countryside are yours to enjoy. The house is beautifully furnished to ensure a delightful and comfortable stay for the non-smoking guest. Centrally heated en suite bedrooms with tea/coffee facilities, shoe cleaning, clock radio and hair dryer. Panoramic views can be enjoyed over the Cumbrian or Pennine Hills. Superb location in five and a half acres of rolling countryside, ideal for the coast, Lakes, Dales, Lancaster bird reserves, historic houses, steam railways or a break en-route London-Scotland. Spacious lounge. Ample parking. Sorry, no pets. Children welcome. Bed and Breakfast from £18; Dinner £8. Open all year. Brochure available. Also small select touring caravan park.

CARNFORTH/KENDAL. Mrs Angie Altham, Tewitfield Farm, Tewitfield, Carnforth LA6 1JH (01524 781598). "Excellent", "A place to remember", "11 out of 10", "Excellent and friendly accommodation", "A1", "Delight to stay here", "Wonderful", "A beautiful farmhouse", "Perfect", "Very comfortable indeed and in a beautiful old farmhouse", "Five star". Just some of the recent comments from our visitors' book. Tewitfield is situated about midway between the villages of Burton, Carnforth and the town of Kendal on the A6070 and two miles or so from Junction 35 of the M6 motorway. The Cumbria Lakes, Yorkshire Dales and Kirkby Lonsdale are all within easy driving distance. Tea/coffee making facilities. Bed and Breakfast from £18.50 to £20 per person. No smoking or pets.

CHORLEY. Mrs Val Hilton, Jepsons Farm, Moor Road, Anglezarke, Chorley PR6 9DQ (01257 481691). Jepsons Farm, formerly a 17th century inn, is a stone built farmhouse with oak beams and wood burning stoves and is situated in Anglezarke, next to Rivington in the West Pennine Moors. Non-working farm apart from horses. It boasts excellent views and is surrounded by beautiful countryside for all outdoor activities including riding, walking, climbing, abseiling, cycling and fishing or simply relaxing. Good food assured and bedrooms have colour TV and tea/coffee trays. Accommodation for horses in spacious looseboxes; bridleways in abundance for all riding requirements. Places of interest include Wigan Pier, Martin Mere, Astley Hall, Camelot and coastal resorts of Blackpool and Southport. Bed and Breakfast from £17; Evening Meal from £7.50. Reductions for children. Special rates for longer stays.

CLITHEROE. Mrs Margaret A. Berry, Lower Standen Farm, Whalley Road, Clitheroe BB7 1PP (01200 424176). 🐾🐾 This farmhouse is situated 20 minutes' walk from town centre, one mile from A59 road. Convenient for M6, 20 minutes' drive from Junction 31. There are two double rooms en suite, one twin-bedded room with washbasin only and an additional single room if required. TV and tea/coffee making facilities; cot also available. Own lounge with electric fire and TV; dining room. Full central heating. Pets and children are welcome, reduced rates for children under 12 years. Open all year except Christmas and New Year. Golf club nearby. Bed and Breakfast from £16 per person, £18 in en suite room.

If you've found
FARM HOLIDAY GUIDES
of service please tell your friends

CLITHEROE near. Mrs Marj Adderley, Rose Cottage, Longsight Road (A59), Clayton-le-Dale, Ribble Valley BB1 9EX (01254 813223; Fax: 01254 813831). A warm welcome awaits at our picturesque cottage situated at the gateway to the Ribble Valley, five miles from Junction 31 of M6 on A59. Excellent night stop travelling to and from Scotland, easy access to Yorkshire Dales, Lake District and Blackpool. Full English breakfast included in price; single occupancy £21, double £18 per person. Three night break to include Sunday night shared occupancy £49 per person. Comfortable well equipped rooms offering tea/coffee, TV and Sky, radio alarms, heated towel rails, hair dryers, shoe cleaning, smoke detectors; all have private facilities. Phone for our brochure. Nearby Ribbleway, cycling, walking. Trace your family at Records Office, Preston.

LANCASTER. Roy and Helen Domville, Three Gables, Chapel Lane, Galgate, Lancaster LA2 0PN (01524 752222). A large detached bungalow, three miles south of Lancaster and 400 yards from Lancaster University. Access from M6 Junction 33 and A6 in Galgate village. Two double bedrooms each with shower, toilet, colour TV and tea/coffee facilities. One bedroom also has a private TV lounge. Open all year with full central heating. A cot and high chair are available. Spacious parking. A good location for visiting Blackpool, Morecambe, the Lake District and Yorkshire Dales. You will be sure of a friendly welcome and a homely atmosphere. Sorry, no pets. Non-smokers only please. Bed and Breakfast £15 per person.

LYTHAM ST. ANNES. Mr J. Soothill, Willow Trees, 89 Heyhouses Lane, Lytham St. Annes FY8 3RN (01253 727235). A warm welcome awaits you in this comfortable detached house with pleasant gardens situated between Blackpool and Lytham, one mile from the sea and backing on to open countryside. Close to all amenities and within easy reach of Lake District, Trough of Bowland and Dales. Convenient for touring, swimming, golf, horse riding, sailing, wind surfing and fishing. The house is in a quiet situation and centrally heated throughout. Guests are accommodated in two double, one twin-bedded and two single rooms, each with tea/coffee making facilities and TV. Bathroom and toilets. Ample parking. Bed and Breakfast from £15 each. Reduced rates for children. No smoking in the house please.

LYTHAM ST. ANNES. Harcourt Hotel, 21 Richmond Road, St. Annes on Sea, Lytham St. Annes FY8 1PE (01253 722299). 🌸🌸 Small 10 bedroomed private Hotel. Perfectly situated adjacent to town centre and 200 yards from sandy beach and Promenade. Open all year with central heating. One mile from Blackpool. Tea making facilities in all rooms. Colour TV in some bedrooms. En suite rooms available. Twin bedded and double rooms, family rooms. Free car park. Licensed. Friendly personal service from **Sue and Andy Royle.** Bed and Breakfast from £16; en suite from £18. Long and short stays available. Special reductions for Senior Citizens on weekly terms. Child reductions for up to 14 year olds, under five years FREE.

MANCHESTER. Margaret and Bernard Satterthwaite, The Albany Hotel, 21 Albany Road, Chorlton-cum-Hardy, Manchester M21 0AY (0161-881 6774; Fax: 0161-862 9405). 🌸🌸🌸 *COMMENDED.* The Albany Hotel, having recently undergone a major refurbishment, offers luxurious and elegant period accommodation with all the comforts of a modern deluxe hotel, plus the personal attention of the owners. Facilities include Erica's Restaurant, licensed bar, games room and full conference facilities. A choice of single (from £39.50 per room), double (from £49.50 per room) or family rooms, all with shower or en suite bathroom, direct-dial telephone, colour TV, hair dryer, radio and tea/coffee. Conveniently located being only 10 minutes from the City and Airport, five minutes Manchester United, L.C.C.C., Salford Quays, Trafford Park and Universities. Directions:- just off the A6010 (Wilbraham Road), approximately one mile from Metrolink, one mile Junction 7 M63 for M62, M61 and M6 North, two miles M56 and M6 South. AA/RAC Two Stars. Brochure and tariff on request.

WHEN MAKING ENQUIRIES PLEASE MENTION
THIS *FHG* PUBLICATION

PILLING. Beryl and Peter Richardson, Bell Farm, Bradshaw Lane, Scronkey, Pilling, Preston PR3

Bell Farm

6SN (01253 790324). Beryl and Peter welcome you to their 18th century farmhouse situated in the quiet village of Pilling, which lies between the Ribble and Lune Estuaries. The area has many public footpaths and is ideal for cycling. From the farm there is easy access to Blackpool, Lancaster, the Forest of Bowland and the Lake District. Accommodation consists of one family room with en-suite facilities, one double and one twin with private bathroom. Tea and coffee making facilities. Lounge and dining room. All centrally heated. Children and pets welcome. Full English Breakfast is served. Open all year, except Christmas and New Year. Bed and Breakfast from £17.50.

PRESTON. Mrs Reynolds-Butler, Butler's Guest House, 6 Stanley Terrace (off Fishergate Hill), Preston PR1 8JE (01772 254486; Fax: 01772 252505). Family-run Grade II Listed Georgian town centre house in cul-de-sac just five minutes' walk from town centre, three minutes from rail station. Private off-road parking with security lighting. All rooms centrally heated with colour TV and tea/coffee. Ground floor en suite rooms; most rooms with private showers. Family, twin/double, single rooms. Special rates for Senior Citizens, students, contractors, long term stays. Pre-booked set evening meal by arrangement.

PRESTON. Mrs M. Jackson, Smithy Farm, Huntingdon Hall Lane, Dutton, Near Longridge, Preston PR3 2ZT (01254 878250). Just a happy home set in the unspoilt beautiful Ribble Valley. 20 minutes from the M6 and 45 minutes to Blackpool. Just come and enjoy the friendly hospitality and good food. No rules. Children, pets and grandmas welcome! Bed and Breakfast from £12.50 per person per night; Evening Meal from £5. Reduced rates for children under 12 years.

PRESTON near. Mrs B. Brown, Wall Mill Farm, Great Eccleston, Blackpool Road, Near Preston PR3 0ZQ (01995 670334). There's a warm welcome when you arrive at Wall Mill Farm. We are eight miles from Blackpool and an hours' drive to the Lakes and the Yorkshire Dales. The lovely village of Great Eccleston is one mile away with many good facilities. Full English breakfast. Lounge with colour TV. Two double and one single room. Bed and Breakfast £15.

ROCHDALE/BURY. Mrs Jane Neave, Leaches Farm, Ashworth Valley, Bamford, Rochdale OL11

5UN (01706 641116/7 or 224307). Tourist Board Listed. Hill farm in the "Forgotten Valley", with magnificent views of the Roch, Irwell and Mersey river valleys; West Yorkshire, Lancashire and Derbyshire hills, Cheshire Plain, Jodrell Bank Telescope, Welsh mountains. At night there are the panoramic twinkling lights of Greater Manchester. Accommodation features oak beams, 18-inch walls, log fires and central heating. Unique rural wildlife in the heart of industrial East Lancashire. Three miles from M62 and M66, 30 miles from Manchester Airport. Ideal for holiday or business visitors. Bed and Breakfast from £19. AA Listed.

SOUTHPORT. Mrs Judith Leck, Sidbrook Hotel, 14 Talbot Street, Southport PR8 1HP (Tel: 01704

530608; Fax: 01704 531198). 🌸 🌸 🌸 *COMMENDED.* A quiet hotel in the centre of this picturesque seaside town, fantastic shopping in Victorian tree-lined boulevard and arcades. We offer select accommodation at a realistic price. All our attractive bedrooms are en suite with remote control TV and satellite, tea/coffee facilities, telephone, radio alarm, hair dryer and toiletries. We have a sauna and sun bed to help you relax, together with a secluded garden and games room in basement with pool table. We have a cosy bar and two lounges. Bed and Breakfast from £19.50. RAC One Star, AA QQQQ Selected.

SOUTHPORT. The Waterford Hotel, 37 Leicester Street, Southport PR9 0EX (01704 530559). Ideally situated overlooking the sea front, The Waterford is only a short walk from the famous Lord Street and its countless variety of shops and restaurants. En suite rooms, most with lake views. Restaurant. Car parking.

SOUTHPORT. Rosedale Hotel, 11 Talbot Street, Southport PR8 1HP (Tel & Fax: 01704 530604). 🌸 🌸 🌸 *COMMENDED.* One of Southport's most centrally situated hotels, ideally placed for the beach, parks, entertainment, golf courses and the famous Lord Street. The perfect location whether you are on holiday or on business. Resident proprietors Joan and Alan Beer make every effort to ensure that all their guests have a happy and comfortable stay. Full central heating and private parking. All rooms have tea/coffee making facilities and colour TV with satellite link. Residents bar and a separate TV lounge. A lovely secluded rear garden is available for guests enjoyment. Children welcome. Sorry no pets. Bed and Breakfast from £18.50.

LEICESTERSHIRE (including Rutland)

BROUGHTON ASTLEY. Mrs A. Cornelius, The Old Farm House, Old Mill Road, Broughton Astley LE9 6PQ (01455 282254). Tourist Board Listed. Quietly situated but within walking distance of the village centre with good pubs and restaurants. Georgian farmhouse with easy access to M1, M69 and A14, good local walks. Children welcome but sorry no pets. No smoking. Accommodation comprises two family rooms, one twin-bedded room and a single room all with TV; two bathrooms; sitting room with TV. Bed and Breakfast from £17 to £19 per night. Advance booking please. Organic home products. Non-smoking.

LUTTERWORTH. Mrs A.T. Hutchinson, The Greenway and Knaptoft House Farm, Bruntingthorpe Road, Near Shearsby, Lutterworth LE17 6PR (Tel & Fax: 01162 478388). ♥♥ *HIGHLY COMMENDED.* **Working farm.** AA QQQQ Selected. M1 Exit 20, M6 Exit 1, A14 Exit 1 (A5199). Nine miles south of Leicester. Very peacefully situated with lovely views across pretty garden to the fields where our sheep and horses graze. Warmth, comfort and good wholesome farmhouse breakfast. Twin/double/single rooms, (some non-smoking, some ground floor). Children over five years. No pets. Each room with colour TV, tea/coffee making facilities, either fully en suite or with adjacent facilities. Sunny dining and sitting room with woodburner and family history memorabilia. Coarse fishing. Parking. Excellent food at local pubs. Bed and Breakfast from £18.50. Phone for brochure. Major credit cards accepted.

MEDBOURNE. Mrs J.A. Wainwright, Homestead House, 5 Ashley Road, Medbourne, Market Harborough LE16 8DL (01858 565724; Fax: 01858 565324). ♥♥ *HIGHLY COMMENDED.* Open all year for Bed and Breakfast, Homestead House is situated in an elevated position overlooking the Welland Valley on the outskirts of Medbourne, a picturesque village dating back to Roman times, with a meandering brook running through the centre. Surrounded by open countryside, the village has two public houses, post office/shop, etc. Local places of interest include Foxton Locks on Grand Union Canal, Rockingham Castle, Rutland Water (sailing, fishing, windsurfing), Eyebrook Reservoir (fishing, bird watching), Naseby Battlefield, various houses and halls, gliding, riding, nature trails and many delightful picnic spots. Accommodation comprises three twin-bedded rooms, all en suite and having TVs, telephones and tea/coffee making facilities; sitting-room, diningroom. Children welcome and pets accepted free of charge. Central heating. Car not essential, although there is parking for four cars. Bed and Breakfast from £19 to £24. Evening Meal available. Reductions for children.

MELTON MOWBRAY. Mrs Linda Lomas, Shoby Lodge Farm, Shoby, Melton Mowbray LE14 3PF (01664 812156). Set in attractive gardens, Shoby Lodge is a spacious, comfortable, tastefully furnished farmhouse. Enjoy an Aga-cooked breakfast and beautiful views of the surrounding countryside. Accommodation comprises two double en suite rooms and one double room with private bathroom. All rooms have tea and coffee making facilities and TV. Close to the market town of Melton Mowbray and ideally situated for Leicester and Nottingham. Coarse fishing available on the farm. Terms from £18 per person.

LEICESTERSHIRE & RUTLAND – THE EPITOMY OF MIDDLE ENGLAND!
A county of undulating farmland containing such delights as Rutland Water, the canal "staircase" at Foxton, the market town of Oakham, Charnwood forest and the estate church at Staunton Harold.

MELTON MOWBRAY. Mr R.S. Whittard, Elms Farm, Long Clawson, Melton Mowbray LE14 4NG (01664 822395; Fax: 01664 823399). Welcome to our 18th century farmhouse in the beautiful Vale of Belvoir! Situated between M1 and A1, 6 miles north of Melton Mowbray, 25 mins drive from Leicester, Nottingham, Grantham and Loughborough. Local attractions include Belvoir Castle, Stamford, Burghley House and Belton House. Enjoy delicious home cooking and attractive, comfortable accommodation with full central heating. One double/family room and one single room; separate dining room and lounge with colour TV. Also our newly renovated self-contained cottage is now available for B&B or weekly for self-catering. Bed and memorable breakfast from £17 per adult; cottage B&B from £22 per adult; dinner (by arrangement) from £8. Open all year except Christmas. No smoking in the house please.

MELTON MOWBRAY (4 miles). Mrs Brenda Bailey, Church Cottage, Main Street, Holwell, Melton Mowbray LE14 4SZ (01664 444255). Church Cottage, an 18th century Listed building, is situated next to Holwell's 13th century church in the heart of the Leicestershire countryside. This is an excellent location for walkers and lovers of the rural scene. The high standard accommodation offers an en suite double room and one twin bedroom, plus own colour TV, radio and tea-making facilities. Guests also have private use of lounge and summerhouse. Full central heating. Children welcome. Bed and Breakfast from £17 per person. No smoking.

MELTON MOWBRAY near. Mrs J.S. Goodwin, Hillside House, 27 Melton Road, Burton Lazars, Near Melton Mowbray LE14 2UR (01664 66312; after February 1998 01664 566312, Fax: 01664 501819; mobile 0585 068956). *COMMENDED.* Hillside House is a charmingly converted 19th century old farm building with views over rolling countryside situated on the outskirts of Burton Lazars. Melton Mowbray, famous for Pork Pies, is close by as is Belvoir Castle, Stamford and Rutland Water. The recently restored accommodation is spacious and very comfortable offering one double en suite, one twin en suite and one twin with own toilet and shower. Prices from £16.50. Children 10 years and over welcome.

UPPINGHAM. The Old Rectory, Belton-in-Rutland, Uppingham, Rutland LE15 9LE (01572 717279; Fax: 01572 717343). *COMMENDED.* On the edge of the picturesque conservation village of Belton in Rutland, 10 minutes from Rutland Water, Launde Abbey, Rockingham Castle and numerous other historical and tourist landmarks. Excellent walks, cycling, golf, bird watching, fishing, water sports and riding locally. This is a relaxed atmosphere to come and go as you please, offering Bed and Breakfast in comfortable en suite rooms with TV and tea/coffee facilities. Arrange an evening meal in or visit one of the local restaurants or pubs (the best in England). Bed and Breakfast from £19 per person. Children half price, under three year olds FREE. Pets welcome. No smoking. RAC Listed.

ONE child admitted free with full-paying adult at SNIBSTON DISCOVERY PARK, Coalville. See the special READERS' OFFER VOUCHER at the front of this guide.

LINCOLNSHIRE

EPWORTH. Mr C.J. Barton, Epworth Old Rectory, 1 Rectory Street, Epworth, Doncaster, South Yorkshire DN9 1HX (01427 872268). AA Recommended

QQ. This handsome Queen Anne period rectory, Grade I Listed, was the boyhood home of John and Charles Wesley, founders of Methodism. Accommodation is in two comfortable twin-bedded rooms (Revd Samuel Wesley's Study and the "Ship's Keel Room") which are equipped with tea and coffee making facilities, washbasins and central heating. Colour TV in the sitting room. There is one bathroom, with bath, shower and WC for the sole use of Bed and Breakfast guests. Not suitable for children or pets. Non-smoking. Terms from £20 to £30 per person per night. Ample parking, pleasant garden. Meals available locally.

GRANTHAM. Shirley Croft Hotel, Harrowby Road, Grantham NG31 9EA (01476 563260). Small, family-run hotel situated on the quiet outskirts of the town, serving excellent English cuisine. Special diets catered for. We pride ourselves of good service and value for money. We have 12 bedrooms all en suite with tea/coffee making facilities and TV. Car essential. Licensed. Children and pets welcome. Prices from £23.75.

GRANTHAM. The Red House, 74 North Parade, Grantham NG31 8AN (01476 579869). Elegant

Grade II Listed Georgian house near town centre. Three en suite rooms with TV and drinks facilities. Excellent food. Special diets catered for. Homely surroundings. Children and pets welcome. Car parking. Bed and Breakfast from £13; Dinner, Bed and Breakfast from £18 per person per night. Minimum stay two nights. Credit cards accepted. For further details contact David or Gillian Parnell.

GRANTHAM. Mrs Helen Porter, Stonepit Farmhouse, Swinstead Road, Corby Glen, Grantham NG33 4NU (Tel & Fax: 01476 550614). ETB Listed

Corby Glen, Lincolnshire

COMMENDED. A picturesque stone house in a quiet corner, on the edge of the village of Corby Glen. Four miles from the A1 trunk road, between Grantham and Stamford. Three minutes' walk to pub/restaurant. Large courtyard and lovely garden with views over rolling countryside. Separate guest wing with TV lounge/breakfast room. Ground floor rooms are one single and one twin-bedded room each with washbasin, shared bathroom and one first floor double en suite bedroom. Radio/alarms, hair dryers. Central heating. Beverages available in the lounge. Full English breakfast. Ample parking. No smoking. Price from £20 per person per night.

GRANTHAM. Mrs Lynne Lewis, The Lanchester Guest House, 84 Harrowby Road, Grantham NG31 9DS (01476 574169). 🐾 🐾 The Lanchester is a well established Edwardian Guest House with a warm and friendly atmosphere. Situated on a pleasant tree-lined road, yet only five minutes to town centre. Single, twin and double rooms (en suite), all with TV and tea/coffee making facilities. Lounge, separate dining room. Bed and Breakfast from £15. Open all year.

HORNCASTLE. Mrs C.E. Harrison, Baumber Park, Baumber, Near Horncastle LN9 5NE (01507

578235; Fax: 01507 578417). Period farmhouse in quiet parkland setting, standing in attractive gardens and on a mixed farm. Situated in the centre of the county and close to the Lincolnshire Wolds, an Area of Outstanding Natural Beauty, this rolling agricultural countryside is little-known and quite unspoilt. The Viking Way long distance footpath passes close by and there is a championship golf course near at hand. There are also a number of interesting market towns within easy reach: Horncastle, only four miles away, has become an important antiques centre for the East Midlands. The historic Cathedral City of Lincoln is 17 miles away. Bed and Breakfast £20 per person. Brochure available.

LINCOLN. Dave Barnes, Ridgeways Guest House, 243 Burton Road, Lincoln LN1 3UB (Tel & Fax:

01522 546878). Ridgeways is an attractive detached guest house with a private car park and pleasant gardens for guests' use. Situated in uphill Lincoln within easy walking distance of the historic heart of Lincoln Cathedral, castle and Lawn Conference Centre. En suite twin, double and family rooms available, all with colour TV, tea/coffee trays, hair dryers; a ground floor room is available for disabled guests. Centrally heated throughout and a non-smoking rule applies for your safety and comfort. Vegetarians are catered for. Bed and Breakfast from £17.50 to £25. Credit cards accepted. Further information available on request.

LINCOLN. Mr David Benson, Mayfield Guest House, 213 Yarborough Road, Lincoln LN1 3NQ

(01522 533732). 👑👑 *COMMENDED.* Small, friendly Victorian guest house with private enclosed parking. Panoramic views of the Trent Valley, yet within a short level walk from the main tourist attractions including Cathedral, Castle, Windmill, Museum and Lawn Visitor Centre. All bedrooms are en-suite with colour TV, clock radio, beverage tray, central heating and double glazing. Spacious dining room with a good breakfast choice. Terms from £17. School-age children welcome at reduced rates. Access to car park at rear from Mill Road. A completely non-smoking establishment. We offer quality bed and breakfast at a comfortable price.

LINCOLN. Edward King House, The Old Palace, Lincoln LN2 1PU (01522 528778; Fax: 01522

EDWARD KING HOUSE

527308). EETB Member. A former palace of the Bishops of Lincoln, Edward King House offers Bed and Breakfast accommodation in a friendly and informal atmosphere. It is in a wonderful setting at the heart of historic uphill Lincoln, next to the Cathedral and Old Palace and overlooking the modern city with views over many miles to the west and south. Single and twin-bedded rooms (non-smoking) are all centrally heated and have washbasins and tea/coffee making facilities. Prices from £18.50 single, £36 twin with Continental breakfast (full breakfast £2 extra per person).

LINCOLNSHIRE – OUTSTANDING NATURAL BEAUTY!

The Lincolnshire Wolds are indeed worthy of their designation as an "Area of Outstanding Natural Beauty". Anybody visiting this county should explore The Wolds and visit such places as Bourne, home of Hereward the Wake, last Saxon noble to resist William the Conqueror; historic Grantham; Gainsborough, Britain's most inland port; and, of course, the historic Cathedral City of Lincoln, site of a Roman military garrison.

LINCOLN. David and Margaret Kaye, Westlyn, 67 Carholme Road, Lincoln LN1 1RT (Tel & Fax: 01522 537468). Westlyn is conveniently situated only a short walk from the city centre with its fine mix of shopping. The historic cathedral area, marina, university and open countryside are close too, as are riding, fishing and other sporting facilities. Stay here and get a warm welcome with clean and comfortable accommodation in spacious bedrooms which have central heating, beverage trays, washbasins, colour TV. Guest lounge with open fire. Pretty garden. Off street parking. Good choice of breakfasts. Price £17 per person per night with discounts for children and stays of three or more nights. Non-smoking house.

LINCOLN near. Mrs Brenda Williams, Gallow Dale Farm, Marton Road, Sturton by Stow, Lincoln LN1 2AH (01427 788387). Situated eight miles north west of Lincoln on the A1500 road between the villages of Sturton by Stow and Marton (one mile west of Sturton by Stow village centre). Tastefully refurbished, centrally heated, Grade II Listed Georgian farmhouse set in 33 acres of grass paddocks. TV lounge with beamed ceiling, pretty bedrooms including en suite room with four-poster bed. Tea/coffee making facilities. Full English farmhouse breakfast. Lunch and evening meals available at three local public houses. Sorry, no smoking. Bed and Breakfast from £16. AA QQQQ Selected.

LOUTH. A.J. Brumpton, Glebe Farm, Church Lane, Conisholme, Louth LN11 7LX (01507 358189). Farmhouse situated in the peaceful village of Conisholme near Louth. Convenient for beaches, nature reserve, fishing, horse racing, Lincoln, Market Rasen, Cleethorpes, Mablethorpe. Ideal countryside for walking and cycling. Accommodation offers the full freedom of the farmhouse with own entrance and includes lounge with TV, two double bedrooms, cot available; own bathroom and private garden. Ample parking. Tea/coffee making facilities. Full English breakfast. Terms £16 per person per night. Reduction for children under 10 years. Sorry no smoking or pets.

PETERBOROUGH. Mrs S.M. Hanna, Courtyard Cottage, 2 West End, Langtoft, Peterborough, Cambridgeshire PE6 9LS (01778 348354). A warm, sincere welcome greets you to our delightful tastefully renovated 18th century stone cottage. We are situated in a small village just 50 yards off A15 at the Langtoft crossroads. We are ideally sited for visiting Peterborough, Stamford, Spalding, Bourne, Sleaford and Lincoln. Our home is maintained to high standards, has double glazing, central heating and we offer a hearty breakfast. Guests accommodated in twin and double room en suite or family suite; rooms have colour TV, tea making facilities and hair dryers. Evening meals (from £5.50) available. Bed and Breakfast from £25 per person per night. Open all year. No smoking. Full details on request.

REEPHAM. Mrs Rollo, The Meadows, 5 Meadow Close, Reepham, Lincoln LN3 4ED (01522 753399). Comfortable family home in quiet unspoilt village, three miles from Lincoln centre. Ideal for wartime airfield tours and visiting Jews House and House of Aaron which date from the 12th century when Jews provided financial services and, of course, Lincoln Cathedral, scene of many TV series. We offer two double bedrooms, each with tea/coffee making facilities. Non smoking. Bed and Breakfast £20. Short Breaks: three nights £40 per person.

SPALDING. Travel Stop RAC Lodge, Cowbit Road, Spalding PE11 2RJ (01775 767290; Fax: 01775

767716). ETB *APPROVED*. A charming riverside motel situated in converted farm and stable block. Cosy and welcoming. Situated on the B1173 half a mile from Spalding town centre. There are 10 bedrooms, all en suite with tea and coffee, and refrigerator. Facilities for disabled visitors. Open fires in Winter. Car park. Room rate: £30 single, £45 double. Weekend Special: two nights, for two persons £70. Credit cards accepted.

STAMFORD. Sue and John Olver, The Old Mill Bed & Breakfast, Mill Lane, Tallington, Stamford

PE9 4RR (01780 740815; Fax: 01780 740280; Mobile: 0802 373326). Recently renovated to provide en suite accommodation of the highest standard without losing any of the atmosphere of bygone years. Many original features are intact including the old mill workings situated in the dining room. Also available is a unique room in barn conversion attached to mill, which can be taken as a double or family room. The historic town of Stamford with its multitude of fine stone buildings is only four miles away, whilst the cathedral city of Peterborough is 10 miles. We are a non smoking establishment. Please send for our brochure.

NORFOLK

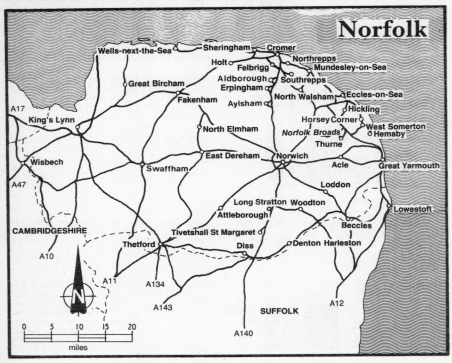

Norfolk

Map showing locations including: Wells-next-the-Sea, Sheringham, Cromer, Holt, Northrepps, Mundesley-on-Sea, Felbrigg, Great Bircham, Aldborough, Southrepps, Erpingham, Fakenham, North Walsham, Eccles-on-Sea, Aylsham, Hickling, King's Lynn, North Elmham, Horsey Corner, West Somerton, Hemsby, Norfolk Broads, Thurne, Wisbech, East Dereham, Norwich, Acle, Great Yarmouth, Swaffham, Loddon, Long Stratton, Woodton, Lowestoft, Attleborough, Beccles, CAMBRIDGESHIRE, Tivetshall St Margaret, Thetford, Diss, Denton Harleston, SUFFOLK.

Roads: A17, A47, A10, A11, A134, A143, A140, A12.

miles: 0 5 10 15 20

ACLE. East Norwich Inn, Old Road, Acle, Norwich NR13 3QN (01493 751112). ♛♛♛

Acle is midway between Great Yarmouth and Norwich. We are ideally situated for visiting all Heritage, National Trust and holiday attractions. The inn is situated on a quiet residential road and has a full 'on' licence with a good local bar trade. All our rooms are situated well away from the bar area and comprise two twin rooms, four double rooms and three family rooms, all have en suite bathrooms, colour TV with Sky and tea/coffee making facilities. Bed and Breakfast from £17.50 per person per night. Three-night break prices available. Ample car parking.

ALDBOROUGH near. The Grange, Harmers Lane, Thurgarton, Near Aldborough NR11 7PF (01263 761588).

A fine rural Victorian country house, former rectory, situated in secluded grounds of two acres offering peace and tranquillity in warm, friendly and comfortable surroundings. Close to Cromer and the coast and central for all the North Norfolk attractions and National Trust properties. The accommodation comprises two spacious double/twinbedrooms with tea and coffee making facilities and private shower/bathrooms. A large guests' dining room and lounge with colour TV. Double bed and full English breakfast from £18 per person per night. Evening meals on request. Two night Short Breaks including evening meals at reduced rates. Private parking. No smoking. No pets. Open March to November. Further information on request.

ATTLEBOROUGH. Hill House Farm, Deopham Road, Great Ellingham, Attleborough NR17 1AQ

(01953 453113). ETB 🏵 COMMENDED. A working farm in quiet rural setting situated within easy reach of all local attractions. We offer our guests a warm welcome, children welcome, pets by arrangement only. Attractions include Banham Zoo, world famous Butterfly Gardens, Snetterton Racing Circuit, riding stables and fishing lakes are close by; seaside resorts and Norfolk Broads are approximately 40 miles distance. Comfortable rooms with washbasins, tea/coffee facilities and colour TV. Ample parking. Open all year. Awarded Good Food Hygiene Certificate. Terms from £16 per person per night. Reduction for children up to 12 years.

ATTLEBOROUGH. Mrs Iris Thomas, Cannells Farm, Bow Street, Great Ellingham, Attleborough

NR17 1JA (Tel & Fax: 01953 454133). ETB Listed *COMMENDED.* A warm friendly welcome awaits you at our 18th century farm house in one acre of delightful gardens overlooking open countryside in a peaceful location at Great Ellingham. Easy reach of local attractions — Snetterton Racing Circuit, Norwich, North Norfolk Coast and the Broads, ideally situated for "Peddars Way" (walkers), several golf courses nearby, good business base. One double, one twin, one single bedrooms, all with central heating, colour TV, tea/coffee facilities, hairdryer. Good farmhouse cooking with full English breakfast. Bed and Breakfast from £16 per person. Evening meals by arrangement. Ample parking. Non smoking. Open all year. Special breaks available. Please send for our brochure.

AYLSHAM. Tim and Janet Bower, Old Mill House, Cawston Road, Aylsham NR11 6NB (Tel & Fax:

01263 732118). Old Mill House is a converted 19th century granary attached to a magnificent disused windmill. There is ample parking and guests are welcome to enjoy the pretty terrace and peaceful gardens. We have one double room with washbasin and one twin room, both sharing a private bathroom. Both rooms have TV, radio and tea/coffee making facilities. Norwich, the Broads and the North Norfolk coast are all only 10 miles. We are on Marriots Way cycle trail and only half a mile from Weavers Way footpath. Warm welcome guaranteed all year. Bed and Breakfast from £15 to £18 per person.

AYLSHAM. The Old Pump House, Holman Road, Aylsham, Norwich NR11 6BY (01263 733789).

🏵 🏵 *HIGHLY COMMENDED.* This comfortable 1750's house, facing the thatched pump a minute from Aylsham's church and historic marketplace, has five bedrooms, four en suite, with colour TV and tea/coffee facilities. English Breakfast with free range eggs and local produce (or vegetarian breakfast) is served in the pine-shuttered sitting room overlooking the peaceful garden. Aylsham is central for Norwich, the coast, the Broads, National Trust houses, steam railways and unspoilt countryside. Well behaved children are very welcome. Bed and Breakfast from £18 to £25. Dinner by prior arrangement from October to May. Non-smoking.

NORFOLK – NOT JUST THE BROADS!

There's more to do in Norfolk than messing about in boats – pleasurable though that may be. Other places of interest include the gardens and steam museum at Bressingham, the Broadland Conservation Centre, the flint mines at Grimes Graves, The Norfolk Rural Life Museum, Sandringham – which is often open to the public – and of course Norwich itself.

BARTON BENDISH. Carole, Rodger and Lucie Gransden, Spread Eagle Country Inn, Church Road, Barton Bendish, Near Swaffham PE33 9DP (Tel & Fax: 01366 347295). Standing in the picturesque Norfolk village of Barton Bendish just off the A1122, adjacent to RAF Marham, twixt Downham Market and Swaffham. 20 minutes from Kings Lynn, Cambridge, Norwich and the coast just under one hour away. Personally run for the past five years, the Inn dates back to the 1700s and is still the hub of the village. There are three spacious bedrooms with all facilities, an attractive lounge bar and two secluded restaurants. Comprehensive menu including home-made desserts. Real Cask Ales. Open all year. Dogs by arrangement. Bed and Breakfast from £15.

BECCLES near. Mrs Rachel Clarke, Shrublands Farm, Burgh St. Peter, Near Beccles, Suffolk NR34 0BB (01502 677241; mobile 0468 313527). 👑👑 COMMENDED. This attractive homely farmhouse offers a warm and friendly welcome and is peacefully situated in the Waveney Valley on the Norfolk/Suffolk border, surrounded by one acre of garden and lawns. The River Waveney flows through the 550 acres of mixed working farmland; opportunities for bird-watching. Ideal base for touring Norfolk and Suffolk; Beccles, Lowestoft, Great Yarmouth and Norwich are all within easy reach. The house has two double rooms with en suite facilities and one twin-bedded room with private bathroom, shower room and toilet. All have satellite colour TV and tea/coffee making facilities; dining room, separate lounge with colour TV. Non-smoking rooms available. Games room for snooker and darts. Tennis court available; swimming pool and food at River Centre nearby.

No pets. Car essential — ample parking. Open all year. Bed and Breakfast from £18 per person, reductions for longer stays. SAE please.

DEREHAM. Mrs Jeanne Partridge, Shilling Stone, Church Road, Old Beetley NR20 4AB (01362 861099). 👑 APPROVED. A friendly welcome awaits you in our comfortable family home with full central heating and parking. Situated on the edge of the village of Beetley (B1146), next to the church and set in its own extensive grounds with an informal garden. Double, twin and single rooms available with washbasin, tea/coffee. Residents' lounge with colour TV, dining room. Non smoking. Pets welcome. The area's small market towns are a short drive away. Ideal base for touring East Anglia, Norwich, Sandringham, Broads, National Trust properties; golf and fishing nearby. Open all year. Bed and full English Breakfast from £15. Reduced rates for children.

DEREHAM. Mrs Pam Gray, Sycamore House, Yaxham Road, Mattishall NR20 3PE (01362 858213). A guesthouse offering friendly, personal service, ideal for overnight stops and short breaks. Quiet rural location in central Norfolk within easy reach of Norwich, the Broads, beaches, country houses, etc. All rooms with colour TV, washbasins, tea/coffee making facilities. Separate WC and shower for guests' use. Traditional home cooking with fruit and vegetables from the garden in season. Early breakfasts if required, served with a smile. Village pub within walking distance. Ample off road parking. We regret no pets. Bed and Breakfast from £14.50; three-course Evening Meal £9.50.

NORFOLK – THE BROADS!

Formed by the flooding of medieval peat diggings, the Broads have a unique quality which attracts thousands of visitors each year. Slow moving waterways are bounded by reed and sedge, and despite the pressures of the modern world are home to rare birds, butterflies and plants. Motor boats and sailing boats can be hired in most towns and villages and there are lots of lively riverbank pubs to round off a day afloat.

DEREHAM. David and Annie Bartlett, Bartles Lodge, Church Street, Elsing, Dereham NR20 3EA

(01362 637177). ✤✤ *COMMENDED*. If you would like a peaceful tranquil stay in the heart of Norfolk's most beautiful countryside yet only a short drive to some of England's finest sandy beaches, then Bartles Lodge could be the place for you, with all rooms tastefully decorated in country style, with full en suite facilities, TVs, tea/coffee making facilities, etc. Overlooking 12 acres of landscaped meadows with its own private fishing lakes. The local village inn is within 100 metres and has a restaurant which serves "pub grub". Bed and Breakfast from £20. Why not telephone David and Annie so that we can tell you about our lovely home.

DISS. Mrs Jill Potterton, Blacksmiths Cottage, Langmere Green Road, Langmere, Diss IP21 4QA

(01379 740982). Friendly relaxed atmosphere in our detached country cottage in pretty hamlet, with three and a half acre meadow, home to our collection of poultry, waterfowl, Shetland sheep and small nursery growing cottage garden plants. Ideal central location for touring being two and a half miles off A140, six miles north of Diss. Guest accommodation comprises one double and one single room with tea/coffee facilities; lounge overlooking a well lawned garden, dining room and bathroom. Hearty breakfasts using free-range eggs and homemade preserves. Children over 10 welcome. No dogs. Packed lunch and evening meals by arrangement. Bed and Breakfast £16. Reduction for long stay. Registered with the East Anglian Tourist Board.

DISS. Strenneth, Airfield Road, Fersfield, Diss IP22 2BP (01379 688182; Fax: 01379 688260; E-mail: ken@mainline.co.uk).

Strenneth is a well established family run business situated in unspoiled countryside just a short drive from Bressingham Gardens and the picturesque market town of Diss. Offering first class accommodation, the original 17th century building has been carefully renovated to a high standard with a wealth of exposed oak beams and a newer single storey courtyard wing. There is ample off road parking and plenty of nice walks nearby. All seven bedrooms, including a four-poster and an Executive, are tastefully arranged with period furniture and distinctive beds. Each has remote control colour TV, hospitality trays, central heating and full en suite facilities. The main house is smoke free and the guest house has a log fire on cold winter evenings. There is an extensive breakfast menu using local produce. Ideal touring base. Pets most welcome at no extra charge. Outside kennels with runs if required. Hair and beauty salons now open. Bed and Breakfast from £20.

DISS near. Oxfootstone Granary, Low Common, South Lopham, Diss IP22 2JS (01379 687490).

ETB ✤ *COMMENDED*. Stay with us at our converted barn, erected in 1822 at Oxfootstone Farm in quiet open countryside with long views but near the A1066 between Thetford and Diss. Our two en suite guest rooms and lounge/breakfast room are at ground level, in former cart sheds gouped around a central courtyard garden and directly overlooking a large pond with waterfowl. Nearby attractions include Redgrave and Lopham Fen Nature Reserve (walking distance), Bressingham Steam Museum and Alan Bloom's Gardens (two miles), Thelnetham windmill and Banham Zoo. Bed and Breakfast from £18. Non-smoking. Well behaved pets and children over five years welcome. Open all year.

· The Old Shop ·

AA QQ

24 London Road, Downham Market, Norfolk PE38 9AW   Tel: 01366 382051   Mrs June Roberts

Charming conversion of three cottages built in 1815. Relaxed, homely atmosphere in a quiet market town approximately 12 miles from the historic towns of King's Lynn and Wisbech, bordering on Lincolnshire and Cambridgeshire. Ideally situated for walking, cycling, fishing, bird watching and touring East Anglia. Two double and one family room, all en suite, with colour TV and tea/coffee making facilities. Guests' lounge. Bed and Breakfast from £16. Evening Meal available. Pets welcome. Open all year.

FELTHORPE. Irene and Dennis Thompson, Spinney Ridge, Hall Lane, Felthorpe, Norwich NR10 4BX (01603 754833). You will find us within easy reach of the Broads, National Trust country houses, North Norfolk coast and just six miles north of Norwich just off the 1149. We are situated down a country lane in a rural and woodland setting but convenient for recommended restaurants. Spinney Ridge has the conveniences of a recently constructed house plus the character of beamed ceilings and waxed polished woodwork. The accommodation consists of one double and one twin bedroom with en suite facilities and one double and one twin bedroom with adjacent bathroom. Each room is equipped with a vanity unit, tea/coffee making facilities, TV and central heating. Children welcome. Sorry no pets. Bed and Breakfast from £15.

FELTWELL. Mrs Joy Day, Bruton Cottage, Lime Kiln Lane, Feltwell IP26 4BJ (01842 828368). 18th century cottage near Thetford Forest. Central heating and log fire. Large garden. Bed and Breakfast from £15 per night; with dinner £20. Self catering prices from £250 per week for two or £300 for four. Please write or telephone for further details.

GARBOLDISHAM. Ingleneuk Lodge, Hopton Road, Garboldisham, Diss IP22 2RQ (01953 681541). COMMENDED. AA QQQ, RAC Highly Acclaimed, Guestaccom Good Room Award. Our modern single level home is set in 10 acres of partly wooded rural countryside. We have seven bedrooms with a choice of single, double or twin with en suite facilities and all have remote control TV, hot drink making facilities, central heating and comfortable easy chairs. Spacious lounge and bar overlooks the garden; the comfortable dining room overlooks the sheltered patio. There is a no smoking policy in the dining room and some bedrooms. Many interesting places to visit are within easy reach — take a week or stay a day or two. Special breaks available. Please send for our colour brochure and full tariff listing. A warm welcome awaits.

GREAT YARMOUTH. Mr and Mrs Brian and Diana Kimber, Anglia House Hotel, 56 Wellesley Road, Great Yarmouth NR30 1EX (01493 844395). This comfortable private hotel is pleasantly situated adjacent to the sea front and near the coach station, just three minutes from pier and town centre. A warm and friendly welcome awaits you. Our reputation and good name have been built on service, a friendly atmosphere and fine food with a choice of menu. Radio, colour TV and tea making facilities in all bedrooms. Most rooms en suite. Own front door keys with access to rooms at all times. Licensed bar. Children welcome. Bed and Breakfast from £13; Bed, Breakfast and Evening Meal from £99 weekly. Open all year. For a happy holiday please send SAE or telephone. RAC Listed.

GREAT YARMOUTH. Mrs E. Dack, 'Dacona', 120 Wellesley Road, Great Yarmouth NR30 2AP (01493 856863 or 855305). Homely guest house with own keys and access at all times. Centrally situated, it is only two/three minutes from the seafront and five minutes from shopping centre. Every amenity provided — tea making facilities in all rooms, comfortable accommodation and an ideal location. Bed and Breakfast terms from £13 to £14 nightly. Small parties (up to 24) welcomed. Children catered for (half price rates). Dogs accepted on enquiry.

GREAT YARMOUTH. Mrs M. Lake, Old Station House, North Road, Hemsby, Great Yarmouth NR29 4EZ (01493 732022). Standing well off the road behind a large front garden, this well-maintained turn-of-the-century house is ideally situated for touring the Norfolk Broads and Great Yarmouth area. The immaculate bedrooms are spacious and have pine vanity units. A large TV lounge contains lots of books and overlooks the garden and patio where guests can sit out on sunny days. Children welcome. Sorry no dogs; no smoking. Terms: single occupancy £24, double £34, family £40 to £45. Reductions for children depending on ages. Open Easter to end October. Please send for further information.

HARLESTON. Mrs June E. Holden, Weston House Farm, Mendham, Harleston IP20 0PB (01986 782206). ❦❦ COMMENDED. 17th century Grade II Listed farmhouse set in one acre garden overlooking pastureland on a mixed farm. Close to Norfolk/Suffolk border, it is within easy reach of Suffolk Heritage Coast, Norfolk Broads, Wild Life Parks and many stately homes. Accommodation comprises one family/double and two twin rooms, all with en suite facilities, shaver points and beverage facilities. Comfortable lounge with colour TV for guests' use, dining room with separate tables. Adequate parking space. Bed and Breakfast from £18. Discount for longer stays. AA Recommended QQQ.

HELHOUGHTON (Near Fakenham). Mrs C. Curtis, Greenlea, Raynham Road, Helhoughton, Fakenham NR21 7BH (01485 528547). Tranquillity and relaxation are assured in this friendly home in a rural setting. Ground floor bungalow accommodation consists of two double and one twin bedrooms; bathroom, two toilets and shower room. All rooms have colour TV, tea/coffee facilities and central heating. Helhoughton can be found five miles from Fakenham and is an ideal base for touring. Close to Sandringham, many attractions and beaches are within easy reach. Bed and Breakfast from £17; Evening Meal available by prior arrangement. Open all year.

KING'S LYNN. Mrs Joan Bastone, Maranatha Guest House, 115 Gaywood Road, Kings Lynn PE30 2PU (01553 774596). ❦❦ APPROVED. Charming Victorian guesthouse within easy walking distance of the town centre and Lynn Sports Centre. Sandringham House and the coast near by. Owned and run by Joan Bastone providing personal service. Accommodation comprises two double (one en suite), three twin (one en suite), two family and one single bedrooms; ground floor room available en suite. Ideal for business travellers or holiday makers alike. Children and pets welcome free of charge. Bed and Breakfast from £14; Evening Meal available. AA QQ, RAC.

KING'S LYNN. Stuart House Hotel, 35 Goodwins Road, King's Lynn PE30 5QX (01553 772169; Fax: 01553 774788). ❀ ❀ ❀ *COMMENDED.* AA Two Star. An elegant Victorian Hotel, quietly situated in its own grounds, just a few minutes' walk from the centre of historic market town and port of King's Lynn. All bedrooms (some four-poster) have en suite facilities, colour TV with satellite channels, refreshment tray and direct-dial telephone. Superb à la carte restaurant. Cosy bar with real ales and varied bar meals. Quiet garden. Private parking. Bed and Breakfast from £22.50. Children and pets welcome. Open all year. Special breaks available.

MATTISHALL, near Dereham. Mrs Betty Jewson, Ivy House Farm, Welgate, Mattishall, Dereham NR20 3PL (01362 850208). Working farm. This architecturally interesting house dates from the Cromwellian period with a strong Jacobean influence and a later Georgian facade. Situated in 17 acres in the village of Mattishall, four miles from East Dereham, 12 from Norwich and within easy reach of the Coast and Norfolk Broads. Guests are accommodated in one double and two twin-bedded rooms; bathroom and toilet; guests' own dining and drawing room. We provide a full English Breakfast, a four course Evening Meal if required, and packed lunches. Bed and Breakfast from £14, Evening Meal from £6. Reductions for children. Pets welcome. Brochure available.

NORFOLK BROADS/NEATISHEAD. Alan and Sue Wrigley, Regency Guest House, The Street, Neatishead, Near Norwich NR12 8AD (01692 630233). ❀ ❀ *COMMENDED.* An 18th century guest house in picturesque, unspoilt village in the heart of Broadlands. Personal service top priority. Long established name for very generous English breakfasts. 20 minutes from medieval city of Norwich and six miles coast. Ideal base for touring East Anglia — a haven for wildlife, birdwatching, cycling and walking holidays. No. 1 centre for Broads sailing, fishing and boating. Guest house, holder of "Good Care" Award for high quality services, has five bedrooms individually Laura Ashley decorated and tastefully furnished. Rooms, including two king-size doubles, and family room, have TV and tea/coffee making facilities and most have en suite bathrooms. Two main bathrooms. Separate tables in beamed ceiling breakfast room. Guests' sitting room. Cot, babysitting, reduced rates children and all stays of more than one night. Pets welcome. Parking. Open all year. Fire Certificate held. AA QQQ. Also self catering cottage, sleeps six, available next to guest house. Bed and Breakfast from £19.50.

NORWICH. The Broads Hotel, Station Road, Wroxham, Norwich NR12 8UR (01603 782869; Fax: 01603 784066). ❀ ❀ ❀ *HIGHLY COMMENDED.* Comfortable hotel renowned for its high standard cuisine. Owned and run by dog-loving family. Ideally situated for boating, fishing and exploring the beautiful Norfolk countryside and coastline. All rooms fully en suite with tea/coffee making, colour TV, etc. RAC/AA Two Stars. Please telephone for brochure.

NORWICH. Mr Brian and Mrs Diane Curtis, Rosedale Guest House, 145 Earlham Road, Norwich NR2 3RG (01603 453743). Tourist Board Listed. Friendly, family-run Victorian Guest House pleasantly situated within short walking distance of city centre and University, on the B1108. All rooms have colour TV, tea/coffee making facilities and own keys for your convenience. A full English breakfast is served in the diningroom and vegetarians are made very welcome. There are several good eating places nearby and once you have parked your car you can relax and enjoy Norwich. The Norfolk Broads are just seven miles away and the coast 20 miles. Full central heating. Bed and Breakfast from £15 per person.

NORWICH. Mrs M. Gilbert, Aberdale Lodge, 211 Earlham Road, Norwich NR2 3RQ (01603 502100). Tourist Board Listed *APPROVED.* Visiting Norwich? Enjoy your overnight accommodation, weekend break or annual holiday at this friendly guest house close to the centre of Norwich, ideally situated for visiting all the historic places of interest for which the city is famous. Within 10 minutes you are on the Norfolk Broads, or you can visit the bird sanctuaries in the depths of the Norfolk countryside. Six bedrooms, all with hot and cold water, colour TVs, tea/coffee making facilities and central heating. There is a pleasant diningroom with separate tables; excellent food and service under the personal supervision of the proprietor. Full Fire Certificate. Guests have access at all times with keys provided. Bed and Breakfast from £15.50. No VAT. Reduced rates for children.

NORWICH. Mrs M.A. Hemmant, Poplar Farm, Sisland, Loddon, Norwich NR14 6EF (01508 520706). Working farm. This 400 acre mixed farm is situated one mile off the A146, approximately nine miles south east of Norwich, close to Beccles, Bungay, Diss and Wymondham. An ideal spot for the Broads and the delightful and varied Norfolk coast. We have a Charolais X herd of cows, with calves born March-June. The River Chet runs through the farm. Accommodation comprises double, twin and family rooms, bathroom, TV sittingroom/dining room. Central heating. Tennis court. Children welcome. A peaceful, rural setting. Car essential. Open all year for Bed and Breakfast. Terms from £15 per person per night.

RACKHEATH. Mr and Mrs R. Lebbell, Manor Barn House, Back Lane, Rackheath, Norwich NR13 6NN (01603 783543). ♥ ♥ *COMMENDED.* 17th century converted barn with a wealth of exposed beams. A family home with lovely gardens in quiet surroundings, situated just off A1151. Very convenient for Norwich (five miles), and two miles from Wroxham, heart of Broadland. Accommodation includes twin/double rooms with central heating, tea/coffee facilities, TV and own bathroom. Separate lounge area with colour TV. We are 100 yards from traditional old Norfolk pub, "The Green Man", where it is possible to eat very well and inexpensively. Open all year for Bed and Breakfast from £18 to £25 single, £35 to £40 double.

RACKHEATH. Julie Simpson, Barn Court, Back Lane, Rackheath NR13 6NN (Tel & Fax: 01603 782536). Tourist Board Listed *COMMENDED.* Friendly and spacious accommodation in a traditional Norfolk Barn conversion built around a courtyard. Situated five miles from the historic city of Norwich and two miles from the heart of the Norfolk Broads at Wroxham. Our accommodation consists of one double en suite room with a four-poster and two double/twin rooms. All rooms have colour TV and facilities for making tea/coffee. We are within walking distance of a very good Norfolk pub which serves reasonably priced meals. Packed lunches and dinners are available on request. Children are very welcome. Bed and Breakfast from £18 to £20.

SHERINGHAM. Pinecones, 70 Cromer Road, Sheringham NR26 8RT (01263 824955). ♥ ♥ *COMMENDED.* Sheringham is an attractive little seaside town with top-class sandy beaches and a nice traditional character. We are surrounded by the best of North Norfolk's tremendously varied countryside. There are woods, hills, cliffs, heaths, historic houses and England's best birdwatching. At Pinecones we have private parking, a sheltered garden to sit in, guests' lounge with open fire, and tea/coffee and TV in your room. Our family room and a double are en suite, the other double and twin have a separate bathroom. Bed and Breakfast from £16.50 to £19. We have tandems and cycles plus detailed routeplans for rides and walks, also special low season "Why Not?" Weekends involving anything from dressmaking to fantasy poker.

SHERINGHAM. Mrs Pat Pearce, The Birches, 27 Holway Road, Sheringham NR26 8HW (01263 823550; e-mail: wwwbroadland.com.thebirches). Small guest house conveniently situated for town and sea front. Ideal centre for touring North Norfolk. Accommodation comprises one double and one twin-bedded rooms, both with luxury bathrooms, tea/coffee making equipment and colour TV. Full central heating. Open March to November. Bed and Breakfast for two nights £37 per person; Evening Meal available on request. Special diets catered for. No children under 12 years. No pets. NON-SMOKING ESTABLISHMENT. EATB registered. Member of the North Norfolk Hotel and Guest House Association. Heartbeat Award for 1994/5 and 1996/97.

SOMERTON. George and Prue Dobinson, White House Farm, The Street, West Somerton NR29 4EA (01493 393991). Welcoming 17th century farmhouse with space, peace and comforts to ensure relaxation, providing an excellent base for exploring the wonderful local beach and nature reserve, the Broads and National Trust Properties (at Horsey, Blickling and Felbrigg). Substantial breakfasts with local produce. Conservatory and sunny, walled garden. Private bath/shower rooms. Log fires. Bicycles. Piles of books and magazines with colour TV/video in comfortable sitting room. Bed and Breakfast from £17. Children welcome. Sorry no pets or smoking in the house.

SWAFFHAM. Mrs Green, "Paget", Lynn Road, Narborough, King's Lynn PE32 1TE (01760 337734). Private house offering Bed and Breakfast. Lounge available, log fire. TV in bedrooms. Ample parking. Pleasant local river, lakes and rural walks. Various water sports and horse riding nearby. Situated between the old market town of Swaffham and King's Lynn. Trout and coarse fishing lakes nearby. Pets welcome. Bed and Breakfast £14 per person. SAE please.

THETFORD. Mrs Marion Ford, Old Bottle House, Cranwich, Mundford, Thetford IP26 5JL (01842 878012). Old Bottle House is a 275 year old former coaching inn, on the edge of Thetford Forest. Guests have a choice of three spacious, colour co-ordinated bedrooms (two twin, one double/family) with tea/coffee making facilities and colour TV. Delicious meals are served in the dining room, which has an inglenook fireplace. A charming house with every comfort, and a warm friendly welcome. An excellent base from which to explore Norfolk. Bed and Breakfast from £17; Dinner from £12. Children welcome, minimum age five years. Open all year. No smoking.

THETFORD/WATTON. Kevin and Yvonne Fickling, Rose Cottage, Butters Hall Lane, Thompson, Thetford IP24 1QQ (01953 488104). EATB Listed *COMMENDED.* Thompson, situated 10 miles north of Thetford, three miles south of Watton off the A1075, is a quiet village on the edge of Thetford Forest in an area noted for its interesting walks, including Peddars Way. Rose Cottage is a spacious and comfortable house in an acre of ground. Excellent breakfasts and evening meals are served in the oak beamed diningroom. Bedrooms, two large double and one single, have colour TV, radio, tea/coffee facilities. There is central heating throughout. Bed and Breakfast from £18 single, £35 double. Three-course Evening Meal £10. Sorry, no smoking. Pets welcome. We are open throughout the year including Christmas. Business people are welcome.

THURSFORD. Mrs Sylvia Brangwyn, The Heathers, Hindringham Road, Thursford, Fakenham NR21 0BL (01328 878352). Very quiet country location ideal for touring, walking and visiting stately homes (ie., Sandringham, Holkham Hall, Blickling and Felbrigg), bird watching at Cley, Titchwell and Blakeney Point; Walsingham Shrine four miles. There is one ground floor double room with one twin and one double on first floor; all rooms have private en-suite with shaver points, colour TV and tea/coffee making facilities. Full central heating. Christmas and New Year Breaks. Car is essential; ample parking facilities. Bed and Breakfast from £19 to £21 per person per night on two people sharing; optional Evening Meals by prior arrangement.

"The Heathers"

THURSFORD, near Holt. John and Jenny Duncan, Mulberry Cottage, Green Farm Lane, Thursford Green, Fakenham NR21 0BX (01328 878968). We are situated six miles from Holt and three miles from Walsingham. The sandy beaches of the North Norfolk coast lie within easy reach. Plenty of walks for the energetic. Accommodation comprises double and twin-bedded rooms (one on ground floor), both are en suite and have TV and tea/coffee making facilities. Log fires in winter to relax by. Wide choice of breakfast. Ample parking. We regret our home is not suitable for children or pets and we would ask guests to kindly refrain from smoking. Bed and Breakfast from £20 per person per night.

WALSINGHAM. The Old Rectory, Waterden, Walsingham NR22 6AT (01328 823298). This charming

rectory is situated in peaceful rural surroundings on the Holkham Estate close to the village of South Creake. Ideally positioned for exploring the North Norfolk coast and countryside and for bird watching, walking, cycling, sailing, golfing and much more. A great place for gourmet restaurants and pubs. Three well appointed en suite rooms are available. A warm welcome awaits guests from your host Mrs Pile. Prices on application. This is a non-smoking house. Open all year.

WATTON. Mrs Sue Baldwin, The Croft, 69 Hills Road, Saham Hills, Watton, Thetford IP25 7EW

(01953 881372). An attractive Victorian farmhouse covered in Virginia creeper and set in large well tended gardens. Situated on the edge of Breckland two miles north of the small town of Watton. Central position makes this an ideal base to explore Norfolk: Norwich, King's Lynn, Sandringham, Bury St. Edmunds and the coast are all within 30 miles. Non-smoking guests are accommodated in one double room en suite and one twin bedroom. Bed and Breakfast from £18. Delicious evening meals by arrangement using home produced vegetables in season. Ample parking. Sorry, no pets.

WELLS-NEXT-THE-SEA. Mrs Dorothy MacCallum, Machrimore, Burnt Street, Wells-next-the-Sea

NR23 1HS (01328 711653). A warm welcome awaits you at this attractive barn conversion. Set in quarter of an acre in quiet location close to the shops and picturesque harbour of Wells. Guest bedrooms at ground floor level. Ample car parking. Sorry no smoking in the bedrooms. Ideal for the bird watching sanctuaries at Cley, Salthouse and Titchwell. Close to Sandringham, Holkham and the Shrines at Walsingham. Prices from £20 to £22 daily; £115 to £130 weekly.

WINTERTON-ON-SEA. Muriel Webster, Tower Cottage, Winterton-on-Sea, Great Yarmouth NR29

4AP (01493 394053). A friendly welcome awaits you at this charming flint cottage overlooked by the 14th century church in this quiet village. Pretty bedrooms (two on the ground floor) have tea/coffee facilities and TV (one bedroom is en suite with its own sittingroom, in a converted barn). Generous breakfasts including home-made preserves, are served amongst the grapevines in the conservatory, during summer. Beautiful, unspoilt sandy beach and traditional village pub with good food are within a few minutes' walk and the Norfolk Broads, Great Yarmouth and Norwich are within easy reach by car. "Which?" entry since 1994. Open all year. Children over eight years. Bed and Breakfast from £16.

NORTHAMPTONSHIRE

PETERBOROUGH. Trudy Dijksterhuis, Lilford Lodge Farm, Barnwell, Oundle, Peterborough PE8 5SA (01832 272230). ♛ ♛ *COMMENDED.* Mixed farm set in the attractive Nene Valley situated on the A605, three miles south of Oundle and five miles north of the A14. Peterborough and Stamford are within easy reach. Guests stay in the recently converted original 19th century farmhouse. All bedrooms have en suite bathrooms, central heating, radio and tea/coffee making facilities. Comfortable lounge with satellite TV and separate dining room. Coarse fishing available. Children welcome. Bed and Breakfast from £19. Reductions for children. Open all year except Christmas and New Year.

THE GLOBE HOTEL

– A Countryside Inn –

Watling Street, Weedon, Northants NN7 4QD
Tel: 01327 340336   Fax: 01327 349058

♛♛♛♛ Commended   RAC ★ ★

Conveniently located three miles west of Junction 16 of the M1, this eighteenth century coaching inn offers attractively furnished and well equipped rooms, all with private bathrooms, colour TV, radio, telephones and tea/coffee making facilities. A comprehensive food operation, OPEN ALL DAY, features home fayre bar meals and value for money à la carte menus. Pies are our speciality. Weedon is centrally located for visiting the many historic places and fascinating market towns in the area also Silverstone Racing Circuit: leisure activities include golf and walking. Weekend Giveaway Breaks – bed and breakfast £22.50 per person per night sharing a double or twin room.

RECOMMENDED SHORT BREAK HOLIDAYS IN BRITAIN

Introduced by John Carter, TV Holiday Expert and Journalist

Specifically designed to cater for the most rapidly growing sector of the holiday market in the UK. Illustrated details of hotels offering special 'Bargain Breaks' throughout the year.

Available from newsagents and bookshops for £4.50 or direct from the publishers for £5.00 including postage, UK only.

FHG PUBLICATIONS LTD
Abbey Mill Business Centre, Seedhill,
Paisley, Renfrewshire PA1 1TJ

NORTHUMBERLAND

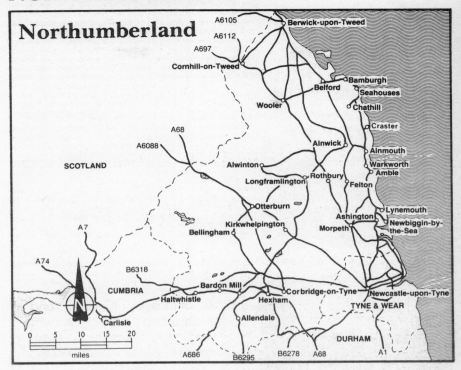

Northumberland

SCOTLAND

CUMBRIA

DURHAM

TYNE & WEAR

(Map of Northumberland showing roads including A6105, A6112, A697, A68, A6088, A7, A74, B6318, B6295, A686, B6278, A68, A1, and towns including Berwick-upon-Tweed, Cornhill-on-Tweed, Bamburgh, Belford, Seahouses, Wooler, Chathill, Craster, Alnwick, Alnmouth, Alwinton, Warkworth, Longframlington, Rothbury, Amble, Felton, Otterburn, Lynemouth, Ashington, Newbiggin-by-the-Sea, Kirkwhelpington, Morpeth, Bellingham, Bardon Mill, Corbridge-on-Tyne, Newcastle-upon-Tyne, Haltwhistle, Hexham, Carlisle, Allendale.)

miles 0 5 10 15 20

ALLENDALE. Mrs Eileen Ross Finn, Thornley House, Allendale NE47 9NH (01434 683255). ♥ ♥ ♥

HIGHLY COMMENDED. Beautiful country house in spacious grounds surrounded by field and woodland, one mile out of Allendale, 10 miles south of Hexham, near Hadrian's Wall. Two large beautifully furnished lounges, one with TV, one with Steinway Grand Piano; three bedrooms all with private facilities, tea makers and home-made biscuits. Marvellous walking country where you don't see anybody. Conducted walks sometimes available. Riding school, golf course nearby. Home baking. Bring your own wine. Packed lunches, vegetarians catered for. Christmas Breaks. Portable TV available. Ample parking. Bed and Breakfast from £18.50. Dinner £11.

ALNMOUTH. Janice and Norman Edwards, "Westlea", 29 Riverside Road, Alnmouth NE66 2SD (01665 830730). ♥ ♥ ♥ *COMMENDED.* We invite you to

relax in the warm, friendly atmosphere of "Westlea" situated at the side of the Aln Estuary. We have an established reputation for providing a high standard of care and hospitality. Guests start the day with a hearty breakfast of numerous choices and in the evening a varied and appetising four-course traditional meal is prepared using local produce. All bedrooms are bright, comfortable and en suite with colour TVs, hot drinks facilities, central heating and electric blankets. Two bedrooms on the ground floor. Large visitors' lounge and diningroom overlooking the estuary. Ideal for exploring castles, Farne Islands, Holy Island, Hadrian's Wall. Fishing, golf, pony trekking, etc within easy reach. Bed and Breakfast from £20; Bed, Breakfast and Evening Meal from £32. Alnwick District Council Hospitality Award 1989/1991/1992. 1994 Award for Overall Contribution to Tourism.

ALNMOUTH. Mrs A. Stanton, Mount Pleasant Farm, Alnmouth, Alnwick NE66 3BY (01665 830215). Mount Pleasant is situated on top of a hill on the outskirts of the seaside village of Alnmouth, with spectacular views of surrounding countryside. We offer fresh air, sea breezes, green fields and beautiful beaches, country roads and peace and quiet. There are two golf courses and a river meanders around the farm with all its bird life. There are also historic castles, Holy Island, the Farnes and the Cheviots to explore. Farmhouse has large rooms, tea making and en suite facilities. Ample parking. Terms from £18.50. Self catering accommodation can be booked. Details on request.

ALNWICK. Mrs Ann Bowden, Roseworth, Alnmouth Road, Alnwick NE66 2PR (01665 603911). 👑👑 *HIGHLY COMMENDED.* A warm Northumbrian welcome awaits you at Roseworth, set in a beautiful situation covered in Virginia creeper and roses. You can enjoy sitting in our large garden. Roseworth is a very clean and comfortable house which is very tastefully decorated to the highest standards. Two en suite rooms, and one with private facilities. All bedrooms have tea trays, colour TV and double glazed windows. Comfortable lounge. Each morning Ann serves a good hearty Northumbrian breakfast to start the day. Alnwick is a good touring area with good, clean beaches four miles to the east and 17 miles north west to the Cheviot Hills. Many castles and good country walks available. Bed and Breakfast from £19. Please telephone for further details.

ALNWICK. Mrs J.W. Bowden, "Anvil-Kirk", 8 South Charlton Village, Alnwick NE66 2NA (01665 579324). A very characterful cottage offering a friendly, homely atmosphere and a welcome to match. Former Smithy built in 1771, completely modernised iñ 1974, affording very comfortable accommodation comprising a double bedroom and one twin bedded room with washbasin, shower and shaver points. Open wood-burning fire in communal lounge. Full English Breakfast. Good value meals at local pubs. A peaceful village surrounded by farmland plus moorland walks with views of the Cheviot Hills, Bamburgh and Dunstanburgh Castles and, of course, our lovely clean beaches. Three-quarters of a mile from the A1 and very easy to locate. Pets welcome. Ample parking. Bed and Breakfast terms from £16 to £18. Also available, a 39 ft. Residential Caravan for hire weekly from £165 to £195. Please phone for details.

ALNWICK. Charlton House, 2 Aydon Gardens, South Road, Alnwick NE66 2NT (01665 605185). 👑👑 *HIGHLY COMMENDED.* Beautiful Victorian town house where guests are always welcomed in a friendly, relaxed, informal atmosphere. There is a real flair for decor with antiques, home-made patchwork quilts and excellent home cooking. Two double, one twin, one family and one single bedrooms have en suite facilities and are complete with colour TV and hospitality trays. Comfortable guests' lounge with satellite TV. We offer a choice of breakfast — full English, Continental, vegetarian, "healthy option", local Craster kippers (when in season), various crepes. Alnwick District Council "Lionheart Award" Winners. Bed and Breakfast from £18 per person. Information leaflet available. Ideally situated to discover the Northumbrian "Secret Kingdom".

ALNWICK. Mrs B. Gaines, Crosshills House, 40 Blakelaw Road, Alnwick NE66 1BA (01665 602518). 👑👑 *HIGHLY COMMENDED.* Come and join us at Crosshills for your stay in historic Northumberland. A friendly guest house situated in a quiet area near golf course and only a short walk into town. We have two double rooms and one twin room, all en suite and having colour TV and tea/coffee making facilities. Twin room has balcony with a beautiful view of coast and countryside. Parking. Sorry, no dogs. Bed and Breakfast from £19 per person. Parking available.

AMBLE near. Mrs L.A. Marshall, Togston Hall Farm House, North Togston, Near Amble NE65 0HR

(01665 712699). ❦❦❦ COMMENDED. Tranquil farmhouse atmosphere and personal service in country setting. En suite bedrooms plus adjacent cottage for four or more. Colour TV. Varied breakfast menu using our own eggs, Craster kippers, etc and traditional home cooked food served for our ever popular five course evening meal at 7pm. Private parking. Bed and Breakfast from £19 per person per night; Dinner, Bed and Breakfast from £29 per person per night. Weekly rates available.

BEADNELL. Marilyn Davidson, 7 Benthall, Beadnell NE67 5BQ (Tel & Fax: 01665 720900). Two

comfy en suite double rooms furnished with family antiques in recently restored non-smoking home. 7 Benthall forms part of a terrace of old stone cottages near the harbour and 2km of sandy beaches. This is glorious country for golfers and walkers, riders and painters, bird watchers and historians to explore and enjoy a relaxing holiday in the clear light of the East Coast's open skies. A few miles off the A1, Beadnell is easily accessible for visiting Edinburgh or Newcastle and is in the midst of Northumberland's "secret kingdom" with its castles, keeps and peel towers.

BELFORD. Jan and David Thompson, The Cott, Belford NE70 7HZ (01668 213233). ❦ COMMEN-

DED. The Cott is situated on the A1 outside the village of Warenford, 12 miles north of the market town of Alnwick. The Cott consists of two cottages, owners living in one, the other — "Etive" — converted into four comfortable bedrooms, two family/twin and two double rooms, all with washbasins, tea/coffee, central heating and double glazing. All rooms are on ground level with use of gardens and private car park. We are an ideal base for exploring the beautiful Northumberland coast or countryside, five miles from Bamburgh and Seahouses. Golf courses nearby. Pets welcome. Bed and Breakfast from £18.

BELSAY (3 miles). Mrs Kath Fearns, Bounder House, Belsay, Newcastle-upon-Tyne NE20 0JR (01661 881267). Stone built farmhouse situated in beautiful Northumbrian countryside off A696 Newcastle/Edinburgh road. Half a mile north of Belsay, turn right onto B6309, follow B&B sign; 15 minutes from Newcastle Airport. Ideally situated for touring Northumberland and the Borders or convenient overnight stop en route for Scotland. Two double rooms (en suite), a family room and a twin room, all with colour TV and tea/coffee facilities. Pets welcome. Open all year round. Terms from £18 per person.

BERWICK-UPON-TWEED. The Cat Inn, Cheswick, Berwick-upon-Tweed TD15 2RL (01289 387251). A Wayside Inn with eight bedrooms situated on the A1, four miles south of Berwick-upon-Tweed. All rooms have full facilities, four of which have en suite facilities. Lunches and dinners available. Real ales served. Pets welcome. Open all year. Please write or telephone for further details.

CORBRIDGE. Mr and Mrs F.J. Matthews, The Hayes, Newcastle Road, Corbridge NE45 5LP (01434 632010). 🐦 *APPROVED.* Spacious, attractive stone-built guesthouse set in seven acres of grounds. Single, double, twin, family bedrooms. Lounge and dining rooms. Open 11 months of the year. Bed and Breakfast from £16. Children's reductions. Stair lift for disabled guests. Also self catering properties — three cottages, flat and caravan. Awarded two Farm Holiday Guide Diplomas. Car parking. For brochure or booking SAE/phone.

EMBLETON. Mr and Mrs K. Robson, Brunton House, Brunton, Near Embleton, Alnwick NE66 3HQ (01665 589238). 🐦🐦 *COMMENDED.* Elegant country house set in large gardens, ideally situated close to miles of clean sandy beaches and the unspoilt and beautiful Cheviot Hills. Excellent centre for walking, golfing, fishing, birdwatching and visiting the numerous castles and stately homes in the area. The accommodation is spacious and comfortable, with twin, double and single rooms, some of which are en suite; a pleasant dining room and two lounges, one for those who wish to smoke. Guests can look forward to a warm welcome and good home cooking (Tourist Board Gourmet Food Award 1997). Open March to October. Bed and Breakfast from £17; Evening Meal by arrangement. Reduction for children under 12 years.

HADRIAN'S WALL. Mr Mark Chaplin, Hadrian Lodge, Hindshield Moss, North Road, Haydon Bridge, Hexham NE47 6NF (01434 688688). Hadrian Lodge is a quality conversion of a stone-built hunting and fishing lodge into Bed and Breakfast and Self Catering accommodation. Set in 18 acres of idyllic Northumberland countryside, Hadrian Lodge provides a friendly social atmosphere with single, twin, double and family rooms; some en suite available. Two miles from the most popular attractions — Hadrian's Wall, Housesteads and Vindolanda Museum. Hadrian Lodge is the ideal base from which to explore the beauty and history of the Hadrian's Wall area and the North Pennines. Licensed lounge/bar. Ample parking. Trout fishing in our well stocked private lake. We offer a high standard of accommodation and service. Bed and Breakfast from £10. Find us two miles north of Haydon Bridge.

HEXHAM. Mrs Margot Fyfe, Morningside, 15 Woodlands, Hexham NE46 1HT (01434 603133). 🐦🐦 Morningside is a spacious, centrally heated Edwardian house situated on the Corbridge Road offering a high standard of cleanliness and comfort, along with personal friendly service. One large double room, one large twin room both fully en suite, one single room with private bathroom. All rooms have colour TV, tea/coffee making facilities and radio clock alarms. Selection of breakfasts available. Overnight off-street parking. Non-smoking establishment. Ideal for visiting Hadrian's Wall, Northumberland National Park, Beamish Museum, Metro Centre and Hexham Abbey. Convenient bus/rail; 10 minute walk to town centre. Prices from £17.50 per person.

HEXHAM. Mrs E. Courage, Rye Hill Farm, Slaley, Hexham NE47 0AH (01434 673259; Fax: 01434 673608). 🏵🏵🏵 *COMMENDED.*

This is a 300-year-old stone farmhouse set in its own 30 acres of rural Tynedale. Rye Hill Farm offers you the freedom to enjoy the pleasures of Northumberland throughout the year while living comfortably in the pleasant family atmosphere of a cosy farmhouse adapted especially to receive holidaymakers. Family, double and single rooms, all with colour TV, hot-beverage facilities and bathrooms en-suite. Full English Breakfast, three-course Evening Meal (optional); table licence. There is even room for your caravan if you prefer not to live in. Well-mannered children and pets are more than welcome. Terms for Bed and Breakfast from £20 plus VAT; Evening Meal from £10 plus VAT. Major credit cards accepted. Brochure available. AA QQQ.

HEXHAM. Mrs D.A. Theobald, Dukeslea, 32 Shaws Park, Hexham NE46 3BJ (01434 602947). 🏵🏵 *HIGHLY COMMENDED.* AA QQQ Recommended. Dukeslea is an unusual modern detached family home situated in a quiet position overlooking Hexham Golf Course, with private parking.

High standards are maintained throughout the tasteful guest accommodation conveniently located on the ground floor. Both comfortable double en suite rooms have central heating, tea/coffee making facilities, hair dryers and radio/alarms. Relax and enjoy excellent breakfasts served in the cosy dining/TV lounge. Approximately one mile from station and town centre. Ideal base for exploring Hexham and its Abbey, Hadrian's Wall, Kielder, Beamish Museum and Gateshead Metro Centre. Totally non-smoking establishment. Open all year. Prices from £17. Brochure on request.

HEXHAM. Mrs Ruby Keenleyside, Struthers Farm, Catton, Allendale, Hexham NE47 9LP (01434 683580). 🏵🏵 *COMMENDED.* Struthers Farm offers a warm welcome in the heart of England with many splendid local walks from the farm itself. Panoramic views. Double/twin rooms, en suite, central heating. Good farmhouse cooking. Ample safe parking. Come and share our home and enjoy beautiful countryside. Children welcome, pets by arrangement. Open all year. Bed and Breakfast from £16.50; Evening Meal from £8.50. Farm Holiday Bureau Member, Tourist Board inspected.

HEXHAM near. Mrs Doreen Cole, Hillcrest House, Barrasford, Hexham NE48 4BY (01434 681426). *AA QQQ Recommended.* Hillcrest House has been specifically extended to provide a high standard of accommodation with a homely, comfortable atmosphere. One family, one double, one twin and one single rooms, all with en-suite shower rooms, colour TV and tea/coffee making facilities. Evening Meal optional; packed lunches on request. Comfortable lounge; separate tables in diningroom. Residential licence. Situated seven miles from historic Hexham in beautiful North Tyne Valley. Ideal for touring Hadrian's Wall and within easy distance of Kielder, the Borders, Newcastle, and Gateshead Metro Centre. Car essential. Bed and Breakfast from £18–£20 Single, £32–£35 Double; Evening Meal £7.

NORTHUMBERLAND – BORDER COUNTRY!

You cannot go any further north and remain in England! There is much outstanding scenery, both inland and on the coast, and a host of interesting places to visit. Border Forest Park has everything you would expect, plus many interesting Roman remains. There are also remains at Housesteads and other places of interest include Lindisfarne, the "conserved" village of Blanchland, Hexham, Heatherslaw Mill and Craster.

PONTELAND near. Mr and Mrs Edward Trevelyan, Dalton House, Dalton, Newcastle-upon-Tyne NE18 0AA (01661 886225). ❦ ❦ We offer our visitors a warm welcome and a high standard of accommodation in this attractive Georgian house, situated in the peaceful little village of Dalton, near Ponteland on the A696. Ideal for touring Northumberland and exploring Hadrian's Wall, Border castles and glorious countryside and coastline. Newcastle, Morpeth and the Airport are within an easy 30-minute drive: this is a convenient place for visiting businessmen who prefer to stay out of town. Bed and Breakfast from £18 per person including bedtime drink; Evening Meal by arrangement from £12; light snacks £5. Excellent home cooking, using own produce when available. Children over 12 welcome. Sorry, no pets. Non-smokers preferred. Open May to October. Directions: four miles from Ponteland A696 follow signs to Dalton.

POWBURN. A. & D. Johnson, Doveburn, Powburn NE66 4HR (Tel & Fax: 01665 578266). ❦ ❦ *HIGHLY COMMENDED.* A warm welcome awaits you at Doveburn which is situated high upon the hill overlooking the village of Powburn with spectacular views of the Cheviot Hills and the Breamish Valley. Converted from 18th century farm buildings the house has retained the charm of a period listed building whilst providing every modern convenience for your comfort. The immaculate well appointed bedrooms all with private facilities have remote control TV, tea making facilities, hair dryer, king size bath towels, top quality toiletries, etc. Delicious traditional English breakfast is served. Bed and Breakfast from £22.50. Breaks available. Dogs welcome by arrangement. Non-smoking establishment. Please write or telephone for our brochure and full tariff.

WARKWORTH. John and Edith Howliston, North Cottage, Birling, Warkworth NE65 0XS (01665 711263). ❦ ❦ *HIGHLY COMMENDED.* Situated on the outskirts of the historic coastal village of Warkworth, we are an ideal base from which to explore Northumberland with its superb beaches and castles. We have four comfortable, well furnished no-smoking rooms — two double and one twin-bedded rooms en suite, and one single with washbasin; all have colour TV. All bedrooms have hospitality trays, central heating and electric overblankets and all are on ground floor. There is of course a bathroom with shower, and a sitting-room with cheery gas fire and colour TV. A full breakfast is served in the diningroom and afternoon tea is served (free of charge) with home-made cakes/biscuits. Large well kept garden and water garden. Warkworth has its own castle, river, golf course and beautiful sandy beaches. Bed and Breakfast from £18.50. Weekly rates from £123. AA Recommended QQQ, RAC Acclaimed.

WARKWORTH. Mo and Brian Halliday, Beck 'n' Call Cottage, Warkworth NE65 0XS (01665 711653). ❦ ❦ *HIGHLY COMMENDED.* This traditional country cottage is set in beautiful terraced gardens with a stream and is only five minutes' walk to the village, castle, river walks and sandy beaches. The accommodation is comfortably furnished and includes two double rooms and one family room. All on ground floor with washbasins, shaver points, colour TV, tea/coffee making facilities and heating; en suite available. Residents' lounge. Warkworth makes an ideal base from which to explore rural Northumberland and the Borders with their unspoilt beauty and historic interest. Bed and Breakfast from £18. Children welcome, reduced rates. Non-smokers. Private parking. Colour brochure available. Open all year.

WARKWORTH. Mrs Sheila Percival, Roxbro House, 5 Castle Terrace, Warkworth NE65 0UP (01665 711416). ❦ A small family guest house overlooking historic Warkworth Castle, and in the centre of this unspoilt village. Half a mile from sandy beach in a designated Area of Outstanding Natural Beauty. Central for touring Northumberland. Plenty of eating places within walking distance. The accommodation is comfortable and includes one family room and two double rooms. All have private shower and washbasin, are centrally heated and have locks on the doors. There is a lounge with TV, and tea/coffee is available. Open all year. Bed and Breakfast from £16.50, reduced rates for children. Non-smokers only.

WOOLER. Mrs J. Allan, Loreto Guest House, 1 Ryecroft Way, Wooler NE71 6BW (01668 281350). A

charming early Georgian house set in its own grounds, occupying a central position in the North Northumberland town of Wooler. For those who wish to explore old ruins, discover wildlife, sample superb beaches, walk through forests or over hills and moors, North Northumberland offers all of these in abundance. All rooms are tastefully decorated and have en suite facilities; guests' lounge with colour TV, cocktail bar. We are well known for our excellent cuisine and our elegant dining room with choice of menus at breakfast and evening meal offers charming surroundings for diners. Licensed. Please telephone, or write, for tariff and brochure.

NOTTINGHAMSHIRE

BLIDWORTH. Ann and Simon Shipside, Holly Lodge, Ricket Lane, Blidworth NG21 0NQ (01623

793853). Attractive 19th century former Hunting Lodge delightfully situated in peaceful country surroundings approximately 10 miles north of Nottingham, quarter of a mile off A60. The Victorian outbuildings have been attractively converted to provide comfortable en suite accommodation. All rooms have colour TV and tea/coffee making facilities. Central heating throughout. Ample car parking. Tennis court, golf, riding, walking available. Good pubs and restaurants nearby. Rates from £21. Non-smoking establishment.

BURTON JOYCE. Mrs V. Baker, Willow House, 12 Willow Wong, Burton Joyce, Nottingham NG14 5FD (0115 931 2070). A large period house (1857) in quiet village location yet only four miles from city. Attractive, interesting accommodation with authentic Victorian ambience. Bright, clean rooms with tea/coffee facilities, TVs. Walking distance of beautiful stretch of River Trent (fishing). Ideally situated for Holme Pierrepont International Watersports Centre; golf course; Trent Bridge (cricket); Sherwood Forest (Robin Hood Centre) and the unspoiled historic town of Southwell with its Minster and Racecourse. Good local eating. Evening Meal by arrangement. Private parking. From £16 per person per night. Reduced rates for children. Please phone first for directions.

LAXTON. Reg and Margaret Rose, Lilac Farm, Laxton, Newark NG22 0NX (01777 870376). 🐾 *APPROVED.* Lilac Farm 1748 Listed building, situated in the medieval village of Laxton. Two family rooms and one double room, all have central heating, washbasin, TV and tea/coffee making facilities. The bathroom is fitted with bath, shower, toilet, hair dryer and shaving pint; additional toilet and shower down stairs. Evening meals to be booked in advance, also special diets. The Heritage Museum is adjacent. The Dovecot Inn is a five minute walk and is noted for its fine beers and wine, good home cooking. The Visitors Centre is nearby. Laxton is within easy reach of many historic places, Lincoln, Nottingham, Chatsworth and Sherwood Forest. Open all year. Large secure car park. Terms from £16 per person per night. Reductions for children.

MANSFIELD. Mrs L. Palmer, Boon Hills Farm, Nether Langwith, Mansfield NG20 9JQ (01623

743862). This is a stone-built farmhouse, standing 300 yards back from A632 on edge of village. It is on a 155-acre mixed farm with dogs, cats, goats, chicks, calves. Situated on the edge of Sherwood Forest, six miles from Visitors' Centre, eight miles from M1, 10 miles from A1. Chatsworth House, Newstead Abbey, Hardwick Hall and Creswell Crags all within easy reach. Two double and one twin-bedded room; bathroom; toilet; fitted carpets throughout. Open fires. Background central heating for comfort all year round. Large sittingroom/diningroom with colour TV. Children welcome, cot and babysitting. Pets allowed. Car essential — parking. Bed and Breakfast from £15 per night, which includes bedtime drink. Evening Meal available nearby. Non-smokers only. Rates reduced for children. Open March to October inclusive.

MANSFIELD. Marion's Manor B&B, Ollerton Road, Edwinstowe, Mansfield NG21 9QF (01623 822135). Tourist Board Listed. Marion and Eric welcome you to the heart of Sherwood Forest. Also situated near Rufford and Clumber Park, Newstead Abbey, only 30 minutes' drive to Nottingham City. From only £18 per person we can offer you a full English breakfast, bright comfortable rooms with colour TV, tea/coffee facilities, hand/bath towels. Central heating for all year round comfort. Private car park with security lights. Downstairs consists of one twin room and one family room with adjoining shower room. Upstairs one double room with adjoining bathroom. All rooms have washbasins and shaver sockets.

NEWARK. Mr Gilmour, The Old Rectory, Church Lane, Averham, Newark NG23 5RB (01636 707655; Fax: 01636 701108). A very imposing English rectory, a beautiful Listed country house standing in three acres of landscaped gardens. There are many mature and varied trees including an American Redwood and a very rare Ginkgo Biloba. The Old Recotry is situated next to the Robin Hood Theatre and has views of the open countryside and the River Trent. Central heating. Prices from £15.

NEWARK. Ken and Margaret Berry, Lockwell House Guest House, Lockwell Hill, Farnsfield, Newark NG22 8JG (01623 883067). Set in 25 acres with 10 acres of woodland and situated on the edge of Sherwood Forest near Rufford Park on the A614, we are within easy reach of Nottingham, Newark, Mansfield, Worksop and all local country parks and tourist attractions. Small family-run Bed and Breakfast offering friendly service and comfort. All bedrooms are en suite and have tea/coffee making facilities, hair dryers, etc. TV room. Full English breakfast. Tariff: Double room (twin/double bed) £38; Double room (single occupancy) £24; Family room (double and single beds) £50. Reductions for children. Brochure available.

NORTON (Sherwood Forest). Fernie Palmer, Norton Grange Farm, Norton, Cuckney, Near Mansfield NG20 9LP (01623 842666). 🐾 *COMMENDED.* **Working farm, join in.** Norton Grange Farm is a Listed Georgian-type farmhouse and is situated on the edge of Sherwood Forest overlooking peaceful open countryside, away from the traffic. The 172 acre mixed farm carries poultry and arable crops, also many domestic farm animals. A car is advantageous for visiting the many places of local interest — ample parking. Accommodation comprises family room, double and twin-bedded rooms with washbasins. All rooms have tea/coffee making facilities. Fitted bathroom with shower, separate toilet. Sitting room, dining room. Bed and full English Breakfast from £17 is provided all year except Christmas. Flasks filled on request. Reductions for children sharing family room.

NORTON GRANGE FARM
Tel. 0623 842666

NOTTINGHAM. Mrs J. Buck, Yew Tree Grange, 2 Nethergate, Clifton Village, Nottingham NG11 8NL (0115 984 7562). Yew Tree Grange is a Georgian residence of great charm and character located five miles from the M1 Junction 24. The house is situated in the quiet rural setting of Clifton Village, only 10 minutes from the City Centre. Accommodation includes single, twin and family bedrooms, some with en suite facilities. There is ample car parking and a mature garden with duck pond. Ideally located for tourists visiting Robin Hood country or for businessmen stopping overnight. Bed and Breakfast from £18 per person per night with reduced rates for small children. Evening Meals by arrangement. A non-smoking establishment.

NOTTINGHAM. Mr and Mrs Binns, The Grantham Hotel, 24-26 Radcliffe Road, West Bridgford, Nottingham NG2 5FW (0115 981 1373; Fax: 0115 981 8567). 🐾 *COMMENDED.* Only a quarter of a mile from Trent Bridge and one and a half miles from the city centre — the Grantham is ideally situated for both the city of Nottingham (shopping and castle), the National Water Sports Centre at Holme Pierrepont and all the sporting facilities at Trent Bridge. It is a 22 bedroom family-run hotel providing comfortable accommodation, mainly en suite, a licensed bar and restaurant (Dinner served 6-7pm). Terms: Single £28 en suite, £21 standard; Double/Twin £40.00 including breakfast and VAT. Family rooms available.

NOTTINGHAM. Masterson's, 3 Melton Road, West Bridgford, Nottingham (0115 9818198). Guesthouse conveniently situated for city centre. All rooms are spacious and comfortably furnished with remote control colour TV and tea/coffee making facilities. Bathroom/shower room adjacent to bedrooms. Children and pets welcome. Central heating. parking. Prices from £17 per person.

NOTTINGHAM. Grace Moffett, "The Hermitage", 150 Perry Road, Sherwood, Nottingham NG5

1GL (0115 9621716). A warm welcome is guaranteed at this delightful family-run guest house. "The Hermitage" is within easy reach of the ring road, close to the city centre, and yet tranquilly set in its own charming gardens. Convenient for exploring Robin Hood country, or cosmopolitan attractions. Spacious bedrooms with tea/coffee making facilities as well as Satellite TV. Home cooked breakfast. Children of all ages catered for. Ample secure parking.

NOTTINGHAM/CLIFTON VILLAGE. Alan and Jane Haymes, Camellia House, 76 Village Road, Clifton Village, Nottingham NG11 8NE (0115 9211653). A quiet picturesque village only three miles from city centre, backing onto the River Trent with riverside wooded walks. Our new traditionally built house in mature setting is double glazed, has central heating and private parking. We offer double, twin and single rooms with colour TV and tea/coffee making facilities. Continental breakfast consisting of fruit juice, cereals, grapefruit, prunes, yoghurt, toast, jams, marmalade, warm rolls, cheeses, tea and coffee. Our rates are from £17.50 per night. We aim to provide a warm welcoming atmosphere at all times.

NOTTINGHAM/NUTHALL. Rodney and Margaret Cains, "Camelot", 22 Watnall Road, Nuthall NG16 1DU (0115 938 2597). Three minutes from Junction 26 of the M1, close to D.H. Lawrence country and convenient for walkers of the Robin Hood Way. Nottingham, the ice arena and sports stadiums are all within easy reach. TV, tea/coffee in rooms. Local pubs and restaurants provide meals at reasonable prices. Our en suite family room is on the ground floor; cot and highchair available. this is a non-smoking house in pleasant gardens. Bed and Breakfast from £15 to £18 per person per night. Reductions for children and room only rates available.

SOUTHWELL. Mrs Erica McGarrigle, Archway House, Kirklington, Newark NG22 8NX (01636

812070; Fax: 01636 812200). Atmospheric Edwardian country house set in 40 acres of parkland, located between A1 and M1, three miles north of Southwell. Close to Sherwood Forest and a wealth of walks and golf courses. Accommodation comprises two double rooms, one with en suite shower, one with private bath; one twin-bedded room with en suite bath. No smoking in bedrooms. Colour TV and tea/coffee facilities in all rooms. Separate drawing room. Bed and Breakfast from £18.50 to £22.50 pp; light suppers available or Dinner (if ordered in advance) £15. Children welcome. Swimming pool, tennis, croquet, snooker and four practice golf holes. Advance booking please.

STANTON-ON-THE-WOLDS. Mrs Val Moffat, Laurel Farm, Browns Lane, Stanton-on-the-Wolds NG12 5BL (0115 937 3488). Laurel Farm is an old farmhouse set in approximately four acres standing on a lane off the main A606. Rooms are spacious, all have shower and washbasin with three having full private facilities; all have colour TV and tea/coffee making. There are pet horses, sheep, cats and dogs and our own free range hens. Children are welcome in the large family room, at reduced rates. Babysitting free. Large garden with unusual plants, pond and bog area. Dogs housed in the stables. All day access to rooms. Bed and Breakfast from £16.50 to £20. No smoking in the house.

SUTTON-IN-ASHFIELD. Dalestorth Guest House, Skegby Lane, Skegby, Sutton-in-Ashfield NG17 3DH (01623 551110). Dalestorth Guest House is an 18th century Georgian family home converted in the 19th century to become a school for young ladies of the local gentry and a boarding school until the 1930s. In 1976 it was bought by the present owners and has been modernised and converted into a comfortable, clean and pleasant guest house serving the areas of Mansfield and Sutton-in-Ashfield, offering overnight accommodation of Bed and Breakfast or longer stay to businessmen, holidaymakers or friends and relations visiting the area. Please send for further information.

UPPER BROUGHTON. Mrs Hilary Dowson, Sulney Fields, Colonel's Lane, Upper Broughton,

Melton Mowbray LE14 3BD (Tel & Fax: 01664 822204). Large country house in quiet position with magnificent views across the Vale of Belvoir. Easy access to Nottingham, Leicester, Loughborough and Melton Mowbray. Centrally placed for day trips to York, Cambridge, Warwick, Chatsworth and the Peak District. Spacious accommodation in twin/double rooms, most of which have private bathrooms and all have tea/coffee making facilities. Large sitting room with TV for guests' use. Bacon and sausages for breakfast come from the Award winning butcher in the village. Good pub/restaurant within walking distance which serves food every evening. Bed and Breakfast from £16 per person.

OXFORDSHIRE

BANBURY. Mrs K.A. Batchelor, The Cotswold Guest House, 45 Oxford Road, Banbury OX16 9AH

(01295 256414). Family-run Georgian town house within walking distance of town centre. Small residents bar available. Freshly prepared evening meals served daily. Healthy eating always a priority. Children welcome, cot available. A warm and friendly welcome assured. Central heating.

BANBURY. Mrs Rosemary Cannon, High Acres Farm, Great Bourton, Banbury OX17 1RL (Tel &

Fax: 01295 750217). New Farmhouse situated on edge of village off A423 Southam Road, three miles north of Banbury overlooking the beautiful Cherwell Valley. Ideally situated for touring Cotswolds, Stratford, Warwick, Oxford, Blenheim Palace. Pub in village serving evening meals Tuesdays to Saturdays. Very comfortable accommodation comprising one twin room, one family room (one double and one single bed). Tea/coffee facilities, hair dryers; central heating; shower room with electric shower; guests' sittingroom with colour TV. All rooms fully carpeted. Non-smoking. Parking. Bed and Breakfast from £16. Child under 10 sharing family room £10. Sorry, no pets. A warm welcome awaits you.

BANBURY. Mrs E.J. Lee, The Mill Barn, Lower Tadmarton, Banbury OX15 5SU (01295 780349). Tadmarton is a small village three miles south-west of Banbury. The Mill, no longer working, was originally water-powered and the stream lies adjacent to the house. The Mill Barn has been tastefully converted, retaining many beams and exposed stone walls and with all the amenities a modern house can offer. Two spacious en suite bedrooms, one downstairs, are available to guests in this comfortable family house. Base yourself here and visit Stratford, Oxford, Woodstock and the Cotswolds, knowing you are never further than an hour's drive away. Open all year round for Bed and Breakfast from £17.50. Reductions for children. Weekly terms available.

BICESTER near. Barbara Hands, The Old Post Office, Church Raod, Ardley, Near Bicester OX6 9NP

(01869 345958). This rural accommodation is set in the garden of the main house giving the rooms their own separate entrances. Both have en suite facilities, are spacious and comfortable. The location is just right for leisure or business.

BLADON near. Tom and Carol Ellis, Wynford Guest House, 79 Main Road, Long Hanborough,

Woodstock OX7 2JX (01993 881402; Fax: 01993 883661). Tourist Board Listed. Wynford Guest House is situated in the village of Long Hanborough only a mile from Bladon, final resting place of Sir Winston Churchill, and three miles from famous Woodstock and Blenheim Palace. The city of Oxford is twelve miles away and the Cotswolds are on our doorstep. We offer personal service, excellent food and comfortable accommodation consisting of a family room en-suite, with colour TV, and double and twin rooms; all have tea/coffee making facilities. Excellent pubs and restaurants less than five minutes' walk. Bed and Breakfast from £19; Evening Meal from £9. Open all year.

CHARLBURY. Mr and Mrs G. Widdows, Banbury Hill Farm, Enstone Road, Charlbury OX7 3JH (01608 810314; Fax: 01608 811891). Banbury Hill Farm offers Bed and Breakfast in Cotswold stone farmhouse with extensive views across Evenlode Valley. Comfortable rooms with tea/coffee and colour TVs. Ideal touring centre for Blenheim Palace, Oxford and Cotswolds. Ample parking. Terms: single from £16 to £25; double from £16 to £20 per person. Brochure available.

Banbury Hill Farm

COMBE. Mrs Rosemary Fox, Mayfield Cottage, West End, Combe, Witney OX8 8NP (01993 898298). ETB Listed *HIGHLY COMMENDED.* Guests are assured of a warm welcome in our home, a delightful Cotswold stone cottage with oak beams and inglenooks, yet providing all home comforts. Combe, a small unspoilt village, is an ideal base for touring the Cotswolds with Blenheim Palace and Woodstock only 10 minutes by car. There are lovely walks and many good pubs and restaurants in the area. Our accommodation comprises a single, a twin and a double room, all furnished in cottage style with bathroom exclusively for guests' use. There is also a comfortable lounge. Children over 12 years welcome. Sorry, no pets. Bed and Breakfast from £17.

DEDDINGTON. Mrs Audrey Fuller, Earls Farm, Deddington, Oxford OX15 0TH (01869 338243). 🐾🐾 **Working farm.** Delightfully situated on edge of village 200 yards from main Banbury to Oxford road, this farm covers 230 acres of cropping fields. Open all year, it has two double, one family bedrooms, all with washbasins; two bathrooms, two toilets; sitting room, dining room. Central heating. Children very welcome and facilities for them include cot, high chair, babysitting and reduced rates; also swing and slide. Fishing available on River Swere, trout fishing on local lake by arrangement. Golf five miles away, tennis two miles, Banbury six miles. This is an ideal touring base. Pets accepted. Car essential, parking. Bed and Breakfast £17 per person per night sharing.

FARINGDON (Oxon). Mr D. Barnard, Bowling Green Farm, Stanford Road, Faringdon, Oxfordshire SN7 8EZ (01367 240229; Fax: 01367 242568). 🐾🐾 Attractive 18th century period farmhouse offering 20th century comfort, situated in the Vale of White Horse, just one mile south of Faringdon on the A417. Easy access to the M4 Exit 13 for Heathrow Airport. An ideal place to stay for a day or longer. This is a working farm of cattle and horse breeding, poultry and ducks. Large twin-bedded/family room (en suite) on ground floor. All bedrooms have colour TV, tea/coffee making facilities and full central heating throughout. Ideal area for riding, golf, fishing and walking the Ridgeway. Interesting places to visit include Oxford, Bath, Windsor, Burford, Henley-on-Thames, Blenheim Palace and the Cotswolds. Open all year. Member of Farm Holiday Bureau.

FREELAND. Mrs B.B. Taphouse, Wrestlers Mead, 35 Wroslyn Road, Freeland, Oxford OX7 2HJ (01993 882003). A warm welcome awaits you at the home of the Taphouses. We are conveniently located for Blenheim Palace (10 minutes), Oxford (20 minutes), and the Cotswolds (25 minutes). Accommodation comprises one double and one single room, both with washbasins and at ground level. Our first floor family room has its own en suite shower room with washbasin and toilet. The double and the family rooms each have a colour television. Cot, highchair and babysitting service available. Pets by arrangement. No hidden extras. Bed and Breakfast from £17.

OXFORDSHIRE – CHILTERNS, COTSWOLDS AND COLLEGES!

Many fine days can be spent studying Oxford's architecture – both old and new. Other interesting pastimes might include trips to Banbury and Europe's biggest cattle market, the Cotswold Wildlife Park near Burford, the Rollright Stones near Chipping Norton and the Vale of the White Horse at Uffington.

HENLEY-ON-THAMES. Mrs K. Bridekirk, 107 St. Marks Road, Henley-on-Thames RG9 1LP (01491 572082). A large comfortable house in a quiet location near town and River Thames. Very good for short breaks and visits to Oxford, Windsor and London, and river trips along the famous Henley Regatta course. Plenty of places to eat. Good area for walking. Easy to get to Heathrow. All rooms have colour TV, tea/coffee making facilities, washbasin. En suite available. Full central heating. Full English breakfast. Children under three years FREE, under 12 years half price. Singles from £26, double/twin from £45. Regret no dogs. Good parking facilities. Open all year.

HENLEY-ON-THAMES. Mrs Liz Roach, The Old Bakery, Skirmett, Near Henley-on-Thames RG9 6TD (01491 638309). This welcoming family house is situated on the site of an old bakery, seven miles from Henley-on-Thames and Marlow; half an hour from Heathrow and Oxford; one hour from London. It is in the Hambleden Valley in the beautiful Chilterns, with many excellent pubs selling good food. Riding school nearby; beautiful walking country. Two double rooms with TV, one twin-bedded and two single rooms; two bathrooms. Open all year. Parking for five cars (car essential). Children and pets welcome. Bed and Breakfast from £20 to £25 single; £40 to £50 double.

LONG HANBOROUGH. Ann Warwick, The Close Guest House, Witney Road, Long Hanborough OX8 8HF (01993 882485). ❤❤ *COMMENDED.* We offer comfortable accommodation in house set in own grounds of one and a half acres. Two family rooms, one double room; all are en suite and have colour TV and tea/coffee making facilities. Lounge. Full central heating. Use of garden and car parking for eight cars. Close to Woodstock, Oxford and the Cotswolds. Babysitting. Open all year except Christmas. Bed and Breakfast from £15.

MILTON-UNDER-WYCHWOOD. Mrs Wendy Jones, Hillborough House, The Green, Milton-under-Wychwood OX7 6JH (01993 830501; Fax: 01993 832005). AA QQQQ Selected — Awarded Best Newcomer 1989. Elegant Victorian house set deep in the Evenlode Valley facing the village green in this delightful Cotswold village. The bedrooms are all en suite, warm and spacious; some are of a cottage character in an annexe across the courtyard from the main house. A guests' lounge with comfy sofas, and secluded, walled, lawned gardens make for a relaxing stay. Dinner may be arranged for you in our adjoining Willows Restaurant from Tuesday to Saturday. The Cotswolds are renowned for good walks and picturesque villages. Explore Shakespeare's Stratford, Warwick and Leamington Spa or the University City of Oxford. Tariff: Double £27 per person Tuesday/Saturday, £21 per person Sunday/Monday. Mid-week reductions for three nights or more.

OXFORD. Diana and Richard Mitchell, Highfield West, 188 Cumnor Hill, Oxfrod OX2 9PJ (01865 863007). ❤❤ *HIGHLY COMMENDED.* Welcome to our comfortable home, which is in a quiet residential area on the western outskirts of Oxford — on a bus route to the centre of Oxford, we are near to the ring road and to Cumnor village where two attractive inns serve meals. Blenheim Palace is nearby — London, Stratford-on-Avon, Bath and the Cotswolds are within comfortable travelling distance. Our well-appointed rooms have central heating, colour TV and refreshment trays. The family, double and twin rooms are en suite, the two single rooms share a bathroom. Our large outdoor pool is heated in season. Non-smoking. Vegetarians welcome.

OXFORD. Mrs B.A. Downes, Bravalla Guest House, 242 Iffley Road, Oxford OX4 1SE (01865 241326 or 250511). ❤❤ AA, RAC Listed. Homely guest house one mile south-east of centre. Majority of rooms en suite with TV and beverage facilities. Parking. From £20 per person. Pets welcome (£1 per night).

OXFORD. Mrs Gwen Absolom, The Old Post Office, 11 Church Road, Sandford-on-Thames, Oxford

OX4 4XZ (01865 777213). A friendly welcome and comfortable accommodation await you in our centrally heated 17th century home. Situated in a Thameside village only four miles from the centre of Oxford (bus stop nearby); river and pub serving good food only five minutes' walk away. Accommodation offered in one double and one twin room, both en suite with colour TV and drinks making facilities; guests' sitting room. Regret no pets. No smoking. Bed and Breakfast from £17.50 per person.

OXFORD. Mr and Mrs L. Price, Arden Lodge, 34 Sunderland Avenue (off Banbury Road), Oxford OX2 8DX (01865 552076; 04020 68697). Modern detached house in select part of Oxford, within easy reach of Oxford Centre. Excellent position for Blenheim Palace and for touring Cotswolds, Stratford, Warwick, etc. Close to river, parks, country inns and golf course. Easy access to London. All rooms have tea/coffee making and private facilities. Parking. Bed and Breakfast from £21 per person per night.

SOULDERN. Toddy and Clive Hamilton-Gould, Tower Fields, Tusmore Road, Near Souldern,

Bicester OX6 9HY (01869 346554; Fax: 01869 345157). 🏵 🏵 *COMMENDED.* Tower Fields is in an unspoilt elevated position with outstanding views, situated half a mile from the village of Souldern. A recently renovated farmhouse and barn provide comfortable en suite bedrooms on the ground floor, all with colour TV and tea/coffee making facilities. This is a working smallholding where you will see rare breeds of cattle, sheep, poultry and pigs. Full English breakfast using home produce is available. Stabling and garaging available on request. No smoking. Disabled guests accommodated. Three miles Junction 10 M40. Ideally situated for Cotswolds, Silverstone, Birmingham, Oxford. Bed and Breakfast from £22. Full details on request.

STANTON HARCOURT. Mrs Margaret Clifton, "Staddle Stones", Linch Hill, Stanton Harcourt OX8 1BB (01865 882256). A chalet bungalow situated in a peaceful location on the outskirts of the village, with four acres of attractive surroundings including a carp pond; visitors are allowed to fish. A full breakfast is offered to satisfy the keenest of appetites. Disabled persons, children and dogs are welcome. In easy reach of the Cotswolds and Oxford. One double or family room en suite, two twin bedrooms with private bathrooms, also a comfortable TV lounge with tea/coffee available. Bed and Breakfast from £17.50.

TETSWORTH, near Thame. Julia Tanner, Little Acre, Tetsworth, Thame OX9 7AT (01844 281423).

A charming, secluded country house retreat, offering every comfort, set in 18 acres of private grounds, nestling under the Chilterns escarpment. Single, twin and double rooms, all with central heating, colour TV, tea/coffee making facilities; some with en suite facilities. Full English or Continental breakfast. A perfect place to relax and enjoy the local countryside in a quiet location, but only three minutes from Junction 6 on the M40. Children and well behaved family dog welcome. Lovely walking area (Oxfordshire Way and Ridgeway Path). Riding, fishing, gliding and excellent golf course nearby. Within easy reach of Blenheim Palace, Cotswold Wildlife Park, historic Oxford, etc. Little Acre offers a warm welcome and REAL VALUE FOR MONEY from just £15 per night. Reductions for weekly bookings and children. Highly recommended by previous guests. Plenty of good restaurants nearby. Open all year.

THAME, near Oxford. Mr and Mrs J. & G. Dean, Heath House, London Road, Milton Common,

Thame OX9 2NR (01844 278904). A tastefully restored Victorian farmhouse set in five acres with beautiful views to the Chilterns yet only three minutes from Junction 7 of M40 and 20 minutes' drive to Oxford's historic city centre. Bedrooms and bathrooms (some en suite) are decorated and furnished to a high specification; all bedrooms have tea/coffee making facilities, some have TV. The house is close to excellent golf courses and local pubs serve very good food. Enjoy a full English breakfast in beautiful surroundings. A friendly welcome is guaranteed. Sorry no smoking. Bed and Breakfast from £20.

PLEASE SEND A STAMPED ADDRESSED ENVELOPE WITH ENQUIRIES

WITNEY. Mrs Elizabeth Simpson, Field View, Wood Green, Witney OX8 6DE (01993 705485). 🐦🐦
HIGHLY COMMENDED. Witney is famous for blankets, made here for over 300 years. Our house was built in 1959, of Cotswold stone. Set in two acres and situated on picturesque Wood Green, with football and cricket pitches to the rear, yet only 10 minutes' walk from the centre of this lively, bustling market town. An ideal touring centre for Oxford University (12 miles), Blenheim Palace (eight miles), Cotswold Wildlife Park (eight miles) and country walks. Ample parking. Three delightful en suite bedrooms with central heating, tea/coffee making facilities and colour TV. No smoking. A peaceful setting and a warm, friendly atmosphere await you. Bed and full English Breakfast from £21.

WITNEY near. The Leather Bottel, East End, North Leigh, Near Witney OX8 6PY (01993 882174).

🐦🐦 *COMMENDED.* Joe and Nena Purcell invite you to The Leather Bottel 16th century Inn situated in the quiet hamlet of East End near North Leigh, convenient for Blenheim Palace, Woodstock, Roman Villa, Oxford and the Cotswolds. Victorian conservatory restaurant, where you can enjoy our extensive home cooked bar snacks, vegetarian and à la carte menus, overlooking pretty gardens. Breathtaking countryside walks. Two double en suite bedrooms, one family room with own bathroom, one single bedroom, all with colour TV and tea/coffee making facilities. Bed and Breakfast £18 per person per night, £26 per night for single room. Children welcome. Open all year. Directions — follow signs to Roman Villa off A4095.

WOODSTOCK. Gorselands Farmhouse Auberge, Near Long Hanborough, Near Woodstock, Oxford OX8 6PU (01993 881895). 🐦🐦

Situated in an idyllic peaceful location in the Oxfordshire countryside, Gorselands has its own grounds of one acre. This Cotswold stone farmhouse has exposed beams, flagstone floors, billiards room (full size table), guest lounge, dining conservatory and tennis court. En suite rooms, family room, double/twin rooms available. Large main bathroom with bath and shower. Near to Oxford, Blenheim Palace, East End Roman Villa, Cotswold villages. Children welcome. Bed and Breakfast from £17.50 per person; Evening Meal from £10.95. Licensed. RAC Listed; Elizabeth Gundrey Recommended.

WOODSTOCK. Mrs Kay Bradford, Hamilton House, 43 Hill Rise, Old Woodstock OX20 1AB (01993 812206; Mobile: 0378 705568). High quality Bed and Breakfast establishment with parking, overlooking Blenheim Park, Blenheim Palace and the town centre with good selection of restaurants, pubs and shops within walking distance. Accommodation offered — one twin-bedded room and two double rooms, all en suite with colour TV and tea making facilities. Pleasant dining room. Excellent selection of Continental and full English breakfast. Comfortable and relaxed atmosphere with informative and very hospitable hostess. Ideal base for Blenheim Palace, Bladon, the Cotswolds, Stratford-upon-Avon, Oxford and major airports. Access off A44 northern end of Woodstock, 200 yards from Rose and Crown pub. Children and pets welcome. Bed and Breakfast from £20.

FOR THE MUTUAL GUIDANCE OF GUEST AND HOST

Every year literally thousands of holidays, short-breaks and overnight stops are arranged through our guides, the vast majority without any problems at all. In a handful of cases, however, difficulties do arise about bookings, which often could have been prevented from the outset.

It is important to remember that when accommodation has been booked, both parties — guests and hosts — have entered into a form of contract. We hope that the following points will provide helpful guidance.

GUESTS: When enquiring about accommodation, be as precise as possible. Give exact dates, numbers in your party and the ages of any children. State the number and type of rooms wanted and also what catering you require — bed and breakfast, full board, etc. Make sure that the position about evening meals is clear — and about pets, reductions for children or any other special points.

Read our reviews carefully to ensure that the proprietors that you are going to contact can supply what you want. Ask for a letter confirming all arrangements, if possible.

If you have to cancel, do so as soon as possible. Proprietors do have the right to retain deposits and under certain circumstances to charge for cancelled holidays if adequate notice is not given and they cannot re-let the accommodation.

HOSTS: Give details about your facilities and about any special conditions. Explain your deposit system clearly and arrangements for cancellations, charges, etc, and whether or not your terms include VAT.

If for any reason you are unable to fulfil an agreed booking without adequate notice, you may be under an obligation to arrange alternative suitable accommodation or to make some form of compensation.

While every effort is made to ensure accuracy, we regret that FHG Publications cannot accept responsibility for errors, omissions or misrepresentation in our entries or any consequences thereof. Prices in particular should be checked because we go to press early. We will follow up complaints but cannot act as arbiters or agents for either party.

SHROPSHIRE

BISHOPS CASTLE. Mrs Ann Williams, Shuttocks Wood, Norbury, Bishops Castle SY9 5EA (01588 650433; Fax: 01588 650492). Shuttocks Wood is a Scandinavian house in woodland setting situated within easy travelling distance of the Long Mynd and Stiperstone Hills. Accommodation consists of two double and one twin-bedded rooms, all en suite and with tea/coffee facilities and colour TV. Good walks and horse riding nearby and a badger set just 20 yards from the door! Ample parking. Non smoking establishment. Children over 12 years welcome. Sorry, no pets. Open all year. Bed and Breakfast from £22 per person per night.

BUCKNELL. Mrs Christine Price, The Hall, Bucknell SY7 0AA (01547 530249). ♛♛ *COMMENDED.* You are assured of a warm welcome at The Hall, which is a Georgian farmhouse with spacious accommodation. The house and gardens are set in a secluded part of a small South Shropshire village, an ideal area for touring the Welsh Borderland. Offa's Dyke is on the doorstep and the historic towns of Shrewsbury, Hereford, Ludlow and Ironbridge are within easy reach as are the Church Stretton Hills and Wenlock Edge. Three bedrooms — one twin en suite, two doubles (with washbasins). All have tea-making facilities and TV. Guest lounge. Ample parking. Bed and Breakfast from £17; Dinner £9. SAE, please, for details.

CHURCH STRETTON. Mrs Isobel Burgoyne, Churchmoor Farm, Marshbrook, Church Stretton SY6 6PU (01694 781365). Situated at the foothills of the Long Mynd, the farmhouse has panoramic views of all the hills of South Shropshire. Ideal for rambling and wildlife. Convenient to the A49 and for local places of interest. Homely atmosphere with personal attention. Two double rooms with own bathroom, tea/coffee facilities. Central heating. Bed and Breakfast from £17.50.

CHURCH STRETTON. Mrs Mary Jones, Acton Scott Farm, Acton Scott, Church Stretton SY6 6QN (01694 781260). ♛♛ *COMMENDED.* Lovely 17th century farmhouse in peaceful village amidst the beautiful hills of South Shropshire, an area of outstanding natural beauty. The house is full of character and the rooms, which are all heated, are comfortable and spacious and have washbasins and beverage making facilities; en suite available. Colour TV lounge. We are a working farm, centrally situated for visiting Ironbridge, Shrewsbury and Ludlow, each being easily reached within half an hour. Visitors' touring and walking information available. No smoking. Bed and full English Breakfast from £15 per person. Farm Holiday Bureau member.

CHURCH STRETTON. Don and Rita Rogers, Belvedere Guest House, Burway Road, Church Stretton SY6 6DP (Tel & Fax: 01694 722232) ♛♛♛ *COMMENDED.* A quiet, family-run guest house pleasantly situated on the slopes of Long Mynd, 200 yards from the centre of Church Stretton, yet only 200 yards from 6000 acres of National Trust hill country. Belvedere is an ideal centre for exploring the Welsh borders or for just enjoying the most beautiful county in England. All 12 rooms are centrally heated and have hairdryers, shaver points and tea making facilities. There are two lounges for guests' use (one with TV) and evening meals and packed lunches are available if required. Well-behaved pets are welcome. Bed and Breakfast from £23; Evening Meal £10. 50% reduction for children under 10, 10% reduction for weekly or party bookings. RAC Acclaimed. AA QQQQ.

CLEOBURY MORTIMER. The Kings Arms Hotel, Cleobury Mortimer DY14 8BS (01299 270252).

★★★ *COMMENDED.* 15th century coaching inn, centre lovely village, excellent touring area, convenient for Ludlow, Worcester, Long Mynd, Shrewsbury, Bridgnorth and Ironbridge. Golf courses, fishing, Severn Valley Railway, Safari Park and many National Trust properties all close by. This is a friendly family run pub famous for superb home cooked food, real ales and exceptional accommodation. Five rooms with en suite facilities, all have TV, central heating, tea/coffee making facilities, shaver points and hair dryers. Oak beamed bars and dining room with inglenook fireplace. Snacks, full meals and vegetarian dishes available. Two nights Bed, Breakfast and Dinner from £60 per person; Bed and Breakfast from £22.50 per person.

CLEOBURY MORTIMER. Robert and Joan Neil, The Old Bake House, 46/7 High Street, Cleobury Mortimer, Near Kidderminster DY14 8DQ (01299 270193).

★★ Situated in the main street, was originally two houses built in the late 18th century and contains oak beams, dormer and bay windows and is Grade II Listed. It is fully heated and each guest room has its own private bath or shower room with tea/coffee making facilities and radios. Residents' lounge with TV and separate dining room. Local amenities include golf, riding, fising, Safari Park, walking and a leisure centre in nearby Stourport. Bed and Breakfast from £18; Evening Meals by arrangement. Coeliacs and vegetarians catered for. 10% reductions for stays of three nights or more. Brochure available.

CLUN. Mrs I.J. Evans, Springhill Farm, Clun, Craven Arms SY7 8PE (01588 640337). A mixed working farm situated on the Offa's Dyke footpath, ideal for walkers and weekend breaks with superb views of the countryside. Local interests include Ludlow with Castle, Ironbridge with delightful museums, Shrewsbury with medieval attractions and Clun, all within easy reach. Accommodation includes one family room with cot, one twin-bedded room and one double room, all with tea/coffee making facilities; guest lounge with TV. Central heating throughout. Full English breakfast provided, evening meals available on request when booking. Packed lunches available, vegetarians catered for. Pets welcome by arrangement. Please telephone for further details.

CLUN. Mrs M. Jones, Llanhedric, Clun, Craven Arms SY7 8NG (01588 640203). HETB Listed ★★

Working farm. A mixed farm just two miles off the A488 road, overlooking the picturesque Clun Valley, near the Welsh Border and Offa's Dyke. Ideal for walking or exploring the many places of historic interest including Ludlow and Shrewsbury. Attractive beamed farmhouse with lawns and garden, spacious accommodation, friendly atmosphere and good food. One twin bedroom and two double rooms, one en suite, with washbasins and tea/coffee facilities; visitors' lounge with inglenook fireplace and separate dining room. Sorry, no dogs. Open Easter to October. Non smoking household. Bed and Breakfast from £16; Bed, Breakfast and Evening Meal from £25. Reductions for children.

CLUNGUNFORD. Mrs Anne Prytz, Knock Hundred Cottage, Abcott, Clungunford SY7 0PX (01588 660594).

★ *HIGHLY COMMENDED.* Knock Hundred Cottage, which is a non-smoking home, is a character stone and half timbered cottage believed to originate from the 16th century, enjoying an open aspect with extensive views. The accommodation consists of a double bedroom with private bathroom and a twin-bedded room en suite; both have TV. We are ideally situated for visiting National Trust/English Heritage properties and gardens. Historic Ludlow is 10 miles away and there is an abundance of walks including the Long Mynd, Offa's Dyke and the Corve Dale. Bed and Breakfast from £22.50 per person. Dinner by prior arrangement.

WHEN MAKING ENQUIRIES PLEASE MENTION THIS *FHG* PUBLICATION

DORRINGTON. Ron and Jenny Repath, Meadowlands, Lodge Lane, Frodesley, Dorrington SY5 7HD (01694 731350). ETB Listed *COMMENDED*. Former

farmhouse newly decorated throughout set in eight acres of gardens, paddocks and woodland. Quiet location in a delightful hamlet seven miles south of Shrewsbury. The guest house lies on a no through road to a forested hill rising to 1000ft. Meadowlands features panoramic views over open countryside to the Stretton Hills. Guest accommodation includes en suite facilities and every bedroom has a colour TV. Guests lounge with maps and guides for loan. Drinks on arrival.Central heating. Plenty of parking space. Strictly no smoking. Bed and Breakfast from £16; Evening Meal from £8 by arrangement. Brochure available.

IRONBRIDGE. Len and Daphne Roberts, Woodlands, Park Lane, Madeley, near Ironbridge, Telford TF7 5HJ (01952 580693). ❀❀ *COMMENDED*. Superior

quality en suite accommodation in large new detached bungalow one mile from Ironbridge. Tea and coffee trays in rooms. Lounge with TV and conservatory for guests use. Hearty breakfasts and delicious evening meals. Vegetarian food if required. Convenient for all museum sites and Telford town centre. Easy private parking. Pretty, secluded garden with waterfall and pond. Ideal base for touring beautiful Shropshire and the perfect place to relax. Open all year. From £16 per person per night. Always a warm welcome for guests.

IRONBRIDGE. Springhill, 2 School Road, Coalbrookdale, Telford TF8 7DY (01952 432210). ❀❀

COMMENDED. Situated amidst the many sites of the Ironbridge Gorge Museums, Springhill Guest House offers three en suite bedrooms in an 18th century Ironmaster's house. Within this conservation area, the River Severn cuts through the South Shropshire hills, by the picturesque village of Ironbridge. Coalport China Museum, Blists Hill Open Air Museum and the Coalbrookdale Museum of Iron are all to be found only minutes from our guest house. The historic towns of Bridgnorth, Ludlow and Shrewsbury are within easy reach. There is a large garden and private parking for the use of guests. Evening Meals can be provided if booked in advance. Brochure available. No smoking. Bed and Breakfast from £19 per person.

IRONBRIDGE. Mrs Virginia I. Evans, Church Farm, Rowton, Wellington, Near Telford TF6 6QY (01952 770381). ❀❀ **Working farm, join in.** Come and

enjoy a large country breakfast in our 300 year old farmhouse where guests are welcome to join in the farming way of life. A real working farm with dairy cows, sheep and free range hens. Guests' TV lounge, dining room, bathroom. Family and four-poster bedrooms en suite, also twin-bedded rooms, all with washbasins and tea/coffee facilities; towels provided. Peacefully situated in a quiet village yet near Ironbridge, Shrewsbury, Chester, Ludlow, Potteries, Alton Towers, Cosford Aerospace, etc. Pets and children welcome. Bed and Breakfast from £18 per person. Reductions for children. Also self-catering cottages and caravans available.

LUDLOW. Malcolm and Margaret Lowe, Lower Hayton Grange, Lower Hayton, Ludlow SY8 2AQ (01584 861296; Fax: 01584 861371). Our beautiful

home in the Corvedale Valley, which is designated an Area of Outstanding Natural Beauty, is three and a half miles from the medieval market town of Ludlow. The period house stands in grounds of four acres well away from busy roads and guests enjoy relaxing in our lovely gardens which include an attractive duck pond. We also have a swimming pool and all-weather tennis court. The accommodation is centrally heated, with tea/coffee facilities, colour TV and en suite. Dine in our magnificent conservatory and relax in our guest lounge. Plenty of off-road parking. Rates from £17.50 to £25 Bed and Breakfast. Evening Meal optional. Non-smoking house. We also offer two self catering cottages in grounds.

LUDLOW. Mrs Kath Lanman, "Red Roofs", Little Hereford, Near Ludlow SY8 4AT (01584 711439).

👑 👑 "Red Roofs" is situated in the lovely Teme Valley in an attractive acre of Herefordshire garden. Comfort and a warm welcome awaits you at this centrally heated bungalow which has a ground floor double bedroom, luxury en suite bathroom (suitable for disabled guests) and a first floor double, twin or family room with adjacent private shower room. Colour TV, hospitaly tray in all rooms. Guests' lounge. Ample parking. An ideal centre for walking, visiting National Trust properties and the historic town of Ludlow with its Norman castle and architecture is five miles north. Bed and Breakfast from £20 per person.

LUDLOW. Mr G. Black, Lower House Farm Guest House, Cleedownton, Ludlow SY8 3EH (01584 823648). 👑 👑 COMMENDED. Situated in an Area of Out-

standing Natural Beauty, this Grade II Listed building dates from the Jacobean period. Six miles from Ludlow. Sensitively restored it retains all the charms of mullioned windows, flagstones, inglenooks and a wealth of oak beams as well as en suite or private facilities with every bedroom. We have a residential licence and evening meals feature local produce. We are ideally placed for our guests to uncover Shropshires secrets whether by walking, cycling or driving. Non-smoking house, well behaved pets welcome. Bed and Breakfast from £20; Evening Meal £12. House parties specially welcome. Telephone for brochure.

LUDLOW. Ted & Pat Hansen, Studley Cottage, Clee Hill, Ludlow SY8 3NP (01584 890990). 👑 👑 👑

COMMENDED. Our warm, spacious home offers two guest lounges, four bedrooms (two en suite), all with views, central heating, colour TV, hospitality trays and many extras. The house is set in two acres of gardens containing a stream, ponds, orchard and a sunny, south-facing terrace with stunning views across the Teme Valley. There is ample parking. Clee Hill Common surrounds us, providing scenic rambling and a haven for wildlife. We are ideally located for visiting Ludlow, Ironbridge and the rest of Shropshire. Fresh, free-range eggs from our chickens; home made jams and local produce. Bed and Breakfast from £20; Evening Meal from £10.

LUDLOW. Patricia and Philip Ross, Number Twenty Eight, Lower Broad Street, Ludlow SY8 1PQ (01584 876996; Fax: 01584 876860). 👑 👑 👑

HIGHLY COMMENDED. AA QQQQQ Premier Selected. Where Shropshire meets Herefordshire, and England meets Wales! The guest house comprises three houses, all within a few yards of each other in Lower Broad Street, between the 13th century Broadgate and the ancient Ludford bridge over the River Teme. Each house has two double en suite bedrooms individually decorated and furnished, providing great comfort. Enjoy book-lined walls, pictures, prints, plates and maps with sitting rooms and gardens. Breakfast is at Number Twenty Eight for guests partaking of full English fare, or Continental in your room. Historic Ludlow has much to offer visitors, all within walking distance, fine period houses, lanes with antique and book shops. Ludlow also has a wealth of really good eating houses! Enough to satisfy both the most catholic and fastidious tastes. A non-smoking house.

SHROPSHIRE – HISTORIC BORDER COUNTY!

The lonely Shropshire Hills – an "Area of Outstanding Natural Beauty" – are much favoured by walkers. Those seeking more traditional tourist activities would do well to visit the Acton Scott Working Museum, Ironbridge, Offa's Dyke, the black and white Tudor town of Shrewsbury or the market town of Bridgnorth.

LUDLOW near. Mrs P. Turner, The Brakes, Downton, Near Ludlow SY8 2LF (Tel and fax: 01584 856485). 🐦🐦 *HIGHLY COMMENDED.* AA QQQ. Set in the

heart of beautiful rolling countryside only five miles from the picturesque historic town of Ludlow, The Brakes offers extremely comfortable accommodation with excellent cuisine. A period farmhouse, tastefully modernised, with central heating throughout; there are three double en suite bedrooms with colour TV and a charming lounge with log fire. Open March to October inclusive. The Brakes stands in three acres of grounds with a beautiful garden. Here is excellent walking country including Offa's Dyke and the Long Mynd not far away. Golf, riding and fishing are available. The area is steeped in history with many places of interest within easy reach. Bed and Breakfast £22.50; Dinner £17.50.

MINSTERLEY. Paul and Debbie Costello, Cricklewood Cottage, Plox Green, Minsterley SY5 0HT (01743 791229). 🐦🐦 *HIGHLY COMMENDED.* AA QQQQ

Selected. A delightful 18th century cottage at the foot of the Stiperstones Hills, retaining its original character with exposed beams, inglenook fireplace and traditional furnishings. The bedrooms are fully en suite with lovely views of the Shropshire countryside. Breakfast is served in the sun room, looking out to the hills, with an attractive blackboard menu. Especially inviting is the pretty cottage garden where guests can wander amongst many old-fashioned and unusual plants and stroll alongside the trout stream. Excellent restaurants/inns nearby — full details supplied to guests. Ideal for visiting Shrewsbury and Ironbridge. Private parking. No smoking. Bed and Breakfast from £19.50. Call for brochure.

OSWESTRY. Mrs Margaret Jones, Ashfield Farm House, Maesbury, Near Oswestry SY10 8JH (01691 653589). 🐦🐦 *HIGHLY COMMENDED.* This warm

and friendly old house was once a coach house and later a Georgian farmhouse originating in the 16th century. Full of warmth, charm and character; set in large gardens and orchard just one mile from Oswestry, A5 and A483 roads. All the spacious rooms are fully equipped and have en suite or luxury bathrooms, decorated and furnished in a true country style with lovely views of Welsh mountains, Payphone and cot available. Log fires in winter. Wealth of castles, mountains, lakes and valleys to explore. Chester, Shrewsbury and Llangollen about 30 minutes' drive. Excellent food, canal and boat hire only five minutes' walk. Relaxing, welcoming atmosphere. Children and well behaved pets welcome. Bed and Breakfast from £18.50 per person per night. Special terms for short breaks. Details on request. Four-berth caravan also available.

OSWESTRY near. Mrs Jill Plunkett, Rhoswiel Lodge, Weston Rhyn, Near Oswestry SY10 7TG (01691 777609). 🐦🐦 Victorian country house in delightful gardens beside the Shropshire Union/Llangollen Canal. We are easy to find — just 400 yards from the A5. A convenient place to stop overnight or better still as a centre to explore the Welsh hills, forests, lakes and castles to the west or the verdant, rural quietness of North Shropshire to the east. We enjoy where we live and would be disappointed should you not enjoy our area and our home — at a price of course! Bed and Breakfast from £17 to £20 per person. Double room is en suite and twin room has its own separate facilities.

SHREWSBURY. Bill and Angela Tudor, Holly Farm, Astley, Shrewsbury SY4 4BP (01939 210446). 🐦 *HIGHLY COMMENDED.* A non-smoking establishment

situated in rural Shropshire near the Shropshire Way public footpath. No longer a working farm but stands in one and a quarter acres of gardens and lawns with ample car parking space. The accommodation offers two double bedrooms with washbasins, radio alarms, hair dryers and tea/coffee facilities; modern bathroom with toilet and bath/shower; a lounge with colour TV, and a cloakroom. Full English breakfast with homemade bread and marmalade. Several local establishments provide evening meals but if you would like to try our home cooking this is offered by prior arrangement. Brochure available.

PLEASE SEND A STAMPED ADDRESSED ENVELOPE WITH ENQUIRIES

SHREWSBURY. Anton Guest House, 1 Canon Street, Monkmoor, Shrewsbury SY2 5HG (01743

359275). ☛ *COMMENDED*. The Anton Guest House is an attractive corner-positioned Victorian house which stands on a main road just 10 minutes' stroll from both Shrewsbury town centre and the 10th century Abbey church. Family owned and run, offering a very friendly welcome to guests. Very tastefully decorated with each of the three bedrooms warm and comfortable (house has double glazing) and with tea/coffee making facilities and TVs. Breakfast is wholesome and delicious. The world famous Brother Cadfael books by the late Ellis Peters (now serialised for TV) are set in the area and visitors may be interested in retracing the intrepid monk's steps in the Brother Cadfael Walks. Open all year. Smoking banned throughout. Children welcome. No pets. Bed and Breakfast from £17.50 to £21.

SHREWSBURY. Mrs Janet Jones, Grove Farm, Preston Brockhurst, Shrewsbury SY4 5QA (01939

220223). ☛ *HIGHLY COMMENDED*. AA QQQ, RAC Acclaimed. This lovely 17th century farmhouse with a beautiful view, offers warmth and comfort to all guests. It is set in a little village on the A49, seven miles north of Shrewsbury. The house has a large lounge and dining room with fires and colour TV; four lovely bedrooms (one double/family, one twin both with showers en suite, one double, one single both with washbasins) with easy chairs and tea/coffee trays. Guests' bathroom. Central heating throughout. Visitors are welcomed with tea and home-made cakes, and there is always a variety of delicious food offered for breakfast. Sorry, no smoking. No pets. Bed and Breakfast from £17. We look forward to welcoming you to our home. Reduced rates for children in family room. Short Breaks and weekly terms available.

SHREWSBURY near. Mrs Gwen Frost, Oakfields, Baschurch Road, Myddle, Shrewsbury SY4 3RX

(01939 290823). ☛ *COMMENDED*. Visiting Shropshire? Why not enjoy the warm welcome and home from home atmosphere at Oakfields, which is in a quiet, idyllic setting located in the picturesque village of Myddle made famous by Gough's "History of Myddle" written in 1700. All ground floor bedrooms, each tastefully decorated and equipped with colour TV, tea-making facilities, washbasin, hair dryers and shaver points; cot and high chair also available; guests' TV lounge. Central heating throughout. Large and pleasant garden for guests to enjoy. 15 minutes from Shrewsbury and Hawkstone Park and convenient for Ironbridge, Wales, Chester, etc. Golf and riding nearby. Extensive car park. No smoking. Bed and Breakfast from £16. Nearest main road A528, also straight road from A5.

STIPERSTONES. Roy and Sylvia Anderson, Tankerville Lodge, Stiperstones, Minsterley, Shrews-

bury SY5 0NB (01743 791401). ☛ *COMMENDED*. A cosy country house nestling below the Devil's Chair and Stiperstones nature reserve in the dramatic Shropshire Hills, Tankerville Lodge has won a reputation for its caring, friendly atmosphere and deliciously different food. Guests love the peaceful setting and the sweeping, unforgettable views the area offers. Rich in lore and legend, it's superb walking country and there's a strategic bonus: just 25 minutes from the Tudor delights of Shrewsbury, Tankerville Lodge is excellently placed for touring across the Welsh Border, too. So in addition to other Shropshire "musts" like historic Ironbridge, the Long Mynd and Ludlow, the lovely terraced gardens of Powis Castle and the beauty of Lake Vyrnwy are within easy reach. Bed and Breakfast from £16.50. AA Recommended QQ. Licensed. Pets welcome.

TELFORD. Mrs Jo Savage, Church Farm, Wrockwardine, Wellington, Telford TF6 5DG (01952 244917). 🌸🌸🌸 *HIGHLY COMMENDED.* Down a lime tree avenue in a peaceful village betwixt Shrewsbury and Telford, lies our superbly situated Georgian farmhouse. Mature gardens with medieval stonework, old roses and unusual plants. Minutes from Ironbridge, Shrewsbury and Telford; one mile M54 Junction 7 and M5. Attractive bedrooms with TV, tea/coffee/chocolate, some en suite with ground floor rooms available. Enormous inglenook fireplace in spacious guests' lounge. Delicious breakfasts helped by free-range hens! Bed and Breakfast from £20; Evening meal available from £15. Children and pets welcome. Open all year. AA QQQQ.

TELFORD. The Old Vicarage, Shop Lane, High Ercall, Telford TF6 6AG (01952 770616). 🌸🌸 *COMMENDED.* This 17th century Listed home in High Ercal village is set in rolling countryside between Shrewsbury and Telford. The large attractive gardens also offer ample private parking. All bedrooms are spacious, comfortable and well furnished, tea/coffee making facilities as well as colour TV, en suite or private bathrooms. Explore and enjoy lovely Shropshire, medieval Shrewsbury, the Ironbridge Gorge, Roman remains, Iron Age forts from this attractive rural spot. A warm welcome, friendly family atmosphere, only a stroll to the local pub for an excellent meal and cheerful company. Open all year. Prices from £17.50 to £25 per head Bed and Breakfast.

TELFORD. Mrs Mary Jones, Red House Farm, Longdon on Tern, Wellington, Telford TF6 6LE (01952 770245). 🌸🌸 *COMMENDED.* Our Victorian farmhouse is on a mixed farm. Two double bedrooms have private facilities, one family room with separate bathroom, all large and comfortable. Excellent breakfast. Farm easily located, leave M54 Junction 6, follow A442, take B5063. Central for historic Shrewsbury, Ironbridge Gorge museums or modern Telford. Several local eating places. Open all year. Families most welcome, reductions for children. Pets also welcome. Bed and Breakfast from £18.

WELSH/SHROPSHIRE BORDER. Mrs Hibbert, Corner House Farm, The Cadney, Bettisfield, Near Whitchurch SY13 2LD (01948 710572). Smallholding in idyllic surroundings, peacefully situated with lovely walks. One single, one twin or family suite with bathroom. Rates start at £15 per person.

WHITCHURCH. Miss J. Gregory, Ash Hall, Ash Magna, Whitchurch SY13 4DL (01948 663151). *Tourist Board Listed APPROVED.* **Working farm.** An early 18th-century house in the small North Shropshire village of Ash Magna. One-and-a-half miles from the A41 with easy access to Chester, Crewe, Shrewsbury, Wrexham, Llangollen: all 20 miles or less. Medium sized mixed farm with pedigree Friesians. The farmhouse has oak panelling in several rooms with a large oak staircase as a particular feature. Accommodation in two bedrooms, one with en suite bathroom. Children are welcome and rates are reduced. Open all year.

SOMERSET

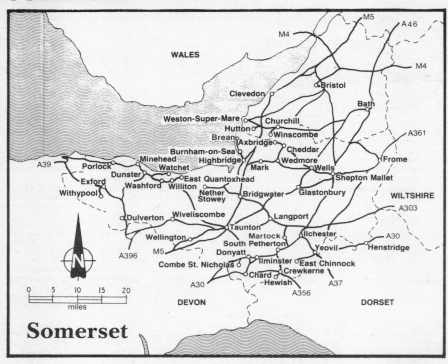

Somerset

ASH. Paterson and Sue Weir, Follys End, 6 Back Street, Ash, Martock TA12 6NY (01935 823073).

Set in an acre of peaceful gardens where ducks and geese idle beside the tranquil pond, Follys End welcomes you with its friendly relaxed atmosphere. All three rooms (two double, one twin) are attractively furnished in period style with central heating, colour TV, tea/coffee making, shaver points and washbasins; the twin room has en suite facilities. Guests are welcome to use the barbecue on summer evenings or improve their golf on the practice bunker and green. Ideal location for nearby National Trust properties, Somerset cider and Willow Craft Centres, Clark's Village Factory Shopping; Lyme Regis, the Dorset coast, Glastonbury, Wells, Cheddar, Stourhead all within easy reach. No smoking. Bed and Breakfast from £17.50 per person. B&B GB Approved, FHG Diploma Award 1997.

ASHBRITTLE. Ann Heard, Lower Westcott Farm, Ashbrittle, Near Wellington TA21 0HZ (01398 361296). ♛♛ *COMMENDED.* AA QQQ Recommended. On Devon/Somerset border, 230 acre family farm with Friesian herd, sheep, poultry and horses. Ideal for walking, touring Exmoor, Quantocks, both coasts and many National Trust properties. Pleasant farmhouse, tastefully modernised but with olde worlde charm, inglenook fireplaces and antique furniture. Set in large gardens with lawns and flower beds in peaceful scenic countryside. Two family bedrooms with private facilities and tea/coffee making; large lounge, separate dining room. Offering guests every comfort, noted for relaxed, friendly atmosphere and good home cooking. Bed and Breakfast from £15; Dinner £8 per person. Reductions for children. Brochure available.

AXBRIDGE near. Miss Jenny Hopkins, Rosewood Cottage, Bridgwater Road, Cross, Near Axbridge BS26 2EB (01934 732694). Situated at the base of the Mendip Hills on the A38 three miles from Cheddar Gorge and five and a half miles from the M5 Junction 22. Ideal base for Wells, Glastonbury, Weston and Bristol Airport. There is a trekking centre next door and foot and cyle paths nearby. There is one double and one family room, each with colour TV and tea making facilities. Private parking. Open all year. Very relaxed atmosphere. Bed and Breakfast from £15. Reduced rates for children; cot available.

AXBRIDGE near. Mrs S. Vincent, Hurdle House, Turnpike Road, Lower Weare, Near Axbridge BS26 2JF (01934 732491). Hurdle House is situated in the beautiful Cheddar Valley, on the A38, four-and-a-half miles from M5 Junction 22. It is within easy reach of Cheddar, Wells, Glastonbury, Weston-super-Mare. Ideal base for a touring holiday; also ideal overnight stop for travellers to Devon and Cornwall. There are two double bedrooms and one family room; bathroom, toilet; sittingroom, diningroom. Children welcome, cot, high chair and babysitting. Open January to November with central heating. Pets are allowed. Car is essential and there is parking space. Bed and Breakfast from £12. Rates reduced for children.

BATH. Mrs Maria Beckett, Cedar Lodge, 13 Lambridge, London Road, Bath BA1 6BJ (01225 423468). Within walking distance of historic city centre, this gracious detached Georgian house offers period elegance combined with modern comfort. Beautiful individually designed bedrooms, one with four-poster, one with half-tester bed and one twin-bedded room. All with TV and en suite/private facilities. Guests may relax in the lovely gardens or by the fire in the drawing room. Choice of breakfasts served with home-made preserves. Secure car parking. This is an ideal base for Bath, Avebury, Stonehenge, Salisbury, Wells, Longleat, Cotswolds, Wales and many other places of interest. Help given with planning your excursions. Children welcome. Sorry, no smoking or pets. Bed and Breakfast from £25 per person per night based on two people sharing.

BATH. The Hollies Guesthouse, Hatfield Road, Bath BA2 2BD (Tel & Fax: 01225 313366). 👑👑 COMMENDED. The Hollies is a lovely old early Victorian family house, built of Bath stone and situated within walking distance of the city. With just three pretty guestrooms, personal attention and hospitality are assured. All rooms either en suite or have private facilities, colour TV, radio alarm cloack and beverage making facilities and overlook parish church and gardens. A wide breakfast menu is served. Private parking. An ideal base for exploring Bath and the Mendip Hills. Non-smoking. Prices from £20 to £25 per person.

BATH. Mrs June E.A. Coward, Box Road Gardens, Box Road, Bathford, Bath BA1 7LR (01225 852071). Homely, comfortable country house in two acres, situated on A4 road three miles east of Bath City Centre. Easy access to M4, local beauty spots. Accommodation in twin, double and family rooms with central heating, vanity units, tea/coffee making facilities; TV. Some with shower en suite. Ample parking and good local "pub food". Open all year for Bed and Breakfast from £15 per person. This is a non-smoking house. Sorry, no pets. Phone June on **01225 852071** for further details.

OAKLEIGH HOUSE

Your comfort is assured at Oakleigh House which is quietly situated only 10 minutes from the city centre. Combining Victorian elegance with today's comforts, Oakleigh gives your stay in Bath that extra special touch. All rooms have private bath/shower and WC, hairdryer, colour TV, clock radio and tea/coffee making facilities. Guests' lounge, telephone and private car park. Double or twin rooms with private bathroom and full English Breakfast £50–£65 per night. 10% reduction on a stay of five nights or more and reduced rates also for Senior Citizens. Winter Breaks available. RAC Highly Acclaimed. AA Selected.

Ms Jenny King, Oakleigh House, 19 Upper Oldfield Park, Bath BA2 3JX Tel: **01225 315698**

ABBEY RISE *AA QQQ*

Very high standard of accommodation in this modernised Victorian town house. Extremely attractively decorated comfortable rooms, all with colour TV and tea/coffee making facilities. En suite rooms available, with panoramic views over the city.

A seven minute walk to the City, National Coach station, railway station and many excellent restaurants. Unlimited unrestricted parking, and some private. English breakfast with a choice of vegetarian or Continental if preferred. From £18 per person.

Proprietor: Jill Heath, Abbey Rise, 97 Wells Road, Bath BA2 3AN
Telephone (01225) 316177

BATH. Mrs Chrissie Besley, The Old Red House, 37 Newbridge Road, Bath BA1 3HE (01225 330464; Fax: 01225 331661). Welcome to our romantic Victorian "Gingerbread" house which is colourful, comfortable and warm; full of unexpected touches and intriguing little curiosities. The leaded and stained glass windows are now double glazed to ensure a peaceful night's stay. Each bedroom is individually furnished with canopied or king size bed, colour TV, complimentary beverages, radio alarm clock, hair dryer and either en suite shower or private bathroom. Generous four course breakfasts are served. Waffles, pancakes or kippers are just a few alternatives to our famous hearty English grill. Dinner is available at the local riverside pub, just a short stroll away. We are non-smoking and have private parking. Prices range from £19.50 to £30 per person. Brochure on request.

BATH. The Old Malt House Hotel, Radford, Timsbury, Near Bath BA3 1QF (Tel & Fax: 01761 470106). ♣ ♣ ♣ *COMMENDED.* Between Bath and Wells in beautiful country surroundings, ideally situated for visiting many places of interest. A relaxing comfortable hotel, built in 1835 as a brewery malt house, now a hotel of character with interesting paintings, furnishings, etc., and with log fires in the colder months. Car park, gardens and lawns. Owned/managed by the same family for over 20 years. All 12 bedrooms (including two on the ground floor suitable for disabled guests) have private facilities, colour TV, telephone and beverage tray. Extensive menus. Restaurant and bar meals served every evening. Full licence, wide choice including draught Bass. Bed and Breakfast from £27.50; Evening Dinner from £5. AA QQQ.

BATH. Mrs D. Strong, Wellsway Guest House, 51 Wellsway, Bath BA2 4RS (01225 423434). ♣ A comfortable Edwardian house with all bedrooms centrally heated; washbasins and colour televisions in the rooms. On bus route with buses to and from the city centre every few minutes or an eight minute walk down the hill. Alexandra Park, with magnificent views of the city, is five minutes' walk. Bath is ideal for a short or long holiday with many attractions in and around the city; Longleat, Wells and Bristol are all nearby. Parking available. Bed and Breakfast from £14, with a pot of tea to welcome you on arrival.

Key to
Tourist Board Ratings

The Crown Scheme
(England, Scotland & Wales)

Covering hotels, motels, private hotels, guesthouses, inns, bed & breakfast, farmhouses. Every Crown classified place to stay is inspected annually. *The classification:* Listed then 1-5 Crown indicates the range of facilities and services. Higher quality standards are indicated by the terms APPROVED, COMMENDED, HIGHLY COMMENDED and DELUXE.

The Key Scheme
(also operates in Scotland using a Crown symbol)

Covering self-catering in cottages, bungalows, flats, houseboats, houses, chalets, etc. Every Key classified holiday home is inspected annually. *The classification:* 1-5 Key indicates the range of facilities and equipment. Higher quality standards are indicated by the terms APPROVED, COMMENDED, HIGHLY COMMENDED and DELUXE.

The Q Scheme
(England, Scotland & Wales)

Covering holiday, caravan, chalet and camping parks. Every Q rated park is inspected annually for its quality standards. The more ✓ in the Q – up to 5 – the higher the standard of what is provided.

BATH. Janet and Barry Thearle, Fairhaven Guest House, 21 Newbridge Road, Bath BA1 3HE (01225 314694). ♛ *COMMENDED.* Beautifully appointed Victorian house with friendly family atmosphere, one mile west of city centre on A4 Junction with A431. Very frequent bus service or pleasant walk (no steep hills) through Voctoria Park or along banks of River Avon to rail and bus stations and city centre. Convenient for exploring Roman and Georgian Bath or easy access to Bristol, Wells, Glastonbury, Cheddar, Stonehenge, etc. All rooms have central heating, colour TV, washbasin, shaver point, tea/coffee making facilities. Lounge available. This is a house for non-smokers. We provide superb traditional English and vegetarian breakfasts. Bed and Breakfast from £15 to £24. Open all year round. Parking.

BATH. Mrs K.M. Addison, Bailbrook Lodge, 35/37 London Road West, Bath BA1 7HZ (01225 859090). ♛♛♛ *COMMENDED.* Bailbrook Lodge is a splendid Georgian hotel and with a warm welcome assured it makes and excellent base to tour the area. Its 12 bedrooms are elegantly furnished, all offering en suite bathrooms or showers, TV, coffee and tea making facilities; some with antique four-poster beds. Dining room and bar. Situated on the A4 London road, Bailbrook Lodge is just one and a half miles from Bath city centre and has ample car parking facilities. It is 100 yards from the A46 which leads to Junction 18 of the M4 and is also close to the beautiful villages of Castle Combe and Lacock. Price per person including full English breakfast is from £24 to £35. RAC Highly Acclaimed, AA QQQQ.

BATH. Geoff and Avril Kitching, Wentworth House Hotel, 106 Bloomfield Road, Bath BA2 2AP (01225 339193; Fax: 01225 310460). ♛♛ *COMMEN-DED.* Imposing Victorian Bath stone mansion (1887) standing in secluded gardens with stunning views of valley. Situated in quiet part of city with free car park. Walking distance Abbey, Baths. High standard of comfort. Licensed bar. Outdoor swimming pool, horse riding, golf nearby. Prices from £25 to £35 per person per night, Bed and full English Breakfast. Light suppers available. RAC Highly Acclaimed, AA Selected.

BATH. Jan and Bryan Wotley, The Albany Guest House, 24 Crescent Gardens, Bath BA1 2NB (01225 313339). Tourist Board Listed *COMMENDED.* A warm welcome awaits you at our Victorian home, ideally placed to enjoy the delights of Bath — just five minutes' level walk from the city centre, Roman Baths, Abbey, etc. Our four attractively decorated bedrooms are equipped with colour TV, tea/coffee making facilities, washbasins and central heating. Enjoy a traditional English breakfast or try our delicious homemade vegetarian sausages! We happily cater for special dietary needs with prior notification. Many of our guests return again and again to enjoy the personal and unpretentious service we offer. Private parking. Non-smoking. Bed and Breakfast from £16 per person.

BATH. Mrs Judith Goddard, Cherry Tree Villa, 7 Newbridge Hill, Bath BA1 3PW (01225 331671). ♛ Friendly Victorian home approximately one mile from centre of Bath, at the start of the A431. Very frequent bus service, or for those who enjoy walking, a stroll through Victoria Park will take you comfortably into the city. Bright comfortable bedrooms, all with washbasin, colour TV and tea/coffee making facilities. Full central heating and off-street parking. Bed and full English Breakfast from £16 per person per night. Children and pets welcome. Tourist Board registered. From city centre take main A4 Upper Bristol road, at Sportsman Pub take A431 and Cherry Tree Villa lies on the left hand side. Winner of an FHG Diploma awarded by readers.

BATH near. Mrs B.M. Martin, The Old Inn Farmhouse, Farmborough, Near Bath BA3 1BY (01761

470250). The Old Inn Farmhouse is very attractive, built 1684, and was at one time a Coaching Inn. It has been extensively modernised to offer every comfort, though retaining its charm and character. It stands on the side of a hill overlooking the valley on the edge of Farmborough Village. Attractive landscaped garden. It is highly recommended and maintains a high standard of home cooked food; a family atmosphere prevails, with personal attention. All bedrooms (doubles, twins, and family size) have washbasins. Lounge with TV. Ample parking space. Very central for touring Bath, Wells, Cheddar, Wookey Hole, Longleat, Chew Lake, Wye Valley. Open all the year. Bed and full English Breakfast. Fire Certificate held. SAE or telephone for terms.

BATH. Ron and Vanessa Pharo, Ashley House, 8 Pulteney Gardens, Bath BA2 4HG (01225 425027). ♥ This charming, wisteria-clad, Victorian house in a quiet location is conveniently situated for all travellers to this beautiful city. We are a short level walk from the Roman Baths, Abbey, Pump Room and Sports Centre, and only 150 yards from the picturesque Kennet and Avon Canal where a stroll along the towpath will take you away from the crowds. All bedrooms have washbasins, shaver points, tea/coffee making facilities; some rooms have private shower and toilet; family rooms are available. Your breakfast is cooked to order and served with home-made marmalade. Double room £32 to £50. No smoking.

BATH. Josie and Brian Surry, Dene Villa, 5 Newbridge Hill, Bath BA1 3PW (01225 427676; Fax: 01225 482684). ♥♥ *COMMENDED*. A friendly welcome is assured in our comfortable family home, with full central heating and parking facilities. It is situated one mile from Bath centre at the start of the A431, with buses passing, and close to the Royal United Hospital and the Caravan Park. Single, double, twin and family rooms, all en suite with colour TV; dining/sitting room with colour TV. Non-smoking rooms if required. Many people pay a return visit. Open all year. From £18 for Bed and full English Breakfast. Reduced rates for children.

BRENT KNOLL. Roy and Lorrayne Page, Old Holt Farm, Edingworth Road, Weston-super-Mare

BS24 0JA (01934 750245). Listed 17th century buildings and grounds in beautiful rural location. Accommodation including double rooms or self-contained luxury stone cottages with central heating, colour TV, private bathroom/kitchenette. Home cooked evening meals available. Well behaved pets welcome and children will love feeding the animals. Situated just five miles from beaches of Burnham or Weston-super-Mare and major attractions such as Cheddar Gorge. We are just 10 minutes from Junction 22 of the M5, just off the A370. Bed and Breakfast from £18. Please telephone for more information.

BRIDGWATER. The Acorns Guest House, 61 Taunton Road, Bridgwater TA6 3LP (01278 445577).

The Acorns is a large guesthouse providing first class accommodation of hotel standard at competitive prices. Situated on the edge of the town centre approximately one mile from the M5 motorway (Junction 24) and on the bank of the Bridgwater and Taunton Canal. There is a private guest lounge with a warm and friendly atmosphere. All bedrooms have colour TV and tea/coffee making facilities; en suite rooms available. Full central heating and double glazing. Ample car parking. Please send for our colour brochure.

SOMERSET HAS IT ALL!

Peaceful thatched cottages, stately homes, sandy beaches, breathtaking caves, churches and cathedrals, romantic legends, heather-covered moorland — Somerset has something for everyone! Much of West Somerset lies within Exmoor National Park, and the county's many areas of upland make it ideal for a walking or nature-study holiday.

THE COTTAGE

A charming country cottage set in 2 acres of garden in an area of outstanding natural beauty and special interest close to rivers and canal where bird and wildlife flourish. A centre not only for the famous Somerset Levels but all of this historic County. We offer you privacy, comfort and tranquillity staying in king-size antique four poster or twin bedded en suite rooms with TV and heating. Easy access with all rooms at ground level opening directly onto the gardens. Ample secure parking. Evening meals available by arrangement. English country cooking at its best using our own fresh vegetables, fruits, honey and free range eggs. Bed & Breakfast from £16 per person per night. Easy access junction 24 M5. Phone or write for brochure and map. No smoking in house please. Open all year. Highly recommended.

Beverley and Victor Jenkins, The Cottage, Fordgate, Bridgwater TA7 0AP
Telephone: 01278 691908

BRIDGWATER. Mr and Mrs Fouracre, Oggshole Farmhouse, Broomfield, Bridgwater TA5 2EJ (01823 451689 or 0850 469220). ETB ✿ All the fun of the farm. Paradise for children and animal lovers at this charming 18th century farmhouse, nestling in the Quantock hills. With the emphasis on friendly, personal attention in a relaxing family atmosphere. Meet all the hand tame animals, join in with feeding. Pony rides for the children. We have two spacious, tastefully furnished rooms, both double/family rooms with washbasins and tea/coffee trays. TV lounge. Good home cooked meals optional. Easy access to M5 motorway. Convenient for walking, riding or fishing and close to Hestercombe Gardens. Well behaved pets welcome. Stabling available. Phone for a brochure.

BRIDGWATER. Mr and Mrs Sally and Norman Hunt, West Town Farm, Greinton, Bridgwater TA7 9BW (01458 210277). ✿ ✿ *COMMENDED.* A warm welcome awaits you at West Town Farm, a comfortable 17th century country house in the village of Greinton. Ideally situated on the A361 Street-Taunton road for exploring the beauties of the Somerset countryside and within easy reach of coastal resorts. Breakfast is served in the flag-stoned diningroom and each bedroom has en-suite shower and toilet, tea/coffee making facilities and colour TV. Guest lounge with inglenook fireplace. Bed and Breakfast from £19 to £21. Reductions for children sharing. Open March to September. Car essential — parking. Non-smokers please.

BRIDGWATER near. Mrs F.S. Filsell, The Cedars, High Street, Othery, Near Bridgwater TA7 0QA (01823 698310).

A warm welcome awaits guests at this small Grade III Listed Georgian house in the centre of Othery village, well placed for touring and coarse fishing. Two twin and one double bedrooms with washbasins and tea/coffee making facilities; shower, bath, two toilets; diningroom; TV lounge; large garden, parking for six cars. Cot, high chair and babysitting available. Central heating. Car essential. Pets by arrangement. Glastonbury, Taunton only 10 miles away. Brendon, Quantock hills 30 minutes; Dorset coast half an hour's drive away. Bed and Breakfast from £32 per double/twin room. Reductions for children when sharing.

BRISTOL. Mr and Mrs J. & M. Horman, The Parsonage, Main Street, Farrington Gurney, Bristol BS18 5UB (01761 453553).

A fine Grade II Listed building with a French influence. Built in the 17th century in its own grounds with ample secure parking, tea room and garden. Three large charming rooms retaining original features, two on ground floor suitable for disabled guests. All rooms have colour TV and complimentary tea trolley. Free laundry service. Special diets welcome. Standing at the foot of the Mendips The Parsonage is an ideal base for exploring Bath, Wells, Cheddar, Glastonbury and South Somerset. Close to airport and motorways. Relaxed home from home atmosphere.

BRISTOL. Downs View Guest House, 38 Upper Belgrave Road, Clifton, Bristol BS8 2XN (0117 9737046). ❧ *APPROVED.*

RAC Approved. A well established, family-run Victorian guest house situated on the edge of Durdham Downs. All rooms have panoramic views over the city or the Downs. We are one and a half miles north of the city centre, just off Whiteladies Road where there are plenty of restaurants, shops and buses. We are within walking distance of Bristol Zoo and Clifton Suspension Bridge. All rooms have tea/coffee making facilities, washbasin, colour TV and central heating. There are four en suite rooms. We offer a varied menu including traditional English breakfast.

BRISTOL near. Mrs Nicky Parsons, Langford Green Farm, Upper Langford, Near Bristol BS18 7DG (01934 852368).

Dairy farm surrounded by fields, situated at the foot of the Mendip Hills. Picturesque farmhouse with lovely views from all rooms and a pleasant garden. Many local amenities including walking, horse riding, dry ski slope, pot-holing, fishing in Blagdon Lake, easy access to Weston-super-Mare, Wells, Cheddar Caves, Bath. M5 (exit 21) approximately 15-17 minutes. Bed and Breakfast from £14.50. Several local pubs with good eating facilities, one within walking distance. Two double bedrooms and one single with tea/coffee making facilities. Separate guests' lounge and diningroom; two bathrooms with showers. Children welcome. Open all year.

CHEDDAR. Market Cross Hotel, Church Street, Cheddar BS27 3RA (01934 742264). *COMMENDED.*

This privately owned, licensed Regency Hotel is situated in the village of Cheddar, five minutes' walk from the famous Gorge, caves and Mendip Hills, making it an ideal centre for rambling, riding, caving, fishing, sightseeing. Wells, Glastonbury, Bath and Bristol are all within easy reach; the seaside is only 10 miles away. Seven bedrooms, some family, some en suite, are all centrally heated to ensure a comfortable stay. Log fires burn in the lounge during colder periods. A choice of excellent fresh home-cooked food and a desire to pleasure ensures our guests a happy stay at moderate prices. Bed and Breakfast from £21.50–£27.00. Open all year. AA QQ. Excellent self catering apartments also available in adjacent Georgian house.

CHEDDAR. P.A. Phillips, The Forge, Cliff Street, Cheddar BS27 3PL (01934 742345). A non-smok-

ing household, this is a comfortable old stone cottage complete with "TRADITIONAL WORKING FORGE". Set in the heart of the village with a five minute walk to famous Gorge and caves, pubs and restaurants. Accommodation comprises one double and one family bedrooms. *Includes Full English Breakfast (vegetarians catered for). *Tea/coffee making facilities in all rooms. *Guests' TV lounge. *Private parking and cycle lock-up. *Ramblers especially welcome. *Local maps and advice on walks available. *Lovely views from all rooms. Bed and Breakfast from £15, reduced rates for children.

CHEDDAR. Mrs Barbara Cook, The Poacher's Table, Cliff Street, Cheddar BS27 3PT (01934 742271). A friendly and warm welcome to all at our family

run guest house and licensed restaurant built in the 17th century and featuring many exposed oak beams. Situated at the foot of Cheddar Gorge within walking distance of caves and gorge, ideally placed to visit the many local places of interest including Bath, Wells, Glastonbury and Bristol. Three double en suite bedrooms and one twin standard bedroom, all have colour TV and tea/coffee making facilities. Pets welcome. Bed and full English Breakfast from £14.50 per person per night. Evening Meal also available in our candlelit restaurant.

CHEDDAR near. Winston Manor Hotel, Bristol Road, Churchill, Near Cheddar BS19 5NL (01934 852348). ❀ ❀ ❀ *COMMENDED.* AA QQQ. This charming manor house stands in one and a half acres of secluded gardens overlooking the Mendip Hills. An ideal stop for visits to Bath, Wells, Longleat and Cheddar. Only a short drive from the beaches of Weston-super-Mare and Burnham-on-Sea. The proprietors Marion Sherrington and Jill Green offer a warm welcome to families, lone travellers and pets. All diets catered for, the cosy restaurant opens every evening. Bedrooms all en suite with tea/coffee making facilities and home made biscuits. The hotel is a member of Logis of Great Britain where hospitality wears a human face. Bed and English Breakfast from £25 per person.

CREWEKERNE. Mr Gilmore, Manor Arms, North Perrott, Crewkerne TA18 7SG (Tel & Fax: 01460 72901). ❀ ❀ *COMMENDED.* AA QQQ. A lovely 16th century

Grade II Listed inn, set in the conservation village of North Perrott and overlooking the village green. The Inn has been lovingly restored retaining much of its olde world charm. There is an inglenook fireplace, flagstone floors and oak beams. The guests' accommodation which consists of five well appointed en suite rooms in the coach house and three in the inn, all with colour TV and tea/coffee making facilities. The Old Coach House is situated behind the Inn away from the road. The Inn is renowned locally for its very high standard of home cooking both from the bar and restaurant menus. Bed and Breakfast from £21, low season breaks from £17.50 per person.

Terms quoted in this publication may be subject to increase if rises in costs necessitate

ETB 🏵🏵🏵 De-Luxe & AA QQQQQ Premier Selected – both top quality awards

BROADVIEW GARDENS

East Crewkerne, Crewkerne, Somerset TA18 7AG
(Dorset Border)

Phone/Fax Mrs Swann 01460 73424

Unusual Colonial bungalow built in an era of quality. Achieving top quality awards for comfort, cooking and friendliness. Carefully furnished in the Edwardian style. Ensuite rooms overlooking acre of beautiful gardens. Traditional English home-cooking. Perfect touring base for country and garden lovers, NT Houses, antique enthusiasts, moors and quaint old villages. Dorset coast 20 minutes. List of 50 places provided. B&B £25-£28. Colour TV, tea facilities. Hair dryer, easy chairs and electric fans. A no smoking house. All year parking.

CREWKERNE. Mrs Sally Gregory, Dryclose, Newbery Lane, Misterton, Crewkerne TA18 8NE (01460 73161). 🏵 *HIGHLY COMMENDED.* Recommended by WHICH? Dryclose is a 16th century former farmhouse set in two acres of garden with swimming pool in a quiet area of the village of Misterton. Close by are historic buildings, beautiful gardens and, within half an hour, the Devon and Dorset coast. Explore Thomas Hardy's countryside with wonderful walks. We offer Bed and Breakfast with optional Evening Meals or light suppers. Three bedrooms: one twin en suite, one twin, one single. Two separate guests' sitting-rooms with TV. All bedrooms have hot drinks facilities. Children over eight years welcome. Non-smokers please. Bed and Breakfast from £18.50. Reductions for weekly bookings. Write or phone for further details.

DUNSTER near. Mr and Mrs R. Brown, ''Green Bay'', Washford, Watchet TA23 0NN (01984 640303). 🏵🏵 *COMMENDED.* Small guesthouse close to Exmoor and sea. All rooms with private facilities, TV and tea/coffee trays. Good home cooking and friendly welcome assured. Bed and Breakfast from £15.50. Reduced rates for weekly stays.

EAST CHINNOCK. Lloyd and Gloria Jones, The Gables Guest House, High Street, East Chinnock, Near Yeovil BA22 9DR (Tel & Fax: 01935 862237). The Gables is a 300 year old cottage, formerly the village bakery. The original oven remains in place in the dining room and tea room. Situated in the picturesque village of East Chinnock midway between Yeovil and Crewkerne it is an ideal touring centre for South Somerset and the Dorset Coast. Lyme Regis is just 15 miles with the historic towns of Sherborne, Dorchester, Blandford Forum and Shaftesbury within easy driving distance. The Gables is well known for its generous cream teas with home cooked scones. A retreat from busy town activity. Car parking available for six cars. Bed and Breakfast from £15 to £18; Evening Meal £8. Brochure available.

Discounted price at Wookey Hole Caves and Papermill, Somerset for maximum of six people. For further details see our READERS' OFFER VOUCHER.

EXFORD. Exmoor House Hotel and Restaurant, Exford TA24 7PY (01643 831304). 👑👑

APPROVED. Small, family-run Bed and Breakfast hotel overlooking the village green in the beautiful village of Exford and situated in the heart of the Exmoor National Park. Exford is an excellent base from which to enjoy riding, fishing, game shooting or just to explore the delights of the Moor. All our bedrooms have tea/coffee making facilities, colour TV, clock radios and offer en suite or private facilities. Children and pets welcome. There is a reading/residents' lounge. Please write or phone for our brochure.

Hunters Moon

Exford, near Minehead TA24 7PP

Tel: 01643 831695   Fax: 01643 831576

Hunters Moon, in the heart of the Exmoor National Park on the edge of the village of Exford. Come and join us in our cosy bungalow smallholding set in five acres with glorious views, comfortable rooms with a large lounge to relax in plus a sun terrace to enjoy. Our dining room enjoys superb views across the Exe Valley to the moor beyond. Open all year including Christmas and New Year. Bed and Breakfast from £16 per person per night; Evening Meal £10. Reductions for children. Seven nights for the price of six. Well behaved dogs are very welcome. **Jane and Bryan Jackson.**

HIGHERCOMBE FARM

Relax and enjoy our special hospitality on a 450 acre working farm (including 100 acres of woodland), in an outstanding, peaceful situation on Exmoor. Off the beaten track yet only four miles from Dulverton. We are an ideal base for exploring coast and moor. There is an abundance of wildlife on the farm including wild red deer. We are happy to take you on a farm tour. The farmhouse enjoys spectacular views, central heating, large visitors' lounge and log fires. Pretty rooms with generous en suite bathrooms. Delicious farmhouse cooking, fresh

produce, home-made marmalade, etc. Bed and Breakfast from £19.50, Dinner, Bed and Breakfast from £34. Private, well equipped self catering wing of farmhouse also available.

Abigail Humphrey, Highercombe Farm,
Dulverton TA22 9PT   Telephone 01398 323616

👑 Highly Commended   ⚘⚘⚘⚘ Commended

EXMOOR. Merton Hotel, Western Lane, Minehead TA24 8BZ (01643 702375). Small friendly hotel in a quiet area offering 10 en suite bedrooms, large oak-panelled dining room, lounge and bar area. Large car park. Approximately half a mile from town and sea front, ideal for exploring Exmoor and villages, walking or by car. Bed and Breakfast from £17 to £20 per night.

AA
★★

RAC
★★

RESTAURANT
AWARD

EXMOOR

THE ROYAL OAK INN

'There is nothing which has yet been contrived by man by which so much happiness is produced as by a good tavern or inn'. Samuel Johnson. Since this quotation, times have certainly changed, but hospitality, comfort and excellent food afforded by the Royal Oak have not. The inn has been renowned for its comfort and sustenance for approximately three centuries and has gained many awards and acknowledgements for its food. Set in the beautiful village of Withypool in the middle of Exmoor it is an ideal base from which to ride, hunt, shoot, fish or simply walk and enjoy the calm and beauty of the moor with its sparkling rivers and fertile valleys. Dogs are welcome in guest rooms or can be accommodated in our stable block free of charge.

THE ROYAL OAK INN, WITHYPOOL, EXMOOR NATIONAL PARK, SOMERSET TA24 7QP
TELEPHONE 01643 831506/7 FAX: 01643 831659

FROME near. Mrs Molly Brown, The Lodge, Fairwood Farm, Standerwick, Near Frome BA11 2QA (01373 823515). The Lodge is situated in pleasant country surroundings with good walks and served by several good local inns. It is on the B3099 within quarter of a mile of the A36. Warminster is three miles and Bath 12 miles. All bedrooms are en suite with tea making facilities and colour TV. One has twin beds, two have double beds. Full breakfast is served and there is central heating throughout. Bed and Breakfast from £18 per person. Ample parking. Sorry no pets.

GLASTONBURY. Mrs L. White, Bradley Batch, 64 Bath Road, Ashcott, Bridgwater TA7 9QJ (01458 210256). Tourist Board Listed. Cottage guest house, five miles from Glastonbury on A39; convenient for M5 Motorway (exit Junction 23). Three comfortable double rooms with washbasins; central heating; colour TV lounge; shower. Car park; attractive garden. Meals available in Inns nearby. Well behaved dogs welcome. Weekly terms, reductions for children on request. 30 minutes from Wells, Wookey and Cheddar, 20 minutes from Fleet Air Arm Museum, one hour to Bath, Exmoor or Dorset coast. Bed and Breakfast from £15; single occupancy from £15.50. Non smokers preferred. Send SAE or telephone for more information.

GLASTONBURY near. Mrs M.A. Bell, New House Farm, Burtle Road, Westhay, Near Glastonbury BA6 9TT (01458 860238). ❦❦ HIGHLY COMMENDED.

Working dairy farm, situated on the Somerset Levels. Large Victorian Farmhouse offering comfortable accommodation, central for touring Wells, Cheddar, Bath, Burnham-on-Sea etc. Accommodation comprises one family room and one double room, each with en suite facilities, colour TV, tea/coffee facilities, hair dryer, clock radio, etc; lounge with colour TV, separate dining room and conservatory. Central heating throughout. Ample parking and warm welcome assured. Bed and full English Breakfast from £19 to £21; Evening Meal £11. Self catering also available. Directions: near Peat Moor Visitor Centre which is signposted from A39 and B3151.

GLASTONBURY. Mrs D.P. Atkinson, Court Lodge, Butleigh, Glastonbury BA6 8SA (01458

850575). A warm welcome awaits at attractive, modernised 1850 Lodge with homely atmosphere. Set in picturesque garden on the edge of Butleigh, three miles from historic Glastonbury. Only a five minute walk to pub in village which serves lovely meals. Accommodation in one double, one twin and one single bedrooms; constant hot water, central heating. Bathroom adjacent to bedrooms. TV lounge. Tea/coffee served. Bed and Breakfast from £13.50; Evening Meal by arrangement. Children welcome at reduced rates.

GLASTONBURY. Mrs J.M. Gillam, Wood Lane House, Butleigh, Glastonbury BA6 8TG (01458 850354). Charming old AA Listed house with lovely views over open countryside and woods. Quiet yet not isolated and only 200 yards from excellent village "local". Ideal touring centre for Cheddar, Wells, Bath and many beauty spots and only 20 miles from coast. Attractions include Butterfly Farm, Fleet Air Arm Museum, Rural Life Museum, cheese making, steam engines and many places of historic interest. Accommodation comprises three double rooms with well equipped en suite facilities, tea/coffee and TV. Comfortable and warm sitting/dining room. Open all year round except Christmas and New Year. Car essential. Parking. Bed and Breakfast £18.50. Half price for children.

FHG DIPLOMA WINNERS 1997

Each year we award a small number of diplomas to holiday proprietors whose services have been specially commended by our readers and the following advertisers were our FHG Diploma winners for 1997.

ENGLAND

Mrs E.R. Elford, Tresulgan Farm, Near Menheniot, Liskeard, Cornwall PL14 3PU (01503 240268)

Mrs Ellis, Efford Cottage, Lymington, Hampshire SO41 0JD (01590 642315)

Mrs Ruby Keenlyside, Struthers Farm, Allendale, Hexham, Northumberland NE47 9LN (01434 683580)

Mrs Doreen Cole, Hillcrest House, Hexham, Northumberland NE48 4BY (01434 681426)

Mrs Sue Weir, Follys End, Back Street, Martock, Somerset TA12 6NY (01935 823073)

Mrs M.A. Bell, New House Farm, Near Glastonbury, Somerset BA6 9TT (01458 860238)

Mr & Mrs Jeffrey, Brymbo, Mickleton, Gloucestershire GL55 6PU (01386 438890)

Helen and Colin Lowes, Wilson House, Richmond, North Yorkshire DL11 7EB (01833 621218)

Mr & Mrs J. Sawley, The Hawthorns, Cowley, Keighley, North Yorkshire BD22 0DH (01535 633299)

David & Jennie Randall, The Coach House, Midhurst, West Sussex GU29 0HZ (01730 812351)

SCOTLAND

Mr Young, Ballachulish Hotel, Ballachulish, Argyll PA39 4HL (01855 811606)
(Isles of Glencoe Hotel & Leisure Centre)

Mr & Mrs R. Baldon, Barbagianni Guest House, Spean Bridge, Inverness-shire PH34 4EU (01397 712437)

Mr & Mrs Howes, Ardoch Lodge, Strathyre, Perthshire FK18 8NF (01877 384666)

WALES

Mrs Sandra Davies, Barley Villa, Walwyn's Castle, Broadhaven SA62 3EB (01437 781254)

GLASTONBURY. Mrs Elizabeth Ruddle, Laverley House, West Pennard, Glastonbury BA8 8NE (01749 890696).

Tony and Liz look forward to welcoming you to their attractive and spacious Listed Georgian farmhouse with superb views, paddock and gardens, all set in a rural area. There are two double bedrooms with en-suite bathrooms and a family bedroom with private bathroom. Colour TV and hospitality trays in all bedrooms. We have a comfortable guests' lounge and diningroom and are happy to provide a cot and high chair for children. Fresh produce is served, traditionally cooked. A good area for touring; Wells six miles, Bath 20 miles. Many National Trust houses and gardens. Bed and Breakfast from £19.50. Please telephone for brochure.

GLASTONBURY. Mrs Dinah Gifford, Little Orchard, Ashwell Lane, Glastonbury BA6 8BG (01458 831620). Tourist Board COMMENDED. This holiday accommodation is centrally positioned for touring the West Country, lying at the foot of historic Glastonbury Tor, with breathtaking views over the Vale of Avalon. Convenient for A361 Glastonbury to Shepton Mallet Road. Cheddar is ten miles away; Weston-super-Mare 18 miles; the "Lions of Longleat" 15 miles; and Wells Cathedral five miles. It is in the heart of the sheepskin and shoe-making industry — both are available at factory prices. Facilities for guests include colour TV lounge, central heating, washbasins, and bathroom with shower. Tea/coffee facilities. Car parking. Children welcome, cot. Pay phone. Open all year. Bed and Breakfast from £15. Fire Certificate.

GREINTON. Mrs M. Tingey, Greinton House, Near Bridgwater TA7 9BW (01458 210307).

Greinton is on the A361 between Taunton and Street where Clarks renowned factory shop village is located. The house is a beautiful Listed former rectory (dating back to the 16th century) with panelling and galleried hall, situated on the southern slopes of the Polden Hills, overlooking Sedgemoor. Accommodation can be arranged to suit individual requirements. There are two bathrooms, one luxury en suite and a shower room. All bedrooms have tea/coffee making facilities. Three sitting rooms; TV. Ample parking. There is a hard tennis court and a croquet lawn. The premises are not suitable for young children and no pets are allowed in the house. No smoking. In winter there is oil-fired central heating and log fires. Open all year for Bed and Breakfast from £20 nightly.

COCKHILL FARM

Marchants Hill, Gurney Slade, Near Bath, Somerset BA3 4TY Tel: 01749 840125

Farmhouse accommodation on a working farm keeping a small beef suckler herd in the heart of the Mendips. A friendly atmosphere is assured in this Victorian farmhouse. Excellent home cooking from local produce. Bed and Breakfast, optional Evening Meal. Spacious rooms with period furnishings. TV, tea/coffee making facilities. One twin, one double and one single bedroom available. Ideally situated for the Cathedral City of Wells, Glastonbury, Cheddar, Georgian Bath and historic Bristol. Royal Bath and West Showground 10 minutes. Magnificent Chew Valley Lake for bird watching, fly fishing and picnicking 20 minutes. Good local pubs and peaceful country walks. Children welcome, baby facilities available.

Open all year • Bed and Breakfast from £14.00
Mrs Jacqueline Hawkins

HENSTRIDGE. Patricia and Brian Thompson, Quiet Corner Farm, Henstridge BA8 0RA (01963 363045; Fax:01963 363400). ♥♥ COMMENDED.

Lovely old stone farmhouse and barns, some converted to self catering cottages sleeping two/four, set in five acres beautiful garden and orchards with sheep and miniature Shetland ponies. The village, 'twixt Shaftesbury and Sherborne, has super pubs, two restaurants, shops and post office. Marvellous centre for touring Somerset, Dorset and Wiltshire with host of National Trust and other houses and gardens. Golf and fishing nearby. The spacious farmhouse is most comfortable with central heating throughout. Bedrooms with washbasins and tea making facilities; one en suite. Safe car parking. Payphone. Bed and Breakfast from £19. Reductions for children under 12 years. SAE, or telephone, for brochure. Special offer: Three days for price of two (subject to availability) October 1st to end May except Public Holidays. Recommended by "Which?" Good Bed & Breakfast Guide.

HIGHBRIDGE. Mrs V.M. Loud, Alstone Court Farm, Alstone Lane, Highbridge TA9 3DS (01278

789417). Working farm. 17th century farmhouse, situated on outskirts of town, two miles from M5 Edithmead interchange, on a mixed farm of 200 acres. The land adjoins Bridgwater Bay, ideal as touring centre for Somerset. Within easy reach of Burnham-on-Sea, Weston-super-Mare, Wells, Cheddar Gorge, Wookey Hole and the Mendips. Ideal for sea and coarse fishing. Horse riding on the farm — qualified instructor. Spacious comfortable bedrooms — two family and one twin-bedded rooms. Lounge with colour TV, large dining room. Central heating. Home produce when available. Children welcome. Ample parking space. Evening Meal, Bed and Breakfast. Terms on request with SAE, please.

HIGHBRIDGE near. Mrs B.M. Puddy, "Laurel Farm", Mark Causeway, Near Highbridge TA9 4PZ (01278 641216) 🏵 *COMMENDED.* **Working farm.** Laurel Farm is over 200 years old with 120 acres and 70 milking cows, Friesian and Holstein. We are about two miles from MARK CHURCH and VILLAGE on the WELLS TO BURNHAM-ON-SEA B3139 road, two miles from M5 Junction 22. Ideal touring centre or halfway house. There is a large sittingroom with a colour TV, log fires September to May. CENTRAL HEATING, ELECTRIC BLANKETS. Washbasins in all bedrooms. Nicely decorated with fitted carpets throughout. Separate tables in dining room. Doubles, singles and family rooms, shower, two baths, three toilets. En suite available. Car essential/or bike. Undercover garages. OPEN ALL THE YEAR. Bed and Breakfast from £13.50 to £17; Bed, Breakfast and Evening Meal £140 to £154 per week only.

ILMINSTER. Mrs G. Phillips, 'Hermitage', 29 Station Road, Ilminster TA19 9BE (01460 53028).

Enjoy the friendly atmosphere of a lovely listed 17th century house with beams and inglenook. Bedrooms, with fourposters, overlook two and a half acres of delightful gardens, woods and hills beyond. Twin or double rooms with washbasins. Lounge with log fire and colour TV. Tea or coffee with homemade biscuits on arrival. Full English breakfast. Traditional inns nearby for evening meals. Ideal touring centre for Quantock Hills, Wells, Glastonbury, Lyme Regis and many picturesque villages. Several National Trust properties, gardens and historic houses within a few miles. Ten miles from M5, one mile from A303. Bed and Breakfast from £15.50; reductions for children.

LOPEN. Mrs Jean Hepworth, September House, Lopen, South Petherton TA13 5JU (01460

240647). 🏵 *COMMENDED.* Our aim is to ensure our guests feel comfortable and at ease in our bright and friendly home. Enjoy our pleasant and well stocked garden. Our standards are high, breakfasts excellent and our welcome is warm. Lopen is a small village just two minutes from the A303. Not only is it a convenient break point when making a long journey but is is a perfect place to spend a few nights whilst exploring the many delights and attractions of Somerset and Dorset. En suite bedrooms with beverage tray. TV lounge. From £15 to £19 per person. Non-smoking.

MARTOCK. Mrs H. Turton, "Wychwood", 7 Bearley Road, Martock TA12 6PG (Tel & Fax: 01935

825601). 🏵🏵 *HIGHLY COMMENDED.* Quality, comfortable accommodation. Excellent home cooking. In quiet position just off A303. Ideal touring location, close to Montacute House, Fleet Air Arm Museum, Tintinhull Gardens and eight other "classic" Gardens. Walk the Leland Trail through Camelot Country and the Legend of King Arthur. Yeovil 10 minutes, Sherborne 15 minutes; Glastonbury, Wells, Taunton and M5, Junction 25, under 30 minutes. TV, radio and tea/coffee making facilities in all bedrooms. Double rooms with en suite, twin with private bathroom. Separate diningroom. Garden. Full central heating. Parking. No smoking. Bed and full English Breakfast from £19. Open all year. AA QQQQ Selected, RAC Acclaimed, FHG Diploma Award. Credit cards accepted. Recommended by "Which?" Good B&B.

FHG PUBLICATIONS LIMITED publish a large range of well-known accommodation guides. We will be happy to send you details or you can use the order form at the back of this book.

NORTON-SUB-HAMDON. Mrs John Fisher, Brook House, Norton-sub-Hamdon TA14 6SR (01935 881789). Comfortable and spacious high quality accommodation with friendly atmosphere in peaceful village one mile off the A303 in South Somerset. Half acre beautiful garden with secure parking. Both rooms colour TV, tea making facilities. Generous English breakfast. Two self catering cottages also available. Adjacent Ham Hill Country Park and wonderful walks. Close classic gardens of Lambrook, Tintinhull, Forde Abbey, Hadspen and Stourhead and additional National Trust properties of Montecute, Lytes Cary and Barrington. Golf, racing, fishing, riding all at hand and near to Fleet Air Museum, Royal Armoured Corps and Haymes Motor Museums. One twin (for one) £25, One double/twin (for two) £45. Bathroom and power shower room (both private). Open all year except Christmas and New Year.

PORLOCK. Margery and Henry Dyer, West Porlock House, West Porlock, Near Minehead TA24 8NX (01643 862880). ♛♛ *HIGHLY COMMENDED.* Imposing country house in Exmoor National Park on the wooded slopes of West Porlock commanding exceptional sea views of Porlock Bay and countryside. Set in five acres of beautiful woodland gardens unique for its variety and size of unusual trees and shrubs and offering a haven of rural tranquillity. The house has large spacious rooms with fine and beautiful furnishings throughout. Two double, two twin and one family bedrooms, all with en suite or private bathrooms, TV, tea/coffee making facilities and shaver points. Licensed. Non-smoking. Private car park. Bed and Breakfast from £24.50 to £26 per person.

PORLOCK. Mrs A.J. Richards, Ash Farm, Porlock, Near Minehead TA24 8JN (01643 862414). Ash Farm is situated two miles off the main Porlock to Lynmouth road (A39) and overlooks the sea. It is two-and-a-half miles from Porlock Weir, and eleven from Minehead and Lynmouth. Only 10 minutes to the tiny church of "Culbone", and Coleridge is reputed to have used the farmhouse which is 200 to 300 years old. The house has double, single and family bedrooms, all with washbasins; toilet; large sittingroom and diningroom. Open from Easter to October. Oare Church, Valley of Rocks, County Gate, Horner Valley and Dunkery Beacon are all within easy reach. Bed and Breakfast from £15 which includes bedtime drink. SAE please.

PURTON/BRIDGWATER. Mrs B. Pipkin, Rockfield House, Purton Hill, Purton, Bridgwater TA7 8AG (Tel & Fax; 01278 683561). ♛♛ *COMMENDED.* AA QQ Recommended. Just off M5 motorway junction 23 on the A39 overlooking motorway and the Bristol Channel. This large family house is a good stopping point for travellers to and from Cornwall or the ideal base to explore the Somerset countryside. Comfortable rooms with washbasins, some en suite, tea/coffee making facilities, colour TV. Central heating. Ample parking. Large garden and patio. Midweek bookings or single night welcome. Evening meals by arrangement or good local pubs nearby. Non smoking.

QUANTOCK HILLS. Susan Lilienthal, Parsonage Farm, Over Stowey, Bridgwater TA5 1HA (01278 733237; Fax: 01278 733511). Traditional 17th century farmhouse and organic smallholding in quiet location in Quantock Hills with delightful walled gardens; orchard; and walks to explore. Delicious meals are prepared using the farm's produce — fresh eggs, home-made breads and jams — and served before an open fire. Three double bedrooms include colour TV and tea/coffee facilities, en suite available. Guests are invited to enjoy the gardens or relax in the log-fired sitting room. Spacious and welcoming, this is an ideal base for rambling and exploring the Quantock Hills, Exmoor, North Somerset Coast, as well as Glastonbury and Wells. No smoking. Bed and full Breakfast from £18, reductions for children. Optional Evening Meal £15.

PLEASE ENCLOSE A STAMPED ADDRESSED ENVELOPE WITH ENQUIRIES

QUANTOCKS. Mrs N. Thompson, Plainsfield Court, Plainsfield, Over Stowey, Bridgwater TA5 1HH (01278 671292; Fax: 01278 671687). Plainsfield Court is the 15th century ancestral home of the Blake family. The farmhouse, is a Listed building of historic interest set in the Quantock Hills, superbly located for walking, riding, fishing and all country pursuits. Magnificent views, walled garden and cider orchards; wild Red Deer are often seen grazing in the surrounding fields. Two stylish double bedrooms with private bathroom, TV, tea/coffee making facilities. Open log fires in the sitting room and ancient beamed dining room. Home cooked meals available. Bed and Breakfast from £20. Pets by arrangement, stabling available. No smoking in B&B. Self catering (The Granary) for four/six also available.

SHEPTON MALLET. Mrs M. White, Barrow Farm, North Wootton, Shepton Mallet BA4 4HL (01749 890245). Working farm. This farm accommodation is AA QQQ Listed. Barrow is a dairy farm of 146 acres. The house is 15th century and of much character, situated quietly between Wells, Glastonbury and Shepton Mallet. It makes an excellent touring centre for visiting Somerset's beauty spots and historic places, for example, Cheddar, Bath, Wookey Hole and Longleat. Guest accommodation consists of two double rooms, one family room, one single room and one twin-bedded room, each with washbasin, TV and tea/coffee making facilities. Bathroom, two toilets; two lounges, one with colour TV; diningroom with separate tables. Guests can enjoy farmhouse fare in generous variety, home baking a speciality. Bed and Breakfast, with optional four course Dinner available. Car essential; ample parking. Children welcome; cot and babysitting available. Open all year except Christmas. Sorry, no pets. Bed and Breakfast from £15 to £16; Dinner, Bed and Breakfast from £140.

SHEPTON MALLET. Mr and Mrs J. Grattan, Park Farm House, Forum Lane, Bowlish, Shepton Mallet BA4 5JL (01749 343673; Fax: 01749 345279). A 17th century house formerly a working farm situated in a conservation area. The accommodation comprises one twin-bedded room (bathroom en suite) and a suite of a double bedroom and a twin bedroom with private bathroom. There is ample discreet car parking. Conveniently situated close to the ancient Cathedral City of Wells (four miles), Cheddar Gorge and Caves, Clarkes village at Street and Longleat within 12 miles. The Georgian city of Bath and Bristol are only 18 miles away. Shepton Mallet has good restaurants, many local pubs and easy access to the scenic Mendip Hills. Bed and Breakfast £17.50 per person per night: no single person supplement.

SOUTH PETHERTON near. Sue and Alastair Rouston, Shores Farm, Frogs Street, Lopen TA13 5JP (Tel & Fax: 01460 240587). AA QQQ Grade 2 non-working farmhouse. Situated in a rural village (minutes from A303), with well stocked walled garden. An ideal base for touring the west country. A relaxing warm and attractive house for summer or winter breaks. Comfortable rooms with en suite, all have tea/coffee facilities with colour TV and central heating. Separate dinning room and lounge heated with inglenook log fire. With plenty of beamed ceilings and interesting old nooks and crannies. Private car parking. Bed and Breakfast from £18; Evening Meal from £7.50. Directions: leave A303 at South Petherton roundabout, follow sign to Lopen, next roundabout, turn left through village, situated on right by Frogs Street.

TAUNTON. Mrs Dianne Besley, Prockters Farm, West Monkton, Taunton TA2 8QN (01823 412269). ♛ ♛ Prockters is a large 17th century oak-beamed farmhouse with open fireplace, only two miles from Taunton and M5 motorway. A cup of tea and a cake welcomes you on arrival at the family farmhouse, set at the foot of the Quantock Hills. All the bedrooms have washbasins, colour TV and tea-making facilities, including ground floor en-suite bedrooms suitable for disabled guests. Only five minutes from the M5, just off the A38 and A361. We are ideally situated to break your journey, or for a farmhouse holiday. Lovely walks and wild life parks and historic houses to see. Bed and Breakfast from £18. Reduction on a week's holiday. Children and pets welcome.

Hall Farm Guest House

Stogumber, Taunton TA4 3TQ Tel: (01984) 656321

Hall Farm is situated on a working farm in the centre of Stogumber Village, surrounded by the Quantocks and Exmoor. Within easy reach of the sea, Minehead, Blue Anchor, Watchet and St. Audries Bay. Accommodation for 12 to 14 guests. The bedrooms are comfortable and have ensuite facilities. The catering is under the personal supervision of the proprietress, whose concern it is to make your holiday a happy one. Dogs are welcome if kept well under control. Good parking. Breakfast at 9am with Evening Dinner at 6.30pm. Traditional Sunday lunches at 1pm. **Proprietress: Christine M. Hayes.**

TAUNTON. Tom and Rowena Kirk, Yallands Farmhouse, Staplegrove, Taunton TA2 6PZ (Tel & Fax: 01823 278979). ✿✿ *COMMENDED.* A delightful 16th century Listed farmhouse which has become an oasis of "Old England" as the town has expanded over the former farmland. Quietly situated one and a half miles north-west of the town centre. Guests are assured of a warm welcome and individual attention. The en suite bedrooms are comfortable, well furnished and attractive with colour TV and tea/coffee making facilities. Ground floor single room available. Ideally situated between the Quantock and Blackdown Hills, with many places of interest within easy reach. A pub serving lunches and evening meals is within easy walking distance. Ample parking. Open all year. Brochure/tariff available.

TAUNTON. Mr and Mrs P.J. Painter, Blorenge House, 57 Staplegrove Road, Taunton TA1 1DG (Tel & Fax: 01823 283005). AA QQQ Recommended. Spacious Victorian residence set in large gardens with a swimming pool and large car park. Situated just five minutes' walking distance from Taunton town centre, railway and bus station. 21 comfortable bedrooms with washbasins, central heating, colour TV and tea making facilities. Five of the bedrooms have traditional four-poster beds, ideal for weekends away and honeymoon couples. Family and twin rooms are available. The majority of rooms have en suite facilities. Large dining room traditionally furnished; full English breakfast and continental breakfasts included in the price. Evening Meals available on request. Please send for our colour brochure.

TAUNTON near. Mrs Pamela Akers, Springfield House, Walford Cross, West Monkton, Taunton TA2 8QW (01823 412116). ✿✿ *HIGHLY COMMENDED.* A country house set in grounds of two acres with a friendly relaxed atmosphere in quiet, tranquil surroundings. The bedrooms are all en suite and they, with a private sitting room, are in a newly converted annexe next to the house. All rooms have tea/coffee making facilities with complimentary tray, TV. Central heating. Toiletries supplied. There is an iron and board, hair dryers and telephone available. Ideal base for touring the area, excellent for walking, fishing and golf. Just five minutes' drive off M5 Junction 25 and Taunton centre. Signposted on A38. Set back up a private drive with private parking. Bed and Breakfast £19.50 per person (double occupancy), £27 single occupancy. Reductions on a weeks holiday. AA QQQQ.

TAUNTON. Ann and John Bartlett, The Spinney, Curland, Taunton TA3 5SE (Tel & Fax: 01460 234362). ✿✿ *HIGHLY COMMENDED.* Six miles from Taunton, convenient for A303 and M5. Ann and John welcome you to their home on the slopes of the Blackdowns. Nestling in a designated area of outstanding natural beauty, enjoying panoramic views of the Quantock and Mendip Hills, it is ideally situated for touring, walking, riding or visiting places of interest. A choice of family, double or twin rooms each with en suite shower, toilet and washbasin, central heating, colour TV and tea/coffee making facilities including ground floor bedrooms. Non-smoking throughout. Traditional evening meals available. Bed and Breakfast from £19.50. Dogs by arrangement. Open all year. Detailed brochure on request. AA QQQQ Selected.

TAUNTON near. Mrs M. Summers, Warrescote, 2 Trendle Lane, Bicknoller, Taunton TA4 4EG (01984 656257). ETB Listed. Situated in this quiet picturesque friendly village at the foot of the Quantock Hills, the house stands in its own large garden just beyond the church. Easily accessible from the M5 motorway and the A39 Exmoor, Bath, Bristol and coast. Comfortable accommodation consisting of one twin bedroom and one single which easily converts to a twin, both with private bathroom and tea/coffee making facilities; lounge with TV. Well behaved pets welcome. Reduced rates for children. Bed and Breakfast from £13.

TAUNTON. Mrs Susan Honeyball, Manor Farm, Waterpitts, Broomfield, Bridgwater TA5 1AT (01823 451266). This 14th century farm house is situated in the folds of the beautiful Quantock Hills, six miles from Taunton and Bridgwater with good food and pubs. It is a working stud farm of 140 acres with a lovely lake and trout fishing available. Ideally situated for most outdoor pursuits including walking, golfing, mountain bikes, horse riding facilities, stables for guests' horses. Storage for bikes. Safe parking area for cars. Large garden. Accommodation itself comprises one double room with balcony and washbasin, one twin-bedded room; dining room with log fire. Children welcome, cot and babysitting available. Open all year. No smoking. Bed and Breakfast from £14; children under 10 years half price.

TAUNTON near. Mrs Pam Parry, Pear Tree Cottage, Stapley Churchstanton, Taunton TA3 7QA (Tel & Fax: 01823 601224; E-mail: colvin.parry@virgin.net). An old thatched country cottage halfway between Taunton and Honiton, set in the idyllic Blackdown Hills which has been designated an area of outstanding natural beauty. Picturesque countryside laced with winding lanes full of natural flora and fauna. Wildlife abounds. Three-quarters of an acre traditional cottage garden leading off to two and a half acres of meadow garden planted with specimen trees. Central for north/south coasts of Somerset, Dorset and Devon. Exmoor, Dartmoor, Bristol, Bath, etc within little more than an hour's drive. Many gardens and National Trust properties encompassed in day out. Double/single — own facilities, TV, tea/coffee. Dining/sitting room. Evening Meals available. Open all year.

TAUNTON near. Mrs J. Greenway, Woodlands Farm, Bathealton, Near Taunton TA4 2AH (01984 623271). A warm, relaxed atmosphere, delicious food and comfortable accommodation are only some of the hallmarks of this cosy farmhouse which welcomes guests from June to September. Ideal for touring Somerset, Devon, Exmoor and the coast, there is also ample opportunity for simply relaxing on the farm or enjoying some carp fishing. Children welcomed at reduced rates. Family room en suite. Also available self-catering wing sleeping five. Bed and Breakfast, including bedtime drink and tea-making facilities, from £14 daily.

WATCHET. Mrs Sarah Richmond, Hungerford Farm, Washford, Watchet TA23 0LA (01984 640285). Hungerford Farm is a comfortable 13th century farmhouse on a 350-acre mixed farm, three-quarters of a mile from the West Somerset Steam Railway. Situated in beautiful countryside on the edge of the Brendon Hills and Exmoor National Park. Within easy reach of the North Devon coast, two and a half miles from the Bristol Channel and Quantock Hills. Marvellous country for walking, riding (STABLING FOR OWN HORSES AVAILABLE), and fishing on the reservoirs. Family room with TV and twin-bedded room; own bathroom, shower, toilet. Own lounge with TV and open fire. Children welcome at reduced rates, cot and high chair. Sorry, no pets. Bed and Breakfast from £16. Evening drink included. Open February to November.

FUN FOR ALL THE FAMILY IN SOMERSET

Cheddar Showcaves; Cricket St. Thomas Wildlife Park, Chard; Glastonbury Abbey; Haynes Sparkford Motor Museum; Peat Moors Visitors Centre, Westhay, near Glastonbury; Somerset Rural Life Museum, Glastonbury; Tropical Bird Gardens, Rode; West Somerset Railway, Minehead; Wookey Hole, near Wells.

WEDMORE. Mrs Sarah Willcox, Townsend Farm, Sand, Near Wedmore BS28 4XH (01934 712342).

Townsend Farm is delightfully situated in peaceful countryside with extensive views of the Mendip Hills. Set on the outskirts of the picturesque Georgian village of Wedmore with easy access to many places of natural and historic interest, such as the famous Cheddar Gorge, Wells Cathedral, Glastonbury Tor and Abbey ruins and only six miles from the M5 motorway, Junction 22 (one night stops welcome). All bedrooms have tea/coffee making facilities and some have portable TVs. Guests can be assured of a warm and pleasant atmosphere. We offer Bed and Breakfast from £15.50 per person, en-suite from £18. Phone for availability. Farm Holiday Bureau member.

WELLS. Mrs Pat Higgs, Home Farm, Stoppers Lane, Coxley, Wells BA5 1QS (01749 672434).
COMMENDED. Pat Higgs offers a relaxed holiday, long or short stay welcome, in a peaceful spot just off the A39. The rooms are well decorated and have TV and tea/coffee making facilities. We are in a very good touring area with Glastonbury, Wookey Hole Caves, Cheddar Gorge, National Trust properties and Bath all within easy reach, also many more places of interest. Good pubs and restaurants very close, within walking distance. Bed and Breakfast from £17.50 en suite. Directions: A39 between Wells and Glastonbury (one and a half miles from Wells, four miles Glastonbury). AA QQ Recommended. Please write or phone for brochure.

WELLS. Mrs Janet Gould, Milton Manor Farm, Old Bristol Road, Upper Milton, Wells BA5 3AH

(01749 673394). *COMMENDED.* **Working farm.** Manor Farm is a Grade II star Listed Elizabethan Manor House superbly situated on southern slopes of Mendip Hills one mile north from Wells. It is a beef farm of 130 acres. Three large rooms for visitors with hot and cold water, central heating and tea/coffee facilities. Full English breakfast with choice of menu served at separate tables in panelled dining room. Colour TV. Large peaceful garden with lovely view towards the sea. Ideal for walking on the Mendip Hills and exploring local places of historic interest. Access to house at all times. AA listed QQQ. No smoking. Closed Christmas and New Year. Bed and Breakfast from £15.50 per person. Reductions for children. Brochure on request.

WELLS near. Mrs Betty Hares, Highcroft, Wells Road, Priddy, Wells BA5 3AU (01749 673446).

COMMENDED. Set in 23 acres of rolling countryside, Highcroft is a new luxury, traditional, natural stone house, fully centrally heated and double glazed. It has two en-suite rooms and one with washbasin, all with tea/coffee making facilities. There is a separate TV lounge and diningroom. Situated in the Mendip Hills with delightful views, Highcroft is ideal for walking and touring. Four miles to Wells and Wookey Hole, six miles Cheddar. Trout fishing, golf, riding and swimming nearby. Bed and Breakfast from £18. Open all year.

WESTON-SUPER-MARE. Mr and Mrs H. Wallington, Braeside Hotel, 2 Victoria Park, Weston-super-

Mare BS23 2HZ (Tel & Fax: 01934 626642).
COMMENDED. AA QQQQ Selected RAC Highly Acclaimed. Delightful family-run hotel, ideally situated near sandy beach; shops and park are close by. All our nine bedrooms have bath/shower and toilet en suite, colour TV and coffee/tea making facilities and are tastefully decorated, creating just the right atmosphere in which to relax after a busy day. Some rooms with sea views. Unrestricted on-street parking. Good base for exploring Mendip and Quantock Hills, Exmoor, etc. Directions: with sea on left, take first right after Winter Gardens, then first left into Lower Church Road, Victoria Park is the cul-de-sac on the right after the left hand bend.

Terms quoted in this publication may be subject to increase if rises in costs necessitate

STAFFORDSHIRE

ECCLESHALL. M. Hiscoe-James, Offley Grove Farm, Adbaston, Eccleshall ST20 0QB (01785 280205). 🏵 *COMMENDED.* AA QQ Recommended, RAC Listed. You'll consider this a good find! Quality accommodation and excellent breakfasts. Small traditional mixed farm surrounded by beautiful countryside. The house is tastefully furnished and provides all home comforts. En suite rooms available. Whether you are planning to book here for a break in your journey, stay for a weekend or take your holidays here, you will find something to suit all tastes among the many local attractions. Situated on the Staffordshire/Shropshire borders we are convenient for Stoke-on-Trent, Ironbridge, Alton Towers, etc. Just 15 minutes from M6 and M54; midway between Eccleshall and Newport, four miles from the A519. Reductions for children. Play area for small children. Open all year. Bed and Breakfast from £16. Many guests return. Self catering cottages available. Brochure on request.

ECCLESHALL. Mrs Sue Pimble, Cobblers Cottage, Kerry Lane, Eccleshall ST21 6EJ (01785 850116). 🏵🏵 A five minute walk from the centre of Eccleshall and just past the 12th century church is Cobblers Cottage, in a quiet lane within the conservation area. We offer three bedrooms (one double, one twin and one family), all en suite with colour TV, tea/coffee facilities and central heating. Eccleshall has seven pubs, five with restaurants for your evening meal. Five miles from Junction 14 of M6, Eccleshall is ideally situated for the Potteries, Wedgwood, Ironbridge, Alton Towers and other attractions. Children and pets welcome. Non-smoking establishment. Bed and Breakfast from £18 per person per night; £26 for single occupancy. Reduction for children sharing.

LEEK. Mrs P. Knott, Lynwood, Westfields, Leek ST13 5LP (01538 384237). Tourist Board Listed *COMMENDED.* A warm welcome awaits you at this family-run guest house. Accommodation comprises double, twin and single bedrooms, all with colour TV, tea/coffee making facilities and individually heated. Double and twin rooms fitted with washbasins. Double en suite room with four-poster bed also available. Bathroom/shower with washbasin and toilet, second shower with washbasin and toilet. Dining room and breakfast room. Private garden with fish pond and fountain. Ideal touring base and convenient for Peak District; 20 minutes' drive to Alton Towers. Bed and Breakfast from £15.50; Bed, Breakfast and Evening Meal from £20.50. Brochure available.

NEWCASTLE-UNDER-LYME. Mary Hugh, The Old Hall, Poolside, Madeley, Near Crewe CW3 9DX (01782 750209). Civic Trust Award. English Heritage Grade II Starred Listed family-owned timbered house of great character and historic interest. Built between 1410 and 1420, predating its inscription "Walke knave what lookest at?" Situated in large attractive gardens with ornamental pool, tennis court and croquet lawn for visitors' use. Excellent accommodation; most rooms en suite; all with tea and coffee facilities, TV and central heating. Situated on A525, close to the Potteries and two of the largest garden centres in Europe — Bridgemere and Stapeley. Children over ten welcome at reduced rates. Bed and Breakfast from £20; Dinner £14; all meals by arrangement. Open all year.

The Old Hall, Madeley

OAKAMOOR. The Laurels, Star Bank, Oakamoor ST10 3BN (01538 702629). 🏵🏵 *COMMENDED.* From our centrally heated guest house with six superbly appointed family or double rooms you can spend a day in romantic Dovedale, get your thrills at Alton Towers or take a walk in the beautiful Churnet Valley. Wild and unspoilt moorland, deep limestone valleys, the antique shops of Leek or the world famous Potteries with names such as Wedgwood, Minton and Spode. All this can be yours within half an hour's drive of The Laurels. And in the evening you can relax with a drink in our bar or lounge. Brochure and terms available on request.

STAFFORD near. Mrs Sue Busby, Littywood Farm, Bradley, Stafford ST18 9DW (01785 780234; Fax: 01785 780770). 🏵🏵 Littywood Farm is a beautiful 14th century double moated manor/farmhouse, secluded yet easily accessible from the M6. Set in its own grounds on the edge of Bradley village in beautiful countryside. One double-bedded room with en suite bathroom from £19 per person Bed and Breakfast, one twin-bedded room with washbasin (bathroom adjacent) from £17.50 per person Bed and Breakfast. Both rooms have tea/coffee making facilities and colour TV. Reductions for children. Open all year except Christmas and New Year.

STOKE-ON-TRENT. Mr and Mrs J. Little, Lee House Farm, Leek Road, Waterhouses, Stoke-on-Trent ST10 3HW (01538 308439). HETB 🏵🏵 *HIGHLY COMMENDED.* Josie and Jim Little welcome you to their charming 18th century farmhouse in the heart of Waterhouses, a village with many amenities set in the Peak District National Park. The house is tastefully furnished and retains many of its original features. Ample off-road parking is available. All rooms are en suite and centrally heated. The non-smoking bedrooms are equipped with TV and drinks facilities. Waterhouses is an ideal centre for visiting the Derbyshire Dales, Staffordshire Moorlands, Alton Towers and the Potteries. Bed and Breakfast from £20 per person.

STAFFORDSHIRE – A STARK CONTRAST!

Staffordshire provides a stark contrast between rural and industrial landscapes. The former being represented by Cannock Chase and Dovedale, the latter by the Black Country and The Potteries. Of interest to the visitor might be the Staffordshire County Museum, Park Hall country park, the Watermills at Cheddleton, the Manifold Valley and the landscape gardens of Alton Towers.

STOKE-ON-TRENT. Mrs Anne Hodgson, The Hollies, Clay Lake, Endon, Stoke-on-Trent ST9 9DD

(01782 503252). ♛♛ *COMMENDED.* Beautiful Victorian house in quiet country setting off the B5051 convenient for the M6, Alton Towers, Staffordshire Moorlands and the Potteries. Five spacious comfortable bedrooms with en suite or private facilities, central heating, TV, tea/coffee makers. Children welcome sharing family room. Dogs by arrangement. Secluded garden, ample parking. Choice of breakfast with own preserves. No smoking, please. Bed and Breakfast from £18 with reductions for longer stays. Guests are assured of a warm friendly welcome. AA QQQ.

STOKE-ON-TRENT (7 miles). Mrs I. Grey, The Old Vicarage, Leek Road, Endon, Stoke-on-Trent ST9

9BH (01782 503686). Convenient stop-over for M6 travellers, Endon is a village on the Potteries to Leek road. North Staffordshire is an area of contrasts from unspoilt moorlands for motoring and walking to the Pottery towns with their wealth of history. Visit Alton Towers, the famous Pleasure Park; Gladstone Pottery Museum and City Museum, both award winners; Wedgwood, Royal Doulton, Spode etc, for visits and purchases. Accommodation is in a quiet situation and centrally heated with one double and two twin-bedded rooms, all with TV, tea/coffee making facilities; guests' lounge; two bathrooms and toilets; ample parking. Bed and Breakfast from £17.50 each, reduced rates for children. No smoking in the house, please.

SUFFOLK

BOXFORD. Mrs Janet Havard-Davies, Cox Hill House, Boxford, Sudbury CO10 5JG (01787

210449). Cox Hill House is a delightful Suffolk country house situated on the top of Cox Hill overlooking the old wool village of Boxford with its Anglo Saxon church and Elizabethan Grammar School. Nearby are the market towns of Sudbury (15 minutes), Hadleigh (10 minutes) and the picturesque village of Kersey (eight minutes). Within easy reach of Colchester, Ipswich, Harwich, Felixstowe, Dedham and Flatford Mill (Constable country), Cambridge and Lavenham. The accommodation comprises two twin-bedded rooms with en suite bathroom and one double bedded room with own facilities. Ample parking. Golf at Stoke-by-Nayland Golf Club by prior arrangement. Bed and Breakfast from £18.50 per person. No smoking.

BUNGAY/BECCLES. Mrs S. Cook, Butterley House, Leet Hill Farm, Yarmouth Road, Kirby Cane,

Bungay NR35 2HJ (01508 518301). A warm welcome awaits at this dairy/arable farm set in the heart of the Waveney Valley, with excellent rural views, situated between the historic towns of Beccles and Bungay, 15 minutes from Norwich, a 20-minute drive from the Suffolk/Norfolk coasts. Nearby is the famous Otter Trust at Earsham. Accommodation comprises one double/family room with en suite facilities, one double with washbasin, one twin room; bathroom and two toilets. Guests have their own sittingroom with TV, separate diningroom. A full English breakfast is served. Evening Meal by arrangement. Farm produce used wherever possible. Car essential. No pets please. Reductions for children. Terms on request. Tourist Board registered.

PLEASE ENCLOSE A STAMPED ADDRESSED ENVELOPE WITH ENQUIRIES

BURY ST. EDMUNDS. Jenny Pearson, Hay Green Farm, Whepstead, Bury St. Edmunds IP29 4UD

Hay Green Farm

(01284 850567). Hay Green Farm, a typical Listed Suffolk farmhouse, is quietly situated off the A143 five miles south of Bury St. Edmunds, close to the National Trust property of Ickworth Park. Ideal base for exploring East Anglia, being close to the picturesque villages of Clare, Kersey, Long Melford and Lavenham to the south; Newmarket and Cambridge to the west. Accommodation comprises a family room, double room and single room, all with TV and tea making facilities. Open all year. As there are horses, sheep and other livestock on the farm, sorry no pets. Paddock and stabling available for horses. Bed and Breakfast from £20. Good evening meals in local pubs.

BURY ST. EDMUNDS. John Kemp, Gifford's Hall, Hartest, Near Bury St. Edmunds IP29 4EX

(01284 830464; Fax: 01284 830229). 🐛🐛 *COMMENDED*. Gifford's Hall is a vineyard and small country living set in some of Suffolk's most beautiful and tranquil surroundings, midway between Bury, Lavenham and Sudbury. It is a listed Georgian farmhouse with large comfortable rooms including two twin and one double with en suite bathrooms. Guests have the use of the large drawing/TV/games room and breakfast is usually taken in the conservatory. You will be welcome to explore our 33 acres which includes 12 acres of vines and a winery, wild flower meadows grazed by rare breed sheep, pigs and pure breed free range hens, an acre rose garden, sweet peas and chrysanthemums, an organic vegetable garden and even a shop and tea room where you can enjoy a cream tea or taste the wines. Bed and Breakfast £40 double, £42 and £44 twin. Brochures on request.

BURY ST. EDMUNDS. Kay Dewsbury, Manorhouse, The Green, Beyton, Near Bury St. Edmunds IP30 9AF (01359 270960). 🐛🐛 *HIGHLY COMMENDED*.

You will find a welcoming and relaxed atmosphere at this lovely timbered 15th century farmhouse, set in large gardens overlooking village green. Pretty, spacious, en suite bedrooms — two twin and two double, all with colour TV, tea-making, radio and hairdryer. Choice of breakfasts at individual tables. A non-smoking house. Parking. Good local inns. Occasional evening meal by arrangement. Terms from £20 to £23 per person. Beyton signposted off A14. AA QQQQ Selected.

CHEDISTON. Mrs Susan Oakford, Blyth Lodge, Chediston, Halesworth IP19 0AR (01986 873067). Blyth Lodge is set back from the road and stands in three-quarters of an acre of garden, a spacious bungalow offering holiday makers an ideal base for the fine city of Norwich, the Suffolk Heritage coast, nearby Minsmere Bird Sanctuary and the Earsham Otter Trust; also convenient for several local golf courses. One double and one twin-bedded rooms, both with en suite facilities and colour TV; large sitting and dining room for residents own use with full central heating suitable for a break any time of the year. Ample private parking. Sorry no children under 10 years or pets and no smoking in the house. A warm and friendly welcome awaits you at Blyth Lodge. Telephone or SAE for terms. Self catering accommodation also available.

CLARE. Mrs Debra Bowles, 22 Callis Street, Clare, Sudbury CO10 8DX (01787 277834; Fax: 01787 277183). 🐛🐛🐛 *COMMENDED*. Situated in the delightful small town of Clare, Ship Stores comprises a small village store, tea room and five bedroomed guest house. All rooms are en suite with colour TV and tea and coffee facilities. A comfortable guests' lounge is available with TV and video (free video hire from shop). As well as being recommended in the "Which?" Guide we are proud of our Tourist Board grading. Ideally situated for Constable country, Cambridge and Bury St. Edmunds. Children welcome. Sorry, no pets. Bed and Breakfast from £18.50 per person; Evening Meal from £7.50 per person.

CLARE. Jean and Alastair Tuffill, "Cobwebs", 26 Nethergate Street, Clare, Near Sudbury CO10 8NP (01787 277539). ETB Listed COMMENDED. Situated in one of the loveliest parts of East Anglia, a friendly welcome awaits you at "Cobwebs" — this Grade II Listed beamed house dates back to the 14th century. Clare is an historic market town and the area abounds in history and ancient buildings — with many antique shops to explore. The house is within easy walking distance of the town centre and the delightful castle and country park. Good restaurants and pubs nearby for evening meals. Accommodation is provided in one twin and one single bedroom in the house, with bathroom, and a charming twin-bedded en suite cottage set within the delightful walled garden. All rooms have central heating, colour TV, handbasins and tea/coffee making facilities. Bed and Breakfast from £20 per person per night. Easy parking.

COLCHESTER. Ryegate House, Stoke-by-Nayland, Colchester CO6 4RA (01206 263679). 👑👑 HIGHLY COMMENDED. Situated on the B1068 within the Dedham Vale, in a quiet Suffolk village, Ryegate House is a modern property built in the style of a Suffolk farmhouse. It is only a few minutes' walk from the local shops, post office, pubs, restaurants and church and an ideal base for exploring Constable country. A warm welcome, good food and comfortable accommodation in a peaceful setting, with easy access to local historic market towns, golf courses and the east coast. Comfortable en suite bedrooms with colour TV, radio alarms, tea/coffee making facilities, shaver points and central heating. Children welcome. Parking for six cars. Open all year except Christmas. Bed and Breakfast from £25 to £29 per night single, double £36 to £42.

FRAMLINGHAM. Brian and Phyllis Collett, Shimmens Pightle, Dennington Road, Framlingham, Woodbridge IP13 9JT (01728 724036). ETB Listed COMMENDED. Shimmens Pightle is situated in an acre of landscaped garden, surrounded by farmland, within a mile of the centre of Framlingham, with its famous castle and church. Ideally situated for the Heritage Coast, Snape Maltings, local vineyards, riding, etc. Cycles can be hired locally. Many good local eating places. Double and twin bedded rooms, with washbasins, on ground floor. Comfortable lounge with TV overlooking garden, central heating and log fires in winter. Morning tea and evening drinks offered. Sorry, no pets or smoking indoors. Bed and traditional English Breakfast, using local cured bacon and home made marmalade. Vegetarians also happily catered for. SAE please. Open all year. Self catering flats at Southwold also available.

FRAMLINGHAM. Mrs C. Jones, Bantry, Chapel Road, Saxtead, Woodbridge IP13 9RB (01728 685578). 👑 👑 👑 Bantry is situated in the picturesque village of Saxtead close to the historic castle town of Framlingham. Saxtead is best known for its working windmill beside the village green. Bantry is set in half an acre of gardens overlooking open countryside and three-quarters of a mile along Tannington Road on right hand side from Saxtead Windmill. We offer you accommodation in one of three purpose-built self-contained apartments, separate from the house. For secluded comfort each comprises an en suite bedroom leading through to its own private lounge/dining room with TV and drink making facilities. Bed and Breakfast from £19 per person. Bed, Breakfast and Evening Meal from £28.50 per person. Non-smoking.

FRAMLINGHAM. Mrs Jennie Mann, Fiddlers Hall, Cransford, Near Framlingham, Woodbridge IP13

9PQ (01728 663729). Working farm, join in. Signposted on B1119, Fiddlers Hall is a 14th century, moated, oak-beamed farmhouse set in a beautiful and secluded position. It is two miles from Framlingham Castle, 20 minutes' drive from Aldeburgh, Snape Maltings, Woodbridge and South-wold. A Grade II Listed building, it has lots of history and character. The bedrooms are spacious, one has en suite shower room, the other has a private bathroom. Use of lounge and colour TV. Plenty of parking space. Lots of farm animals kept. Traditional farmhouse cooking. Bed and Breakfast from £20.

HITCHAM. Mrs Philippa McLardy, Hill Farmhouse, Bury Road, Hitcham IP7 7PT (01449 740651).

Hill Farmhouse is "Which?" Recommended and has lovely views. Set in its own grounds of three acres. It is an ideal touring centre, close to Lavenham, Constable and Gains-borough country. The coast, Cambridge, Norwich, Ipswich and Colchester are within an hour's drive. Restaurant and three pubs serving food all within two miles. Accommo-dation is in the main farmhouse and adjoining oak-beamed Tudor cottage. Twin and double suites all have private or en suite bathrooms, colour TV and tea/coffee making facilities. Pets by arrangement. Special diets catered for. Bed and Breakfast £18; Dinner £11. Tuesdays and Thursdays supper only (set menu) £6.50. £2 supplement for single nights, £2 discount for stays of five or more nights. Reductions for children. Closed November to beginning March.

IPSWICH. Mrs Rosanna Steward, High View, Back Lane, Washbrook, Ipswich IP8 3JA (01473

730494). A comfortable modernised Edwardian house set in a large secluded garden located four miles south of Ipswich the county town of Suffolk. Ideally situated to explore the Suffolk heritage coast and countryside, we are within easy reach of "Constable Country", Lavenham, Kersey, the his-toric market town of Bury St. Edmunds plus many other picturesque locations. There is a maze of public footpaths in and around the village providing a good variety of walks through woodland and open countryside. Twin and double bedrooms; guests bathroom with shower and toilet, lounge with TV. Good pub meals available in the village. £17.50 per person per night.

SAXMUNDHAM. Mrs Ann Ratcliffe, Fir Tree Farm, Kelsale, Saxmundham IP17 2RH (01728

668356). A warm welcome awaits you at this Tudor farm-house which has been modernised for your comfort, yet retains its olde worlde charm. Overlooking fields, gardens and pond. Accommodation comprises a self-contained wing including a double bedroom, with extra single bed, sitting room with TV, tea-making facilities, own shower and toilet, shaver point. Breakfast is in the main part of the house (beams and inglenook) overlooking the garden. Mid-way Aldeburgh and Southwold, 10 minutes Minsmere Bird Sanctuary, Dunwich beach, Snape (Aldeburgh Music Festi-val) and sports centre with indoor heated swimming pool. Yoxford with its pottery, art gallery, pubs and restaurants one mile. Bed and Breakfast from £17.50 per person per night. Self catering accommodation also available. SAE, or tele-phone, for further information.

STOWMARKET. Mrs Mary Noy, Red House Farm, Station Road, Haughley, Stowmarket IP14 3QP

(01449 673323). 🌸🌸 COMMENDED. Working farm. A warm welcome and homely atmosphere awaits you at our attractive farmhouse set in the beautiful surroundings of mid Suffolk. Comfortably furnished bedrooms with en suite shower rooms. Tea/coffee making facilities. One double, one twin and two single rooms. Central heating. Guests' own lounge with TV and dining room. Ideal location for exploring, walking, cycling and birdwatching. No smoking or pets. Open January to November.

WOODBRIDGE. Leslie and Jean Kelly, Grove House Hotel, 39 Grove Road, Woodbridge IP12 4LG (01394 382202). 🌸🌸🌸 Grove House is conveniently situated on the main A12 at Woodbridge. There are excellent opportunities close by for bird-watching, walking, golf and fishing. We offer a warm welcome and excellent service. All our bedrooms are comfortably furnished and include colour TVs and welcome trays. Most bedrooms have en-suite facilities. We are also able to offer ground floor accommodation for the partially disabled. Separate lounge/bar. Ample car parking. Open all year. Superb à la carte breakfast menu. Bed and Breakfast from £19.50. Special rates for Short Break holidays. AA QQ. Brochure on request.

SURREY

DORKING. The Waltons, 5 Rose Hill, Dorking RH4 2EG (Tel & Fax: 01306 883127; Mobile: 0802 469953). Tourist Board Listed. The Waltons is a listed house of historic interest situated in a conservation area. All the rooms are centrally heated with colour TV and tea/coffee facilities. Children are welcome, we can provide a cot and high chair. Evening meals and packed lunches are available if pre-booked, vegetarian diets are no problem. Smoking is discouraged but not totally forbidden in some areas. Prices for Bed and Breakfast start at £17.50, rising to £22.50 for a single with full English breakfast. Evening meals range between £8 for a snack or £12.50 for a three-course meal.

LINGFIELD. Mrs Vivienne Bundy, Oaklands, Felcourt, Lingfield RH7 6NF (01342 834705). Oaklands is a spacious country house of considerable charm dating from the 17th century. It is set in its own grounds of one acre, about one mile from the small town of Lingfield, and three miles from East Grinstead, both with rail connections to London. It is convenient for Gatwick Airport and ideal as a stop-over or as a base to visit the many places of interest in south-east England. Dover and the Channel Ports are two hours' drive away whilst the major towns of London and Brighton are about one hour distant. One en-suite room; one double and one single bedrooms, with washbasins; two bathrooms, two toilets; sittingroom; diningroom. Cot, high chair, babysitting and reduced rates for children. Gas central heating. Open all year. Parking. Bed and Breakfast from £18. Evening Meal by arrangement.

LINGFIELD. Mrs Vanessa Manwill, Stantons Hall Farm, Eastbourne Road, Blindley Heath, Lingfield RH7 6LG (01342 832401).

Stantons Hall Farm is an 18th century farmhouse, set in 18 acres of farmland and adjacent to Blindley Heath Common. Family, double and single rooms, most with WC, shower and wash-hand basins ensuite. Separate bathroom. All rooms have colour TV, tea/coffee facilities and are centrally heated. There are plenty of parking spaces. We are conveniently situated within easy reach of M25 (London Orbital), Gatwick Airport (car parking for travellers) and Lingfield Park racecourse. Enjoy a traditional English breakfast in our large farmhouse kitchen. Bed and Breakfast from £18 per person, reductions for children sharing. Cot and high chair available. Well behaved dogs welcome by prior arrangement.

OXTED. Pinehurst Grange Guest House, East Hill (A25), Oxted RH8 9AE (01883 716413).

Victorian ex-farmhouse offers one double, one twin and one single bedroom. All with washbasin, tea/coffee making facilities, colour TV; residents' dining room. Private parking. Close to all local amenities. Only 20 minutes' drive from Gatwick Airport and seven minutes' walk to the station with good trains to London/Croydon. Also close to local bus and taxi service. There are many famous historic houses nearby including "Chartwell", "Knole", "Hever Castle", and "Penshurst Place". Very handy for Lingfield Park racecourse. WALKERS NOTE: only one mile from North Downs Way. No smoking.

WALTON-ON-THAMES. Mrs Joan Spiteri, Beechtree Lodge, 7 Rydens Avenue, Walton-on-Thames KT12 3JB (01932 242738/886667). Tourist Board Listed *COMMENDED.* A comfortable Edwardian home situated in a quiet avenue, plenty of parking. Minutes from local shops and restaurants; station 10 minutes' walk, Waterloo 25 minutes. Easy access by bus to Heathrow and handy for Hampton Court, Chessington World of Adventure, Thorpe Park, Kempton and Sandown Exhibition Centres, Brooklands Aero/Motor Museum and glorious countryside. All rooms warm and comfortable with washbasins, colour TV, tea/coffee. Families catered for and business people welcome. French, Italian and Greek spoken. Coach trips can be booked. Bed and Breakfast from £16; family rates available. Sorry, no smoking.

SUSSEX

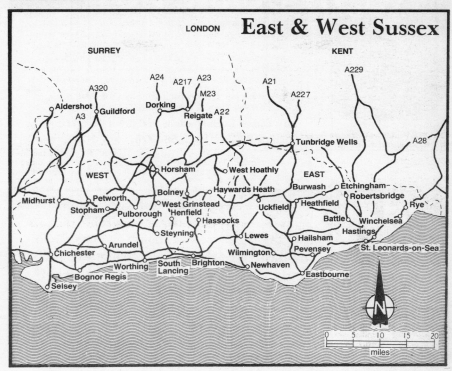

LONDON **East & West Sussex**

SURREY   KENT

A320 · A24 · A217 · A23 · M23 · A22 · A21 · A227 · A229

Aldershot · Guildford · Dorking · Reigate · A3

Tunbridge Wells · A28

Horsham · West Hoathly

WEST · Bolney · Haywards Heath · EAST · Burwash · Etchingham · Robertsbridge

Midhurst · Petworth · West Grinstead · Uckfield · Heathfield · Rye

Stopham · Pulborough · Henfield · Battle · Winchelsea

Steyning · Hassocks · Hastings

Arundel · Lewes · Hailsham

Chichester · Wilmington · Pevensey · St. Leonards-on-Sea

Worthing · South Lancing · Brighton · Newhaven · Eastbourne

Bognor Regis · Selsey

N

0   5   10   15   20
miles

EAST SUSSEX

BATTLE. Mrs Fay Ramsden, Brakes Coppice Farm, Telham Lane, Battle TN33 0SJ (Tel & Fax: 01424 830347).

Brakes Coppice Farmhouse is set in the midst of 70 acres of pasture and woodland with panoramic views to the sea five miles away. The house is modernised to a high standard and all bedrooms have en suite bath or shower rooms. A warm welcome and a hearty breakfast are provided by Fay Ramsden. The large towns of Hastings and Eastbourne are nearby and the surrounding area is famous as "1066 Country" with the Battle of Hastings actually having been fought within a mile of the farm. One double, one twin and one single bedrooms, all en suite with colour TV and tea/coffee making facilities; separate guests' lounge and dining room. No smoking or pets. Bed and Breakfast £30 single, £45 double. AA QQQQQ, RAC Highly Acclaimed.

EAST SUSSEX – 1066 AND ALL THAT!

The story of the famous battle can be traced from Pevensey, where William the Conqueror first landed; to Hastings, where the Norman and Saxon armies met and King Harold was slain; to Battle, where the victorious William founded an abbey. Visit too the Cinque Port of Rye (now a hilltop town), Michelham Priory and the magnificent moated Bodiam Castle.

BRIGHTON. Mrs M.A. Daughtery, Maon Hotel, 26 Upper Rock Gardens, Brighton BN2 1QE (01273 694400).

This completely non-smoking Grade II Listed building is run by proprietors who are waiting with a warm and friendly welcome. Our standard of food has been highly commended by many guests who return year after year. Two minutes from the sea and within easy reach of conference and main town centres. All nine bedrooms are furnished to a high standard and have colour TV, hospitality trays, radio alarm clocks and hair dryers; most en suite. A lounge with colour TV is available for guests' convenience. Dining room. Full central heating. Access to rooms at all times. Terms from £22. Brochure on request with a SAE.

BRIGHTON. Amber House, 4 East Drive, Brighton BN2 2BQ (01273 682920; Fax: 01273 676945).

A NON SMOKING HOUSE located on a quiet position overlooking the beautiful Queens Park Victorian Gardens, with tennis courts, bowling greens, duck pond, etc. Ample free street parking. Close to the sea with Brighton's historic Lanes, the Royal Pavilion, conference centre and marina only a stroll away. Attractively designed rooms both with and without en suite facilities (shower and toilet). Full central heating, colour TV and complimentary tea/coffee in all rooms. We want to make your stay enjoyable. Bed and Breakfast from £17.

BRIGHTON. Brighton Marina House Hotel, 8 Charlotte Street, Marine Parade, Brighton BN2 1AG (01273 605349 or 679484; Fax: 01273 605349).

ꗃ ꗃ ꗃ AS SHOWN ON BBC TV. Your comfort and that of your children is our first concern. Cosy, clean, comfortable, caring, family-run, highly recommended, beautifully maintained, elegantly furnished, well equipped — we care for and cater to children's individual needs. Single, double, twin, triple and family bedrooms — standard and en suite with colour TV, tea/coffee making facilities, washbasin, radio, alarm, clock, telephone, hairdryer. Our own pets — fish, birds, cats. Near sea front and fun fair, central for Palace Pier, Royal Pavilion, Lanes (for antiques), tourist attractions, conference/exhibition halls and Marina. 24 hour access and check in/out. Bed and Breakfast from £15 to £39.50 per night. Please write or phone for further details.

BRIGHTON. Amblecliff Hotel, 35 Upper Rock Gardens, Brighton BN2 1QF (01273 681161; Fax: 01273 676945).

ꗃ ꗃ ꗃ A NON-SMOKING HOTEL. AA QQQQ Selected, RAC Highly Acclaimed. This stylish hotel, highly recommended as the place to stay when in Brighton by a national newspaper and two television programmes, has been awarded the AA's coveted Select QQQQ, only given to two or three hotels in Brighton and the RAC's Highly Acclaimed for quality and customer satisfaction. Excellent location, close to the seafront, with historic Brighton, the Conference Centre, Royal Pavilion and the Marina only a stroll away. All double, twin and family rooms are en suite. Individually designed rooms with four poster and king size beds. Best in its price range, we believe you deserve an excellent service, comfortable accommodation and value for money. Bed and Breakfast from £21 to £30. Special offer — seven nights for the price of six!

BRIGHTON. Mr & Mrs P. Edwards, Four Seasons, 3 Upper Rock Gardens, Brighton BN2 1QE (01273 681496).

A 200 year old Grade II Listed Guest House recently refurbished offering a warm and comfortable stay. Character rooms, some with sea views; all with central heating, colour TV, radio alarms, hospitality trays, showers and some with full en-suite. 100 yards to sea, close to Conference and Exhibition Centre, shops, Lanes and theatres. Excellent full English breakfast, vegetarian or Continental as preferred. All major credit cards accepted. Pets by arrangement. Children welcome (50% discount for children under 12 years sharing). Access at all times. Open all year. Prices from £15 per person.

BURWASH. Mrs E. Sirrell, Woodlands Farm, Burwash, Etchingham TN19 7LA (01435 882794).

Working farm, join in. Woodlands Farm stands one third of a mile off the road surrounded by fields and woods. This peaceful and beautifully modernised 16th century farmhouse offers comfortable and friendly accommodation. Sitting/dining room; two bathrooms, one en suite, double or twin bedded rooms (one has four-poster bed) together with excellent farm fresh food. This is a farm of 55 acres with mixed animals, and is situated within easy reach of 20 or more places of interest to visit and half an hour from the coast. Open Easter to October. Central heating. Literature provided to help guests. Children welcome. Dogs allowed if sleeping in owners' car. Parking. Evening meal optional. Bed and Breakfast from £17.50 to £20 per person per night. AA Listed. Telephone or SAE, please.

EASTBOURNE. The Alfriston Hotel, 16 Lushington Road, Eastbourne BN21 4LL (01323 725640).

🛆🛆🛆 *COMMENDED*. Trevor and Brenda Gomersall welcome you to the Alfriston Hotel — a friendly, comfortable, family-run hotel in the centre of Eastbourne. Most bedrooms are en suite and all are non-smoking with colour TV and tea/coffee making facilities. Full English breakfasts are served with free range eggs cooked to your requirements. Vegetarians welcome. Home-cooked evening dinners are available if booked, but there are also plenty of eating places nearby. We are very close to the shopping centre and railway station, while the seafront, theatres and Devonshire Park are less than half a mile away. Licensed. Bed and Breakfast from £18.50. Open March to October.

EASTBOURNE. Farrar's Hotel, Wilmington Gardens, Eastbourne BN21 4JN (01323 723737; Fax: 01323 732902).

🛆🛆🛆🛆 AA/RAC Two Star. Quitely situated yet within 200 yards of the seafront and promenade. All 45 attractively furnished bedrooms are centrally heated and have either bathroom or shower en suite, direct dial telephone, radio, colour TV and complimentary tea/coffee facilities. We have three lounges, cocktail bar serving bar snacks at lunchtime and our fully licensed restaurant offers extensive luncheon and dinner meal. Large private car park. Children welcome, sorry no pets. Bed and Breakfast from £22 to £32 per person per night. Full colour brochure available on request.

EASTBOURNE. Mr & Mrs J. Frost, "Sainvia", 19 Ceylon Place, Eastbourne BN21 3JE (Tel & Fax: 01323 725943).

A warm welcome awaits you at "Sainvia". Three minutes from Pier, five minutes from a lovely shopping centre, approximately 10 minutes from theatres (walking). We are central for all your entertainment. Regular bus service to beautiful Beachy Head. All our rooms have colour TV and tea making facilities. Enjoy a drink in our comfortable bar. Open all year. Bed and Breakfast from £16 per night. Special Christmas three-day Breaks available. Enquiries welcome.

EASTBOURNE. The Mayvere Guest House, 12 Cambridge Road, Eastbourne BN22 7BS (01323 729580). 🛆🛆 Lorna and Bob Brett welcome you to The Mayvere, just a few steps from the seafront and a short walk to the centre and all amenities, the bowling greens, Treasure Island for the children, the Redoubt Fortress with its historical museum, aquarium and tea rooms. All this and more at Mayvere, with its seven comfortable rooms and friendly caring atmosphere, with TV, washbasins and tea/coffee making facilities. Excellent food served at separate tables. Comfortable lounge. Licensed. Separate bath and shower rooms. Full central heating in winter. Bed and Breakfast from £14.50 to £16 per person. Optional Evening Dinner £5. Send SAE for colour brochure. Directions: A22 Eastbourne seafront (east) turn right at Seafront, pass Redoubt Fortress, turn right at Langham Hotel into Cambridge Road.

PUBLISHER'S NOTE

FAIRLIGHT. Mrs Adams, Fairlight Cottage, Warren Road (via Coastguard Lane), Fairlight TN35

4AG (01424 812545). A warm welcome awaits you at our comfortable country house, delightfully situated alongside Hastings Country Park with cliff top walks and magnificent coastal views. Bedrooms are tastefully furnished, with central heating, en suite facilities and tea/coffee trays. Large, comfortable TV lounge. Good home cooking served in the elegant dining room. Evening meals by prior arrangement; guests may bring their own wine. An ideal base for exploring the ancient towns of Rye, Winchelsea, Battle and Hastings. No smoking in house. Ample parking and use of garden. Dogs kept. Pets welcome. Bed and Breakfast £18 to £22.50; Bed, Breakfast and Dinner £28 to £32.50.

HAILSHAM near. David and Jill Hook, Longleys Farm Cottage, Harebeating Lane, Hailsham BN27 1ER (Tel & Fax: 01323 841227). Situated in quiet private country lane one mile north of the market town of Hailsham with its excellent amenities including modern sports centre and leisure pool, surrounded by footpaths across open farmland. Ideal for country lovers. Dogs and children welcome. The coast at Eastbourne, South Downs, Ashdown Forest and 1066 Country are all within easy access. The non-smoking accommodation comprises one single, one twin and one family room with en suite and tea-making facilities. Bed and Breakfast £16. Reductions for children.

HASTINGS. Pat and Tim Lowe, Bell Cottage, Vinehall, Robertsbridge TN32 5JN (Tel & Fax: 01580

881164). 16th century converted Inn full of charm and character with inglenooks and beams throughout. Guests are assured of a warm welcome and are invited to sit in our lovely garden. Breakfast is a feast with homemade preserves. We are situated in 1066 Country close to Battle, Hastings and Rye; Canterbury, Brighton and Sissinghurst Gardens within driving distance. We are on the A21, nine miles from Hastings between Whatlington and Robertsbridge. One double bedrom with private bathroom, one twin en suite and one twin with shared bathroom, all have colour TV and tea-making facilities. Rates £34 to £40 per room (two persons). B&B of the Year 1997. Brochure on request.

HASTINGS. Mr and Mrs R. Steele, Amberlene Guest House, 12 Cambridge ardens, Hastings TN34 1EH (01424 439447). Hastings town centre, two minutes' walk from the beach, shops, entertainments, rail/bus stations and central car park. Single, double, twin and family rooms; some with en suite. Very clean, comfortable, well carpeted and decorated. All with central heating, colour TV, washbasins, power and shaver points. Guests have their own front door keys and access to rooms and facilities at all times. Bed and full four-course English Breakfast £13 to £18 per night (room only, £2 less); half price for children sharing. All prices include tea/coffee and biscuits in your room. Baby cots free. No extra charges. Sorry, no pets. Tourist Board registered. Also holiday flats available nearby.

HASTINGS. Peter Mann, Grand Hotel, Grand Parade, St. Leonards, Hastings TN38 0DD (Tel & Fax: 01424 428510). 🐾🐾 Seafront family-run hotel, half a mile west of Hastings Pier on the A259. Spacious lounge, licensed bar, central heating. All bedrooms have radio/room call/baby listening and some rooms have en suite facilities and colour TV. Free access at all times. Unrestricted/disabled parking. Non-smoking restaurant. In the heart of 1066 country close to Battle Abbey, Bodiam and Hever Castles, Kiplings' Bateman and historic Cinque Ports plus Hasting Castle Caves, Sealife Centre, local golf courses and leisure centres. Open all year. Bed and Breakfast from £14; Evening Meal from £8. Children welcome, half price when sharing room. SAE for further information.

HASTINGS. Mrs Afroditi G. Wall, Beechwood Hotel, 59 Baldslow Road, Hastings TN34 2EY (01424

420078). 🐾🐾 Beechwood is a typical example of late Victorian architecture with this atmosphere retained in the bedrooms, lounge, diningroom and bar. It is a small, family run hotel with full central heating, large south-facing garden and unrivalled views of Alexandra Park, situated in quiet surroundings adjacent to good bus routes or 15 minutes' walk to town centre, seafront or station. Off the A2101 and ideal for touring South East England. On and off the road parking. Tea/coffee making facilities on request. Open all year. Bed and English Breakfast from £15. Evening Dinner can be provided at £9. Bargain Breaks available. RAC Listed. Resident Proprietor: Afroditi G. Wall MHCIMA MRSH.

HASTINGS. Mr and Mrs S. York, Westwood Farm, Stonestile Lane, Hastings TN35 4PG (01424 751038). Working farm. Farm with pet sheep, chickens, etc. Quiet rural location off country lane half a mile from B2093 approximately two miles from seafront and town centre. Golf course nearby. Central position for visiting places of interest to suit all ages. Elevated situation with outstanding views over Brede Valley. All bedrooms have washbasins, tea making facilities and TV; some en suite and two bedrooms on ground floor. Full English breakfast. Off-road parking. Bed and Breakfast from £15 to £25 per person for two persons sharing. Reduced rates for weekly booking. Also available six-berth self catering caravan — details on request.

HEATHFIELD. Mrs Jean Morren, "Iwood", Mutton Hall Lane, Heathfield TN21 8NR (01435 863918). Secluded bungalow in delightful large garden with distant views of South Downs and English Channel. Main accommodation comprises double bedroom with en suite sitting room with TV, video, radio and coffee/tea making facilities plus private bathroom. A further two persons in party can be accommodated on double sofa bed in sitting room at additional discretionary charge. A further double bedroom with TV is also available. A cot and high chair can be provided and babysitting facilities are available. A wide choice of breakfast menu. First class non smoking accommodation in a quiet and peaceful setting. Bed and Breakfast from £18 to £20.

HEATHFIELD. Mrs Angela Wardell, Yew Tree Cottage, Street End Lane, Broad Oak, Heathfield TN21 8SA (01435 864053). Yew Tree Cottage dates back to 1750 having been extensively modernised. Situated one mile east of Heathfield off the A265 and having glorious views over the Rother Valley. Close to the Sussex/Kent border making an ideal touring centre. South Coast and the historic towns of Battle, Rye and Hastings together with many other places of interest within easy reach; Dover two hours, Ashford one hour's drive. Many attractive eating houses in the vicinity. Accommodation comprises two double rooms (one with twin bed option) and one single. Tea-making facilities and TV. No pets. Ample parking. Open all year. Log fires. A warm welcome. Bed and Breakfast £17.50 per person.

FOR THE MUTUAL GUIDANCE OF GUEST AND HOST

Every year literally thousands of holidays, short-breaks and overnight stops are arranged through our guides, the vast majority without any problems at all. In a handful of cases, however, difficulties do arise about bookings, which often could have been prevented from the outset.

It is important to remember that when accommodation has been booked, both parties — guests and hosts — have entered into a form of contract. We hope that the following points will provide helpful guidance.

GUESTS: When enquiring about accommodation, be as precise as possible. Give exact dates, numbers in your party and the ages of any children. State the number and type of rooms wanted and also what catering you require — bed and breakfast, full board, etc. Make sure that the position about evening meals is clear — and about pets, reductions for children or any other special points.

Read our reviews carefully to ensure that the proprietors you are going to contact can supply what you want. Ask for a letter confirming all arrangements, if possible.

If you have to cancel, do so as soon as possible. Proprietors do have the right to retain deposits and under certain circumstances to charge for cancelled holidays if adequate notice is not given and they cannot re-let the accommodation.

HOSTS: Give details about your facilities and about any special conditions. Explain your deposit system clearly and arrangements for cancellations, charges, etc. and whether or not your terms include VAT.

If for any reason you are unable to fulfil an agreed booking without adequate notice, you may be under an obligation to arrange alternative suitable accommodation or to make some form of compensation.

While every effort is made to ensure accuracy, we regret that FHG Publications cannot accept responsibility for errors, omissions or misrepresentation in our entries or any consequences thereof. Prices in particular should be checked because we go to press early. We will follow up complaints but cannot act as arbiters or agents for either party.

Cleavers Lyng Country Hotel

For excellent home cooking in traditional English style, comfort and informality, this small family-run hotel in the heart of rural East Sussex is well recommended. Peacefully set in beautiful landscaped gardens extending to 1.5 acres featuring a rockpool with waterfall. Adjacent to Herstmonceux Castle's West Gate, the house dates from 1577 as its oak beams and inglenook fireplace bear witness. This is an ideal retreat for a quiet sojourn away from urban clamour. The castles at Pevensey, Scotney, Bodiam and Hever are all within easy reach as are Battle Abbey, Kipling's House, Bateman's, Michelham Priory and the seaside resorts of Eastbourne, Bexhill and Hastings. Bedrooms are all fully ensuite and all have central heating, direct-dial telephone and tea and coffee-making facilities with some having separate siting area with colour television. On the ground floor there is an oak-beamed non-smoking restaurant with a fully licensed bar, lounge bar, cosy residents' lounge with television and an outer hall with telephone and cloakrooms. Peace, tranquillity and a warm welcome await you. Attraction: Badger Watch. Room rate from £22.50 p.p. upwards sharing double/twin room. No single rooms available however at certain times of the year we offer a reduced single occupancy rate for double/twin bedroom.

Church Road, Herstmonceux, East Sussex BN27 1QJ. Telephone: 01323 833131; Fax: 01323 833617
For further information call Talking Pages on Freephone 0800 600 900

RYE. Mrs J.P. Hadfield, Jeake's House, Mermaid Street, Rye TN31 7ET (01797 222828). 🌸🌸

HIGHLY COMMENDED. This beautiful listed building, originally built as a wool store and later converted to a Baptist School, was built by Samuel Jeake in 1689. It stands in one of England's most famous streets, renowned for its cobblestoned charm and association with notorious gangs of smugglers. It was once the "deeply cherished" home of American author Conrad Aiken. Breakfast, traditional or vegetarian, is served in the 18th century galleried former chapel. Oak beamed and panelled bedrooms, overlooking the marsh and roof tops to the sea, are furnished with brass or mahogany bedsteads, linen sheets and lace. En-suite facilities. TV, telephones and hot drinks trays. Four poster honeymoon suite available. Residential licence. Terms from £22.50 to £29.50 per person.

RYE. Rita Cox, Four Seasons, 96 Udimore Road, Rye TN31 7DY (01797 224305). Four Seasons is situated on Cadborough Cliff with spectacular views across the south facing garden to the Brede Valley, Rye and the sea. We offer excellent B&B in our attractive house which is decorated to reflect the changing seasons. Centrally heated rooms are en suite or have private facilities and have TV and hot drinks tray. Breakfasts are full English or vegetarian, with home-made preserves and local produce. Evening Meals on request. Four Seasons is a short walk from the town centre, has private parking, is an excellent centre for touring East Sussex and Kent, and is convenient for the Channel Ports and Tunnel. Rates are £16 to £18 per person with special winter bargain breaks mid-November to February. Brochure on request.

RYE. Mrs Dawn Keay, Aviemore Guest House, 28/30 Fishmarket Road, Rye TN31 7LP (Tel & Fax: 01797 223052). 🌸🌸 *APPROVED.* Guests are assured of a genuinely warm welcome and clean, comfortable accommodation at Aviemore, which overlooks the park and the River Rother, just two minutes' walk from the town centre. Four rooms have private shower and WC, four have shared facilities; Kenya tea/coffee. Fully licensed. Guests' lounge, dining room, TV. 24 hour access. Car park nearby. Excellent breakfasts, evening meals by prior arrangement. Credit cards accepted. Bed and Breakfast from £17.

Children go FREE with full paying adult on visits to WILDERNESS WOOD, near Uckfield on production of our READERS' OFFER VOUCHER.

CADBOROUGH FARM

Udimore Road, Rye, East Sussex TN31 6AA
Tel: 01797 225426 Fax: 01797 224097
Jane Apperly

A lovely country house set in 24 acres with outstanding views towards the sea overlooking Camber Castle and the medieval towns of Rye and Winchelsea. Spacious sunny bedrooms with ensuite facilities and sea views. Self contained suite with inner hall, bedroom, sitting room and bathroom. Colour TV's, radio/alarms, hairdryers and hot drinks tray. Drawing room with log fire. Superb English, continental and vegetarian breakfast. Ample parking. Short walk from town centre. B&B from £22.50-£25.00 pppn.

RYE. Pat and Jeff Sullivin, Cliff Farm, Iden Lock, Rye TN31 7QE (Tel & Fax: 01797 280331, long

ring please). Our farmhouse is peacefully set in a quiet elevated position with extensive views over Romney Marsh. The ancient seaport town of Rye with its narrow cobbled street is two miles away. We are an ideal touring base although the town and immediate district have much to offer — golden beaches, quaint villages, castles, gardens etc. Comfortable guest bedrooms with washbasins and tea/coffee facilities; two toilets; own shower; diningroom and sittingroom. Home produce. Open March to October for Bed and Breakfast from £15 to £16. Reduced weekly rates. AA and RAC Recommended.

RYE. Mrs Heather Coote, "Busti", Barnetts Hill, Peasmarsh, Rye TN31 6YJ (01797 230408).

Comfortable and clean accommodation in detached house on the edge of the rural village of Peasmarsh. Ideally located for touring both East Sussex and Kent and for visiting Bodiam Castle, the historic town of Rye, Great Dixter, Sissinghurst, Battle Abbey and many other seasonal attractions; lake fishing locally. Guest lounge/dining room with TV. Guests' shower/toilet. Bedrooms have tea/coffee making facilities. Central heating throughout. Hairdryer available. Friendly service and tourist advice provided. Full English breakfast or alternative. Ample off road parking. Bed and Breakfast from £15. No smoking in the house. Member of Rye and District Hotels and Caterers Association.

RYE near. David and Eliane Griffin, Kimblee, Main Street, Peasmarsh, Near Rye TN31 6UL (01797

230514 or 0831 841004 mobile). 🐾🐾 *COMMENDED.* Friendly country house with views from all aspects. Rye five minutes' drive, beaches 15 minutes. Ample off road parking. Ideal base for visiting Kent and Sussex. Two large rooms with shower, toilet, washbasin en suite. Smaller room with en suite bathroom. Single room possible. All rooms have colour TV, radio alarm, tea/coffee facilities, hair dryers. Locally renowned pub/restaurant 250 metres. Generous English breakfast, vegetarian on request. Reduction for substantial Continental breakfast. French spoken. On A268 three miles from Rye in the direction of London. £18 to £19 per person. Reductions for three nights or more. Mid week breaks November to March: three nights for the price of two. Brochure on request.

SEAFORD. Mrs Roberts, Sunnyside, 23 Connaught Road, Seaford BN25 2PT (01323 895850).

Comfortable Victorian family house approximately 120 yards from the seafront, between Eastbourne and Brighton. An ideal overnight stop three miles from the Newhaven/Dieppe ferry and South Downs Way. TV, tea/coffee making facilities and washbasins in all bedrooms. Separate bath and shower rooms. Choice of continental or full English breakfast. No smoking. Within easy reach of many good restaurants and places of historic interest. Please write or telephone for further details.

UCKFIELD. Mrs Fiona Brown, The Cottage, Chillies Lane, High Hurstwood, Near Uckfield TN22 4AA (Tel & Fax: 01825 732804). A pretty stone cottage in a quiet lane in a valley of outstanding natural beauty with beautiful views at the rear — on the edge of Ashdown Forest with its extensive views, open spaces and many walks. Many National Trust houses and gardens to visit locally and within easy reach of Tunbridge Wells and the South Coast. One twin/family room en suite, one twin and one single room, all have TV and tea/coffee facilities. Children welcome. Bed and Breakfast from £16 to £20 per person per night.

WINCHELSEA. A.N. Roche, The Strand House, Winchelsea, Near Rye TN36 4JT (Tel & Fax: 01797 226276). ❀❀❀ COMMENDED. Nestling beneath the cliff

of the ancient medieval town of Winchelsea lies the 15th century Strand House. Full of atmosphere with oak beams and inglenook fireplaces, but with the comfort of en suite facilities, central heating, colour TV and hot drinks tray. Romantic four-poster bedroom available. A lounge with log fires in winter leads onto a pretty garden for your enjoyment in summer. A residential licence, payphone, and ample parking in the grounds make your visit relaxed and enjoyable. An ideal place to stay while you explore the many places of interest within easy reach. AA QQQQ Selected, RAC Acclaimed. Tariff from £22.50 to £29 per person. Visa/Mastercard/Eurocard accepted.

WEST SUSSEX

ALDWICK. Nigel and Fiona Pickett, Bramley Bed and Breakfast, 34 Inglewood Drive, Aldwick, Bognor Regis PO21 4JZ (01243 268966). Nigel and

Fiona will quickly make you feel at home in their comfortable family house situated at the very end of a quiet cul-de-sac, but within easy reach of the city of Chichester, Goodwood, Bognor Regis and beaches. There are two double bedrooms, one with king-size bed and king-size shower room and the other with a private bathroom. All rooms are superbly furnished and have colour TV and tea/coffee trays. In summer months a delicious full English breakfast is served in our south-facing conservatory overlooking a delightful garden. Bed and Breakfast from £16 to £22.50 per person per night.

ARUNDEL. Swan Hotel, 27-29 High Street, Arundel BN18 9AG (01903 882314; Fax: 01903 883759). ❀❀❀ HIGHLY COMMENDED. RAC/AA Three

Star. Situated in the heart of historic Arundel the Swan Hotel has been lovingly restored to its former Victorian splendour. Many of the hotel's original features, including English oak flooring and wall-panelling, are still very much in evidence creating a wonderful ambience throughout. Both table d'hôte and à la carte menus are available in the hotel's popular award-winning restaurant where local and seasonal produce is used extensively, and wines can be selected from the original 200 year old cellar. Local real ales can be sampled in the bar. All bedrooms have en suite bathroom, colour TV, hairdryer, telephone, tea/coffee making, room service. Prices from £30 per person per night including full English breakfast. Arundel is an enchanting place with its castle, Cathedral and parks; well placed for touring the lovely West Sussex countryside. All major credit cards accepted.

ARUNDEL near. Peter and Sarah Fuente, Mill Lane House, Slindon, Arundel BN18 0RP (01243 814440). ✿ ✿ *COMMENDED.* Magnificent views to the coast. 17th century house with three acres of grounds, in pretty National Trust village on South Downs. Direct access to many miles of footpaths including South Downs Way; superb bird watching locally, at coastal harbours and Amberley Brooks. Easy reach Arundel Castle, Goodwood, Chichester with Roman Palace, Cathedral and Festival Theatre. Sandy beach six miles. Pubs within easy walking distance. Rooms en suite and with TV; central heating and log fires in winter. One mile Junction A27/A29. Bed and Breakfast (double/twin room) £20 per person per night. Single occupancy and family rooms on request. Three course Evening Meals from £10.25 by arrangement. Weekly terms available.

BOGNOR REGIS. Mrs B.M. Hashfield, Taplow Cottage, 81 Nyewood Lane, Bognor Regis PO21 2UE

"TAPLOW COTTAGE"

(01243 821398). This cottage lies in a residential part, west of the town centre, 600 yards from the sea and shops. Proximity to many beaches and contrasting towns and countryside makes this an ideal touring centre. Chichester, Goodwood Racecourse, Arundel Castle, Brighton, Portsmouth and Southsea are but a few of the places of interest within easy reach. Accommodation comprises one double, one twin, and one family bedrooms, all with vanity units, tea/coffee making facilities and colour TVs. Lounge, dining-room; central heating throughout. The cottage is well appointed and the area is served by public transport. Parking space available. Dogs by arrangement. Bed and Breakfast only from £15 nightly. SAE, please.

BOGNOR REGIS. Deborah S. Collinson, The Old Priory, 80 North Bersted Street, Bognor Regis PO22 9AQ (01243 863580; Fax: 01243 826597).

✿ ✿ ✿ *HIGHLY COMMENDED.* A charming 17th century Priory restored to its former glory with a blend of historic charm. Situated in a picturesque rural village close to Bognor Regis, Chichester, Arundel, Goodwood, Fontwell and within easy access of Portsmouth, Brighton, Continental ferry port and all major commuting routes. Facilities include superb en suite rooms equipped to 4 star standard, four-poster water bed with jacuzzi bath, secluded outdoor swimming pool, Cordon Bleu cuisine, residential licence, open all year. Tariff from £22.

BURY. Mrs Jane Hare, Eedes Cottage, Bignor Park Road, Bury Gate, Pulborough RH20 1EZ (01798 831438). Eedes Cottage is situated in unspoilt countryside just north of the Downs, yet convenient for the A29 which is only half a mile away. There are interesting places to visit including Arundel, Petworth, Chichester and Bignor Roman Villa. There is very good walking and riding, and dogs are welcome. Accommodation comprises two twin bedded rooms and one double bedroom with ensuite bathroom, all with colour TV. Also separate bathroom and toilet. Terms from £20 to include full English Breakfast.

CHICHESTER. Mrs Jenny Parfoot, The Meadows, 2 Meadow Close, Hunston, Chichester PO20 6PB

(01243 788504 or 0585 790564). Country chalet bungalow. A warm welcome and friendly relaxed atmosphere, close to Chichester, Hunston Golf Course, Goodwood, Festival Theatre, good pub with restaurant. Ideal touring base. Accommodation comprises two double/twin bedrooms with central heating, one en suite the other with private facilities. Microwave and fridge to self cater light meals. No smoking. Open January to December. Bed and Breakfast from £16.

CHICHESTER (Hambrook). Mrs Edna Bailey, 14 The Avenue, Hambrook, Chichester PO18 8TY (01243 573199). A genuinely warm welcome awaits you if you choose to stay with us. Our quiet and comfortable accommodation has two rooms — one twin and one double, both with TV and tea/coffee facilities. Shared bathroom. Central heating. Bed and full English Breakfast from £16 per person, reductions for children under 10 years. 10 minutes' drive to Chichester Cathedral and Festival Theatre, 20 minutes' drive to Portsmouth, Singleton Open Air Museum. We have a large garden. No smoking. Several good public houses and restaurants in the area.

WEST SUSSEX – COASTAL RESORTS AND DOWNS!

Although dominated perhaps by Chichester and Bognor Regis, West Sussex does have much to offer. Places like Arundel, Marden-Stoughton Forest, Midhurst, and its historic inn, the open-air museum at Singleton and the National Butterfly Museum at Bramber are worth a visit.

HENFIELD. Mrs J.A. Pound, The Squirrels, Albourne Road, Woodmancote, Henfield BN5 9BH

(01273 492761). The Squirrels is a country house with lovely large garden set in a secluded area convenient for south coast and downland touring. Brighton and Gatwick 20 minutes. Good food at pub five minutes' walk. One family, one double, one twin and one single rooms, all with colour TV, washbasin, central heating and tea/coffee making facilities. Ample parking space. A warm welcome awaits you. Open all year. Directions: from London take M25, M23, A23 towards Brighton, then B2118 to Albourne. Turn right onto B2116 Albourne/Henfield Road — Squirrels is approximately one and a half miles on left. Bed and Breakfast £16.

HENFIELD. Mrs J. Forbes, Little Oreham Farm, off Horne Lane, Near Woodsmill, Henfield BN5 9SB

(01273 492931). Delightful old Sussex farmhouse situated in rural position down lane, adjacent to footpaths and nature reserve. One mile from Henfield village, eight miles from Brighton, convenient for Gatwick and Hickstead. Excellent base for visiting many gardens and places of interest in the area. The farmhouse is a Listed building of great character; oak-beamed sitting room with inglenook fireplace (log fires), and a pretty dining room. Three comfortable attractive bedrooms with en suite shower/bath; WC; colour TV; tea making facilities. Central heating throughout. Lovely garden with views of the Downs. Situated off Horne Lane, one minute from Woodsmill Countryside Centre. Winner of Kellog's award: "Best Bed and Breakfast" in the South East. You will enjoy a friendly welcome and pleasant holiday. Sorry, no children under 10. Bed and Breakfast from £18 per person. Evening Meals by arrangement. No smoking. Open all year.

HURSTPIERPOINT. Philip and Suzanne Norris, Bankyfield, 21 Hassocks Road, Hurstpierpoint BN6 9QH (01273 833217). Bankyfield is a Grade II Listed Georgian house. Hurstpierpoint is a charming Downland village with restaurants and pubs three minutes' walk away. We are close to the South Downs, a walkers paradise. Brighton and the gardens of Leonardslee, Nymans, Sheffield Park and Wakehurst Place are all near. We offer one twin room overlooking our garden. A full English breakfast is served (in our courtyard garden on warmer days). There is central heating, a private bathroom is available and an elegant drawing room. BR station, Hassocks is one and a quarter miles away to Victoria, one hour. Open all year. £17.50 per person.

MIDHURST. Sue and Mike Hook, The Old Cottage, Didling, Near Midhurst GU29 0LQ (Tel & Fax:

01730 813680). Garden designer's characterful 16th century shepherd's cottage in idyllic, peaceful hamlet south west of Midhurst. Newly restored, architect-designed accommodation surrounded by beautiful downland views. Ideal stopover en route to Portsmouth ferries, or for racing at Goodwood, polo, golf, yachting. 15 minutes' walk from South Downs Way. Two centrally heated twin rooms with washbasins, clock-radios and tea/coffee making facilities. Bathroom immediately adjacent. Large garden, wildlife pond, free-range chickens. Vegetarians catered for. On site parking. Warm and friendly welcome, but regret cannot accommodate children or smokers. Bed and Breakfast £20 per person.

MIDHURST/HEYSHOTT. Annabelle Costaras, Amberfold, Heyshott, Midhurst GU29 0DA (01730

812385). Charming 17th century cottage with self-contained annexe set in beautiful countryside. Private entrance, en suite double bedroom with TV and self catering facilities for continental breakfast. No smoking please. Bed and Breakfast from £20 per person. Open January to December.

PETWORTH. Phyl Folkes, "Drifters", Duncton, Petworth GU28 0JZ (01798 342706). Welcome to a

quiet, friendly, comfortable house overlooking countryside. One double en suite, two twin and one single rooms. Duncton is three miles from Petworth on the A285 Chichester Road, South Downs Way close by and many interesting places to visit. Petworth House and Gardens, Roman Villa, Chichester Cathedral and Theatre, Goodwood House and racecourse, Wheld and Downland Museum and mnay more. TV and tea/coffee making facilities in all rooms. Sorry no young children and no smoking. Bed and Breakfast from £17.50 to £21 per person.

STEYNING. Mrs A. Shapland, Wappingthorn Farm, Horsham Road, Steyning BN44 3AA (01903

813236). Working farm. Delightful traditional farmhouse with oak-beamed lounge, open log fire and pretty dining room. Situated in rural position viewing "South Downs", four miles from seaside, seven miles Worthing, 12 miles Brighton, Gatwick and Hickstead convenient. Comfortable, attractive, spacious bedrooms with en suite shower/bath; WC; colour TV; tea/coffee making facilities. Lovely garden with heated swimming pool. Many footpaths surround the farm and old market town. Bed and Breakfast from £15. Evening meal and picnic baskets available. Children welcome. Babysitting possible. There is also a converted barn with two self contained cottages. Fully equipped, sleeps two/four, from £110 per week. Short breaks available. Open all year.

STORRINGTON/PULBOROUGH. Mrs M. Smith, Willow Tree Cottage, Washington Road, Storrington RH20 4AF (01903 740835). Family-run B&B situated at the foot of South Downs Way surrounded by fields and horses. Large off road parking area. Twin or double rooms, all en suite with colour TV, tea making facilities. Centrally heated. Full choice English breakfast. Ideally situated for walking holidays; Arundel Castle 10 minutes by car, Parham House five minutes. Worthing 15 minutes, Storrington village 15 minutes' walk with good choice of restaurants and pubs. Open all year except Christmas Day and Boxing Day. No smoking. Terms from £20 per person. Reduced rates for three or more nights. Brochure available.

TYNE & WEAR

GATESHEAD. Mrs Joan Douglas, Dunster Lodge, Earls Drive, Low Fell, Gateshead NE9 6AB (0191

4879078). Detached property situated in a quiet area with large garden (excellent for children to play in) and ample parking. Accommodation comprises one double, two twin, one family and four single bedrooms, three of which are en suite, all have TV and tea/coffee making facilities. Ground floor accommodation available, suitable for disabled guests. Private residents' lounge. Children welcome, babysitting available. Dogs welcome. Ironing facilities. Near to Metro Centre, Newcastle and main motorways. Bed and Breakfast from £15 to £20; Evening Meal from £5 to £9.

WARWICKSHIRE

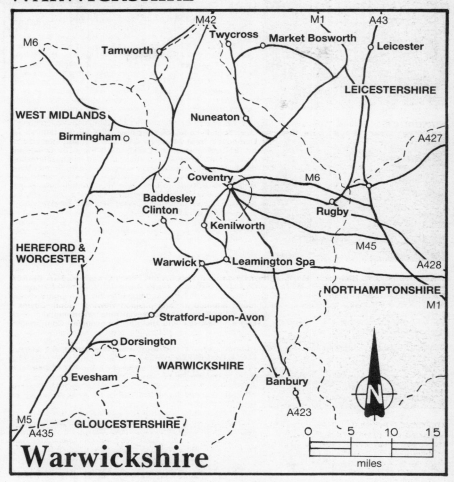

Warwickshire

BURTON DASSETT. Ros Thompstone, Grove Farm, Burton Dassett, Near Leamington Spa CV33 0AB (01295 770204). Grove Farm is situated on the edge of Burton Dassett Country Park with superb panoramic views and only three miles from M40. The house is built of local stone and is surrounded by gardens set amidst its rolling pastures. Children and pets welcome. Parking. Bed and Breakfast from £15. En suite family room available. Please write or telephone for further details.

PLEASE SEND A STAMPED ADDRESSED ENVELOPE WITH ENQUIRIES

COVENTRY near. Mrs Sandra Evans, Camp Farm, Hob Lane, Balsall Common, Near Coventry CV7

7GX (01676 533804). Tourist Board Listed COMMEN-DED. Camp Farm is a farmhouse 150 to 200 years old. It is modernised but still retains its old world character. Nestling in the heart of England in Shakespeare country, within easy reach of Stratford-upon-Avon, Warwick, Kenilworth, Coventry with its famous Cathedral, and the National Exhibition Centre, also the National Agricultural Centre, Stoneleigh. Camp Farm offers a warm homely atmosphere and good English food, service and comfortable beds. The house is carpeted throughout. Dining room and lounge with colour TV. Three double rooms or three single rooms, all with washbasins. The house is suitable for partially disabled guests. All terms quoted by letter or telephone.

COVENTRY near. Mrs Barbara Chamberlain, Mill Farmhouse Country Residence, Mill Lane,

Fillongley, Near Coventry CV7 8EE (Tel and Fax: 01676 541898). ETB ✺ ✺ ✺ COMMENDED. Experience the peace and tranquillity of our beautiful country home offering exceptional standards of comfort in idyllic surroundings. All rooms are centrally heated and immaculately furnished with comfortable new beds and hostess tray. Ample private car parking and gardens. No smoking. Tariff: Luxury double/twin en suite rooms with colour TV £40 to £45, single occupancy £25 including full English breakfast. 15 minutes NEC, Coventry; 30 minutes Birmingham, Stratford; convenient for Forest of Arden and Belfry Golf Courses. Special rates for lodgings. Brochure on request.

FENNY COMPTON. Mrs C.L. Fielder, Willow Cottage, Brook Street, Fenny Compton, Leamington Spa CV33 0YH (01295 770429). HETB Listed. A warm welcome awaits you in the centre of this attractive village near the Oxfordshire/Northamptonshire borders. Character cottage with delightful garden and terrace in rural situation. Easy access to the Cotswolds and Shakespeare country and, for the businessman, to the NEC, Warwick, Leamington and Banbury. Very tasteful twin-bedded and single accommodation with own washing facilities, colour TV and radio. Family atmosphere. Dinner by previous arrangement from £10; Bed and Breakfast from £17.

LEAMINGTON SPA. Miss Deborah Lea, Crandon House, Avon Dassett, Leamington Spa CV33 0AA

(Tel & Fax: 01295 770652). ✺ ✺ HIGHLY COMMENDED. **Working farm.** Guests receive a specially warm welcome at our comfortable farmhouse offering an exceptionally high standard of accommodation. Set in 20 acres with beautiful views over unspoilt countryside this is a small working farm with rare breeds of cattle, sheep and poultry. Five attractive bedrooms with en suite/private facilities, (one ground floor), tea/coffee making equipment and colour TV. Guests' dining room and sitting rooms, one with colour TV. Full central heating and log fire in chilly weather. Car essential, ample parking. Peaceful and quiet yet offers easy access for touring the Heart of England, Warwick, Stratford-upon-Avon, the Cotswolds RIAC and NEC. Open all year. Extensive breakfast menu. Bed and Breakfast from £19. Winter breaks available. Farm Holiday Bureau member. Write or ring for further details.

LEAMINGTON SPA. Mrs Rebecca Gibbs, Hill Farm, Lewis Road, Radford Semele, Leamington Spa

CV31 1UX (01926 337571). ✺ ✺ COMMENDED. This friendly, comfortable farmhouse is set in 350 acres of mixed farmland in beautiful Shakespeare country, one mile from A425 on east of Leamington Spa. Pretty bedrooms with full facilities, some en suite, all have TV. Excellent food. Guests' private bathroom, TV lounge and dining room. Children welcome, reduced rates. AA award winner. FHG Diploma. Bed and Breakfast from £17. Spacious five caravan site also available.

WHEN MAKING ENQUIRIES PLEASE MENTION
THIS *FHG* PUBLICATION

White Horse Inn

Sun Patio
Beer Garden

We extend a warm welcome to guests in our traditional oak-beamed pub where you are assured of personal service. We offer Bed and Breakfast at reasonable prices and have a restaurant where good food and real ale are always served. All of our bedrooms are tastefully furnished and ensuite with colour TV, central heating, and tea/coffee making facilities.

Set in the heart of Shakespeare country, The White Horse Inn is ideal for Stratford-upon-Avon and the Cotswolds, and also close to NEC Birmingham, Royal Show Ground at Stoneleigh and Warwick Castle.

Weekend Break reductions from November to April.

**Banbury Road, Ettington,
near Stratford-upon-Avon CV37 7SU**

**Proprietors: Roy & Valerie Blower
Telephone: 01789 740641**

LIGHTHORNE, near Warwick. Mrs J. Stanton, Redlands Farm, Banbury Road, Lighthorne, Near Warwick CV35 0AH (01926 651241).

🐾 🐾 A beautifully restored 15th century farmhouse built of local stone, the Old Farmhouse is set in two acres of garden with its own swimming pool, well away from the main road, yet within easy travelling distance of Stratford and Warwick; two miles Junction 12 M40. Handy for the Cotswolds. Guest accommodation in one double (with bathroom), one single and one family bedrooms, all with tea making facilities; bathroom, beamed lounge with TV, dining room. Rooms are centrally heated and the farmhouse also has open fires. Bed and Breakfast from £17.50. Children welcome, facilities available and reduced rates. No pets. A car is recommended to make the most of your stay. AA QQQ.

OXHILL. Nolands Farm and Country Restaurant, Oxhill CV35 0RJ (01926 640309; Fax: 01926 641662).

🐾 🐾 Working farm situated in tranquil valley surrounded by fields. All rooms en suite (four-posters, double, twin, family, singles) with TV, hostess trays and central heating. Most of these are on the ground floor, in converted stables, overlooking the old stableyard. We can offer fishing in the lake, clay pigeon shooting, bikes for hire or horse riding nearby. Everything for those who want to relax and enjoy the peace and quiet of the countryside! Dinner is by arrangement. Plenty of parking. Stratford is eight miles. Prices from £18 per person; single room from £20. AA QQQQ Selected. RAC Highly Acclaimed.

PILLERTON HERSEY. Mrs Carolyn Howard, Docker's Barn Farm, Oxhill, Bridle Road, Pillerton Hersey, Warwick CV35 0RL (01926 640475; Fax: 01926 641747).

Idyllically situated 18th century stone barn conversion surrounded by its own land, handy for Warwick, Stratford-upon-Avon, Cotswolds, NAC, NEC, Heritage Motor centre and six miles from Junction 21 M40. The house is full of character with antiques and interesting collections. The warm, attractive en suite bedrooms have tea/coffee trays and colour TV, and the four-poster suite has its own front door. Wildlife abounds and lovely walks lead from the barn, and we keep a few sheep, horses and pultry. If you are looking for total peace with friendly attentive service from £18.50 per person, Docker's Barn is for your. No-smoking establishment. AA QQQ.

SHAKESPEARE COUNTRY. Elizabeth Hughes, Hither Barn, Star Lane, Claverdon, Warwick CV35 8LW (01926 842839).

Peaceful bed and full English breakfast with home made bread (coeliacs welcome, home made g/f bread). Enjoy Warwick Castle, Stratford-upon-Avon (super shops), visit the theatre, Shakespear properties and National Trust Gardens. The National Exhibition Centre and Stoneleigh Royal Showground are within easy reach, as are the Cotswolds and Oxford. Really pretty here Spring/Summer, Autumn and Winter, lovely and warm open fires. Adjacent to a Country Club with excellent facilities. Usual prices: single person in double/twin room £29 and couple, double room £45. Discounted rates for people who stay for four weeks or more.

SHIPSTON-ON-STOUR near. Mrs Posy MacDonald, Brook House, Stourton, Near Shipston-on-Stour CV36 5HQ (Tel and Fax: 01608 686281). A very warm welcome awaits you at this 19th century farmhouse with lovely views on the edge of this quiet unspoilt north Cotswold village two miles from the A34. Furnished with antiques, the bedroom accommodation includes family room, double room and single room. There is a guest sitting room with log fire and TV and guests' dining room. Parking. Stratford-upon-Avon, Oxford, Broadway, Kiftsgate and Hidcote Gardens all within easy distance. Open all year. Bed and Breakfast from £17.50. Evening meal if booked in advance or several good local pubs.

STRATFORD-UPON-AVON. Hampton Lodge, 38 Shipston Road, Stratford-upon-Avon CV37 7LP (Tel & Fax: 01789 299374). ♛ ♛ *COMMENDED.* Paul and Pru Williams welcome you to Hampton Lodge wich is situated within five minutes walking distance of the centre of this historic town and world famous theatre. The accommodation comprises cosy residents lounge, six comfortable rooms including two family, two double, one twin and one four-poster, all are en suite and have colour TV, tea/coffee trays and direct-dial telephones. Traditional English breakfasts are served in our large, relaxed conservatory overlooking attractive gardens and summer house. Ideal base for Cotswolds, Blenheim Palace, Warwick Castle, National Trust properties. Plentiful private parking. Prices from £18 per person per night.

STRATFORD-UPON-AVON. Mrs M. Turney, Cadle Pool Farm, The Ridgway, Stratford-upon-Avon CV37 9RE (01789 292494). ♛ ♛ ♛ Working farm. Situated in picturesque grounds, this charming oak-panelled and beamed family house is part of a 450-acre mixed farm. It is conveniently situated two miles from Stratford-upon-Avon town, between Anne Hathaway's Cottage and Mary Arden's House, also only eight minutes from The Royal Shakespeare Theatre. Ideal touring centre for Warwick, Kenilworth, Oxford, the Cotswolds and Malvern Hills. Accommodation comprises family, double and twin bedrooms, one en suite and one with private bathroom, all with central heating and tea/coffee making facilities. There is an antique oak dining room, and lounge with colour TV. The gardens and ornamental pool are particularly attractive, with peacocks and ducks roaming freely. Children over 10 years welcome at reduced rates. Sorry, no pets. Non-smoking accommodation available. Bed and Breakfast from £20 to £25 per person. Open all year.

STRATFORD-UPON-AVON. Mrs Gillian Hutsby, Thornton Manor, Ettington, Stratford-upon-Avon CV37 7PN (01789 740210). ♛ ♛ *COMMENDED.* **Working farm.** Enjoy the peace and beautiful surroundings of this late 16th century stone manor house whilst taking a pleasant walk over the farm and scenic lanes. We are ideal for visiting Warwick, Stratford and the Cotswolds, with numerous houses and gardens of interest to visit in the area. Relax in our lounge by the splendid inglenook fireplace, or on the lawn in the garden. There are two double bedrooms with en suite facilities and a twin bedded room with a private bathroom. All rooms have tea/coffee making facilities. Stabling for horses is also available. Bed and Breakfast from £18.50 per person per night.

Moonraker House

You'll feel at home at the Moonraker©!

English Tourist Board
COMMENDED
♛ ♛

- All rooms have been thoughtfully styled by a professional Interior Designer with your comfort in mind.
- All rooms have en-suite bathrooms, colour TV, clock radio, tea and coffee making facilities, hairdryers.
- Enjoy an excellent English breakfast including seasonal preserves prepared and served by the resident proprietors Mike and Mauveen Spencer.

- Moonraker is just 5-10 minutes' walk from the town centre.
- Car park (open and garage).
- Ideal centre for exploring the Cotswolds, Shakespeare's countryside, Warwick Castle and Shakespeare's Theatres
- There are also extra special luxury rooms with Four-Poster Beds, lounge area and garden patio (non smoking).

AA QQQ
Michelin

**40 Alcester Road, Stratford-upon-Avon CV37 9DB
Tel: (01789) 299346/267115   Fax: (01789) 295504
Web site: www.stratford-upon-avon.co.uk/moonraker.htm**

MinOtels
Les Routiers

HELP IMPROVE BRITISH TOURIST STANDARDS

You are choosing holiday accommodation from our very popular FHG Publications. Whether it be a hotel, guest house, farmhouse or self-catering accommodation, we think you will find it hospitable, comfortable and clean, and your host and hostess friendly and helpful. Why not write and tell us about it?

As a recognition of the generally well-run and excellent holiday accommodation reviewed in our publications, we at FHG Publications Ltd. present a diploma to proprietors who receive the highest recommendation from their guests who are also readers of our Guides. If you care to write to us praising the holiday you have booked through FHG Publications Ltd. – whether this be board, self-catering accommodation, a sporting or a caravan holiday, what you say will be evaluated and the proprietors who reach our final list will be contacted.

The winning proprietor will receive an attractive framed diploma to display on his premises as recognition of a high standard of comfort, amenity and hospitality. FHG Publications Ltd. offer this diploma as a contribution towards the improvement of standards in tourist accommodation in Britain. Help your excellent host or hostess to win it!

FHG DIPLOMA

We nominate ....

....

Because ....

Name ....

Address ....

.... Telephone No. ....

STRATFORD-UPON-AVON. Bill and Veronica Stevenson, "Dosthill Cottage", 2 The Green, Wilmcote, Stratford-upon-Avon CV37 9XJ (01789 266480). ♛♛ *COMMENDED.* One of the original properties situated in the centre of this Shakespearean village, overlooking Mary Arden's House and gardens. Walk three miles past 14 locks into Stratford-upon-Avon, take an easy drive to the NEC, Royal Show Ground or tour the Cotswolds. There are double and twin rooms, all with private facilities and TV. Non-smoking accommodation available. Car parking, garage if required. Bed and Breakfast from £20, family reductions.

STRATFORD-UPON-AVON. Mrs Karen Cauvin, Penshurst Guest House, 34 Evesham Place, Stratford-upon-Avon CV37 6HT (01789 205259; Fax: 01789 295322). ETB Listed *COMMENDED.* You'll get an exceptionally warm welcome at this prettily refurbished, totally non-smoking Victorian townhouse, five minutes' walk from the centre of town. Attention to detail is obvious and the proprietors, Karen and Yannick will go out of their way to make you feel at home. You'd like a lie-in while on holiday? No problem!! Delicious English or Continental breakfasts are served from 7.00 right up until 10.30 in the morning. Rooms have been individually decorated and are well-equipped with many little extras apart from the usual TV and beverages. Home-cooked evening meals by arrangement. Brochure available on request. Excellent value for money is obtained at Penshurst with prices ranging from £15 to £20 per person.

STRATFORD-UPON-AVON. Mrs Pat Short, Nando's Guest House, 18/20 Evesham Place, Stratford-upon-Avon CV37 6HT (Tel & Fax: 01789 204907). A warm welcome awaits you at Nando's where Pat and Peter pride themselves on a high standard of cleanliness, good home cooking and a friendly atmosphere. Nando's is AA and RAC Acclaimed and a member of "Best Bed and Breakfast in the World" Association. It is ideally located only five minutes' walking distance from the town centre and famous Royal Shakespeare Theatre. It is also conveniently placed for the Cotswolds, Warwick Castle, Blenheim Palace and the National Exhibition Centre. Nando's has 21 rooms, 17 of which are en suite and four of these are located on the ground floor. All rooms are centrally heated, double glazed and have colour TV and tea/coffee making facilities. Private parking is available. Room charges (including full English breakfast and VAT) start from £14 per person. Visa/Mastercard, Amex welcome.

STRATFORD-UPON-AVON. Mrs E. Hunter, Hill House, Hampton Lucy, Warwick CV35 8AU (01789 840329). HETB Listed *COMMENDED.*

Idyllically situated midway between Stratford and Warwick, both of which are only five minutes away, this charming Georgian country house stands in two acres of private grounds and enjoys fine rural views. Traditionally furnished to a high standard, accommodation includes one double room with adjoining single, and one twin room with washbasin, each with private bathroom and tea/coffee making facilities; comfortable TV sittingroom with open fire and dining room where full breakfast is served. Ideal base for touring the Cotswolds, Oxford, Stratford, NEC or NAC. You will be assured of a very peaceful stay and warm hospitality. No smoking. Bed and Breakfast from £20.

STRATFORD-UPON-AVON. Mrs A. Cross, Lemarquand, 186 Evesham Road, Stratford-upon-Avon CV37 9BS (01789 204164).

Small homely accommodation, highly recommended, friendly atmosphere and personal attention. Providing full English Breakfast and comfortable beds. All rooms centrally heated, with washbasins, some with private shower; tea/coffee making facilities and pleasant views. Separate tables in dining room. Parking on own private forecourt of house. Close to town centre, theatres, leisure centre, river and local places of interest including Shakespeare's birthplace and Anne Hathaway's Cottage; Warwick Castle and Cotswold villages are easily accessible and there are numerous golf courses for the golfing enthusiast. Local inns provide good food. Open all year.

STRATFORD-UPON-AVON. Allors, 62 Evesham Road, Stratford-upon-Avon CV37 9BA (01789 269982). ETB Listed *COMMENDED.*

Detached house on the B439 Stratford/Evesham road, 15 minutes' walk from town centre. Well situated for visiting Royal Shakespeare Theatre, Stratford Racecourse, Shakespeare properties, Warwick Castle and the Cotswolds. We offer non-smokers comfortable centrally heated en suite accommodation. Each bedroom has its own sitting area with tea/coffee making facilities and colour TV. Pleasant dining room overlooking secluded garden. Private car parking. Bed and Breakfast from £18.50 per person. SPECIAL RATE FOR THREE NIGHT BREAKS THROUGHOUT THE YEAR.

STRATFORD-UPON-AVON. Highcroft, Banbury Road, Stratford-upon-Avon CV37 7NF (01789 296293). 🐝🐝 *COMMENDED.* **AA QQQ.**

Highcroft visitors are assured of a warm welcome and an informal atmosphere, only two miles from Stratford on A422 in two acres of gardens surrounded by open countryside. We have two large rooms, double/family, adjacent to house with own access and suitable for disabled guests; one double in main house with the benefit of its own stairs (an adjoining room available for families). Both rooms enjoy en-suite facilities, central heating, colour TV and tea/coffee making facilities. Excellent country pubs nearby for eating out. Ideally situated for Cotswolds, Stratford, Warwick. Terms from £35 double room; discounts for children. Telephone for more details.

WARWICKSHIRE – SHAKESPEARE'S COUNTY

Stratford-upon-Avon is the county's, and indeed one of the country's biggest attractions. Make time however to explore Northern Warwickshire and George Eliot Country around Nuneaton and "England's Historic Heartland" – the three very individual towns of Warwick, Royal Leamington Spa and Kenilworth, together with their surrounding villages.

STRATFORD-UPON-AVON. Janet and Keith Cornwell, "Midway", 182 Evesham Road, Stratford-upon-Avon CV37 9BS (01789 204154). Relax, enjoy Stratford's attractions and surrounding area with us. Clean, centrally heated rooms — three double, one single, all en-suite, with colour TV, clock radio, tea/coffee facilities, tastefully and comfortably furnished. Superb English breakfast. Pleasant diningroom with separate tables. Keys provided, access at all times. Park your car on our forecourt and take a 10/15 minute walk to town centre, theatres, Anne Hathaway's Cottage or race course. Personal friendly service. Map and information on attractions provided in rooms. Fans in bedrooms during summer. Full Fire Certificate. Open all year. Sorry no dogs. Arthur Frommer recommended.

HOLLY TREE COTTAGE

STRATFORD-UPON-AVON. Mrs Julia Downie, Holly Tree Cottage, Birmingham Road, Pathlow, Stratford-upon-Avon CV37 0ES (Tel & Fax: 01789 204461). Period cottage dating back to 17th century, with beams, antiques, tasteful furnishings and friendly atmosphere. Gardens with views over the countryside. Situated three miles north of Stratford towards Henley-in-Arden on A3400 (was A34), convenient for overnight stops or longer stays, and ideal for theatre visits. Excellent base for touring Shakespeare country, Heart of England, Cotswolds, Warwick Castle and Blenheim Palace. Well situated for National Exhibition Centre. Double, twin and family accommodation with en suite and private facilities; colour TV and tea/coffee in all rooms. Full English Breakfast. Restaurant and pub meals nearby. Bed and Breakfast from £20; reductions for children sharing. Telephone for information.

PLEASE SEND A STAMPED ADDRESSED ENVELOPE WITH ENQUIRIES

STRATFORD-UPON-AVON. Mrs R.M. Meadows, Monk's Barn Farm, Shipston Road, Stratford-upon-Avon CV37 8NA (01789 293714; Fax: 01789 205886). Working farm. One-and-a-half miles south of Stratford-upon-Avon on the A3400 (formerly A34) is Monk's Barn, a 75 acre mixed farm welcoming visitors all year. Monk's Barn dates back to the 16th century and succeeds in combining real traditional character with first class amenities. One double room with washbasin and three twin/double rooms with en suite facilities (two on ground floor suitable for some disabled guests) and one single room. Visitors lounge. Beautiful riverside walk to village. Bed and Breakfast from £15.50. Tea/coffee facilities and colour TVs in rooms. Sorry no pets. Non-smokers preferred. AA QQ. Details on request.

STRATFORD-UPON-AVON. Mrs J. Wakeham, Whitfield Farm, Ettington, Stratford-upon-Avon CV37 7PN (01789 740260). Working farm. Situated down its own private drive, off the A429, this 220-acre mixed farm (wheat, cows, sheep, geese, horses, hens) is ideal for a quiet and relaxing holiday. Convenient for visiting the Cotswolds, Warwick, Coventry, Stratford, Worcester. Near M40. Fully modernised centrally heated house with separate lounge having colour TV. Accommodation in one double room with washbasin, one double and one twin en suite, all with tea/coffee making facilities. Parking. Open all year (except Christmas) for Bed and Breakfast from £15 per night. Home produced food served. Full English Breakfast. AA registered. SAE please.

STRATFORD-UPON-AVON. Ms Diana Tallis, Linhill, 35 Evesham Place, Stratford-upon-Avon CV37 6HT (Tel & Fax: 01789 292879). HETB Listed. Linhill is a comfortable Victorian Guest House run by a friendly young family. It is situated only five minutes' walk from Stratford's town centre with its wide choice of fine restaurants and world famous Royal Shakespeare Theatres. Every bedroom at Linhill has central heating, colour TV, tea/coffee making facilities and washbasin. En suite facilities are also available, as are packed lunches and evening meals. Bicycle hire and babysitting facilities if desired. Leave the children with us and re-discover the delight of a candlelit dinner in one of Stratford's inviting restaurants. Bed and Breakfast from £13 to £18; Evening Meal from £5 to £7.50. Reduced rates for Senior Citizens.

STRATFORD-UPON-AVON. Mrs D.M. Hall, "Acer House", 44 Albany Road, Stratford-upon-Avon CV37 6PQ (01789 204962). 🏵 *COMMENDED.* Quality Bed and Breakfast, non-smoking establishment. Situated in a quiet road, within five minutes' walk from railway station and to town centre. Guest rooms overlook pleasant garden. Central heating, TV lounge. Enjoy a hearty English breakfast with choices, or Continental and vegetarian menus; early breakfasts on request. Double, twin, family and single rooms available. Tariff £15 to £17 per person Bed and Breakfast inclusive of tea/coffee making facilities. Street parking available. French spoken.

STRATFORD-UPON-AVON near. Jane Weldon, Bridge House, Alderminster, Stratford-upon-Avon CV37 8NY (01789 450521; Fax: 01789 414681). 🏵🏵 Set in the heart of Shakespeare's country our charming Georgian house with "Hayloft" dates from 1812 and has uninterrupted views across open countryside to the meandering River Stour and to the Cotswold Hills in the distance. Accommodation in either the Hayloft, the Blue and White Room or the Tulip Room. All have colour TV and tea/coffee facilities and have been recently stylishly redecorated, some have private facilities. Beautiful gardens. Alderminster is five miles south of Stratford-upon-Avon on the main Stratford to Oxford road (A3400). Bridge House is the perfect place for a relaxing break. Bed and Breakfast from £20 per person per night to include full breakfast. Ample car parking. Licensed.

WHEN MAKING ENQUIRIES PLEASE MENTION
FARM HOLIDAY GUIDES

TANWORTH IN ARDEN. Monica and Brian Palser, Mungunyah, Poolhead Lane, Tanworth in Arden, Near Solihull B94 5EH (01564 742437).

Monica and Brian Palser welcome you to their attractive home set in the peaceful Warwickshire countryside overlooking a golf course on the outskirts of the pretty village of Tanworth in Arden. It is centrally located for the National Exhibition Centre and major tourist attractions (Stratford-upon-Avon, Warwick Castle, National Trust Houses, etc) being only five minutes' drive from M42 Junction 3. They offer two twin-bedded rooms (one with washbasin), guests' private bathroom and sittingroom with TV. Tea/coffee making facilities plus hospitality tray on arrival and evening drink are included. Ample parking. Non-smokers please. Bed and Breakfast from £22 per person. Twin occupancy.

WARWICK. Mr and Mrs D. Clapp, The Croft, Haseley Knob, Warwick CV35 7NL (Tel & Fax: 01926 484447).

COMMENDED. Join David and Pat on their four acre smallholding and share the friendly family atmosphere, the picturesque rural surroundings, home cooking and very comfortable accommodation. Bedrooms, most en-suite, have colour TV, tea/coffee making equipment. Ground floor en-suite bedrooms available. Bed and Full English Breakfast from £20. Centrally located for touring Warwick (Castle), Stratford (Shakespeare), Coventry (Cathedral), and Birmingham. Also ideal for the businessman visiting the National Exhibition Centre or Birmingham Airport, both about 15 minutes inside. Ample parking. Mobile home available, also caravan park. Large gardens. Open all year. RAC Acclaimed. French spoken.

WARWICK. Ian and Dawn Kitchen, The Old Rectory, Vicarage Lane, Sherbourne, Warwick CV35 8AB (01926 624562; Fax: 01926 624995).

AA QQQQ Selected. A licensed Georgian country house, rich in beams, flagstones and inglenooks. Situated in a gem of an English village, half a mile from the M40 Junction 15. 14 elegantly appointed en suite bedrooms, thoughtfully provide all possible comforts. Some antique brass beds, four poster bedroom and some wonderful Victorian-style bathrooms. Try our Honeymoon Suite with hand-carved antique French bed and a spa bath. Choice of menu for breakfast and dinner in the oak and elm dining room. Ideally situated for Warwick Castle, Shakespeare's Stratford, the Cotswolds and many National Trust properties. NEC 20 minutes, Stoneleigh 10 minutes. Recommended by all major guides.

WARWICK. Mrs D.E. Bromilow, Woodside, Langley Road, Claverdon, Warwick CV35 8PJ (Tel & Fax: 01926 842446).

Woodside Guest House offers its guests something very special. Situated amidst acres of gardens and privately owned conservation woodland, it is perfect for families and those wishing to get away from traffic, yet is only 15 minutes from Warwick and Stratford-upon-Avon. Each of the large bedrooms have garden and woodland views and are comfortably and individually furnished providing tea and coffee making facilities (one en suite). Claverdon Village only five minutes away has a choice of pubs offering evening meals, alternatively dinner can be arranged at Woodside. Pets and children welcome. Open all year. Bed and Breakfast from £18. Reductions for children.

WEST MIDLANDS

BIRMINGHAM. Mrs Pamela E. Lendon, "Abberley", 51 Victoria Road, Acocks Green, Birmingham B27 7YB (0121 707 2950). "Abberley" is a mid-Victorian house set among tall trees. Situated off the A41, midway between Birmingham and Solihull, about five miles from Birmingham International Airport and Station, National Exhibition Centre and New Convention Centre. Convenient for theatres in Birmingham, Coventry and Stratford-upon-Avon. Homely, welcoming atmosphere, with comfortable centrally-heated rooms, one with en-suite luxury bathroom including bidet. All rooms with washbasins, tea and coffee making facilities, radio and colour TV. Ample parking. If using us as a staging-post for holidays abroad we offer parking for your car while away. Bed and Breakfast from £20. Member Solihull Tourism Association.

BIRMINGHAM. Ian and Angela Kerr, Awentsbury Hotel, 21 Serpentine Road, Selly Park, Birmingham B29 7HU (0121-472 1258). 🐦🐦 A Victorian country house set in its own large garden. Close to buses, trains, Birmingham University, BBC Pebble Mill, Queen Elizabeth and Selly Oak Hospitals, and only two miles from the city centre. All rooms have colour TV, telephones, tea/coffee making facilities, washbasins and central heating. Some rooms ensuite, some with showers. TV lounge. Ample car parking. Open all year. Pets and children welcome. Reductions for children. AA and RAC Listed. Terms from £26 single room, from £40 twin room, inclusive of breakfast and VAT; Evening Meals if required. Light supper or bedtime drink at small charge.

SOLIHULL near. Mrs Kathleen Connolly, Holland Park Farm, Buckley Green, Henley in Arden, Near Solihull B95 5QF (01564 792625). 🐦🐦 A Georgian style farmhouse set in 300 acres of peaceful farmland, including the historic grounds of "The Mount" and other interesting walks. Three large en suite bedrooms (two with bath/shower, other with shower). Large garden with pond. Livestock includes cattle and sheep. Ideally situated in Shakespeare's country, within easy reach of Birmingham International Airport, NEC, NAC, Stratford-upon-Avon, Warwick and the Cotswolds. Open all year. Children and pets welcome. Bed and Breakfast from £18.

WILTSHIRE

CHIPPENHAM near. Mrs Diana Barker, Manor Farm, Sopworth, Near Chippenham SN14 6PR (01454 238676). Working farm, join in. Manor Farm is a working mixed farm on the Beaufort estate near Badminton. The Jacobean farmhouse was updated in Georgian and Victorian times. It is very quietly situated in lovely countryside yet near many places of interest: Malmesbury, Tetbury and South Cotswolds, Berkeley Castle, Bristol, Bath, Castle Combe, Lacock Abbey, Avebury. Ideal overnight stop for travellers to South West. Junction 18, M4 six miles and close to Fosse Way and M5. Spacious comfortable rooms with heating and en-suite available. Lounge/diningroom with open fires in winter. Personal attention and a warm welcome. Bed and Breakfast from £12 to £25 per person.

DEVIZES. Colin and Cynthia Fletcher, Lower Foxhangers, Canalside Farm, Rowde, Devizes SN10 1SS (Tel & Fax: 01380 828254). 🐾🐾 *COMMENDED.*

Enjoy your holiday with us on our small farm/marina with its many diverse attractions. Hear the near-musical clatter of the windlass heralding the lock gate opening and the arrival of yet another narrowboat. Bed and Breakfast available in spacious 18th century farmhouse — double, family and twin rooms with TV, all en suite or with private bathrooms. From £18 per person. Self catering mobile homes sleep four/six, also available. Weekly holidays or short breaks with our narrowboat holidays; small campsite.

DEVIZES near. Rob and Jacqui Mattingly, The Old Coach House, 21 Church Street, Market Lavington, Devizes SN10 4DU (01380 812879). 🐾🐾 *COMMENDED.*

A warm welcome awaits you at this delightful 18th century coaching house. Attractive rooms with en suite facilities and colour TV ensure your stay will be relaxed and comfortable. Whether you enjoy a traditional English breakfast or choose a speciality from the menu you can be sure it will be freshly prepared using the finest local ingredients. Situated a few miles south of Devizes it is a perfect location from which to explore the surrounding area. Bath, Salisbury, Stonehenge and many other places of interest are all within easy reach. Excellent for walking and cycling and ideal for Short Breaks. Children welcome but sorry no pets. Bed and Breakfast from £21.75 to £26. No smoking. AA QQQ.

MALMESBURY. Mrs Susan Barnes, Lovett Farm, Little Somerford, Near Malmesbury SN15 5BP (Tel & Fax: 01666 823268). 🐾🐾 *COMMENDED.*

Working farm. AA QQQ. Situated in the beautiful Wiltshire countryside close to Malmesbury, England's oldest Borough, and within easy reach of the Cotswolds, Bath, Badminton, Avebury and Stonehenge. Our farmhouse, with delightful views, has full central heating. Guest accommodation in one double room and one twin room, both en suite, each offering tea/coffee making facilities, radio and colour TV. The lounge/dining room with a traditional log fire creates a warming atmosphere for our winter visitors who wish to enjoy an evening by the fireside. Enjoy a hearty farmhouse breakfast! Bed and Breakfast from £18 to £22. Reduced rates for children. Open all year except Christmas. Farm Holiday Bureau member.

MARLBOROUGH. Mrs Clarissa Roe, Clench Farmhouse, Malborough SN8 4NT (01672 810264).

Attractive 18th century farmhouse set in its own grounds with lovely views. There are three double bedrooms, two en suite and one single room. The house has a relaxed and happy atmosphere and a warm welcome awaits guests. Tennis court, heated pool and croquet lawn are all available. Three course dinner may be provided by prior arrangement. We are within easy reach of Stonehenge, Salisbury and Bath and close to the Avon and Kennet Canal. Children and pets welcome. Bed and Breakfast from £22; Dinner from £16.50.

MERE. Mrs Jean Smith, The Beeches, Chetcombe Road, Mere BA12 6AU (01747 860687). 🐝

COMMENDED. A comfortable, old Toll House with interesting carved stairway and gallery, standing in beautiful garden at entrance to Early English village. Centrally situated for Bath, Wells, Salisbury, Bournemouth, New Forest and Sherborne. In close proximity to the famous Stourhead Gardens and Longleat House and Wildlife Park. We have two double and family rooms. The house is furnished to a very high standard, is centrally heated with TV, tea/coffee making facilities, washbasin and shaver points in all rooms, one room having en suite shower, another room en suite bath and bidet. Large lounge. Large enclosed car park. Open all year. Bed and Breakfast from £17.50. Reductions for children.

MERE. Mrs Jane Hurd, Willowdown House, Wet Lane, Mere BA12 6BA (01747 860218). 18th

century farmhouse situated one mile from town centre, set in four acres, surrounded by open fields and country footpaths. Convenient for Stourhead Gardens, Shaftesbury, Salisbury and Bath. There is a twin-bedded room with en suite bathroom and a double bedroom, both have TV, radio and tea/coffee facilities. Open all year. Dinner by arrangement. Bed and Breakfast £17 per person. Reductions for children, who are very welcome.

NEW FOREST. Jim and Glenda Hickman, Springfields, Lyndhurst Road, Landford, Salisbury SP5

2AS (01794 390093). ETB Listed *COMMENDED.* Situated on the edge of the New Forest Springfields is a large house offering an ideal touring location. Salisbury with its famous cathedral is just 10 miles away whilst Southampton, Lyndhurst, Bealieu and the coast are all within easy reach. the New Forest starts within a few minutes' walk. Watch out for all the animals! Horse riding, golf, pretty pubs serving home made food, walking all close by. Springfields offers two double rooms each able to accommodate an extra bed for accompanying children and with colour TV, radio and tea/coffee making facilities. Payphone. Garden. Off road parking. Bed and Breakfast from £17 per person per night.

SALISBURY. Mrs K. Robinson, Michaelmas Cottage, Guilder Lane, Salisbury SP1 1HW (01722

329580/325335). Two very pretty medieval cottages two minutes from town centre, Old Chequers dating from the 14th century and Michaelmas Cottage from the 16th. Both offer a warm welcome, good food and comfort in a non-smoking environment. One double bedded room, oak-beamed, in each house. Parking. Tea/coffee facilities and TV in both. Excellent pub food and restaurants two/three minutes away. This is a perfect centre for exploring Bath and Winchester, each less than one hour away, as well as this ancient beautiful city. Bed and Breakfast in both cottages £32 to £34 double. Enquire about special discounts.

SALISBURY. Violet and Victor Bath, "Beulah", 144 Britford Lane, Salisbury SP2 8AL (01722 333517). Tourist Board Listed. "Beulah" is a pretty bungalow on the outskirts of Salisbury overlooking meadows, 25 minutes' walk from the city centre, 16 minutes from Salisbury Cathedral with its beautiful surrounding close and the tallest spire in England (404 ft). Situated at the end of a quiet lane, no passing traffic. Within one hour by car of Stonehenge, Bournemouth, the New Forest and Southampton. A friendly welcome awaits you. English or Continental breakfasts, all home made preserves. TV lounge, gas central heating; TV, washbasins and tea/coffee making facilities in all bedrooms; bathroom and shower. Children over three years welcome, reduced rates. Bed and Breakfast from £16. Open all year. Directions: bungalow at end of lane (no through traffic), off A338 main road Salisbury to Bournemouth.

SALISBURY. Audrey Jerram, Chicklade Lodge, Chicklade, Hindon, Salisbury SP3 5SU (01747 820389). Ideally situated for exploring this interesting area — Salisbury, Stonehenge, Shaftesbury, Stourhead, Longleat, Bath, Wells, Glastonbury, etc. This is a 19th century house of character set amidst lovely countryside. Charming twin-bedded rooms with washbasins, shaver points and tea/coffee making facilities. Pets welcome. Open all year. Painting Holidays are also available, full details on request. Ample parking space. Location: A303 nearby, about 28 miles west of Andover. Going through Chicklade turn right at the small cross road (signposted Hindon on left). Bed and Breakfast from £15; optional Evening Meal.

SALISBURY. Dawn and Alan Curnow, Hayburn Wyke Guest House, 72 Castle Road, Salisbury SP1 3RL (Tel & Fax: 01722 412627). ❀ *COMMENDED.* Hayburn Wyke is a Victorian house, situated adjacent to Victoria Park, half a mile from the city centre on the A345 Salisbury to Amesbury road. Salisbury and surrounding area has many places of interest to visit, including Salisbury Cathedral, Old Sarum, Wilton House and Stonehenge. Some bedrooms have en suite facilities, all have washbasins, televisions, and tea/coffee making equipment. Children are welcome at reduced rates. Sorry, no pets (guide dogs an exception). Private car parking for guests. Open all year. Bed and full English Breakfast from £16. Credit cards and Switch accepted. AA QQQ and RAC Accredited.

SALISBURY. Mrs Sue Combes, Manor Farm, Burcombe, Salisbury SP2 0EJ (01722 742177; Fax: 01722 744600). Tourist Board Listed *COMMENDED.* **Working farm.** An attractive stone built farmhouse with a lovely walled garden, set in a quiet village amid downland and water meadows, five miles west of Salisbury. The two bedrooms are very comfortable with en suite facilities, tea trays and clock radios. A large lounge has colour TV and access to the garden. This is an ideal location for Salisbury, Wilton and Stonehenge and easy access to many places of historic interest and gardens. For those seeking peace this is an idyllic place to stay with various walks and the local pub only a five minute stroll. Children welcome. Bed and Breakfast from £20 to £22.

SALISBURY. Mrs Suzi Lanham, Newton Farmhouse, Southampton Road, Whiteparish, Salisbury SP5 2QL (01794 884416). ❀❀ *COMMENDED.* This historic listed 16th century farmhouse on the borders of the New Forest, was formerly part of the Trafalgar Estate and is situated 8 miles south of Salisbury, convenient for Stonehenge, Romsey, Winchester, Portsmouth and Bournemouth. All rooms have pretty en suite facilities and are delightfully decorated, three with genuine period four poster beds. The beamed dining room houses a collection of Nelson memorabilia and antiques and has flagstone floors and an inglenook fireplace with an original brick-built bread oven. The superb English breakfast is complimented by fresh fruits, home-made breads and preserves and free range eggs. Dinner is available by arrangement, using home-grown kitchen garden produce wherever possible. A swimming pool is idyllicly set in the extensive, well stocked gardens and children are most welcome in this non smoking establishment.

WILTSHIRE – "WHITE" HORSE COUNTY!

Many "White" horses adorn the Wiltshire chalk downs and the prehistoric theme continues with Stonehenge and Avebury. Also of interest are the landscape gardens at Studley, Chiselbury Camp, the Kennet and Avon canal with lock "staircase", Salisbury Plain, and the abandoned city Old Sarum.

SALISBURY near. The Compasses Inn, Chicksgrove, Tisbury, Near Salisbury SP3 6NB (01722 714318). A 14th century thatched Freehouse maintaining all the olde worlde charm that is in keeping with its setting in the depths of the Wiltshire countryside. The Inn, with its unique oak-beamed and traditionally furnished bar, offers excellent home cooked food, ales and wine. There are gardens at the front and an enclosed children's play area to the rear. There are four double en suite bedrooms and one twin-bedded room with use of bathroom across hall; separate lounge with tea/coffee making facilities and a well stocked book case. All rooms are comfortable, well appointed and centrally heated. Children welcome. Open all year round. Prices per person per night for Bed and full English Breakfast from £35 per night twin room, £45 per night double room for two. Please write, or telephone for brochure.

SWINDON. County View Guest House, 31/33 County Road, Swindon SN1 2EG (01793 610434/ 618387; Fax: 0118 9394100). This Victorian property is situated on the main road and is only five minutes' walk from town centre, coach and rail stations and only five minutes' drive from Junction 15 and 16 M4. It is ideally placed for business and leisure visits to Swindon and Wiltshire area. All rooms have tea/coffee making facilities and TV. En suite and shower rooms. Private parking. Evening meals. It is like home from home. Children and pets accepted by arrangement. Cot and high chair available. Ground floor bedrooms. Bed and Breakfast single room from £18, twin room from £30 per night. Pilgrims Progress Commendation.

SWINDON near. Mrs Claire Read, Leighfield Lodge Farm, Cricklade, Near Swindon SN6 6RH (Tel & Fax: 01666 860241). ♛♛ *COMMENDED.* Comfortable farmhouse accommodation half a mile from the main road offering seclusion and tranquillity. Two rooms available, both with en suite facilities, maintained to a high standard. Guests dining room and a separate sitting room with roaring fire for cooler evenings. Local pubs provide evening meals. We are well situated for exploring the Cotswolds, Wiltshire Downs ands Swindon's new designer outlet village. No pets, no smoking. Open all year except Christmas and New Year.

WARMINSTER. Mrs Sarah Coward, Manor Farm Bed and Breakfast, Mere, Warminster BA12 6HR (01747 860242). Not the usual B&B. This elegant farmhouse nestling under the Wiltshire Downs is very much a working family farm. We have an unusual variety of family pets including hawks and falcons. The bedrooms and guests areas are spacious and well furnished. Two double rooms/ family room, one twin, all with washbasins, tea/coffee facilities and colour TV. Totally non-smoking. Within the farm there are excellent walks, mountain bike tracks, clay pigeon shooting and ideal hand-gliding conditions. Bed and Breakfast from £17 to £20.

YORKSHIRE

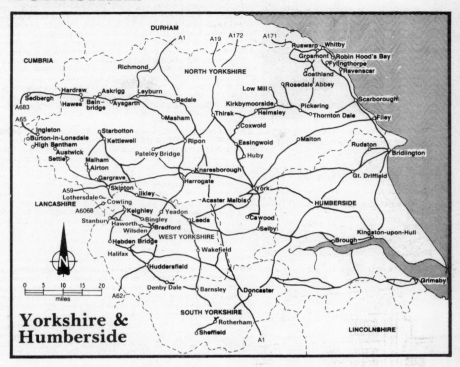

Yorkshire &
Humberside

EAST YORKSHIRE

BRIDLINGTON. Mrs Pat Cowton, The Grange, Bempton Lane, Flamborough, Bridlington YO15 1AS (01262 850207). For a relaxing holiday come and stay in our Georgian farmhouse situated in 450 acres of stock and arable land on the outskirts of Flamborough village. Ideally situated for bird watching at RSPB Sanctuary at Bempton, sandy beaches, cliffs and coves on our Heritage Coast. Golf and sea fishing nearby. Children and pets welcome. Open all year except Christmas and New Year. Bed and Breakfast from £15.

BRIDLINGTON. Christine and Peter Young, The White Rose, 123 Cardigan Road, Bridlington YO15 3LP (01262 673245). 👑 👑 👑 We are a small hotel situated in a quiet residential area close to the South Beach and within walking distance of the Spa and Harbour. We offer comfortable accommodation with most bedrooms en suite with colour TV, hospitality tray and gas heating. We have a non-smoking bedroom and dining room. We offer choice of menus at all meals; choice of early or late evening dinner. Open all year including Christmas. Special breaks available out of season. Bed and Breakfast from £20 per person.

POCKLINGTON near. Mrs A. Pearson, Meltonby Hall Farm, Meltonby, Near Pocklington YO4 2PW (01759 303214). Working farm, join in. Meltonby Hall Farm is in a small village at the foot of the Yorkshire Wolds, offering a relaxed and homely atmosphere. It provides a good base for historic York 13 miles, coast 30 miles, as well as the beautiful North York Moors with their forest drives, also for stately homes. Pocklington with its magnificent water lilies is two and a half miles away. Gliding/golf nearby. Double and twin rooms with tea/coffee making facilities, cot and high chair if required; guests' own bathroom with electric shower; dining room/lounge. Central heating. Own and local produce used and free-range eggs. Car essential, parking. Children welcome. Sorry, no pets. Open Easter to October. Bed and Breakfast from £15; Evening Meal available in nearby Pocklington. Reduced rates for children under 12 years. AA Recommended.

NORTH YORKSHIRE

AMPLEFORTH. Mrs L.K. Chambers, The Old Summerhouse, East End, Ampleforth, York YO6 4DA (01439 788722). The original old stone summerhouse has been transformed into exclusive en suite accommodation for two guests only. Set in an attractive private garden, this very comfortable, tastefully furnished cottage ensures peace, privacy and almost everything you could need to make your holiday here memorable. The property lies within Ampleforth, well away from traffic. Very good evening meals available locally. Ryedale offers lovely countryside, abbeys and historic houses. So much to see and do (painting, walking) or just relax and forget the world — the choice is yours. NON-SMOKERS ONLY PLEASE. Brochure by request. Bed and Breakfast from £17.50.

ASKRIGG. Mrs Kate Empsall, Whitfield, Helm, Askrigg, Near Leyburn DL8 3JF (Tel & Fax: 01969 650565). 🐾🐾 *COMMENDED.* Whitfield is a superb 350 year old converted barn situated at 285m in Upper Wensleydale, all rooms facing south with uninterrupted views, and surrounded by meadows in a very peaceful setting. The double en suite and the twin room with a washbasin have hair dryers, colour TV and a tea/coffee tray, books and magazines. Guests are welcome to use the lounge with an open fire and a comprehensive range of books, guides and maps. A full cooked breakfast with home made preserves. Non-smoking and pets are welcome. One mile to Herriot locations in Askrigg. Bed and Breakfast from £18.

ASKRIGG. Mrs B. Percival, Milton House, Askrigg, Leyburn DL8 3HJ (01969 650217). 🐾🐾 *COMMENDED.* Askrigg is situated in the heart of Wensleydale and is within easy reach of many interesting places — Aysgarth Falls, Hardraw Falls, Bolton Castle. Askrigg is one of the loveliest villages in the dale. This is an ideal area for touring or walking. Milton House is a lovely spacious house with all the comforts of home. There are three pretty double bedrooms, all with private facilities, TV and tea/coffee making facilities. Visitors' lounge with TV, dining room. Central heating. Children are welcome. Private parking. Milton House is open all year for Bed and Breakfast. Evening Meal by arrangement. You are sure of a friendly welcome and a homely atmosphere. Please write or phone Mrs Beryl Percival for details and brochure.

BEDALE. Mrs Valerie Anderson, Ainderby Myers Farm, Near Hackforth, Bedale DL8 1PF (01609 748668/748424). 🐾 *COMMENDED.* Historic manor house set amidst moors and dales with orgins going back to the 10th century. Terrific atmosphere. Once farmed by the monks of Jervaulx Abbey. Sheep, crops, pastures and a stream. Walk the fields and discover the wildlife. Visit castles and abbeys. Excellent base for walkers. Pony trekking and fishing by arrangement. Children welcome. Traditional Yorkshire breakfasts. Picnic facilities. Open all year. Bed and Breakfast from £16; Evening Meal from £10.

BEDALE. Bobbies XVIIth Century Cottage, Aiskew, Bedale DL8 1DD (01677 423385). Charming beamed cottage with inglenook fireplace, surrounded by old cottage gardens. Situated on A684 midway between Bedale and A1. Easy walking distance to the old market town of Bedale and a good base for exploring Herriot's Yorkshire Dales and Moors. Numberous historic attractions can be reached easily by car and Lightwater Valley Theme Park is approximately 15 minutes' drive away. Pretty rooms — one double and two twin, have washbasins, colour TV, tea/coffee making facilities, razor points and central heating. Personal, friendly welcome and full English breakfast included, making good value at prices from £16 per person per night. Open all year — this is our 20th year!

BEDALE. Mrs M. Keighley, Southfield, 96 South End, Bedale DL8 2DS (01677 423510). This is a quiet country town only five minutes from A1, so is ideal for breaking journey from South to Scotland. With the Dales immediate and the Lakes only one hour away, it is a good base for touring. Area attractions include Fountains Abbey, Ripon Cathedral, Harewood House, Bolton Castle, Lightwater Valley (as on TV) and many more. Two 18-hole golf courses and swimming, to keep husband and children happy. Free off-road parking for four/five cars. One double, one single, twin and family bedrooms, all fully en suite; tea/coffee making facilities and sittingroom. Bed and Breakfast from £16. SAE please. Now open all year. "Which?" Recommended.

BEDALE. Mrs Patricia Knox, Mill Close Farm, Patrick Brompton, Bedale DL8 1JY (01677 450257). 🐾🐾 *HIGHLY COMMENDED.* Mill Close is a secluded 17th century working farm surrounded by beautiful rolling countryside at the foothills of the Yorkshire Dales and Herriot Country, and is situated two miles from the A1. Charming bedrooms with tea/coffee making facilities, guests' private bathrooms, dining and sitting room with log fires. Highland cattle, sheep, calves, pony, wild flowers and woodland. A relaxing peaceful atmosphere with romantic walled garden, pond and waterfall. Sumptuous breakfasts cooked on the Aga and served in our conservatory dining room. Open March to November. Colour brochure available.

BEDALE. John and Freda Coppin, Richmond House, 6 Beech Close, Scruton, Northallerton DL7 0TU (01609 748369). Welcome Host establishment. Our detached house is in a lovely rural village between Bedale and Northallerton, yet only three miles from A1. Ideal for North/South travellers. One double and one single room, both with colour TV, tea/coffee making facilities, central heating, double glazing. Large luxury bathroom with shower, shaver point. Home cooked full English breakfast is served in our dining room/lounge. Private parking. Centrally located for touring Yorkshire Dales and Moors. Several stately homes and gardens within easy reach. Bed and Breakfast from £14 per person. special reduced rates during July and August. Open April to October. Brochure available.

BEDALE. Mrs Sheila Dean, 88 South End, Bedale DL8 2DS (01677 422334). 🐾🐾 *HIGHLY COMMENDED.* An attractive large detached house in the delightful market town of Bedale in lovely North Yorkshire. One large double bedroom with en suite bathroom, one double with adjacent private bathroom or can be shared with twin. Excellent well cooked varied breakfast of your choice (separate tables). Colour TV and tea/coffee in all rooms. Off street parking for four cars. Bar meals and restaurants in Bedale or surrounding villages. Ideal for holidays and north/ south stopover. Enquire for Bargain Breaks. Bed and Breakfast £17 to £21, single in double £25. £20 deposit secures room. Completely non smoking, no pets.

BEDALE. Mrs D. Hodgson, Little Holtby, Leeming Bar, Northallerton DL7 9LH (01609 748762). 🐾🐾 *HIGHLY COMMENDED.* A period farmhouse with beautiful views at the gateway to the Yorkshire Dales, within easy distance of many places of great interest, just 100 yards off the A1 between Bedale and Richmond. Little Holtby has been restored and furnished to a high standard whilst still retaining its original character; polished wood floors, open fires and original beams in many of the rooms. All bedrooms have colour TV, tea/coffee making facilities and are centrally heated. One double bedroom (en suite), two twin-bedded rooms with washbasins and one family room (en suite). Bed and Breakfast from £17.50; Evening Meal available.

BEDALE. David and Thea Smith, Waterside, Glenaire, Crakehall, Bedale DL8 1HS (01677 422908). A warm and friendly welcome awaits you at Waterside where you can relax and enjoy the mature one acre gardens running down to the trout stream. As a holiday centre it is ideal for exploring by car or on foot the glories of the Yorkshire Dales and Moors . . . "The Gateway to Herriot Country" . . . Bed and Breakfast with private facilities £20 per person; reductions for longer stays. Room only from £20 (two sharing). Evening Meal optional £12. Full details on request. Central heating, TV, tea and coffee facilities, radio in all rooms. No smoking.

BEDALE near. Mrs J. Rudd, Tentrees, Exelby, Near Bedale DL2 2HF (01677 426541). Warm welcome guaranteed in our dormer bungalow situated in the quiet hamlet of Exelby, two miles from Bedale and three-quarters of a mile from A1. Large garden with fishpond. One double/ family room en suite, one double and single room. Tea/ coffee facilities. Comfortable, homely rooms. Sitting room with open fire, TV, maps and guides. Central heating. Ramblers/cyclists welcome — drying facilities. Vegetarian breakfast available (please ask). Parking spaces. Central for Yorkshire Dales and Moors. Good en route stop for Scotland. Eating places few minutes away. Bus two miles away, lifts possible. Completely non-smoking. Fishing, golf, tennis, swimming and riding nearby. Bed and Breakfast from £16 per person per night. Deposit required. Discounted breaks. SAE for brochure please. Open all year.

CARLTON (Leyburn). Mrs P. Suttill, "Coverlea", Carlton (Coverdale), Leyburn DL8 4AY (01969 640248). A private house situated in the picturesque village of Carlton. Ideal for walking and touring around the Yorkshire Dales. Accommodation comprises one double and one family bedrooms, both with washbasin and tea/coffee making facilities. Ful central heating. Pets welcome. Open from February to November. A warm welcome awaits you.

Terms quoted in this publication may be subject to increase if rises in costs necessitate

CASTLE HOWARD. Mrs Janet Foster, Grange Farm, Bulmer, York YO6 7BN (01653 618376). A

warm Yorkshire welcome awaits you at Grange Farm which is a family-run 500 acre dairy/arable farm forming part of the Castle Howard (Brideshead) Estate. The farmhouse set in a large secluded garden has spectacular views across open countryside and woodlands. The spacious farmhouse is centrally heated, there is a sitting room with TV and a games room where you can play table tennis and pool. The three bedrooms, double/family and twin with vanity units, all have tea/coffee making facilities. Guests have their own bathroom complete with shower. The farm is in an ideal location with easy access to the east coast, North Yorkshire Moors, the historic city of York and much more. We look forward to meeting you. £16 per person with reductions for children.

CROPTON/PICKERING. The New Inn, Cropton, Near Pickering YO18 8HH (01751 417330; Tel & Fax: 01751 417310). 👑 👑 👑 *COMMENDED.* Traditional

country inn perched on the edge of the North Yorkshire Moors National Park. Warm and friendly with a high standard of food and accommodation. No smoking restaurant serving à la carte and table d'hôte, bar meals also served. Special two day Dinner, Bed and Breakfast breaks available. Home of the award winning Cropton Brewery. Children welcome. Bed and Breakfast £25 per person.

EASINGWOLD. Mrs Christine Kirman, The Old Vicarage, Market Place, Easingwold YO6 3AL (01347 821015). 👑 👑 *COMMENDED.* This 18th century

house sits in a corner of this quiet Georgian market town just off the A19 halfway between York and Thirsk. It provides an excellent touring centre for York, the Dales and the moors. The centrally heated "no smoking" accommodation comprises two twin, two double and one single bedrooms, all enjoying en suite facilities, colour TV, radio alarm and beverage tray. A large sitting room is available solely for guests and the private grounds include a croquet lawn and walled rose garden. Tea and Yorkshire biscuits await you on arrival. Bed and Breakfast from £22.50 per person per night.

EASINGWOLD. Mrs Rachel Ritchie, The Old Rectory, Thormanby, Easingwold, York YO6 3NN (01845 501417). 👑 👑 A warm welcome awaits you at this

interesting Listed Georgian rectory built in 1737 and furnished with many antiques including a four-poster bed. Three comfortable and very spacious bedrooms, two en suite, with tea/coffee making facilities; charming lounge with colour TV and open fire. Separate diningroom. Large mature garden. An excellent base for touring the Moors, Dales and York. This is the centre of "James Herriot" country with many historic houses and abbeys to visit in the area. Thormanby is a small village between Easingwold and Thirsk. Historic York is 17 miles away. Many delightful inns and restaurants serving good food locally. Bed and Breakfast from £13, reductions for children under 12 years. Reduced weekly rates. Ample private parking. SAE for brochure or telephone. Open all the year.

FILEY. Mayfield Guest House, 2 Brooklands, Filey YO14 9BA (01723 514557). 👑 👑 👑 Close to all

amenities. Five bedrooms, all en suite and have TV and tea/coffee facilities (one ground floor). Ideal centre for touring. Bed and Breakfast from £18; Dinner £8. Open all year.

HARROGATE. Pauline and Robert McKay, Parnas Hotel, 98 Franklin Road, Harrogate HG1 5EN (Tel & Fax: 01243 564493). A family-run licensed, spacious 10 bedroomed Hotel where a friendly atmosphere is our priority plus comfort and a hearty breakfast. An easy walk to town and conference centre. Single, double, twin or family rooms, mostly en suite or with private bathroom. All have TV and tea/coffee facilities. Harrogate is a sophisticated Spa Town with beautiful buildings and exclusive shops (where Kim Tate really shops!). Enjoy a drink in the garden or take an evening stroll to beautiful valley gardens. Ideal base for touring — York 17 miles and near Dales. Ample parking. Prices from £22.50. Children's rates available. Brochure on request.

HARROGATE. Davina Webb, Glenayr, 19 Franklin Mount, Harrogate HG1 5EJ (01423 504259). Whether you visit Harrogate for business or pleasure you won't find a warmer welcome or enjoy genuine hospitality anywhere to match the comfortable Victorian home of Davina Webb; who treats her guests as invited friends. Harrogate's elegant town centre is a leisurely five minute' walk and the International Conference and Exhibition Centre a mere 200 yards from the hotel. Six light and pleasantly furnished bedrooms with en suite bathroom offer home from home comfort. You can savour a traditional and substantial English breakfast and fresh home-cooked dinners can be prepared to order. Brochure available. AA QQQ, RAC Acclaimed.

HARROGATE. Mrs Janet Anderson, Croft House, Little Croft, Markington, Harrogate HG3 3TU (01765 677782). 🐦 *HIGHLY COMMENDED.* Lovely farm house style comfortable home in pleasant village two miles from Fountains Abbey and four miles from Ripon. Busy Harrogate is a 20 minute drive away and all the best of Nidderdale is close by. The accommodation comprises one twin room with en suite facilities and a double room with private bathroom, each has own colour TV, hair dryer, radio alarm and courtesy tray. Car parking. Open March to end October. Bed and Breakfast £22.50 per night. A non-smoking house where a friendly welcome is always assured.

HARROGATE. Mrs Alison Harrison, Garden Cottage, Moor Park, Norwood Lane, Beckwithshaw, Harrogate HG3 1QN (01423 530197). ETB Listed. Set in secluded woodland grounds, three miles west of Harrogate with pastoral views. Two luxury twin en suite ground floor apartments with private patio. Purpose built from converted pottery to high standard. Comfy beds, electric blankets, TV, beverage trays, gas and convector heating. Roomy non-slip power showers, large windows, own entrance. Breakfast in Listed cottage dining room. Pub in village and good dining places within 15 minutes. A good base for touring and walking. Harrogate is 10 minutes' drive, York, Leeds and Dales 25 minutes. Reasonably disabled friendly. Open all year. Bed and Breakfast from £22.50 per person. A warm welcome assured.

NORTH YORKSHIRE – RICH IN TOURIST ATTRACTIONS!

Dales, moors, castles, abbeys, cathedrals – you name it and you're almost sure to find it in North Yorkshire. Leading attractions include Castle Howard, the moorlands walks at Goathland, the Waterfalls at Falling Foss, Skipton, Richmond, Wensleydale, Bridestones Moor, Ripon Cathedral, Whitby, Settle and, of course, York itself.

HARROGATE. Mrs C.E. Nelson, Nidderdale Lodge Farm, Fellbeck, Pateley Bridge, Harrogate HG3

5DR (01423 711677). ETB ♨♨ *COMMENDED*. Homely, comfortable, Christian accommodation. Spacious stone built bungalow in beautiful Nidderdale which is very central for touring the Yorkshire Dales; Pateley Bridge two miles, Harrogate 14 miles, Ripon nine miles. Museums, rocks, caves, fishing, bird watching, beautiful quiet walks, etc all near by. En suite rooms (one twin, two double), TV. Private lounge. Tea making facilities available. Choice of breakfast. Evening meals available one mile away. Ample parking space on this working farm. Open Easter to end of October.

HARROGATE. Argyll House, 80 Kings Road, Harrogate HG1 5JX (01423 562408). Visit Harrogate the North Yorkshire Spa Town with many places of historic interest and excellent shopping centre. Stay with Jacqueline and Jeff at the Argyll, a mid Victorian garden fronted stone-built hotel within two minutes' walking distance from the town centre and famous valley gardens. All rooms have colour TV, central heating, direct dial telephone, alarm clock radio, hairdryer and generous hospitality tray. Most rooms have en suite facilities. There is a private car park if you are touring the North Yorkshire Dales and other places of interest. Full English breakfast is provided, evening meals are available if required. Bed and Breakfast from £20 per person.

HARROGATE. Gillmore Hotel, 98 Kings Road, Harrogate HG1 5HH (Tel & Fax: 01423 503699; Tel: 01423 507122). A family-run hotel, ideally positioned within easy walking distance of the Conference Centre and Exhibition Complex, with the shops, cafes, theatres, cinemas and all the many amenities of Harrogate town centre very close at hand. 20 bedrooms comprising doubles, twins, singles — some en suite and all with colour TV, shaver points, hairdrying points and tea/coffee making facilities. Family rooms available. Access at all times. Comfortable TV lounge; licensed bar; spacious dining room. Private car park. Pets welcome by arrangement. Open all year. A warm welcome and friendly atmosphere await all guests. Please send for our brochure and tariff.

HARROGATE. Mrs Murray's Guest House, 67 Franklin Road, Harrogate HG1 5EH (01423 505857;

Fax: 01423 530027). ♨ ♨♨ *COMMENDED*. Anne Marie and Tom will welcome you to "Mrs Murray's Guest House". It is the only place to stay in Harrogate. We offer hotel service at guest house prices, whether you are on holiday or business. We are located within a few minutes' stroll of the town centre. Phone Anne Marie and she will send you our brochure with our special offers from only £20 per person. RAC Acclaimed.

HARROGATE. Mr Derek and Mrs Carol Vinter, Spring Lodge, 22 Spring Mount, Harrogate HG1

2HX (01423 506036). ♨ Attractive Edwardian guest house situated in a quiet cul-de-sac, yet close to all the amenities of Harrogate, Britain's floral spa town, with its elegant and outstanding architecture and gardens, antique shops and restaurants. Five minutes' walk from the International Conference and Exhibition Centre. Ideal for the business visitor or tourist, with the beautiful Yorkshire Dales within easy access. All year round a warm welcome awaits you from the resident proprietors. Accommodation comprises four double rooms, one triple and one single. En suite rooms available. Coffee and tea making facilities in all rooms. Dinner provided on request. Residential licence and no smoking. Bed and Breakfast from £16.

HARROGATE. Mr and Mrs P. Bell, Dene Court Guest House, 22 Franklin Road, Harrogate HG1 5EE (01423 509498). Friendly family-run guest house offering comfortable Bed and Breakfast accommodation. A good traditional English breakfast served, with a good choice for vegetarians too. Standard single, twin, double and family rooms available all with washbasins, tea/coffee facilities, radio/alarm clocks and central heating. TV in guest lounge, two bathrooms and third toilet. Private parking for three/four cars at rear of Victorian terrace house. Very close to town centre, exhibition halls, Valley Gardens, railway and bus station and other amenities. Bed and Breakfast from £16 per person; optional Evening Meal from £8. Reductions for children. Discount for weekly bookings.

HARROGATE. Mrs Christine Ryder, Scaife Hall Farm, Blubberhouses, Otley, West Yorkshire LS21

2PL (01943 880354). ☙☙ *HIGHLY COMMENDED.* Farm Holiday Bureau member. Scaife Hall is a working farm set in picturesque countryside on the edge of the Yorkshire Dales. Ideal location for visiting the Dales, Harrogate, Fountains Abbey, York, Skipton and Emmerdale country. Sheep and beef cattle are kept and guests are free to roam and even take part in some seasonal activities such as lambing, etc. One twin-bedded and two double rooms, each tastefully decorated and having en suite facilities, central heating and beverage tray. Guests' private sittingroom with colour TV and log fires on chilly nights. Open all year. Local inns provide excellent evening meals. Bed and Breakfast from £20.

HARROGATE. Charles and Gill Richardson, The Coppice, 9 Studley Road, Harrogate HG1 5JU

(01423 569626; Fax: 01423 569005). ☙☙☙ *COMMENDED.* A high standard of comfortable accommodation awaits you at The Coppice, with a reputation for excellent food and a warm friendly welcome. All rooms en suite with telephones. Quietly located off Kings Road, five minutes' walk from the elegant shops and gardens of the town centre. Just three minutes' walk from the Conference Centre. Ideal location to explore the natural beauty of the Yorkshire Dales. Midway stop Edinburgh — London. Bed and Breakfast £23 single, £40 double, family from £54; Evening Meal from £13.50.

HARROGATE. Alvera Court Hotel, 76 Kings Road, Harrogate HG1 5JX (01423 505735; Fax: 01423

507996). ☙☙☙ *COMMENDED.* Overlooking the new Harrogate Conference Centre, the Alvera Court is a private, luxury, licensed hotel owned and run by Marion and Craig Simpson who offer guests individual attention and hospitality in a relaxed, comfortable atmosphere. All rooms are en suite with colour TV, radio, direct dial telephone, tea/coffee making facilities and hair dryer. After a busy day, relax in our elegant lounge, cosy bar or sample our delicious cuisine in our licensed restaurant. We have full central heating, our own car park and are open all year round. Bargain Breaks available from £29 per person per day. AA and RAC One Star; Yorkshire Tourist Board member; Member of British Hospitality Association. Please ring for details and full colour brochure.

HARROGATE. Mrs Joan Smith, Dalriada, Cabin Lane, Dacre Banks, Harrogate HG3 4EE (01423 780512). Homely hospitality awaits you at Dalriada, situated on a country lane in a small Nidderdale village four miles from Pateley Bridge and nine miles from Harrogate, famous for its beautiful gardens. Fountains Abbey, Ripley Castle, Newby Hall and Harewood House are just some of the nearby attractions. A very good centre for touring the Yorkshire Dales and excellent walking country (on Nidderdale Way). Comfortable rooms — one double, one twin with washbasins and tea making facilities, one en suite single and TV lounge. Ample private parking. Good home cooking and inns nearby. Bed and Breakfast from £15. Open all year.

HARROGATE. Hazel and Michael Leatherdale, Imbercourt Hotel, 57 Valley Drive, Harrogate HG2 0JW (01423 502513). A Yorkshire stone building in a sylvan setting overlooking Harrogate's famous Valley Gardens yet only minutes' walk from the towns shopping centre and a short drive from the Yorkshire Dales. The hotel is family-run, the owners living on the premises where pets and children are welcome. All 10 rooms have central heating, colour TV, radio and kettles and half have en suite facilities. The public rooms include a TV lounge, well stocked bar and a restaurant where meals are served at any hour. Yorkshire breakfasts are a speciality. Bed and Breakfast charges range from £22 to £26; Dinner from £10 to £15. Special rates apply to weekend breaks and longer stays.

HARROGATE. Mrs H.M. Phillips, Shutt Nook Farm, Chain Bar Lane, Killinghall, Harrogate HG3 2BS (01423 567562). Working farm. Shutt Nook Farm is a mixed 150 acre family-run farm, ideally situated for touring the Yorkshire Dales; the spa town of Harrogate is just three miles away and Ripley Castle, Fountains Abbey and the ancient city of York are all within easy reach. Good home cooking, colour TV. There are one double, one twin and one family bedrooms, all with washbasins; bathroom, toilet; sitting room, dining room. Sorry no pets. Open May to December. A car is recommended and there is parking. Bed and Breakfast. Reduced rates for children.

HARROGATE. Mrs Judy Barker, Brimham Guest House, Silverdale Close, Darley, Harrogate HG3 2PQ (01423 780948). The family-run guest house is situated in the centre of Darley, a quiet village in unspoilt Nidderdale. All rooms en suite and centrally heated with tea/coffee making facilities and views across the Dales. Full English breakfast served between 7am and 9.30am in the dining room; a TV lounge/conservatory is available for your relaxation. Off street parking. Central for visits to Harrogate, York, Skipton and Ripon, or just enjoying drives through the Dales and Moors where you will take in dramatic hillsides, green hills, picturesque villages, castles and abbeys. Children welcome. Bed and Breakfast from £17 (double room) to £25 (single room).

HARROGATE. Mrs M. Thomson, Knox Mill House, Knox Mill Lane, Harrogate HG3 2AE (01423 560650). 👑👑 *COMMENDED.* AA QQQ. A delightfully renovated 200-year-old Millhouse, standing on the banks of a stream in a rural setting less than two miles from Harrogate's centre. Situated along a quiet country lane just off the A61 Ripon road, it is highly recommended for touring Yorkshire Dales and Moors, seeing York itself or for visiting conference and exhibition facilities in town. Inglenook fireplace and original oak beams give a 'farmhouse' atmosphere to the Residents' Lounge which faces south overlooking beautiful rolling meadow. All bedrooms are attractively furnished, some en suite, with complimentary tea/coffee making facilities, and there is ample private parking for residents. No smoking. Bed and Breakfast only (a wide choice of pubs, restaurants are close by) £20 per person. Brochure available.

HARROGATE. Mrs A. Wood, Field House, Clint, Near Harrogate HG3 3DS (01423 770638). In beautiful gardens, five miles from Harrogate. Ideal for exploring the Dales and Moors, with ancient abbeys, castles and country houses. The market towns of Skipton, Ripon and Knaresborough and the historic City of York are within easy reach. Accommodation is in one twin and one double room with private bathroom. Private sittingroom with TV etc. Open all year. Car essential — private parking. Bed and Breakfast from £15 with Evening Meal readily available nearby. A warm welcome guaranteed in a peaceful, friendly atmosphere. Telephone or SAE, please, for further details.

HARROGATE. Anne and Bob Joyner, Anro Guest House, 90 King's Road, Harrogate HG1 5JX (01423 503087). AA and RAC Listed. "Excellent!", "Exceptional value!", "Good food!", "Quiet!", "Never had it so good!" — just a few of the testimonials visitors have written in our book on leaving. Situated in a tree-lined avenue in a central position close to all amenities. Conference and Exhibition Centre two minutes' walk. Valley Gardens, town and local swimming baths close by. Our house is centrally heated, with tea/coffee making facilities and colour TV in all rooms, hot and cold throughout. Some rooms en-suite. Home cooking. Bed and Breakfast from £22. Four-course Dinner plus tea or coffee upon request £12.50. Ideal centre for touring Dales/Herriot country. Well recommended.

HELMSLEY. Mrs Margaret Wainwright, Sproxton Hall, Sproxton, Helmsley YO6 5EQ (01439 770225; Fax: 01439 771373). 👑👑 *HIGHLY COMMENDED.* Enjoy the peaceful atmosphere, magnificent views and comfort of Sproxton Hall, a 17th century Listed farmhouse on a 300-acre family farm. A haven of peace and tranquillity, lovingly and tastefully furbished with antiques and co-ordinating fabrics giving the warm, cosy, elegance of a country home. Set amidst idyllic countryside, one and a half miles from Helmsley. Excellent base for touring North Yorkshire Moors, Dales, Coast, National Trust properties and York. One double room en suite, one twin room with private bathroom, double and twin with shared luxury shower room. Colour TV, central heating, drinks facilities, washbasins and razor points in all rooms. Laundry facilities. "A non-smoking household". No children under 10 years. Bed and Breakfast from £20 per person. Brochures available. Five self catering award-winning cottages also available.

HELMSLEY. Mrs Jenny Oakley, Rose Cottage, Oswaldkirk, York YO6 5XT (01439 788339; Fax: 01439 788037). Rose Cottage is an 18th century village house situated three miles south of Helmsley on the B1363 in the National Park. You will be given a warm welcome and keys to your own two guest self-contained accommodation in the Coach House. Breakfast is taken in Rose Cottage just across the yard. The newly converted luxury double-bedded room has king-size bed, bathroom en suite, tea/coffee making facilities, colour TV, radio, central heating and is non-smoking. Much to see and do in the area, and local pubs serving good bar meals. Open all year. Bed and Breakfast £20 per person. Brochure available.

HELMSLEY. Mrs Elizabeth Easton, Lockton House Farm, Bilsdale, Helmsley YO6 5NE (01439 798303). Working farm. 16th century farmhouse on mixed family-run farm of 400 acres with sheep, cattle and ponies, ideally situated for touring North Yorkshire Moors and the many other attractions of this area. There are peaceful panoramic views from the farm. Guest accommodation is in two double and one family rooms all with washbasins; lounge with colour TV. Good home cooking in abundance. Open March to October. Bed and Breakfast from £15; Bed, Breakfast and Evening Meal (optional) from £25. Reduced rates for children. Horses welcome, stables and grazing available.

HELMSLEY. Mrs J. Milburn, Barn Close Farm, Rievaulx, Helmsley YO6 5LH (01439 798321). 🐾 🐾 *COMMENDED.* **Working farm.** Farming family offer homely accommodation on mixed farm in beautiful surroundings near Rievaulx Abbey. Ideal for touring, pony trekking; good walking terrain! Home-made bread, own home produced meat, poultry, free range eggs — in fact Mrs Milburn's excellent cooking was praised in "Daily Telegraph". En suite double and one family bedrooms; bathroom; toilets; sitting room and dining room. Children are welcome, cot, high chair and babysitting available. Sorry, no pets. Open all year round. Open log fires. Storage heaters in bedrooms. Car essential — parking. Bed and Breakfast from £20 to £22; Dinner £12. Reduced rates for children under 10 sharing parents' room. Farm Holiday Bureau Member.

HORTON-IN-RIBBLESDALE. Marilyn Pilkington, Middle Studfold Farm, Horton-in-Ribblesdale, Settle BD24 0ER (01729 860236). 18th century Dales farmhouse superbly situated on the lower slopes of Pen-y-ghent (one of the famed "Three Peaks") and overlooking the lovely valley of Upper Ribblesdale and scenic Settle to Carlisle railway. Middle Studfold provides an ideal base for exploring the Yorkshire Dales National Park. We have a homely lounge with open fire and an oak beamed dining room where you can choose from a variety of breakfasts to start the day, and enjoy fine food and wine in the evening. All bedrooms with washbasins and tea making facilities. Our quiet location with private approach offers ample parking. Bed and Breakfast from £17; Dinner £8 to £10. Pets by arrangement. Open all year. SAE for brochure.

HUTTON LE HOLE. Ann Willis, Hammer and Hand House, Hutton le Hole, York YO6 6UA (01751 417300; Fax: 01751 417711). Charming Listed Georgian property, built in mellow York Stone as the village beer house, stands in a sheltered spot on the east side of this idyllic village, facing the green and beck and within North York Moors National Park. It is within easy striking distance of Heartbeat and Herriot country, the coastal resorts of Whitby and Scarborough and the magnificent city of York. Comfortable guest sitting room has handsome Georgian fireplace with open log fire and the en suite bedrooms, with their canopied beds and beamed ceilings, are prettily decorated and furnished with antiques or reproduction furniture. The surroundings are as memorable as the meals presented in the oak panelled dining room. Bed and Breakfast from £20; Evening Meals £12.50. A non-smoking establishment.

INGLETON. Mrs Claire Faraday, Langber End Farm, Ingleton, Via Carnforth LA6 3DT (015242

41776). Quietly situated one and a half miles out of Ingleton. The house is centrally heated and has one double, one twin and one single bedrooms, all with washbasins, shaver points and tea-making facilities; one room en-suite. Comfortable sittingroom with access at all times. A good four-course breakfast is served; vegetarian and special diets catered for. Good pubs and restaurants in the area serve Evening Meals at reasonable prices. Good centre for touring Lakes, Dales and coast. No smoking in the house. Bed and Breakfast from £13.50 (£15.50 en-suite).

INGLETON. Mrs Mollie Bell, Langber Country Guest House, Ingleton, via Carnforth LA6 3DT (015242 41587). ♛ ♛ Ingleton, "Beauty Spot of the North" in the Three Peaks/Dales National Park area. Renowned for waterfalls, glens, underground caves, magnificent scenery and Ingleborough Mountain (2,373 feet), an excellent centre for touring Lakes, Dales and coast. Golf, fishing, swimming and tennis in vicinity; pony trekking a few miles away. Guests are warmly welcomed to "Langber", a detached country guest house with beautiful views and 82 acres of gardens, terrace and fields. Lambs and sheep kept. Ample parking space available. Three family, three double/twin and one single bedrooms, all with washbasins, some en-suite. Bathroom and two toilets. Sunny comfortable lounge and separate diningroom. Central heating; fire precautions. Babysitting offered. Open all year except Christmas. Fire Certificate granted. AA and RAC Listed. Bed and Breakfast from £15.50; Bed, Breakfast and Evening Meal from £21.50. Reductions for children under 13 sharing parents' room.

INGLETON. Allan and Louise Bruns, Ferncliffe Guest House, Ingleton, Carnforth LA6 3HJ (015242

42405). ♛ ♛ ♛ *COMMENDED.* A spacious late Victorian house refurbished by present owners Allan and Louise with the comfort of their guests in mind. All rooms are en suite with TV and tea/coffee trays. Dinner by owner chef should not be missed. Ferncliffe House stands on the edge of the village of Ingleton known as the beauty spot of the north with its waterfalls, glens and walks and Ingleborough Hill as a back drop. All this makes an ideal base for touring the Dales. Bed and Breakfast £22; Dinner £12.50. Weekly and Short Break prices on request. AA QQQQ, RAC Acclaimed, Les Routiers. Ring or write for brochure.

LEYBURN. Mrs H.M. Richardson, Sunnyridge, Argill Farm, Harmby, Leyburn DL8 5HQ (01969

622478). Situated on a small sheep farm in Wensleydale, Sunnyridge is a spacious bungalow in an outstanding position. Magnificent views are enjoyed from every room. In the heart of the Yorkshire Dales and the midst of Herriot country, it is an ideal centre for exploring the wide variety of activities and attractions; or a restful stop-over for travellers to Scotland. Sample Yorkshire hospitality and relax in comfortable ground floor accommodation comprising one double or twin-bedded room with washbasin, one family room with/without en suite shower room; each with colour TV and tea/coffee facilities. Guest lounge. Children welcome. Pets by arrangement. Evening meal optional. Prices from £12.

MALHAM. Sparth House Hotel, Malham, Skipton BD23 4DA (01729 830315). Malham is an ideal

base for the Yorkshire Dales, and several of the National Park's major attractions are only a short walk away. York, the Settle — Carlisle Railway, Bronte country and the Lake District are easy days out. Sparth House has an enviable reputation for imaginative freshly prepared meals — you should not miss Dinner! The accommodation is attractive and comfortable. All rooms have tea/coffee facilities and most have high quality en-suite bathrooms and colour TV. One ground floor bedroom is equipped for disabled guests. Two lounges (one for non-smokers) and a well stocked bar complete this delightful country hotel. Bed and Breakfast from £18.50; Evening Meal £13.50.

PLEASE SEND A STAMPED ADDRESSED ENVELOPE WITH ENQUIRIES

MALHAM (near Skipton). Keith and Patricia Dyball, Malham Cafe, The Green, Malham, Near Skipton BD23 4DB (01729 830348). 🏵

17th century building situated in the centre of Malham village offering three olde worlde en-suite bedrooms with colour TV and tea/coffee making facilities. Homely atmosphere and a true Yorkshire welcome. Residential licence. Bed and Breakfast from £18. Reduced rates for children. Pets welcome. Ideally situated for touring the popular Yorkshire Dales and National Park. Skipton nearby, also the interesting old village of Gargrave. Within easy reach of Harrogate, York and Bronte country. Lovely walking countryside.

MALTON. Mrs Ann Hopkinson, The Brow, 25 York Road, Malton YO17 0AX (01653 693402). The Brow is a large house with beautiful views. It was the home of the Walker family who owned the oldest of the five breweries for which Malton was famous. Captain Walker of Whitby (to whom Captain Cook was apprenticed) was a member of the same Walker family. A visit to The Brow should not be missed. A warm welcome awaits you here with TV and tea/coffee making facilities in all rooms. Children welcome, reduced rates. Bed and Breakfast from £14 to £25.

MALTON. Mrs C.R. Neuff, North's Farm, 2 Westgate, Rillington, Malton YO17 8LN (Tel & Fax: 01944 758620).

A warm welcome awaits you at this non working early 19th century farmhouse with beamed lounge and open fire. Accommodation comprises one twin-bedded room and one single. Open all year, it is suitable as a one night stop for walkers or cyclists or as a base for a wide range of visits and activities including the Wolds Way, the North York Moors, the East Coast and the ancient walled city of York. Coastliner buses stop outside and off road parking is available. Spinning and rug weaving courses are available on request. Bed and Breakfast from £14; Evening Meal by prior arrangement. Visa/Access cards accepted.

NORTH YORKSHIRE MOORS NATIONAL PARK. Mrs Marion N. Cockrem, Dale End Farm, Green End, Goathland, Whitby YO22 5LJ (01947 895371). Working farm.

140 acre working farm, 500 year old stone built farmhouse in North Yorkshire Moors National Park. Generous portions of home cooked food. Rare breeds of animals kept including llama, emus and Vietnamese pot-bellied pigs. Children and pets welcomed. An excellent children's playground. Guests' lounge with TV and log fire. Homely olde worlde interior, oak beams and panelling. Many repeat bookings. Sensible prices. SAE for brochure.

NORTHALLERTON. The White Rose Hotel, Leeming Bar, Northallerton DL7 9AY (01677 422707/424941; Fax: 01677 425123). 🏵🏵🏵 COMMENDED. RAC/AA Two Star. 18 bedroom private hotel situated in village on A684, half a mile from A1 motorway. Ideal base for touring North Yorks Moors, Dales and coastal resorts. All bedrooms have en suite bathrooms, colour TV, radio, telephone, trouser press and tea/coffee making facilities. Private residents' lounge. Fully licensed; restaurant. Pets welcome. Please write or telephone for further details.

PICKERING. Stan and Hilary Langton, Vivers Mill, Mill Lane, Pickering YO18 8DJ (01751 473640).

Vivers Mill is an ancient watermill situated in peaceful surroundings, quarter mile south of Pickering Market Place on Pickering Beck. The Mill is a listed building constructed of stone, brick and pantiles, part of which possibly dates back to the 13th century. The building with its characteristic beamed ceilings has been renovated and most of the machinery is being preserved (including the water wheel and millstones). Pickering is an excellent centre from which to explore the North York Moors National Park, Ryedale and the spectacular Heritage Coast. It is the terminal station for the preserved North York Moors Railway and is only 26 miles from historic York. Visitors are assured of a friendly welcome with nourishing, traditional breakfasts. Large lounge and six comfortable en suite bedrooms with tea/coffee making facilities. Bed and Breakfast £23 daily; from £145 weekly. Reductions for family room. Pets welcome.

WHEN MAKING ENQUIRIES PLEASE MENTION
THIS *FHG* PUBLICATION

PICKERING. Mrs Livesey, Sands Farm Country Hotel, Wilton, Pickering YO18 7JY (01751

474405). Enjoy a relaxing holiday in a friendly atmosphere where food, rooms and service are of the highest standard. Laura Ashley style bedrooms, with flowers, colour TV and tea-making facilities; all en-suite and some with four-poster beds. Full English Breakfast; tea-trays in front of a log fire. Many sporting facilities and places of interest nearby — we are happy to suggest many places to visit. NO SMOKING. No children under 10 years. No dogs. Terms from £17.50 per person per night. Special low fat diets on request. Private parking. Special low season breaks. Self catering cottages also available, set in 15 acres. Write or phone for full details.

PICKERING. Mrs Sandra M. Pickering, "Nabgate", Wilton Road, Thornton-le-Dale, Pickering

YO18 7QP (01751 474279). ✿✿ *COMMENDED.* Situated at the eastern end of this beautiful village, "Nabgate' was built at the turn of the century. Accommodation comprises two double en suite rooms, one twin with private bathroom, all with TV, tea making facilities, shaver points. Central heating. Dining room/lounge. Keys provided for access at all times. Car park. Children and pets welcome. Thornton Dale has three pubs all providing meals, also cafes, fish and chip shop and bistro. Situated in the North Yorkshire Moors National Park it is an ideal base for East Coast, Steam Railway, Flamingoland, Castle Howard, York and "Heartbeat" village. Open all year. Bed and Breakfast from £17. Welcome Host and Hygiene Certificate held.

PICKERING. Mrs Ella Bowes, Banavie, Roxby Road, Thornton-le-Dale, Pickering YO18 7SX (01751

474616). ✿✿ *COMMENDED.* Banavie is a large stone built semi-detached house set in Thornton-le-Dale, one of the prettiest villages in Yorkshire with a stream flowing through the centre. Situated in an attractive part of the village off the main road, it is ideal for touring coast, moors, Castle Howard, Flamingo Park, Eden Camp, North Yorkshire Moors Railway and "Heartbeat" country. A real Yorkshire breakfast is served by Mrs Bowes herself which provides a good start to the day. One family en suite bedrooms, one double en suite and one double room with private bathroom, all with shaver points, colour TV and tea-making facilities. Dining room. Lounge with TV, central heating. Children and pets welcome; cot, high chair, babysitting. Own door keys. Car park. Open all year. Bed and Breakfast (including tea and biscuits at bedtime) from £16.50. SAE, please. Thornton-le-Dale has three pubs, two restaurants and fish and chip shop for meals. Welcome Host, Hygiene Certificate held.

RICHMOND. Helen and Colin Lowes, Wilson House, Barningham, Richmond DL11 7EB (01833

621218). ✿✿ *COMMENDED.* Wilson House is ideally situated enjoying magnificent views over open countryside. Located one mile from A66, this is an ideal base for exploring the Yorkshire and Durham Dales and the Lake District; Durham City, Newcastle and the Beamish Museum are all within one hour's drive. The historic towns of Richmond and Barnard Castle are both under 10 miles away and offer castle, museums, galleries, antiques, shops and sports facilities. This charming farmhouse is tastefully decorated, clean, comfortable and centrally heated throughout. Accommodation comprises double and twin rooms en suite with colour TV and tea/coffee facilities, guests' lounge with colour TV. Non-smoking accommodation available. We offer good farmhouse cooking, Evening Meal by arrangement. Bed and Breakfast from £16; Evening Meal from £10. Children welcome at reduced rates.

RICHMOND. Mrs Dorothy Wardle, Greenbank Farm, Ravensworth, Richmond DL11 7HB (01325 718334). This 170-acre farm, both arable and livestock, is four miles west of Scotch Corner on the A66, midway between the historic towns of Richmond and Barnard Castle, and within easy reach of Teesdale, Swaledale and Wensleydale. Only an hour's drive from the Lake District. The farm is one mile outside the village of Ravensworth, with plenty of good eating places within easy reach. Guests' own lounge, diningroom; two double rooms and one en suite room, one family room. All bedrooms have washbasins, tea/coffee facilities, heating and electric blankets. Children welcome; play area with swings, slides, trampoline, etc. Sorry, no pets. Car essential. Bed and Breakfast from £12.50 includes light supper/bedtime drink. Evening Meals available. Reductions for children and Senior Citizens. Open all year. Luxury mobile home available.

RICHMOND. Mrs L. Brooks, Holmedale, Dalton, Richmond DL11 7HX (01833 621236).

COMMENDED. Holmedale is a Georgian house set in a quiet village midway between Richmond and Barnard Castle. Seven miles from Scotch Corner and ideally situated for touring Swaledale, Wensleydale and Teesdale. One double and one family room, both with washbasins and central heating. Comfortable sittingroom with open fire when necessary. Good plain home cooking with plentiful Yorkshire helpings. Tea/coffee making facilities available. Bed and Breakfast from £13.50 per person; Bed, Breakfast and Evening Meal from £22, single room from £15.

RIPON. Mrs S. Gordon, St. George's Court, Old Home Farm, High Grantley, Ripon HG4 3EU (01765 620618).

At beautifully situated St. George's Court sleep in our renovated cow byre and dairy. Modern comfort with old world charm. Five bedrooms — three double, one twin and one family suite, all with private bathrooms, colour TV and tea making facilities. Each room has superb views over farmland and woods. All rooms on ground level. Peace and tranquillity is our password. We are 200 yards from any road. We have a third of an acre pond where wildlife and flora are encouraged to flourish. Breakfast in our 17th century farmhouse, before a log fire. Only fresh local food cooked to a very high standard. A warm and friendly welcome guaranteed. Open all year. Children and dogs welcome.

RIPON. Valerie Leeming, Bay Tree Farm, Aldfield, Near Fountains Abbey, Ripon HG4 3BE (Tel & Fax: 01765 620394).

HIGHLY COMMENDED. As featured in "Which? B&B", this 17th century converted stone hay barn combines character with comfort in quiet hamlet. Beautiful Fountains Abbey, half a mile to York, Harrogate and Dales all in easy reach. Lovely circular walks from our door returning to open fires and super cooking (HE trained). All rooms en suite, central heating, beverages, TV. Kettle always on the boil. Ideal for "get togethers" or just a peaceful few days. Colour brochure. Open all year. Bed and Breakfast from £18.50; Evening Meal from £11.50. Children and pets welcome.

RIPON. Mrs Dorothy Poulter, Avenue Farm, Bramley Grange, Ilton Road, Grewelthorpe, Ripon HG4 3DN (01765 658348). Small dairy farm offering quiet, homely farmhouse accommodation at the foot of the Yorkshire Dales set in lovely countryside with beautiful views. Near James Herriott country. Within easy reach of A1, Ripon, York, Fountains Abbey and just three miles from Masham with the taste of Black Sheep Ale, golf, fishing and pony trekking nearby. Avenue Farm guarantees a warm welcome with a cup of tea on arrival and bedtime drink. TV lounge. Bed and Breakfast from £14 per night.

ROBIN HOOD'S BAY. David and Angela Pattinson, Hogarth Hall, Boggle Hole Road, Robin Hood's Bay, Near Whitby YO22 4QQ (01947 880547).

Hogarth Hall is a newly built farmhouse set in 145 acres of habitat, situated at the top of the valley with wonderful views of sea, farmland, moors and sky. Experience the wonder of glorious sunrises and sunsets, June being the loveliest month for these. Bring your binoculars to study the wildlife all around. All rooms are en suite with whirlpool baths and showers, and TV. Tea/coffee making facilities available. There is a large lounge for relaxing and enjoying these views and we also have a sauna. Scarborough 15 miles, Whitby nine miles, York 40 miles, Durham 60 miles, Hornsea 50 miles. Please write, or telephone, for further details.

ROBIN HOOD'S BAY. Mrs G. Hogdson, Low Farm, Fylingthorpe, Whitby YO22 4QF (01947 880366). Robin Hood's Bay, where the North York Moors roll down to the sea. A real Yorkshire welcome awaits you in our traditional Georgian farmhouse. We offer guests a large south facing family room with washbasins and central heating, comfortably furnished in country style. Exclusive use of spacious lounge with period oak furniture and a large fireplace built of local stone. A working farm in beautiful countryside, we are ideal for walking, riding or cycling, with Whitby five miles, Scarborough 14 miles or "Heartbeat" country 10 miles.

ROBIN HOOD'S BAY. Mrs B. Reynolds, Gilders Green, Raw, Robin Hood's Bay, Whitby YO22 4PP (01947 880025). Comfortable accommodation in 17th century farm cottage on a sheep-rearing and stock farm. Pleasantly situated in the hamlet of Raw, overlooking Robin Hood's Bay and close to the Moors, it is ideal for walking and touring. One mile from the A171, it is within easy reach of Whitby, Scarborough and many more places of interest. There is one family room, with children welcome. Bed and Breakfast from £15, with bedtime drink included. Open Easter to October. Also available, self catering house in village.

ROSEDALE ABBEY. Mrs Alison Dale, Five Acre View, Rosedale, Near Pickering YO8 8RE (01751 417213). Working farm. This 150 acre farm is within easy

driving distance from Scarborough, Whitby, York and various leisure parks. Nearer to home there is a wide range of walks set in the North Yorkshire Moors National Park. A small golf course within walking distance is a challenge for any enthusiast. Three quarters of a mile of trout fishing is also nearby. The "Olde Worlde" farmhouse has all modern-day comforts and offers one family, one twin and one double bedrooms, all with washbasins, tea/coffee making facilities and colour TV. The open-beamed lounge, complete with log fire, has colour TV and satellite. Bed and Breakfast from £14.50; Evening Meal from £7.50. Reductions for children. Pets welcome.

ROSEDALE EAST. Maureen and John Harrison, Moordale House, Dale Head, Pickering YO18 8RH (01751 417219). ♛♛ COMMENDED. Dating back to the

mid 17th century Moordale House once served the local iron ore mining community as a granary and general stores. Today after extensive refurbishment and modernisation Maureen and John offer you a visit they hope will remain in your heart and memory for years to come. Accommodation is available in one family, two double, two twin bedded rooms, all with en suite facilities, one double bedded room with washbasin. Tea/coffee making facilities. Full central heating. Separate shower room, bathroom and toilets. Guests are offered Bed and full English Breakfast, five course Evening Dinner optional in the spacious diningroom which benefits from magnificent views over the valley. Comfortable, relaxing lounge with open fire and colour TV, also quiet lounge. A family-run licensed guest house offering good home cooking, every comfort and a happy, friendly atmosphere. Members of the Yorkshire and Humberside Tourist Board. Full Fire Certificate. Brochure and terms on request.

SCARBOROUGH. Ivyholme Hotel, 30 West Street, Scarborough YO11 2QP (01723 360649).

Charming Victorian cottage hotel situated close to Spa and Esplanade. Comfortable en suite bedrooms with TV, teasmaid. Bed and Breakfast from £14 per person; Dinner, Bed and Breakfast from £21 per person. Reductions for full weeks and Senior Citizens.

SCARBOROUGH. Maureen and Ron Jacques, The Premier Hotel, 66 Esplanade, Scarborough

YO11 2UZ (01723 501062). This lovely Victorian licensed Hotel overlooking the sea and coastline has all the warmth and hospitality of a bygone era. It is conveniently situated for all Scarborough's attractions and is near the Italian, Rose and Holbeck Gardens; also convenient for the historic city of York, North Yorkshire Moors, Whitby and many stately homes in the area. The Premier has a high reputation for its standards of food and service, specialising in traditional English cuisine using the very best local produce. Peaceful, relaxing atmosphere; lift to comfortable bedrooms, some with magnificent sea views and all with private facilities en suite, colour TV, tea tray, clock radio and hairdryer. Private car park. Pets very welcome. AA, RAC Highly Acclaimed.

SCARBOROUGH. Sylvia and Chris Kirk, The Terrace Hotel, 69 Westborough, Scarborough YO11 1TS (01723 374937). A small family-run Hotel situated between North and South Bays, close to all Scarborough's many attractions and only a short walk from the town centre, rail and bus stations. Private car park. Three double bedrooms (one en suite), three family rooms (one en suite) and one single bedroom, all with colour TV and tea making facilities. Licensed bar. Full Fire Certificate. Non-smoking accommodation available. Bed and full English Breakfast from £15; Evening Meal £6. En suite facilities £3 extra per person per night. Children (sharing room with adults) under four years FREE, four to 11 years half price.

SCARBOROUGH. Sue Batty, Wheatcroft Lodge, 156 Filey Road, Scarborough YO11 3AA (01723 374613). Wheatcroft Lodge is situated on the southern outskirts of Scarborough and offers comfortable centrally heated accommodation. Rooms, majority non-smoking, are all en suite, with colour TV, direct dial telephone, clock radio with alarm, hair dryer and tea/coffee making facilities. High standards throughout. Private car park. Guests have the choice of room only, traditional cooked breakfast in the dining room, or continental breakfast which, if wished, can be served directly into bedrooms through specially constructed hatches. Day time coffee shop serving refreshments and light meals. RAC Listed, Roy Castle Good Air Award. Open most of the year. From £17 per person.

SCARBOROUGH. Sue and Tony Hewitt, Harmony Country Lodge, Limestone Road, Burniston, Scarborough YO13 0DG (01723 870276). DISTINC-

TIVELY DIFFERENT HARMONY COUNTRY LODGE is a peaceful and relaxing retreat, octagonal in design and set in two acres of private grounds overlooking the National Park and sea. An ideal centre for walking or touring. Three miles from Scarborough and within easy reach of Whitby, York and the beautiful North Yorkshire countryside. Comfortable standard or en suite centrally heated rooms with colour TV and all with superb views. Attractive dining room, guest lounge and relaxing conservatory. Traditional English breakfast, optional evening meal including vegetarian. Fragrant massage available. Bed and Breakfast from £18.50 to £25.50. Non smoking, licensed, private parking facilities. Personal service and warm, friendly Yorkshire hospitality. Spacious eight berth caravan also available for self-catering holidays. Cycle hire. Open all year. Please telephone or write for brochure.

BRIDGE END FARM

Threshfield, Skipton, North Yorkshire BD23 5NH – *Eileen and Allan Thompson* – 01756 752463

Eileen and Allan Thompson invite you to share their idyllic 17th century riverside cottage, recently restored to original style, yet having the benefit of modern amenities. Home cooking and log fires help to create a relaxing and friendly atmosphere. A large garden with natural flora and wildlife runs down to the banks of the River Wharfe with private fishing. Pets and smoking not permitted in the house. Colour brochure showing the wide range of tariffs available on request. Situated in the heart of the Yorkshire Dales, yet easily accessible to the Lake District, historic York, and beautiful countryside.

SKIPTON. Sandra and Michael Wade, Grassington Lodge, 8 Wood Lane, Grassington, Skipton BD23 5LU (01756 752518).

Grassington Lodge is a quiet and cosy family-run guest house in its own grounds, yet only 100 yards from Grassington village square in the heart of the Yorkshire Dales. Grassington village boasts many good shops, pubs and restaurants, making an ideal base for walkers, cyclists and tourists alike. Most rooms at the lodge are en suite with colour TV. There is adequate private parking and a cycle shed. Breakfast is a feast!

SKIPTON. Mrs Heather Simpson, Low Skibeden Farmhouse, Skibeden Road, Skipton BD23 6AB (01756 793849; Fax: 01756 793804; Mobile 0411 275683). ETB

"Welcome Host", "Which?" Detached 16th century farmhouse in private grounds one mile east of Skipton off the A59/A65 gateway to the Dales, eg Bolton Abbey — Malham, Settle. Luxury bed and breakfast with fireside treats in the lounge. All rooms are quiet, spacious, have panoramic views, washbasins, tea facilities and electric overblankets. Central heating October to May. All guests are warmly welcomed and served tea/coffee and cakes on arrival, bedtime beverages are served from 9.30pm. Breakfast is served from 7am to 8.45am in the dining room. No smoking. No pets and no children under 12 years. Safe parking. New arrivals before 10pm. Quality and value guaranteed. Bed and Breakfast from £16 to £17.50 per person per night; en suite from £18 per person per night; full en suites single occupancy from £25 to £40. A deposit secures a room. Open all year. AA QQQ Recommended.

SKIPTON. Mrs Phillis Sapsford, Alton House, 5 Salisbury Street, Skipton BD23 1NQ (Tel & Fax:

01756 794780). An elegant Victorian town house situated in a quiet area off the main Gargrave Road, only a few minutes' walk from the town centre with its many attractions. You are assured of a warm and friendly welcome, comfortable beds in one twin and two triple rooms, and a delicious breakfast. Special rates for out of season breaks. Ideal base for touring the beautiful Yorkshire Dales. Children 10 years and over welcome. Prices from £17.50.

THIRSK. Mrs R. Dawson, Long Acre, 86a Topcliffe Road, Sowerby, Thirsk YO7 1RY (01845

522360). Tourist Board Listed *COMMENDED.* A warm welcome awaits you at Long Acre, a small family smallholding offering you a comfortable stay — just like home. Situated on the edge of Thirsk, ideal for touring the Dales/Moors. Our comfortable rooms have tea/coffee making facilities and colour TV. Relax in our lounge. Children and pets welcome. Bed and Breakfast from £15.

THIRSK. Joyce Ashbridge, Mount Grace Farm, Cold Kirby, Thirsk YO7 2HL (01845 597389). 🌸🌸

HIGHLY COMMENDED. A warm welcome awaits you on working farm surrounded by beautiful open countryside with magnificent views. Ideal location for touring or exploring the many walks in the area. Luxury en suite bedrooms with tea/coffee facilities. Spacious guests' lounge with colour TV. Garden. Enjoy delicious, generous helpings of farmhouse fayre cooked in our Aga. Children welcome. No smoking. Bed and Breakfast from £20; Evening Meal from £12. Weekly rates available. Open all year except Christmas.

THIRSK. Mrs Julie Bailes, Glen Free, Holme-on-Swale, Sinderby, Near Thirsk YO7 4JE (01845

567331). Glen Free is an old Lodge Bungalow set in a very peaceful situation, but still only one mile from A1 motorway (off the B6267 Masham/Thirsk road). Approximately seven miles from Ripon, Thirsk, Bedale, York and Harrogate 40 minutes approximately. One double, one twin rooms with central heating, tea making facilities and TV. Children welcome. All rooms ground floor. Golf, fishing, swimming and riding available locally. Ideal for touring the Dales and Herriot country. Bed and Breakfast fron £13 per person.

THIRSK. Mrs Lynda Dolan, Fourways Guest House, Town End, Thirsk YO7 1PY (01845 522601; Fax: 01845 522131). 🌸🌸 *APPROVED.* FOURWAYS is a comfortable family home with the advantage of being only two minutes' walk from the Town Centre and James Herriot's veterinary practice. Ideal for touring North Yorkshire Moors and Yorkshire Dales. All rooms have colour TV, tea/coffee facilities, washbasins; some rooms have en suite facilities. Traditional English Breakfast with Evening Meal available if booked in advance. Licensed. Open all year. Ample parking provided. Bed and Breakfast from £16 per person with reductions for children. Evening Meal from £7.

Terms quoted in this publication may be subject to increase if rises in costs necessitate

THIRSK. Mrs Barbara Ramshay, Garth House, Dalton, Near Thirsk YO7 3HY (01845 577310).

Tourist Board Listed. Working farm, join in. Garth House is situated in Herriot country amidst beautiful scenery. Near to York, Harrogate and many historic buildings this area with its many attractions is ideal for touring. Guest accommodation is in one family room with washbasins and one twin room, both with TV and tea/coffee making facilities; TV in lounge; central heating. Large gardens and lawns, children's pets and toys. Access to badminton court and other sporting facilities. Bed and Breakfast from £12 to £14. Easy access — from A1 turn off onto A168 and follow signposts for Dalton. Brochure on request.

THIRSK. Mrs T. Williamson, Thornborough House Farm, South Kilvington, Thirsk YO7 2NP (01845 522103). ₩₩ *COMMENDED*. **Working farm.** Ideally

positioned farmhouse, one and a half miles north of Thirsk on the fringe of the North Yorkshire Moors, 35 minutes from the Pennine Dales and beautiful, historic York itself. Guests can be assured of a traditional warm Yorkshire welcome in comfortable, homely accommodation. Three bedrooms, two en-suite. Tasty home cooking, special diets catered for. Children and pets welcome. A perfect centre for walking and touring the beautiful surrounding area. Golf course half a mile, fishing and riding available locally. Open all year, Bed and Breakfast from £15 per person. Reductions for children, and for Senior Citizens — out of high season. Evening Meals can be provided.

THORNTON-LE-DALE. Mrs S. Wardell, Tangalwood, Roxby Road, Thornton-le-Dale, Pickering YO18 7SX (01751 474688). Tangalwood is a large

detached family house providing a warm welcome, clean comfortable accommodation and good food. Situated in a quiet part of this picturesque village, which is in a good central position for Moors ("Heartbeat" country), coast, North Yorkshire Moors Railway, Flamingo Park Zoo and forest drives, mountain biking and walking. Good facilities for meals provided in the village. Accommodation in one twin room en suite and two doubles (one with washbasin), all with tea/coffee making facilities and TV; bathroom, two toilets and washroom; diningroom; central heating. Open Easter to October for Bed and Breakfast from £14 each. Private car park.

THORNTON-LE-DALE. Mrs Ella Bowes, Banavie, Roxby Road, Thornton-le-Dale, Pickering YO18 7SX (01751 474616). ₩₩ *COMMENDED*. Banavie is a

large stone built semi-detached house set in Thornton-le-Dale, one of the prettiest villages in Yorkshire with a stream flowing through the centre. Situated in an attractive part of the village off the main road, it is ideal for touring coast, moors, Castle Howard, Flamingo Park, Eden Camp, North Yorkshire Moors Railway and "Heartbeat" country. A real Yorkshire breakfast is served by Mrs Bowes herself which provides a good start to the day. One family en suite bedroom, one double en suite and one double room with private bathroom, all with shaver points, colour TV and tea-making facilities. Dining room. Lounge with TV, central heating. Children and pets welcome; cot, high chair, baby-sitting. Own door keys. Car park. Open all year. Bed and Breakfast (including tea and biscuits at bedtime) from £16.50. SAE, please. Thornton-le-Dale has three pubs, two restaurants and fish and chip shop for meals. Welcome Host, Hygiene Certificate held.

♛♛ Highly Commended

BRIDGEFOOT GUEST HOUSE

Thornton Le Dale, Pickering
North Yorkshire YO18 7RR
Telephone 01751 474749

Bridgefoot House is situated in the village of Thornton-le-Dale, by the trout stream in a wall-enclosed garden next to the thatched cottage. Ideal touring base for the moors, east coast, countryside, forestry and York. Centrally heated throughout, open fires in season. Family room; several double and twin-bedded rooms; ground floor double (most rooms en-suite), tea and coffee facilities, shaver points, electric blankets. Colour TV. Guest lounge; diningroom. Bed and Breakfast from £17.50 to £20. Registered with ETB. Car parking. Open Easter to November. Contact **Mr and Mrs B. Askin** for brochure.

THRESHFIELD. Long Ashes Inn, Threshfield, Near Skipton BD23 5PN (01756 752434). ♛♛♛ *HIGHLY COMMENDED.* You will receive a warm welcome and personal attention in this charming, traditional old Dales Inn, set in picturesque Wharfedale in the Yorkshire Dales National Park. A tranquil retreat in an idyllic setting, perfect for relaxing or as a base from which to enjoy everything the Yorkshire Dales have to offer at any time of the year. The de luxe accommodation includes en suite bathrooms, central heating, tea and coffee making facilities and TV. There is a wide range of hand-pulled ales and freshly prepared food, as well as a heated indoor pool, sauna, squash courts, etc adjacent for use by residents.

WENSLEYDALE. Barbara and Barrie Martin, The Old Star, West Witton, Leyburn DL8 4LU (01969 622949). ♛♛ *APPROVED.* Formerly a 17th century coaching inn, now a family-run guest house. You are always welcome at the Old Star. The building still retains many original features. Comfortable lounge with oak beams and log fire. Dinner available if ordered in advance. Bedrooms mostly en suite with central heating and tea/coffee facilities. In the heart of the Yorkshire Dales National Park we are ideally situated for walking and touring the Dales. Large car park. Open all year except Christmas. Bed and Breakfast from £15 to £19 with special breaks available.

WHITBY. The George Hotel, Baxtergate, Whitby YO21 1BN (01947 602565). Superbly furnished hotel central for all amenities. Licensed busy bar serving quality ales and lagers. Ideal for fishing parties. Children welcome. Central heating. Telephone for full details and brochure. Bed and Breakfast from £20 per person.

WHITBY. Mrs Avril Mortimer, Hollins Farm, Glaisdale, Whitby YO21 2PZ (01947 897516). Hollins Farm is 10 miles from Whitby, surrounded by beautiful countryside and moorland, with lots of lovely walks. Moors Steam Railway, Pickering market town with castle, National Park Centre at Danby are places of interest nearby, as also Whitby, Staithes, Robin Hood's Bay and other coastal villages to visit; choice of pony trekking and fishing. The 16th century farmhouse provides comfortable accommodation comprising one large family or double room with washbasin and TV, sleeps four/five, also twin room, both with tea-making facilities and storage heaters; bathroom; sitting/diningroom with colour TV. Conservatory. In winter peat and log fires are cosy. Cot and high chair. Access to rooms at all times. Camping facilities available. Phone or send SAE for terms.

WHITBY near. Mrs Pat Beale, Ryedale House, Coach Road, Sleights, Near Whitby YO22 5EQ (01947 810534). Welcoming non-smoking Yorkshire house of charm and character at the foot of the Moors, National Park and "Heartbeat" country, three and a half miles from Whitby. Rich in history, magnificent scenery, picturesque harbours, cliffs, beaches, scenic railways, superb walking. Three double/twin beautifully appointed bedrooms with private facilities. Guests' lounge and dining room (separate tables) with breathtaking views over Eskdale. Enjoy our large sun terrace and gardens, relax, we're ready to pamper you! Long established for delicious Yorkshire fare; extensive breakfast menu, picnics (traditional and vegetarian). Recommended local inns and restaurants. Parking, near public transport. Regret no pets. Bed and Breakfast £17.50 to £18.50 per person, minimum two nights. Weekly reductions, special Spring and September/October breaks. Tourist Board Member.

WHITBY near. Mrs G. Watson, The Bungalow, 63 Coach Road, Sleights, Whitby YO22 5BT (01947 810464). Be sure of a warm Yorkshire welcome at this large, comfortable, well appointed bungalow in the picturesque village of Sleights, just three miles from historic Whitby, half an hour's drive from Scarborough, close to North Yorkshire Moors National Park, Moors Railway, "Heartbeat" country, River Esk for fishing and boating; bowling nearby. Superb area for walkers. We offer two double and one twin room, all large, with en suite bathrooms, colour TV and tea/coffee making equipment. Central heating. Large lounge, separate diningroom. Substantial breakfast. Large parking area. Suitable for disabled. Bed and Breakfast from £18 to £19. Open Easter to October. Car not essential, near bus route.

WHITBY near. Mrs M. Bradshaw, Hawthorn Farm, Ellerby, Hinderwell, Whitby TS13 5JD (01947 840228). A pleasant farmhouse situated on the B1266 road, link road between A171 moors road and A174 coast road. Set in the beautiful North Yorkshire National Park, two miles from Runswick Bay, it makes an ideal base for all Yorkshire beauty spots and places of interest. Whitby is only seven miles away. Hawthorn Farm has central heating, dining room cum sitting room with colour TV, two double bedrooms (twin beds), shower room with washbasin and toilet. Tea/coffee making facilities. Bed and Breakfast from £12.50 per night.

YORK. Mrs Helen Butterworth, Wellgarth House, Wetherby Road, Rufforth, York YO22 3QB (01904 738592 or 738595). ♥♥ AA Listed. A warm welcome awaits you at Wellgarth House, ideally situated in Rufforth (B1224) three miles from York, one mile from the Ring Road (A1237) and convenient for "Park and Ride" into York City. This country guest house offers a high standard of accommodation with en suite Bed and Breakfast from £16. All rooms have complimentary tea/coffee making, colour TV with Sky. Rooms with four-poster or king-size beds also available. Excellent local pub just two minutes' walk away which serves lunches and dinners. Large private car park. Telephone or write for brochure. Access/Visa accepted.

YORK. Mrs Cynthia Fell, The Hall Country Guest House, Slingsby, York YO6 7AL (01653 628375).

♥♥♥ COMMENDED. The Hall is a Regency house of character set in five acres of delightful grounds, with croquet lawn and stream, situated in a 'real' English village with a ruined castle. A genuine Yorkshire welcome awaits every guest, many of whom return year after year. Excellent varied cuisine with fresh produce. Ideally situated for visiting York, the North Yorkshire Moors, coast and stately homes such as Castle Howard (three miles). We also have bicycles for hire. Double rooms, twin and family rooms, all en suite. A car is essential. Ample parking. Pets welcome. Brochure available. Open Easter to October. Table Licence. Bed and Breakfast from approximately £20; Dinner, Bed and Breakfast from £29.50 (£170 weekly).

YORK. Carol & Baz Oxtoby, Clifton View Guest House, 118/120 Clifton, York YO3 6BQ (01904 625047). ♥ Family-run guest house overlooking picturesque Clifton Green. Situated on main A19 (north), leave your car in our secure car park and enjoy a short 12 minute walk into the city. We have 13 comfortable bedrooms, all non-smoking and with colour TV, tea/coffee facilities, clock radio alarm and hairdryer. Most have a shower cubicle and en suite available. English breakfast menu. Comfortable residents' lounge where smoking is permitted. Children and pets welcome. Bed and Breakfast from £13 to £18 per person, according to room and season.

HOLLY HOUSE

Broad Lane, Appleton Roebuck, York YO5 7DS
Eunice and Bill Whitehead – Tel: 01904 744314
Fax: 01904 744546

Situated in open countryside close to York, this attractive house offers quiet relaxation. It is an ideal base for touring the Yorkshire Dales, Moors, Wolds and Coast. Holly House has five bedrooms (three en-suite) including one family room, a sitting room and separate TV lounge; central heating throughout; a heated indoor swimming pool and jacuzzi; pleasant gardens and ample parking will enhance your stay at Holly House. All bedrooms non-smoking: vegetarians can be catered for. Terms from £20.00

**Eunice and Bill Whitehead
Telephone: 01904 744314**

YORK. Mrs S. Hare, Chimneys, 18 Bootham Crescent, Bootham, York YO3 7AH (01904 644334).

Beautifully decorated house less than five minutes' walk from the city centre, on the north side of York on the A19. All rooms have central heating and washbasins, tea/coffee making facilities and colour TV. Access to rooms at all times. Enjoy breakfast in our olde worlde dining room. You will feel cosy and relaxed in between your sightseeing around historic York. We will guarantee you the wonderful Yorkshire welcome that is world-famous. Open all year. Bargain Winter Breaks for three nights or more. Sorry, no pets. Ample parking. Ground floor rooms and toilet available. Family-run thus ensuring personal attention. No smoking establishment.

YORK. Ron and Susie Spencer, The Grange Farmhouse, Skelton, York YO3 6YQ (Tel & Fax: 01904 470780; Mobile: 0585 432780). The Grange Farmhouse in York is an idyllic choice for a weekend away from it all or mid-week break. Commended by Yorkshire Tourist Board and Which? Good B&B Guide, it nestles in the tranquil village of Skelton (just three miles from the city centre) and is a lovely place to unwind and relax, with its walled garden and the solitude of the surrounding countryside to admire and soothe away your worldly cares. Five cottage-style rooms occupying a tranquil courtyard setting, each is en suite and has tea/coffee making facilities and colour TV. Full English breakfast is served in the main farmhouse.

YORK. Mrs Margaret Munday, Cornmill Lodge, 120 Haxby Road, York YO3 7JP (01904 620566).
👑👑 *COMMENDED.* The Cornmill Lodge is a deceptively large Victorian town house situated 12 minutes' walk from York Minster and city centre. We are AA and ETB Inspected. The beautifully refurbished house offers colour TVs, tea/coffee trays, clock radios; most rooms are en suite. A hearty full breakfast is served though we offer a vegetarian alternative. We have central heating, tourist information, full Fire Certificate and a guests' car park. A bank, post office and launderette are close by. Bed and Breakfast from £17 per person. We are a non-smoking guest house.

YORK. Mrs B. Lazenby, Rossmoor Park Farm, Melbourne, York YO4 4SZ (01759 318410). Working

farm. An attractive farmhouse standing in large gardens, park and woodland, 10 miles east of York. Comfortable accommodation in one double room with en suite shower room and one family room with private bathroom. Each has central heating, colour TV, tea/coffee facilities and hair dryers. There are separate tables in the dining room and a large lounge leading to a sunny patio overlooking the park. Ideally situated for exploring Yorkshire, being close to historic York and only a short drive from the east coast, Yorkshire Moors, Wolds and Dales. Golf, riding, swimming, fishing nearby. Sorry no pets and no smoking in the house. Bed and Breakfast from £20. Reductions for children.

YORK. Mr and Mrs G. Steel, Alder Carr House, York Road, Barmby Moor, York YO4 5HU (01759

380566; mobile 0585 277740). ♛ ♛ A spacious country house situated between the villages of Wilberfoss and Barmby Moor, set in 10 acres of grounds and enjoying lovely views of the Yorkshire Wolds. Close to the historic city of York, Castle Howard, the Moors, etc., also the unspoilt and uncrowded delights of the Wolds. A gliding club and the National Collection of Water Lilies are only three miles away. All bedrooms are en suite or with private bathroom. They are spacious and tastefully furnished; centrally heated and with TV and tea/coffee making facilities. An excellent range of local restaurants and village pubs offer evening meals. Open all year. Bed and full farmhouse Breakfast from £20 single, £34 double with en suite or private facilities.

YORK. Mrs K. Rhodes, Beckside House, Bolton Percy, York YO5 7AQ (01904 744246). Relax in the

peace and quiet of an unspoilt, small village (no through traffic); Bolton Percy is eight miles south of York and about three miles from Tadcaster. Accommodation consists of a comfortable twin-bedded room with private bathroom in a self-contained ground floor wing with own entrance and hall. Central heating; colour TV; tea/coffee making facilities. Cemetery Garden, featured on "Gardeners World", etc is nearby. Very convenient base for visiting York (20 minutes away) and for touring the Dales, North York Moors and East Coast. No smoking in house. Bed and Breakfast from £16.

YORK. Mr Roy Dodd, Charlton House, 1 Charlton Street, Bishopthorpe Road, York YO2 1JN

(01904 626961). Charlton House, built 1913, is a well established Guest House within easy walking distance of the rail and bus stations, City Centre, Minster, Castle Museum, Viking Centre and Racecourse. Personally managed to a high standard, it offers "Yorkshire hospitality" at its very best. Full English breakfast in a relaxed and friendly atmosphere, with no restrictions. Single, twin, double, family en suite spacious rooms with TV, tea/coffee facilities. Ground floor en suite bedroom available. Double glazed and centrally heated. Close to local shops, good restaurants and childen's play-park. Enclosed garden. Parking facilities. No smoking. Open all year. Bed and Breakfast from £15 per person. Reduced rates for children. Highly recommended.

YORK. Mrs R. Foster, Brookland House, Hull Road, Dunnington, York YO1 5LW (01904 489548).

Private house where a warm welcome awaits you. Beautiful appointed and spacious double rooms, one twin, one double, each with vanity units, washbasins, shaver points and a small single room. All have hostess tray, colour TV and are double glazed. Bathroom plus additional toilet for guests use only. Enjoy full English breakfast with homemade preserves in dining room overlooking delightful garden. No smoking. Five minute walk to pub serving evening meals from 6pm. Park and ride nearby. Private parking. Within easy reach of Eluington Air Museum, Castle Howard, North Yorkshire Moors and coastal resorts. Bed and Breakfast from £15.

YORK. Mrs Parker, Bridge House, Haxby Road, York YO3 7JL (01904 636161). Comfortable friendly guest house, 12 minutes' walk from Minster and city centre. Ideally situated for touring Yorkshire Moors, Dales and Coast, all within one hour's drive. All rooms have central heating, colour TV and tea/coffee facilities, also some en suite available. Bed and Breakfast from £15 per person.

THE GREEN GUEST HOUSE
31 BEWLAY ST., BISHOPTHORPE ROAD, YORK YO2 1JT
Telephone: (01904) 652509

Norma and Ted welcome you to their small Non-Smoking Guest House and offer you a full English or Vegetarian breakfast. Open all year with en suite rooms available. Colour TV and hospitality tray in all rooms. Only 10 minutes' walk to city centre. Evening meal on request. Children welcome at reduced rate. Bargain Breaks from November to March. A warm welcome awaits you with tea and biscuits on arrival. Bed and Breakfast from £16. Proprietors: Norma and Ted Long.

Member Yorkshire and Humberside Tourist Board 👑 Commended

YORK. Mrs Lorna Edmondson, The Lodge, 302 Strensall Road, Earswick, York YO3 9SW (01904 761387). 👑 👑 *COMMENDED.* The best for less, where guests become friends. This "no smoking" house surrounded by open fields is only three miles north of York. Large, well kept gardens where guests can sit and children play in safety. The upper floor of this modern house has two exceptionally large en suite bedrooms, shower room and toilet. Twin room on ground floor near main bathroom for those who cannot manage stairs. Full English Breakfast with own free-range eggs. We understand the needs of "allergy" diets and cater willingly for all others. Bed and Breakfast from only £17 with reductions for children.

YORK. Mr Mike Cundall, Orillia House, 89 The Village, Stockton on Forest, York YO3 9UP (01904 400600). 👑 👑 *COMMENDED.* A warm welcome awaits you at Orillia House, conveniently situated in the centre of the village, three miles north east of York, one mile from A64. The house dates back to the 17th century and has been restored to offer a high standard of comfort with modern facilities yet retaining its original charm and character. All rooms have private facilities, colour TV and tea/coffee making facilities. Our local pub provides excellent evening meals. We also have our own private car park. Bed and Breakfast from £18. Telephone for our brochure.

YORK. Four Poster Lodge Hotel, 68/70 Heslington Road, off Barbican Road, York YO1 5AU (01904 651170). 👑 👑 👑 Four Poster Lodge, imaginatively named and unique in its conception, is a Victorian house lovingly restored and furnished. We are almost a whisper away from historic York with all its fascinations — the Castle, the Shambles, the Viking Centre — invitingly close. When on holiday dream of the exciting days to come, and plan the tasks ahead amidst the lush covers of a four-poster bed. En suite facilities, hair dryers, colour TV, radio and hospitality trays. Licensed. Car park. Bed and hearty English Breakfast from £25 to £28 per person. Brochure available.

NORTH YORKSHIRE – RICH IN TOURIST ATTRACTIONS!
Dales, moors, castles, abbeys, cathedrals – you name it and you're almost sure to find it in North Yorkshire. Leading attractions include Castle Howard, the moorlands walks at Goathland, the Waterfalls at Falling Foss, Skipton, Richmond, Wensleydale, Bridestones Moor, Ripon Cathedral, Whitby, Settle and, of course, York itself.

YORK. Mont-Clare Guest House, 32 Claremont Terrace, Gillygate, York YO3 7EJ (01904 627054; Fax:01904 651011; E-mail: FredaRob32@aol.com).

👑 👑 👑 Take advantage and enjoy the convenience of City Centre accommodation in a quiet location close to magnificent York Minster. A warm and friendly welcome awaits you at the Mont-Clare. All rooms are en-suite, tastefully decorated, with colour TV (Satellite), Radio Alarm, Direct Dial Telephone, Hairdryer, Tea/Coffee Tray, Shoe Cleaning, etc. All of York's attractions are within walking distance and we are ideally situated for the Yorkshire Dales, Moors and numerous Stately Homes. Fire and Hygiene Certificates. Cleanliness, good food, pleasant surroundings and friendliness are our priorities. Private car park. Open all year. Reduced rates for weekly stay. Bed and Breakfast from £17.50 per person per night.

YORK. Pauleda House Hotel, 123 Clifton, York YO3 6BL (01904 634745; Tel & Fax: 01904 621327). Enjoy superb accommodation centrally situated only minutes away from all the historic attractions. A warm and friendly welcome awaits you at Pauleda, a small family-run hotel offering excellent value for money. All rooms are en suite and tastefully equipped, some with four-poster beds, colour TV with satellite, tea/coffee tray, etc. Car park. Bed and Breakfast from £20 to £35.

YORK. Tree's Hotel, 8 Clifton Green, York YO3 6LH (01904 623597). 👑 👑 👑 Small, elegant hotel, privately owned and managed. Attractive location overlooking Clifton Green. Just 10 minutes' walk to the city centre and York Minster. Spacious bedrooms, some with en-suite bathrooms and all with colour televisions. Children welcome. Private car parking. Bed and Breakfast from £17.50. Reductions for children and Senior Citizens. Bargain Short Breaks between November and March. AA and RAC Listed. Contact: Mr D.G. Tree.

YORK. Gordon and Trudi Smith, Rosedale Guest House, Wetherby Road, Rufforth, York YO2 3QB (01904 738297). 👑 👑 *COMMENDED*. Rufforth is a delightful village situated three and a half miles west from the historic city of York, ideally situated for touring Yorkshire Moors and Dales. Rosedale offers you the comfort of a family guest house; all our rooms are furnished to a high standard, some with en suite facilities, and for the comfort of our guests we provide tea/coffee making facilities and TV in all bedrooms. Guest lounge. Full central heating. Private parking. Children welcome, reduced rates available. Low season rates available. Open all year. Bed and full English Breakfast from £19.

YORK. Mrs Barbara Curtis, Cumbria House, 2 Vyner Street, Haxby Road, York YO3 7HS (01904

636817). ETB Listed COMMENDED. AA QQQ. A warm and friendly welcome awaits you at Cumbria House — an elegant, tastefully decorated Victorian guest house, where comfort and quality is assured. We are convenient for the city, being only 12 minutes' walk from York's historic Minster and yet within minutes of the northern by-pass (A1237). A launderette, post office and children's park are close by. All rooms have colour TV, radio alarms and tea/coffee facilities. Most are en suite or have certain private facilities. Central heating. Fire Certificate. Guests' car park. Full English breakfast or vegetarian alternative. £17 to £21 per person. "You arrive as guests but leave as friends".

YORK. Mav and Maureen Davidson, "Oaklands" Guest House, 351 Strensall Road, Old Earswick,

York YO3 9SW (01904 768443). ♛♛ COMMENDED. A warm welcome awaits you at our attractive family house set in open countryside, yet only three miles from York with easy access to the A64, A1 and A1237. Ideally situated for City, Coast, Dales and Moors. Our comfortable bedrooms are centrally heated with vanity unit, colour TV, razor point, tea-making equipment and radio alarms. En-suite facilities available. A more than ample Breakfast is served in a light, airy dining room. Your hosts, Maureen and Mav, look forward to seeing you. Bed and full English Breakfast from £17. Discounts available. Open all year. No pets. Smoking in garden only.

YORK. Peggy Swann, South Newlands Farm, Selby Road, Riccall, York YO4 6QR (01757 248203).

Friendliness, comfort and good traditional cooking are always on offer to our guests. The kettle's always on the boil in our kitchen, and a comfortable lounge is yours to relax in at any time. Easy access to York and the Dales and Moors. No smoking please. Dogs welcome; day kenneling available.

YORK. Mrs J.Y. Tree, Inglewood Guest House, 7 Clifton Green, York YO3 6LH (01904 653523).

♛♛♛ The Inglewood Guest House has a warm and friendly atmosphere where guests will really feel at home. The bedrooms all have colour TV and some have en suite bathrooms. Open all year with central heating. Breakfast is an enjoyable experience in our pleasant dining room with dark wooden tables and chairs. Helpful information is given on where to go and what to see. It is an ideal centre for exploring York and making day excursions to many market towns and attractive villages around York. Places of historic interest also to visit. Children are welcome. Sorry, no pets. A car is not essential, but there is parking. Bed and Breakfast from £17.50; reductions for children.

YORK. Mrs Susan Viscovitch, The Manor at Acaster Malbis, Acaster Malbis, York YO2 1UL (Tel &

Fax: 01904 706723). ♛♛♛ HIGHLY COMMENDED. Atmospheric Manor in rural tranquillity with our own private lake set in five and a half acres of beautiful mature grounds. Preservation orders on all trees with abundant bird life. Fish in the lake, cycle or walk, bring your own boat for river cruising. Close to racecourse and only 10 minutes' car journey from the city or take the leisurely river bus (Easter to October). Conveniently situated to take advantage of the Dales, Moors, Wolds and splendid coastline. Find us via A64 exiting for Copmanthorpe, York, Thirsk, Harrogate or Bishopthorpe (Sim Balk Lane). 10 centrally heated en suite bedrooms with direct-dial phones, hair dryers, TV, courtesy tray; dining room with open coal fire. Licensed. Optional Evening Meal. Bed and Breakfast from £24 to £32 per person per night. For details SAE or telephone. See our Colour Advertisement on the Outside Back Cover of this guide.

YORK. Keith Jackman, Dairy Guesthouse, 3 Scarcroft Road, York YO2 1ND (01904 639367).

Beautifully appointed Victorian townhouse that was once the local dairy! Well equipped cottage-style rooms that include colour TV, CD players, hair dryers and hot drinks facilities. Some en suite rooms, one four-poster room. Informal and relaxed, non smoking environment. Offers traditional or vegetarian menu. Bed and Breakfast from £17 per person. Please write or phone for a colour brochure or reservation.

GUESTHOUSE
Traditional and Wholefood

YORK. Mr N. Douthwaite and Family, The Bedford Hotel, 108/110 Bootham, York YO3 7DG (01904 624412). 🐾 🐾🐾 *COMMENDED*.

Family-run licensed hotel with guaranteed space in private car park. A short walk along historic Bootham takes you to the heart of the city and York Minster. Rooms en suite with colour TV and tea/coffee making facilities. Full central heating. Children welcome. Sorry no pets. Evening meals served. Bed and Breakfast from £23 per person per night. AA Listed QQQ. RAC Acclaimed. Mastercard/Visa/Switch/American Express cards accepted. Winter mini breaks available.

YORK. Feversham Lodge, 1 Feversham Crescent, York YO3 7HQ (01904 623882). 🐾 🐾

Bob and Jill Peacock, the proprietors of Feversham Lodge, offer you a warm welcome and a pleasant stay in York. Conveniently situated for the Yorkshire Moors and "Herriot" country, yet only ten minutes' walk from the Minster and city centre. Frequent bus service almost from the door to the city, bus and rail stations. The Lodge was converted from a 19th century manse in 1981 and retains much of its grandeur. Some rooms en suite. Central heating. Diningroom, TV lounge. Colour TV in bedrooms. Car park. Full Fire Certificate. Tea/coffee making facilities. Bed and Breakfast from £16 to £20. Enjoy your stay with us.

YORK. Mrs J.W. Harrison, Fairthorne, 356 Strensall Road, Earswick, York YO3 9SW (01904 768609; Fax: 01904 768609). 🐾 🐾 *COMMENDED*. John and Joan Harrison invite you for a restful holiday in a peaceful country setting — a dormer bungalow with central heating, TV, shaver points, tea making facilities and en suite in bedrooms; TV lounge and dining room. Pleasant family atmosphere. Situated three miles north of York, within easy reach of East Coast and Yorkshire Moors and near golf course. Bus stop 50 yards if required. Bed and Breakfast from £15 per night. Reductions for children. Private car park and large garden. Open all year.

YORK. Stanley House, Stanley Street, York YO3 7NW (01904 637111). 👑👑 *COMMENDED.* Stanley

House is situated just 10 minutes' walk from Britain's most beautiful and fascinating city. Our aim is to provide you with comfort and a friendly base from which you can discover the history and ancient charm of York. All rooms have en-suite facilities with colour TV and courtesy tray. There is off street car parking and payphone for guests' use. We are open all year except Christmas and Boxing Day. Sorry, no smoking or pets. Bed and Breakfast from £18.

YORK. Mrs Diana S. Tindall, Newton Guest House, Neville Street, Haxby Road, York YO3 7NP

(01904 635627). 👑 *APPROVED.* Diana and John offer all their guests a friendly and warm welcome to their Victorian end townhouse, a few minutes' walk from city centre, York's beautiful Minster, city walls and museums. Situated near an attractive park with good bowling greens. York is an ideal base for touring Yorkshire Moors, Dales and coastline. One bedroom (private facilities outside), all other rooms en suite and have colour TV, tea/coffee making tray. Full central heating, Fire Certificate. Private car park. Personal attention. We are a non-smoking house.

YORK. The Palm Court, 17 Huntington Road, York YO3 7RB (01904 639387). 👑👑 *COMMENDED.* A

very warm welcome awaits you at our elegant Victorian family-run hotel which offers excellent value for money. Overlooking the River Foss and only five minutes' walk to the city centre. Spacious double, twin and family en suite rooms with colour TV, tea/coffee making facilities and hairdryer; private car park. The Collier family assure you of a comfortable and enjoyable stay. Bed and Breakfast from £20 per person. Weekly rates available. Please write or telephone for colour brochure.

YORK. Carolyn and Ian McNabb, The Hazelwood, 24-25 Portland Street, Gillygate, York YO3 7EH

(01904 626548; Fax: 01904 628032). 👑👑 *COMMEN-DED.* AA QQQQ Selected, RAC Acclaimed. Non-smoking. Situated in the centre of York only 400 yards from York Minster yet in an extremely quiet location and with private car park the Hazelwood is an elegant Victorian townhouse offering excellent value for money. Our comfortable bedrooms (some with four-poster beds) are all en suite and have colour TV, hairdryer, radio alarm and tea/coffee making facilities. Relax in our secluded garden or in our peaceful guests' lounge with its range of books and visitor information and where tea and coffee are always available. Our quality breakfasts cater for all tastes including vegetarian. Bed and Breakfast from £19.50.

YORK. Mrs S. Jackson, Victoria Villa Guest House, 72 Heslington Road, York YO1 5AU (01904

631647). 10 minutes' walk from city centre. Comfortable double, twin, single and family bedrooms, all with TV. Children and pets welcome. Open all year. Bed and Breakfast from £13 to £18.

YORK near. Mrs Jean A. Tomlinson, Wheelgate Guest House, 7 Kirkgate, Sherburn-in-Elmet, Near

York LS25 6BH (01977 682231). Wheelgate Guest House is set in the attractive village of Sherburn-in-Elmet, only 20 minutes' drive from York, Selby or Leeds. Easy access to M62 and M1 motorways and an ideal stop when travelling north/ south. Sherburn is easily accessible, only three miles off the AI on the B1222 road. The house is olde worlde, set in attractive gardens; central heating throughout; guests' lounge; washbasins, tea/coffee making facilities, colour TV in all rooms. Superb home cooking; Evening Meals and packed lunches available. Car parking. Children and pets welcome. Open all year. Licensed. Terms on request.

SOUTH YORKSHIRE

HOLMFIRTH (Penistone). Ann Unitt, Aldermans Head Manor, Hartcliffe Hill Road, Langsett,

Stocksbridge, Sheffield S30 5GY (Tel and Fax: 01226 766209). ♛♛♛ *HIGHLY COMMENDED.* Award-winning Licensed Guest House. Set in 50 acres of dramatic countryside, the Manor enjoys panoramic views across the Langsett, Midhopestones reservoirs and the Peak District moorland beyond. Seven centuries ago the monks of Kirkstead Abbey owned the farm, and today the welcoming atmosphere of peace and tranquillity still prevails — just right for relaxing and unwinding. Four bedrooms, some en suite, TV and tea/coffee making facilities in all rooms; full central heating. Home cooking with local produce. Bed and Breakfast from £22.50. Ideal centre for walking and exploring the Derbyshire and Yorkshire countryside. A non smoking household. Brochure on request.

WEST YORKSHIRE

HAWORTH. Newsholme Manor Hotel and Restaurant, Slaymaker Lane, on to Slack Lane, Oakworth, Near Haworth BD22 0RQ (01535 642964; Fax: 01535 645629). ETB Listed.  The Tudor style restaurant has retained its oak beams from the original 15th century building, whilst the en suite bedrooms offer the utmost in modern comfort. Lunches and bar meals served daily from 12 noon — 2pm. Evening meals Tuesday — Saturday, also Traditional Sunday Lunch. Fully licensed bar — open to non residents. Large car park. For further details please contact: **Mr C.T. Sexton**.

PONTEFRACT. Jennifer and Richard Adams, Bridge Guest House, Wentbridge, Pontefract WF8 3JJ (01977 620314). Situated in a quiet village just off A1, half-way between London and Scotland; handy for the Dales and Peak District or touring East Coast. Family-run guest house with a warm welcome. Accommodation comprises two en suite rooms downstairs; one double, three twin and one single bedrooms upstairs, all with washbasin, colour TV and tea/coffee making facilities; two bathrooms. Central heating. Off-street parking. Children and pets welcome. Bed and Breakfast from £20 to £24. Directions: four miles from M62 just off A1 on the Old Great North Road.

PONTEFRACT/WENTBRIDGE. Mrs I. Goodworth, The Corner Cafe, Wentbridge, Pontefract WF8 3JJ (01977 620316). Tourist Board Listed. A sixteenth century cottage featuring oak beams and a lovely secluded garden with plenty of car parking space, set in a small village but within easy reach of main roads (a quarter-of-a-mile A1). Accommodation includes two single, one double, one twin with private bathroom and two family rooms en suite, all with washbasins, TV, tea and coffee making facilities and full central heating. Non-smoking accommodation available. Two family rooms en suite in annexe. This picturesque village has three very nice old Inns and restaurants where evening meals or snacks can be obtained. Children welcome. Terms from £18. Open all year round, except Christmas.

ISLE OF WIGHT

CARISBROOKE. Mrs V.A. Skeats, The Mount, 1 Calbourne Road, Carisbrooke, Near Newport PO30 5AP (01983 522173/524359). "The Mount" is superbly situated in the charming village of Carisbrooke, overlooking Carisbrooke Castle. Ideally located for all amenities. Delightful lanes and downs for walking. Information/requirements of maps and details on local activities can be provided. Rooms are comfortably furnished with washbasins/razor points. Own keys. Private car park. Lock-up cycle shelter. Children welcome. We offer homely accommodation in a Victorian house with personal service. Bed and Breakfast from £16. Reductions for children. Any day bookings accepted. For further details, please write or telephone.

FRESHWATER. Mr and Mrs Reynolds, Brookside Forge Hotel, Brookside Road, Freshwater PO40 9ER (01983 754644).

♛♛♛ A substantial detached property recently converted and extended to meet the hotel requirements of today. Ideally located for the beautiful West Wight countryside and the three coastal bays of Freshwater, Colwell and Totland. All bedrooms are en suite and have colour TV, tea/coffee making facilities and hair dryers. Lounge has colour TV and is available at all times. We serve an excellent standard of cuisine and enjoy an enviable reputation on the Island. Terraced lawns with sun chairs, games lawn and patio provide a peaceful haven after your day's activities. Bed and Breakfast from £19.50 per night; Bed, Breakfast and three-course Evening Meal from £27.45 per night. Reduced rates for groups and off season rates. We also have a self catering bungalow with two bedrooms sleeping four to six persons. From £200 per week. Brochure available.

RYDE. Mr David D. Wood, Seaward Guest House, 14/16 George Street, Ryde PO33 2EW (Tel & Fax: 01983 563168). ETB Listed *COMMENDED*. Seaward is a friendly, family-run, 200 year old guest house. All rooms have colour TV, tea/coffee facilities, washbasins and razor points. Some en suite rooms available. Telephone, hair dryer and ironing facilities available for guests' use. Mini bus for collection from ferries or island tours. An excellent base from which to tour the island, with bus, train stations and ferry/hovercraft terminals, as well as shops and sea front within three minutes' walk. Open all year. Special rates for Senior Citizens. Full English, Continental or vegetarian breakfast. Bed and Breakfast from £14; Bed, Breakfast and Evening Meal from £21.

TOTLAND BAY. Mrs Vera F. McMullan, Strang Hall, Uplands, Totland Bay PO39 0DZ (Tel & Fax: 01983 753189).

Strang Hall is an Edwardian family home decorated in the arts and crafts style with splendid views over the downs and the Solent. Set peacefully in the hills above Totland Bay, the house has recently been modernised to provide spacious comfortable accommodation. The two acre garden leads onto a short walk to the beach at Totland. The village of Freshwater (with swimming pool and other amenities) is one mile away and Yarmouth ferry port is two miles. One double, one twin/family and one single rooms; en suite available. Children welcome, but sorry, no pets. Bed and Breakfast from £18 to £20. Evening meals by arrangement. Closed Christmas. Non-smokers please.

PLEASE SEND A STAMPED ADDRESSED ENVELOPE WITH ENQUIRIES

Full Board • Bed & Breakfast • Self-Catering

Campus Holidays

How about a University holiday this year, or perhaps you'd fancy a College?

If you are interested, you'll be joining thousands of non-students who have discovered the delights of the Campus as a value-for-money holiday destination.

For 1997 around 100,000 places are available during the summer and even during term-time many campuses can offer holiday facilities. The various establishments have organised themselves into two marketing groups, both of which will be more than happy to provide you with brochures and information on request.

THE BRITISH UNIVERSITIES ACCOMMODATION CONSORTIUM (BUAC)

First in the field, the members of BUAC can now offer accommodation at over 60 venues nationwide for individual and family holidays, for conferences and study vacations. From Aberdeen to Exeter, from Aberystwyth to Norwich, you will find comfortable and modern accommodation at affordable prices. *Further details from: Carole Formon, BUAC Ltd., University Park, Nottingham NG7 2RD (0115 950 4571).*

THE HIGHER EDUCATION ACCOMMODATION CONSORTIUM (HEAC)

Representing a wider range of institutions as the name suggests, HEAC now has over 70 members with around 30,000 beds available throughout Britain, in seaside, rural and city centre locations.

For further information you should contact: HEAC Ltd., 36 Collegiate Crescent, Sheffield S10 2BP (0114 268 3759).

LONDON. King's Campus Vacation Bureau, 98/2, King's College London, 127 Stamford Street, Waterloo, London SE1 9NQ (0171-928 3777; Fax: 0171-928 5777). Affordable accommodation with some en suite and some parking in Halls of Residence in central and inner London for individuals, families and groups during College vacations. Bed and Breakfast from £17.50 per person; Room only from £13.25 per person per night.

Dumfries from the River Nith.

SCOTLAND

ABERDEENSHIRE

ABERDEEN. Terrace Private Hotel, 1 Springbank Terrace, Aberdeen AB11 6LS (Tel & Fax: 01224

581278). A family-run establishment with a warm and friendly atmosphere offering clean and comfortable accommodation for the non-smoker. The hotel is in a central position within 10 minutes' walking distance of the main shopping centres, rail and bus stations, and His Majesty's Theatre. Also nearby is Duthie Park and Winter Gardens. An ideal base for exploring this unique corner of Scotland with its Whisky and Castle Trails and Royal Deeside. All rooms have TV and tea/coffee making facilities; en suite available. Access at all times. Off-street parking. Colour brochure available.

ABERDEEN. John and Beth Fraser, Abbian Guest House, 148 Crown Street, Aberdeen AB11 6HS

(Tel & Fax: 01224 575826). STB 🦢🦢 *COMMENDED.* John and Beth Fraser give a friendly family welcome at this Victorian, terraced city centre town house. It is the ideal starting point for exploring Royal Deeside and the Grampian Region with its unique Whisky and Castle Trails. Situated within 400 yards of Union Street, the main shopping area, it is convenient for the cinemas and varied night life of this popular Granite City. The bus and rail stations and the sea ferry terminal are nearby. The popular Duthie Park, with its magnificent Winter Gardens open all year, is also easily accessible. Recently totally refurbished, all bedrooms have en suite facilities and teletext TV. There is a free video, cassette and book library for guests.

PUBLISHER'S NOTE

While every effort is made to ensure accuracy, we regret that FHG Publications cannot accept responsibility for errors, omissions or misrepresentation in our entries or any consequences thereof. Prices in particular should be checked because we go to press early. We will follow up complaints but cannot act as arbiters or agents for either party.

BALLATER. The Alexandra Hotel, 12 Bridge Square, Ballater AB35 5QJ (013397 55376; Fax: 013397 55466). 🦢🦢🦢 *HIGHLY COMMENDED.* Situated in the centre of Ballater on Royal Deeside the Alexandra Hotel offers guests the hospitality of a small country hotel whilst providing luxury accommodation, service and outstanding cuisine. Our seven centrally heated bedrooms are all en suite and have colour TV, direct-dial telephone, tea/coffee facilities and the many little extras found in a quality hotel. Our new lounge provides the perfect atmosphere to relax. Ballater is the ideal holiday centre for touring and enjoying natural beauty and pleasures. Colour brochure available.

BANFF. Anne and Jim Mackie, The Orchard, Duff House, Banff AB45 3TA (01261 812146). A warm and friendly welcome is assured. Our traditional house stands within three-quarters of an acre of grounds and enjoys complete privacy due to the surrounding woodland area. We are within comfortable walking distance of Banff, Duff House Royal Golf Club, Duff House and surrounding walks. Centrally heated accommodationm comprises visitors lounge, one double and three twin-bedded rooms, all with shower en suite, colour TV, alarm clock, hair dryer and hostess tray. Children welcome. Ample parking. Bed and Breakfast from £19.50 per person.

HUNTLY. Mrs D. Ingram, Strathlene, MacDonald Street, Huntly AB54 8EW (01466 792664). STB 🦢 *COMMENDED.* A warm welcome awaits you at Strathlene, a detached Granite house close to town centre and railway station. Ideal base for touring, Castle and Whisky Trails and coast. Accommodation copmprises one double and one twin bedrooms with washbasin, central heating, tea/coffee facilities and hair dryer. Shared bathroom with shower. Lounge with TV. On arrival guests are given a pot of tea and home-baked scones. Bed and Breakfast from £14 to £16 per person.

Key to Tourist Board Ratings

The Crown Scheme
(England, Scotland & Wales)

Covering hotels, motels, private hotels, guesthouses, inns, bed & breakfast, farmhouses. Every Crown classified place to stay is inspected annually. *The classification:* Listed then 1-5 Crown indicates the range of facilities and services. Higher quality standards are indicated by the terms APPROVED, COMMENDED, HIGHLY COMMENDED and DELUXE.

The Key Scheme
(also operates in Scotland using a Crown symbol)

Covering self-catering in cottages, bungalows, flats, houseboats, houses, chalets, etc. Every Key classified holiday home is inspected annually. *The classification:* 1-5 Key indicates the range of facilities and equipment. Higher quality standards are indicated by the terms APPROVED, COMMENDED, HIGHLY COMMENDED and DELUXE.

The Q Scheme
(England, Scotland & Wales)

Covering holiday, caravan, chalet and camping parks. Every Q rated park is inspected annually for its quality standards. The more ✓ in the Q – up to 5 – the higher the standard of what is provided.

HUNTLY. Mrs R. Shand, "Newmarnoch", 48 King Street, Huntly AB54 8HP (01466 792018). Detached bungalow in own grounds, spacious parking area, all local amenities within five minutes' walking distance to town centre. A warm welcome to the market town, located for places of interest — Whisky and Castle Trails, Falconry Centre, outdoor bowling green, golf course, rainbow trout fishing, etc. Accommodation comprises one double room en suite, one twin room, tea/coffee making facilities and TV. En suite room £16 per person, twin room £14 per person. Open January to December.

RHYNIE. Gordon Arms Hotel, Main Street, Rhynie AB54 4HB (01464 861615). Country village Hotel offering Bed and Breakfast. All home cooking. Clean and comfortable. Separate TV lounge. Under personal supervision of proprietors at all times. Ideal for touring Whisky/Castle Trails, hill walking, fishing, shooting and golf nearby. Falconry, Archaeolink Prehistoric Park and swiming pool approximately nine miles. Aberdeen 37 miles, Inverness 56 miles. Rates from £14.50; Evening Meal available. Further details available on request.

STONEHAVEN. Mrs Aileen Paton, Woodside of Glasslaw, Stonehaven AB39 3XQ (01569 763799). ✿✿ *COMMENDED.* Modern extended bungalow set in one acre of gardens with ample safe parking. Four centrally heated en suite bedrooms with colour TV and hospitality trays. Lounge/dining room and fitted kitchen are available to guests. Accommodation is accessible for disabled guests. The guest house is situated two miles south of the seaside town of Stonehaven and close to the spectacular Dunnottar Castle. Aberdeen is 15 miles away and Stonehaven is a good base for touring Royal Deeside. Bed and Breakfast from £18 per person.

STONEHAVEN. Mrs C. Pollock, Ormesby Guest House, 26 Dunnottar Avenue, Stonehaven AB39 2JJ (01569 763840). Quiet family-run guest house offering Bed and Breakfast accommodation in clean comfortable bedrooms, all with colour TV and tea/coffee facilities. Accommodation consists of one family/double room with en suite facilities, one double and one twin rooms with washbasin; bath, shower and two toilets. Non-smoking. Parking available. Harbour, town centre, bowling green, swimming pool, tennis courts and golf courses all within walking distance. Stovehaven is just 15 miles south of Aberdeen and makes an ideal base for touring Royal Deeside. Prices from £16 to £18 double, £18 to £20 single per person per night.

TURRIFF. Mrs Christina Roebuck, Lendrum Farm, Birkenhills, Turriff AB53 8HA (Tel & Fax: 01888 544285). ✿✿ *COMMENDED.* Situated halfway between Fyvie and Turriff, Lendrum is an historic working farm set in the lovely Buchan countryside. Visit the picturesque fishing villages and breathtaking coastal scenery of the unspoilt north east coast or spend a day or two touring historic castles, houses and gardens and whisky distilleries. Fyvie Castle, Duff House, Haddo House are all nearby. We offer a warm welcome, comfortable farmhouse accommodation, furnished with antiques, good food and peace and quiet. En suite bathroom, central heating, guests' sitting room, tea/coffee making facilities and TV in bedrooms. Bed and full Scottish Breakfast from £20 per person.

ARGYLL & BUTE

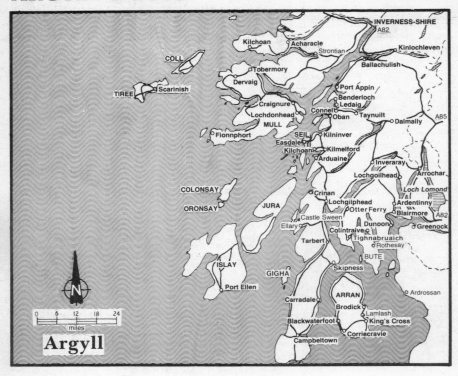

INVERNESS-SHIRE
A82
Kilchoan
Acharacle
Strontian
Kinlochleven
Tobermory
Ballachulish
COLL
Dervaig
Port Appin
Benderloch
Ledaig
Scarinish
Craignure
Connel
TIREE
Lochdonhead
Oban
Taynuilt
Dalmally
MULL
A85
Fionnphort
Kilninver
SEIL
Easdale
Kilmelford
Kilchoan
Arduaine
Inveraray
Lochgoilhead
Arrochar
Loch Lomond
COLONSAY
Crinan
Ardentinny
ORONSAY
Lochgilphead
Otter Ferry
Blairmore
JURA
A82
Castle Sween
Dunoon
Greenock
Ellary
Colintraive
Tighnabruaich
Tarbert
Rothesay
BUTE
ISLAY
Skipness
GIGHA
Ardrossan
ARRAN
Brodick
Port Ellen
Carradale
Lamlash
Blackwaterfoot
King's Cross
Corriecravie
Campbeltown

0   6   12   18   24
miles

Argyll

BALLACHULISH (near Glencoe). Craiglinnhe Guest House, Ballachulish PA39 4JX (Tel & Fax: 01855 811270; E-mail: craiglinnhe@ballachulish. almac.co.uk). STB ♛ ♛ ♛ *COMMENDED*. Craiglinnhe is an enchanting Victorian villa on a splendid spot outside the village on the shores of Loch Linnhe, surrounded by spectacular loch and mountain scenery. All bedrooms are fully en suite. A warm welcome, relaxed atmosphere, excellent food and a residents' licence. Beautiful gardens and private parking. Ideal base for exploring the Western Highlands. Bed and Breakfast from £20 to £23 per person per night. Dinner £11 (optional). Pets by arrangement. Closed November. Ask for colour brochure.

BALLACHULISH (near Glencoe). Mr and Mrs J.A. MacLeod, Lyn-Leven Guest House, Ballachulish PA39 4JW (01855 811392; Fax: 01855 811600). ♛ ♛ ♛ *COMMENDED*. Lyn-Leven, a superior licensed guest house overlooking Loch Leven, with every comfort, in the beautiful Highlands of Scotland, situated one mile from historic Glencoe village. Four double, two twin and two family bedrooms, all rooms en suite; sitting room and dining room. Central heating. Excellent and varied home cooking served daily. Children welcome at reduced rates. An ideal location for touring. Fishing, walking and climbing in the vicinity. The house, open all year, is suitable for disabled guests. Car not essential but private car park provided. Dinner, Bed and Breakfast from £17 to £19.50 per person. AA QQQQ Selected, RAC Acclaimed.

Tigh nan Lochan Guest House

Assapol, Bunessan, Isle of Mull PA67 6DW
Telephone 01681 700 541

Tigh nan Lochan is a modern, family run Guest House with large garden and private parking overlooking Loch Assapol. All bedrooms are tastefully decorated and have en suite facilities, with colour TV and tea/coffee trays. Breakfast is served in the conservatory off the resident's lounge. We are in an ideal situation for fishing, wildlife, bird watching and walking, half mile from Bunessan and six miles from Iona/Staffa Ferries. A warm friendly welcome awaits you.

Open all year. Bed and Breakfast from £19–£22. Tourist Board ♥♥ Commended.

AA **Rockhill Farm Country House** RAC
Est. 1960
Ardbrecknish, by Dalmally, Argyll PA33 1BH

17th century guesthouse in spectacular waterside setting on Loch Awe with breathtaking views to Ben Cruachan where comfort, peace and tranquility reign supreme. Small private Highland Estate breeding Hanoverian competition horses. 1200 metres free trout fishing. 5 delightful rooms with all modern facilities. First class highly acclaimed home cooking with much home grown produce. Wonderful area for touring the western Highlands, Glencoe, the Trossachs and Kintyre. Ideal for climbing, walking, bird and animal watching. Boat trips locally and from Oban (30 miles) to Mull, Iona, Fingal's Cave and other Islands. Early booking discount scheme. **Telephone 01866 833218.**

DALMALLY. Jinty and John Burke, Orchy Bank Guest House, Stronmilchan, Dalmally PA33 1AS **(01838 200370). STB Listed** *COMMENDED.* You will be sure to receive a friendly, warm welcome at this 110 year old Victorian house with eight guest rooms. Situated on the bank of the River Orchy with a 200 year old bridge at the bottom of the large garden. The area has very good river and loch fishing, a nine hole golf course and is ideal for bird watching, hill walking and deer stalking. All rooms have tea making facilities, heaters and electric blankets. Large guest lounge with log fire. Bed and full Breakfast from £17 per person.

DUNOON. Mrs M. Kohls, Ashgrove Guest House, Wyndham Road, Innellan, Dunoon PA23 7SH **(01369 830306; Fax: 01369 830776).** Situated in the village of Innellan, four miles south of Dunoon, in four acres of grounds Ashgrove has ponies, goats, hens, ducks, geese and other small animals. Guests can enjoy leisurely woodland walks, boat or coach trips, or simply relax in the secluded gardens with outstanding views over the Firth of Clyde. Golf, tennis, bowls, fishing, pony trekking are all nearby. Family run guesthouse with a friendly, informal atmosphere. All rooms have en suite shower, WC and washbasin, colour TV, tea/coffee making facilities. Dogs and other pets welcome. Open all year. Bed and Breakfast from £19 daily. Reductions for children. Self catering flat also available.

PLEASE SEND A STAMPED ADDRESSED ENVELOPE WITH ENQUIRIES

KILMARTIN. Kilmartin Hotel, Kilmartin, By Lochgilphead PA31 8RQ (01546 510250; Fax: 01546

606370). Kilmartin Hotel welcomes you to the glorious splendours of mid Argyll's countryside. Surrounded by the finest examples of standing stones and cairns, the Hotel provides the ideal centre from which to explore this area of particular historical and archeological importance. The hotel offers Scottish hospitality at its best. Excellent quality home cooked food is available thoughout the day, with comfortable accommodation at very affordable prices for those wishing to extend their visit. CEUD MILE FAILTE — a hundred thousand welcomes.

KINLOCHLEVEN. Elsie Robertson, Edencoille, Garbhien Road, Kinlochleven PA40 4SE (01855

831358). 🏵 *COMMENDED.* A warm welcome and excellent home cooking at our family-run Bed and Breakfast. All five rooms centrally heated and have tea/coffee facilities, colour TV, washbasins and hair dryers. Perfect base for touring, fishing, ski-ing, climbing, walking or relaxing. We are situated opposite the Mamores which are famous for their 12 Munros which are within five minutes' walk from Edencoille. Bed and Breakfast £16 per person; Evening Dinner £9 per person. Extensive menu.

LOCHGOILHEAD. Mrs Rosemary Dolan, The Shorehouse Inn, Lochgoilhead PA24 8AJ (01301 703340). Friendly informal Inn, fully licensed, has seven letting rooms, central heating and double glazing. There are two family, three twin, one single and one double bedrooms. Residents' lounge, a bar of unusual character and licensed restaurant. Home cooking, bar meals. Formerly the old manse on a historic site with lochside and panoramic views looking southward down Loch Goil, situated in the village on the shore. Local amenities include water sports, fishing, pony trekking, tennis, bowls, golf, swimming pool, curling in winter and a good area for hill walking. Some rooms with private facilities. Fully licensed. One hour travel time from Glasgow. Open all year round. Ideal for winter or summer breaks. Rates from £14 Bed and Breakfast.

OBAN. Mrs J. Waugh, Foxholes Hotel, Cologin, Lerags, Oban PA34 4SE (01631 564982). 🏵 🏵 🏵

HIGHLY COMMENDED. Enjoy peace and tranquillity at Foxholes, situated in its own grounds in a quiet glen, three miles from Oban. We have magnificent views of surrounding countryside, all bedrooms en suite, colour TV, tea/coffee making facilities. Enjoy our supberb six-course table d'hôte menu and large selection of wines. Send for colour brochure and tariff. Bed and Breakfast from £25. Please write or telephone for further information.

OBAN. Mrs C. MacDonald, Bracker, Polvinister Road, Oban PA34 5TN (01631 564302). ❦ ❦
COMMENDED. Bracker is a modern bungalow built in 1975 and extended recently to cater for visitors. We have three guest rooms — two double and one twin-bedded, all en suite with TV and tea/coffee making facilities. Small TV lounge and dining room. Private parking. The house is situated in a beautiful quiet residential area of Oban and is within walking distance of the town (approximately eight to 10 minutes) and the golf course. Friendly hospitality and comfortable accommodation. Bed and Breakfast £16 to £18. Non-smoking.

OBAN. Mrs Gill Cadzow, Duachy Farm, Kilninver, Oban PA34 4QN (Tel & Fax: 01852 316244).
Duachy Farm is situated 10 miles south of Oban on the B844 overlooking Loch Seil. One large double room with two double beds and adjoining bathroom on the ground floor with a beautiful view over Loch. Door out to garden and small patio. Tea/coffee making faciltiies, colour TV. Use of rowing boat on loch. Private beach one mile. Pubs and shops four miles away. Open April to end October. Prices from £18 per person. Cot and camp bed available.

OBAN. Donra Holiday Properties. ❦ ❦, ❦ ❦ ❦ **and** ❦ ❦ ❦ ❦ COMMENDED. Offers the best of both worlds — town and country. Comfortable self catering properties in Oban sleeping two to six persons, or relax at Torlin House with tastefully decorated en suite rooms. Also our properties on the Isle of Luing offer a tranquil and beautiful location for quality relaxation. Wildlife abounds, and there is a richness of Celtic and Norse myths to explore. Ideal for water sports enthusiasts while ensuring a sanctuary of calm for those of a less vigorous temperament. Boat trips and bicycles available. Open all year. Self catering from £150 to £295 per week; Bed and Breakfast from £15 to £22. Reductions for three nights or more. Details from **Mrs S. Russell, Torlin, Glencruitten Road, Oban PA34 4EP (01631 564339).**

OBAN. Tony and Carol Ridley, Briarbank, Glencruitten Road, Oban PA34 4DN (Tel & Fax: 01631 566549). ❦ ❦ ❦ COMMENDED. AA QQQQ Selected, RAC Acclaimed. Briarbank is set in secluded gardens just a few minutes' walk from ferry terminals and town centre. Accommodation costs from £22 to £25 per person including a breakfast of your choice. Comfortable, centrally heated, en suite bedrooms, two with four-poster beds enjoy views over Oban. All are furnished in a tradtional manner and each has colour TV and hospitality tray. Payphone in lobby. Guest lounge (TV free!) with a selection of games and reading material. A non-smoking establishment although guests may smoke in garden. Guests taking dinner are sure to enjoy our international cuisine. Special diets are given sympathetic consideration. Open all year.

SOUTH & WEST SCOTLAND – WHERE TO START?
Scotland's most densely populated region houses more people than many small countries. At its centre is Glasgow where you will find many attractions including the Art Gallery and the Burrell Collection. Heading further out this Region includes such popular places as Oban, the Mull of Kintyre, the Clyde Valley, the Ayrshire Coast and Argyll Forest Park.

OBAN. John and Maureen Simons (MHCIMA), Braeside Guest House, Kilmore, Near Oban PA34 4QR (01631 770243). STB ❤ ❤ ❤ COMMENDED. Beautifully set overlooking Loch Feochan, superb views of local hills. Three miles south of Oban on the A816 this family-run guest house provides excellent home-cooked foods and fine wines in comfortable surroundings. Ideal base for touring, walking, trips to the Isles, etc. Non-smoking. All rooms on ground floor and tastefully decorated. Private parking. Satellite TV. Extended stay, early and late season reductions. Please write or telephone for further information.

OBAN. Mr and Mrs I. Donn, Palace Hotel, Oban PA34 5SB (01631 562294). A small family hotel offering personal supervision situated on Oban's main street with a panoramic view over the Bay. All rooms en suite, several non-smoking. The Palace is an ideal base for a real Highland holiday. By boat you can visit the islands of Kerrera, Coll, Tiree, Lismore, Mull and Iona, and by road Glencoe, Ben Nevis and Inveraray. Fishing, golf, horse riding, sailing, tennis and bowls all nearby. Pets welcome. Please write or telephone for brochure.

OBAN. Mr and Mrs E. Hughes, "Sgeir-Mhaol" Guest House, Soroba Road, Oban PA34 4JF (Tel & Fax: 01631 562650). Family-run guest house situated only an approximate five minutes' walk from town centre, bus/rail stations, main ferry terminal for sailings to the islands of Mull, Iona, Staffa, Coll, Tiree and Colonsay. Bedrooms comprise double, twin and family, all colour co-ordinated and furnished to a high standard with colour TV, tea/coffee makers, etc and most with en suite facilities. The lounge and diningroom overlook a pleasant garden and, like the bedrooms, are on the ground floor. There is a spacious private car park within the grounds. Open all year. The area has a wealth of natural beauty with opportunities for walks, golf, fishing, sailing, pony trekking and a sports complex where swimming, tennis, squash and bowling are available. Oban is an excellent base for day trips by coach or car to many places including Campbeltown, Fort William, Glencoe, etc., or for a day's sailing to the Islands. Bed and Breakfast from £17 to £23.

FOR THE MUTUAL GUIDANCE OF GUEST AND HOST

Every year literally thousands of holidays, short-breaks and overnight stops are arranged through our guides, the vast majority without any problems at all. In a handful of cases, however, difficulties do arise about bookings, which often could have been prevented from the outset.

It is important to remember that when accommodation has been booked, both parties — guests and hosts — have entered into a form of contract. We hope that the following points will provide helpful guidance.

GUESTS: When enquiring about accommodation, be as precise as possible. Give exact dates, numbers in your party and the ages of any children. State the number and type of rooms wanted and also what catering you require — bed and breakfast, full board, etc. Make sure that the position about evening meals is clear — and about pets, reductions for children or any other special points.

Read our reviews carefully to ensure that the proprietors you are going to contact can supply what you want. Ask for a letter confirming all arrangements, if possible.

If you have to cancel, do so as soon as possible. Proprietors do have the right to retain deposits and under certain circumstances to charge for cancelled holidays if adequate notice is not given and they cannot re-let the accommodation.

HOSTS: Give details about your facilities and about any special conditions. Explain your deposit system clearly and arrangements for cancellations, charges, etc. and whether or not your terms include VAT.

If for any reason you are unable to fulfil an agreed booking without adequate notice, you may be under an obligation to arrange alternative suitable accommodation or to make some form of compensation.

While every effort is made to ensure accuracy, we regret that FHG Publications cannot accept responsibility for errors, omissions or misrepresentation in our entries or any consequences thereof. Prices in particular should be checked because we go to press early. We will follow up complaints but cannot act as arbiters or agents for either party.

AYRSHIRE & ARRAN

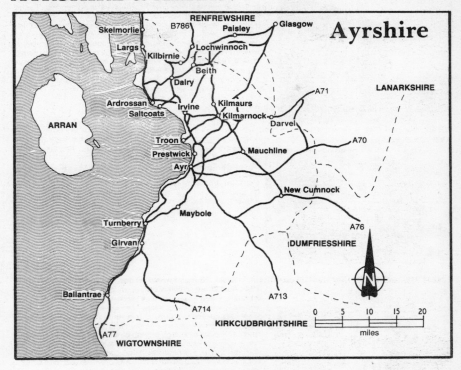

AYR. Tom and Marie Mitchell, Glenmore Guest House, 35 Bellevue Crescent, Ayr KA7 2DP (01292 269830). Charming Victorian terrace house situated in a delightful tree-lined conservation area, very close to the town centre and seafront. Ayr is Scotland's premier coastal resort with sandy beaches and all round entertainment for the family. All bedrooms have colour TV, tea/coffee making facilities and are either en suite or have private facilities. Ground floor and family rooms available. Traditional Scottish breakfast served in the intimate dining room and the elegant residents lounge has TV and video. Rates from £18 to £22.50 per person (two person sharing), £20 to £25 single. Please send for our colour brochure.

AYR. Mrs Wilcox, Fisherton Farm, Dunure, Ayr KA7 4LF (Tel & Fax: 01292 500223). ♛♛ *COMMENDED.* Traditional stone-built farmhouse on working mixed farm with extensive sea views to Arran. Convenient for golf, walking and Burns Country. From Ayr take A719 coast road past Wonderwest World; farm is five miles south of Ayr. Accommodation comprises one double and one twin en suite, ground floor bedrooms with TV and tea/coffee making facilities. Central heating throughout. Children and pets welcome. Please write, telephone or fax for further information.

AYR. Roy and Georgie Gibson, Iona, 27 St. Leonards Road, Ayr KA7 2PS (Tel & Fax: 01292 269541). 🐾🐾 *COMMENDED.* Ideally situated for both town and countryside. A warm Scottish welcome awaits you at Iona where we will help you to make the most of your holiday by advising on visitor attractions and providing routes for day trips and excursions. Close by are Burns Cottage and Heritage Trail, while Culzean Castle is just a short drive away, as are a large number of top class golf courses including two "Open" venues. All our comfortable bedrooms have colour TV and welcome trays, and our hearty Scottish breakfast provides a good choice. Bed and Breakfast from £16 to £19. Stay seven nights for the price of six.

AYR. Charles and Ann Johnston, Chaz-Ann Guest House, 17 Park Circus, Ayr KA7 2DJ (01292 611215; Fax: 01292 285491). 🐾🐾 *COMMENDED.* Charles and Ann welcome you to their refurbished Victorian house. Comfortable accommodation comprises two twin and one family bedrooms, three with private shower/toilet en suite. Quiet surroundings, close to town centre, railway station, beach and other amenities. Open January to December. Single £21 to £25. One person sharing £16 to £20. Please write or telephone for further information.

AYR. Peter and Julia Clark, Eglinton Guest House, 23 Eglinton Terrace, Ayr KA7 1JJ (01292 264623). 🐾🐾 *COMMENDED.* In Welcome Host Scheme. Situated within a part of Ayr steeped in history, within a few minutes' walk of the beach, town centre and many other amenities and entertainment for which Ayr is popular. There are sea and fishing trips available from Ayr Harbour, or a cruise "Doon the Water" on the "Waverley"; golf, swimming pool, cycling, tennis, sailing, windsurfing, walking, etc all available nearby; Prestwick Airport only three miles away. We have family, double and single rooms, all with wash-basins, colour TV and tea/coffee making facilities. En suite facilities and cots available on request. We are open all year round. Please send for our brochure for further information.

AYR near. Mrs Agnes Gemmell, Dunduff Farm, Dunure, Ayr KA7 4LH (01292 500225). 🐾🐾 *HIGHLY COMMENDED.* Welcome to Dunduff Farm where a warm friendly atmosphere awaits you. Situated just south of Ayr at the coastal village of Dunure, this family-run beef and sheep unit of 600 acres is only 15 minutes from the shore providing good walks and sea fishing and enjoying close proximity to Dunure Castle and Park. Accommodation is of a high standard yet homely and comfortable. Bedrooms have washbasins, radio alarm, tea/coffee making facilities, central heating, TV, hair dryer and en suite facilities (the twin room has private bathroom). There is also a small farm cottage available sleeping two/four people. Bed and Breakfast from £20 per person, weekly rate £130. Cottage £230 per week. Colour brochure available.

SOUTH & WEST SCOTLAND – WHERE TO START?

Scotland's most densely populated region houses more people than many small countries. At its centre is Glasgow where you will find many attractions including the Art Gallery and the Burrell Collection. Heading further out this Region includes such popular places as Oban, the Mull of Kintyre, the Clyde Valley, the Ayrshire Coast and Argyll Forest Park.

BEITH. Mrs Joan Wilson, Manor Farm, Burnhouse, Beith KA15 1LJ (01560 484006). STB ✿✿

COMMENDED. **Working farm.** We extend a warm welcome to all our guests — old and new. Our farm guest house offers well appointed standard and en suite rooms, with welcome trays and views over the farm or surrounding countryside. An evening meal is available by prior arrangement and a hearty Ayrshire breakfast is served. Located 15 miles (20 minutes) south of Glasgow Airport on Irvine Road A737, then Dunlop Road B706, Manor Farm is an ideal "home" for business trips to Glasgow. Only 10 miles north of Irvine (on A736) and the many attractions of Ayrshire and Arran are nearby. Bed and Breakfast from £15 per person per night. Brochure available.

BEITH. Mrs Jane Gillan, Shotts Farm, Beith KA15 1LB (01505 502273). STB Listed *COMMENDED.*

Comfortable friendly accommodation is offered on this 160 acre dairy farm situated one and a half miles from the A736 Glasgow to Irvine road; well placed to visit golf courses, country parks, leisure centre or local pottery, also ideal for the ferry to Arran or Millport and for many good shopping centres all around. A high standard of cleanliness is assured by Mrs Gillan who is a first class cook holding many awards, food being served in the diningroom with its beautiful picture windows. Three comfortable bedrooms (double en suite, family and twin), all with tea-making facilities, central heating and electric blankets. Two bathrooms with shower; sitting-room with colour TV. Children welcome. Bed and Breakfast from £12. Dinner can be arranged. AA QQ.

CATACOL, Arran. Catacol Bay Hotel, Catacol (01770 830231; Fax: 01770 830350). Escape from the

pressures of mainland life. Stay awhile by clear shining seas, rocky coast, breathtaking hills and mountains in the comfortable, friendly atmosphere of our small country house hotel where good cooking is our speciality. Fully licensed; bar open all day with extensive bar menu served daily 12 noon to 10pm. Special Sunday buffet. Entertainment during the summer. Centrally heated. Open all year. Island Breaks (October to December and January to April) any three nights Bed and Breakfast. Reduced rates for children. Brochure available. Les Routiers.

DARVEL. Mrs J. Seton, Auchenbart Farm, Darvel, Near Priestland KA17 0LS (01560 320392). ✿

COMMENDED. **Working farm.** Auchenbart Farmhouse is situated in an elevated position overlooking the Irvine Valley. A pleasant house offering comfortable and quiet accommodation of a high standard. One family and one double (cot available) rooms, both with washbasins, tea/coffee making facilities and electric blankets. Bathroom with shower. Guests' sittingroom with colour TV. Heating throughout. Access to Auchenbart is at the east end of Darvel, one mile off the A71 to Edinburgh. We are central for Kilmarnock, Prestwick and Glasgow. Reductions for children. Car essential. Pets welcome. Open Easter till end of October. Bed and Breakfast from £16 per person per night.

KILMARNOCK near. Mr and Mrs P. Gibson, Busbiehill Guest House, Knockentiber, Near Kilmarnock KA2 0DJ (01563 532985). Situated in a rural setting almost in the centre of Ayrshire, looking westwards towards the Arran hills on the Firth of Clyde. Within easy reach of all the popular seaside towns, Burns Country, Culzean Castle. Day trips available to Loch Lomond, Edinburgh and Isle of Arran; sailings on Firth of Clyde. Also many golf courses. Kilmarnock four miles, Ayr 25, Troon 10, Irvine five miles, Ardrossan 13. Eight rooms, five bathrooms; two double rooms with own bathrooms. Tea making facilities, electric blankets. Bed and Breakfast from £12.50. No pets. 35 years service to tourists.

If you've found
FARM HOLIDAY GUIDES
of service please tell your friends

KILMARNOCK. Mrs M. Howie, Hill House Farm, Grassyards Road, Kilmarnock KA3 6HG (01563 523370). ❦❦ *COMMENDED.* Enjoy a peaceful holiday on a working dairy farm two miles east of Kilmarnock. We offer a warm welcome with home baking for supper, choice of farmhouse breakfasts with own preserves. Three large comfortable bedrooms with lovely views over Ayrshire countryside, en suite facilities, tea/coffee, electric blankets, central heating; TV lounge, sun porch, dining room and garden. Excellent touring base with trips to coast, Arran, Burns country and Glasgow nearby. Easy access to A77 and numerous golf courses. Children very welcome. Bed and Breakfast from £16 (including supper). Self catering cottages also available.

LARGS. Mrs M. Watson, South Whittlieburn Farm, Brisbane Glen, Largs KA30 8SN (01475 675881). ❦❦ *HIGHLY COMMENDED.* **Working farm.** AA QQQQ Selected, RAC Listed, chosen by "Which?" Best Bed and Breakfast, Welcome Host. Why not try our superb farmhouse accommodation? With lovely peaceful panoramic views, we are two miles north east of the popular tourist resort of Largs, which is only five minutes' drive away. Also near the ferries for the Islands of Arran, Bute, Cumbrae and Dunoon. Enjoy day trips to Loch Lomond, Inveraray or Culzean Castle; 45 minutes from Glasgow or Ayr. Golf, horse riding, fishing, sailing, diving, shooting, hill walking nearby. All rooms have TV, washbasins, tea/coffee facilities, central heating, hair dryers, radio alarms, toiletries etc; en suite available. TV lounge. Payphone. Large car park. No smoking in bedrooms or dining room. Packed lunches and vegetarian meals can be provided. Bed and Breakfast from £17.50. Reduced rates for children under 11 years. Open all year. Certified caravan and camping site on farm with electric hook-ups, toilet, shower, hot and cold washbasins etc. From £5 per night. Enormous delicious breakfasts and warm friendly hospitality from Mary Watson. Highly recommended!

MAUCHLINE. Mrs J. Clark, Auchenlongford, Sorn, Mauchline KA5 6JF (01290 550761). The farm is situated in the hills above the picturesque village of Sorn, with its Castle set on a promontory above the River Ayr, and nearby its 17th century church. It is only 19 miles east from the A74 and 20 miles inland from the town of Ayr. Accommodation can be from a choice of three attractive, furnished bedrooms and there is also a large well appointed residents' lounge. Full Scottish breakfast is served with home made jams and marmalade; traditional High Tea and/or Dinners are also available on request. Bed and Breakfast £15; Bed, Breakfast and Evening Meal £25. Brochure available.

SHISKINE, Arran. Eileen and Colin Mills, Roadend Christian Guesthouse, Shiskine, Arran KA27 8EW (01770 860448). ❦ *COMMENDED.* Small and homely, situated on the western side of Arran. Superb views from the guests' bedrooms — family room and double room with en suite shower, both with TV, radio/alarm, hair dryer, tea/coffee making facilities and washbasin. Continental or varied full breakfast. Packed lunches and evening meals available — vegetarians, diabetics, coeliacs and Crohn's disease sufferers catered for. Maps and books about the island's archaeology, geology, natural and social history, also those describing walks, freely loaned. Bicycles for hire. Pets not accepted. No smoking. Babysitting and laundering service. Parking.

WHITING BAY. Burlington Hotel, Shore Road, Whiting Bay KA27 8PZ (01770 700255; Fax: 01374 595327; E-mail: 100525.151@compuserve.com). Experience traditional Scottish hospitality in this sea-front Edwardian hotel situated opposite stairs to the sandy beach. Recently refurbished, the bedrooms have private facilities, hospitality trays, hair dryers and colour TV. The Burlington Restaurant offers varied table d'hôte and à la carte menus in a stylish relaxed atmosphere. Comfortable residents' lounge with outstanding views of the Bay, Holy Isle and the Ayrshire coast. Arrangements can be made for pony trekking, sailing, golf, paragliding, boat trips and guided tours of the island. Children and pets welcome.

BORDERS
(Berwickshire, Peeblesshire, Roxburghshire, Selkirkshire)

ASHKIRK. Mrs Betty Lamont, Ashkirktown Farm, Ashkirk, Selkirk TD7 4PB (Tel & Fax: 01750 32315). Working farm. Situated off the A7 midway between Hawick and Selkirk. Ashkirktown Farm offers a warm welcome in a peaceful and tranquil setting. Whether en route to Edinburgh or exploring the beautiful Borders area of Scotland a comfortable stay is assured. The old farmhouse has been tastefully furnished. Large private lounge with colour TV, tea/coffee making facilities. Open all year. Bed and Breakfast from £16; free bedtime drink. Reduced rates for children. Non-smoking accommodation available.

COCKBURNSPATH. Mrs B. Russell, Townhead Farm, Cockburnspath TD13 5YR (01368 830465). Townhead is a 440 acre stockrearing farm situated on an elevated site overlooking the sea, going down to Pease Bay. Nine miles from Dunbar, 15 miles from Berwick-upon-Tweed and 40 miles from Edinburgh, all having good shopping centres and Dunbar having new swimming pool and Leisure Centre. Two family rooms available. Open April to October. Charges from £14 per person per night. Please write or telephone for further details.

DUNS. Mrs W.M. Kenworthy, St. Albans, Clouds, Duns TD11 3BB (01361 883285 — free call diversion maybe in operation; Fax: 01361 883775). ✿✿ *HIGHLY COMMENDED.* Recommended in "Staying Off The Beaten Track". Pleasant Georgian house with secluded south-facing garden. Magnificent views over small country town to Cheviot Hills. Excellent centre for touring. Very quiet location but only three minutes from town centre. Open all year. Colour TV, tea/coffee making facilities, towelling bath robes and hot water bottles in all bedrooms. Private bathroom available. Excellent varied breakfast served in gracious surroundings. Bed and Breakfast from £17. Credit cards accepted. Directions:- Clouds is a lane running parallel to and to the North of Newtown Street where the police station and county offices are situated.

DUNS. Mrs G.E. Burrough, Harelawside Farm, Grants House, Duns TD11 3RP (01361 850380). Working farm. A 550 acre family farm situated in the picturesque Lammermuir foothills very close to St. Abb's Head Nature Reserve and the East Coast fishing villages — ideal for a Borders holiday. The farmhouse has an outstanding view of the wooded Eyewater Valley. It has electric central heating for chilly evenings. Traditional farmhouse cooking. Children welcome. Regretfully we cannot take dogs in the house and would appreciate no smoking. Open all year. Bed and Breakfast from £15 to £19 per person per night. Evening meals available in the village. Brochure available.

BORDERS REGION – ABBEYS, ROLLING HILLS AND RUGBY.
For many the home of Scottish rugby, the rolling Border hills are dissected by the salmon rivers of the Tweed and the Teviot, whilst the towns of Melrose, Selkirk, Jedburgh, Kelso and Peebles thrive on their daily business. On any tourist's itinerary should be the fishing village of St Abb's, Walter Scott country, Traquair House, Walkerburn and, of course, the Border Abbeys.

DUNS near. Mrs Alison Landale, Cranshaws House, Cranshaws Farm, Near Duns TD11 3SJ (01361 890242; Fax: 01361 890295). 👑👑 *COMMENDED.* A warm, friendly, spacious farmhouse situated in beautiful surroundings in Lammermur Hills. Perfect for relaxing, walking and visiting all Scottish Borders attractions. Next door to East Lothian and only one hour from Scotland's capital Edinburgh. Accommodation comprises one twin, one twin en suite and one double bedrooms (double and twin room can become a family unit). Outdoor heated swimming pool and the hens and ducks keep children amused. Golf course and beautiful beaches within easy reach. Bed and Breakfast from £20; Dinner by arrangement. Special packages available for families. Also self-catering cottage nearby, sleeping six.

HAWICK. Mrs Sheila Shell, Wiltonburn Farm, Hawick TD9 7LL (01450 372414; mobile 0374 192551). Wiltonburn is a friendly, working, mixed farm situated in a sheltered valley and surrounded by fields, hills and a small stream. Relax in the garden, or use the local facilities, including fishing, riding, swimming, golf, squash, tennis or hill walking. An ideal base for visiting castles, museums and stately homes or for buying knitwear. Farm shop selling designer cashmere knitwear, costume jewellery; art gallery, small gifts. Good selection of eating places nearby. Open all year. Family room en suite, shower available. Two bathrooms. TV lounge and garden with furniture and barbecue. Dogs by arrangement. Cot available. Listed "Commended". Bed and full Scottish Breakfast from £15. Self catering unit available.

JEDBURGH. Mrs Janet Butt, Lethem Farm, Camptown, Jedburgh TD8 6PS (01835 840255). 👑👑 *COMMENDED.* A friendly welcome awaits all at this comfortable farmhouse situated in large woodland gardens in the peaceful surroundings of the Cheviot Hills. Only one mile off the A68, this is an ideal location for exploring the beautiful countryside both north and south of the Border, within easy reach of Hadrian's Wall, Kielder Water and Edinburgh. Accommodation comprises ground floor en suite rooms, one double, one twin and one family, all with tea/coffee making facilities and colour TV, also guest lounge in a self contained wing of the house. From £17 to £19; Evening Meal £11; reductions for children; pets welcome.

PEEBLES. Mrs A. Waddell, Lyne Farm, Peebles EH45 8NR (01721 740255). Tourist Board Listed *COMMENDED.* A warm welcome is assured at Lyne Farm situated in an area of scenic beauty. Located only four miles on the A72 from the picturesque town of Peebles. Guests can walk around the farm, relax in walled garden or go hill walking up the Black Meldon. The tastefully decorated Georgian Farmhouse accommodation consists of one twin room and two double rooms with tea/coffee making facilities; two bathrooms; dining room and sitting room for guests. Also available, spacious cottage which sleeps two to eight persons. Traquair House, Kailzie, Neidpath Castle and Dawyck Botanical Gardens within a few miles. Bed and Breakfast from £16 to £18 per person, reductions for children.

ST. ABBS. Mrs Barbara Wood, Castle Rock Guest House, Murrayfield, St. Abbs TD14 5PP (018907 71815; Fax: 018907 71520; E-mail: boowood@compuserve.com). 👑👑👑 An attractive Victorian house situated on a wonderful cliff top with views of the harbour and the bay from each room. The village of St. Abbs is an unspoilt village in the Border country, there is a safe sandy beach nearby and birdwatching and rambling on St. Abbs nature reserve. All rooms have en suite facilities, TV, direct dial telephone, hospitality tray, electric blanket, hairdryer and clock radio. There is a public whirlpool bath on the mezzanine floor. Four poster room available. Bed and Breakfast £23 per person per night; with four-course Evening Meal £39. Two course meal £11.50. Open February to October. Castle Rock is highly recommended by the STB and by "Which?" as well as various other guide books.

DUMFRIES & GALLOWAY
(Dumfriesshire, Kirkcudbrightshire, Wigtownshire)

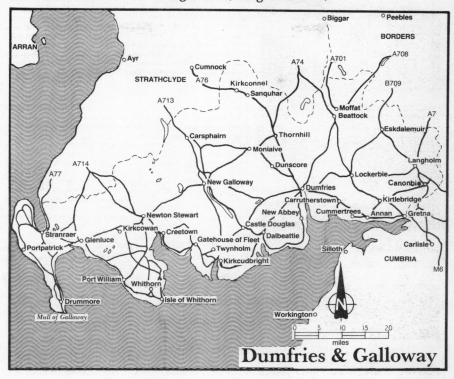

Dumfries & Galloway

CANONBIE. Mrs Steele, North Lodge, Canonbie DG14 0TA (013873 71409). A warm welcome awaits

you at this small family-run guest house situated approximately one mile south of the village of Canonbie, on the tourist route A7 to Edinburgh. Canonbie village is renowned for its fishing — private fishing on the "Willow Pool" can be arranged. NORTH LODGE is a 19th century cottage set in beautiful gardens and was recently extended to include five double/twin bedrooms, four en suite, the other has private facilities. The ground floor en suite room is suitable for the disabled traveller (Grade 1 classification). Within easy reach of Hadrian's Wall, the Lake District, Carlisle, Dumfries, Moffat, Kielder Dam, Hawick, Gretna and many more interesting places. An ideal touring base. Breaks available. Please telephone for further details.

DUMFRIES. Mr & Mrs G. Hood, Wallamhill House, Kirkton, Dumfries DG1 1SL (Tel & Fax: 01387

248249; Mobile: 0850 750150). ♥ ♥ *HIGHLY COMMEN-DED.* A charming country house, tastefully furnished, with a warm, friendly, welcoming atmosphere. The spacious en suite bedrooms — two double/family and one twin, have lovely views over garden and countryside. Beautifully appointed, each room has colour and satellite TV plus video, tea/coffee making faciliies, shower and toilet and full central heating. Situated in peaceful countryside only three miles from Dumfries town centre with excellent shopping, swimming pool, ice bowl for curling, green bowling, fishing and golf. Hill and forest walks, birdwatching, cycling and mountain bike trails all nearby. Bed and Breakfast from £16 to £18. Please send for our brochure for further information.

LOCKERBIE. Mrs Marion Cornthwaite, Balgray Home Farm, Lockerbie DG11 2JT (01576 610244; 0378 551959 mobile).

A large working hill farm off the beaten track yet only three miles from Lockerbie and the M74. Central heating, own sitting/dining room with TV and games, etc. Tea/coffee making facilities, towels, hairdryers and other extras. Access at all times. Large garden for relaxation or ball games. See the farm, enjoy walks, there's plenty to see and do in the area. A substantial breakfast, evening meals by arrangement; all home made, though plenty of good eating places locally. Reductions for children under 12 years. Well behaved pets welcome. Bed and Breakfast from £15; Dinner if requested. A warm welcome awaits you!

LOCKERBIE. Mrs Cecilia Hislop, Carik Cottage, Waterbeck, Lockerbie DG11 3EU (01461 600652).

🐾🐾 *HIGHLY COMMENDED.* Bed and Breakfast accommodation set in peaceful village of Waterbeck with beautiful views where you can see our Belted Galloways. Twin or double tastefully decorated rooms, two en suite, one with private bathroom. TV and tea/coffee making facilities, central heating, visitors' lounge. Ideal for touring south west Scotland and Cumbria or an overnight stop between north and south. 10 miles north of Gretna, seven miles south of Lockerbie, situated three miles from M74, exit Junction 20 on to B722 east, turning left at Post Office in Eaglesfield. We are first cottage in Waterbeck village. Bed and Breakfast £19; Dinner (booked in advance) £10. Three nights Bed and Breakfast break £50; Three nights Dinner, Bed and Breakfast £75.

LOCKERBIE. Miss J. Foster, Dryfe View, Boreland, Lockerbie DG11 2LH (01576 610341).

Set in beautiful rural setting yet only 15 minutes from M74 London/Glasgow motorway. Family room with private bathroom available — suit one, two or three adults plus one cot. Tea/coffee making facilities. Good parking space. Bed and Breakfast £18 per person per night. Children under 12 years £5. This is a non-smoking household. Sorry, no pets unless kept in owner's car.

MOFFAT. Mr and Mrs W. Gray, Barnhill Springs Country Guest House, Moffat DG10 9QS (01683 220580). 🐾🐾 *COMMENDED.* AA QQ. Barnhill Springs is an early Victorian country mansion standing in its own grounds overlooking Upper Annandale. Situated half-a-mile from the A74/M, the house and its surroundings retain an air of remote peacefulness. Internally it has been decorated and furnished to an exceptionally high standard of comfort. Open fire in lounge. Accommodation includes family, double, twin and single rooms, some en suite. Children welcome. Pets welcome free of charge. Open all year. Bed and Breakfast from £18.50; Evening Meal (optional) from £13.

DUMFRIES AND GALLOWAY REGION – BURNS' COUNTRY.

A fair sprinkling of castles, the Solway Firth coast and, of course, Burns' Country makes this region an interesting tourist destination. Other attractions include the Grey Mare's Tail, Galloway Forest Park, Caerlaverock and Clatteringshaws deer museum.

MOFFAT. Mrs Jean McKenzie, "Hidden Corner", Beattock Road, Moffat DG10 9SE (01683

220243). Hidden Corner stands in an acre of ground only half a mile from the A74 and half a mile from Moffat. An ideal base for exploring the Borders and South West Scotland; Edinburgh, Glasgow, The East and West Coasts are within one hour's drive. Accommodation comprises two double and one twin-bedded rooms, all with washbasins, shaver points and tea/coffee making facilities; bath/shower room; lounge with TV; dining room. Open all year except Christmas and New Year. Ample parking. Bed and Breakfast £15 to £17.

MOFFAT. Mr and Mrs A. Armstrong, Boleskine, 4 Well Road, Moffat DG10 9AS (01683 220601). *HIGHLY COMMENDED.* A fine Victorian town house in a quiet street offering comfortable accommodation only two minutes' walk from town centre. All rooms are centrally heated, have washbasins, colour TV, tea/coffee making facilities, electric blankets and hair dryer. En suite rooms available, including twin room on ground floor. Private parking. Ideal stopover, or base for walking or touring. Open all year. Bed and Breakfast from £16. No single supplement. AA QQQ. Directions: from High Street turn into Well Street beside Nisa grocery, at end of Well Street turn right into Well Road. Also self-catering cottage available.

MOFFAT. Mr Gary Hall, The Lodge, Sidmount Avenue, Moffat DG10 9BS (01683 220440). The Lodge is a late Victorian stone house situated in a quiet cul-de-sac, about a quarter of a mile from the centre of Moffat. Surrounded by superb lawned gardens with fine mature trees, there is a splendid view spanning the valley. Ample parking space. Selection of twin, single and double bedrooms and a family suite with two rooms. Children welcome, cot and high chair available. Tea making facilities and colour TV in all bedrooms. Comfortable lounge; large diningroom. Two bathrooms, one with shower. Central heating in all rooms. Spacious garden which is perfect for ball games and croquet. Open all year. Local attractions include golf, putting, boating, fishing, riding, tennis, bowls. Numerous castles, abbeys, forests and hills within easy reach. Bed and Breakfast from £14. Reduced rates for children.

MOFFAT. T.J. Hull, Alton House, Moffat DG10 9LB (01683 220903; mobile 0850 129105). Alton is

an historic country house situated in several acres of secluded grounds at the end of a long private lane. The property is a former home of Chiefs of the Clan Moffat and is of considerable historic and architectural interest. The present property dates from circa 1650 and has evolved over several centuries. It contains many period features including elegant public rooms, marble fireplaces, fine plasterwork and woodwork with period furnishings throughout and has wonderful views. All bedrooms have washbasins, TV, tea making facilities and welcome tray; en suite available. There is full central heating. Bed and Breakfast from £16.

NEWTON STEWART. The Stables Guest House, Corsbie Road, Newton Stewart DG8 6JB (01671

404224). Byron and Janet welcome you to their home which is comfortably furnished having en suite and private facilities. Only five minutes' walk from town. Good home cooking and selection of wines available. Ample parking. Ground floor bedrooms. Ideal base for touring, ferry stopovers, exploring Galloway. Golf, fishing and walking available locally. Bed, Breakfast and Evening Meal from £29. Relax in comfort.

NEWTON STEWART. Miss K.R. Wallace, Kiloran, 6 Auchendoon Road, Newton Stewart DG8 6HD

(01671 402818). Spacious, luxury bungalow set in secluded landscaped garden, with panoramic views of Galloway Hills, in quiet area of Newton Stewart. Enjoy comfortable accommodation on one level in two double bedrooms (one twin-bedded); bathroom with shower; cloakroom with WC. Soap and towels supplied. Lounge (colour TV), dining room where good home cooking is served (menu changed daily). Central heating. Children over 10 years welcome. Dogs allowed, but not in house. Ideal centre for touring Galloway. Safe, sandy beaches 12 miles. Within easy reach of hill walking, golf, riding and trekking. Terms on request. SAE, please, for Evening Dinner, Bed and Breakfast or Bed and Breakfast only. For Auchendoon Road, turn at Dashwood Square to Princess Road, then second on right. Ample parking available.

WHITHORN. Barbara Fleming, Belmont, St. John Street, Whithorn, Newton Stewart DG8 8PG

(01988 500890). Belmont is ideal for a quiet relaxing holiday in a very beautiful and historically interesting part of Galloway — the Whithorn Dig is nearby. There is an attractive sitting/dining room, colour TV is available downstairs and in bedrooms. There are two bathrooms. Various and generous meals are provided, with tea/coffee making facilities in all bedrooms. All guests (maximum five) are given a warm welcome and well behaved pets are allowed (two resident cats and one dog). Prices from £15 to £18 per person per night.

DUNBARTONSHIRE

ARROCHAR. Jean and Jim Preston, Fascadail Country Guest House, Shore Road, Arrochar G83 7AB (Tel & Fax: 01301 702344). ♛ ♛ ♛ *COMMENDED.* Enjoy a warm welcome in this mid 19th century country residence set in beautiful grounds with panoramic views of Loch Long and the Arrochar Alps. Discover peace and tranquillity five minutes from Loch Lomond and only 45 minutes from Glasgow. Ideal base for walking and touring and then return to a friendly and relaxing atmosphere. Large comfortable lounge. All bedrooms have en suite facilities, full central heating, TV, clock radio alarm, tea/coffee making, etc. If you prefer something different we can offer rooms with either a four-poster bed or a jacuzzi or spa bath. Ample private car parking. Bed and Breakfast from £20 per person.

Key to Tourist Board Ratings

The Crown Scheme
(England, Scotland & Wales)

Covering hotels, motels, private hotels, guesthouses, inns, bed & breakfast, farmhouses. Every Crown classified place to stay is inspected annually. *The classification:* Listed then 1-5 Crown indicates the range of facilities and services. Higher quality standards are indicated by the terms APPROVED, COMMENDED, HIGHLY COMMENDED and DELUXE.

The Key Scheme
(also operates in Scotland using a Crown symbol)

Covering self-catering in cottages, bungalows, flats, houseboats, houses, chalets, etc. Every Key classified holiday home is inspected annually. *The classification:* 1-5 Key indicates the range of facilities and equipment. Higher quality standards are indicated by the terms APPROVED, COMMENDED, HIGHLY COMMENDED and DELUXE.

The Q Scheme
(England, Scotland & Wales)

Covering holiday, caravan, chalet and camping parks. Every Q rated park is inspected annually for its quality standards. The more √ in the Q – up to 5 – the higher the standard of what is provided.

DUNDEE & ANGUS

FORFAR. Mrs Allison Clanton, 4 Westfield Loan, Forfar DD8 1EJ (01307 462424). Comfortable accommodation in modern bungalow with gas central heating, off street parking and a warm welcome. Fofar is a busy market town close to Dundee and Aberdeen. Glamis Castle, our Queen Mothers birthplace, is five miles away. Pony trekking and hill walking are popular pastimes available nearby. Choice of traditional or cold breakfast. Complementary tea and coffee. En suite facilities available. We operate a non-smoking policy. Children welcome. Sorry, no pets. Bed and Breakfast from £16 to £18.50 per person per night.

MONTROSE near. Mrs Alison Coates, Burnmouth Guest House, St. Cyrus, Near Montrose (01674

850430). 200 year old property, country/seaside house with access to beautiful glens and beaches. Local golf courses, nature reserve, fishing and rough shooting. All rooms have tea/coffee facilities; TV lounge; two double bedrooms with private bathroom, family room en suite, twin room en suite; single room; shower room. Relaxed friendly atmosphere. Home cooking. Adequate parking. Just off Aberdeen coast road (A92), eight miles north of Montrose, 15 miles south Stonehaven. Follow sign for "Burnmouth B&B By the Sea".

MONTROSE near. Mrs Moyra Braes, Ballochy House, West Ballochy, Near Montrose DD10 9LP

(01674 810207; Fax: 01674 810739). This lovely Victorian house has wonderful views over open countryside and Montose Basin and Wildlife Centre. One hours' drive from Royal Deeside, St. Andrews and close to Angus Glens. Beach at Montrose is being upgraded, golf courses and fishing rivers are close by; shooting can be arranged. National Trust Scotland house of Dun with its lovely gardens and walks all very near. Ballochy House has full central heating, all en suite facilities, colour TV, radio alarms, tea/coffee making facilities and electric blankets. An execellent licensed restaurant five minutes' walk where all tastes are catered for. Children welcome. Bed and Breakfast from £16 to £18.

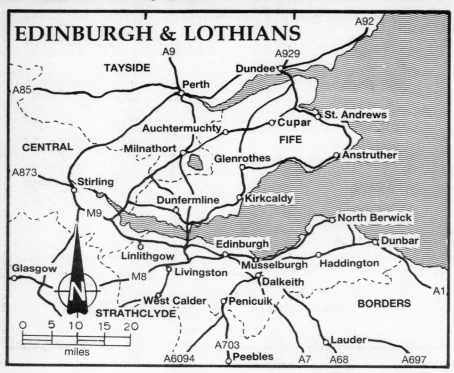

EDINBURGH & LOTHIANS

EAST CALDER (near Edinburgh). Mrs Jan Dick, Overshiel Farm, East Calder EH53 0HT (01506 880469; Fax: 01506 883006). ♛♛ *COMMENDED.*

Working farm in a peaceful country setting yet only six miles west of Edinburgh. Easy access into city centre by car, bus or train (station one and a quarter miles). Comfortable rooms (one double, one twin, one family) look onto a large attractive garden. All have colour TV, washbasins, tea/coffee making facilities and two are en suite. Ample private parking. Sorry no smoking. Excellent local pubs and restaurants. Bed and Breakfast from £16.

EDINBURGH. Kildonan Lodge Hotel, 27 Craigmillar Park, Edinburgh EH16 5PE (0131-667 2793; Fax: 0131-667 9777). ♛♛♛ *HIGHLY COMMENDED.*

Kildonan Lodge is an outstanding example of Victorian elegance providing the perfect setting for your visit to Scotland's capital. With its ideal location you can leave your car (private car park) and take the frequent local transport to nearby city centre (one and a half miles away) for a carefree holiday. Well appointed non-smoking bedrooms have for your comfort en suite facilities, direct-dial telephone, colour TV, radio alarms and welcome tea/coffee trays. Delicious wholesome Scottish breakfasts. Bed and Breakfast en suite from £28 to £45 per person. A warm friendly welcome assured.

EDINBURGH. Lorne Villa Guest House, 9 East Mayfield, Edinburgh EH9 1SD (Tel & Fax: 0131-667 7159). Tourist Board Listed *COMMENDED.* Calum and Mandy McCulloch welcome you to Lorne Villa. This "Festival" city centre guest house offer you superb Scottish hospitality and cuisine. We offer en suite and standard facilities and all our rooms are decorated to a high standard with TV and complimentary hospitality trays. We are situated one mile from city centre and all other visitor attractions. Ample off street parking. Bed and Breakfast from £18 per person per night. Reduced rates for children sharing parents room and under fives go FREE. Open all year. Special rates for out of season breaks.

Southdown Guest House

A warm welcome and personal service is assured at the Southdown Guest House. Conveniently situated on a main bus route in a prime residential area just ten minutes from Princes Street, The Castle, Holyrood Palace and several golf courses are within easy reach. We have several full en suite rooms available while all others have private showers. Cable/Sky/Satellite TV, tea/coffee making facilities. There is a comfortable residents' lounge with colour TV. Full Scottish Breakfast  with home produce our speciality. Bed and Breakfast from £17.50 (singles from £22.50). Reduced rates for families and groups. Own key access all day. Full central heating and Fire Certificate. Private car park. Cot, high chair and babysitting service available. **Access/Visa accepted.**

20 Craigmillar Park, Edinburgh EH16 5PS
Telephone: 0131-667 2410   Fax: 0131-667 6056
STB ♛♛ Commended

EDINBURGH. Norah Alexander, Tiree Guest House, 26 Craigmillar Park, Edinburgh EH16 5PS (0131-667 7477; Fax: 0131-662 1608). STB Listed *COMMENDED.* AA QQ. Terraced Victorian villa situated on main bus route to city centre, 10 minutes from historic High Street and Princes Street. All rooms have tea/coffee making and colour TV. Private parking. Full Scottish breakfast.

EDINBURGH. Kenvie Guest House, 16 Kilmaurs Road, Edinburgh EH16 5DA (Tel & Fax: 0131-668 1964). ♛♛ *COMMENDED.* Comfortable house situated in quiet residential area 10 minutes from city centre. Excellent bus service. We have five rooms, two of which are en suite. Terms: weekend extra night £17; mid-week £17.

Terms quoted in this publication may be subject to increase if rises in costs necessitate

EDINBURGH. Mrs Maureen Sandilands, Sandilands House, 25 Queensferry Road, Edinburgh EH4 3HB (Tel & Fax: 0131-332 2057). ❦ *COMMENDED.*

Sandilands House is ideally located five minutes from Edinburgh's city centre by bus with its own guests' private parking. A distinctive and attractive detached bungalow in its own gardens with excellent bus service to the city centre or a short walk to the city's West End; also near to Murrayfield Stadium. Enjoy the friendly welome and relax in the well furnished and tastefully decorated accommodation with en suite facilities. All rooms are equipped with central heating, colour TV, hair dyrer, tea/coffee making facilities, etc. Full Scottish breakfast is included. Family rooms available and discounts of 50% apply for children under 12 years sharing with adults. Open all season. Terms from £38 to £60 for en suite double/twin room or from £25 to £40 for single occupancy.

EDINBURGH. O. Lyons, Ard-na-Said, 5 Priestfield Road, Edinburgh EH16 5HH (Tel & Fax: 0131-667 8754). A real Scottish welcome awaits you at Ard-na-Said, situated in a quiet residential area 2 kilometres south of the city centre; Airport 10 kilometres. For those wishing to explore Edinburgh we are only 100 metres from an excellent bus service. Within walking distance we can offer golf, swimming, Holyrood Park, University halls of residence and a selection of good pubs/restaurants. One family room en suite, three twin (one en suite, one with private facilities), one double en suite and one single bedrooms, all furnished to a high standard ensuring your stay in Edinburgh will be as comfortable as possible. Vegetarians are catered for in our varied breakfast menu. Ample free parking. Children welcome.

EDINBURGH. Harold and Alison Levey, St. Margarets Guest House, 18 Craigmillar Park, Edinburgh EH16 5PS (Tel & Fax: 0131-667 2202). St. Margarets is an elegant and characterful Victorian stone built terraced villa situated on A701 A722 on the south side of Edinburgh only minutes from city by-pass, city centre and train station (Waverley). A warm house with warm welcome from new owners (June 1997) and typically full Scottish breakfast with menu choice. All bedrooms, most en suite, are clean and comfortable, centrally heated and have colour TV and tea/coffee trays. Tasteful dining room and residents lounge. Open all year. Bed and Breakfast from £22 to £35. We also offer Winter Break specials and Christmas and New Year Breaks. Private car park. Excellent bus service. Credit cards accepted.

EDINBURGH. Mrs Rhoda Mitchell, Hopetoun Guest House, 15 Mayfield Road, Edinburgh EH9 2NG (0131-667 7691). ❦❦ *COMMENDED.* AA QQ. "Which?" Books Good Bed and Breakfast Guide. COMPLETELY NON-SMOKING. Hopetoun is a small, friendly, family-run guest house situated close to Edinburgh University, one and a half miles south of Princes Street, and with an excellent bus service to the city centre. Very comfortable accommodation is offered in a completely smoke-free environment. Having only three guest bedrooms, and now offering private facilities, the owner prides herself in ensuring personal attention to all guests in a friendly, informal atmosphere. All rooms have central heating, washbasins, colour TV and tea/coffee making facilities. Parking is also available. Bed and Breakfast from £17 to £30. Visa/Access.

INTERNATIONAL GUEST HOUSE

30 Mayfield Gardens, Edinburgh EH9 2BX
Tel: 0131 667 9833   Dr. M. Eltorkey

The International is an attractive, stone-built Victorian terrace house conveniently situated one and a half miles south of Princes Street on the main A707 and only four miles from the Straiton junction on the Edinburgh city by-pass. Lying on the main bus route, access to the city centre is easy. **The International** has ample private parking. Visitors who require a touch of luxury a little out of the ordinary can do no better than visit **The International**. All bedrooms have en suite facilities, colour television and tea/coffee makers. The decor is outstanding with ornate plasterwork on the ceilings as fine as in 'The New Town'. Some rooms enjoy magnificent views across to the extinct volcano of Arthur's Seat. The full Scottish breakfasts served on the finest bone china are a delight.

19th century setting with 21st century facilities!

In Britain magazine has rated **The International** as their 'find' in all Edinburgh.

EDINBURGH. Mr and Mrs John and Rita Veitch, Dunstane House Hotel, 4 West Coates, Edinburgh EH12 5JQ (0131-337 6169). ❦❦❦ *COMMENDED.* A beautiful detached mansion of historic and architectural interest, set in delightful gardens. Handy for town centre, good bus service, railway station, golf courses and 15 minutes by car to airport, five minutes to Princes Street. A friendly welcome awaits you at this private, family-run hotel, open all year. Rooms are comfortable with en suite facilities, each having tea/coffee making facilities, shaver/hairdryer points, radio and colour TV. Family and single rooms available. Licensed residents' bar. Private, secluded car park. Bed and Breakfast from £25 to £36 per person. AA QQQ.

EDINBURGH. Villa San Monique, 4 Wilton Road, Edinburgh EH16 5NY (0131-667 1403; Fax: 0131-662 1608). ❦❦ *APPROVED.* Lovely Victorian villa situated in a quiet residential area, one and a half miles south of the city centre, just off the main bus route into town. The bedrooms are generally large and well equipped. We have basic accommodation as well as en suite. Private parking. Open April to October. Bed and Breakfast from £16 to £28 per person per night.

EDINBURGH. Angus Beag Guest House 5 Windsor Street, Edinburgh EH7 5LA (0131-556 1905). City centre Georgian guest house close to all amenities. 10 minutes Princes Street, adjacent Playhouse Theatre, and 10 minutes from railway station and airport buses. All rooms have washbasins, shower TV, tea/coffee facilities; one en suite. Delicious full Scottish breakfast available. Terms from £19 per person per night.

EDINBURGH. Alan and Angela Vidler, Rowan House, 13 Glenorchy Terrace, Edinburgh EH9 2DQ

(0131-667 2463). 👑👑 *COMMENDED*. Elegant Victorian home, quietly located in an attractive area of the city only 10 minutes by bus from the centre. Rooms have colour TV, tea/coffee making facilities and are mostly en suite. Children welcome at reduced rates. Convenient for Castle, Royal Mile, University, theatres and restaurants. Located just off the A701 from the south (turn left at Bright's Crescent, just off Mayfield Gardens) and close to major roads A1, A7 and A702. Unrestricted street parking. Bed and Breakfast from £20 per person. From October to March inclusive (excluding New Year). 10% reduction on production of this guide.

EDINBURGH. The Ivy Guest House, 7 Mayfield Gardens, Edinburgh EH9 2AX (0131-667 3411). STB

👑👑 *COMMENDED*. AA QQQ Recommended, RAC Acclaimed. Bed and Breakfast in a comfortable Victorian villa. Open all year round. Private car park. Close to city centre and all its cultural attractions with excellent public transport and taxi services available on the door step. Many local sports facilities (booking assistance available). All rooms have central heating, washbasins, colour TV and tea/coffee making facilities. Choice of en suite or standard rooms, all power showers. Public phone. Large selection of eating establishments nearby. A substantial Scottish breakfast and warm welcome is assured, courtesy of Don and Dolly Green. Terms from £18 per person per night.

EDINBURGH. Classic Guest House, 50 Mayfield Road, Edinburgh EH9 2NH (0131-667 5847; Fax:

0131-662 1016). 👑👑 *HIGHLY COMMENDED*. Good value Bed and Breakfast accommodation is offered at this friendly, well-run guest house. All bedrooms are tastefully decorated and thoughtfully equipped and have shower en suite, hair dryer, garment press, TV and welcome tray. Conveniently located for bypass and city centre, so come and explore this historic city. Breakfast is served at individual tables in the large dining room. The Classic proudly displays a host of certificates such as "Welcome Host", Customers Come First, Guest Courtesy and Health and Hygiene. TOTALLY NON-SMOKING. AA Selected. Bed and Breakfast from £18 to £30. Brochure.

EDINBURGH. Bryan and Margaret Love, Highland Park Guest House, 16 Kilmaurs Terrace,

Edinburgh EH16 5DR (0131-667 9204). 👑 *COMMENDED*. Friendly family run Guest House situated in quiet area off Dalkeith Road (A68/A7). Unrestricted street parking. Close to Royal Commonwealth Swimming Pool, Cameron Toll Shopping Centre, Holyrood Park and local golf course with shops and launderette easily accessible. Excellent bus service to city centre (one and a half miles). Accommodation comprises two family, two twin (one en suite) and two single bedrooms, all with washbasin, tea/coffee making facilities and colour TV, central heating. Open all year except Christmas. Terms for Bed and Breakfast from £16 to £25. Reductions for children sharing with two adults.

EDINBURGH. Harvest Guest House, 33 Straiton Place, Portobello, Edinburgh EH15 2BA (0131-657 3160; Fax: 0131-468 7028). 👑👑 Georgian house beside Portobello beach with easy access to Edinburgh City Centre. Close to shops, restaurants, swimming pool and A1. Parking. Central heating. Tea/coffee facilities and colour TV in rooms, en suite available. £15 to £25 per night. Directions: from city centre — Princess Street, London Road, Portobello Road, Portobello High Street, Bath Street then to Straiton Place; or from city centre by-pass — A1 Edinburgh direction look for sign Portobello, Portobello Road, then as above.

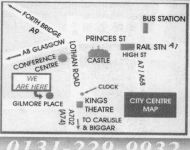

EDINBURGH. Mardale Guest House, 11 Hartington Place, Edinburgh EH10 4LF (0131-229 2693).

🏅🏅 *COMMENDED.* Elegant Victorian villa situated in central but quiet residential cul-de-sac. Theatres, restaurants and city centre are all within easy reach whether by foot or by use of the excellent bus service. The extremely comfortable bedrooms are individually decorated with care and flair and have private bathrooms, TV, tea/coffee facilities, hair dryer and telephone. Choice of breakfast is served at individual tables in the cosy lounge/dining room. Visitors' comments include "A cosy, friendly amd most beautiful home", "Excellent 10/10". AA QQQ Recommended.

EDINBURGH. Mrs H. Donaldson, "Invermark", 60 Polwarth Terrace, Edinburgh EH11 1NJ (0131-337 1066).

🏅 *COMMENDED.* "Invermark" is a Georgian semi-detached villa situated in quiet suburbs on the main bus route into the city and only five minutes by car. Edinburgh bypass — Lothianburn Junction — two miles — left Balcarres Street, right Myreside Road — Grays Loan — right into Polwarth Terrace. Edinburgh is one of Europe's most splendid cities, famous for its dramatic beauty, historic interest, extensive shopping and dining facilities. There is a park to the rear of the house. Accommodation consists of one single, one twin and one family rooms (with tea/coffee making facilities); TV lounge/diningroom; toilet; bathroom/ shower. Non-smoking accommodation available. Friendly atmosphere. Children and dogs welcome. Bed and Breakfast from £17. Reductions for children.

HELP IMPROVE BRITISH TOURIST STANDARDS

You are choosing holiday accommodation from our very popular FHG Publications. Whether it be a hotel, guest house, farmhouse or self-catering accommodation, we think you will find it hospitable, comfortable and clean, and your host and hostess friendly and helpful. Why not write and tell us about it?

As a recognition of the generally well-run and excellent holiday accommodation reviewed in our publications, we at FHG Publications Ltd. present a diploma to proprietors who receive the highest recommendation from their guests who are also readers of our Guides. If you care to write to us praising the holiday you have booked through FHG Publications Ltd. – whether this be board, self-catering accommodation, a sporting or a caravan holiday, what you say will be evaluated and the proprietors who reach our final list will be contacted.

The winning proprietor will receive an attractive framed diploma to display on his premises as recognition of a high standard of comfort, amenity and hospitality. FHG Publications Ltd. offer this diploma as a contribution towards the improvement of standards in tourist accommodation in Britain. Help your excellent host or hostess to win it!

FHG DIPLOMA

We nominate ....

....

Because

Name ....

Address ....

.... Telephone No. ....

EDINBURGH (14 miles). Mrs Janet Burke, Patieshill Farm, Carlops, Penicuik EH26 9ND (01968 660551; Fax: 01968 661162). 🐑🐑 *COMMENDED.* This is a working hill sheep and cattle farm set in the midst of the Pentland Hills with panoramic views of the surrounding countryside yet only 20 minutes' drive from the city of Edinburgh. It is situated near the main A702 Edinburgh — Carlisle road close to the village of Carlops. Accommodation, all in separate guest wing, consists of two double and one twin-bedded rooms, all with full en suite facilities. Each room has tea/coffee making facilities, central heating and TV. This is an ideal base for many activities including fishing, golf, ski-ing, hill walking and pony trekking. A very warm and friendly welcome is extended to all guests. Bed and Breakfast from £18 with reductions for children.

GULLANE. Mrs Mary Chase, Jardini Garden, Goose Green, Gullane EH31 2BA (01620 843343). Jardini Garden is in a very secluded walled garden, with private parking. The main room has its own patio door, and guests are welcome to use the garden. Gullans is a charming coastal village, well known for its famous golf courses. The three public courses are just minutes walk from Jardini Garden and Muirfield is at the other end of the village. The beautiful sandy beach bordered by cliffs and dunes provides spectacular walks in both directions. Edinburgh is only 30 minutes by car. Children and pets welcome. Bed and Breakfast from £17.50 to £22.50 per person; Dinner from £10.

INVERESK. 16 Carberry Road, Inveresk, Musselburgh EH21 7TN (0131-665 2107). A lovely Victorian

stone detached house situated in a quiet conservation village seven miles east of Edinburgh, overlooking fields and close to a lovely river walk and seaside with harbour. Buses from door to city, very close to sports centre with swimming pool and within easy distance of many golf courses. Spacious accommodation comprises one family room and two double rooms, all have central heating, colour TV and tea/coffee making facilities. Two large, full equipped bathrooms adjacent. Parking in quiet side road or in garden if required by arrangement. Full cooked breakfast included from £18 per person per night; reduction for children.

LINLITHGOW. Mrs J. Erskine, Woodcockdale Farm, Lanark Road, Linlithgow EH49 6QE (01506 842088). 🐑🐑 *COMMENDED.* **Working farm, join in.** Look no further, be among one of the many guests who return to Woodcockdale — a busy dairy and sheep farm. Ideal base for touring central Scotland. The accommodation comprises two double and two family en suite rooms, one family and one twin-bedded basic room. Tea/coffee making facilities, radio alarm and TV in all rooms. Children and pets welcome. Non-smoking accommodation available. Situated one and a half miles from Linlithgow on Lanark A706 Road. Bed and Breakfast from £16 to £22 per person per night. Phone now!

LINLITHGOW. Mr and Mrs R. Inglis, Thornton, Edinburgh Road, Linlithgow EH49 6AA (01506 844216). STB 🐑🐑 *HIGHLY COMMENDED.* Comfortable

family-run Victorian house with original features retained. Centrally situated in a peaceful location near the Union Canal in historic Linlithgow, only five minutes' walk from town centre, Linlithgow Palace and railway station. This is a real home-from-home offering quality accommodation and friendly personal attention in a relaxing atmosphere. One double and one twin room, both en suite and furnished to high standards with colour TV etc. Ample off-street parking and large garden. Excellent base for visiting Edinburgh, Stirling, Glasgow and Central Scotland; Edinburgh Airport 10 miles. Open all year except Christmas and New Year. Early booking advisable.

LOTHIAN REGION – THE CAPITAL ATTRACTION.

Although your first stop will probably be Edinburgh – and with every justification – you should endeavour to get out of town and visit the likes of South Queensferry, the Bass Rock, Haddington and Preston Mill.

LINLITHGOW. Mrs Mary Mitchell, The Cedars, 135 High Street, Linlithgow EH49 7EJ (01506 845952). Small comfortable house with double, twin and single bedrooms, all with washbasin and tea/coffee making facilities. Lounge for guests' use. Historic Linlithgow, birthplace of Mary, Queen of Scots, is an ideal location for visiting the many attractions in Central Scotland. Good rail and bus links to Edinburgh, Glasgow, Stirling, etc. 11 miles from Edinburgh Airport, nine miles from the Forth Bridge. Bed and Breakfast from £17 per person per night. Reductions for children under 10 years. Pets by arrangement.

LIVINGSTON (West Lothian). Ms M. Easdale, 3 Cedric Rise, Dedridge East, Livingston EH54 6JR (Tel & Fax: 01506 413095). Open all year except Christmas and New Year, with central heating, a friendly welcome is assured in this New Town accommodation situated 15 miles from Edinburgh, one of Europe's most splendid cities. Easy access to the motorway for visitors touring north or south. Fife, Borders, Trossachs, Loch Lomond, country parks in Lothian and Central regions, recreation park at Falkirk, all within easy driving distance. Four golf courses in the surrounding area. Accommodation comprises one twin-bedded, one single, one room with double and single beds and a triple bedded room (these rooms are located on the first and second floors). Tea/coffee making facilities and TV in all bedrooms. Bathroom with shower, two toilets; shared sitting/diningroom. Children welcome, but sorry, no pets. Parking nearby. Bed and Breakfast £17; reductions for children under 10 years.

NORTH BERWICK. "Craigview", 5 Beach Road, North Berwick EH39 4AB (01620 892257).

Margaret and Willie Mitchell — British Institute of Innkeeping, Welcome Host, AA QQ Recommended, RAC Caradon. "Craigview" is situated in the centre of North Berwick with views over the West Bay, the Harbour and the Firth of Forth. Overlooking a sandy beach and 100 yards from the West Links Golf Course it is ideally placed for both activity and leisure breaks in and around North Berwick including bird-watching, historic castles, golf courses, boat trips, good restaurant and excellent sports facilities. Good train and bus links. Private facilities, four-poster beds, central heating, colour TV, tea/coffee and biscuits, hi-power hairdryers, irons and ironing boards. Full cooked breakfast with alternative healthy or vegetarian options. Open all year. Bed and Breakfast £20 to £25 single, £16 to £20 double. No smoking. Also self catering flat. Brochure available.

PATHHEAD. Mrs Margaret Winthrop, "Fairshiels", Blackshiels, Pathhead EH37 5SX (01875 833665). We are situated on the A68, three miles south of Pathhead at the picturesque village of Fala. The house is an 18th century coaching inn (Listed building). All bedrooms have washbasins and tea/coffee making facilities; one is en suite. The rooms are comfortably furnished. We are within easy reach of Edinburgh and the Scottish Borders. A warm welcome is extended to all our guests — our aim is to make your stay a pleasant one. Cost is from £15 per person; children two years to 12 years £8.50, under two years FREE.

ROSLIN. Mrs Rosemary Noble, Glenlea House, Hawthornden, Lasswade EH18 1EJ (0131-440 2079). Glenlea is one mile from the picturesque village of Roslin. Large 150 year old family house standing in one acre of garden, overlooking historic Rosslyn Chapel and the Pentland Hills. Plenty of good eating places in the area also walking and riding but within easy reach of Edinburgh which is seven miles away. Accommodation comprises one large family room, two double and one single. One of the double rooms is on the ground floor with bathroom adjacent. Full Scottish breakfast. Fully centrally heated. Ample parking. Bed and Breakfast from £18 to £20.

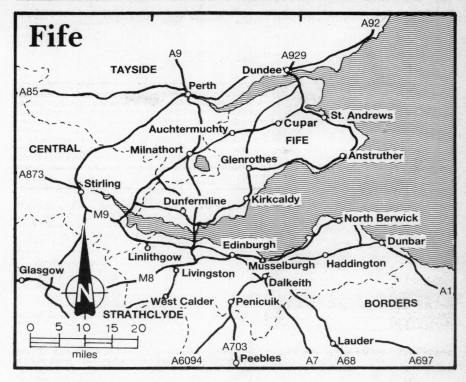

Fife

(Map of Fife and surrounding areas showing: A92, A929, A9, TAYSIDE, Dundee, Perth, A85, St. Andrews, Cupar, Auchtermuchty, FIFE, CENTRAL, Milnathort, Glenrothes, Anstruther, A873, Stirling, Dunfermline, Kirkcaldy, M9, North Berwick, Dunbar, Edinburgh, Linlithgow, Glasgow, Livingston, Musselburgh, Haddington, M8, Dalkeith, BORDERS, A1, West Calder, Penicuik, STRATHCLYDE, 0 5 10 15 20 miles, N, Lauder, A6094, A703, Peebles, A7, A68, A697)

CULROSS. Jim and Brenda Ferguson, The Old Manse, 136 Main Street, Newmills, Culross KY12 8SX (01383 880150). STB Listed *COMMENDED.* Built around 1840, situated in secluded surroundings overlooking the River Forth with ample parking, yet close to major tourist and golf attractions (St. Andrews), with easy access to Edinburgh and Glasgow for shopping. All day access; tea, coffee and TV in rooms. Three en suite rooms, three with shared bathroom, all with electric showers. Bed and Breakfast from £15 per person, en suite from £20 (sharing). Discounts for more than two nights. Open January to December.

CUPAR by. Mrs Gill Donald, Todhall House, Dairsie, By Cupar KY15 4RQ (Tel & Fax: 01334 656344). 👑👑👑 *HIGHLY COMMENDED.* AA PREMIER SELECTED QQQQQ. Traditional Scottish country home surrounded by superb scenery and only seven miles from historic St. Andrews. Ideally situated for pursuing sporting activities and exploring the many places of interest in the Kingdom of Fife and beyond. There is something for everyone! Guests enjoy comfortable bedrooms en suite, an elegant guests' lounge, traditional food and the opportunity to relax and unwind. On site facilities include ample parking, a walled garden, outdoor swimming pool and golf practice net. This is a home for non-smokers. Open April to October. Bed and Breakfast from £22; Dinner by arrangement. Children over 12 years welcome. Contact Gill Donald for a brochure/booking.

CUPAR (near St. Andrews). Mrs Morna Chrisp, Scotstavit Farm, By Cupar KY15 5PA (Tel & Fax: 01334 653591). ♥♥ COMMENDED. Working farm.

Make this unusually quiet and scenic spot a must to enjoy the stunning unspoilt views over and beyond the Bonnie Howe of Fife to the Lomond Hills, the Sidlaws and the Grampian Mountains. Nestled beside National Trust places of interest our traditional working farm is a few minutes from the county town of Cupar and the historic village of Ceres with St. Andrews 10 minutes' drive away. Comfortable characteristic farmhouse where you can gaze on panoramic views whilst enjoying a hearty breakfast or preparing for bed — the wonderful scenery is endless. Perfectly situated for golfing or touring. Open all year. Realistic prices.

CUPAR. Rathcluan Guest House, Carslogie Road, Cupar KY15 4HY (Tel & Fax: 01334 657857/6).

Views overlooking the park and mature landscaped gardens, private courtyard parking. Secluded but not isolated. Access and rooms for disabled visitors. Private leisure facilities package. Hourly Intercity service to Aberdeen, Edinburgh or London. 10 miles to St. Andrews on the A91, yet miles from city prices. Bed and Breakfast from £18 per person. All major credit cards accepted. Highly commended self-catering accommodation also available in the heart of old St. Andrews. Please write, or telephone, for further details.

DAIRSIE. Mrs Rena Keiller, "Osnaburgh", 84 Main Street, Dairsie, Cupar KY15 4SS (01334 870603). Old cottage set on the edge of the small country village of Dairsie (only 10 minutes from St. Andrews) which has been extended to a high standard to accommodate guests. Three bedrooms two en suite and one with private bathroom. Dairsie is central for touring the area with many tourist attractions nearby. Golfers welcome as there are many golf courses in the area. Special rates for three or four night breaks and weekly rates available, based on two sharing double room. Please write or telephone for further details.

DALGETY BAY. Mr & Mrs Mead, The Coach House, 1 Hopeward Mews, Dalgety Bay KY11 5TB (01383 823584). STB Listed COMMENDED. Comfortable bungalow with beautiful views of River Forth and Edinburgh. Large waterfront gardens with access to Fife Coastal Path. One twin, one double/family and one single bedrooms. No smoking. No pets. Bed and Breakfast from £18 per person. Open January to December.

FALKLAND. Mrs C. Wilson, The Red House, Freuchie, Falkland KY15 7EZ (01337 857555). Built in 1736, this traditional house is situated in a lovely village in the rural heart of the Kingdom. Less than one hours' drive from Edinburgh, Stirling and Pitlochry and a stone's throw from St. Andrews, Perth and Dundee. Golfers love it here — over 50 courses within a 30 mile radius including Ladybank, Carnoustie and the Old Course. National Trust properties, especially Falkland Palace, convenient, as are clean beaches, sports facilities, entertainment, crafts and shops. Start your day with a wholesome breakfast served in the conservatory overlooking our beautiful mature gardens. Come and savour Scottish hospitality at its best.

FIFE REGION – THE KINGDOM PERSISTS!
Sandwiched between the Firth of Forth and the Firth of Tay, Fife Region has much to commend it to the tourist. The home of golf at St Andrews, the restored National Trust village of Culross, Falkland Palace, the Fife Folk Museum and the East Neuk, a delightful stretch of coastline, where days can be spent exploring.

FREUCHIE. Mrs Duncan, Freuchie Farmhouse, Little Freuchie Farm, Freuchie near Falkland, Cupar

KY15 7HU (01337 857372). 👑 *COMMENDED.* 19th century farm house where Janice Duncan would like to make you welcome. Porridge, home-made preserves and substantial breakfast served in surroundings guaranteed to make you feel at home. Tea/coffee and home baking available. Facilities include sun lounge with TV, secluded garden. Bedrooms have washbasins, central heating and electric blankets. Ideal centre for sightseeing, golf, walking or simply relaxing, with good restaurants nearby. St Andrews, Dundee and Perth only 30 minutes away. Bed and Breakfast £16 to £18 per person, single room supplement £4 to £5. Open March till October. Welcome Host Certificate.

LEVEN BY. Mrs Audrey Hamilton, Duniface Farm, By Leven KY8 5RH (01333 350272). Working

farm. Situated on the A915 between Windygates and Leven, Duniface is well placed for exploring historic Fife, playing the numerous golf courses and visiting the endless places of interest within the county and in the surrounding shires; St. Andrews 25 minutes' drive, Forth Road Bridge 30 minutes' drive. The elegant, spacious Victorian farmhouse with its lovely gardens is particularly beautiful, a place where comfort combined with hospitality, relaxed atmosphere and personal attention is assured. Open all year.

NEWBURGH. Mrs Kathleen Baird, East Clunie Farmhouse, Easter Clunie, Newburgh KY14 6EJ

(01337 840218). 👑👑 *COMMENDED.* **Working farm.** David and Kathleen Baird warmly welcome you to their 18th century centrally heated farmhouse. Easter Clunie is an arable farm with stock situated on the Fife and Perth border. Home baking and tea served on arrival in the resident's lounge. All rooms have eithe private facilities or en suite and tea/coffee trays. Relax in the walled garden, enjoy panoramic views of the River Tay. Ideal touring base for Fife and Perthshire, only 45 minutes from Edinburgh. Children welcome. Bed and Breakfast from £15 to £17. Open April to October.

ST. ANDREWS. Mrs M. Allan, 2 King Street, St. Andrews KY16 8JQ (01334 476326). STB Listed,

APPROVED. This is a family-run B&B situated in a quiet residential area of the historic town of St. Andrews. It is within easy walking distance of the town centre and the golf courses. Accommodation comprises one double and one twin-bedded room, both have TV, radio and tea/coffee making facilities. The house is centrally heated. Early breakfasts are available for golfers. Well behaved dogs are most welcome by arrangement. Open all year. Non-smokers preferred. Bed and Breakfast from £15 to £18 per person. A warm welcome awaits you.

PUBLISHER'S NOTE

While every effort is made to ensure accuracy, we regret that FHG Publications cannot accept responsibility for errors, omissions or misrepresentation in our entries or any consequences thereof. Prices in particular should be checked because we go to press early. We will follow up complaints but cannot act as arbiters or agents for either party.

ST. ANDREWS. Mrs Anne Duncan, Spinkstown Farmhouse, St. Andrews KY16 8PN (01334 473475). STB *HIGHLY COMMENDED.* Only two miles from St. Andrews on the picturesque A917 coast road to Crail, Spinkstown is a uniquely designed farmhouse with views of the sea and surrounding countryside. Bright and spacious, it is furnished to a high standard. Accommodation consists of double and twin rooms, all are en suite and have tea/coffee making facilities; diningroom and lounge with colour TV. Substantial farmhouse breakfast to set you up for the day, evening meals by arrangement only. The famous Old Course, historic St. Andrews and several National Trust properties are all within easy reach, as well as swimming, tennis, putting, bowls, horse riding, country parks, nature reserves, beaches and coastal walks. Plenty of parking available. Bed and Breakfast from £18; Evening Meal £11. AA Selected.

UPPER LARGO. Mr and Mrs D. Law, Monturpie Guest House, Upper Largo, Leven KY8 5QS (01333 360254 & 01333 360850). Superior quality guest house beautifully situated with magnificent views over Firth of Forth. Ideally suited for both golfers wishing to sample some of Scotland's finest courses and others simply wanting to experience the many varied attractions in the East Neuk. All rooms non-smoking with en suite, colour TV and tea/coffee facilities. Large private lounge with colour TV. Bed and Breakfast from £17.50 to £19.50. A very warm welcome awaits — a real home from home.

GLASGOW and District

AIRDRIE. Mrs Elsie Hunter, Easter Glentore Farm, Slamannan Road, Greengairs, By Airdrie ML6 7TJ (Tel & Fax: 01236 830243). 🐛🐛 *HIGHLY COMMENDED.* Best B&B Award Winner. Come and enjoy peace and quiet with a warm, friendly, homely relaxed atmosphere (home from home) with good traditional food and hospitality. Working farm with 18th century ground floor farmhouse offering one double/twin en suite, two double rooms with washbasins; guests' own bathroom. Tea/coffee facilities with homemade shortbread and radio alarms in all rooms. Central heating throughout. Lounge with colour TV, separate dining room. Evening tray with home baking. Telephone on request. Excellent touring base — Glasgow and Stirling 15 miles, Edinburgh 28 miles, Airdrie, Cumbernauld and Falkirk all 10 minutes' drive, Strathclyde Leisure Park 13 miles. Museums, sports and parks too numerous to mention nearby. Non-smoking only. Bed and Breakfast from £18,

single supplement £5. Evening meal optional £10. Reductions for long stays. Open all year.

BEITH. Mrs Joan Wilson, Manor Farm, Burnhouse, Beith KA15 1LJ (01560 484006). STB 🐛🐛 COMMENDED. **Working farm.** We extend a warm welcome to all our guests — old and new. Our farm guest house offers well appointed standard and en suite rooms, with welcome trays and views over the farm or surrounding countryside. An evening meal is available by prior arrangement and a hearty Ayrshire breakfast is served. Located 15 miles (20 minutes) south of Glasgow Airport on Irvine Road A737, then Dunlop Road B706, Manor Farm is an ideal "home" for business trips to Glasgow. Only 10 miles north of Irvine (on A736) and the many attractions of Ayrshire and Arran are nearby. Bed and Breakfast from £15 per person per night. Brochure available.

FINTRY. Mrs M. Mundell, Craigton Farm, Denny Road, Fintry G63 0XQ (0136-086 0426). One mile from the beautiful village of Fintry, this new farmhouse sits on the banks of the Endrick Water. The house looks onto the Campsie Fells and the Fintry Hills which we farm. There are two comfortable bedrooms, bathroom, large TV lounge. Local amenities include trout fishing and scenic hill and river walks. Ideal centre for touring Loch Lomond, Trossachs, Callander, Stirling (all 20 minutes by car); Glasgow 35 minutes; Perth, Loch Tay, Lochearnhead, Crieff, Edinburgh all within one hour by car. A cup of tea and a very warm welcome greets guests on arrival. Bed and Breakfast from £14.

GLASGOW. Mr Douglas Rogen, Kirklee Hotel, 11 Kensington Gate, Glasgow G12 9LG (0141-334 5555; Fax: 0141-339 3828). 🌊 🌊 *HIGHLY COMMENDED.* The Kirklee is set in Glasgow's West End Conservation Area and is an Edwardian townhouse. The character of the building has been retained and there is an extensive collection of paintings, drawings and etchings. As we are away from the main roads all our rooms are quiet. The hotel wins many awards for its gardens and there is a private park facing the hotel which can be used by hotel guests. All rooms have en suite bathrooms, TVs, telephones and much more. The hotel is only a short walk from many restaurants and bars in the centre of the "West End".

GLASGOW. Park Hotel, 960 Sauchiehall Street, Glasgow G3 7TH (0141-337 3000). Small, comfortable and friendly Hotel situated near town centre, good bus service. Only 10 minutes into town for bus and railway stations plus the Royal Concert Hall, Exhibition and Conference Centre, not forgetting our modern variety theatres with all the well known popular artistes appearing there. The Hotel is only five minutes' walk to Kelvingrove Park with its tennis courts and bowling greens; the Botanic Gardens with all its splendour is worth a visit — 10 minutes from hotel by bus. Heating, colour TV, biscuits/tea/coffee facilities in all bedrooms. Bed and Breakfast from £15 to £17.50 per person per night.

GLASGOW. Ms McAlpine, Avonbank Guest House, 132 Yokermill Road, Glasgow G13 4HN (0141-952 1637). STB Listed *COMMENDED.* Situated in excellent location for airport, Glasgow Centre, Clydebank Centre, 15 minutes Loch Lomond, 15 minutes Highland Walkway and many tourist attractions. Train and bus two minutes, SECC 10 minutes, Kelvin Sports Arena 10 minutes, Scotstoun Sports Arena four minutes. All rooms have colour TV, tea/coffee making facilities, towels and are cleaned daily. Parking for eight cars. Own key. Full three course breakfast. Singles from £18, twin from £17 per person. Family rooms available with reduced rates for under 12s.

GLASGOW. Margaret and George Ogilvie, Lochgilvie House, 117 Randolph Road, Glasgow G11 7DS (Tel & Fax: 0141-357 1593). Lochgilvie is a luxurious Victorian townhouse situated in Glasgow's prestigious West End. All bedrooms are very comfortable, well furnished with colour TV, tea/coffee facilities and en suite showers. Centrally heated throughout. Adjacent to rail/station convenient for art galleries, international airport. Eight minutes by train to city centre. Our visitors are assured of warm and friendly service in pleasant surroundings. Open all year. Prices from £22.50 per person.

HIGHLANDS (North) — Caithness & Sutherland

BRORA. Duncan and Marjory Robertson, Braes Hotel, Fountain Square, Brora KW9 6NX (Tel & Fax: 0108 621217). Welcome to the Braes Hotel, with eight bedrooms (two en suite), all have heaters, colour TV, tea/coffee making facilities, radio and duvets. We serve a full Scottish breakfast and evening meals to order. Brora is an ideal centre for North Scotland, John O'Groats and Scrabster (Orkey ferry) are one and a quarter hours' drive. Golf courses in abundance including Royal Dornoch, miles of deserted sandy beaches, sea, river and loch fishing, hill walking, bird watching. Bed and Breakfast from £18 to £22 per person per night. Reduced rates for children under 10 years.

DORNOCH. Mrs Audrey Hellier, Achandean, Meadows Road, Dornoch IV25 3SF (Tel & Fax: 01862 810413). 🌺🌺 *COMMENDED.* RAC Acclaimed. One hour's drive above Inverness. We offer a warm welcome in our delightful bungalow set back off road in secluded feature garden just off town centre in quiet location. Our pleasant, airy bedrooms, en suite and private facilities, have colour TV, tea/coffee tray, comfortable beds. Cosy lounge, separate dining room. Bed and Breakfast from £19. Tea/coffee on arrival. Golf, 13th century Cathedral, other attractions. Excellent for touring/exploring superb far north scenery. Ideally situated for birdwatching, fishing, drives, walking or relaxing. Senior Citzens and disabled persons always welcomed. Evening meal available. Special rates available. Guests return time after time. Renowned for our hospitality.

ROGART. Mrs A. Nicolson, Dalbhioran, 177 Muie, Rogart IV28 3UB (01408 641345). Visitors made very welcome at this award-winning Croft House, situated in the lovely valley of Strathfleet on the main A839 road. Quiet and peaceful location. Guests are accommodated in two family rooms and one single room, all usual amenities. Car park. Golf course and swimming pool within easy reach. Central for touring. Highland cattle can be seen nearby. Children and pets welcome. Award-winning Bed and Breakfast from £14 to £16; Evening Meal on request.

HIGHLANDS (Mid) — Ross-shire

BALINTORE. Mrs J. Palfreman, Rowchoish, East Street, Balintore, Near Tain IV20 1UE (01862 832422). Welcome Host Award. Bed and Breakfast in Balintore overlooking the Moray Firth, north-east of Inverness. Comfortable homely accommodation in one double and one twin room with tea-making facilities; separate shower and toilet. Visitors' lounge. Packed lunches available. Guests can enjoy sea angling, golf and riding in the area, plus the unique Dolphin Watch. Bed and Breakfast £14.50 per person per night. Longer stay reductions. Brochure on request.

GAIRLOCH. Mrs V. Mullaney, Wayside, Strath, Gairloch IV21 2BZ (01445 712008). Set amidst the spectacular scenery of the Scottish Highlands, in the lovely village of Gairloch overlooking Gairloch Bay. Ideally situated for walking, touring, fishing and sandy beaches; six miles away is the world famous National Trust's Inverewe Gardens. Wayside provides central heating, tea/coffee making facilities, TV and wash-basins in all rooms — two double and one twin-bedded. Bed and Breakfast from £13.50 to £16 per person. A warm welcome awaits you.

GAIRLOCH. Mrs McKenzie, "Duisary", 24 Strath, Gairloch IV21 2DA (01445 712252). ♛♛

COMMENDED. A true Highland welcome awaits you in this modernised croft house situated on the outskirts of the village. Superb views of the sea and Torridon Hills. Close to the famous Inverewe Gardens. Idyllic setting with beaches, watersports, golf course, swimming pool and leisure centre all nearby. Ideal spot for hill walking, bird watching, fishing or just relaxing. Lounge with colour TV. Full central heating. Open April to October. Further details available on request.

TAIN. Mrs K.M. Roberts, Carringtons, Morangie Road, Tain IV19 1PY (Tel & Fax: 01862 892635).

STB ♛♛ *COMMENDED.* Welcome Host. Situated two/three minutes' walk from town centre, Carringtons is an attractive Victorian house with magnificent views over Dornoch Firth. Family, double, twin, single rooms available; some en suite, all with tea/coffee facilities, colour TV, shaver points, hair dryers. Public telephone available. Guest lounge with colour TV. Extensive breakfast menu. Washing/drying facilities. Reduced rates for children and under two year olds FREE — cot and babysitting service available. Tain has numerous hotels and restaurants serving food and drink, boasts its own golf course and is close to other courses. Excellent spot for touring; West Coast, Ullapool, John O'Groats, Inverness are within a day's reach. Tariff from £13 per person per night.

TAIN. Mrs S. Ross, Dunbius, Morangie Road, Tain (Tel & Fax: 01862 893010; E-mail: dunbius@

cali.co.uk). ♛♛ *COMMENDED.* Quiet, friendly guest house run by local couple. Good restaurants and a variety of shops all within walking distance. Great selection of golf courses in the area. John O'Groats only one and three-quarters of an hour away so we would make a good base for touring. Twin, double and family rooms, all en suite, colour TV, tea/coffee making facilities and hair dryer. Plenty of off-road parking. Prices from £16 per person per night.

FOR THE MUTUAL GUIDANCE OF GUEST AND HOST

Every year literally thousands of holidays, short-breaks and overnight stops are arranged through our guides, the vast majority without any problems at all. In a handful of cases, however, difficulties do arise about bookings, which often could have been prevented from the outset.

It is important to remember that when accommodation has been booked, both parties — guests and hosts — have entered into a form of contract. We hope that the following points will provide helpful guidance.

GUESTS: When enquiring about accommodation, be as precise as possible. Give exact dates, numbers in your party and the ages of any children. State the number and type of rooms wanted and also what catering you require — bed and breakfast, full board, etc. Make sure that the position about evening meals is clear — and about pets, reductions for children or any other special points.

Read our reviews carefully to ensure that the proprietors you are going to contact can supply what you want. Ask for a letter confirming all arrangements, if possible.

If you have to cancel, do so as soon as possible. Proprietors do have the right to retain deposits and under certain circumstances to charge for cancelled holidays if adequate notice is not given and they cannot re-let the accommodation.

HOSTS: Give details about your facilities and about any special conditions. Explain your deposit system clearly and arrangements for cancellations, charges, etc. and whether or not your terms include VAT.

If for any reason you are unable to fulfil an agreed booking without adequate notice, you may be under an obligation to arrange alternative suitable accommodation or to make some form of compensation.

While every effort is made to ensure accuracy, we regret that FHG Publications cannot accept responsibility for errors, omissions or misrepresentation in our entries or any consequences thereof. Prices in particular should be checked because we go to press early. We will follow up complaints but cannot act as arbiters or agents for either party.

HIGHLANDS (South) — Inverness-shire

CARR-BRIDGE. Lynn and Dave Benge, The Pines Country House, Duthil, Carr-Bridge PH23 3ND (01479 841220). Relax and enjoy our Highland hospitality, offering you personal service in a friendly family atmosphere. Situated in the peaceful surroundings of a pine forest, two miles from the village of Carr-Bridge, we are open all year. All rooms en suite with TV and tea/coffee facilities, central heating throughout. Enjoy our home cooking with traditional or vegetarian meals. Special diets can be arranged. Children and pets are welcome. This is an ideal base for birdwatching, fishing, golf, hill walking, pony trekking, ski-ing plus lots more. A car is essential, parking available. Bed and Breakfast from £17 daily; Dinner, Bed and Breakfast from £155 weekly.

CULLODEN MOOR. Mrs Margaret Campbell, Bay View, Westhill, By Inverness IV1 2BP (01463 790386). 🐾🐾 *COMMENDED.* Bay View is set in a rural area on famous Culloden Moor, offering comfortable homely accommodation in one twin-bedded room with en suite shower, one double room en suite and one double room with private bathroom. An excellent touring base for the Highlands of Scotland and many famous historic sites. All home made food, local produce used. Bed and Breakfast from £16.

DAVIOT. Torguish House, Daviot, Inverness (01463 772208). Torguish House, once the local manse and childhood home of the late author Alistair MacLean of "Guns of Navarone" fame, has now been converted into a very homely Guest House, with generous rooms, most en suite. All rooms have TV and tea/coffee facilities. Guests' lounge. Ample parking, large garden and play area for children. Pets welcome. Bed and Breakfast £18 to £22. Reductions for children. The STEADING has recently been converted into self catering cottage sleeping 2/4 with extra bed settee in lounge. Fully equipped kitchen and bathroom. Lighting included in the rent, all other electricity by £1 coin meter. Cot and high chair available. Rent £110 to £195 (one bedroom) and £150 to £295 (two bedrooms) per week.

DULNAIN BRIDGE. Cheryl and Tim Shouesmith, Rosegrove Guest House, Skye of Curr, Dulnain Bridge, Grantown-on-Spey PH26 3PA (01479 851335). 🐾🐾 *COMMENDED.* Situated close to the famous Heather Centre, in the beautiful Spey Valley, 10 miles from Aviemore. Ideal for birdwatching, walking, fishing, golfing and exploring the mountains and glens of the Scottish Highlands. The food is something special, venison, salmon and Scotch beef. After dinner relax by the log fire enjoying the view over the valley to the Cairngorms. Accommodation is in double, twin, single and family rooms, some en suite. Rosegrove is a holiday for the whole family, children and pets are welcome and there is ample parking. Open New Year. Bed and Breakfast from £15.50; Dinner, Bed and Breakfast from £24. Weekly terms available.

HIGHLAND REGION – AND THE ISLANDS TOO!

From the genteel town of Inverness to the ragged formations of the west-coast and on, over the sea to Skye and many more islands – yes Highland Region is vast! You'll probably not find that many people but places that most definitely should be found include, the Caledonian Canal, Culloden, Mallaig, Loch Ness, Inverewe, Duncansby Head, Ben Nevis, the Cairngorms, Golspie, and the Islands themselves.

FORT WILLIAM. Mrs Catherine Smith, Ben View Guest House, Belford Road, Fort William PH33 6ER (01397 702966). ✤✤ *COMMENDED.* Family-run guest house on A82 Glasgow/Fort William/Inverness road, five minutes' walk from town centre, bus and rail stations, town gardens and sports centres. Bedrooms have en suite facilities, central heating, tea/coffee makers, radio and colour TV. There are two comfortable lounges and spacious dining-room. Car parking available within grounds. Excellent touring area. Full fire precautions. Member of Tourist Board and Automobile Association. Bed and full Scottish Breakfast £17 to £23 per person. AA QQQQ.

FORT WILLIAM. Mrs Mary MacLean, Innishfree, Lochyside, Fort William PH33 7NX (01397 705471). ✤✤ *HIGHLY COMMENDED.* Set against the background of Ben Nevis, this spacious Bed and Breakfast house offers a high level of service. Just two miles from the town centre and three miles from Glen Nevis. Visitors are guaranteed a warm friendly welcome and excellent accommodation. All rooms have en suite facilities and also offer remote control colour TV and tea/coffee making facilities. Breakfast is served in the conservatory, which is overlooked by panoramic views. Enthusiastic advice on pursuits and activities are given. Access to private car park is available. This house has a no-smoking policy and pets are not allowed. Open all year. Prices range from £17 to £21.

FORT WILLIAM. Mrs A. Grant, Glen Shiel Guest House, Achintore Road, Fort William PH33 6RW (01397 702271). ✤✤ *COMMENDED.* Modern purpose built guest house situated near the shore of Loch Linnhe with panoramic views of the surrounding mountains. Accommodation comprises three en suite double bedrooms, one twin-bedded room and one family room (to suit three adults), all with colour TV and tea making facilities. Non smoking. Large car park. Garden. Bed and Breakfast from £15. Directions: on the A82 one and a half miles south of Fort William.

FORT WILLIAM. Patricia Jordan, "Beinn Ard", Argyll Road, Fort William PH33 6LF (01397 704760). ✤✤ *COMMENDED.* Situated in a quiet street in an elevated position just above the town with panoramic views of Loch Linnhe and surrounding hills. Only five minutes' walk from town centre, pier and station. This is a most attractive wooden house which has recently been extended and renovated to a high standard. We offer our guests a pleasant informal and comfortable base from which to view the magnificent local scenery and experience the many attractions Fort William has to offer. One family room en suite, one double room en suite, one twin room and two single rooms; all have colour TV and tea/coffee making facilities. Open 28th December to end October. Skiers welcome. Bed and Breakfast from £16 to £18.50.

INVERGARRY. Caroline Francis, Drynachan Cottage, Invergarry PH35 4HL (01809 501225). STB ✤✤ *COMMENDED.* A friendly welcome awaits you all year round at our 17th century Highland cottage, visited by Bonnie Prince Charlie in 1746, idyllically situated in the Great Glen. All rooms are either en suite (bath and shower) or with washbasins, together with comfortable seating, central heating and tea/coffee making. There is a cosy sitting room with log fire, colour TV and comfortable armchairs and a separate dining room where breakfast and home cooked evening meals are served. There is also a large garden and ample parking. Drynachan is ideal for touring, hillwalking and cycling; outdoor activities packages are also available.

INVERNESS. Miss Storrar, Abb Cottage, 11 Douglas Row, Inverness IV1 1RE (01463 233486). A

historic Listed terraced cottage in a quiet, central riverside street. Within easy walking distance of coach and train stations. No smoking policy throughout. Three twin bedrooms have washbasins, shaver points; lounge/dining room has books, puzzles, games, tourist information and time-tables, etc. All ground floor rooms are wheelchair accessible, one step only at front door. Evening meals by arrangement, vegetarians and special diets catered for. Packed breakfasts are provided for early departures. Sorry no children under 12 years and no pets.

INVERNESS. Mrs A. MacLean, Waternish, 15 Clachnaharry Road, Inverness IV3 6QH (01463 230520). 🐾🐾 *COMMENDED.* Delightful bungalow in beautiful setting overlooking Moray Firth and Black Isle. On main A862 road to Beauly, and just five minutes to Inverness town centre. Ideal touring centre for North and West. Canal cruises five minutes' walk away, lovely walks by banks of Caledonian Canal. Golf course is also nearby, and Loch Ness is just 15 minutes' drive. Accommodation comprises three double/twin rooms, one ensuite, all with tea/coffee making facilities. Comfortable TV lounge, full Scottish breakfast. Private car park. Open March to October. Bed and Breakfast from £14.

INVERNESS. Mrs Marion Singer, Balvonie Cottage, Drumossie Hill, Inverness IV1 2BB (Tel & Fax:

01463 230677). Situated downhill from the Drumossie Hotel (two miles approximately south east of Inverness). Guests are accommodated in a charming fully en suite spacious bedsittingroom (twin) convertible to a family bedroom (twin and double) with colour TV, tea/coffee making, etc. Graded Superior by international operator. From Balvonie Cottage, an attractive residence between two farms, guests enjoy panoramic views of mountains and firths with all the advantages of town nearby. Ideal touring centre for Loch Ness and convenient for Culloden Battlefield Visitor Centre. Bed and Breakfast from £16.50 or three night breaks from £15 per person per night (May and October) in this non-smoking residence. Tariff including single and family occupancy rates and illustrated brochure on application. Loan video £5 (returnable). NB accommodation unsuitable for very young children.

INVERNESS. Mrs E. Alexander, Culdoich Farm, Culloden Moor IV1 2EP (01463 790268). 🐾

COMMENDED. AA QQ. Come and enjoy a holiday in our 18th century farmhouse on a working farm with breeding cattle and sheep, collie dogs and farm cat; free-range eggs. We are seven miles from Inverness near Culloden Battlefield and Clava Cairns; Cawdor Castle and Loch Ness not far away. An ideal centre for touring. Come and try my home cooking with Bed and Breakfast or Dinner, Bed and Breakfast; bedtime drink free plus home baking. Bed and Breakfast from £16. Farm Holiday Guide Diploma Winner.

INVERNESS. Mrs Joan Hendry, 'Tamarue', 70A Ballifeary Road, Inverness IV3 5PF (01463

239724). 🐾 *COMMENDED.* Comfortable Bed and Breakfast base whilst you tour the many beauty spots and places of interest in the Highlands, or if you are simply passing through. Guests are accommodated in one double with private facilities and one double and one twin; all rooms overlook attractive garden to rear and have washbasins and tea-making facilities; central heating; TV lounge; separate shower for visitors' use. Near to riverside walks, golf course and Loch Ness cruises; 10 minutes' walk to Eden Court Theatre and 15 minutes to shops, restaurants, bus and railway station. Ample parking. Long established reputation for cleanliness and attractive surroundings. Completely non-smoking house. Bed and Breakfast from £13.50, no VAT.

INVERNESS. Mrs E. MacKenzie, The Whins, 114 Kenneth Street, Inverness IV3 5QG (01463 236215). Comfortable, homely accommodation awaits you here 10 minutes' walking distance from town centre, bus and railway stations. Inverness being an excellent touring base for North, West and East bus and rail journeys. Bedrooms have TV and tea-making facilities, washbasins and heating off-season. Bathroom has a shared shower and toilet. Pensioners welcome at slightly reduced rate. Two double/twin rooms from £14 per person per night. Write or phone for full details.

INVERNESS. Mrs F. McKendrick, Lyndale Guest House, 2 Ballifeary Road, Inverness IV3 5PJ

(01463 231529). Lyndale Guest House, adjacent to the A82 on entering Inverness from Loch Ness, is delightfully situated in an exclusive residential area close to the River Ness and within eight minutes' walk from town centre. Eden Court Theatre and Restaurant 200 yards, the municipal golf course and Loch Ness Cruise departure point five minutes' walk. Standing in private grounds Lyndale is well appointed, with an attractive diningroom; all bedrooms with colour TV and tea/coffee facilities; several en suite. Guests have full use of amenities of the house all day. Private parking in grounds. Bed and Breakfast from £15; en suite £20.

KINCRAIG/INSH. Ian and Pamela Grant, Greenfield Croft, Insh PH21 1NT (01540 661010). 🌸🌸

HIGHLY COMMENDED. Nestled on the edge of Insh village, with panoramic views over Insh Marshes Bird Reserve to the Monadhliath Mountains. A working croft set in quiet, peaceful countryside, ideal for all outdoor pursuits including bird-watching, climbing, shooting, gliding, fishing, mountaineering, pony trekking, riding, golf, cycling, mountain biking, downhill and cross-country ski-ing and watersports. There are many forest trails from the doorstep, rivers, glens and mountains to explore. Relax in the evening by our cosy log fire. Double and twin rooms available, all with en suite shower room. Bed and Breakfast from £15. Dinner by arrangement from £11. Reduced weekly rates.

KINGUSSIE. John and Elrine Jarratt, St. Helens, Ardbroilach Road, Kingussie PH21 1JX (01540 661430). 🌸🌸 *HIGHLY COMMENDED.* Non-smoking,

centrally heated throughout, St. Helens is an elegantly furnished Victorian house c.1890, situated within half an acre of garden in an elevated position overlooking the village with magnificent views of the Cairngorm Mountains beyond. We have two large comfortable bedrooms, twin en suite and double with private bathroom, tea/coffee trays and large private lounge with TV. Ample parking. An ideal base for playing golf, fishing, walking, water sports, horse riding, ski-ing, etc., and touring the Highlands. Open all year. Terms from £20 per person (special rates for out of season breaks). We look forward to welcoming you.

NAIRN. Mrs B. Fraser, Sandown House, Sandown Farm Lane, Nairn IV12 5NE (01667 454745). STB

Listed *COMMENDED.* Situated on the outskirts of Nairn offering comfortable B&B accommodation. Double, twin, family and single rooms available, all have washbasins and are centrally heated. Visitors are welcome to make themselves at home in our very comfortable TV lounge or if you are feeling more energetic a swim in our indoor swimming pool. Tea/coffee facilities available. Ample off street parking. Enjoy the tranquillity of the countryside while being only five minutes' drive to town centre. Two championship golf courses and beautiful clean sandy beaches nearby. Bed and Breakfast from £14 to £16.

NEWTONMORE. Mr Dennis Hugh Blackburn, The Aspens, Speybridge, Newtonmore PH20 1DA

(01540 673264; Fax: 01540 662494). In the beautiful Scottish Highlands by the banks of the River Spey, Dennis and Isobel Blackburn are pleased to welcome you to our luxury Bed and Breakfast home. Our three spacious en suite, fully centrally heated bedrooms all have mountain views, TV and tea/coffee facilities. Full Scottish or Continental breakfast and four-course dinner (book by 3pm) are served in our garden room. All meals are freshly prepared using wherever possible, local produce. Many outdoor pursuits including golf, fishing and hill walking available locally. Children and pets are welcome. Bed and Breakfast from £20; Dinner £15. Details available on request.

SMITHTON. Mrs M.B. Mansfield, 3A Resaurie, Smithton, By Inverness (01463 791714). STB ♕ ♕

COMMENDED. Three miles east of Inverness. Views across open farmland to Moray Firth, Ross-shire Hills. Double with en suite facilities; double and twin with shared bathroom. Non-smoking. Car parking. Home baking. High Tea from 6. Evening Meal from £12. Public transport nearby. Bed and Breakfast from £15.

TOMATIN. Mhorag and Tony Lucock, Glenan Lodge (Licensed), Tomatin (01808 511217; Fax:

01808 511356). The Glenan Lodge is a typical Scottish Lodge situated in the midst of the Monadhliath Mountains in the valley of the Findhorn River, yet only one mile from the A9. It offers typical Scottish hospitality, home cooking, warmth and comfort. The 10 bedrooms all have central heating, tea making facilities and washbasins; some have en suite facilities. There is a large comfortable lounge and a homely dining room. The licensed bar is well stocked with local malts for the guests. Glenan Lodge caters for the angler, birdwatcher, hillwalker, stalker and tourist alike whether passing through or using as a base. Open all year round. Bed and Breakfast from £16; Dinner £9.50 (optional). Fishing is available at a modest price on our own two mile private beat.

LANARKSHIRE

CALDERBANK. Mrs Betty Gaines, Calderhouse, 13 Main Street, Calderbank ML6 9SG (01236

769077). Calderhouse is situated five minutes from the M8 motorway, 12 miles from Glasgow and 30 miles from Edinburgh, close to Strathclyde Park and many other attractions. A very spacious Victorian sandstone house which is over 100 years old and has been tastefully refurbished over the last three years. Twin en suite room, family room and singles, all with shower and washbasins, satellite TV and tea making facilities. Guest lounge with satellite TV. Ample parking. Bed and Breakfast from £22 per person. Reduced rates for children.

ELVANFOOT. Mrs Marian Iles, Glenelvan, Dumfries Road, Elvanfoot ML12 6TF (01864 505254).

Situated in peaceful Lowther Hills just three minutes from the M74 Junction 14, this is the ideal halfway house when travelling North or South or the perfect centre for touring the lovely Border countryside. Many local places of interest — Drumlanrig Castle, Lead Mining Museum, restored railway and scenic passes are but a few. Excellent walking area. Accommodation is centrally heated, spacious and comfortable. All bedrooms (one double, two twin) have washbasins, electric blankets and clock radios — sharing three shower/bathrooms. Lounge with TV. A very warm welcome and good home cooking is guaranteed, home-made bread a speciality. Open all year. Bed and Breakfast from £16; Evening Meals by arrangement. NON-SMOKING.

HARTHILL. Mrs M. Ireland, Blair Mains Farm, Harthill ML7 5TJ (01501 751278). Working farm.

Attractive farmhouse on small farm — 72 acres. Immediately adjacent to Junction 5 of M8 motorway. Has horses and various other animals. Ideal centre for touring, with Edinburgh, Glasgow, Stirling 30 minutes' drive. Fishing (trout and coarse) and golf nearby. Clay pigeon shooting. One family, one double, two twin and four single bedrooms; bathroom; sittingroom, diningroom; sun porch. Central heating. Children welcome — babysitting offered. Pets welcome. Car essential — parking. Bed and Breakfast from £16; weekly rates available. Reduced rates for children. Open all year.

LESMAHAGOW. Mrs Hamilton, Kerse Farm, Lesmahagow ML11 0HX (01555 894545; Fax: 01555

894646). STB *HIGHLY COMMENDED.* The farm is situated in quiet peaceful surroundings yet only five minutes from Junction 10 on M74. It is an ideal base for touring in the south of Scotland. Accommodation is in two twin bedrooms, both have washbasins and tea/coffee making facilities. Guests bathroom with bath, shower, WC and washbasin. Sorry no pets. It is a no smoking house. Bed and Breakfast from £18.

SKIRLING. Mrs Marion McIntyre, Forest Edge, Muirburn Farm, Skirling, Near Biggar ML12 6HL

(01899 860284). Set half a mile from road in beautiful surroundings. Dog walking in adjacent forest. Good home cooking. Lounge with log fire. Ample parking. Convenient for Glasgow and Edinburgh. Bed and Breakfast £14 double/family room, single £12; Children five to 11 years half price, under five years FREE. Three-course Evening Meal £6. Pets welcome.

MORAY

ELGIN. Mr W.G. Ross, The Bungalow, 7 New Elgin Road, Elgin IV30 3BE (01343 542035). 👑

COMMENDED. Family-run guest house, 15 minutes walk from town centre, five minutes from railway station. Convenient for touring, six to 10 miles to beaches, Whisky Trail and historic Castle Trail near by. Links and inland golf courses and river or loch fishing available locally. There are one single, one double and one twin-bedded rooms, two with shared bathroom, all with TV, radio and tea making facilities. Open January to December. Children and pets welcome. Central heating. Bed and Breakfast from £15. Please write, or telephone, for further details.

ELGIN. Nonsmokers Haven, 37 Duff Avenue, Elgin IV30 1QS (01343 541993; Mobile: 07050 371891). STB Listed COMMENDED. AA Recommended.

Isobel and Mac welcome guests to their comfortable bungalow, which stands on the corner of a tree lined avenue. Centrally located in a pleasant residential area, only minutes' walk from railway station and town amenities. The two bedrooms with "guests only" shower and toilet room are on the ground floor, (no long corridors or stairs to climb). Bedrooms have washbasins, TV, tea/coffee facilities and small posies of flowers from the garden. Ideal base for touring. Whisky Trail, golf, trout and salmon fishing, ornithology or just relaxing. Private parking. Non-smokers delight. Phone bookings taken.

FORRES. Louise Nuttall-Halliwell, Neptune Guest House and Verdant Restaurant, 22/24 Tolbooth Street, Forres IV36 0PH (Tel & Fax: 01309 674387). 👑👑👑 COMMENDED.

Neptune Guest House is a 17th century modernised Scottish townhouse offering every modern convenience in traditional surroundings. It is situated in a quiet location just off Forres town centre within easy walking distance of all local amenities. All rooms are beautifully appointed and have colour TV, tea/coffee making facilities, radio alarms and washbasins; some rooms also have en suite bathrooms. Children and pets are welcome, and we accept all major credit cards. We also boast a fully licensed restaurant specialising in vegetarian and vegan cuisine which offers a range of meals and snacks throughout the day and into the evening.

NAIRN. Marie and Blair Cruickshank, The Briaighe, Albert Street, Nairn IV12 4HQ (Tel & Fax: 01667 453285).

FHG award-winning "B&B on the Golf Trail". Ideal base for Dornoch, Lossiemouth and many other courses within one hours' drive. Nairn Golf Club hosting 1999 Walker Cup three minutes away. Inverness Airport 10 miles. Quiet residential area. Short Breaks and out of season reductions. Open all year. Bed and Breakfast from £16 to £20 per person per night.

PERTH & KINROSS

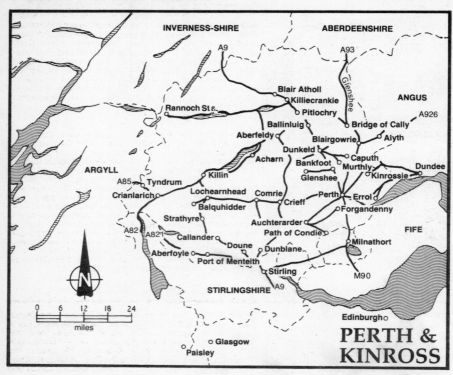

PERTH & KINROSS

BRIDGE OF CALLY. Mrs Josephine MacLaren, Blackcraig Castle, Bridge of Cally PH10 7PX (01250 886251 or 0131-551 1863). A beautiful castle of architectural interest situated in spacious grounds. Free trout fishing on own stretch of River Ardle. Pony trekking can be arranged. Excellent centre for hill walking, golf and touring — Braemar, Pitlochry (Festival Theatre), Crieff, Dunkeld, etc., Glamis Castle within easy reach by car. Four double, two twin, two family and two single bedrooms, eight with washbasins; two bathrooms, three toilets. Cot, high chair. Dogs welcome free of charge. Car essential, free parking. Open for guests from July to early September. £21.50 per person per night includes full breakfast plus tea/coffee and home baking served at 10pm in the beautiful drawing room which has a log fire. Reduced rates for children under 14 years. Enquiries November to end June to **1 Inverleith Place, Edinburgh EH3 5QE.**

Blackcraig Castle, Bridge of Cally, Perthshire

CALLANDER. Betty McLeod, Craigroyston, 4 Bridge Street, Callander FK17 8AA (01877 331395; E-mail: craigroy@world-traveler.com). ♥♥ *COMMENDED.* Craigroyston is in the oldest part of Callander and is adjacent to the Meadows and shops. You can be sure of a warm welcome and good home cooking when you stay at Craigroyston. All rooms have central heating, tea/coffee making facilities, en suite facilities and colour TV. Centrally located within an hour's drive of Edinburgh, Glasgow and Perth, Callander is an ideal touring centre, long considered as the most convenient starting point for touring the Trossachs. Children and well behaved dogs welcome. Bed and Breakfast from £18. Brochure available.

CALLANDER. LenyMede Bed & Breakfast, Leny Road, Callander FK17 8AJ (01877 330952; E-mail: jamesgreen@msn.com Website: http://www. lenymede.demon.co.uk). ♛♛ *COMMENDED.* A non-smoking family home, this Victorian house in a rural setting overlooking the River Leny has extensive views of forest and hills. Ideally situated for the Southern Highlands and Trossachs, an area of lochs, forests, rivers and mountains with woodland and hill trails for walkers and cyclists. Three well appointed double rooms, one en suite, one family. King size beds, central heating, tea/coffee maker, colour TV. Facilities include bathroom, shower room, drying area, packed lunches by arrangement, off road parking and guided walks. Close to Stirling, Edinburgh and Glasgow. Children welcome. From £18.

CALLANDER. Lynne and Alistair Ferguson, Roslin Cottage Guest House, Lagrannoch, Callander FK17 8LE (01877 330638). Situated on the outskirts of Callander, the Gateway to the Trossachs, Roslin Cottage has recently been restored yet still retains many original features including stone walls, beams and an open fireplace in the lounge. We offer a varied Scottish Breakfast with Evening Meals on request. We use our own produce when available which includes eggs from our hens, ducks or geese, and honey from our apiary. We have three double, one twin and two single bedrooms, all with central heating, washbasins and tea/coffee makers. Bed and Breakfast from £15.50 per person per night; four-course Evening Meal from £12.50 per person. Single occupancy £18.50. Brochure on request. Ideal touring base, with sailing, fishing, walking, climbing, mountain biking, etc all on the doorstep. Reduced weekly rates. Dogs especially welcome and stay FREE.

CRIANLARICH. Mr & Mrs A. Chisholm, Tigh Na Struith, The Riverside Guest House, Crianlarich FK20 8RU (01838 300235). Voted the Best Guest House in Britain by the British Guild of Travel Writers in 1984, this superbly sited Guest House comprises six bedrooms, each with unrestricted views of the Crianlarich Mountains. The three-acre garden leads down to the River Fillan, a tributary of the River Tay. Personally run by the owners, Janice and Sandy Chisholm, Tigh Na Struith allows visitors the chance to relax and enjoy rural Scotland at its best. To this end, each bedroom is centrally heated, double glazed, with colour TV and tea/coffee making facilities. Open March to November. Bed and Breakfast from £16 per person.

INCHTURE. "The Orchard", Easter Ballindean, Inchture PH14 9QS (01828 686318). STB *COMMENDED.* Attractive south-facing country cottage set in its own spacious grounds offering comfortable Bed and Breakfast accommodation in peaceful panoramic location, half way between Perth and Dundee. Accommodation comprises two double and one twin bedrooms, all with private shower rooms and tea/coffee making facilities; two rooms with colour TV. Enjoy breakfast in a relaxed and spacious conservatory overlooking the tranquil garden, Tay Valley and Fife hills beyond. Bed and Breakfast from £20. Reductions for children under 12 years. Private safe parking. The Orchard is an ideal base for walking, fishing or golf being only 40 minutes from at least 12 golf courses, including St. Andrews, Carnoustie, Rosemount and Gleneagles.

KIRKMICHAEL by. Malcolm & Jacky Catterall, "Tulloch", Enochdhu, By Kirkmichael PH10 7PW (01250 881404). STB *COMMENDED*. Peace and quiet guaranteed in this friendly, family-run, former farmhouse situated on the A924 Braemar/Kirkmichael Road from Pitlochry. We have three bedrooms — one double en suite and two with washbasins. There are lots of walks and wildlife and birds to be seen from the house. We are members of the RSPB and can show you where many sites of interest are. We are central (geographically) to the Highlands and within an hour or two you can drive to most towns and cities in Scotland. Ideal base for walking or touring. Bed and Breakfast £16; three-course Dinner if required £9.

METHVEN. Mrs Mary Jackson, Sunnylea, Methven PH1 3RF (01764 683354). Comfortable cottage in lovely garden, adjacent A85. 10 miles Perth, seven miles Crieff. Large twin bed/sitting room with private bathroom adjoining, tea/coffee facilities and fridge. Remote control colour TV, electric blankets, central heating, double glazing. Breakfast room. Use of laundry. All ground floor. Ample parking. Beautiful area for touring and visiting many and varied attractions and activities. Bed and Breakfast from £17 per person. Discount for full week. Open April to October. Also self-catering apartment for two with all facilities, available all year.

PERTH. Mrs Mary Fotheringham, Craighall Farmhouse, Forgandenny, Near Bridge of Earn, Perth PH2 9DF (01738 812415). 👑👑 *COMMENDED*. **Working farm.** Come and stay in a modern and warm farmhouse with a cheerful, friendly atmosphere situated in lovely Earn Valley, half a mile west of village of Forgandenny on B935 and only six miles south of Perth. True Highland hospitality and large choice for breakfast served in diningroom overlooking fields where a variety of cattle, sheep and lambs graze. Farm produce used. Open all year, the 1000 acre arable and stock farm is within easy reach of Stirling, Edinburgh, St. Andrews, Glasgow and Pitlochry. Fishing, golf, tennis, swimming locally. Hill walking amid lovely scenery. Rooms with private facilities, others all en suite. Tea making facilities. Sittingroom. Cot and reduced rates for children. Sorry, no pets. Central heating. Car not essential, parking. Bed and Breakfast from £16.50. Mid-week bookings taken. AA/RAC Acclaimed.

PERTH. Mr and Mrs Rennie, Auld Manse Guest House, Pitcollen Crescent, Perth PH2 7HT (Tel & Fax: 01738 629187). 👑 *COMMENDED*. Victorian semi-villa, former manse just a short walk from city centre, parks and sport amenities. Situated on the A94 Coupar Angus road the Manse offers comfortable rooms all with private facilities, colour TV and hospitality tray. Guest lounge with satellite TV. Payphone and fax for guests' use. Ample car parking. Fire and Food Hygiene Certificates. Perth is an ideal base for touring and is only a short drive from most major cities; or try our many beautiful golf courses with a choice of nine or 18 hole play. Open all year. Bed and Breakfast from £18.50. Reductions for party bookings.

Dalshian House STB ♨♨♨ Commended

Quiet, secluded and set in its own parklands only one and a half miles south of Pitlochry, Dalshian House is an early 19th century farmhouse built in 1812. The original public rooms are elegantly furnished and the spacious bedrooms retain their original character. Four double, one twin and two family bedrooms, all en suite with colour TV and welcome tea/coffee tray. The resident owners Malcolm and Althea Carr have created an atmosphere of comfort and quality with a reputation for good food. Bed and Breakfast from £20.50 to £24 per person; Dinner, Bed and Breakfast from £30.50 to £34. Pets welcome. Brochure available.

Old Perth Road, Pitlochry PH16 5JS   Telephone: 01796 472173

PITLOCHRY. Mrs Ruth MacPherson-MacDougall, Dalnasgadh House, Killiecrankie, By Pitlochry PH16 5LN (01796 473237). Attractive country house in grounds of two acres amidst magnificent Highland scenery. Close to National Trust Centre in Pass of Killiecrankie, historic Blair Castle nearby. Only seven minutes from Pitlochry with its famous Festival Theatre. Easy touring distance to Queen's View, Loch Tummel, Balmoral, Braemar, Glamis Castle, Scone Palace and Aviemore. Centrally heated throughout. Lounge with colour TV. All bedrooms have washbasins, shaver points, electric blankets and tea/coffee making facilities. Convenient toilets, showers, bathroom. Sorry no pets. No smoking. Open Easter to October. AA and RAC Listed. Fire Certificate Awarded. Write, telephone or just call in to enquire about terms.

PITLOCHRY. Mrs Barbara Bright, Craig Dubh Cottage, Manse Road, Moulin, Pitlochry PH16 5EP (01796 472058). We invite you to come and stay with us for Bed and Breakfast in our family home which is in the historic conservation village of Moulin, one mile from Pitlochry. Set in one and a half acres of garden, our accommodation comprises one twin room (ground floor) en suite £15 per person per night, one double room (with washbasin) £14 per person per night, two single rooms £14 per night. Disabled guests can be accommodated and most diets catered for on request. All rooms have tea/coffee making facilities and electric blankets. There is a TV lounge. Cot is available. Dogs are welcome. Public transport can be met by arrangement. Open mid-April to mid-October. Come to the heart of the Highlands and relax with us.

STANLEY. Mrs Ann Guthrie, Newmill Farm, Stanley PH1 4QD (01738 828281). ♨ ♨ ♨ *COMMEN-DED.* This 330 acre farm is situated on the A9, six miles north of Perth. Accommodation comprises twin room, double room and family rooms, most en suite; lounge, sittingroom, dining room; bathroom, shower room and toilet. Bed and Breakfast from £17; Evening Meal on request. The warm welcome and supper of excellent home baking is inclusive. Reductions and facilities for children. Pets accepted. The numerous castles and historic ruins around Perth are testimony to Scotland's turbulent past. Situated in the area known as "The Gateway to the Highlands" the farm is ideally placed for those seeking some of the best unspoilt scenery in Western Europe. Many famous golf courses and trout rivers in the Perth area.

PLEASE SEND A STAMPED ADDRESSED ENVELOPE WITH ENQUIRIES

STRATHYRE. Mrs Catherine B. Reid, Coire Buidhe, Strathyre FK18 8NA (01877 384288). Tourist

Board Listed *APPROVED.* Run by the longest established hosts in Strathyre, Coire Buidhe sits in the beautiful valley of Strathyre, nine miles from Callander. An excellent base for touring Loch Lomond, Trossachs, Stirling, Edinburgh, with both east and west coasts within easy reach. Two single, two twin, two double (one with en suite bathroom), two family rooms, all with heaters, washbasins, electric blankets, shaver points and tea making facilities; two showers, bathroom, three toilets. Sitting and dining rooms. Open all year. Parking. Regret no dogs. Children welcome at reduced terms; cot, high chair and babysitting offered. All water sports and shooting available plus trekking, tennis, hill walking, golf and putting. Bed and Breakfast from £14; Dinner from £11. All food personally prepared; home baking. Special diets catered for. Well recommended. Full Fire Certificate. Reduced weekly terms.

RENFREWSHIRE & INVERCLYDE

JOHNSTONE. Mrs Capper, Auchans Farm, Johnstone PA6 7EE (01505 320131). Family-run working farm with large farmhouse offering Bed and Breakfast accommodation. All bedrooms are centrally heated and have colour TV and tea/coffee making facilities. Only five minutes from Glasgow Airport; convenient for City Centre and for touring Burns Country, Loch Lomond, Trossachs, etc. Excellent salmon and trout fishing on River Gryffe close by, permits available. Children welcome. Parking. Open all year. Bed and Breakfast from £15 to £20 per person per night.

LOCHWINNOCH. Mrs Janet Blair, East Kerse Farm, Lochwinnoch PA12 4DU (01505 502400). An

attractive farmhouse with sun lounge and panoramic views over Kilbirnie Loch. A warm welcome awaits you on this 200 acre family-run dairy farm situated just off the A760 Lochwinnoch to Largs road and just 15 minutes from Glasgow Airport. Close by are Muirshiel Country Park RSPB Centre and canoeing at Lochwinnoch, Burns Country within easy reach; Kelburn Country Park; many golf courses; fishing in the Maich burn and Kilbirnie Loch. Accommodation comprises one double room, one twin and one single bedroom. Home baking. Bed and Breakfast from £11.

FOR THE MUTUAL GUIDANCE OF GUEST AND HOST

Every year literally thousands of holidays, short-breaks and overnight stops are arranged through our guides, the vast majority without any problems at all. In a handful of cases, however, difficulties do arise about bookings, which often could have been prevented from the outset.

It is important to remember that when accommodation has been booked, both parties — guests and hosts — have entered into a form of contract. We hope that the following points will provide helpful guidance.

GUESTS: When enquiring about accommodation, be as precise as possible. Give exact dates, numbers in your party and the ages of any children. State the number and type of rooms wanted and also what catering you require — bed and breakfast, full board, etc. Make sure that the position about evening meals is clear — and about pets, reductions for children or any other special points.

Read our reviews carefully to ensure that the proprietors you are going to contact can supply what you want. Ask for a letter confirming all arrangements, if possible.

If you have to cancel, do so as soon as possible. Proprietors do have the right to retain deposits and under certain circumstances to charge for cancelled holidays if adequate notice is not given and they cannot re-let the accommodation.

HOSTS: Give details about your facilities and about any special conditions. Explain your deposit system clearly and arrangements for cancellations, charges, etc, and whether or not your terms include VAT.

If for any reason you are unable to fulfil an agreed booking without adequate notice, you may be under an obligation to arrange alternative suitable accommodation or to make some form of compensation.

While every effort is made to ensure accuracy, we regret that FHG Publications cannot accept responsibility for errors, omissions or misrepresentation in our entries or any consequences thereof. Prices in particular should be checked because we go to press early. We will follow up complaints but cannot act as arbiters or agents for either party.

SCOTTISH ISLANDS

ISLE OF MULL

CRAIGNURE. Pennygate Lodge Guest House, Craignure PA65 6AY (01680812 333/444). 🐾 🐾 🐾

COMMENDED. Georgian house in four and a half acres of landscaped garden with magnificent views of Sound of Mull, 500 yards from ferry point. Eight bedrooms, four en suite, all with tea/coffee making facilities. Delicious home cooking. Children welcome. No dogs. Parking; car and bus hire arranged. Bed and Breakfast from £18 to £30. A la carte Dinner optional, non-resident meals also available.

ISLE OF SKYE

LUIB, by Broadford. Harvey and Gill Willett, Laimhrig, Luib, By Broadford IV49 9AN (01471 822686). With its own access to the sea and magnificent views of the Red Cuillin Hills and the islands of Raasay and Scalpay, this centrally situated bungalow on the shores of Loch Ainort is perfect for exploring Skye. Walking, climbing, bird watching, sailing and golf are popular pastimes in this peaceful area. Explore at will or let us help you plan your days to gain the most from your visit. Bed and Breakfast (English or Continental) from £11.50. Three-day breaks (Bed, Breakfast and Evening Meal) from £58. Vegetarians welcome. Sorry, no smoking.

PORTREE by. Mrs M. MacKenzie, Caberfeidh, 2 Heatherfield, Penifiler, By Portree IV51 9NE (01478 612820). This farmhouse is situated on a croft three miles from Portree on the Isle of Skye. It is in a beautiful setting beside the sea, overlooking Portree Bay, and with views of the Old Man of Storr and the magnificent Cuillins. Two double, one en suite, one twin; shower room, bathroom; sitting room; dining room. Children welcome, babysitting available. Pets permitted. Central heating. Car essential, parking. Open from April to October for Bed and Breakfast from £16. Reduced rates for children. Further details gladly sent on request.

SLEAT. Rosemary Houlton, Home Leigh, Ardvasar, Sleat IV45 8RU (Tel & Fax: 01471 844361).

Home Leigh is an attractive modern home with extensive views across the Sound of Sleat, surrounded by spectacular scenery — the "Garden of Skye". Relax and enjoy the breathtaking views and wildlife. Five minutes' drive to Skye, Armadale Ferry, one mile to Clan Donald Visiting Centre. Most bedrooms have private facilities. All rooms have tea/coffee and TV. Car park. Full Scottish breakfast. Children welcome. Sorry no pets. Open from February to December. Bed and Breakfast from £16.50 to £18.

STAFFIN. Mrs MacDonald, Gairloch View, 3 Digg, Staffin IV51 9LA (01470 562718). Built in 1997 "Gairloch View" is a modern bungalow on the north coast of Skye with magnificent sea and mountain views overlooking Gairloch on the mainland and nestling below the famous Quiraing Mountain. An ideal base for touring, walking, fishing (sea and loch), golf and beach. Day trips to Outer Isles from Uig (eight miles). Hotels and restaurants nearby. One en suite family room sleeping up to four persons, one en suite family room sleeping up to three persons. Central heating, tea/coffee making facilities. Large guest lounge with sea views, open fire, TV and video. Private car park. Double/twin/family from £18 per person per night. Reduced rates for children.

UIG. Mrs G.J. Wilson, Garybuie Guest House, 4 Balmeanach, Glennhinnisdal, Snizort IV51 9UX

(01470 542310). Tourist Board Listed *APPROVED.* Situated in the glen by the side of the River Hinnisdal. Turn off A856 at Hinnisdal Bridge, over cattle grid to telephone box next to house. Accommodation can be provided in two family rooms, one double, one twin, one single. Warm family house, home cooking. Dinner on request. Tea/coffee trays and TV all rooms. Lounge. 10 minutes Uig ferry to Outer Hebrides. River fishing, walking Trotternish Ridge, scenic area. From £15 for Bed and Breakfast; Evening Dinner (3 course) £10; Evening Supper £5. Special winter rates. Brochure available, please ring.

ORKNEY ISLES

SANDWICK. Mrs Hourie, Flotterston House, Sandwick KW16 3LP (01856 841700). Flotterston

House Bed and Breakfast is a former manse, built in the 1850s set in the heart of Orkneys main tourist and fishing attractions. With outstanding views overlooking Skaill Loch, Skara Brae and Skaill Beach. We always welcome children at Flotterston and have a play area and large family rooms which have recently been refurbished to a high standard. At breakfast you can enjoy a full Scottish breakfast or a locally smoked traditional kipper. Flotterston is a few miles from Stromness and is very convenient for catching the St. Ola sailing. We look forward to meeting you. Bed and Breakfast from £14 to £18.

SHETLAND ISLES

BRAE. Mrs E. Wood, Westayre Bed and Breakfast, Muckle Roe, Brae ZE2 9QW (01806 522368).

🌼🌼🌼 *HIGHLY COMMENDED.* A warm welcome awaits you at our working croft on the picturesque island of Muckle Roe, where we have breeding sheep, pet lambs, ducks and cats. The island is joined to the mainland by a small bridge and is an ideal place for children. The accommodation is of a high standard and has en suite facilities and guests can enjoy good home cooking and baking. In the evening sit by the open peat fire and enjoy the views looking out over Swarbacks Minn. Spectacular cliff scenery and clean safe sandy beaches, bird watching and hill walking and also central for touring North Mainland and North Isles. Bed and Breakfast from £16; Dinner, Bed and Breakfast from £24.

WALES

WALES

ANGLESEY & GWYNEDD

ABERDARON. Mrs V. Bate, Bryn Mor, Aberdaron LL53 8BS (01758 760344). Bryn Mor is a family run

Guest House. Full English breakfast, evening meal optional. Comfortable lounge and separate diningroom. Access to rooms at all times. TV and tea making facilities in all rooms. Bathroom and shower facilities. The house overlooks the Bay a few minutes from village and beach. Ample parking space in our own grounds. Bryn Mor is situated in the village of Aberdaron at the tip of the Lleyn Peninsula. Around the Bay are numerous walks with panoramic views, also fishing, sailing and golf in the locality. Assuring you of our best endeavours to make your holiday a pleasant one. Sorry, no pets. Bed and Breakfast £16; Bed, Breakfast and Evening Meal £23.

ABERDOVEY. Jim and Marion Billingham, Preswylfa, Aberdovey LL35 0LE (01654 767239). ♛ ♛ ♛ *HIGHLY COMMENDED.* Preswylfa is a non-smoking very attractive Edwardian family home, private and secluded with a lovely mature garden filled with old fashioned fragrant flowers and safe car parking area. A footpath leads down to the old fishing village of Aberdovey, also famous for its sailing, walking and golf. All three luxury en suite bedrooms have full facilities, two of which enjoy breathtaking views over Cardigan Bay. A relaxing guest lounge with period furniture and grand piano awaits you, the dining room beyond leading into the garden. Evening meals are available by arrangement. Excellent cuisine and a warm welcome guaranteed.

ANGLESEY. Mrs Kirkland, "Carreg Goch", Llanedwen, Llanfairpwll, Anglesey LL61 6EZ (01248

430315). ♛ *HIGHLY COMMENDED.* "Carreg Goch" is quietly situated in the south of Anglesey and is set well back off the A4080 in four acres of gardens and paddock. Easy access to the coast, National Trust properties, Snowdonia and many places of interest makes it a convenient centre. Two centrally heated ground floor rooms have washbasins and tea making facilities. There is a shared guest bathroom/shower but two separate toilets. Both rooms have French windows opening onto a private patio and garden with magnificent views of Snowdonia. Separate guest sitting room with colour TV. Bed and Breakfast £16. Weekly rates available.

Terms quoted in this publication may be subject to increase if rises in costs necessitate

ANGLESEY. Mrs Ritson, "Ger-y-Coed", Gaerwen, Anglesey LL60 6BS (01248 421297; Fax: 01248 421400). ✿ ✿ *HIGHLY COMMENDED.* Homely guest house situated six miles from Bangor on main Holyhead road (A5). Comfortably furnished. Tea/coffee making facilities, washbasins, shaver points and colour TVs in all rooms. Some rooms en suite. Sky TV in lounge. Nice garden, with off-road parking. Good and plentiful food. Double, twin and family rooms available. Central heating. Open all year. Close to all amenities and ferry. Ideal for touring and discovering Snowdonia. Warm welcome assured. Bed and Breakfast from £17. Access and Visa accepted. Full Fire Certificate.

ANGLESEY. Mrs Gwen McCreadie, Deri Isaf, Dulas Bay, Anglesey LL70 9DX (01248 410536). ✿ ✿ ✿ Beautiful Victorian country house standing in 20 acres of woodland, garden and fields, surrounded by lovely countryside, overlooking the bay. Easily accessible, excellent base for touring the island and exploring the coastline with its many lovely beaches. Local amenities include golf, swimming pool and sports centre. Accommodation of a very high standard in two family rooms and one double all en suite with TV and tea/coffee making facilities. Guests' own sitting-room with TV, video, etc. Separate diningroom. Full central heating. Pets welcome; horse stabling available. Car advisable. Bed and Breakfast from £19; Bed, Breakfast and Evening Meal from £26. Reductions for children. Holder of FHG Diploma.

BALA. Glynn and Wenda Jones, Frondderw, Stryd-y-Fron, Bala LL23 7YD (01678 520301). ✿ ✿ ✿ *COMMENDED.* A period mansion situated in own grounds overlooking Bala town and Lake, with views of the Berwyn Mountains. Ideally situated for walking, sailing, golfing and general sightseeing around North and Mid Wales. Accommodation consists of eight bedrooms, four with en suite facilities and two with showers. All bedrooms have washbasins, central heating, tea/coffee making facilities. Guests' lounge. Separate TV lounge, colour TV. Residential licence. Free parking. Sorry, NO PETS. Open March to November inclusive. Bed and Breakfast from £16 to £22 daily per person. Optional three course Dinner £10, including tea/coffee. Home cooked meals. Special diets catered for by prior arrangement. Weekly terms. AA QQ, WTB Welcome Host.

BALA. Mrs C.A. Morris, Tai'r Felin Farm, Frongoch, Bala LL23 7NS (01678 520763). WTB *COMMENDED.* Tai'r Felin Farm is situated three miles north of Bala (A4212 and B4501 roads). Double and twin bedrooms with washbasins, tea/coffee facilities, clock radio; bathroom with shower; lounge with colour TV and log fire when weather is cool. Separate tables in the dining room. Recommended for excellent cooking and friendly atmosphere. Ideal base for walks, sailing (Bala Lake) and for touring Snowdonia Mountains and coast. National White Water Centre is nearby. Relax and enjoy a homely welcome. Please write or telephone for further information.

Cwm Hwylfod

BALA near. Mrs J. Best, Cwm Hwylfod, Cefn-Ddwysarn, Bala LL23 7LN (01678 530310). ✿ *HIGHLY COMMENDED.* **Working farm.** Remote, peaceful 400-year-old farmhouse on working sheep farm. Beautiful countryside and wonderful views. Two double rooms, one large family room, all with washbasins and tea making facilities. Two bathrooms, clothes washing and drying machines. Guests' lounge with colour TV. Full central heating. Cot, high chair available. Parking space. All meals are home cooked. Special diets catered for. Ideal centre for touring, walking, fishing, pony trekking and watersports. Bala Lake 10 minutes by car. Snowdon and many beaches can be reached in 40 minutes. Bed and Breakfast from £16 to £18; Evening Meal by arrangement. Reductions for long stays and children under 10 years. Brochure available. Children most welcome.

BEAUMARIS. Mrs E. Roberts, Plas Cichle, Beaumaris, Anglesey LL58 8PS (Tel & Fax: 01248 810488).

❦ ❦ *HIGHLY COMMENDED.* Welcome Host Gold Award, Farmhouse Award. We welcome you to Plas Cichle, a large period farmhouse set in 200 acres, one and a half miles from the historic town of Beaumaris and the Menai Straits. Accommodation is offered in spacious, comfortable rooms, most are en suite, all have hospitality tray, colour TV and hair dryers. Most have panoramic views over to Snowdonia. Start your day in our elegant dining room and enjoy a hearty breakfast. Relax in the comfortable guest lounge, sit out in the garden or stroll around the farm to see the animals. Plas Cichle is an ideal base from which to explore Anglesey and Snowdonia. Many guests return year after year. Come along and find out why! Bed and Breakfast from £21.50 to £25. Open February to November. Brochure available.

AA
★★★
RAC

plas hall hotel & restaurant

♕♕♕♕
COMMENDED

Snowdonia National Park

Standing in its own gardens offering PEACE and SECLUSION on the banks of the River Lledr off the main A470 road, this magnificent stone built hall is ideally placed for the tourist, walker, fisherman or golfer.

All bedrooms are ensuite, with colour TV, telephone, clock radio and central heating. Licensed bar and superb restaurant. Bed and Breakfast from £19.95, Evening Meal from £10. 2 day Breaks DBB from £47.95. Write or phone for colour brochure B.M. Williams.

Plas Hall Hotel & Restaurant, Dolywyddelan, near Betws-y-Coed, Gwynedd LL25 0PJ. Telephone: 01690 750206. Fax: 01690 750526.

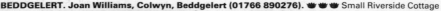

BEDDGELERT. Joan Williams, Colwyn, Beddgelert (01766 890276).

❦ ❦ ❦ Small Riverside Cottage Guesthouse, C1700. Beamed lounge. En suite bedrooms, fresh white linen. Warm, comfortable and friendly. In the centre of a pretty village right at the foot of Snowdon. Wooded mountains, lakes and streams. At the heart of the National Park. With little village shops, inns and cafes. Booking usually essential. Bed and Breakfast £16 to £19. Walkers (muddy boots) and wet dogs welcome. Also tiny cottage, sleeps two, £165 per week.

BLAENAU FFESTINIOG. Mrs B.A. Griffiths, Afallon, Manod Road, Blaenau Ffestiniog LL41 4AE (01766 830468).

❦ *HIGHLY COMMENDED.* Family run guesthouse situated in Snowdonia National Park. Good friendly atmosphere. One double, one twin and one single bedrooms, all are spacious and centrally heated and have colour TV with Sky, tea/coffee facilities, shaver points and washbasins; separate bathroom, toilet and shower. Narrow gauge railways, slate mines, historic castles nearby. Portmeirion, Swallow Falls, sandy beaches, climbing all within easy reach. A choice of Welsh, Continental or vegetarian breakfast. Children and pets welcome. Bed and Breakfast from £14 to £16. Reduced rates for children. Private parking. A Welsh welcome awaits all our guest.

FREE and REDUCED RATE Holiday Visits!
See our READERS' OFFER VOUCHER for details.

BLAENAU FFESTINIOG. Mrs G.E. Hughes, Bryn Celynog Farm, Cwm Prysor, Trawsfynydd, Blaenau Ffestiniog LL41 4TR (01766 540378). A true Welsh welcome awaits you on this working beef/sheep farm surrounded by beautiful scenery in the centre of Snowdonia National Park. Choice of spacious twin, double or family bedrooms, all with washbasins and tea/coffee facilities, one room en suite. Guest bathroom. Lounge with colour TV, open fire. Reputation for excellent food and friendliness. Bed and Breakfast from £17.50 to £19. SAE please.

CAERNARFON. Gwyndaf and Jane Lloyd Rowlands, Pengwern, Saron, Llanwnda, Caernarfon LL54 5UH (Tel & Fax: 01286 831500; Mobile: 0378 411780). ♛ ♛ ♛ *DE LUXE.* Charming spacious farmhouse of character, situated between mountains and sea. Unobstructed views of Snowdonia. Well appointed bedrooms, all en suite. Set in 130 acres of land which runs down to Foryd Bay. Jane has a cookery diploma and provides excellent meals with farmhouse fresh food, including home-produced beef and lamb. Excellent access. Children welcome. Open February to November. Bed and Breakfast from £20 to £25; Evening Meal from £12.

CAERNARFON. Mrs Lilian Wyn Griffiths, Meifod, Bontnewydd, Caernarfon LL55 2TY (01286 673351). ♛ ♛ ♛ Lilian and Rodney welcome you to Meifod in the Royal town of Caernarfon, set in five acres of mature gardens with own tennis court, plus games room. The en suite bedrooms (two double, one twin and one family) have TV and tea/coffee facilities. Beach, golf, Snowdonia and many more attractions only a few minutes' drive away. We will assure you a comfortable stay with real Welsh hospitality. From £15 per night.

CAERNARVON. Mrs S. Williams, Tal Menai Guest House, Bangor Road, Caernarvon LL55 1TP (01286 672160). ♛ ♛ *COMMENDED.* Victorian house standing in its own grounds off the A487 to Bangor (about one mile from Caernarfon Castle), Tal Menai enjoys panoramic views over Menai Straits and Anglesey. It is an ideal centre for touring Snowdonia. Off the road private parking. Locked garages for bicycles. Twin and double rooms, all en suite, colour TV, tea/coffee making facilities and central heating. Access to house at all times. Packed lunches available and special diets catered for. Special terms for four nights stay and out of season bookings. Sorry no pets and no smoking. From £19 per person.

ANGLESEY AND GWYNEDD – OUTSTANDING NATURAL BEAUTY!

With Snowdonia National Park and the Lleyn Peninsula, Gwynedd well deserves its designation as an 'Area of Outstanding Natural Beauty'. The tourist is spoiled for choice in this county but should endeavour to visit the hill-fort at Tre'r Ceiri, the Llugwy Valley, Cwm Pennant, Dinas Dinlle hill-fort, the gold mine at Clogau and the railways and quarries at Blaenau Ffestiniog.

CAERNARVON near. Paula and David Foster, Tan y Gaer, Rhosgadfan, Near Caernarvon LL55 7LE (01286 830943). Set in spectacular scenery with views to the top of Snowdon and over the Irish Sea, this farmhouse with beams and open fires offers a restful atmosphere from which to enjoy beautiful North Wales. Riding, climbing, walking and beaches are all close by. The home-made bread and farmhouse cooking are done on the 'Aga' and much of the food is home produced. Guests have their own dining-room and lounge with TV, books, etc. The ensuite bedrooms are spacious and the family room is comfortable with double bed and bunks. Evening Meal with Bed and Breakfast from £15. Reductions for weekly stays. Telephone/SAE for details, please.

CRICCIETH. Mrs A. Reynolds, Glyn-y-Coed Hotel, Porthmadoc Road, Criccieth LL52 0HL (01766 522870; Fax: 01766 523341). 🌸🌸🌸 *HIGHLY COMMENDED.* Lovely Victorian family run hotel overlooking sea, mountains, Criccieth and Harlech Castles. Fully centrally heated, cosy bar, parking in our grounds. Special diets catered for, highly recommended home cooking. Separate tables in our pretty pink restaurant. All bedrooms are en-suite with colour TV, tea/coffee making facilities. Fire Certificate. Moderate rates, from £20 for Bed and Breakfast. Good reductions for children. One ground floor bedroom with facilities available. Self catering accommodation also available. Les Routiers, AA, RAC. SAE please. Brochure sent with pleasure.

DOLGELLAU. Mr and Mrs J.S. Bamford, Ivy House, Finsbury Square, Dolgellau LL40 1RF (01341 422535). 🌸🌸🌸 A country town Guest House offering a welcoming atmosphere and good food. Guest accommodation consists of six double rooms, three with en suite toilet facilities, all with TV and tea/coffee making. In the evening the dining room is open to non-residents as well as residents offering an extensive menu of HOME MADE FOOD including many vegetarian dishes. There is a bar in the cellar. The lounge has tourist information literature and there are maps available to borrow. Dolgellau is an ideal touring and walking centre in the Snowdonia National Park. Bed and Breakfast from £18.

DOLGELLAU. Mrs G.D. Evans, "Y Goedlan", Brithdir, Dolgellau LL40 2RN (Tel and Fax: 01341 423131). 🌸 *COMMENDED.* Guests are welcome at "Y Goedlan" from February to October. This old Vicarage with adjoining farm offers peaceful accommodation in pleasant rural surroundings. Three miles from Dolgellau on the B4416 road, good position for interesting walks (Torrent, 400 yards from the house), beaches, mountains, narrow gauge railways and pony trekking. All bedrooms are large and spacious; one double, one twin and one family room, all with colour TV, tea/coffee facilities and washbasins; bathroom, two toilets; shower; lounge with colour TV; separate tables in dining room. Reduced rates for children under 10 years. Central heating. Car essential, parking. Comfort, cleanliness and personal attention assured, with a good hearty breakfast; Bed and Breakfast from £15.50.

DYFFRYN ARDUDWY. Mrs A. Jones, Byrdir Farm, Dyffryn Ardudwy LL44 2EA (01341 247200). 🌸🌸🌸 *HIGHLY COMMENDED.* Dragon Awarded, Welsh stone farmhouse in peaceful setting in Snowdonia National Park with coastline in front, mountains to rear. Woods, streams, beaches, lovely walks, golf, swimming pools, fishing, riding nearby. Double and family bedrooms (three en suite); sitting room with colour TV; dining room. Children welcome at reduced rates. Bed and Breakfast from £17 to £19 per person. Open March to September.

Terms quoted in this publication may be subject to increase if rises in costs necessitate

FAIRBOURNE. John and Ann Waterhouse, Einion House, Friog, Fairbourne LL38 2NX (01341 250644). 🌺🌺🌺 *COMMENDED.* Lovely old house between mountains and sea, set in beautiful scenery. Comfortable rooms, double, twin or single, en suite available. Reputation for good home cooking — vegetarians catered for. All rooms with colour TVs, clock/radios, hairdryers, teamakers, sea or mountain views. Separate dining tables. Guests' TV lounge. Restaurant and residential licence. Wonderful sunsets, marvellous walking — maps and Land Rover lifts available. Pony trekking, fishing and bird watching. Good centre for Narrow Gauge Railways. Castle within easy reach. Safe sandy beach few minutes' walk from house. Children and dogs welcome. Bed and Breakfast from £19; optional three-course Dinner £10. Weekly terms.

HARLECH. Gillian and Eric Davies, Noddfa Hotel, Fford Newydd, Harlech LL46 2UB (01766 780043; Fax: 01766 781105). 🌺🌺🌺 *COMMENDED.* Noddfa means place of safety. The orignal Burgers cottage was within bowshot of Harlech Castle and was under its protection. It was modernised by Samuel Holland MP in 1850 as a Victorian country house with magnificent views over Tremadog Bay and the Snowdonia National Park. Eric and Gillian are keen historians and are pleased to explain the displayed medieval weapons, conduct tours of the Castle (World Heritage Site) or turn the clock back 700 years for a traditional archery lesson. All rooms have TV, tea/coffee facilities; some en suite. Close to beach, theatre and public indoor swimming pool. Bed and Breakfast from £16 to £23; Evening Meal from £12.50 to £15.

Key to
Tourist Board Ratings

The Crown Scheme
(England, Scotland & Wales)

Covering hotels, motels, private hotels, guesthouses, inns, bed & breakfast, farmhouses. Every Crown classified place to stay is inspected annually. *The classification:* Listed then 1-5 Crown indicates the range of facilities and services. Higher quality standards are indicated by the terms APPROVED, COMMENDED, HIGHLY COMMENDED and DELUXE.

The Key Scheme
(also operates in Scotland using a Crown symbol)

Covering self-catering in cottages, bungalows, flats, houseboats, houses, chalets, etc. Every Key classified holiday home is inspected annually. *The classification:* 1-5 Key indicates the range of facilities and equipment. Higher quality standards are indicated by the terms APPROVED, COMMENDED, HIGHLY COMMENDED and DELUXE.

The Q Scheme
(England, Scotland & Wales)

Covering holiday, caravan, chalet and camping parks. Every Q rated park is inspected annually for its quality standards. The more √ in the Q – up to 5 – the higher the standard of what is provided.

LLANBEDR. Mrs L. Howie, Gwyn Fryn Farm, Llanbedr LL45 2NY (01341 241381). Stone built 17th century farmhouse set in 20 peaceful acres of beautiful scenery half a mile outside the village of Llanbedr. Accommodation comprises two double, family/twin, one double/twin bedrooms, two rooms en suite and one with shower; all have tea/coffee making facilities. Lounge with colour TV. Full Welsh breakfast. Warm welcome. Parking available. Children welcome and they will love the animals — friendly ponies, goat, hens and ducks. Bed and Breakfast from £18 per person. Self catering accommodation also available.

LLANBERIS. Dolafon Hotel, High Street, Llanberis LL55 4SU (01286 870993). 👑 👑 A small family-run NON SMOKING HOTEL, all rooms are en suite with colour TV and tea/coffee making facilities. We have a small licensed restaurant and bar which offers a varied menu including home made Welsh dishes and a good vegetarian selection. DOLAFON is situated on the main street of Llanberis and is separated from the road by a large lawned garden bordered by mature trees and a small mountain stream offering ample secluded private parking. Llanberis has many places of interest, the slate museum, Dinorwic Hydro Electric Power Station, Dolbardarn Castle and nearby Caernarfon and Beaumaris Castles. Bed and Breakfast from £16.

LLANFAIR. Fron Deg Guest House, Llanfair, Harlech LL46 2RE (01766 780448). Small Georgian cottage overlooking the magnificent beach at Harlech. Central for unspoiled beaches and countryside, yet within easy reach of Porthmadog and Lleyn Peninsula. Good home cooking. Dinner, Bed and Breakfast at reasonable prices. Pretty bedrooms overlooking sea. Pets welcome. Please write or telephone for further information.

LLANGAFFO. Mrs Lamb, Plas Llangaffo Farmhouse, Llangaffo, Anglesey LL60 6LR (01248 440452). Peaceful location situated near to Newborough Forest and Llandwyn Bay with its miles of golden sands. Large garden for visitors' use. Free range eggs and home made marmalade for breakfast. Dinner optional. Tea/coffee making facilities. Sheep, horses and hens kept. Horse riding available in our outdoor manege or a hack out. Lessons can be arranged. We can accommodate your own horse. We are half a mile from cycle route 8 and we have bicycles for hire. Approximately 20 miles from Holyhead, so use us as a base to visit Ireland. Please send for further information.

LLANNERCH-Y-MEDD (Anglesey). Mrs J. Bown, Drws-y-Coed, Llanerch-y-Medd, Anglesey LL71 8AD (01248 470473). 👑 👑 Drws-y-Coed, a beautifully appointed farmhouse on 550 acres of beef, sheep and arable farmland, is set in beautiful wooded countryside with panoramic views of Snowdonia, near to picturesque Bodafon Mountain. Centrally located for beaches, fishing, golf, riding, leisure centres. Tarmac drives. A warm welcome awaits our guests who are accommodated in beautifully decorated and furnished bedrooms, all en suite with colour TV, tea-making facilities and clock radios. Full central heating. Spacious lounge with log fire. Dining room with separate tables; delicious meals. Games room. Lovely walks in vicinity. WTB Rural Tourism Award. Farm Holiday Guide Diploma Award. Reductions for children. Bed and Breakfast from £20 to £23. Non-smoking establishment. Open all year. Brochure available.

MENAI BRIDGE. Ms. Rosemary Ann Abas, Bwthyn, Bryn Afon, Menai Bridge, Isle of Anglesey LL59 5HA (Tel & Fax: 01248 713119).

👑👑 *HIGHLY COMMEN-DED.* Warm, welcoming, non-smoking Bed and Breakfast one minute from beautiful Menai Straits and bowling green, close by Telford's elegant suspension bridge. Bwthyn ("dear little house" in Welsh), a former quarryman's Victorian terraced cottage offers character, comfort, genuine hospitality. Two very pretty en suite double rooms, power showers, etc (one plus bath), colour TV, tea/coffee makers, scrumptious home cooking. Bed and Breakfast £16 per person per night (double) one or two nights; £15 per person per night three nights or more. Delicious four-course dinner £12.50 per person. Special Breaks for over 45's three nights' Dinner, Bed and Breakfast £79 per person. Ideal base for coast, country, castles, Snowdonia; one and a half miles A5/A55, two miles rail, coaches, 40 minutes Holyhead ferry. Come as guests, leave as friends.

NEFYN. Mrs E. Jones, "Terfyn", Morfa Nefyn, Pwllheli LL53 6BA (01758 721332).

Detached house situated at the end of quiet seaside village, only seven miles from Pwllheli, popular market town. Beach and 26 hole golf course 10 minutes' walk away. Caernarfon Castle, Portmeirion Italian Village and Anglesey only 30/40 minutes' drive away. Tea and coffee making facilities in all rooms. TV in sitting room. Light refreshments served at 9pm included in the price. Table and chairs in garden. Open all year except family holidays. Children welcome. Private parking. Sorry no pets. Bed and full cooked Breakfast from £15 adults, children under five year FREE, up to 13 years £7.

PORTHMADOG. Tyddyn Du Farm Holidays (FHG), Gellilydan, Near Ffestiniog LL41 4RB (Tel & Fax: 01766 590281).

👑👑👑 *HIGHLY COMMENDED.* Enchanting old world farmhouse set amidst spectacular scenery in the heart of the Snowdonia National Park with a friendly relaxed atmosphere. One superb private ground floor cottage suite. Delicious candle-lit dinners with excellent farmhouse cuisine. Working sheep farm — feed the ducks on our mill pond, bottle feed pets lambs and fuss over Polly the pony. Excellent central base. Weekly Dinner, Bed and Breakfast from £160 to £200; bed and Breakfast from £16 to £20. AA QQQQ. Luxury self-catering suites also available.

FOR THE MUTUAL GUIDANCE OF GUEST AND HOST

Every year literally thousands of holidays, short-breaks and overnight stops are arranged through our guides, the vast majority without any problems at all. In a handful of cases, however, difficulties do arise about bookings, which often could have been prevented from the outset.

It is important to remember that when accommodation has been booked, both parties — guests and hosts — have entered into a form of contract. We hope that the following points will provide helpful guidance.

GUESTS: When enquiring about accommodation, be as precise as possible. Give exact dates, numbers in your party and the ages of any children. State the number and type of rooms wanted and also what catering you require — bed and breakfast, full board, etc. Make sure that the position about evening meals is clear — and about pets, reductions for children or any other special points.

Read our reviews carefully to ensure that the proprietors you are going to contact can supply what you want. Ask for a letter confirming all arrangements, if possible.

If you have to cancel, do so as soon as possible. Proprietors do have the right to retain deposits and under certain circumstances to charge for cancelled holidays if adequate notice is not given and they cannot re-let the accommodation.

HOSTS: Give details about your facilities and about any special conditions. Explain your deposit system clearly and arrangements for cancellations, charges, etc, and whether or not your terms include VAT.

If for any reason you are unable to fulfil an agreed booking without adequate notice, you may be under an obligation to arrange alternative suitable accommodation or to make some form of compensation.

While every effort is made to ensure accuracy, we regret that FHG Publications cannot accept responsibility for errors, omissions or misrepresentation in our entries or any consequences thereof. Prices in particular should be checked because we go to press early. We will follow up complaints but cannot act as arbiters or agents for either party.

NORTH WALES

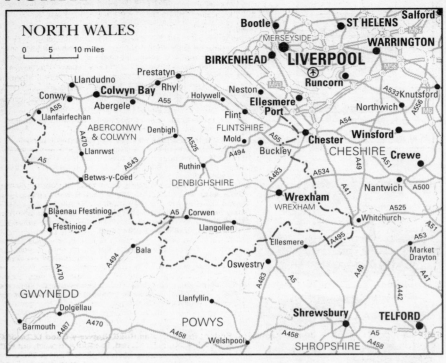

NORTH WALES

0   5   10 miles

Salford
Bootle   ST HELENS
MERSEYSIDE   WARRINGTON
BIRKENHEAD   LIVERPOOL
Prestatyn   Neston   Runcorn   Knutsford
Llandudno   Rhyl   A533
Conwy   Colwyn Bay   Holywell   A55   Northwich
Abergele   A55   Ellesmere   A556
Llanfairfechan   Flint   Port   A54
ABERCONWY   Denbigh   FLINTSHIRE   Winsford
& COLWYN   Mold   Chester   Crewe
Llanrwst   A525   A55   CHESHIRE   A51
A543   Buckley   A494   Nantwich   A500
Betws-y-Coed   Ruthin   A483   A534   Whitchurch
DENBIGHSHIRE   A49   A525
Blaenau Ffestiniog   A5   Corwen   Wrexham   A41
Ffestiniog   Llangollen   WREXHAM   A53
Bala   Ellesmere   A495   Market
A494   Drayton
GWYNEDD   Oswestry   A41
Dolgellau   Llanfyllin   A483   A5   A49
Barmouth   A470   POWYS   Shrewsbury   TELFORD
A458   A458   A5
Welshpool   SHROPSHIRE   A458

BETWS-Y-COED. David and Jean Pender, Bryn Bella Guest House, Llanrwst Road, Betws-y-Coed LL24 0HD (01690 710627). ✿✿ *HIGHLY COMMENDED.*

Bryn Bella is a small but select Victorian guest house enjoying an elevated position overlooking the beautiful village of Betws-y-Coed and the surrounding mountains of the Snowdonia National Park. All rooms are pleasantly furnished and most have en suite shower rooms. All rooms have colour TV and tea/coffee making facilities. Guests can enjoy glorious views from the front patio and there is ample private parking. Garaging for motorcycles and mountain bikes is also available. If travelling by train or bus there is a free pick up service from the local station. Non smoking throughout. Bed and Breakfast from £18 per person.

BETWS-Y-COED. Mrs M. Jones, Tyddyn Gethin Farm, Penmachno, Betws-y-Coed LL24 0PS (01690 760392). Working farm. 80 acre mixed farm situated 200 yards off B4406 quarter of a mile from village, one mile from

woollen mill and falls. Very central for touring and within easy reach of the sea and mountains. Pony trekking nearby; walks. Stone farmhouse with lovely views, clean and comfortable and serving good breakfasts. Always a warm welcome. All bedrooms have washbasins and shaving points; bathroom with shower and separate shower room; two lounges, one with colour TV; log fires when needed; dining room with separate tables. Ample parking. Bed and Breakfast from £15. Self catering cottage nearby (sleeps four) also available from £90 to £258 per week.

BETWS-Y-COED. Mrs Joyce Melling, Mount Pleasant, Betws-y-Coed LL24 0BN (01690 710502).

WTB 👑👑 *HIGHLY COMMENDED.* A warm Welsh welcome awaits you at our Victorian stone-built house only a few minutes' walk from the centre of Betws-y-Coed, yet overlooking open fields and woodland. Our four comfortably furnished centrally heated bedrooms (two en suite) all have colour TV and beverage trays. Enjoy a hearty breakfast at individual tables in our breakfast room, where you can choose between a vegetarian or more traditional breakfast. Walkers are welcome and packed lunches are available on request. No children under 10 years old. No pets. Some off-road parking available. Totally non-smoking. Bed and Breakfast from £15 per person per night. Special rates for out of season breaks. AA QQQ.

BETWS-Y-COED. Mrs E.A. Jones, Pant Glas, Padoc, Pentrefoelas Road, Betws-y-Coed LL24 0PG

(01690 770248). WTB Listed. Peaceful and quiet, but with a friendly atmosphere, this beef and sheep farm of 181 acres, with scenic views, is situated five miles from Betws-y-Coed. Ideal for touring, within easy reach of Snowdon, Bodnant Gardens, Caernarvon Castle, Llandudno, Black Rock Sands, Ffestiniog Railway, Llechwedd Slate Mines, Swallow and Conwy Falls and woollen mills. Accommodation comprises two double and one twin bedrooms, all with washbasins and tea/coffee making facilities; bath and shower, two toilets. Use of colour TV lounge. Sorry no pets. Car essential, parking for three/four cars. Bed and Breakfast from £12.50 to £13.50. Open Easter to November.

BETWS-Y-COED. Mrs Florence Jones, Maes Gwyn Farm, Pentrefoelas, Betws-y-Coed LL24 0LR

(01690 770668). WTB Listed *HIGHLY COMMENDED.* Maes Gwyn is a mixed farm of 90-97 hectares, situated in lovely quiet countryside, about one mile from the A5, six miles from the famous Betws-y-Coed. The sea and Snowdonia Mountains about 20 miles. Very good centre for touring North Wales, many well-known places of interest. Houses dates back to 1665. It has one double and one family bedrooms with washbasins and tea/coffee making facilities; bathroom with shower, toilet; lounge with colour TV and diningroom. Children and Senior Citizens are welcome at reduced rates and pets are permitted. Car essential, ample parking provided. Good home cooking. Six miles to bus/railway terminal. Open May/November for Bed and Breakfast from £15. SAE, please, for details.

BETWS-Y-COED. Summer Hill Non-Smokers' Guest House, Coedcynhelier Road, Betws-y-Coed LL24 0BL (01690 710306). 👑👑 *COMMENDED.* Especially for the non-smoker, Summer Hill is delightfully situated in a quiet, sunny location overlooking the River Llugwy and Fir Tree Island; 150 yards from main road, shops and restaurants. Seven comfortable bedrooms (four en suite), washbasins and tea/coffee making facilities. Residents' lounge with colour TV. Singles, children and pets welcome. Flasks filled, packed lunches provided, evening meals bookable in advance. Vegetarians, special diets catered for. Private car parking. Betws-y-Coed is the gateway to Snowdonia, with spectacular mountains, forests and rivers. Golf, fishing, gardens, castles all accessible. Bed and Breakfast from £16; Evening Meal from £9.50.

BETWS-Y-COED. Mrs E. Jones, Maes-y-Garnedd Farm, Capel Garmon, Llanrwst, Betws-y-Coed

(01690 710428). Tourist Board Listed *APPROVED.* **Working farm.** This 140-acre mixed farm is superbly situated on the Rooftop of Wales as Capel Garmon has been called, and the Snowdonia Range, known to the Welsh as the "Eyri", visible from the land. Two miles from A5. Surrounding area provides beautiful country scenery and walks. Safe, sandy beaches at Llandudno and Colwyn Bay. Salmon and trout fishing (permit required). Mrs Jones serves excellent home produced meals with generous portions including Welsh lamb and roast beef. Gluten-free and coeliacs' wheat-free diets can be arranged. Packed lunches, with flask of coffee or tea. One double and one family bedrooms with washbasins; bathroom, toilet; sittingroom, dining room. Children welcome; cot, high chair and babysitting available. Regret, no pets. Car essential, ample parking. Open all year. Bed and Breakfast; Evening Meal optional. SAE brings prompt reply with details of terms. Reductions for children. Bala Lakes, Bodnant Gardens, Ffestiniog Railway, slate quarries, Trefriw Woollen Mills nearby. Member of AA.

BETWS-Y-COED. Jim and Lilian Boughton, Bron Celyn Guest House, Lon Muriau, Llanrwst Road, Betws-y-Coed LL24 0HD (01690 710333; Fax: 01690

710111). 🌺🌺🌺 *HIGHLY COMMENDED.* A warm welcome awaits you at this delightful Guest House overlooking the Gwydyr Forest and Llugwy/Conwy Valleys and village of Betws-y-Coed in Snowdonia National Park. Ideal centre for touring, walking, climbing, fishing and golf. Also excellent overnight stop for Holyhead ferries. Easy walk into village and close to Conwy/Swallow Falls and Fairy Glen. Most rooms en-suite. All with colour TV and beverage makers. Full central heating, lounge. Garden, car park. Open all year. Full hearty breakfast, packed meals, snacks, Evening Meals. Special diets catered for. Bed and Breakfast from £18 to £24. Reduced rates for children under 12 years and out of season breaks.

BETWS-Y-COED near. Mrs Eleanore Roberts, Awelon, Plas Isa, Llanrwst LL26 0EE (01492

640047). 🌺 Awelon once formed part of the estate of William Salisbury, translator of the New Testament into Welsh in the 16th century. With three-foot thick outer walls, it has now been modernised and is an attractive small guest house. Three bedrooms (one en suite) with colour TV and teamakers; cosy lounge; central heating ensures a comfy stay. Private parking. Llanrwst, a busy market town at the centre of the beautiful Conway Valley, is close to Snowdonia, Bodnant Gardens and North Wales coast. A warm Welsh welcome awaits all guests. Bed and Breakfast from £15; en suite from £18. Dinner optional. All home cooking. Children and pets welcome.

CHESTER near. Mrs P. Davies, Bryn Yorkin Manor, Caergwrle, Flintshire LL12 9HT (01978

760346). 14th century manor house set in walled garden and surrounded by 140 acres of private woodland and pasture with superb views. Friendly family home, tastefully furnished to a very high standard offering double, twin or family room with either en suites and private bathrooms, tea/coffee making facilities and colour TV. Lounge and snooker room for guests' use. Only 15 minutes' drive from Chester and an ideal base for exploring Shropshire and North Wales. Regret no smoking. Please send for further information and prices.

CHESTER near. Mrs Christine Whale, Brookside House, Brookside Lane, Northop Hall, Mold CH7 6HN (01244 821146). 👑 👑 *HIGHLY COMMENDED.* Relax and enjoy the hospitality of our recently refurbished 18th century Welsh stone cottage. The home-from-home accommodation offers a double, twin or family room with private bathroom upon request. All rooms have colour TV and tea making facilities. Within a short walk the village has an excellent restaurant and two pubs (one of which serves bar meals). Suitable for touring North Wales and Chester or just a short break away from it all. Bed and Breakfast from £17.

CONWY. Mr Anderton, Bodlwyfan, Conway Road, Penmaenmawr, Conwy LL34 6BL (01492 623506). Come and visit our beautiful Victorian home with breathtaking views of Conwy Bay, Puffin Island and the mountains of Snowdonia National Park. A warm friendly welcome awaits all our guests. An ideal base for exploring Snowdon, with sailing, windsurfing, jet ski-ing, sea and freshwater fishing, golf, bowls, climbing and many walks within easy reach. Beach quarter of a mile, Llandudno and Anglesey close by. Wonderful quaint shops and many castles to visit. Enjoy our comfortable rooms with tea making facilities and TV. Tasty home cooked meals. Private off-road parking. Bed and Breakfast from £15; Evening Meal £7.50.

CONWY. Mrs Sylvia Baxter, Glyn Uchaf, Conwy Old Road, Dwygyfyichi, Penmaenmawr, Conwy LL34 6YS (01492 623737). 👑 👑 👑 *HIGHLY COMMENDED.* Enjoy a quiet, peaceful holiday at this old mill house set in 11 acres of National Parkland in beautiful mountainous countryside. Ideal touring centre for Snowdonia. Accommodation comprises three bedrooms, all en suite and having lovely views. Lounge with colour TV; diningroom. Excellent cuisine with varied menus and home produce. Tea/coffee making facilities. Children welcome. Two-and-a-half miles to Conwy, five to Llandudno and Colwyn Bay — three minutes' walk to village. Pony trekking, golf and fishing locally. Ample parking. Guests have access to house at all times. Bed and Breakfast from £19, or Bed, Breakfast and Evening Meal. Moderate terms, reductions for children under 12. Highly recommended. SAE or phone please.

CONWY. Glan Heulog Guest House, Llanrwst Road, Conwy LL32 8LT (01492 593845). 👑 👑 👑 AA QQQ. Spacious Victorian house, close to historic walled town of Conwy and its castle. All rooms have TV and tea/coffee facilities. There is off-street parking, en suite facilities are available and we have a lounge for guests with games and books available and a residential licence. There is a large garden with good views. We are conveniently situated for Snowdonia National Park, Anglesey, Bodnant Gardens and other well-known attractions. Our guests say "great rooms", "excellent service", "wonderful meals", "charming hosts", "lovely warm welcome", "best place I've stayed", "we will be back". Book early to avoid disappointment. Bed and Breakfast from £13.

CONWY. Mrs E. Wagstaff, Pinewood Towers Country Guest House, Sychnant Pass Road, Conwy LL32 8BZ (01492 592459). Victorian Country House with residential licence set in 10 acres, gardens, woods and paddocks on Conwy mountainside situated in the Snowdonia National Park. Tea/coffee making facilities and washbasins in all rooms. Plentiful home cooked food. Reduction for children sharing, children under five years not accepted. Dogs in owners' rooms or kennels available if required. Ideal for real country lovers and people liking peace and quiet — yet not isolated. Open April to September. Stamp for brochure please.

CORWEN. Bob and Kit Buckland, Corwen Court Private Hotel, London Road, Corwen LL21 0DP (01490 412854). 👑 👑 *COMMENDED.* Situated on the main A5, this converted old police station and courthouse has six prisoners' cells turned into single bedrooms. Hot and cold in each, with a bathroom to service three on the first floor and a shower room for three on the ground floor. All double bedrooms have bathrooms en suite. The dining room in the old courthouse is where the local magistrates presided, and the comfortable lounge spreads over the rest of the court. Central heating throughout and colour TV in the lounge. Fire Certificate. Bed and Breakfast from £14 to £16; Evening Meal £8. Children and pets welcome. AA listed. Convenient base for touring North Wales.

LLANDUDNO. Mr & Mrs S.J. Probert, St. Hilary Hotel, Promenade, Llandudno LL30 1BG (01492

875551). WTB ♥♥ *HIGHLY COMMENDED.* AA QQQ, RAC Acclaimed. This well appointed promenade hotel offers comfortable, refined accommodation at realistic prices. The St. Hilary's position on the seafront affords magnificent views of Llandudno's sweeping bay and Great Orme headland. For those wishing to venture further afield the St. Hilary is an ideal centre for touring North Wales and the Snowdonia National Park. All our individually styled bedrooms (mostly en suite) have colour TV and hospitality trays to make your stay with us all the more relaxing and enjoyable. Bed and Breakfast from £15.50 per person. You can be assured of a warm Welsh welcome at the St. Hilary!

LLANDUDNO. Mrs T. Williams, Roselea, Deganwy Avenue, Llandudno (01492 876279). Situated a few minutes from sea front and shops, entertainments, etc. Near to ski slope and Great Orme Tram. Access to house at all times with own front door and bedroom keys. Colour TV in all rooms. Children welcome; small dogs welcome by arrangement. Car park. Bed and Breakfast £13 per person per night. Please write or telephone for further details.

LLANDUDNO. Mrs Ruth Hodkinson, Cranleigh, Great Orme's Road, West Shore, Llandudno LL30 2AR (01492 877688). A comfortable, late Victorian private residence and family home situated on the quieter West Shore of Llandudno. Only yards from beach and magnificent Great Orme Mountain. Parking: no problem. Town centre is a short pleasant walk away. Many places of interest in surrounding area, and opportunities for sports and recreational activities. Excellent home cooked food. Two en suite rooms available, both with views of sea and mountains. Conforms to high standards of S.I. 1991/474. Most highly recommended.

LLANDUDNO. Mrs E. Jones, Gloddaeth Isa Farm, Derwen Lane, Penrhynside, Llandudno LL30 3DP

(01492 549209). A warm welcome awaits you at Gloddaeth Isa Farm, situated close to the village of Penrhynside, two miles from the popular Victorian holiday resort of Llandudno with its many and varied attractions. The Great Orme and Happy Valley are always a source of interest. Ideally located for touring the North Wales Coast and Anglesey, within easy reach of the famous Bodnant Gardens and the historic town of Conway. We offer spacious and comfortable bedrooms with tea/coffee making facilities. TV lounge. Two bathrooms. Ample car parking space. Children welcome. Bed and Breakfast; Evening Meal by arrangement. Enquiries to Mrs Eirwen Jones.

LLANFAIRFECHAN. Mrs K.M. Coleman, Plas Heulog, Mount Road, Llanfairfechan LL33 0HA (Tel &

Fax: 01248 680019). ♥ *COMMENDED.* A Snowdonia mountainside retreat in private woodland with breathtaking views over the sea, Plas Heulog is peaceful and secluded yet only two miles from the A55 expressway, station and beach. An ideal touring centre for the famous castles and National Trust properties of North Wales. It is also an excellent WTB Approved walking and mountain biking base. Horse riding, mountain bike hire and guided walks can be arranged. Evening meal and packed lunches are available by arrangement. The centrally heated en suite bedrooms have panoramic views from their elevated position above the house. Warm welcome, friendly family atmosphere. Children and pets welcome. Bed and Breakfast from £17.50. Non-smoking.

LLANGOLLEN. Mrs A. Dennis, Oaklands Guest House, Llangollen Road, Trevor, Llangollen LL20

7TG (01978 820152). ♥♥ Situated in the beautiful Vale of Llangollen, Oaklands is a charming Victorian house set in lovely gardens. All rooms are warm, spacious and comfortably furnished, with tea-making facilities, washbasins, and very comfortable beds. Guests' television lounge. Nearby are places of interest such as Telford's Aqueduct, Llangollen Steam Railway, swimming baths, and National Trust properties at Chirk and Erddig. Ideal base for touring, golf, climbing, pony trekking, walking Offa's Dyke or on Berwyn Mountains. On bus route to Chester and coast. Bed and hearty English Breakfast from £16. Three nights Bed and Breakfast from £42 per person. Families welcome at reduced rates. Sorry, no pets. Ample parking. Open all year.

LLANRWST. Mr Michael John Bucknall, Pickwicks Hotel, Bridge Street, Llanrwst LL26 0ET (01492 640275). 🐾🐾 A 400 year old, family-run guest house/tea-room, oak beamed and retaining its "olde worlde" character, whilst offering modern facilities: central heating, en suite rooms, tea/coffee makers, etc. Centrally situated in Llanrwst, a small market town nestling in the beautiful Conwy Valley, an ideal base for exploring Snowdonia, lakes, forests, coastal resorts and popular local attractions. Friendly and informal, a haven for walking and climbing enthusiasts with drying area, storage for equipment and comfortable lounge for relaxation. Parking. Packed lunches, evening meals available (with vegetarian options). Open all year. Bed and Breakfast from £14.50.

LLANSILIN. Mrs G. Jones, Lloran Ganol Farm, Llansilin, Oswestry SY10 7OX (01691 791287). WTB 🐾 **Working farm, join in.** A friendly welcome is assured at this modern farm set in 300 acres in Welsh valley. A busy working farm of dairy, sheep and cattle, it has surrounding garden and lawns. Fly fishing, rough shooting and horse riding locally. Tastefully furnished farmhouse has three bedrooms — one double, one twin each with wash-basin, TV and tea/coffee making facilities and one single with tea/coffee facilities; modern bathroom. Large lounge, dining room and conservatory; colour TV. English Breakfast and Evening Meal. Bed and Breakfast from £15; Dinner, Bed and Breakfast (by arrangement) from £24. Weekly self catering from £80.

RHOS-ON-SEA, near Llandudno. Mr and Mrs Mike Willington, Sunnydowns Hotel, 66 Abbey Road, Rhos-on-Sea, Near Llandudno LL28 4NU (01492 544256; Fax: 01492 543223). 🐾🐾🐾 A family-run hotel. All rooms en suite with colour TV, video and Satellite channels, clock radio, tea/coffee facilities, hair dryer, mini-bar refrigerator, direct dial telephone and central heating. Hotel facilities also include bar, pool room, restaurant, sauna and car park. Situated just a five minute walk from Rhos-on-Sea Golf Club and with four more Championship courses close by. Telephone or Fax for brochure and special group terms.

RUTHIN. Mrs I. Henderson, Esgairlygain, Llangynhafal, Ruthin LL15 1RT (01824 704047). 🐾🐾🐾 Stone barn conversion. En suite rooms. Direct access to Clwydian hills. Convenient for Llangollen, Chester, Snowdonia, castles and coast. Well behaved dogs welcome free. Owners £16.50!

RUTHIN. Gill Buxbaum, The Old Rectory, Clocaenog, Ruthin LL15 2AT (01824 750740). 🐾🐾 *HIGHLY COMMENDED.* Clocaenog is in a quiet valley just off the B5105 10 minutes from Ruthin. We enjoy sharing our comfortable Georgian family home with guests who appreciate personal service and like relaxing in peaceful surroundings. Ideal for walking or touring the beautiful North Wales countryside with Chester, Llangollen, Snowdonia and many varied places of interest within easy reach. Rooms include a single and twin, adjoining bathroom, two double en suite bedrooms (one a family room sleeping four), all with tea/coffee making facilities. Lounge with colour TV. Bed and Breakfast from £16; Evening Meal by prior arrangement. Children welcome. Sorry no smoking or pets in the house.

RHIWLAS

RHIWLAS sits high on the Clwydian range with magnificent views of the old market town of Ruthin, Snowdonia and the Irish Sea. All bedrooms are en suite and a comfortable guests' sitting room, with open fire, is available throughout the day. Dinner is offered with complementary wine, and medieval banquets are held in Ruthin Castle on most evenings throughout the year. Pets Welcome. Prices from £20. 👑👑👑 Highly Commended.

RHIWLAS, LLANBEDR, RUTHIN, DENBIGHSHIRE LL15 1US
TELEPHONE: 01824 702482

RUTHIN. Mrs Anna V. Meadway, Firgrove, Llanfwrog, Ruthin LL15 2LL (01824 702677 ansaphone). 👑👑 *HIGHLY COMMENDED.* A Listed Georgian country house set in one and a half acres of mature gardens with panoramic views of the Vale of Clwyd, Firgrove is situated one and a half miles from the medieval market town of Ruthin on the B5105, conveniently centred for visiting Chester and Snowdonia, only one and a half hours from Manchester Airport and Holyhead, the Irish Ferry Port. We offer Bed and Breakfast in comfortable surroundings with two tastefully decorated double rooms in the house sharing one bathroom and an attached ground floor cottage offering full en suite facilities. All rooms have colour TV and tea/coffee facilities. Please ring for further details.

ST. ASAPH. Mrs Eirlys Jones, Rhewl Farm, Waen, St. Asaph, Denbighshire LL17 0DT (01745 582287). 👑 *COMMENDED.* Enjoy Welsh hospitality on our 180 acre farm, conveniently situated three-quarters of a mile from A55 expressway in peaceful and beautiful setting. Comfortable bedrooms with radiators and tea/coffee making facilities. Double room has en suite facilities, twin and family rooms have washbasins. Spacious lounge with inglenook fireplace and colour TV. Convenient for Chester, coast and Snowdonia. Free fishing. Reductions for children. Bed and Breakfast from £16 to £17. This is a non-smoking household. Welcome Host Certificate. Please send SAE for brochure.

ST. ASAPH. Mrs N. Price, Plas Penucha, Caerwys, Mold CH7 5BH (01352 720210). 👑👑👑 *HIGHLY COMMENDED.* One family has owned this unique farmhouse for over 400 years. Over the centuries it has been altered and modernised, but always with the aim of retaining its sense of history and serenity. Extensive gardens overlook the Clwydian Hills. A spacious lounge has large library, grand piano and Elizabethan panelling. Full central heating. There are four bedrooms, two en suite, all with washbasins, shaver points, hairdryers and tea/coffee making facilities. Two miles from A55 expressway — 30 minutes Chester and North Wales Coast — one hour Snowdonia. Open all year. Bed and Breakfast £18.50; Evening Meal from £10.50. Discounts available. Brochure on request.

TREFRIW. Mrs B. Cole, Glandwr, Trefriw, Near Llanrwst LL27 0JP (01492 640 431). Large country

house on the outskirts of Trefriw Village overlooking the Conway River and its Valley, with beautiful views towards the Clwydian Hills. Good touring area; Llanrwst, Betws-y-Coed and Swallow Falls five miles away. Fishing, walking, golfing and pony trekking all close by. Comfortable rooms, lounge with TV, dining room. Good home cooking using local produce whenever possible. Parking. Bed and Breakfast from £16; Dinner if required.

TREFRIW. Arthur and Ann Eaton, Crafnant Guest House, Trefriw LL27 0JH (01492 640809). Quality

accommodation and service can be enjoyed at Crafnant, an elegant Victorian residence in the charming village of Trefriw, Conwy Valley. The village is known for its Woollen Mill, Roman Spa, fishing, lakes and forest walks. The RSBP Nature Reserve, Snowdon, Bodnant Gardens and other attractions are within easy reach. Five en suite double/twin rooms with drinks tray and TV. Bed and Breakfast from £15 to £16; children up to 12 years £8. Special discount — book seven nights, pay only for six. Non-smoking, private parking. Open all year except Christmas and Boxing Days.

WREXHAM. Mrs M.A. Smith, Aldersey Guest House, 25 Hightown Road, Wrexham LL13 8EB

(01978 365687). 🏵 *HIGHLY COMMENDED.* A warm friendly welcome awaits you at this small family-run guest house situated minutes from the town centre, an ideal base for exploring the Welsh and English borderlands. The historic city of Chester and the beauty of the Vale of Llangollen are within easy travelling distance. Full central heating, TV lounge, tea and coffee making facilities. One double bedroom, a spacious twin/family room and three single rooms, all with washbasins and shaver points. Three bath/shower rooms with toilets. Large parking area. Bed and Breakfast £15 to £17 per person per night.

FOR THE MUTUAL GUIDANCE OF GUEST AND HOST

Every year literally thousands of holidays, short-breaks and overnight stops are arranged through our guides, the vast majority without any problems at all. In a handful of cases, however, difficulties do arise about bookings, which often could have been prevented from the outset.

It is important to remember that when accommodation has been booked, both parties — guests and hosts — have entered into a form of contract. We hope that the following points will provide helpful guidance.

GUESTS: When enquiring about accommodation, be as precise as possible. Give exact dates, numbers in your party and the ages of any children. State the number and type of rooms wanted and also what catering you require — bed and breakfast, full board, etc. Make sure that the position about evening meals is clear — and about pets, reductions for children or any other special points.

Read our reviews carefully to ensure that the proprietors you are going to contact can supply what you want. Ask for a letter confirming all arrangements, if possible.

If you have to cancel, do so as soon as possible. Proprietors do have the right to retain deposits and under certain circumstances to charge for cancelled holidays if adequate notice is not given and they cannot re-let the accommodation.

HOSTS: Give details about your facilities and about any special conditions. Explain your deposit system clearly and arrangements for cancellations, charges, etc, and whether or not your terms include VAT.

If for any reason you are unable to fulfil an agreed booking without adequate notice, you may be under an obligation to arrange alternative suitable accommodation or to make some form of compensation.

While every effort is made to ensure accuracy, we regret that FHG Publications cannot accept responsibility for errors, omissions or misrepresentation in our entries or any consequences thereof. Prices in particular should be checked because we go to press early. We will follow up complaints but cannot act as arbiters or agents for either party.

CARDIGAN

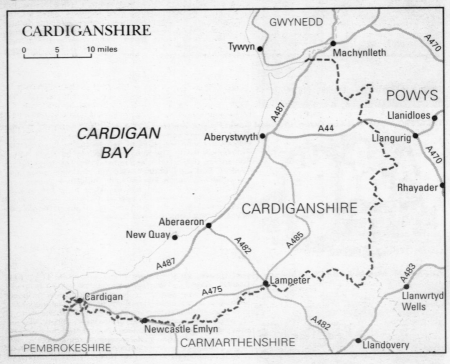

CARDIGANSHIRE

0   5   10 miles

GWYNEDD

Tywyn

Machynlleth

A470

POWYS

Llanidloes

A487

A44

Llangurig

CARDIGAN
BAY

Aberystwyth

A470

Rhayader

CARDIGANSHIRE

Aberaeron

New Quay

A482

A485

A487

A483

Lampeter

Llanwrtyd
Wells

A475

Cardigan

A482

Newcastle Emlyn

PEMBROKESHIRE

CARMARTHENSHIRE

Llandovery

ABERYSTWYTH. Mrs E. Jones, Ael-y-Bryn Guest House, Capel Bangor, Aberystwyth SY23 3LR (01970 880681; Mobile: 0374 631439). 🏵 *HIGHLY COMMENDED.* Small family-run guest house situated 100 yards off the A44 road, five miles east of Aberystwyth. It has lovely views overlooking the Rheidol Valley and is an ideal base from which to explore beautiful beaches and many other places of interest. All rooms have washbasin, TV, radio and tea/coffee facilities; dining room with separate tables; TV lounge. Central heating. Bed and Breakfast from £16 to £18 each per night. There is safe parking within the grounds. Sorry no pets. No smoking. SAE for brochure.

ABERYSTWYTH. Mrs F.J. Rowlands, Tycam Farm, Capel Bangor, Aberystwyth SY23 3NA (01970 84662). 🏵🏵 *COMMENDED.* Peaceful dairy and sheep farm situated seven and a half miles from Aberystwyth and just two and a half miles off A44 road. Accommodation comprises one double bedroom and one family room en suite; lounge and diningroom with separate tables and colour TV. Central heating. Perfect centre for walking, sightseeing, bird watching, fishing, golf, swimming and many beaches within easy reach. Ample car parking. Bed and Breakfast from £15 to £17.50 per person. Reduction for children over five years sharing parents' room.

ABERYSTWYTH. Sarah and Lester Ward, Sinclair Guest House, 43 Portland Street, Aberystwyth SY23 2DX (Tel & Fax: 01970 615158). 🏵🏵🏵 *HIGHLY COMMENDED.* Centrally situated in a peaceful tree-lined street close to the seafront and shopping and convenient for the University and the National Library of Wales. Sinclair is a late Victorian terraced house of character with three spacious en suite bedrooms individually designed and decorated and equipped to the highest standard. Whether you are visiting Aberystwyth for business or pleasure Sinclair combines comfort and cleanliness, personal service and value for money and is totally smoke-free. Bed and Breakfast is £22.50 per person.

CARDIGAN. Joy Evans, Garth Guest House, Park Place, Gwbert Road, Cardigan SA43 1AE (01239 613085). Tourist Board *COMMENDED.* Informally run and conveniently situated in a pleasant area. All bedrooms have colour TV, radio alarm, tea/coffee facilities, full central heating. Payphone, private parking. Cot and high chair. Family and en suite rooms available. Evening meals on request. High standard of comfort assured in a relaxed and friendly atmosphere. Pets welcome. Open January to December. Bed and Breakfast from £16 per person.

LAMPETER. Mrs J.P. Driver, Penwern Old Mills, Cribyn, Lampeter SA48 7QH (01570 470762). A former rural woollen mill set in a quiet valley alongside a small stream. Penwern, after its demise in 1953 when it subsequently lay derelict for 20 years, is now enjoying a new lease of life. Renovated and converted to living accommodation, the Old Mill now offers a comfortable, interesting and relaxing base from which to enjoy your sojourn in Mid Wales. Double, single and twin rooms. Cot and high chair available. Trout lakes nearby. Bed and Breakfast £13 per person; Evening Meal by arrangement. Reduced rates for children and weekly bookings. Totally non-smoking.

LAMPETER. Mrs Eleanor Marsden-Davies, Brynog Mansion, Felinfach, Lampeter SA48 8AQ (01570 470266). 🐾🐾 *HIGHLY COMMENDED.* Enjoy a relaxing holiday in the friendly atmosphere of this spacious 250 year old country mansion. Brynog is a 170 acre grazing farm situated in the beautiful Vale of Aeron, midway between Lampeter market town and the unique Aberaeron seaside resort, just 10 minutes by car. The mansion is approached by a three-quarter-mile rhododendron-lined drive. Spacious en suite bedrooms with bathroom or shower, other room with washbasin, near bathroom. Tea making facilities on request. Central heating and a welcoming woodburner in cold weather. Full Welsh breakfast provided, served in the grand old well-furnished dining room. There is a spacious comfortable lounge with TV. Rough shooting, private fishing, bird-watching and riverside walk nearby. Children over six years welcome. Sorry, no dogs. Bed and Breakfast from £18.50 to £19.50. Tourist Board "Welcome Host" Award.

PONTERWYD. Dyffryn Castell Hotel, Ponterwyd, Aberystwyth SY23 3LB (01970 890237). A 400 year old coaching inn on the A44 London to Aberystwyth road. Well stocked bar, friendly atmosphere, wide range of bar food. Central heating, TV lounge, games room, beer garden, children's play area. Tea/coffee facilities. Ideal rambling (5 Rivers Walk, Cambrian Way), bird watching, trekking, fishing and magnificent scenery. Drying facilities. Please write or telephone for more details.

CARMARTHENSHIRE

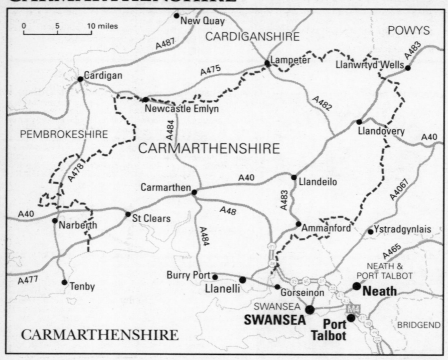

CARMARTHEN. Mrs Heather E. Rodenhurst, Glôg Farm, Llangain, Carmarthen SA33 5AY (01267 241271). ✿✿ *COMMENDED.* **Working farm.** Welcome Host. Glôg is a working farm, a traditional Welsh longhouse set in the lovely Dylan Thomas countryside. Five miles from the market town of Carmarthen and five miles from beach and castle at Llanstephan. Open all year Glôg offers a warm welcome. We have four bedrooms, all en suite with tea/coffee making facilities. Separate lounge and dining room. Wide breakfast choice, evening meal by arrangement. All home cooking. Central heating throughout, log fires in colder months. Children welcome. Ideal base offering peace and tranquillity. Bed and Breakfast £20 per person. AA QQQ.

CARMARTHEN. Colin and Jacquie Rouse, Allt-y-golau Uchaf, Felingwm Uchaf, Carmarthen SA32 7BB (01267 290455). ✿✿ *HIGHLY COMMENDED.* Traditional Welsh breakfasts and cosy oak beams in a peaceful rural setting that offers excellent walking, fishing, riding and birdwatching. Our Georgian stone-walled farmhouse has been furnished and decorated to a very high standard retaining many original features. Spacious first floor lounge with panoramic views over the Tywi Valley, equipped with colour TV and radio. The house is fully centrally heated and all bedrooms (non-smoking) have washbasins and tea/coffee trays. The guest wing has two large bathrooms. Situated on the B4310 two miles north of Nantgaredig off the A40. Open all year. Terms from £17.50 per person.

CARMARTHEN. Mrs Margaret Thomas, Plas Farm, Llangynog, Carmarthen SA33 5DB (01267 211492). ✿✿ *COMMENDED.* **Working farm.** Welcome Host. Situated six miles west of Carmarthen town along the A40 towards St. Clears. Quiet location, ideal touring base. Working farm run by the Thomas family for the past 100 years. Very spacious, comfortable farmhouse. En suite rooms available, all with tea/coffee making facilities, colour TV and full central heating. TV lounge. Evening meals available at local country inn nearby. Good golf course minutes away. Plas Farm is en route to Fishguard and Pembroke Ferries. Bed and Breakfast from £15 per person. Children under 16 years sharing family room half price. Special mid-week breaks available. A warm welcome assured.

PEMBROKESHIRE

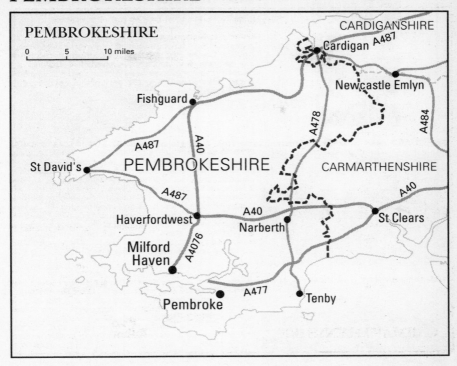

PEMBROKESHIRE

0 5 10 miles

CARDIGANSHIRE
Cardigan A487
Newcastle Emlyn
Fishguard
A487 A40 A478 A484
St David's PEMBROKESHIRE CARMARTHENSHIRE
A487
A40 A40
Haverfordwest A40 St Clears
Narberth
Milford Haven A4076
A477 Tenby
Pembroke

BLAENFFOS. Castellan House, Blaenffos, Boncath SA37 0HZ (01239 841644). ♥♥♥ Castellan

nestles on the edge of the Preseli Hills with spectacular panoramic views and our own valley with badger setts, fox and buzzard lairs. We are 10 minutes from Cardigan market town and Cardigan Bay, home of the famous bottle nose dolphins. We have salmon, sewin and trout fishing within five miles, several golf courses within 10 miles, beaches rivalling the Mediterranean, National Trust walks; riding available on premises plus delightful tea rooms, gardens and antique shop. Quality ground floor bedrooms with own front door, en suite, central heating, TV, tea making facilities. Pets welcome. Bed and Breakfast from £17 per person; optional Evening Meal £12. Reductions for children. RAC Acclaimed.

BROAD HAVEN near. Sandra Davies, Barley Villa, Walwyn's Castle, Near Broad Haven, Haverfordwest SA62 3EB (01437 781254). WTB ♥♥ *COMMEN-*

DED. Situated in peaceful, attractive countryside, our comfortable modern house overlooks a small nature reserve and is an ideal base for touring Pembrokeshire's beautiful coastline and sandy bays, suitable for sailing, surfing and swimming. Visit the bird islands famous for puffins, Manx shearwaters, kittiwakes and many other species. We have one double room and one twin en suite room with tea/coffee making facilities; spacious lounge/dining room has TV, board games and coal fire on chilly evenings. Comfort, cleanliness and personal attention assured. Substantial breakfasts; packed lunches; special diets catered for. Off road parking. Bed and Breakfast from £15.50. Comfortable two bedroomed caravan also available for hire.

DUDWICK. Mrs M.P. Miller, Siriole Guest House, 2 Siriole, Quay Road, Goodwick SA64 0BS

(01348 872375). Beautifully run Bed and Breakfast with spacious accommodation overlooking Fishguard Bay and the Preseli Hills. In a quiet location with ample parking and close to Goodwick village and a short walk to the main ferry terminal to Rosslare — ideal for day trips to Ireland. We are centrally located for walks along the splendid Pembrokeshire National Coastal Path and numerous attractions. All rooms are en suite with shower/toilet, tea/coffee facilities and colour TV; some have sea views. Children and pets welcome. Prices range from £14 to £18 per person. Reductions for longer stays. Open all year.

FISHGUARD near. Heathfield Mansion, Letterston, Near Fishguard SA62 5EG (01348 840263).

WTB ♛ ♛ ♛ *HIGHLY COMMENDED.* A Grade II Listed Georgian country house in 16 acres of pasture and woodland, Heathfield is the home of former Welsh rugby international, Clive Rees and his wife Angelica. This is an ideal location for the appreciation of Pembrokeshire's many natural attractions. There is excellent golf, riding and trout fishing in the vicinity and the coast is only a few minutes' drive away. The accommodation is very comfortable and two of the three bedrooms have en suite bathrooms. The cuisine and wines are well above average. This is a most refreshing venue for a tranquil and wholesome holiday. Bed and Breakfast from £18 per person; Dinner by prior arrangement.

HAVERFORDWEST. Joyce Canton, Nolton Haven Farm, Nolton Haven, Haverfordwest SA62 1NS

(01437 710263). The farmhouse is beside the beach on a 200 acre mixed farm, with cattle, calves and lots of show ponies. It has a large lounge which is open to guests all day, as are all the bedrooms. Single, double and family rooms, two family rooms ensuite, four other bathrooms. Pets and children most welcome, babysitting free of charge. 50 yards to the beach, 75 yards to the local inn/restaurant. Pony trekking, surfing, fishing, excellent cliff walks, boating and canoeing all available nearby. Riding holidays, and short breaks all year, a speciality. Colour brochure on request.

HAVERFORDWEST. Mrs M.E. Davies, Cuckoo Mill Farm, Pelcomb Bridge, St. David's Road, Haverfordwest SA62 6EA (01437 762139). Tourist

Board Listed. Working farm. This farm is situated in central Pembrokeshire, two miles out of Haverfordwest on St. David's Road. It is within easy reach of many beaches and coastline walks. Peaceful country walks on the farm, also a small trout stream. Children are welcome at reduced rates and cot, high chair and babysitting provided. The house is cosy with open fires and welcomes guests from January to December. Car is not essential, but parking available. Home-produced dairy products; poultry and meats all home-cooked. Mealtimes arranged to suit guests. Well appointed, warm, comfortable bedrooms with washbasins and tea making facilities. Pets permitted. Evening Dinner/Meal, Bed and Breakfast or Bed and Breakfast only. Rates also reduced for Senior Citizens.

MYNACHLOGDDU. Mrs Ann Barney, Yethen Isaf, Mynachlogddu, Clynderwen SA66 7SW (Tel & Fax: 01437 532256). ♛ ♛ *COMMENDED.* Nestling on the southern slopes of the Preseli Hills, Yethen Isaf awaits you with a warm welcome. Our working farm with sheep and cattle surrounds the house and garden. The open moorland of the Preseli Hills is immediately outside the farm gate and the walks are fabulous. We provide cosy, friendly accommodation with pretty welcoming bedrooms offering all facilities. Our 250 year old farmhouse has many interesting features including an inglenook fireplace with a wood-burning stove for chilly evenings. Hearty farmhouse breakfasts give you a good start for enjoying the beautiful coast and countryside of Pembrokeshire. Come and visit us soon. Sorry no pets.

Yethen Isaf

NARBERTH. Naomi James, Highland Grange Farm, Robeston Wathen, Narberth SA67 8EP (01834

860952). A most relaxing place to stay, beautifully situated in central south Pembrokeshire, bordering the National Park. Excellent central location, easily found, with good access on A40 amidst scenic countryside. Panoramic views, castles, woodland walks, picnic sites, country inn and river nearby. Endless amenities including Oakwood Theme Park, Megaphobia, Crystal Maze, bowling, golf and riding. Coastal paths, sandy beaches, reservoir, Preseli Hills and convenient for ferry ports (half hour drive). Delightfully spacious and well appointed ground floor accommodation, guest lounge and unrestricted access. En suite rooms are available. Delicious meals using garden produce. Residential licence. Family pony in paddock. Further details on request.

PEMBROKE. Mrs Ruth Smith, Chapel Farm, Castlemartin, Pembroke SA71 5HW (01646 661312).

WTB Welcome Home *HIGHLY COMMENDED*. Chapel Farm offers comfortable accommodation for a relaxing holiday. The 260 acre dairy farm is a mile from the coast in Pembrokeshire Coast National Park and has splendid views out to sea. The large bedrooms, one en suite, are equipped with radios and tea making facilities. The TV lounge with its inglenook fireplace has a grand piano for guests to enjoy. Good tasty farmhouse food is prepared; packed lunches on request. The long distance footpath passes the farm and within five miles are wild surfing beaches, quiet bathing coves, riding and fishing. Bed and Breakfast from £16 to £20; Dinner, Bed and Breakfast from £165 to £180 per week.

SAUNDERSFOOT. Mrs Joy Holgate, Carne Mountain Farm, Reynalton, Kilgetty SA68 0PD (01834

860546). WTB Listed *COMMENDED*. **Working farm.** A warm welcome awaits you at our lovely 200 year old farmhouse set amidst the peace and tranquillity of the beautiful Pembrokeshire countryside. Distant views of Preseli Hills, yet only three and a half miles from Saundersfoot. Pretty, picturesque bedrooms with colour TV, washbasins, tea/coffee tray, central heating. Separate dining room with interesting plate collection, books and maps. Delicious traditional or light farmhouse breakfast; vegetarians very welcome. Let the strain and stress slip away as you enjoy the peaceful atmosphere and friendly farmyard animals. Bed and Breakfast from £14. Welcome Host and Farmhouse Award. Quality six-berth caravan also available in pretty, peaceful setting from £90 per week. SAE please.

SOLVA. Mrs Julia Hann, Min-yr-Afon, 11 Y Gribin, Solva, Haverfordwest SA62 6UY (01437

721752). Charming cottage/self-contained annexe, surrounded by flowers. Tucked away in a peaceful hamlet with the River Solva winding its way down to the harbour. Restaurants, coastal path, pubs and shops are just a short walk away. The Annexe is suitable for partially disabled guests. All rooms are en suite. Twin bedroom, lounge/kitchen for refreshments, fridge/microwave, with an upstairs double bedroom. A full choice breakfast is served in the low beamed dining room in the cottage next door. Upstairs is a double room with its sloping ceiling and chintzy decor. Refreshment tray, TV and washbasin. From £16 per person per night. "Which?" Recommended.

TENBY. Emilio and Roberta Romeo, Pen Mar, New Hedges, Tenby SA70 8TL (01834 842435). *HIGHLY COMMENDED*. RAC Acclaimed. Situated between Tenby (one mile) and Saundersfoot (one and a half miles) in Pembrokeshire National Park, having sea views of Carmarthen Bay. Waterwynch Bay is just a few minutes' walk. South Pembrokeshire with its beautiful coastline, unspoiled beaches, golden sands and sheltered bays is ideal for sailing, sea fishing, horse riding, golfing or touring. There are many interesting walks along the coastal paths. Comfortable, relaxing atmosphere awaits offering "a touch of Italy" at Pen Mar, our friendly fully licensed family-run Hotel. We have a pleasant diningroom with separate tables, a well stocked bar, table d'ho3te and a2 la carte menus offering a wide choice of English and Continental cuisine. Recommended by Guild of Master Caterers. Open all year. Reductions for children. Bed and Breakfast £17 to £22. Some rooms en suite. Private car park. All credit cards accepted.

POWYS

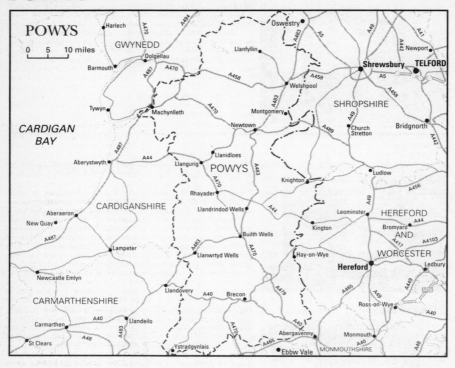

POWYS

0   5   10 miles

GWYNEDD

CARDIGAN
BAY

POWYS

CARDIGANSHIRE

CARMARTHENSHIRE

SHROPSHIRE

HEREFORD
AND
WORCESTER

MONMOUTHSHIRE

BRECON. Mrs Theresa Jones, Trehenry Farm, Felinfach, Brecon LD3 0UN (01874 754312). 🌸🌸🌸

DE LUXE. Enjoy the beauty of the Welsh countryside at our 200 acre farm, situated six miles east of Brecon, with panoramic views of the Black Mountains and the Brecon Beacons. An 18th century farmhouse offering select accommodation, en suite bedrooms with tea/coffee making facilities, TV lounge, separate dining tables, pay phone, large gardens. Brecon, Hay-on-Wye and Builth Wells close by and sport and lesiure are well catered for with golf, swimming, boating, pony trekking, water ski-ing and beautiful walks. Personal service and a warm welcome await you at Trehenry. Please send for our brochure.

BRECON. Mrs Marion Meredith, Lodge Farm, Talgarth, Brecon LD3 0DP (01874 711244). 🌸🌸🌸

HIGHLY COMMENDED. Welcome to the "Lodge", a working family farm nestling in the Black Mountains in the eastern section of the Brecon Beacons National Park, one and a half miles from Talgarth off A479. Hay-on-Wye/Brecon eight miles, Llangorse Lake four miles. The house enjoys mountain views and is set in a large garden where guests are welcome to relax. This 18th century house with original oak beams offers quality en suite rooms with tea making facilities; lounge with TV, dining room with separate tables, original inglenook fireplace and flagstone floor. Freshly prepared "real food", including vegetarian choice using local and home grown produce, is a speciality. A non-smoking establishment. Bed and Breakfast from £19 to £21 per person; Evening Meal from £12.

BRECON. The Beacons, 16 Bridge Street, Brecon LD3 8AH (01874 623339). ♛♛♛ *HIGHLY*

COMMENDED. AA QQQ, RAC Acclaimed. In the heart of the National Park surrounded by magnificent scenery, an elegant Georgian house with well-equipped rooms (mostly en suite). Luxury four-poster and king-size coronet rooms also available. Licensed restaurant with superb cuisine by award-winning chef. The Beacons is just two minutes' walk from the centre of Brecon where you can discover its cathedral, castle, museums, marina, theatre and River Usk. Bargain Breaks available. Ring **Peter or Barbara.**

BRECON. Mrs Eileen Williams, Upper Farm, Llechfaen, Brecon LD3 7SP (01874 665269). WTB Listed *COMMENDED.* **Working farm.** A modernised farmhouse offering Bed and Breakfast only, situated just off the A40 Brecon to Abergavenny road, two miles from Brecon town. A 64 acre dairy farm in the heart of the National Park directly facing Brecon Beacons. Ideal for touring, with golf, trekking and fishing nearby and many Welsh craft shops to visit. Two double and one family bedrooms with washbasins and tea/coffee facilities; bathroom, toilet; sittingroom; dining room. Cot, babysitting, reduced rates for children. Open all year. Car essential, parking. No pets.

BRECON near. Gwyn and Hazel Davies, Caebetran Farm, Felinfach, Brecon LD3 0UL (01874

754460). ♛♛♛ *HIGHLY COMMENDED.* **Working farm, join in.** "Welcome Host". A warm welcome, a cup of tea and home-made cakes await you when you arrive at Caebetran. Visitors are welcome to see the cattle and sheep on the farm. There are breathtaking views of the Brecon Beacons and the Black Mountains and just across a field is a 400 acre Common, ideal for walking, bird watching or just relaxing. Ponies and sheep graze undisturbed, while buzzards soar above you. The farmhouse dates back to the 17th century and has been recently modernised to give the quality and comfort visitors expect today. There are many extras in the rooms to give that special feel to your holiday. The rooms are all en suite and have colour TV and tea making facilities. Comfortable lounge with colour TV for guests' use. Caebetran is an ideal base for exploring this beautiful unspoilt part of the country with pony trekking, walking, birdwatching, wildlife, hang gliding and so much more. For more details, a brochure and terms please write or telephone. "Arrive as visitors and leave as friends".

BRECON. Mrs Pamela Boxhall, The Old Mill, Felinfach, Brecon LD3 0UB (01874 625385). ♛♛

HIGHLY COMMENDED. A 16th century converted corn mill peacefully situated in its own grounds. Inglenook fireplace, exposed beams, en suite rooms, beverage trays, TV lounge. Ideal for country pursuits or just relaxing. Within easy reach of Brecon Beacons, Black Mountains, Hay-on-Wye. Local pubs within walking distance. Packed lunches by arrangement. Children welcome. Terms: Double Room from £15 per person; Twin en suite from £16.50 per person; Single from £16 to £18. Reductions for weekly stays.

BUILTH WELLS. Derek Johnson, Halcyon House, Cilmery, Builth Wells LD2 3NU (Tel & Fax: 01982

552838). "Relaxed atmosphere", "Superb", "The ambience", "Delicious breakfast", and that's the visitors' book! Tranquil with panoramic southerly views. Short Breaks specialist. Centrally situated for touring the "secret" heart of Wales, Severn Bridge, Cardiff, Worcester and West/South Wales. Beaches within one and a half hours. Silver service breakfast. All rooms remote control colour TV, tea/coffee making, central heating. Billiard room. Shower and jacuzzi bathrooms. Conference facility for 30. Dormitory accommodation available. Adjacent inn/restaurant. Nearby (two miles) golf, fishing, riding, bowls, tennis, swimming, theatre, sports centre, Wales Showground. Under one hour to Hay-on-Wye, Hereford, Brecon Beacons and Elan Valley Reservoirs. Convenient for railway station (200 yards) and bus services. Terms from £17 for Bed and Breakfast.

PLEASE SEND A STAMPED ADDRESSED ENVELOPE WITH ENQUIRIES

BUILTH WELLS near. Mrs Margaret Davies, The Court Farm, Aberedw, Near Builth Wells LD2 3UP

(01982 560277). WTB *HIGHLY COMMENDED.* Non smokers please. We welcome guests into our home on a family-run livestock farm situated away from traffic in a peaceful, picturesque valley surrounded by hills. Lovely walking, wildlife area, central to Hay-on-Wye, Brecon Beacons, Elan Valley and very convenient for Royal Welsh Showground. We offer comfort, care and homeliness in our spacious stone-built farmhouse with traditional cooking using home produce where possible. Bedrooms have adjustable heating, hospitality trays and electric blankets. En suite or private bathroom available. Guests lounge with TV. Bed and Breakfast from £16.

BUILTH WELLS. C. Davies, Gwern-y-Mynach, Llanafan Fawr, Builth Wells LD2 3PN (01597

860256). Gwern-y-Mynach Farm is a mixed sheep and dairy working farm near Builth Wells in mid-Powys where golf, rugby, bowls, cricket and a new sports hall are all available. Our house is centrally heated throughout. Guest accommodation comprises one single room and one double room with bathroom en suite. Situated in a lovely area, ideal for walking, enjoying the open mountains and watching the Red Kites in flight. Close to the farm in the forest we have Greenwood chair making, steam bending, coracle making which attract people from overseas to the classes. Please write, or telephone, for further information and tariff.

HAY-ON-WYE. Peter and Olwen Roberts, York House, Cusop, Hay-on-Wye HR3 5QX (01497

820705). From January to December enjoy a relaxing holiday in this elegant Victorian guest house, quietly situated on the B4348, five minutes' walk from Hay-on-Wye, the famous "town of books". Accommodation comprises four comfortable bedrooms all with en suite facilities. Dining room and separate lounge. All rooms are furnished and equipped to a very high standard including TV and overlook beautiful one-acre gardens towards the mountains. Full English Breakfast served, packed lunches and evening meals by arrangement; complimentary hot bedtime drinks. Large private car park. Secure cycle shed. Heated drying room. Hay is an ideal walking base and a good centre for touring the lovely Border country. Bed and Breakfast from £22. Further details from resident proprietors. AA QQQQ Selected, RAC Highly Acclaimed. No smoking indoors.

LLANBADARN FYNYDD. Barbara and Bill Ainsworth, Hillside Lodge Guest House, Llanbadarn

Fynydd LD1 6TU (01597 840364). ♥♥♥ *HIGHLY COMMENDED.* A small, family-run, country guest house catering for non-smokers exclusively. Situated between Newtown and Llandrindod Wells. All bedrooms are en suite and have colour TV and tea making facilities, hair dryers, irons and ironing boards on request. For those who don't want to go out to visit the many interesting attractions nearby, there is always the snooker room, a large private room with full size snooker table. Children welcome. Bed and Breakfast from £19 per person. Please send for our brochure.

LLANDRINDOD WELLS. Mrs Ruth Jones, Holly Farm, Howey, Llandrindod Wells LD1 5PP (01597

822402). ♥♥♥ *HIGHLY COMMENDED.* Holly Farm, set in beautiful countryside, offers guests a friendly welcome. Situated one and a half miles south of the spa town of Llandrindod Wells, it is an excellent base for exploring lakes and mountains and for birdwatching. Most rooms are en suite with beverage trays. There is a TV lounge with log fire; in the dining room, which has separate tables, superb meals are served using home produce. Safe car parking. Brochure on request. Bed and Breakfast from £17; Bed, Breakfast and Evening Meals from £25 to £27. Weekly rates from £170 to £180. AA QQQ.

LLANGURIG. Nigel and Jean Felstead, Pant-y-Benny, Llangurig, Llanidloes SY18 6RT (01686 440212). An extended 16th century farmhouse situated on A44 one and a half miles west of Llangurig in the Upper Wye Valley. Activities available locally include fishing, mountain biking, narrow gauge railways; horse riding on site with facilities for your own horse/pony. Many local motor sport (car and bike) events take place throughout the year. Three twin rooms, one downstairs being en suite, all with tea/coffee trays. Residents' lounge with TV, video, board games. Separate dining room. Open all year. Bed and Breakfast £15 to £18 per person. Dinner by arrangement £8 per person. Self-catering six-berth mobile home also available.

LLANIDLOES. Mrs Janet Evans, Dyffryn Glyn, Llanidloes SY18 6NE (01686 412129). Dyffryn is centrally situated in an Area of Natural Beauty two miles from the friendly market town of Llanidloes, one mile from Clywedog Lake with its spectacular views where sailing, fishing, birdwatching and walking can be pursued. Ideal area for touring. Accommodation comprises one en suite room and one twin-bedded room with washbasin and use of bathroom; both rooms have towels and tea making facilities. Visitors' own sitting room with TV, separate dining room. Ample parking. Bed and Breakfast from £15.

LLANIDLOES. Jean Bailey, Glangwy, Llangurig, Llanidloes SY18 6RS (01686 440697). Local river stone (Wye) built house offering comfortable Bed and Breakfast accommodation in beautiful countryside. Traditional English breakfast served with all home cooked evening meals; special diets catered for, vegetarians included. Accommodation comprises two doubles (can be used as family rooms as single bed also in each) and one twin bedrooms with washbasins, tea/coffee facilities and storage heaters (all beds have electric underblankets); bathroom, separate shower room; dining room (separate tables per party); lounge with colour TV. Pets welcome. Parking. Central for touring and local walks. Bed and Breakfast £14 per person; reductions for children under nine years.

MACHYNLLETH. Jill and Barry Stevens, Yr Hen Felin, Abercegir, Machynlleth SY20 8NR (01650 511868). 👜 *HIGHLY COMMENDED.* AA QQQQ Selected. Relax at our converted stone watermill, built in 1820 on the peaceful banks of the River Gwydol, where you can listen to the sound of the river from your bedroom window. The walking and scenery are some of the finest in Wales and the coast with its fine sandy beaches can be reached in 20 minutes by car. Heavily beamed throughout with original pine floors, the character has been enhanced with antique furniture and an interesting collection of china and clocks. Our double and two twin-bedded rooms have en suite facilities and there is a large comfortable guests' sitting room with TV. Private parking. Traditional or vegetarian breakfast. The mill is not suitable for smokers. Bed and Breakfast £19 per person per night. Brochure available.

PUBLISHER'S NOTE

MACHYNLLETH near. Monica and David Bashford, Gelli-graean Farmhouse, Cwrt, Pennal, Near Machynlleth SY20 9LE (Tel & Fax: 01654 791219).

Nestling at the foot of a wooded hillside in the southernmost tip of the Snowdonia National Park, the farmhouse is in a secluded and sheltered spot. Handy for the Centre for Alternative Technology, Ynys Hir Bird Reserve and the beach at Aberdovey. Stunning panoramic views of the Dovey Valley can be seen from the hill walks behind the house. Stream with migratory salmon and sea trout nearby; otters in autumn. Vernacular architecture and massive timbers date from the seventeen hundreds, a huge log fire in the handsome inglenook flickers in the polished slate hearth. One double and one twin bedrooms, both en suite. Fully centrally heated. Totally non-smoking. Open all year. Bed and Breakfast from £19.50 to £23.50. Special Breaks out of season available.

NEWTOWN. Mrs Vi Madeley, Greenfields, Kerry, Newtown SY16 4LH (01686 670596; Fax: 01686 670354). 🌸 🌸 🌸 A warm welcome awaits you at Greenfields. All rooms are tastefully decorated and are spacious in size, each having panoramic views of the rolling Kerry hills. There is a good choice of breakfast menu and evening meals can be provided by prior arrangement; packed lunches are also available. Licensed for residents. Accommodation available in one double and two twin-bedded rooms, all en suite (twin rooms let as singles if required). Hostess trays and TVs in all rooms. The dining room has individual tables. A good place for stopping for one night, a short break or longer holiday. Excellent off road parking. Bed and Breakfast from £17.50 to £20 per person; Evening Meal £4.50 to £10. Brochure available.

Greenfields

PENYBONT-FAWR. Mrs Anne Evans, Glanhafon, Penybont-Fawr, Oswestry SY10 0EW (01691 860377). 🌸 🌸 *HIGHLY COMMENDED.* **Working farm, join in.** Glanhafon is a working sheep farm situated in the heart of the magnificent Tanat Valley. The traditional Welsh farmhouse offers good home cooking with fresh farm produce which makes it attractive to families or those who seek the peace and quiet of the countryside. Bordering the Berwyn Mountains with easy access to Lake Vyrnwy and Bala Lake, both offering water sports. You may wish to spend a day browsing in the old market towns of Oswestry and Welshpool. Accommodation comprises three bedrooms, all en suite with own sitting room. Tea making facilities in bedrooms. Full central heating. Ample parking. Children and pets welcome. Open Easter till October. Bed and Breakfast from £15.

RHAYADER. Mrs Lena Powell, Gigrin Farm, South Road, Rhayader LD6 5BL (01597 810243). WTB Listed. Gigrin is a 17th century longhouse, retaining original oak beams and cosy atmosphere. Peacefully situated overlooking the Wye Valley and half a mile from the market town of Rhayader with its numerous inns and new leisure centre. The spectacular Elan Valley dams, which supply Birmingham with water — home of the Red Kite — are three miles away. The sea is only an hour's drive away over the Cambrian Mountains to Aberystwyth. A two mile Nature Trail on the farm; Red Kite feeding station November to March. The farmhouse is centrally heated and guests have shared use of a bathroom with shower. There are two bedrooms, each with double bed, washbasins and hospitality trays. Residents' sittingroom and dining room. Bed and Breakfast from £15. No smoking. Restaurant nearby (200 yards) for Evening Meals. Children welcome. Self catering accommodation also available. Brochure on request.

TALGARTH. Mrs Bronwen Prosser, Upper Genfford Guest House, Talgarth LD3 0EN (01874 711360). The cottages are situated amongst the most spectacular scenery of the Brecon Beacons National Park. An excellent location for walking and exploring the Brecon Beacons, Black Mountains and Wye Valley. An Area of Outstanding Natural Beauty, rich in historic and archaeological interest. The cottages are beautifully furnished with fitted carpets, oil-fired Rayburn, oak-beamed lounges, antique furniture, open log fires, Calor gas heaters and colour TVs. In Bed and Breakfast cottage bedrooms are en suite with colour TV and beverage trays. Tea and home made cakes served on arrival at both cottages. Pets welcome. Linen provided. A warm friendly welcome awaits you. Children enjoy our friendly pony ''Topsy''. Bed and Breakfast from £16. Weekend breaks available. Highly recommended. Self catering available from £100 to £150 per week. Caravan also for hire. Mrs Prosser has been nominated one of the top 20 proprietors for the AA Landlady of the Year Competition 1996 and is also one of the only two winners from Wales of the FHG Diploma 1995/6. AA QQQQ Selected.

WELSHPOOL. Mrs Freda Emberton,Tynllwyn Farm, Welshpool SY21 9BW (01938 553175/ 553054). WTB 🌼🌼 *HIGHLY COMMENDED.* **Working**

farm. A warm welcome is assured at Tynllwyn Farm, built 1861, which stands on a hillside with breathtaking views of the Long Mountain and Severn Valley. We are a working beef and sheep farm. Large comfortable lounge with open fires in winter. Also licensed bar. All bedrooms have colour TV, tea/coffee facilities and central heating. All home cooking; plentiful farmhouse meals served. Large parking area. Nearby are the lovely market town of Welshpool, Powys Castle, Welshpool and Llanfair Steam Railway, canal trips also exciting quad trekking and mountain bike hire. Easy reach of the lakes and mountains of Mid Wales. Children welcome, pets by arrangement. Bed and Breakfast from £15.50 to £18; Evening Meal £8.50.

WELSHPOOL. Mrs Jane Jones, Trefnant Hall, Berriew, Welshpool SY21 8AS (01686 640262).

🌼🌼🌼 *HIGHLY COMMENDED.* Trefnant Hall offers a warm welcome in a Grade II Listed farmhouse built in 1742. All rooms are comfortably furnished with tea/coffee making facilities, colour TV and are en-suite. This sheep and beef farm is set in beautiful peaceful countryside away from the busy roads with superb views and gardens. Powis Castle and gardens are just two miles away with the market town of Welshpool close by. An ideal centre for exploring mid-Wales with the seaside less than an hour away. Bed and Breakfast from £17.

WELSHPOOL near. Mrs E.E. Sheridan, Cross Lane Farm, Berriew, Near Welshpool SY21 8AU (01686 640233). Bill and Lucy welcome you with tea, scones and a friendly chat when you visit them at their spacious farmhouse near the best kept village in Wales, just five miles from the market town of Welshpool. We have enjoyed 18 years of providing accommodation in unspoilt countryside, ideal for walking, golfing, fishing, etc. Accommodation comprises two large double and one single bedrooms; visitors' lounge. Ample parking. Children welcome, cot available. Good plain home cooking comes recommended. Bed and Breakfast from £13.50. Reduced rates for children under 11 years. Packed lunches by prior request.

SOUTH WALES

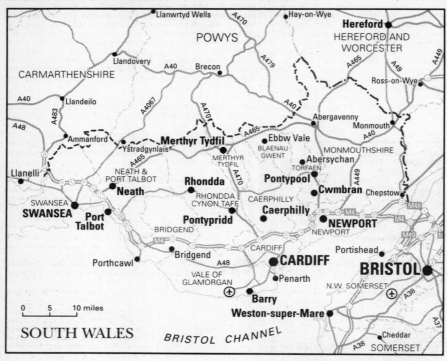

SOUTH WALES

0 5 10 miles

BRISTOL CHANNEL

BLAINA. Mr J.W. Chandler, Lamb House, Westside, Blaina NP3 3DB (01495 290179). ♛♛
COMMENDED. Lamb House nestles amongst trees in its own well kept gardens with private off-road parking. Set in the Upper Gwent Valleys, close to all major tourist attractions in South Wales. Activities in the area include walking, fishing, golfing, boating, etc. Accommodation comprises two double en suite rooms on ground floor suitable for partially disabled guests and one twin/double room on first floor with washbasin; all rooms have radio alarms. Tea/coffee available at all times. TV lounge, separate dining room. No smoking in bedrooms. Full central heating throughout. Local public house for excellent food only a five minute walk. Children welcome but sorry, no pets. Bed and Breakfast from £15 per person per night.

BLAINA. Malcolm and Betty Hancocks, Chapel Farm, Blaina NP3 3DJ (01495 290888). ♛♛
COMMENDED. Guests are assured of a warm welcome when they visit this 15th century renovated farmhouse and many return each year. A good base for touring Big Pit, Blaenavon; Bryn-Bach Park, Brecon Beacons, Abergavenny. Family and double rooms; one bedroom has shower en suite. Packed lunches available; Evening Meal on request. There is a drinks licence. No smoking in bedrooms. Bed and Breakfast from £17 to £20. Full details available.

CAERPHILLY. Watford Fach Farm Guest House, Watford Road, Caerphilly CF83 1NE (01222 851500). ♛ Open all year. Seven bedrooms, four with bathrooms, all with washbasins, TV and tea/coffee making facilities. Central heating. Parking. Good home cooking. Bed and Breakfast from £16. Fire Certificate held.

CARDIFF. Mrs Sarah Nicholls, Preste Gaarden Hotel, 181 Cathedral Road, Cardiff CF1 9PN (01222

228607). 🏵🏵 *COMMENDED*. "Welcome Host". This spacious Victorian family home offers olde worlde charm with modern amenities, including en suite facilities in most rooms. You will immediately feel relaxed by the warm welcome given by Sarah. Situated in the heart of the City, close to the Castle, museums, shops and an international array of restaurants and only 100 yards from Sophia Gardens offering walking, fishing and horse riding. Bed and Breakfast from £17.50 to £27 per person includes tea/coffee and biscuits in your room. Well established and independently recommended.

CARDIFF. Paul and Annette Howard, Marlborough Guest House, 98 Newport Road, Roath, Cardiff CF2 1DG (Tel & Fax: 01222 492385). This cosy and impeccably maintained Victorian guesthouse is just an easy five minute stroll from the city centre. It has nine tastefully decorated bedrooms, all with TV; lounge with satellite TV, and a small bar. A laundry service can be provided and a hot drink and complimentary sandwiches are offered upon arrival. Breakfasts are very large, enough to set the heartiest eater up for the day. Children welcome. Sorry, no pets. Car park. Terms available on request. Children's reductions. Please send for further information.

CARDIFF. Austins Hotel, 11 Coldstream Terrace, City Centre, Cardiff CF1 8LJ (01222 377148). 🏵🏵 Situated in the centre of Cardiff, 300 yards from the Castle. Five single and six twin-bedded rooms, five with full en-suite facilities, all with washbasins, shaver points, fixed heating, colour TV and tea/coffee making facilities. Full English Breakfast. Only 10 minutes' walk from central bus and train stations. Fire Certificate held. Warm welcome offered to all. Bed and Breakfast from £16. Reduced rates for children and Senior Citizens.

CHEPSTOW. Mr Lewis Bell, The Coach and Horses Inn, Welsh Street, Chepstow NP6 5LN (01291

622626). Chepstow's first traditional pub. Take advantage of your stay here by visiting the Chepstow Racecourse (just two miles) or simply by enjoying the Welsh countryside; Offa's Dyke Walk nearby. Accommodation comprises seven bedrooms; ample bath and toilet facilities. Restaurant, licensed. Children welcome. Sorry, no pets. Bed and Breakfast accommodation offered (breakfast served between 7am and 9am). CAMRA Gwent Pub of the Year 1992. Real Ale Festival yearly — live music, darts, quiz.

COWBRIDGE near. Mrs Sue Beer, Plas Llanmihangel, Llanmihangel, Near Cowbridge CF7 7LQ

(01446 774610). WTB Listed *COMMENDED*. Plas Llanmihangel is the finest medieval Grade I Listed manor house in the beautiful Vale of Glamorgan. We offer a genuine warmth of welcome, delightful accommodation, first class food and service in our wonderful home. The baronial hall, great log fires, the ancient tower and acres of beautiful historic gardens intrigue all who stay in this fascinating house. Its long history and continuous occupation have created a spectacular building in romantic surroundings unchanged since the 16th century. A great opportunity to experience the ambience and charm of a past age. Three double rooms. Bed and Breakfast £25. High quality home cooked evening meal on request.

GOWER. Mrs Anne Main, Tallizmand, Llanmadoc, Gower SA3 1DE (01792 386373). 🏵🏵🏵

HIGHLY COMMENDED. Located near the splendid Gower coastline surrounded by beautiful countryside. Miles of unspoilt beaches, pine woods and salt marshes. Ideal for walking, surfing, bird watching and wild flowers. Tallizmand has tastefully furnished en suite bedrooms with tea/coffee making facilities; TV lounge. Home cooking, packed lunches, vegetarians catered for. Ample parking. Bed and Breakfast from £16; Evening Meal available.

PLEASE SEND A STAMPED ADDRESSED ENVELOPE WITH ENQUIRIES

GOWER PENINSULA. Chris and Joanne Allder, Heathfield, Llethryd, Gower SA2 7LH (01792 390198).

All guests are welcomed by a friendly family atmosphere, our house is set in an acre of garden with a swimming pool that visitors are welcome to use by arrangement. Llethryd village is in a quiet hamlet on the B4271 on the Gower Peninsula which is an area of outstanding natural beauty, within minutes of lovely tranquil woodland walks and unspoiled sandy beaches. We are also only 20 minutes from Swansea's extensive shopping centre, theatre and restaurants. All rooms have TV and tea/coffee making facilities. Children welcome. Non-smokers preferred. Bed and Breakfast £15 to £18.

GOWER PENINSULA. Mrs M. Valerie Evans, The Old Rectory, Reynoldston, Swansea SA3 1AD (01792 390129).

A warm welcome awaits visitors to our home in this beautiful peninsula. The village is 12 miles west of Swansea and the area offers lovely coast and hill walks, wild flowers, birdwatching, pony trekking, golf and sea activities. We offer comfort, peace and quiet, a lovely secluded garden and good food grown in own garden or locally. Tea/coffee facilities in all bedrooms. Central heating. Open most of the year. Bed and Breakfast £18; Evening Meals to order £10. Non-smokers preferred.

KNELSTON (Gower). Mrs C.W. Ashton, Fairfield Cottage, Knelston, Gower SA3 1AR (01792 391013).

Fairfield Cottage is an 18th century Gower cottage set in attractive gardens in the hamlet of Knelston. Approximately 12 miles west of Swansea with its marina, theatres and excellent shopping and entertainment facilities. The Cottage has comfortable lounge with wood fires set in an inglenook fireplace, pretty double bedrooms with wash-basins, tea/coffee making facilities and full central heating. Home cooking is to a high standard with locally produced vegetables and fruit when in season. Elizabeth Gundry recommended. There is also ample parking. Sorry no dogs unless prepared to leave in cars. No smoking. Bed and Breakfast £16/£17 per person; Dinner £12. Brochure available.

MONMOUTH. Rosemary and Derek Ringer, Church Farm Guest House, Mitchel Troy, Monmouth NP5 4HZ (01600 712176). ❦❦ COMMENDED. AA QQQ.

A spacious and homely 16th century former farmhouse with oak beams and inglenook fireplaces, set in large attractive garden with stream. An excellent base for visiting the Wye Valley, Forest of Dean and Black Mountains. All bedrooms have washbasins, tea/coffee making facilities and central heating; most are en suite. Own car park. Terrace, barbecue. Colour TV. Non-smoking. Bed and Breakfast from £18 to £21 per person, Evening Meals by arrangement. We also offer a programme of guided and self-guided walking holidays and short breaks. Separate "Wysk Walks" brochure on request.

MONMOUTH near. Mrs Smith, New House Farm, Dingestow, Near Monmouth NP5 4EB (Tel & Fax: 01600 740245). Tourist Board COMMENDED. New House Farm is a 300 acre working farm set in peaceful countryside with magnificent views. Ideally situated for touring Wye Valley, Brecon Beacons and Forest of Dean. A warm welcome awaits you with a high standard of comfort and cooking. Children are welcome with animals to see, circular walks start on the farm. Open January to December. Bed and Breakfast from £17 per person.

NEATH. Mr S. Brown, Green Lantern Guest House, Hawdref Ganol Farm, Cimla, Neath SA12 9SL

(01639 631884). 🌸🌸🌸 *HIGHLY COMMENDED.* West Glamorgan's only AA QQQQQ Premier Selected House. Family-run 18th century luxury centrally heated farmhouse set in its own 45 acres with beautiful scenic views over open countryside. Safe off road parking. Close to Afan Argoed and Margam Parks; 10 minutes from M4; one mile from birthplace of Richard Burton. Ideal for walking, cycling, horse riding from farm. Perfect base for touring South Wales valleys and the beautiful Gower Coast. Large guest room with inglenook fireplace and TV; colour TV and tea/coffee facilities in all rooms. En suite available. Terms from £18 per person. Reductions for children. Pets welcome. Please telephone for colour brochure.

NEWPORT. Mr and Mrs R. Evans, "Westwood Villa Guest House", 59 Risca Road, Crosskeys, Newport NP1 7BT (01495 270336).

🌸🌸🌸 *HIGHLY COMMENDED.* Six miles M4; close Newport, Cardiff, Wye Valley. Brecon Beacons one hour's drive, Ebbw Vale 20 minutes. Scenic drives, walks, sport and leisure entertainment. Guest House has central heating and is double glazed. Single, double and family rooms available, en suite rooms can be supplied, all with colour TV, washbasin, tea/coffee making facilities, radio alarm clocks; two bathrooms. Tasty home cooking; evening meals. Licensed bar. Garden and play area. Children, contractors and pets very welcome. Set in beautiful valleys with outstanding scenery "Westwood Villa", originally a manse, offers beautiful accommodation with that personal touch which makes all the difference and a holiday to remember. Bed and Breakfast from £22 single, £38 double. Bar meals from £5 served 6pm to 9pm. A warm welcome from hosts Robert and Maureen awaits guests. Visa accepted.

FOR THE MUTUAL GUIDANCE OF GUEST AND HOST

Every year literally thousands of holidays, short-breaks and overnight stops are arranged through our guides, the vast majority without any problems at all. In a handful of cases, however, difficulties do arise about bookings, which often could have been prevented from the outset.

It is important to remember that when accommodation has been booked, both parties — guests and hosts — have entered into a form of contract. We hope that the following points will provide helpful guidance.

GUESTS: When enquiring about accommodation, be as precise as possible. Give exact dates, numbers in your party and the ages of any children. State the number and type of rooms wanted and also what catering you require — bed and breakfast, full board, etc. Make sure that the position about evening meals is clear — and about pets, reductions for children or any other special points.

Read our reviews carefully to ensure that the proprietors you are going to contact can supply what you want. Ask for a letter confirming all arrangements, if possible.

If you have to cancel, do so as soon as possible. Proprietors do have the right to retain deposits and under certain circumstances to charge for cancelled holidays if adequate notice is not given and they cannot re-let the accommodation.

HOSTS: Give details about your facilities and about any special conditions. Explain your deposit system clearly and arrangements for cancellations, charges, etc, and whether or not your terms include VAT.

If for any reason you are unable to fulfil an agreed booking without adequate notice, you may be under an obligation to arrange alternative suitable accommodation or to make some form of compensation.

While every effort is made to ensure accuracy, we regret that FHG Publications cannot accept responsibility for errors, omissions or misrepresentation in our entries or any consequences thereof. Prices in particular should be checked because we go to press early. We will follow up complaints but cannot act as arbiters or agents for either party.

NEWPORT near. West Usk Lighthouse, St. Brides, Wentloog, Near Newport NP1 9SF (01633 810126/815860; Fax: 01633 815582). ＷＷ Grade II

Listed, The West Usk Lighthouse is a real lighthouse built in 1821 to a unique design. Rooms are wedge-shaped within a circular structure. The entrance hall is slate-bedded and leads to a central stone spiral staircase and the internal collecting well! The views are panoramic from the roof patio. Three double bedrooms, all en suite, which have been individually furnished to include a king size waterbed and four-poster bed. Guests can try the flotation tank for deep and immediate relaxation. Most amenities are close by and there are many interesting places to visit in the area. Distinctly different. Bed and Breakfast from £30 per person. No smoking. Open all year.

SOUTHGATE/GOWER/SWANSEA. Mrs Joyce Churchill, Heatherlands, 1 Hael Lane, Southgate, Gower, Swansea SA3 2AP (01792 233256). ＷＷ

HIGHLY COMMENDED. Delightfully situated Heatherlands is an immaculate non-smoking residence. Pretty garden, 100 yards from cliffs and sea, spectacular scenery, lovely walks to Pobble and Three Cliff Bays, golf course 500 yards away (18 holes). Three double bedrooms, one a twin, washbasins, shaver points, one bedroom en suite the other two each with private bathroom; tea/coffee making facilities. All rooms have TV. Dining room with separate tables, TV lounge for guests' use. Open all year. Bed and Breakfast from £18 per person. Children over eight years welcome. Single person occupying double room supplement £3 to £5. Parking. Excellent breakfast. Warm welcome.

ST. BRIDES WENTLOOG (Near Newport). Mr David W. Bushell, Chapel Guest House, Church Road, St. Brides Wentloog, Near Newport NP1 9SN (01633 681018; Fax: 01633 270470). ＷＷ *COMMENDED.* Comfortable accommodation in a converted chapel situated in a village between Newport/ Cardiff, near Tredegar House. Restaurant and inn adjacent, car park available. Guest lounge with TV. Single, double and twin rooms en suite or private bathroom. Beverage trays, TV, shaver points in all rooms. From £18. Children under three years FREE, three to 12 year olds half price sharing parents' room. Pets by arrangement. Leave M4 at Junction 28, take A48 towards Newport, at roundabout take third left exit signposted St. Brides, B4239. Drive to centre of village, turn right into Church Road and left into Church House Inn car park; the guest house is on the left and a warm welcome awaits.

TINTERN. Anne and Peter Howe, Valley House, Raglan Road, Tintern, Near Chepstow NP6 6TH (01291 689652). ＷＷ *COMMENDED.* Valley House is a

fine Georgian residence situated in the tranquil Angidy Valley 800 yards from the A466 Chepstow to Monmouth road and within a mile of Tintern Abbey. Numerous walks through picturesque woods and valleys right from our doorstep. The accommodation is of a very high standard; all rooms are en suite, have tea/coffee making facilities and colour TV. The guests' lounge has a wealth of exposed beams and a working range whilst the dining room has an arched stone ceiling. Numerous places to eat nearby. Bed and Breakfast from £19 per person. Open all year. Non-smoking preferred. AA QQQ, RAC Acclaimed.

REPUBLIC OF IRELAND

KERRY

ABBEYDORNEY, Near Tralee. Mrs Mary O'Connor, The Abbey Tavern, Abbeydorney (00 353 66 35145). Country village pub ideal for touring Ring of Kerry and Dingle Peninsula, five miles from sandy beaches. Five bedrooms, two en suite. Situated near Tralee, Killarney and Ballybunion Golf Courses. Children welcome. Bed and Breakfast is £13. Licensed. Bar snacks available. Four-bedroomed self catering house and apartments also available. Please write or telephone for further details.

KILLARNEY. Eden Villa Farm, Loreto Road, Killarney (064 31138; from UK 00 353 64 31138).

Lovely old country house in extensive gardens in peaceful farmland surroundings overlooking the lakes, mountains and Killarney town. One mile from Glen Eagle Hotel Complex, the National Park with forest and nature walks, pony trekking, boating and fishing nearby. Two double bedrooms and two single ones, electric blankets on beds. Bathroom with shower and two toilets. Lounge cum dining room. Tea on arrival to welcome you and also night snacks up to 10.30pm. Car essential. Three miles to Killarney town.

KILLARNEY. Noreen Sheahan, Countess House, Killarney (00353 64 34247). ITB *APPROVED.*

Situated in a quiet peaceful location three minutes' walk from town centre and railway station; 200 metres from East Avenue Hotel on Countess Road.. All rooms are en suite and have tea/coffee making facilities. TV lounge. Private car park. Special rate for three sharing. Please write or telephone for further details.

KILLARNEY. Torc Falls, Church Road, Muckross, Killarney (00 353 6433566). ITB *APPROVED.*

Modern house situated two miles from town centre in a quiet location with Killarney Lakes, Muckross House and Gardens within half a mile and close to the National Park and Kerry Way. En suite rooms available. Private car park. Please write or telephone for further details.

KILDARE

CASTLEDERMOT. Mr G.D. Greene, Kilkea Lodge Farm, Castledermot (00 353 50345112). Kilkea

Lodge has belonged to the Greene family since 1740. Set in 260 acres of prime tillage and rolling parklands this tranquil setting offers guests the opportunity to relax in the comfort of log fires and traditional Irish hospitality. Accommodation comprises two double and one twin-bedded rooms en suite, and one single room and one family suite. First class traditional home cooking. Riding Centre on site run by Marion Greene and offering a variety of instructional and fun holidays under qualified supervision. Children welcome. French spoken. Open all year round except Christmas. Bed and Breakfast from £25; single supplement £5. Dinner from £15. Advance booking essential. Brochure available.

Key to
Tourist Board Ratings

The Crown Scheme
(England, Scotland & Wales)

Covering hotels, motels, private hotels, guesthouses, inns, bed & breakfast, farmhouses. Every Crown classified place to stay is inspected annually. *The classification:* Listed then 1-5 Crown indicates the range of facilities and services. Higher quality standards are indicated by the terms APPROVED, COMMENDED, HIGHLY COMMENDED and DELUXE.

The Key Scheme
(also operates in Scotland using a Crown symbol)

Covering self-catering in cottages, bungalows, flats, houseboats, houses, chalets, etc. Every Key classified holiday home is inspected annually. *The classification:* 1-5 Key indicates the range of facilities and equipment. Higher quality standards are indicated by the terms APPROVED, COMMENDED, HIGHLY COMMENDED and DELUXE.

The Q Scheme
(England, Scotland & Wales)

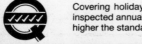

Covering holiday, caravan, chalet and camping parks. Every Q rated park is inspected annually for its quality standards. The more ✓ in the Q – up to 5 – the higher the standard of what is provided.

The Countryman

Discover the countryside that belongs to us all.

There's always plenty to read in *The Countryman*, the little green book that first appeared back in 1927. Every issue of this bi-monthly magazine brings you stories of country ways and insights into country life, as well as keeping a keen eye open for changes that threaten our glorious British countryside.

Our offices at Burford in the Cotswolds are in a former coaching inn and readers are always welcome to visit our delightful garden with views of the Windrush valley across the stone roofs of the village.

Subscribe now, and for just £13.80 we will deliver *The Countryman* direct to your door six times a year.

CREDITCARD SUBSCRIPTIONS CALL
0181 646 6672
quote ref FHG98

The Countryman makes the perfect gift for anyone who loves the countryside. If you make a gift subscription we send the recipient a greeting to tell them you have thought of them.

For a sample copy send two first class stamps to
The Countryman, Sheep Street, Burford, Oxon OX18 4LM.

For holidays in Scotland
why not try
FHG
Scotland 1998

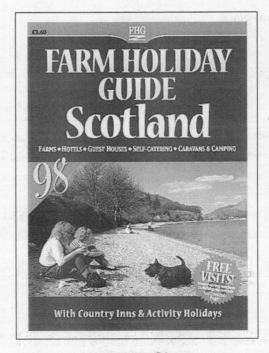

SPECIAL WELCOME SUPPLEMENT

Are you looking for a guest house where smoking is banned, a farmhouse that is equipped for the disabled, or a hotel that will cater for your special diet? If so, you should find this new supplement useful. Its three sections, NON-SMOKERS, DISABLED, and SPECIAL DIETS, list accommodation where these particular needs are served. Brief details of the accommodation are provided in this section; for a full description you should turn to the appropriate place in the main section of the book.

NON-SMOKERS

LONDON, CHISWICK. Mrs A. Louis, 18 Silver Crescent, Chiswick, London W4 5SE (0181-994 6265). Situated two minutes from Gunnersbury Underground station, M4 and A4. Central heating and colour TV in all rooms. Non-smokers preferred.

LONDON, GREENWICH. Marshall Mordew, Oakfield, 36 Southend Crescent, London SE9 2SB (Tel & Fax: 0181-859 8989). A large luxurious Victorian house in the London Borough of Greenwich conveniently located for travel to central London and Kent. Oakfield is entirely non smoking and especially welcomes vegetarians.

LONDON, HIGHGATE/CROUCH END. Penny and Laurence Solomons, The Parkland Walk Guest House, 12 Hornsey Rise Gardens, London N19 3PR (0171-263 3228; Fax: 0171-263 3965; email: parkwalk@monomark.demon.co.uk). Friendly Bed and Breakfast in pretty, comfortable Victorian family house. Totally non-smoking.Bed and Breakfast from £26 nightly.

LONDON, KENSINGTON. Mowbray Court Hotel, 28-30 Penywern Road, Earls Court, London SW5 9SU (0171-370 3690; Fax: 0171-370 5693). Listed Bed and Breakfast Tourist Class Hotel. Non-smoking rooms available. The hotel is close to all the major shopping areas and tourist sights. We accept well behaved pets.

BEDFORDSHIRE, SANDY. Mrs. Joan M. Strong, Orchard Cottage, 1 High Street, Wrestlingworth, Near Sandy SG19 2EW (01767 631355). 🏵 *COMMENDED*. Picturesque 16th Century thatched cottage with modern extension, situated in a quiet, country location. Reduced terms for children. No smoking establishment.

BERKSHIRE, HENLEY-ON-THAMES near. Mrs H. Carver, Windy Brow, 204 Victoria Road, Wargrave RG10 8AJ (01189 403336). *HIGHLY COMMENDED*. Detached Victorian family house ideal for touring the Thames valley, Windsor and Oxford. Plenty of off-road parking. Children welcome. Tourist Board Listed and graded. Please phone for more details.

CAMBRIDGESHIRE, CAXTON. The Old Vicarage, Gransden Road, Caxton CB3 8PL (01954 719585). Beautiful old vicarage in an acre of garden. Quiet and peaceful, approximately 8 miles from Cambridge city centre. Large spacious theme room bedrooms. Central heating throughout.

CAMBRIDGESHIRE, ELY. Jenny Farndale, Cathedral House, 17 St. Mary's Street, Ely CB7 4ER (01353 662124). Cathedral House is situated in the centre of Ely. An ideal base for touring East Anglia, within easy reach of Cambridge. All rooms en suite with TV.

CAMBRIDGESHIRE, HEMINGFORD GREY. Maureen and Tony Webster, The Willow Guest House, 45 High Street, Hemingford Grey, St. Ives, Cambs PE18 9BJ (01480 494748). Large private guest house in centre of this picturesque village. Family, twin, double and single rooms available. All bedrooms en suite and non-smoking. Sorry no pets.

CAMBRIDGESHIRE, WYTON. Robin and Marion Seaman, The Elms, Banks End, Wyton PE17 2AA (01480 453523). Edwardian house with cottage garden. All rooms en-suite or with vanity units. No pets. No smoking.

CHESHIRE, CHESTER. Nigel and Clare Hill, Cotton Farmhouse, Cotton Edmunds, Chester CH3 7PT (Tel & Fax: 01244 336699). Large farmhouse only four miles from Chester yet set in beautiful open countryside. The house has recently undergone extensive, sympathetic, internal renovation. We are a non-smoking house.

CHESHIRE, SANDBACH. Mrs Helen Wood, Arclid Grange, Arclid Green, Sandbach CW11 0SZ (01270 764750). Some of our rooms are strictly non-smoking. Please confirm when booking. ETB Category 3 Disabled.

CORNWALL, BUDE. Mr and Mrs M.J. Whattler, Markhayes Manor, Marhamchurch, Bude EX23 0HJ (Tel & Fax: 01228 341321 or mobile 0831 742508). Grade II Listed farmhouse dating from Domesday set in 100 acres of countryside. Kitchen facilities, private walled garden. Ample parking. Non-smoking.

CORNWALL, CAMBORNE. Mrs Christine Peerless, Highdowns (formerly Cargenwen Farm), Blackrock, Praze-an-Beeble, Camborne TR14 9PD (01209 831442). Set on a hillside with extensive country views towards St. Ives Bay. A non-smoking household offering Bed and Breakfast and optional Evening Meal.

CORNWALL, FALMOUTH. Celia and Ian Carruthers, Harbour House, 1 Harbour Terrace, Falmouth TR11 2AN (01326 311344). Enjoy quality Bed and Breakfast accommodation with some of the most fantastic harbour views in Cornwall. We welcome guests for long or short stays, especially non-smokers. Please call for brochure.

CORNWALL, PENZANCE. Mr and Mrs G.W. Buswell, Penalva Private Hotel, Alexandra Road, Penzance TR18 4LZ (01736 369060). ❦ ❦ ❦ *APPROVED.* AA QQQ. Non-smoking hotel — immaculate fresh interior — excellent position close to amenities. Total ban on smoking on premises. Open all year. Highly recommended.

CORNWALL, ST. AGNES. Cleaderscroft Hotel, 16 British Road, St. Agnes TR5 0TZ (01872 552349). Heart of village. Mature gardens. Children's play area. Lounge, Bar, Dining and Games rooms. Private parking. Non-smokers welcomed. Bed and Breakfast from £19.50.

CORNWALL, TRURO. Mrs Shirley Wakeling, Rock Cottage, Blackwater, Truro TR4 8EU (01872 560252). ❦ ❦ ❦ *HIGHLY COMMENDED.* AA QQQQ Selected. RAC Acclaimed. 18th century beamed cottage, two double rooms and one twin, all en suite. Haven for non-smokers. Dinner by arrangement. A la carte menu. Open all year.

CORNWALL, TRURO. Andrew and Catherine Webb, Tregony House, 15 Fore Street, Tregony, Truro TR2 5RN (01872 530671). Grade II Listed building on main street of Tregony, nine miles Truro, many beaches close by. Ideally situated for exploring all of Cornwall. Children over seven years welcome.

CORNWALL, TRURO. Marcorrie Hotel, 20 Falmouth Road, Truro TR1 2HX (01872 277374; Fax: 01872 241666). ❦ ❦ ❦ *APPROVED.* Victorian town house in conservation area, five minutes' walk from the city centre and cathedral. Non-smokers welcome.

CUMBRIA, ALSTON. Clare and Mike Le Marie, Brownside House, Leadgate, Alston CA9 3EL (01434 382169; Fax: 01434 382100). Ideal centre for walking, cycling, birdwatching and exploring old lead mines. Easy reach for Lake District, Hadrian's Wall, Northumberland. Children and pets welcome (babysitting available).

CUMBRIA, AMBLESIDE. Colin and Rosemary Haskell, Borwick Lodge, Outgate, Hawkshead, Ambleside LA22 0PU (015394 36332). ❦ ❦ *HIGHLY COMMENDED.* Charming 17th century country house with magnificent panoramic lake and mountain views. Peaceful perfection. Non-smoking throughout.

CUMBRIA, AMBLESIDE. ❦ ❦ *COMMENDED.* **Bob and Anne Jeffrey, The Anchorage, Rydal Road, Ambleside LA22 9AY (015394 32046).** Modern guest house, with private car park. Bedrooms with pleasant views over parkland or surrounding fells, en suite available. Ideal base for walkers. Non-smoking. Sorry, no pets.

CUMBRIA, BOWNESS-ON-WINDERMERE. Mrs Susan Lewthwaite, Beech Tops, Meadowcroft Lane, Storrs Park, Bowness-on-Windermere LA23 3JJ (015394 45453). Modern detached house near lake offers first class, spacious accommodation in double/twin/family suites. Sorry, no smoking.

CUMBRIA, DENT (Yorkshire Dales/Cumbria). Mrs Mary Ferguson, Scow Cottage, Cowgill, Near Dent, Sedbergh LA10 5RN (015396 25445). Situated at the head of Dentdale ideal for touring the Lake District and the Yorkshire Dales. Large bedrooms with washbasins and central heating. Lounge.

CUMBRIA, HAWKSHEAD. Colin and Rosemary Haskell, Borwick Lodge, Outgate, Hawkshead, Ambleside LA22 0PU (015394 36332). ❦ ❦ *HIGHLY COMMENDED.* Charming 17th century country house with magnificent panoramic lake and mountain views. Peaceful perfection. No smoking throughout.

CUMBRIA, KENDAL. Mrs Val Sunter, Higher House Farm, Oxenholme Lane, Natland, Kendal LA9 7QH (015395 61177). ❦ ❦ ❦ *HIGHLY COMMENDED.* AA QQQQ Selected. 17th century farmhouse offers comfortable bed and breakfast accommodation in tranquil village. TV, hair dryer, and tea/coffee making facilities in all bedrooms. Pets welcome. NO SMOKING.

CUMBRIA, KESWICK. Alan & Jean Redfern, Heatherlea, 26 Blencathra Street, Keswick CA12 4HP (017687 72430). This charming "no-smoking" guest house offers all guests a friendly welcome. A full and varied breakfast menu is served in our delightful dining room. AA QQQ.

CUMBRIA, KESWICK. Annie Scally and Ian Townsend, Latrigg House, St. Herbert Street, Keswick CA12 4DF (017687 73068). 🐾🐾 An attractive detached Victorian house situated in a quiet area, only a few minutes' walk from the town centre and Lake, offering a no smoking environment for the well-being and comfort of guests.

CUMBRIA, KESWICK. Mr & Mrs J.M. Pepper, Beckstones Farm, Thornthwaite, Keswick CA12 5SQ (017687 78510). 🐾🐾 COMMENDED. Comfortable, Georgian farmhouse situated in peaceful surroundings. Regret no pets. No children under five years. No smoking in dining room.

CUMBRIA, KESWICK. David and Margaret Raine, Clarence House, 14 Eskin Street, Keswick CA12 4DQ (017687 73186). 🐾🐾🐾 COMMENDED. A lovely Victorian house ideally situated for the Lake, parks and market square. A warm welcome and hearty breakfast await you. Non smoking. Brochure sent on request.

CUMBRIA, KESWICK. Mr and Mrs J.A. McMullan, Jenkin Hill Cottage, Thornthwaite, Keswick CA12 5SG (017687 78443). 🐾🐾 HIGHLY COMMENDED. Each room is tastefully decorated and furnished with matching en-suite shower rooms. Tea/coffee making facilities, colour TV, central heating are available in all the rooms. We have a no smoking policy throughout.

CUMBRIA, KESWICK. David and Valerie Fisher, Howe Keld Lakeland Hotel, 5-7 The Heads, Keswick CA12 5ES (Tel & Fax: 017687 72417). 🐾🐾 COMMENDED. Delightful Lakeland hotel in beautiful and convenient location in Keswick. Home cooked meals, vegetarian food a speciality. En suite bedrooms with colour TV. Licensed.

CUMBRIA, KESWICK. Mrs Sharon Helling, Beckside Guest House, 5 Wordsworth Street, Keswick CA12 4HU (017687 73093). 🐾🐾 COMMENDED. AA QQQ, RAC Highly Acclaimed. Small very comfortable guest house for non-smokers situated close to town centre and convenient for the shops, Fitz Park, pool, Lake, walking and touring.

CUMBRIA, KESWICK. Mr. Jack Jenkins, Bay Tree, Wordsworth Street, Keswick CA12 4HU (017687 73313). 🐾🐾 Small family-run licensed guesthouse. Non-smoking.

CUMBRIA, KESWICK. Gladys & David Birtwistle, Kalgurli Guest House, 33 Helvellyn Street, Keswick CA12 4EP (017687 72935). 🐾🐾 COMMENDED. Be assured of a warm and friendly welcome at this comfortable non-smoking four-bedroomed guest house. Ideal location for touring and walking.

CUMBRIA, LEVENS/KENDAL. Mrs A.H. Parsons, Olde Peat Cotes, Sampool Lane, Levens, Kendal LA8 8EH (015395 60096). Modern comfortable bungalow with every facility. Handy distance to seaside, Lakes or Scotland. No smoking.

CUMBRIA, LOWICK (near Coniston). Garth Row, Lowick Green, Ulverston LA12 8EB (01229 885633). Tourist Board Listed COMMENDED. Traditional, beamed cottage only three miles from Coniston Water. Good food, tea/coffee in rooms, dogs welcome, wonderful walking, drying room, no smoking. Super quiet holiday spot or overnight stay.

CUMBRIA, MUNGRISDALE. Mike and Penny Sutton, Bannerdale View, Mungrisdale, Near Penrith CA11 0XR (017687 79691). Centrally heated 17th century Lakeland cottage. Idyllic, peaceful mountain and riverside location. Superb breakfasts. Non smokers only.

CUMBRIA, PENRITH. Jean and Ron Forrester, Lonnin End, Pallet Hill, Penrith CA11 0BY (017684 83453). Situated in a quiet hamlet on the Penrith to Greystoke road. One double, one family room. Full central heating, colour TV and tea and coffee facilities. No smoking, no pets.

CUMBRIA, PENRITH. Angela and Ivor Davies, Woodland House Hotel, Wordsworth Street, Penrith CA11 7QY (01768 864177; Fax: 01768 890152). 🐾🐾 COMMENDED. Small, friendly and elegant licensed private hotel situated at the foot of Beacon Hill and only five minutes from centre of town. Hotel is NO SMOKING throughout.

CUMBRIA, PENRITH. Mrs S.E. Bray, Norcroft Guest House, Graham Street, Penrith CA11 9LQ (01768 862365). 🐾🐾🐾 COMMENDED. Victorian house in quiet area. Large and comfortable en-suite bedrooms. No smoking in bedrooms and diningroom.

CUMBRIA, TROUTBECK. Gwen and Peter Parfitt, Hill Crest, Troutbeck, Penrith CA11 0SH (017684 83935). A unique warm and friendly Lakeland home, with non smoking lounge/dining room, where children and dogs are welcome. En suite rooms available.

CUMBRIA, WINDERMERE. Diane and David Weatherley, Crookleigh Guesthouse, 15 Woodland Road, Windermere LA23 2AE (Tel & Fax: 015394 48480; Mobile: 0410 538061). A comfortable high quality Victorian home, tastefully furnished and close to the village and station. Rooms have colour TV, generous hospitality trays and represent Excellent Value for Money.

CUMBRIA, WINDERMERE. Mrs L. Christopherson, Villa Lodge, Cross Street, Windermere LA23 1AE (Tel & Fax: 015394 43318). 🐾 COMMENDED. AA QQQ. Extremely comfortable non-smoking accommodation in peaceful area overlooking Windermere village. Open all year. Non-smokers welcomed.

CUMBRIA, WINDERMERE. Roger Wallis and James Peters, Holly Park House, 1 Park Road, Windermere LA23 2AW (015394 42107). 🐾🐾🐾 COMMENDED. A warm welcome is assured. Convenient for shops, train, bus and restaurants. Non-smokers appreciated.

CUMBRIA, WINDERMERE. Brian and Margaret Fear, Cambridge House, 9 Oak Street, Windermere LA23 1EN (015394 43846). ETB Listed COMMENDED. A traditional Lakeland guest house situated in Windermere village centre, convenient for all amenities. Modern, comfortable rooms with en suite facilities. Full English, Continental or vegetarian breakfast is provided.

CUMBRIA, WINDERMERE. Mick & Angela Brown, Haisthorpe Guest House, Holly Road, Windermere LA23 2AF (Tel/Fax: 015394 43445). 🐾🐾 COMMENDED. Comfortable family house situated in a quiet part of Windermere yet close to the village centre and local amenities. Special breaks October to June. No smoking in bedrooms. AA QQQ, RAC Highly Acclaimed.

CUMBRIA, WINDERMERE. Mrs B.J. Butterworth, Orsett Head House, Windermere LA23 1JG (015394 44315). 17th century house nestling above Windermere village enjoying superb views of the Lake and mountains. Non-smokers welcome.

DERBYSHIRE, ASHBOURNE. Paula and Alan Coker-Mayes, The Coach House, The Firs, Ashbourne DE6 1HF (01335 300145; Fax: 01335 300958). ETB Listed *DELUXE*. Former Victorian Coach House, offering accommodation and warm hospitality. Three ground floor double rooms. All the usual facilities are offered. Parking. Open all year. Non-smoking. Brochure available.

DERBYSHIRE, ASHBOURNE. Mr and Mrs A. Kingston, Old Boothby Farm, The Green, Ashbourne DE6 1EE (01335 342044). Bed and Breakfast accommodation in an idyllic location, the "Gateway to the Peak District". Handy for visiting Alton Towers, Dovedale, Buxton, etc. Non-smoking accommodation available.

DERBYSHIRE, ASHOVER. Mrs Ann Brookes, The Red Lion Inn, Ashover S45 0EW (01246 590271). A picturesque Tudor Inn in the very historic, pretty village of Ashover. Recently refurbished, with an extensive menu of cooked foods. Activities nearby — fishing, shooting (clays), riding and country walks.

DERBYSHIRE, BAKEWELL. Mrs Julia Finney, Mandale House, Haddon Grove, Bakewell DE45 1JF (01629 812416). ♥ ♥ Relax in the warm and friendly atmosphere of our peaceful farmhouse situated on the edge of Lathkill Dale. Completely non-smoking. Telephone for brochure.

DERBYSHIRE, BAKEWELL. Mrs Jenny Spafford, Barleycorn Croft, Sheldon, Near Bakewell DE45 1QS (01629 813636). Converted barn accommodating 2,3 or 4 people in twin and/or double rooms making a private apartment with independent access and key. Non-smokers welcomed — see main section.

DERBYSHIRE, BAKEWELL near. Mr and Mrs R.H. Tyler, Sheldon House, Chapel Street, Monyash, Near Bakewell DE45 1JJ (01629 813067). 18th century listed building in Peak District. Three doubles en-suite available. No smoking in bedrooms and public rooms.

DERBYSHIRE, BELPER. Mrs C. Emery, The Hollins, 45 Belper Lane, Belper DE56 2UQ (01773 823955). AA Recommended. Family run guest house in semi-rural location. Ideally situated for Peak District, Amber Valley and Alton Towers. Non smoking establishment.

DERBYSHIRE, BUXTON. Maria and Roger Hyde, Braemar, 10 Compton Road, Buxton SK17 9DN (01298 78050). Accommodation comprises comfortable double and twin rooms fully en-suite with colour TV and tea/coffee making facilities. Non-smokers preferred. Diets catered for.

DERBYSHIRE, HATHERSAGE. Mrs Jean Wilcockson, Hillfoot Farm, Castleton Road, Hathersage, Hope Valley S32 1EG (01433 651673). Tourist Board Listed *COMMENDED*. Welcome Host. Newly built accommodation offering comfortable, well appointed en suite rooms. Current Fire Certificate held. Non smokers please.

DERBYSHIRE, TIDESWELL. Mrs Pat Harris, Laurel House, The Green, Litton, Near Buxton SK17 8QP (01298 871971). ♥ ♥ *COMMENDED*. Overlooking the village green. One double with en-suite facilities and a twin room with washbasin and private use of bathroom and toilet; tea/coffee making facilities in both. Private lounge. No smoking.

DERBYSHIRE, TIDESWELL. Mr D.C. Pinnegar, "Poppies", Bank Square, Tideswell, Buxton SK17 8LA (01298 871083). Situated in attractive Derbyshire village. Bed, Breakfast and Evening Meal available. No smoking in bedrooms or dining room.

DEVON, ASHBURTON. Mrs Anne Torr, Middle Leat, Holne, Near Ashburton TQ13 7SJ (01364 631413). Very comfortable accommodation with wonderful views. Sorry, no smoking in the house. SAE for details or telephone for brochure.

DEVON, BUCKLAND MONACHORUM. Store Cottage B&B, The Village, Buckland Monachorum PL20 7NA (01822 853117). ♥ *HIGHLY COMMENDED*. Comfort and tranquillity in the centre of historic Devon village. Store Cottage is a non-smoking household.

DEVON, CHAGFORD. Jeanette and Graham Smitheram, Throwleigh Manor, Throwleigh, Near Chagford, Okehampton EX20 2JF (01647 231630). ♥ ♥ *COMMENDED*. Beautiful country house situated in 12 acres of parkland within Dartmoor National Park. Renowned for our excellent breakfasts. Heated swimming pool and games room. Ideally situated to explore West Country.

DEVON, CLOVELLY. Mrs P. Vanstone, The Old Smithy, Slerra Hill, Clovelly, Bideford EX39 5ST, (01237 431202). A 16th century cottage and converted forge, situated one mile from the sea and the unspoilt picturesque village of Clovelly. No smoking in public rooms, i.e. dining room.

DEVON, CLOVELLY. Mrs J. Johns, Dyke Green Farm, Clovelly, Near Bideford EX39 5RU (01237 431699 or 431279). ETB ♥ *COMMENDED*. Tastefully converted barn offering beautiful accommodation. Ideal base for Devon and Cornwall. No smoking in bedrooms.

DEVON, CROYDE BAY. Chris and Roslyn Gedling, West Winds Guest House, Moor Lane, Croyde Bay EX33 1PA (01271 890489). ♥ ♥ ♥ AA QQQ Recommended. Small guest house located by picturesque water's edge. Comfortable, relaxing atmosphere. Open all year. No smoking in dining room, lounge and some bedrooms.

DEVON, DAWLISH. Dave and Pat Badcock, West Hatch Hotel, 34 West Cliff, Dawlish (Tel & Fax: 01626 864211). ♥ ♥ *HIGHLY COMMENDED*. AA QQQQ Selected/RAC Highly Acclaimed. Small, friendly quality hotel guarantees a warm welcome and relaxed stay. Well equipped en suite rooms. Bar and separate lounge. Parking.

DEVON, EXETER. Janet Bragg, Marianne Pool Farm, Clyst St. George, Exeter EX3 0NZ (01392 874939). Tourist Board Listed. Thatched Devon Longhouse in peaceful rural location midway between Exmouth and Exeter. Large lawned garden, ideal for children. Car essential. Open March to November. Smoking allowed in lounge only.

DEVON, LYNTON. Fernleigh, Park Street, Lynton EX35 6BY (01598 753575). 🐛🐛 *HIGHLY COMMENDED.* Purpose-built guesthouse standing on a quiet side street within walking distance of restaurants, pubs, shops and the harbour. Luxury accommodation in pretty and spacious en suite bedrooms. Vegetarians can be catered for. Totally non-smoking. Private car park. Please write or telephone for further information.

DEVON, LYNTON. Christine and John Kuczer, Woodlands, Lynbridge Road, Lynton EX35 6AX (01598 752324). 🐛🐛🐛 *COMMENDED.* Ideal base for exploring Exmoor and the stunning coastal scenery. Private parking. Licensed, cosy lounge. Non-smoking. Delicious home cooking.

DEVON, OKEHAMPTON. Mrs E.G. Arney, The Old Rectory, Bratton Clovelly, Okehampton EX20 4LA (01837 871382). Thoroughly modernised property ideally situated for touring Devon and Cornwall. A warm welcome, friendly atmosphere and personal attention. Pets welcome.

DEVON, PLYMOUTH near. Slade Barn, Netton, Noss Mayo, Near Plymouth PL8 1HA (01752 872235). WCTB Listed *COMMENDED.* Sandy Cherrington assures you of a warm welcome to Slade Barn. All rooms have central heating, TV/radio and hair dryers. Tea/coffee on request. Indoor pool, games room, tennis court and private gardens. Plenty of parking. Open all year.

DEVON, SIDMOUTH. Mrs Bridget Hopkinson, Bovett's Farm, Roncombe Lane, Sidbury, Sidmouth EX10 0QN (01395 597456). Beautifully situated in lovely Roncombe Valley, within easy reach of Exeter and coast. 3 double/twin rooms with en suite showers. No smoking in house.

DEVON, TORQUAY near. Jackie and Bill Kirkham, Walmer Towers, Moles Lane, South Whilborough, Kingkerswell, Newton Abbot TQ12 5LS (01803 872105; Fax: 01803 875477). Two large en suite double/family rooms, centrally heated with colour TV and tea and coffee facilities. Delicious breakfast.

DORSET, BLANDFORD near. Mrs Lucienne Sumner-Fergusson, Stocklands House, Hilton, Near Blandford DT11 0DE (01258 880580; Fax: 01258 881188). 🐛🐛 *HIGHLY COMMENDED.* Sumptuous breakfasts, candlelit dinners and cream teas. Heated outdoor pool, table tennis, badminton and clay shooting.

DORSET, BOURNEMOUTH. Cherry View Hotel, 66 Alum Chine Road, Bournemouth BH4 8DZ (01202 760910). RAC Acclaimed, AA Listed Quality Award. Over 50% of our bedrooms and dining room are reserved for non-smokers. See our main advert under Dorset.

DORSET, BOURNEMOUTH. Gervis Court Hotel, 38 Gervis Road, East Cliff, Bournemouth BH1 3DH (01202 556871). 🐛🐛 Centrally located hotel with ample parking. All en suite. Non smoking accommodation.

DORSET, BOURNEMOUTH. Bournecliff House, 31 Grand Avenue, Southbourne, Bournemouth BH6 3SY (01202 426455). Enjoy a happy holiday in the comfort of our small family hotel. Open all year. Off-season bargain breaks. Non-smokers appreciated. Please telephone for further details.

DORSET, CHARMOUTH. Ann and Andy Gorfin, Kingfishers, Newlands Bridge, Charmouth DT6 6QZ (01297 560232). Secluded setting only a short stroll from the beach and village. Great food, friendly atmosphere. No smoking in bedrooms and dining room.

DORSET, DORCHESTER. Michael and Jane Deller, Churchview Guest House, Winterbourne Abbas, Near Dorchester DT2 9LS (01305 889296). 🐛🐛🐛 *COMMENDED.* Beautiful 17th Century Non Smoking licensed Guest House set in the heart of West Dorset. Character bedrooms, delightful period dining room, two lounges and a bar. Pets welcome. AA QQQ.

DORSET, DORCHESTER near. Mr Howell, Appletrees, 23 Affpuddle, Dorchester DT2 7HH (01929 471300). '60's character home with one double, two single and one twin-bedded room with TV and tea making facilities. Use of kitchen if required. Non smoking accommodation available.

DORSET, LYME REGIS. Mrs S.G. Taylor, Buckland Farm, Raymonds Hill, Near Axminster EX13 5SZ (01297 33222). Smallholding of five acres, three miles from Lyme Regis and Charmouth offering Bed and Breakfast accommodation. No smoking in bedrooms. SAE for details.

DORSET, PORTLAND/WEYMOUTH. Alessandria Hotel & Italian Restaurant, Portland, Weymouth DT5 1HW (01305 822270/820108; Fax: 01305 820561). 🐛🐛🐛 *APPROVED.* Hotel and Italian Restaurant situated in a quiet location. Most rooms en suite, colour TV, tea/coffee making facilities, soft towels and toiletries. Ground floor bedrooms level with lounge and restaurant.

DORSET, WAREHAM. Mr and Mrs Axford, Sunnyleigh, Hyde, Wareham BH20 7NT (01929 471822). Situated in the quiet hamlet of Hyde five miles west of Wareham. Accommodation comprises double and twin bedrooms. Open all year. No smoking.

DURHAM, TEESDALE. Mrs M. Rabbitts, Glendale, Cotherstone, Barnard Castle DL12 9UH (01833 650384). 🐛🐛 *HIGHLY COMMENDED.* Beautiful house situated in superb open countryside. En suite double rooms with TV etc. No smoking. No children under 10. Brochure on request.

ESSEX, CASTLE HEDINGHAM. Mrs Heather Hutchings, Fishers, Castle Hedingham CO9 3EW (Tel & Fax: 01787 460382). Attractive Georgian Listed property offering peaceful stay in this medieval village. Twin-bedded room. Completely non-smoking.

ESSEX, COLCHESTER. Mrs Wendy Anderson, The Old Manse, 15 Roman Road, Colchester CO1 1UR (01206 545154). A friendly welcome to this elegant and spacious town centre Victorian family home. Accommodation completely non-smoking.

ESSEX, KELVEDON. Mr & Mrs R. Bunting, Highfields Farm, Kelvedon CO5 9BJ (01376 570334). 🐛 *COMMENDED.* Peaceful overnight stop on the way to Harwich or as a base to visit historic Colchester and Constable country. Three twin rooms, all with en suite facilities. No smoking.

GLOUCESTERSHIRE, AMBERLEY. The Dial Cottage, Amberley, Near Stroud GL5 5AL (01453 872563). We are well positioned to explore Cheltenham, Bath, Cirencester and Tetbury. Children welcome. Non-smoking and sorry, no pets.

GLOUCESTERSHIRE, CHELTENHAM. Cressy Guest House, 44 St. Stephens Road, Cheltenham GL51 5AD (01242 525012). ♥ ♥ Comfortable Edwardian house offering accommodation in one double room with shower, two twin bedrooms, all with washbasins, colour TV and tea/coffee facilities. No smoking in bedroooms. Reduced rates for children.

GLOUCESTERSHIRE, CHELTENHAM near. Mr and Mrs Rooke, Frogfurlong Cottage, Frogfurlong Lane, Down Hatherley GL2 9QE (01452 730430). Exclusive accommodation for one couple. The 18th century cottage is surrounded by fields. No smoking.

GLOUCESTERSHIRE, CHEW MAGNA. Mrs Judi Hasell, Woodbarn Farm, Denny Lane, Chew Magna, Bristol BS18 8SZ (01275 332599). Woodbarn Farm is a working farm five minutes from Chew Valley Lake and is central for touring. Open March to December (closed Christmas). Children welcome. Non smokers preferred. Brochure on request.

GLOUCESTERSHIRE, MINSTERWORTH. Mrs S. Carter, Severn Bank, Minsterworth GL2 8JH (01452 750357). ♥ ♥ A fine country house standing in its own six acre grounds on the bank of the River Severn. Completely non-smoking.

GLOUCESTERSHIRE, PAINSWICK. Jean Hernen, Brookhouse Mill Cottage, Tibbiwell Lane, Painswick GL6 6YA (Tel & Fax: 01452 812854). Beautiful 17th century cottage in an area of outstanding natural beauty. Indoor swimming pool. Plenty of parking. Brochure available.

GLOUCESTERSHIRE, STOW-ON-THE-WOLD. Mrs F.J. Adams, Aston House, Broadwell, Moreton-in-Marsh GL56 0TJ (01451 830475). ETB Listed *COMMENDED.* (Formerly at Banks Farm, Oddington). Chalet bungalow in peaceful village overlooking fields. Bed & good English Breakfast, bedtime drinks. No smoking. Car essential — parking.

GLOUCESTERSHIRE, TEWKESBURY. Keith and Caroline Page, Corner Cottage, Stow Road, Alderton, Tewkesbury GL20 8NH (01242 620630). Close to Cotswolds with easy access North and South. Rooms decorated in cottage style with views over surrounding countryside. Ample parking.

GLOUCESTERSHIRE, WOODCHESTER. Mrs Wendy Swait, Inschdene, Atcombe Road, South Woodchester, Stroud GL5 5EW (01453 873254). Comfortable family house with magnificent views across the valley, set in an acre of garden. No smoking in the house.

GLOUCESTERSHIRE, WOTTON-UNDER-EDGE. Gloria Gomm, Beech Cottage, Southend, Wotton-Under-Edge GL12 7PD (01453 545771). Spacious self contained en suite accommodation in Annexe of 18th century cottage. Private parking. Full English breakfast, Vegetarian by request. No smoking.

HAMPSHIRE, BURLEY. Mrs Gina Russell, Charlwood, Longmead Road, Burley BH24 4BY (01425 403242). Situated in the midst of beautiful New Forest. Ideal walking/touring base. No smoking on premises.

HAMPSHIRE, LYMINGTON. Our Bench, Lodge Road, Lymington SO41 8HH (Tel & Fax: 01590 673141). ♥ ♥ ♥ *COMMENDED.* AA QQQQ RAC Aclaimed, Welcome Host, FHG Diploma Winner. Regional Nominee — England for Excellence. Indoor heated swimming/exercise pool, jacuzzi and sauna. All rooms en suite. Evening meal if required. Non-smokers only. Sorry, no children. National Accessibility Scheme Category 3.

HAMPSHIRE, NEW FOREST. Jim and Glenda Hickman, Springfields, Lyndhurst Road, Landford SP5 2AS (01794 390093). ETB Listed *COMMENDED.* Large house on the edge of New Forest. Two double rooms. Home comforts. Non smoking.

HAMPSHIRE, NEW FOREST. Mrs Pauline Harris, Little Heathers, 13 Whitemoor Road, Brockenhurst SO42 7QG (01590 623512). Warm welcome for all non-smokers. Ground floor bedrooms with limited wheelchair use. Special diets can be catered for.

HAMPSHIRE, NEW FOREST. Mrs M. Stone, Heathlands, Lepe Road, Langley SO45 1YT (01703 892517). New Forest bungalow near Beaulieu, offering Bed and Breakfast in comfortable rooms for non-smoking couples only.

HAMPSHIRE, PORTSMOUTH/SOUTHSEA. Mr and Mrs Willett, Oakleigh Guest House, 48 Festing Grove, Southsea PO4 9QD (01705 812276). Southern Tourist Board Listed *COMMENDED.* Small family-run guest house two minutes' from sea. Double, twin, family or single rooms available. Open all year including Christmas and Easter.

HAMPSHIRE, RINGWOOD (New Forest). Mrs Yvonne Nixon, "The Nest", 10 Middle Lane, Ringwood BH24 1LE (Tel & Fax: 01425 476724; Mobile 0589 854505). This lovely Victorian house is situated in a quiet residential lane within five minutes' walk of Ringwood town centre. This is an excellent base to explore the New Forest. No smoking in the bedrooms.

HAMPSHIRE, WINCHESTER. Mrs S. Buchanan, "Acacia", 44 Kilham Lane, Winchester SO22 5PT (01962 852259; 0585 462993 mobile). ♥ ♥ *HIGHLY COMMENDED.* Accommodation consists of one double and two twin bedrooms, all of which have en-suite or private bathroom, plus tea and coffee making facilities. Off street parking. Non-smokers only.

HAMPSHIRE, WINCHESTER. Susan and Richard Pell, The Lilacs, 1 Harestock Close, off Andover Road North, Winchester SO22 6NP (01962 884122). A non-smoking family home offering an excellent English Breakfast, including vegetarian meals. Country views.

HEREFORD & WORCESTER, OMBERSLEY. Mrs M. Peters, Tytchney, Boreley, Ombersley WR9 0HZ (01905 620185). 16th Century medieval Hall House cottage in peaceful country lane, two and a half miles from Ombersley. Ideal walking, touring Heart of England, fishing in River Severn and just half a mile to Ombersley Golf Course. Double, family and single rooms; cot available.

HEREFORD & WORCESTER, PERSHORE. Jim and Margaret Coward, Oldbury House, George Lane, Wyre Piddle, Pershore WR10 2HX (01386 553754, e-mail:james.coward@virgin.net). Warm friendly welcome assured in modern, centrally heated house. Meals available at nearby Anchor Inn. Full computer facilities available on request. No smoking please.

HEREFORD & WORCESTER, ROSS-ON-WYE. Mrs M.E. Drzymalska, Thatch Close, Llangrove, Ross-On-Wye HR9 6EL (01989 770300). ❀❀ *COMMENDED.* Traditional farmhouse offering Bed and Breakfast, evening meal optional, using mainly home grown produce. Non-smokers please.

HEREFORD & WORCESTER, VOWCHURCH. The Old Vicarage, Vowchurch HR2 0QD (Tel & Fax: 01981 550357). Attractive en suite single/family/double rooms. Quality breakfasts. Dinners by arrangement. Warm hospitality guaranteed in one-time home of Lewis Carroll's brother. Completely non smoking.

HEREFORD & WORCESTER, WINFORTON. Mrs Jackie Kingdon, Winforton Court, Winforton HR3 6EA (01544 328498). Set in old world gardens close to the Black Mountains. Luxurious drawing room, open fires and good books. We appreciate non-smoking visitors.

KENT, ASHFORD near. Pam and Arthur Mills, Cloverlea, Bethersden, Ashford TN26 3DU (01233 820353). Spacious new country bungalow in lovely peaceful location with large garden. Patio area for breakfast (when fine). Full central heating. Excellent breakfast, home made bread everyday. Ample safe parking. Close to village pubs. No smoking.

KENT, MAIDSTONE. Mrs Burbridge, Waterkant Guest House, Moat Road, Headcorn, Ashford TN27 9NT (01622 890154). Small guest house offering a warm and friendly welcome to all our visitors, many of whom return year after year. No smoking in the diningroom.

LANCASHIRE, LYTHAM ST. ANNES. Mr J. Soothill, Willow Trees, 89 Heyhouses Lane, Lytham St. Annes FY8 3RN (01253 727235). Warm welcome awaits you in this comfortable detached house with pleasant gardens. No smoking in the house please.

LEICESTERSHIRE, MELTON MOWBRAY. Mrs Brenda Bailey, Church Cottage, Holwell, Melton Mowbray LE14 4SZ (01664 444255). 18th century listed building in the heart of the Leicestershire countryside. No smoking in bedrooms. Excellent food and accommodation.

LEICESTERSHIRE, MELTON MOWBRAY. Mrs R.S. Whittard, Elms Farm, Long Clawson, Melton Mowbray LE14 4NG (Tel: 01664 822395). A warm welcome awaits you in this non-smoking 17th century farmhouse situated in the beautiful Vale of Belvoir. Open all year except Christmas.

NORFOLK, ATTLEBOROUGH. Iris Thomas, Cannells Farm, Bow Street, Great Ellingham, Attleborough NR17 1JA (01953 454133). 18th Century farmhouse, ideal Snetterton Racetrack, Pedlars Way. Friendly welcome, comfortable rooms, home cooking. Ample parking, non smoking.

NORFOLK, AYLSHAM. David Newman & Hazel Stringer, Old Pump House, Holman Road, Aylsham NR11 6BY (01263 733789). ❀❀ *HIGHLY COMMENDED.* Creature comforts, home cooking, modern facilities. 1750's house near church and market place. Breakfast in pine-shuttered sitting room overlooking peaceful garden. Dinner by arrangement October to May. No smoking.

NORFOLK, GREAT YARMOUTH. Mrs M. Lake, Old Station House, North Road, Hemsby, Great Yarmouth NR29 4EZ (01493 732022). Well-maintained turn-of-the-century house is ideally situated for touring the Norfolk Broads and Great Yarmouth area. A large TV lounge contains lots of books and overlooks the garden and patio where guests can sit out on sunny days. Children welcome. Sorry no dogs; no smoking.

NORFOLK, NORWICH. Mr Brian and Mrs Diane Curtis, Rosedale Guest House, 145 Earlham Road, Norwich NR2 3RG (01603 453743). Friendly Victorian guest house. Full English Breakfast served. Vegetarians catered for. Non-smoking breakfast room.

NORFOLK, RACKHEATH. Mr and Mrs R. Lebbell, Manor Barn House, Back Lane, Rackheath NR13 6NN (01603 783543). ❀❀ *COMMENDED.* A family home with lovely gardens in quiet surroundings. Accommodation includes double rooms with central heating, tea/coffee facilities, TV and own bathroom. Open all year for Bed and Breakfast. Non-smoking.

NORFOLK, RACKHEATH. Julie Simpson, Barn Court, Back Lane, Rackheath NR13 6NW (01603 782536). Friendly and spacious accommodation in a traditional Norfolk barn conversion built around a courtyard. Accommodation includes a double en suite with a four-poster. All bedrooms are non smoking.

NORTHUMBERLAND, ALLENDALE. Mrs Eileen Ross Finn, Thornley House, Allendale NE47 9NH (01434 683255). ❀❀❀ *HIGHLY COMMENDED.* Beautiful country house in spacious grounds. 3 bedrooms, all with private facilities. Home baking, packed lunches. Near Hadrians Wall.

NORTHUMBERLAND, HEXHAM. Mrs D.A. Theobald, Dukeslea, 32 Shaws Park, Hexham NE46 3BJ (01434 602947). ❀❀ *HIGHLY COMMENDED.* AA QQQ Recommended. Open all year. Totally non-smoking establishment. Reduced rates for children and stays of four or more nights.

NORTHUMBERLAND, PONTELAND. Mr and Mrs Edward Trevelyan, Dalton House, Dalton, Ponteland NE18 0AA (01661 886225). ❀❀ Warm welcome extended, high standard of accommodation offered in this attractive Georgian house. No smoking in bedrooms or public rooms.

NORTHUMBERLAND, POWBURN. A. & D. Johnson, Doveburn, Powburn NE66 4HR (01665 578266). ❀❀ *HIGHLY COMMENDED.* Situated high upon the hill overlooking the village of Powburn with spectacular views of the Cheviot Hills and the Breamish Valley. Dogs welcome by arrangement. Non-smoking establishment. Please write or telephone for our brochure and full tariff.

NORTHUMBERLAND, WARKWORTH. Mrs Sheila Percival, Roxbro House, 5 Castle Terrace, Warkworth NE65 0UP (01665 711416). Completely non-smoking establishment overlooking castle. Bed and Breakfast. Open all year.

NOTTINGHAMSHIRE, NOTTINGHAM. Mrs J. Buck, Yew Tree Grange, 2 Nethergate, Clifton Village, Nottingham NG11 8NL (0115 9847562). Georgian residence of great charm and character located ten minutes from the City Centre. No smoking.

NOTTINGHAMSHIRE, STANTON-ON-THE-WOLDS. Mrs Val Moffat, Laurel Farm, Browns Lane, Stanton-on-the-Wolds, Nottingham NG12 5BL (0115 9373488). An old farmhouse in approximately four acres on a lane off the main A606. Spacious rooms all have colour TV and tea/coffee facilities. Children welcome, babysitting FREE. Large garden. No smoking in the house.

OXFORDSHIRE, OXFORD. Diana and Richard Mitchell, Highfield West, 188 Cumnor Hill, Oxford OX2 9PJ (01865 863007). ♥♥ *HIGHLY COMMENDED.* Comfortable home in quiet residential area. Well appointed rooms with colour TV, central heating and refreshment trays. Large outdoor pool. No smoking. Vegetarians welcome.

OXFORDSHIRE, SOULDERN. Toddy and Clive Hamilton-Gould, Tower Fields, Tusmore Road, Near Souldern, Bicester OX6 9HY (01869 346554). ♥♥ *COMMENDED.* Recently renovated farmhouse. Full English Breakfast using home produce when available. No smoking.

OXFORDSHIRE, WITNEY. Mrs Elizabeth Simpson, Field View, Wood Green, Witney OX8 6DE (01993 705485). ♥♥ *HIGHLY COMMENDED.* Set in two acres and situated on picturesque Wood Green, yet only ten minutes from the centre of town. No smoking.

SHROPSHIRE, CLUN. Mrs Jones, Llanhedric, Clun, Craven Arms SY7 8NG (01588 640203). Working farm. Attractive old stone house with lawns and garden overlooking the picturesque Clun Valley, near the Welsh border and Offa's Dyke. Spacious accommodation, friendly atmosphere and good food.

SHROPSHIRE, FRODESLEY. Ron and Jenny Repath, Meadowlands, Lodge Lane, Frodesley, Dorrington SY5 7HD (01694 731350). ETB Listed *COMMENDED.* Former farmhouse newly decorated throughout. Quiet location in delightful hamlet with panoramic views to Stretton Hills. Central heating. Parking. Colour TV in bedrooms. Guests' lounge. En suite available. No smoking. Brochure.

SHROPSHIRE, IRONBRIDGE. Len and Daphne Roberts, Woodlands, Park Lane, Madeley, near Ironbridge, Telford TF7 5HJ (01952 580693). ♥♥ *COMMENDED.* Quality en suite accommodation one mile from Ironbridge. Tea and coffee trays in rooms. Lounge with TV. Private parking. Secluded garden with waterfall and pond. Ideal base for touring Shropshire. Open all year.

SHROPSHIRE, IRONBRIDGE. Mrs Rosemary Clegg, Springhill, 2 School Road, Coalbrookdale, Telford TF8 7DY (01952 432210). ♥♥ *COMMENDED.* Three en-suite bedrooms in an 18th century Iron Master's house. Large garden and private parking. Evening meals if booked in advance. Brochure available. No smoking.

SHROPSHIRE, LUDLOW. Mr and Mrs Lowe, Lower Hayton Grange, Lower Hayton, Ludlow SY8 2AQ (01584 861296; Fax: 01584 861371). Centrally heated accommodation with tea/coffee facilitiies, colour TV and en suite facilities. Guest lounge. Conservatory. A non smoking house.

SHROPSHIRE, LUDLOW. Mrs Kathy Lanman, "Red Roofs", Little Hereford, Near Ludlow SY8 4AT (01584 711439). ♥♥ *AA QQQQ.* Situated in the lovely Teme Valley overlooking glorious open countryside. Central heating throughout. Ample parking. Hospitality trays. Non-smoking accommodation available.

SHROPSHIRE, MINSTERLEY. Paul and Debbie Costello, Cricklewood Cottage, Plox Green, Minsterley SY5 0HT (01743 791229). ♥♥ *HIGHLY COMMENDED,* **AA QQQQ Selected.** Delightful 18th century cottage at foot of Stiperstones Hills. All rooms en suite. Pretty cottage garden with trout stream. No smoking.

SHROPSHIRE, SHREWSBURY. Mrs Gwen Frost, Oakfields, Baschurch Road, Myddle, Shrewsbury SY4 3RX (01939 290823). ♥♥ *COMMENDED.* Situated in a quiet, idyllic setting in the picturesque village of Myddle. 15 minutes from Shrewsbury and Hawkstone Park. A non-smoking establishment.

SHROPSHIRE, SHREWSBURY. Anton Guest House, 1 Canon Street, Monkmoor, Shrewsbury SY2 5HG (01743 359275). ♥♥ *COMMENDED.* Tony and Anne Sandford offer a very friendly welcome to guests at their completely non-smoking home. Special diets can be accommodated by arrangement.

SOMERSET, BATH. Mrs Maria Beckett, Cedar Lodge, 13 Lambridge, London Road, Bath BA1 6BJ (01225 423468). Beautiful individually designed bedrooms, one with four-poster, one with half-tester bed and one twin-bedded room. All with TV and en suite/private facilities. Choice of breakfasts served with home-made preserves. Children welcome. Sorry, no smoking, no pets.

SOMERSET, BATH. Mrs Chrissie Besley, The Old Red House, 37 Newbridge Road, Bath BA1 3HE (01225 330464). Tourist Board *HIGHLY COMMENDED.* Our romantic "Gingerbread House" has stained glass windows. The cosy double bedrooms have canopied beds, colour TVs, showers, etc. Private parking. This is a non-smoking house.

SOMERSET, BATH. The Old Malt House Hotel, Radford, Timsbury, Near Bath BA3 1QF (01761 470106). ♥♥♥ *COMMENDED.* Between Bath and Wells, ideally situated for touring. No smoking in the dining room. Suitable for disabled guests.

SOMERSET, BATH. Jan and Bryan Wotley, The Albany Guest House, 24 Crescent Gardens, Bath BA1 2NB (01225 313339). Non smoking accommodation at our friendly Victorian home. Just five minutes' walk from city centre.

SOMERSET, BATH. Jill and Rob Fradley, "Sarnia", 19 Combe Park, Bath BA1 3NR (01225 424159). Welcome to our lovely Victorian home, rooms individually decorated, with all facilities. Ample parking, main bus route to city. No smoking please.

SOMERSET, BATH. Ron and Vanessa Pharo, Ashley House, 8 Pulteney Gardens, Bath BA2 4HG (01225 425027). 🐾 Charming Victorian house in quiet location conveniently situated for all travellers to this beautiful city. Non-smoking establishment.

SOMERSET, BRENT KNOLL. Roy and Lorrayne Page, Old Holt Farm, Edingworth Road, Weston-super-Mare BS24 0JA (01934 750245). Listed 17th century buildings and grounds in beautiful rural location. Accommodation in double rooms or self-contained luxury stone cottages. Home cooked evening meals available. Please telephone for more information.

SOMERSET, CHEDDAR near. Winston Manor Hotel, Bristol Road, Churchill, Near Cheddar BS19 5NL (01934 852348). Charming manor house standing in one and a half acres of secluded gardens overlooking the Mendip Hills. The hotel is a member of Logis of Great Britain where hospitality wears a human face.

SOMERSET, CREWKERNE. Mr Gilmore, Manor Arms, North Perrott, Crewkerne TA18 7SG (Tel & Fax: 01460 72901). 🐾🐾 *COMMENDED.* Lovely 16th century grade II Listed inn set in conservation village. Five well appointed en suite bedrooms. Renowned locally for very high standard of home cooking from both bar and restaurant. No smoking.

SOMERSET, GLASTONBURY. Mrs L. White, Bradley Batch, 64 Bath Road, Ashcott, Bridgwater TA7 9QJ (01458 210256). Cottage guest house, five miles from Glastonbury has Bed and Breakfast accommodation. Meals available from local Inn. Vegetarian breakfast can be provided. Non-smokers preferred.

SOMERSET, GREINTON. Sally and Norman Hunt, West Town Farm, Greinton, Bridgwater TA7 9BW (01458 210277). 🐾🐾 *COMMENDED.* Bed and Breakfast accommodation. Open March to September. Non-smokers only please.

SOMERSET, PURTON/BRIDGWATER. Mrs B. Pipkin, Rockfield House, Purton Hill, Purton, Bridgwater TA7 8AG (Tel & Fax; 01278 683561). 🐾🐾 *COMMENDED.* AA QQ Recommended. This large family house is a good stopping point for travellers to and from Cornwall, or the ideal base to explore the Somerset countryside. Ample parking. Large garden and patio. Midweek bookings or single night welcome. Non smoking.

SOMERSET, TAUNTON. Ann and John Bartlett, The Spinney, Curland, Taunton TA3 5SE (01460 234362). 🐾🐾 *HIGHLY COMMENDED.* Modern country home in area of outstanding natural beauty. En-suite bedrooms including ground floor. Non-smoking throughout.

SOMERSET, WELLS. Mrs. Janet Gould, Milton Manor Farm, Old Bristol Road, Upper Milton, Wells BA5 3AH (01749 673394). 🐾 **Working farm.** Grade II star Listed Elizabethan Manor House offering no smoking accomodation. Ideal for walking on the Mendip Hills and exploring local places of historic interest. Brochure on request. AA listed QQQ.

STAFFORDSHIRE, ECCLESHALL. Mrs Sue Pimble, Cobblers Cottage, Kerry Lane, Eccleshall ST21 6EJ (01785 850116). 🐾🐾 A five minute walk from the centre of Eccleshall situated within the conservation area. Children and pets welcome but we are non-smoking.

STAFFORDSHIRE, STOKE-ON-TRENT. Mr and Mrs Little, Lee House Farm, Leek Road, Waterhouses, Stoke-on-Trent ST10 3HW (01538 308439). HETB 🐾🐾 *HIGHLY COMMENDED.* Charming 18th century farmhouse in the heart of Waterhouses, a village with many amenities set in the Peak District National Park. Tastefully furnished. Ample off-road parking. All rooms are en suite and centrally heated. No smoking in bedrooms.

STAFFORDSHIRE, STOKE-ON-TRENT. Mrs I. Grey, The Old Vicarage, Leek Road, Stoke-on-Trent ST9 9BH (01782 503686). Convenient stopover for M6 travellers. Accommodation is centrally heated with one double and two twin-bedded rooms. Children welcome. Ample parking. No smoking in the house please.

SUFFOLK, CLARE. Jean and Alastair Tuffill, "Cobwebs", 26 Nethergate Street, Clare, Near Sudbury CO10 8NP (01787 277539). A friendly welcome awaits you at this Grade II Listed beamed house. Within walking distance of town centre, the delightful castle and country park. Non-smokers very welcome.

SURREY, DORKING. Mrs. M. L. Walton, The Waltons, 5 Rose Hill, Dorking RH4 2EG (Tel/Fax: 01306 883127). Listed house of historical interest situated in a conservation area. Vegetarian meals available. Smoking is discouraged but not totally forbidden in some areas.

SUSSEX (EAST), BRIGHTON. Ms M.A. Daughtery, Ma'on Hotel, 26 Upper Rock Gardens, Brighton BN2 1QE (01273 694400). Completely non smoking Grade II Listed building. Tourist Board approved. Two minutes from the sea and within easy reach of conference and main town centres. Access to rooms at all times. Brochure on request with SAE.

SUSSEX (EAST), EASTBOURNE. Farrar's Hotel, 3-5 Wilmington Gardens, Eastbourne BN21 4JN (01323 723737; Fax: 01323 732902). 🐾🐾🐾🐾 AA/RAC Two Star. Attractively furnished bedrooms, centrally heated with either bathroom or shower en suite, direct dial telephone, radio, colour TV tea/coffee facilities. Large private car park. Children welcome, sorry no pets. Full colour brochure on request.

SUSSEX (EAST), FAIRLIGHT. Mrs Adams, Fairlight Cottage, Warren Road (via Coastguard Lane), Fairlight TN35 4AG (01424 812545). Comfortable country house, delightfully situated alongside Hastings Country Park. Tastefully furnished, with central heating, en suite facilities and tea/coffee trays. No smoking in house. Ample parking and use of garden.

SUSSEX (EAST), RYE. Mrs P.M. Hadfield, Jeake's House, Mermaid Street, Rye TN31 7ET (01797 222828). 🐦🐦 *HIGHLY COMMENDED.* Beautiful Listed building standing in one of England's most famous streets. Traditional or vegetarian breakfast served. Non smokers welcome.

SUSSEX (EAST), RYE. Mrs Heather Coote, "Busti", Barnetts Hill, Peasmarsh, Rye TN31 6YJ (01797 230408). Bed and Breakfast in country area. One double, one twin bedded room. No smoking in the house.

SUSSEX (EAST), WINCHELSEA. A.N. Roche, The Strand Hotel, Winchelsea, Near Rye TN36 4JT (Tel & Fax: 01797 226276). 🐦🐦🐦 *COMMENDED.* AA QQQQ Selected, RAC Acclaimed. Nestling beneath the cliff of the ancient medieval town of Winchelsea lies the 15th century Strand Hotel. An ideal place to stay while exploring many places of interest nearby.

SUSSEX (WEST), MIDHURST. Annabelle Costaras, Amberfold, Hayshott, Midhurst GU29 0DA (01730 812385). Accommodation in private, self-contained annexe situated in quiet countryside yet only five minutes from town centre. Attractive garden; ample car parking. No smoking, no pets please. Open all year.

WARWICKSHIRE, LIGHTHORNE. Mrs J. Stanton, Redlands Farm, Banbury Road, Near Warwick CV35 0AH (01926 651241). 🐦🐦 AA QQQ Farmhouse set in two acres of garden with its own swimming pool. Children welcome, facilities available and reduced rates. No pets. Non-smoking rooms available.

WARWICKSHIRE, STRATFORD-UPON-AVON. Mrs Karen Cauvin, Penshurst Guest House, 34 Evesham Place, Stratford-upon-Avon CV37 6HT (01789 205259). Prettily refurbished Victorian townhouse. Town centre five minutes' walk. Totally non-smoking establishment.

WARWICKSHIRE, STRATFORD-UPON-AVON. Mrs S.E. Hunter, Hill House, Hampton Lucy, Warwick CV35 8AU (01789 840329). HETB Listed *COMMENDED.* Idyllically situated midway between Stratford and Warwick, this charming Georgian country house stands in two acres of private grounds. You will be assured of a very peaceful stay and warm hospitality. No smoking.

WARWICKSHIRE, STRATFORD-UPON-AVON. Mrs D.M. Hall, "Acer House", 44 Albany Road, Stratford-upon-Avon CV37 6PQ (01789 204962). 🐦🐦 *COMMENDED.* Quality non-smoking establishment, quiet location near railway station and town centre. Hearty English breakfast with choices or vegetarian. Early breakfasts available.

WARWICKSHIRE, STRATFORD-UPON-AVON. Mrs R.M. Meadows, Monk's Barn Farm, Shipston Road, Stratford-Upon-Avon CV37 8NA (01789 293714). AA QQ Bed and Breakfast. Non-smokers preferred and guests are particularly requested not to smoke in public rooms.

WARWICKSHIRE, TAMWORTH IN ARDEN. Monica and Brian Palser, Mungunyah, Poolhead Lane, Tamworth in Arden B94 5EH (01564 742437). Set in peaceful Warwickshire countryside overlooking golf course on the outskirts of the pretty village of Tamworth in Arden. Two twin-bedded rooms. Tea/coffee making facilities plus hospitality tray on arrival and evening drink are included. Ample parking. Non-smokers please.

WILTSHIRE, DEVIZES near. The Old Coach House, 21 Church Street, arket Lavington, Devizes SN10 4DU (01380 812879). 🐦🐦 *COMMENDED.* This completely non-smoking house also offers guests the option of a vegetarian breakfast.

WILTSHIRE, SALISBURY. Mr and Mrs V. Bath, "Beulah", 144 Britford Lane, Salisbury SP2 8AL (01722 333517). Bed and Breakfast accommodation offered in pretty bungalow on outskirts of Salisbury. Totally non-smoking establishment.

YORKSHIRE (NORTH), HARROGATE. Mrs Janet Anderson, Croft House, Little Croft, Markington, Harrogate HG3 3TU (01765 677782). 🐦 *HIGHLY COMMENDED.* Comfortable home in pleasant village. Car parking. Open March to October. A non smoking house where a friendly welcome is always assured.

YORKSHIRE (NORTH), HARROGATE. Mrs Allison Harrison, Garden Cottage, Moor Park, Norwood Lane, Beckwithshaw, Harrogate HG3 1QN (01423 530197). ETB Listed. Our two luxury ground floor, en suite rooms are non smoking, reasonably disabled friendly, with own entrance. Vegetarian breakfast if required.

YORKSHIRE (NORTH), HARROGATE. Carol and Derek Vinter, Spring Lodge, 22 Spring Mount, Harrogate HG1 2HX (01423 506036). 🐦 All year round a warm welcome awaits you from the resident proprietors. Tea and coffee making facilities in all rooms. Dinner provided on request. Residential licence, no smoking.

YORKSHIRE (NORTH), MALHAM. Sparth House Hotel, Malham, Skipton BD23 4DA (01729 830315). Country hotel of charm and individuality. All bedrooms no smoking. Separate no smoking lounge.

YORKSHIRE (NORTH), SCARBOROUGH. Sue and Tony Hewitt, Harmony Country Lodge, Limestone Road, Burniston, Scarborough YO13 0DG (01723 870276). Relaxing octagonal retreat, superb views overlooking National Park and sea. Licensed, private parking, completely non-smoking. Warm and friendly.

YORKSHIRE (NORTH), SELBY. Peggy Swann, South Newlands Farm, Selby Road, Riccall, York YO4 6QR (01757 248203). Friendliness, comfort and traditional cooking are always on offer to our guests. Easy access to York and the Dales and Moors. No smoking please.

YORKSHIRE (NORTH), SKIPTON. Mrs Heather Simpson, Low Skibeden Farmhouse, Skibeden Road, Skipton BD23 6AB (01756 793849; Fax: 01756 793804). 16th century farmhouse set in private grounds. Open all year. Plenty of parking. No pets. No smoking. No children under 12 years.

YORKSHIRE (NORTH), THIRSK. Joyce Ashbridge, Mount Grace Farm, Cold Kirby, Thirsk YO7 2HL (01845 597389). 🐞🐞 *HIGHLY COMMENDED.* A warm welcome awaits you on working farm, surrounded by beautiful open countryside, ideal touring location. Open all year except Christmas. No smoking.

YORKSHIRE (NORTH), WHITBY near. Mrs Pat Beale, Ryedale House, Coach Road, Sleights, Near Whitby YO22 5EQ (01947 810534). Friendly Yorkshire house of charm and character at the foot of the moors and amid magnificent scenery. Totally non-smoking accommodation — always country-fresh and clean.

YORKSHIRE (NORTH), WHITBY near. Mrs G. Watson, The Bungalow, 63 Coach Road, Sleights, Whitby YO22 5BT (01947 810464). Large bungalow, ample parking. One double room and one twin, both en suite, TV and tea making facilities. Disabled guests welcome.

YORKSHIRE (NORTH) YORK. Mrs Margaret Munday, Cornmill Lodge, 120 Haxby Road, York YO3 7JP (01904 620566). 🐞🐞 *COMMENDED.* Deceptively large Victorian town house situated 12 minutes' walk from York Minster and city centre. The beautifully refurbished house offers colour TVs, tea/coffee trays, clock radios; most rooms are en suite. We are a non-smoking guest house.

YORKSHIRE (NORTH), YORK. Four Poster Lodge Hotel, 68/70 Heslington Road, off Barbican Road, York YO1 5AU (01904 651170). 🐞🐞🐞 *COMMENDED.* RAC Acclaimed, AA QQQ. Victorian house lovingly restored and furnished. Close to historic York with all its fascinations. En suite four-poster bedrooms. Licensed. Non-smokers welcomed.

YORKSHIRE (NORTH), YORK. Mrs R. Foster, Brookland House, Hull Road, Dunnington, York YO1 5LW (01904 489548). Private house where a warm welcome awaits you. All rooms have hostess tray, colour TV and are double glazed. No smoking. Park and ride nearby. Private parking. Within easy reach of Eluington Air Museum, Castle Howard, North Yorkshire Moors and coastal resorts.

YORKSHIRE (NORTH), YORK. Mrs Barbara Curtis, Cumbria House, 2 Vyner Street, Haxby Road, York YO3 7HS (01904 636817). ETB Listed *COMMENDED.* AA QQQ. An elegant, tastefully decorated Victorian guest house, where comfort and quality is assured. All rooms have colour TV, radio alarms and tea/coffee facilities. Central heating. Fire Certificate. Guests' car park. Full English breakfast or vegetarian alternative.

YORKSHIRE (NORTH), YORK. Mrs D.S. Tindall, Newton Guest House, Neville Street, Haxby Road, York YO3 7NP (01904 635627). 🐞 *APPROVED.* Victorian town house, 10 minutes' walk from city centre. Ideal base for touring moors, dales and coast. No smoking policy.

YORKSHIRE (NORTH), YORK. Mr Whitehead, Holly House, Broad Lane, Appleton Roebuck, York YO5 7DS (01904 744314). Approximately seven miles from York centre. Conveniently placed for Yorkshire Dales, Moors, Wolds and coast. All bedrooms non-smoking.

YORKSHIRE (NORTH), YORK. Mr D.R. Dawson, Stanley House, Stanley Street, York YO3 7NW (01904 637111). 🐞🐞 *COMMENDED.* All rooms have en-suite facilities with colour television and courtesy tray. Off street parking and a pay phone. Sorry, no pets or smoking.

YORKSHIRE (NORTH), YORK. Ian and Carolyn McNabb, The Hazelwood, 24-25 Portland Street, Gillygate, York YO3 7EH (01904 626548; Fax: 01904 628032). 🐞🐞 *COMMENDED.* AA QQQQ Selected. Only 400 yards from York Minster, yet in extremely quiet location. Non smoking, quality accommodation with private car park. All rooms en suite. Quality breakfasts catering for all tastes, including vegetarian.

SCOTLAND

ABERDEENSHIRE, ABERDEEN. Terrace Private Hotel, 1 Springbank Terrace, Aberdeen AB11 6LS (Tel & Fax: 01224 581278). A family-run establishment with a warm and friendly atmosphere offering clean and comfortable accommodation for the non-smoker. Central position. Off-street parking. Colour brochure available.

AYRSHIRE & ARRAN, BEITH. Mrs Jane Gillan, Shotts Farm, Beith KA15 1LB (01505 502273). STB Listed *COMMENDED.* Comfortable friendly accommodation. High standard of cleanliness, first class cooking. Three comfortable bedrooms (double, family and twin), all with tea-making facilities, central heating and electric blankets. Children welcome. AA QQ.

AYRSHIRE & ARRAN, KILMARNOCK. Mrs Agnes Hawkshaw, Aulton Farm, Kilmaurs, Kilmarnock KA3 2PQ (01563 538208). 200 year old farmhouse ideally situated for the West Coast of Scotland and a footpath to the Highlands. Only 10 minutes from Prestwick Airport and 25 minutes from Glasgow. Guests are assured of a good Scottish welcome.

DUMFRIES & GALLOWAY, MOFFAT. T.J. Hull, Alton House, Moffat DG10 9LB (01683 220903; mobile 0850 129105). Historic country house situated in several acres of secluded grounds at the end of a long private lane. Bed and breakfast from £16. En suite available.

DUNDEE & ANGUS, MONTROSE (near). Moira Braes, Ballochy House, West Ballochy, Near Montrose DD10 9LP (Tel: 01674 810207; Fax: 01674 810739). Victorian House with wonderful views over open countryside. Full central heating and en suite rooms with colour TV, radio alarm and tea/coffee facilities.

EDINBURGH & LOTHIANS, EDINBURGH. Arden House, 26 Linkfield Road, Musselburgh, Edinburgh EH21 7LL (Tel & Fax: 0131-665 0663). AA/QQQ Ten minutes from city centre overlooking Musselburgh Racecourse. All rooms have colour TV, tea & coffee facilities and are centrally heated. Non smokers welcome.

EDINBURGH & LOTHIANS, EDINBURGH. Mrs H. Donaldson, "Invermark", 60 Polwarth Terrace, Edinburgh EH11 1NJ (0131-337 1066). ♛ COMMENDED. Non-smoking accommodation ive minutes' drive from city centre. Reductions for children.

EDINBURGH & LOTHIANS, EDINBURGH. Kildonan Lodge Hotel, 27 Craigmillar Park, Edinburgh EH16 5PE (0131 667 2793). ♛ ♛ ♛ HIGHLY COMMENDED. Well appointed non-smoking bedrooms with en suite facilities. Frequent local transport to city centre. Private car park. Warm, friendly welcome.

EDINBURGH & LOTHIANS, EDINBURGH. Mrs Janet Burke, Patieshill Farm, Carlops, Penicuik EH26 9ND (01968 660551; Fax: 01968 661162). ♛ ♛ COMMENDED. Working hill sheep and cattle farm set in the midst of the Pentland Hills offering Bed and Breakfast. No smoking.

EDINBURGH & LOTHIANS, EDINBURGH. Classic Guest House, 50 Mayfield Road, Edinburgh EH9 2NH (0131-667 5847; Fax: 0131-662 1016). ♛ ♛ HIGHLY COMMENDED. Good value Bed and Breakfast accommodation. Tastefully decorated, thoughtfully equipped. Convenient for bypass and city centre. TOTALLY NON SMOKING. Brochure on request.

EDINBURGH & LOTHIANS, EDINBURGH. Mrs Maureen Sandilands, Sandilands House, 25 Queensferry Road, Edinburgh EH4 3HB (0131-332 2057). ♛ ♛ ♛ A distinctive and attractive detached bungalow in its own gardens with excellent bus service to the city centre. Open all season. Family rooms available.

EDINBURGH & LOTHIANS, EDINBURGH. Mrs Rhoda Mitchell, Hopetoun Guest House, 15 Mayfield Road, Edinburgh EH9 2NG (0131-667 7691). ♛ ♛ COMMENDED. AA QQ Which? Good Bed & Breakfast Guide. Completely smoke-free environment situated close to Edinburgh University. Personal attention in a friendly, informal atmosphere.

EDINBURGH & LOTHIANS, LINLITHGOW. Mr and Mrs R. Inglis, Thornton, Edinburgh Road, Linlithgow EH49 6AA (01506 844216). Family-run Victorian house in peaceful location near town centre. Both rooms en suite. Off-street parking, friendly, relaxed, non smoking home.

EDINBURGH & LOTHIANS, NORTH BERWICK. "Craigview", 5 Beach Road, North Berwick EH39 4AB (01620 892257). British Institute of Innkeeping, Welcome Host, AA QQ Recommended, RAC Caradon. Private facilities, four-poster beds, central heating, colour TV, tea/coffee and biscuits. No smoking. Also self catering flat. Brochure available.

EDINBURGH & LOTHIANS, ROSLIN. Mrs Rosemary Noble, Glenlea House, Hawthornden, Lasswade EH18 1EJ (0131-440 2079). Glenlea is one mile from the picturesque village of Roslin, seven miles from Edinburgh. Four bedrooms, one on ground floor with bathroom adjacent.

FIFE, UPPER LARGO. Mr & Mrs D. Law, Monturpie Guest House, Upper Largo KY8 5QS (Tel: 01333 360254; Fax: 01333 360850). Superior quality guest house beautifully situated with magnificent views over the Firth of Forth. All rooms non-smoking with en suite, colour TV and tea/coffee facilities.

HIGHLANDS (SOUTH), INVERNESS. Mrs Singer, Balvonie Cottage, Inverness IV1 2BB (Tel & Fax: 01463 230677). Bungalow approximately two miles south east of Inverness offers fully en suite bedsittingroom (twin) convertible to family bedroom. See main advertisement for this non-smoking residence.

HIGHLANDS (SOUTH), INVERNESS. Mrs Joan Hendry, 'Tamarue', 70A Ballifeary Road, Inverness IV3 5PF (01463 239724). ♛ COMMENDED. Comfortable Bed and Breakfast base while you tour the many beauty spots of the Highlands. Completely non-smoking house.

HIGHLANDS (SOUTH), KINGUSSIE. John and Elrine Jarratt, St. Helens, Ardbroilach Road, Kingussie PH21 1JX (01540 661430). ♛ ♛ HIGHLY COMMENDED. Non-smoking, centrally heated throughout. Elegantly furnished Victorian house within half an acre of garden. Ample parking. Open all year.

HIGHLANDS (SOUTH), NEWTONMORE. Dennis & Isobel Blackburn, The Aspens, Speybridge, Newtonmore PH20 1DA (Tel: 01540 673264; Fax: 01540 662494). Luxury Bed & Breakfast. Three spacious bedrooms, all en suite, TV and tea/coffee facilities. Details on request.

MORAY, BANFF. Anne and Jim Mackie, The Orchard, Duff House, Banff AB45 3TA (01261 812146). Traditional house stands within three-quarters of an acre of grounds enjoying complete privacy due to surrounding woodland. Centrally heated accommodation comprising lounge, one double and three twin-bedded rooms, all with shower en suite, colour TV, alarm clock, hair dryer and hostess tray. Children welcome. Ample parking.

PERTH & KINROSS, CALLANDER. Lenymede Bed & Breakfast, Leny Road, Callander FK17 8AJ (01877 330952; Email: jamesgreen@msn.com; Website: http://www.lenymede.demon.co.uk ♛ ♛ COMMENDED. A non smoking family home in rural setting. Ideally situated for Southern Highlands and Trossachs. Children welcome.

ISLE OF ORKNEY, SANDWICK. Mrs Hourie, Flotterston House, Sandwick KW16 3LP (01856 841700). Former manse, built in the 1850s, set in the heart of Orkney's main tourist and fishing attractions. Play area and large family rooms recently refurbished.

WALES

ANGLESEY & GWYNEDD, ABERDOVEY. Jim and Marion Billingham, Preswylfa, Aberdovey LL35 0LE (Tel & Fax: 01654 767239). ✿✿✿ *HIGHLY COMMENDED.* Attractive non-smoking Edwardian house with wonderful views of sea. Luxury en sutie rooms. Excellent cuisine. Garden and parking.

ANGLESEY & GWYNEDD, ANGLESEY. Ms. Rosemary A. Abas, Bwthyn, Brynafon, Menai Bridge, Isle of Anglesey LL59 5HA (Tel & Fax: 01248 713119). ✿✿ *HIGHLY COMMENDED.* Welcoming, century-old terraced house close to Straits. For our mutual comfort and health — wholly and positively non-smoking.

ANGLESEY & GWYNEDD, BALA. Mr T.G. Jones, Frondderw Private Hotel, Stryd-y-Fron, Bala LL23 7YD (01678 520301). ✿✿✿ *COMMENDED.* Delightful period mansion, five minutes from Bala. Non-smoking areas available. Open March to November inclusive. AA QQ. WTB Welcome Host.

ANGLESEY & GWYNEDD, CAERNARFON. Sylvette Williams, Tal Menai Guest House, Bangor Road, Caernarfon LL55 1TP (01286 672160). ✿✿ *COMMENDED.* Victorian house standing in its own grounds off the A487. An ideal centre for touring Snowdonia. Access to house at all times. No smoking.

ANGLESEY & GWYNEDD, CRICCIETH. Mrs S.A. Reynolds, Glyn-y-Coed Hotel, Porthmadoc Road, Criccieth LL52 0HL (01766 522870; Fax: 01766 523341). ✿✿✿ *HIGHLY COMMENDED.* Lovely Victorian, family-run hotel and self catering accommodation overlooking the sea. Vegetarian, diabetic, low-fat and low-cholesterol diets catered for. Ground floor bedroom suitable for disabled guests, also non smoking room available.

ANGLESEY & GWYNEDD, LLANFAIRFECHAN. Mrs K.M. Coleman, Plas Heulog, Mount Road, Llanfairfechan LL33 0HA (Tel & Fax: 01248 680019). ✿✿ *COMMENDED.* Situated in the Snowdonia region with breathtaking views of both sea and mountains. Offering total seclusion yet is easily accessible. Wales Tourist Board Approved for walkers and cyclists. Non-smoking establishment.

CARDIGANSHIRE, ABERYSTWYTH. Sarah and Lester Ward, Sinclair Guest House, 43 Portland Street, Aberystwyth SY23 2DX (Tel & Fax: 01970 615158). ✿✿✿ *HIGHLY COMMENDED.* Immaculate en suite accommodation in totally smoke free guest house.

CARDIGANSHIRE, LAMPETER. Mrs J.P. Driver, Penwern Old Mills, Cribyn, Lampeter SA48 7QH (01570 470762). Formerly a rural woollen mill set in a quiet valley alongside a small stream. Idyllic surroundings. Comfortable lounge. Double, single, twin rooms, cot. Washbasins in all rooms. High chair available. Totally non-smoking.

CARMARTHENSHIRE, CARMARTHEN. Colin and Jacquie Rouse, Allt-y-golau Uchaf, Felingwm Uchaf, Carmarthen SA32 7BB (01267 290455). ✿✿ *HIGHLY COMMENDED.* Our Georgian stone-walled farmhouse has been furnished and decorated to a very high standard retaining many original features. The house is fully centrally heated and all bedrooms (non-smoking) have washbasins and tea/coffee trays. Open all year.

NORTH WALES, BETWS-Y-COED. Summer Hill Non-Smokers' Guest House, Betws-y-Coed LL24 0BL (01690 710306). ✿✿ *COMMENDED.* Especially for the non-smoker, Summer Hill is delightfully situated in a quiet sunny location. Bed, Breakfast and Evening Meals offered.

NORTH WALES, BETWS-Y-COED. Mrs Joyce Melling, Mount Pleasant, Betws-y-Coed LL24 0BN (01690 710502). WTB ✿✿ *HIGHLY COMMENDED.* AA QQQ. A warm Welsh welcome awaits you at our Victorian stone built house. Vegetarian breakfast available. Some off road parking. Totally non-smoking.

NORTH WALES, ST. ASAPH. Mrs N. Price, Plas Penucha, Caerwys, Mold CH7 5BH (01352 720210). ✿✿✿ *HIGHLY COMMENDED.* Bed and Breakfast, Evening Meal available. No smoking in bedrooms and discouraged in the rest of the house.

NORTH WALES, ST. ASAPH. Mrs Jones, Rhewl Farm, Waen, St. Asaph, Denbighshire LL17 0DT (01745 582287). ✿✿ *COMMENDED.* 18th century farmhouse on 180 acre farm in peaceful setting. Comfortable bedrooms double en suite, family/twin. Spacious lounge with inglenook fireplace, colour TV. Coast six miles, three-quarters of a mile to A55. Excellent breakfasts.

NORTH WALES, TREFRIW. Ann and Arthur Eaton, Crafnant Guest House, Trefriw LL27 0JH (01492 640809). Totally non-smoking Victorian country home in charming village setting. Five en suite double/twin rooms with drinks tray and TV. Traditional/vegetarian menu. Private parking.

POWYS, BUILTH WELLS near. Mrs Margaret Davies, The Court Farm, Aberedw, Near Builth Wells LD2 3UP (01982 560277). We welcome guests into our home on a family run livestock farm. All bedrooms have washbasins, shaver points, electric blankets and adjustable heating. Lounge with TV. Non-smokers please.

POWYS, HAY-ON-WYE. Peter and Olwen Roberts, York House, Cusop, Hay-on-Wye HR3 5QX (01497 820705). Totally non-smoking, elegant, quiet Victorian Guest House on the edge of Hay-on-Wye (town of books). Excellent touring and walking centre. No smoking indoors.

POWYS, MACHYNLLETH. Mrs Monica Bashford, Gelli-graean, Cwrt, Pennal, Near Machynlleth SY20 9LE (Tel & Fax: 01654 791219). Farmhouse situated in a secluded and sheltered spot. Stunning panoramic views. Open all year, special breaks out of season. Fully centrally heated. Totally non smoking.

POWYS, WELSHPOOL. Mrs Jane Jones, Trefnant Hall, Berriew, Welshpool SY21 8AS (01686 640262). ✿✿✿ *HIGHLY COMMENDED.* Warm welcome in Grade II Listed farmhouse. All rooms en suite with tea/coffee making facilities and colour TV. No smoking.

SOUTH WALES, BLAINA. Mr J.W. Chandler, Lamb House, Westside, Blaina NP3 3DB (01495 290179). ♛ ♛ *COMMENDED*. Set in the Upper Gwent Valleys close to all major tourist attractions in South Wales. Children welcome. No smoking in bedrooms.

SOUTH WALES, GOWER PENINSULA. Mrs M. Valerie Evans, The Old Rectory, Reynoldston, Swansea SA3 1AD (01792 390129). A warm welcome awaits visitors to our home in this beautiful peninsula. Non-smoking household. Visitors asked to refrain from smoking in the house. Bed and Breakfast £18; Evening Meal available, £10.

SOUTH WALES, NEWPORT near. Mrs D. Sheahan, The West Usk Lighthouse, St. Brides, Near Newport NP1 9SF (01633 810126/815860; Fax:01633 815582). ♛ ♛ A real lighthouse with superb accommodation in peaceful and serene surroundings. Great hospitality. Distinctly different. Non-smokers very welcome.

SOUTH WALES, ST. BRIDES WENTLOOG. Mr. David W. Bushell, Chapel Guest House, Church Road, St. Brides Wentloog, Near Newport NP1 9SN (01633 681018). ♛ ♛ *COMMENDED*. Comfortable, non smoking accommodation in a converted chapel situated in a village between Newport and Cardiff. Children under three years FREE.

SOUTH WALES, ST. BRIDES WENTLOOG. Mr. David W. Bushell, Chapel Guest House, Church Road, St. Brides Wentloog, Near Newport NP1 9SN (01633 681018). ♛ ♛ *COMMENDED*. Comfortable, non smoking accommodation in a converted chapel situated in a village between Newport and Cardiff. Children under three years FREE.

SOUTH WALES, TINTERN. Anne and Peter Howe, Valley House, Raglan Road, Tintern, Near Chepstow NP6 6TH (01291 689652). ♛ ♛ *COMMENDED*. Accommodation of a very high standard in a fine Georgian residence. Open all year. Non-smoking preferred.

DISABLED

CAMBRIDGESHIRE, CAMBRIDGE (Caxton). Mr and Mrs Salt, The Old Vicarage, Gransden Road, Cambridge CB3 8PL (01954 719585). Beautiful old Vicarage in acre of gardens approximately eight miles from centre of Cambridge. Large spacious theme room bedrooms and central heating throughout.

CHESHIRE, BALTERLEY. Mrs Joanne Hollins, Green Farm, Deans Lane, Balterley, Near Crewe CW2 5QJ (01270 820214). ✿ ✿ *COMMENDED.* **Working farm.** Jo and Pete Hollins offer guests a friendly welcome to their home on a 145-acre farm in quiet and peaceful surroundings on the Cheshire/Staffordshire border — an excellent stopover. Children and pets welcome. Accommodation suitable for disabled visitors.
CHESHIRE, SANDBACH. Mrs Helen Wood, Arclid Grange, Sandbach CW11 0SZ (Tel: 01270 764750; Fax: 01270 759255). Category 3 Accessible Scheme. Three of our rooms are on the ground floor. Easy access to car park by ramp. No steps into the house.

CORNWALL, TRURO. Marcorrie Hotel, 20 Falmouth Road, Truro TR1 2HX (01872 277374; Fax: 01872 241666). ✿ ✿ *APPROVED.* Victorian town house in conservation area, five minutes' walk from city centre and cathedral. All rooms are en suite and have central heating, colour TV, tea making facilities and telephone. Accommodation suitable for disabled visitors. Open all year.

CUMBRIA, CARLISLE. Mrs L. Young, 7 Hether Drive, Lowry Hill, Carlisle CA3 0ED (01228 27242). ✿ Detached bungalow in quiet location. One room specially adapted for disabled guests — ramped access, wheel-in shower, six grab rails, adjustable toilet seat, all light switches and sockets at wheelchair height.
CUMBRIA, COCKERMOUTH. Hundith Hill Hotel, Lorton, Cockermouth CA13 9TH (01900 822092; Fax: 01900 828215). Comfortable, quiet family Hotel. Ideal centre for Lakes. We can accommodate disabled/wheelchair users. Dogs welcome. Write or telephone for brochure.
CUMBRIA, KESWICK. David and Valerie Fisher, Howe Keld Lakeland Hotel, 5-7 The Heads, Keswick CA12 5ES (Tel & Fax: 017687 72417). ✿ ✿ *COMMENDED.* Delightful Lakeland hotel situated in one of the most beautiful and convenient locations in Keswick. Home cooked meals, vegetarian food a speciality. Well appointed en suite bedrooms. Licensed bar.
CUMBRIA, LEVENS/KENDAL. Mrs A.H. Parsons, Olde Peat Cotes, Sampool Lane, Levens, Kendal LA8 8EH (015395 60096). Modern, comfortable bungalow with all facilities. Situated in peaceful surroundings with lovely views. Parking space. Accommodation suitable for disabled visitors.
CUMBRIA, PENRITH. Mr S.E. Bray, Norcroft Guest House, Graham Street, Penrith CA11 9LQ (01768 62365). ✿ ✿ ✿ *COMMENDED.* This spacious Victorian house, set in a quiet location and with en-suite ground floor twin room, is ideal for disabled guests.

DERBYSHIRE, BAKEWELL. Mrs Julia Finney, Mandale House, Haddon Grove, Bakewell DE45 1JF (01629 812416). ✿ ✿ Peaceful farmhouse offers bedrooms with colour TV and tea-making facility. Two rooms on the ground floor with en suite facilities suitable for disabled guests.
DERBYSHIRE, CASTLETON. Mrs B. Johnson, Myrtle Cottage, Market Place, Castleton, Near Sheffield, S30 2WQ (01433 620787) Accommodation includes ground floor en suite bedrooms with level access from car park. Disabled visitors welcome.

DEVON, ASHBURTON. Mrs Anne Torr, Middle Leat, Holne, Near Ashburton TQ13 7SJ (01364 631413). A warm welcome and relaxed friendly atmosphere assured in very peaceful surroundings. Accommodation in three ground floor bedrooms, suitable for disabled visitors.
DEVON, CLOVELLY. Mrs P. Vanstone, The Old Smithy, Slerra Hill, Clovelly, Bideford EX39 5ST, (01237 431202). A 16th century cottage and converted forge, situated one mile from the sea and the village of Clovelly. One ground floor en suite double/twin/family room. Not suitable for wheelchair in bathroom.
DEVON, DAWLISH. West Hatch Hotel, 34 West Cliff, Dawlish (Tel & Fax: 01626 864211). ✿ ✿ *HIGHLY COMMENDED.* AA QQQQ Selected, RAC Highly Acclaimed. Small friendly quality hotel. Centrally situated, overlooking the sea. Well equipped, en suite rooms on the ground or first floor. Bar and separate lounge. Extensive menu.
DEVON, ILFRACOMBE. Sunnymeade Country House Hotel, Dean Cross, West Down, Ilfracombe EX34 8NT (01271 863668). ✿ ✿ ✿ A charming country house hotel in its own large gardens set in the rolling Devonshire countryside. 10 pretty en suite bedrooms; some on the ground floor for those less mobile guests.

DORSET, BLANDFORD near. Mrs Lucienne Sumner-Fergusson, Stocklands House, Hilton, Near Blandford DT11 0DE (01258 880580; Fax: 01258 881188). ✿ ✿ *HIGHLY COMMENDED.* One double, one twin, both en suite, both ground floor. Sumptuous breakfasts, candlelit dinners and cream teas. Heated outdoor pool, table tennis, badminton and clay shooting.
DORSET, BRIDPORT. Ann and Dan Walker MHCIMA, Britmead House, West Bay Road, Bridport DT6 4EG (01308 422941). ✿ ✿ ✿ *HIGHLY COMMENDED.* AA QQQQ Selected, RAC Acclaimed. Facilities offered include one full en suite ground floor twin bedroom, limited wheelchair use. Optional Dinner. Open all year.

DORSET, LYME REGIS. Mrs S.G. Taylor, Buckland Farm, Raymonds Hill, Near Axminster EX13 5SZ (01297 33222). Smallholding of five acres, three miles from Lyme Regis and Charmouth. En suite accommodation with shower available on ground floor suitable for disabled visitors.

DORSET, PORTLAND/WEYMOUTH. Alessandria Hotel & Italian Restaurant, Portland, Weymouth DT5 1HW (01305 822270/820108; Fax: 01305 820561). 👑👑👑 *APPROVED.* Hotel and Italian Restaurant situated in a quiet location. Most rooms en suite, colour TV, tea/coffee making facilities, soft towels and toiletries. Ground floor bedrooms level with lounge and restaurant.

ESSEX, COLCHESTER. Mrs Wendy Anderson, The Old Manse, 15 Roman Road, Colchester CO1 1UR (01206 545154). This elegant and spacious town centre Victorian home provides one ground floor double bedded room with separate toilet/shower suitable for partially disabled visitors.

HAMPSHIRE, LYMINGTON. Our Bench, Lodge Road, Lymington SO41 8HH (Tel & Fax: 01590 673141). 👑👑 *COMMENDED.* Welcome Host, FHG Diploma Winner, Regional Nominee — England for Excellence. Large bungalow situated between New Forest and the Coast. Indoor heated swimming/exercise pool, jacuzzi and sauna. RAC Acclaimed, AA QQQQ Selected. Non-smokers only, no children. National Accessibility Scheme Category 3.

HAMPSHIRE, NEW FOREST. Mrs M. Stone, Heathlands, Lepe Road, Langley SO45 1YT (01703 892517). Comfortable accommodation in a large bungalow. All rooms have washbasins, central heating, tea-making facilities and colour TV. There is a shower room and WC. Suitable for disabled guests.

HAMPSHIRE, NEW FOREST. Mrs Pauline Harris, Little Heathers, 13 Whitemoor Road, Brockenhurst SO42 7QG (01590 623512). Warm welcome for all non-smokers. Ground floor bedrooms with limited wheelchair use. Special diets can be catered for.

HEREFORD & WORCESTER, KIDDERMINSTER. Granary Hotel, Heath Lane, Shewstone, Near Kidderminster DY10 4BS (01562 777535). 👑👑👑 *COMMENDED.* A friendly, independently owned hotel with 18 modern en suite bedrooms. Easy access for disabled visitors — single storey building. Fully licensed. Room service available.

NORFOLK, GREAT YARMOUTH. Mr and Mrs Brian and Diana Kimber, Anglia House, 56 Wellesley Road, Great Yarmouth NR30 1EX (01493 844395). RAC Listed. Our reputation and good name have been built on service, a friendly atmosphere and fine food with a choice of menu. Partially disabled guests can be accommodated in ground floor en suite.

NORFOLK, RACKHEATH. Mr and Mrs R. Lebbell, Manor Barn House, Back Lane, Rackheath, Norwich NR13 6NN (01603 783543). 👑👑 *COMMENDED.* Family home with lovely gardens in quiet surroundings. Open all year for bed and breakfast. Accommodation available for disabled visitors.

OXFORDSHIRE, SOULDERN. Mrs C. Hamilton-Gould, Tower Fields, Tusmore Road, Near Souldern, Bicester OX6 9HY (01869 346554; Fax: 01869 345157). 👑👑 *COMMENDED.* A recently renovated farmhouse and barn. All bedrooms on the ground floor (not designed for wheelchairs).

SHROPSHIRE, IRONBRIDGE. Len and Daphne Roberts, Woodlands, Park Lane, Madeley, near Ironbridge, Telford TF7 5HJ (01952 580693). 👑👑 *COMMENDED.* Quality en suite accommodation one mile from Ironbridge. Lounge with TV. Private parking. Secluded garden with waterfall and pond. Ideal base for touring Shropshire. Open all year.

SHROPSHIRE, LUDLOW. Mrs Kathy Lanman, "Red Roofs", Little Hereford, Near Ludlow SY8 4AT (01584 711439). 👑👑 Situated in the lovely Teme Valley overlooking glorious open countryside. Ample parking. Accommodation suitable for disabled guests. AA QQQQ.

SHROPSHIRE, SHREWSBURY. Gwen Frost, Oakfields, Baschurch Road, Myddle, Near Shrewsbury SY4 3RX (01939 290823). 👑 *COMMENDED.* Situated in a quiet, idyllic setting. All bedrooms are on the ground floor, suitable for less mobile guests, and have colour TV, tea making facilities, radio, washbasin, hairdryer and shaver point. Central heating throughout.

SOMERSET, BRENT KNOLL. Roy and Lorrayne Page, Old Holt Farm, Edingworth Road, Weston-super-Mare BS24 0JA (01934 750245). Listed 17th century buildings and grounds in beautiful rural location. Accommodation in double rooms or self-contained luxury stone cottages. Home cooked evening meals available. Please telephone for more information.

SOMERSET, TAUNTON near. Ann and John Bartlett, The Spinney, Curland, Taunton TA3 5SE (01460 234362). En-suite ground floor bedrooms suitable for elderly or less able guests. Ideal for convalescence. Adjacent and easy parking.

SUSSEX (EAST), EASTBOURNE. Farrar's Hotel, 3-5 Wilmington Gardens, Eastbourne BN21 4JN (01323 723737; Fax: 01323 732902). 👑👑👑👑 AA/RAC Two Star. Bedrooms are centrally heated with own bathroom or shower en suite, direct dial telephone, radio, TV and tea/coffee facilities. Three lounges, cocktail bar and fully licensed restaurant. There are two lifts and porters on duty day and night. Private car park. Brochure.

SUSSEX (WEST), ARUNDEL. Peter and Sarah Fuente, Mill Lane House, Slindon, Arundel BN18 0RP (01243 814440). 🐾🐾 Rooms en-suite and with TV; central heating and log fires in winter. Special unit for disabled guests available.

SUSSEX (WEST), MIDHURST. Annabelle Costaras, Amberfold, Hayshott, Midhurst GU29 0DA (01730 812385). Accommodation comprises a private, self-contained annexe situated in quiet countryside yet only five minutes from town centre. Attractive garden; ample car parking. No smoking, no pets please. Open all year.

WARWICKSHIRE, STRATFORD-UPON-AVON. Mrs Karen Cauvin, Penshurst Guest House, 34 Evesham Place, Stratford-upon-Avon CV37 6HT (01789 205259). Prettily refurbished Victorian townhouse. One ground floor en suite room specially adapted for disabled guests. ETB Category 2 Accessibility symbol awarded.

WILTSHIRE, SWINDON. County View Guest House, 31/33 County Road, Swindon SN1 2EG (01793 610434/618387). Situated on the main road and five minutes' walk from rail and coach stations and the town centre. Ground floor rooms available, suitable for less mobile guests.

YORKSHIRE (NORTH), HARROGATE. Mrs Allison Harrison, Garden Cottage, Moor Park, Norwood Lane, Beckwithshaw, Harrogate HG3 1QN (01423 530197). ETB Listed. Our two luxury ground floor, en suite rooms are non smoking, reasonably disabled friendly, with own entrance. Vegetarian breakfast if required.

YORKSHIRE (NORTH), MALHAM. Sparth House Hotel, Malham, Skipton BD23 4DA (01729 830315). Relaxing country Hotel in heart of Yorkshire Dales. One ground floor en-suite bedroom equipped for disabled guests. Tourist Board Accessible Scheme Category 3.

YORKSHIRE (NORTH), WHITBY near. Mrs G. Watson, The Bungalow, 63 Coach Road, Sleights, Whitby YO22 5BT (01947 810464). Large bungalow, ample parking. Two double rooms and one twin, all en suite, TV and tea making facilities. Disabled guests welcome.

SCOTLAND

AYRSHIRE & ARRAN, KILMARNOCK. Mrs Agnes Hawkshaw, Aulton Farm, Kilmaurs, Kilmarnock KA3 2PQ (01563 538208). Tourist Board Listed COMMENDED. AA QQQ. 200 year old farmhouse situated only 10 minutes from Prestwick Airport and 25 minutes from Glasgow; ideal for touring the West Coast of Scotland and a footpath to the Highlands. Disabled visitors welcome.

DUMFRIES & GALLOWAY, CANONBIE. Mrs Steele, North Lodge, Canonbie DG14 0TA (01387 371409). A warm welcome awaits you at this 19th century cottage set in beautiful gardens. A ground floor en suite bedroom is available, suitable for the disabled traveller. Grade 1 Classification awarded by the STB.

DUMFRIES & GALLOWAY, MOFFAT. Mr T.J. Hull, Alton House, Moffat DG10 9LB (01683 220903; mobile: 0850 129105). Historic country house situated in several acres of secluded grounds. All bedrooms have washbasins, tea making facilities and welcome tray. Full central heating.

DUNDEE & ANGUS, MONTROSE near. Moira Braes, Ballochy House, West Ballochy, Near Montrose DD10 9LP (Tel: 01674 810207; Fax: 01674 810739). Victorian House with wonderful views over open countryside. Full central heating and en suite rooms with colour TV, radio alarm and tea/coffee facilities.

EDINBURGH & LOTHIANS, EDINBURGH. Mrs Janet Burke, Patieshill Farm, Carlops, Penicuik EH26 9ND (01968 660551; Fax: 01968 661162). 🐾🐾 COMMENDED. A very warm and friendly welcome is extended to all guests. Ground floor accommodation available.

EDINBURGH & LOTHIANS, LINLITHGOW. Mr and Mrs R. Inglis, Thornton, Edinburgh Road, Linlithgow EH69 6AA (01506 844216). Family-run Victorian house in peaceful location near town centre. Both our en suite rooms are on ground floor — no steps. Off-street parking. Friendly, relaxed non-smoking home.

EDINBURGH & LOTHIANS, ROSLIN. Mrs Rosemary Noble, Glenlea House, Hawthornden, Lasswade EH18 1EJ (0131-440 2079). Glenlea is one mile from the picturesque village of Roslin, seven miles from Edinburgh. Comfortable bedrooms including one on ground floor with bathroom adjacent.

FIFE, CUPAR. Rathcluan Guest House, Carslogie Road, Cupar KY15 4HY (Tel & Fax: 01334 657857/6). Views overlooking the park and mature landscaped gardens, private courtyard parking. Access and rooms for disabled visitors. Private leisure facilities package.

PERTH & KINROSS, PITLOCHRY. Mrs Barbara Bright, Craig Dubh Cottage, Manse Road, Moulin, Pitlochry PH16 5EP (01796 472058). One ground floor twin room, en suite, no steps. Car can be parked at door for easy access.

WALES

ANGLESEY & GWYNEDD, BALA. Mr T. Glynn Jones, Frondderw Private Hotel, Stryd-y-Fron, Bala LL23 7YD (01678 520301). ♛ ♛ ♛ *COMMENDED.* One downstairs double bedroom en suite available for the mobile partially disabled or elderly guests. Bed and Breakfast; optional Evening Meal. AA QQ. WTB Welcome Host.

ANGLESEY & GWYNEDD, CRICCIETH. Mrs S.A. Reynolds, Glyn-y-Coed Hotel, Porthmadoc Road, Criccieth LL52 0HL (01766 522870; Fax: 01766 523341). ♛ ♛ ♛ *HIGHLY COMMENDED.* Lovely Victorian, family-run hotel and self catering accommodation overlooking the sea. Vegetarian, diabetic, low-fat and low-cholesterol diets catered for. Ground floor bedroom suitable for disabled guests, also non smoking room available.

CARMARTHENSHIRE, CARMARTHEN. Colin and Jacquie Rouse, Allt-y-golau Uchaf, Felingwm Uchaf, Carmarthen SA32 7BB (01267 290455). ♛ ♛ *HIGHLY COMMENDED.* Traditional Welsh breakfasts and cosy oak beams in a peaceful rural setting. The house is fully centrally heated and all bedrooms (non-smoking) have washbasins and tea/coffee trays. The guest wing has two large bathrooms. Open all year.

PEMBROKESHIRE, SOLVA. Mrs Julia Hann, Min Yr Afon, Y Gribin, Solva SA62 6UY (01437 721752). Set in a peaceful hamlet, easy access to harbour, shops, restaurants, pubs. Annexe suitable for partially disabled guests. All on ground floor. Twin en suite, kitchen, lounge. Upstairs double en suite.

SOUTH WALES, BLAINA. Mr J.W. Chandler, Lamb House, Westside, Blaina NP3 3DB (01495 290179). ♛ ♛ *COMMENDED.* Set in the Upper Gwent Valleys close to all major tourist attractions. Accommodation includes two double en suite rooms on ground floor suitable for partially disabled guests.

SOUTH WALES, ST. BRIDES WENTLOOG. Mr. David W. Bushell, Chapel Guest House, Church Road, St. Brides Wentloog, Near Newport NP1 9SN (01633 681018). ♛ ♛ *COMMENDED.* Comfortable, non smoking accommodation in a converted chapel situated in a village between Newport and Cardiff. Children under three years FREE.

SPECIAL DIETS

LONDON, GREENWICH. Marshall Mordew, Oakfield, 36 Southend Crescent, London SE9 2SB (Tel & Fax: 0181-859 8989). A large luxurious Victorian house in the London Borough of Greenwich conveniently located for travel to central London and Kent. Oakfield is entirely non smoking and especially welcomes vegetarians.

LONDON, HIGHGATE/CROUCH END. Mr and Mrs L. Solomons, The Parkland Walk Guest House, 12 Hornsey Rise Gardens, London N19 3PR (0171-263 3228; Fax: 0171-263 3965; email: parkwalk@monomak. Value for money Bed and Breakfast in pretty, comfortable Victorian house. Special diets catered for by arrangement. Brochure available.

LONDON, HYDE PARK. Mr R.S. Bhasin, Barry House Hotel, 12 Sussex Place, Hyde Park, London W2 2TP (0171-723 7340/0994; Fax 0171-723 9775). ❀ *APPROVED.* Family-run guest house situated close to many tourist attractions. Vegetarian breakfast available if ordered.

CORNWALL, CAMBORNE. Mrs Christine Peerless, Highdowns, Blackrock, Praze-an-Beeble, Camborne TR14 9PD (01209 831442). Set on hillside with extensive country views towards St. Ives Bay. Bed and Breakfast; optional evening meal. Special and vegetarian diets catered for.

CORNWALL, CAMELFORD. John & Angie Lapham, Sea View Farm, Otterham Station, Camelford PL32 9SW (01840 261355). Friendly guest house. Bed and Breakfast, Evening Meal optional. Vegetarian menu, diabetics catered for on request. Good home cooking. Children and dogs welcome. Set in 10 acres.

CORNWALL, FALMOUTH. Celia and Ian Carruthers, Harbour House, 1 Harbour Terrace, Falmouth TR11 2AN (01326 311344). Enjoy quality Bed and Breakfast accommodation with some of the most fantastic harbour views in Cornwall. Delicious home cooking with generous and varied menus. Special diets catered for.

CORNWALL, LOOE. Mrs Jean Henly, Bucklawren Farm, St. Martin-by-Looe PL13 1NZ (01503 240738; Fax: 01503 240481). ❀ ❀ *HIGHLY COMMENDED.* **Working farm.** Situated deep on unspoilt countryside yet only one mile from the beach, two and a half miles from Looe. Excellent accommodation with en suite rooms and farmhouse cooking; special diets can be catered for. Open March to October. Brochure.

CORNWALL, TINTAGEL. Cate West, Chilcotts, Bossiney, Tintagel PL34 0AY (01840 770324). Friendly, old, listed cottage with beamed ceilings. Vegetarian, vegan, wholefood or special diet breakfasts.

CORNWALL, TRURO. Marcorrie Hotel, 20 Falmouth Road, Truro TR1 2HX (01872 277374; Fax: 01872 241666). ❀ ❀ *APPROVED.* Victorian town house just five minutes' walk from city centre and cathedral. All rooms en suite. Special diets can be catered for. Open all year.

CUMBRIA, ALSTON. Clare and Mike Le Marie, Brownside House, Leadgate, Alston CA9 3EL (01434 382169; Fax: 01434 382100). Ideal centre for walking, cycling, birdwatching and exploring old lead mines. Easy reach for Lake District, Hadrian's Wall, Northumberland. Children and pets welcome (babysitting available).

CUMBRIA, AMBLESIDE. Mr D. Sowerbutts, 2 Swiss Villas, Vicarage Road, Ambleside LA22 9AE (015394 32691). A full English Breakfast or vegetarian meal available. We are open all year round and you are sure of a friendly welcome and good home cooking.

CUMBRIA, APPLEBY. Mrs K.M. Coward, Limnerslease, Bongate, Appleby CA16 6UE (017683 51578). Family-run guesthouse five minutes' walk from town centre. A good half-way stopping place on the way to/from Scotland. Special diets are catered for.

CUMBRIA, BOWNESS-ON-WINDERMERE. Vivien and Howard Newham, Langthwaite, Crook Road, Ferry View, Bowness-on-Windermere LA23 3JB (015394 43329). Large bungalow set in delightful gardens with an elevated patio area. Double and twin rooms are en suite and furnished to a high standard with TV, etc. A wholesome breakfast is served in the conservatory. Open February to November. Sorry no pets or smoking.

CUMBRIA, DENT (Yorkshire Dales/Cumbria). Mrs Mary Ferguson, Scow Cottage, Cowgill, Near Dent, Sedbergh LA10 5RN (015396 25445). Ideal for touring the Lake District and the Yorkshire Dales. Large, comfortable bedrooms with washbasins and central heating. Evening meals available.

CUMBRIA, KENDAL. Mrs V.T. Sunter, Higher House Farm, Oxenholme Lane, Natland LA9 7QH (015395 61177). ❀ ❀ *HIGHLY COMMENDED.* AA QQQQ Selected. 17th century beamed farmhouse offers comfortable bed and breakfast accommodation in tranquil village. Self catering accommodation also available. No smoking. Pets welcome.

CUMBRIA, KESWICK. Annie Scally and Ian Townsend, Latrigg House, St. Herbert Street, Keswick CA12 4DF (017687 73068). ❀ ❀ We promise a very warm welcome, good food, comfort and hospitality (vegetarian and vegan meals provided if required).

CUMBRIA, KESWICK. David and Valerie Fisher, Howe Keld Lakeland Hotel, 5-7 The Heads, Keswick CA12 5ES (Tel & Fax: 017687 72417). ❀ ❀ *COMMENDED.* Delightful Lakeland hotel situated in one of the most beautiful and convenient locations in Keswick. Home cooked meals, vegetarian food is a speciality and there is an exceptional choice for breakfast.

CUMBRIA, KESWICK. Gladys & David Birtwistle, Kalgurli Guest House, 33 Helvellyn Street, Keswick CA12 4EP (017687 72935). ❀ ❀ *COMMENDED.* Be assured of a warm and friendly welcome. Excellent grilled breakfast served between 8am and 9am, menu choice, vegetarians catered for; packed lunches available.

CUMBRIA, LEVENS/KENDAL. Mrs A.H. Parsons, Olde Peat Cotes, Sampool Lane, Levens, Kendal LA8 8EH (015395 60096). Modern, comfortable bungalow with every facility. Situated in peaceful surroundings with lovely views. Special diets catered for; all local pubs do excellent bar snacks.

CUMBRIA, LOWICK (near Coniston). Garth Row, Lowick Green, Ulverston LA12 8EB (01229 885633). Tourist Board Listed COMMENDED. Traditional, beamed cottage only three miles from Coniston Water. Good food, tea/coffee in rooms, dogs welcome, wonderful walking, drying room, no smoking. Super quiet holiday spot or overnight stay.

CUMBRIA, PENRITH. Jean and Ron Forrester, "Lonnin End", Pallet Hill, Penrith CA11 0BY (017684 83453). Pallet Hill is a quiet hamlet on the Penrith to Greystoke road. One double, one family room, all with central heating, colour TV and tea/coffee facilities including biscuits. No smoking. No pets. A friendly welcome with that personal touch, a substantial English breakfast, vegetarians catered for.

CUMBRIA, PENRITH. Angela and Ivor Davies, Woodland House Hotel, Wordsworth Street, Penrith CA11 7QY (01768 864177; Fax: 01768 890152). 🐾🐾 COMMENDED. Licensed hotel situated at foot of Beacon Hill. Special diets catered for by prior arrangement.

CUMBRIA, TROUTBECK. Gwen and Peter Parfitt, Hill Crest, Troutbeck, Penrith CA11 0SH (017684 83935). A unique warm and friendly Lakeland home with vegetarian and healthy eating menus, where children and dogs are welcome. En suite rooms available.

CUMBRIA, WINDERMERE. Mrs Christopherson, Villa Lodge, Cross Street, Windermere LA23 1AE (015394 43318). 🐾🐾 COMMENDED. AA QQQ. Extremely comfortable accommodation in peaceful area overlooking Windermere village. Access to rooms at all times. Vegetarian/Special diets catered for.

CUMBRIA, WINDERMERE. Diane and David Weatherley, Crookleigh Guesthouse, 15 Woodland Road, Windermere LA23 2AE (Tel & Fax: 015394 48480; Mobile: 0410 538061). Victorian home, tastefully furnished and close to the village and station. Our four course breakfast consists of fruit juices, cereals/fresh fruit, full English/vegetarian or our Special Healthy alternative. Combined with freshly brewed coffee, speciality teas, home baked rolls, free-range eggs, local produce, makes our breakfast both memorable and long lasting! Family, double and twin rooms available. Pets welcome by arrangement.

CUMBRIA, WINDERMERE. Mr Brian Fear, Cambridge House, 9 Oak Street, Windermere LA23 1EN (015394 43846). ETB Listed COMMENDED. A traditional Lakeland guest house situated in Windermere village centre, convenient for all amenities. Modern, comfortable rooms with en suite facilities. Full English, Continental or vegetarian breakfast is provided.

CUMBRIA, WINDERMERE. Mick & Angela Brown, Haisthorpe Guest House, Holly Road, Windermere LA23 2AF (Tel/Fax: 015394 43445). 🐾🐾 COMMENDED. AA QQQ, RAC Acclaimed. Comfortable family-run house situated in a quiet part of Windermere yet close to the village centre and local amenities. Ideal location for touring the Lakes. Special diets catered for.

DERBYSHIRE, BAKEWELL. Mrs Julia Finney, Mardale House, Haddon Grove, Bakewell DE45 1JF (01629 812416). 🐾🐾 Vegetarians catered for, other special diets by arrangement.

DERBYSHIRE, BUXTON. Maria and Roger Hyde, Braemar, 10 Compton Road, Buxton SK17 9DN (01298 78050). Accommodation comprises comfortable, fully en suite double and twin rooms with colour TV and tea/coffee making facilities. Non-smokers preferred. Diets catered for.

DERBYSHIRE, BUXTON. Mrs Ann Oliver, "Westlands", Bishop's Lane, St. John's Road, Buxton SK17 6UN (01298 23242). ETB Listed COMMENDED. Close to Staffordshire and Cheshire borders, this well established Bed and Breakfast is for non-smokers. Situated on country lane one mile from town centre. Special diets catered for by arrangement.

DERBYSHIRE, HATHERSAGE. Mrs Jean Wilcockson, Hillfoot Farm, Castleton Road, Hathersage, Hope Valley S32 1EG (01433 651673). Tourist Board Listed COMMENDED. Welcome Host. Newly built accommodation onto exisiting farmhouse offering comfortable, well appointed en suite rooms. Excellent home cooked food including vegetarian meals. Open all year.

DERBYSHIRE, TIDESWELL. Mr D.C. Pinnegar, Poppies, Bank Square, Tideswell, Buxton SK17 8LA (01298 871083). Comfortable accommodation. Restaurant. Vegetarians/vegans, diabetics catered for, other diets by arrangement.

DERBYSHIRE, TIDESWELL. Mrs Pat Harris, Laurel House, The Green, Litton, Near Buxton SK17 8QP (01298 871971). 🐾🐾 COMMENDED. Overlooking the village green. One double with en-suite facilities, and a twin room with washbasin and private use of bathroom and toilet. Tea/coffee making facilities in both. Private lounge. Special diets catered for.

DEVON, ASHBURTON. Mrs Anne Torr, Middle Leat, Holne, Near Ashburton TQ13 7SJ (01364 631413). Comfortable accommodation with wonderful views. Full English Breakfast, vegetarians/vegans welcome. Special diets catered for.

DEVON, BUCKLAND MONACHORUM. Store Cottage B&B, The Village, Buckland Monachorum PL20 7NA (01822 853117). 🐾🐾 HIGHLY COMMENDED. Comfort and tranquillity in the centre of historic Devon village. We are pleased to offer special diets by previous arrangement.

DEVON, CLOVELLY. Mrs J. Johns, Dyke Green Farm, Clovelly, Near Bideford EX39 5RU (01237 431699 or 431279). ETB 🐾 COMMENDED. Tastefully decorated barn offering beautiful accommodation. Ideal base for touring Devon and Cornwall. Many amenities close by. Vegetarians catered for.

DEVON, CLOVELLY. Mrs P. Vanstone, The Old Smithy, Slerra Hill, Clovelly, Bideford EX39 5ST, (01237 431202). A 16th century cottage and converted forge, situated one mile from the sea and the unspoilt picturesque village of Clovelly. Vegetarian breakfast if notified in advance.

DEVON, CREDITON. Mr and Mrs R. Barrie-Smith, Great Leigh Farm, Crediton EX17 3QQ (01647 24297). This outstandingly comfortable accommodation is fully centrally heated. Children welcome. Special diets catered for if prior notice is given. Bed and Breakfast £15, Bed, Breakfast and Evening Meal £21. Children half price.

DEVON, DAWLISH. West Hatch Hotel, 34 West Cliff, Dawlish (Tel & Fax: 01626 864211). 🐦🐦 *HIGHLY COMMENDED.* AA QQQQ Selected, RAC Highly Acclaimed. Small, friendly quality hotel. Centrally situated and well equipped. Extensive English and Continental menu. Private parking.

DEVON, EXETER. Janet Bragg, Marianne Pool Farm, Clyst St. George, Exeter EX3 0NZ (01392 874939). Tourist Board Listed. Thatched Devon Longhouse in peaceful rural location midway between Exmouth and Exeter. Large lawned garden, ideal for children. Car essential. Open March to November. Smoking allowed in lounge only.

DEVON, ILFRACOMBE. Sunnymeade Country House Hotel, Dean Cross, West Down, Ilfracombe EX34 8NT (01271 863668). 🐦🐦🐦 A charming country house hotel in it own large gardens set in the rolling Devonshire countryside. There is always a vegetarian choice on the menu and any special diets can be accommodated.

DEVON, LYNTON. Christine and John Kuczer, Woodlands, Lynbridge Road, Lynton EX35 6AX (01598 752324). 🐦🐦🐦 *COMMENDED.* Ideal base for exploring Exmoor and the stunning coastal scenery. Private parking, licensed, cosy lounge, log fire and central heating. Vegetarians catered for.

DEVON, OKEHAMPTON. Mrs E.G. Arney, The Old Rectory, Bratton Clovelly, Okehampton EX20 4LA (01837 871382). Ideal centre for visiting Devon and Cornwall. Comfortable accommodation and good food.

DORSET, BLANDFORD near. Mrs Lucienne Sumner-Fergusson, Stocklands House, Hilton, Near Blandford DT11 0DE (01258 880580; Fax: 01258 881188). 🐦🐦 *HIGHLY COMMENDED.* One double, one twin, both en suite, both ground floor, one double with private bathroom. Sumptuous breakfasts, candlelit dinners and cream teas. Heated outdoor pool, table tennis, badminton and clay shooting.

DORSET, BOURNEMOUTH. Mayfield Private Hotel, 46 Frances Road, Bournemouth BH1 3SA (01202 551839). 🐦🐦 Sandra and Mike Barling welcome you to this AA Listed hotel, offering a high standard of catering and comfort. Most diets and vegetarians can be catered for with prior notice.

DORSET, BOURNEMOUTH. Bournecliff House, 31 Grand Avenue, Southbourne, Bournemouth BH6 3SY (01202 426455). Enjoy a happy holiday in the comfort of our small family guest house offering excellent food with friendly personal service. Optional evening meal. Vegetarians catered for.

DORSET, CHARMOUTH. Ann and Andy Gorfin, Kingfishers, Newlands Bridge, Charmouth DT6 6QZ (01297 560232). Secluded setting only a short stroll from the beach and village. Great food, friendly atmosphere. Special diets catered for on request.

DORSET, DORCHESTER near. Mr Howell, Appletrees, 23 Affpuddle, Dorchester DT2 7HH (01929 471300). Ideal stopover for Devon/Cornwall (A35 2km); cyclists and walkers especially welcome. One double, two single and one twin bedded rooms. Use of kitchen if required. Special diets catered for.

DORSET, LULWORTH COVE. Mrs Jan Ravensdale, Elads-Nevar, West Road, West Lulworth, Near Wareham BH20 5RZ (01929 400467). Set in the beautiful village of West Lulworth, half a mile from Lulworth Cove. The rooms are large enough for a family and all have tea/coffee making facilities and colour TV. Open all year. Central heating. Vegetarians and vegans catered for.

DORSET, LYME REGIS. Mrs S.G. Taylor, Buckland Farm, Raymonds Hill, Near Axminster EX13 5SZ (01297 33222). Smallholding of five acres, three miles from Lyme Regis and Charmouth. Full English breakfast served, special diets catered for. SAE for details.

DORSET, PORTLAND/WEYMOUTH. Alessandria Hotel & Italian Restaurant, Portland, Weymouth DT5 1HW (01305 822270/820108; Fax: 01305 820561). 🐦🐦🐦 *APPROVED.* Unique Hotel and Italian Restaurant situated in a quiet location. Most rooms en suite with colour TV, tea/coffee making facilities, soft towels and toiletries. Excellent fresh food cooked to order by chef/proprietor Giovanni Bisogno (award winner). Children welcome.

ESSEX, COLCHESTER. Mrs Wendy Anderson, The Old Manse, 15 Roman Road, Colchester CO1 1UR (01206 545154). A friendly welcome to this elegant spacious town centre Victorian home. Most special diets catered for.

GLOUCESTERSHIRE, AMBERLEY near Stroud. The Dial Cottage, Amberley, Near Stroud G15 5AL (01453 872563). 🐦🐦 *HIGHLY COMMENDED.* Tastefully decorated rooms, en suite, and all modern facilities. Non-smoking. Bed and Breakfast from £25 per person. Special Diets catered for.

HAMPSHIRE, BURLEY. Mrs Gina Russell, Charlwood, Longmead Road, Burley BH24 4BY (01425 403242). Situated in an ideal walking and touring area. Riding and golf nearby. Bed and Breakfast. Vegetarian/special diets catered for.

HAMPSHIRE, LYMINGTON. Mrs Patricia J. Ellis, Efford Cottage, Everton, Lymington SO41 0JD (Tel & Fax: 01590 642315). 🐦🐦🐦 *COMMENDED.* AA QQQQ Selected, RAC Acclaimed, Welcome Host, FHG Diploma Winner. Spacious Georgian Cottage in an acre of garden. All rooms en suite. Home grown produce. Special diets catered for.

HAMPSHIRE, LYMINGTON. Our Bench, Lodge Road, Pennington, Lymington SO41 8HH (Tel & Fax: 01590 673141). 🐦🐦🐦 *COMMENDED.* Welcome Host, FHG Diploma Winner, Regional Nominee — England for Excellence. Welcome Host. Indoor heated swimming/exercise pool, jacuzzi and sauna. All rooms en suite. Evening meal if required. RAC Acclaimed, AA QQQQ Selected. Non-smokers only. Sorry, no children. National Accessibility Scheme Category 3.

HAMPSHIRE, NEW FOREST. Mrs Pauline Harris, Little Heathers, 13 Whitemoor Road, Brockenhurst SO42 7QG (01590 623512). A warm welcome for all non-smokers. Ground floor bedrooms with limited wheelchair use. Special diets can be catered for. Brochure.

HAMPSHIRE, PORTSMOUTH/SOUTHSEA. Mr and Mrs Willett, Oakleigh Guest House, 48 Festing Grove, Southsea PO4 9QD (01705 812276). Southern Tourist Board Listed. Small family-run guest house two minutes from sea. Double, twin, family or single rooms available. Central heating. Children welcome. Open all year. Special diets catered for.

HAMPSHIRE, WINCHESTER. Mrs S. Buchanan, Acacia, 44 Kilham Lane, Winchester SO22 5PT (01962 852259; 0585 462993 mobile). ❦❦ *HIGHLY COMMENDED.* Accommodation consists of one double and two twin bedrooms, all of which have en-suite or private bathroom, plus tea and coffee making facilities. Off street parking. Excellent choice of breakfast.

HAMPSHIRE, WINCHESTER. Susan and Richard Pell, The Lilacs, 1 Harestock Close, off Andover Road North, Winchester SO22 6NP (01962 884122). A non-smoking family home offering an excellent English Breakfast, including vegetarian meals. Country views.

HEREFORD & WORCESTER, OMBERSLEY. Mrs M. Peters, Tytchney, Boreley, Ombersley WR9 0HZ (01905 620185). 16th Century medieval Hall House cottage in peaceful country lane, two and a half miles from Ombersley. Ideal walking, touring Heart of England, fishing in River Severn and just half a mile to Ombersley Golf Course. Double, family and single rooms; cot available.

HEREFORD & WORCESTER, WINFORTON. Mrs Jackie Kingdon, Winforton Court, Winforton HR3 6EA (01544 328498). A warm welcome and country hospitality at its best awaits you at 16th century Winforton Court set in its old-world gardens close to the Black Mountains. Special diets are catered for.

KENT, CANTERBURY. Mr and Mrs Martin, The Tanner of Wingham Restaurant, 44 High Street, Wingham, Canterbury CT3 1AB (01227 720532). Family run restaurant with bed and breakfast accommodation. Relax and enjoy evening meals from our monthly changing menu — which includes the largest selection of vegetarian and vegan options in East Kent. Coeliac and diabetic friendly.

KENT, MAIDSTONE. Mrs D. Burbridge, Waterkant Guest House, Moat Road, Headcorn, Ashford TN27 9NT (01622 890154). ❦ Small guest house offering a warm and friendly welcome. Special diets catered for.

LANCASHIRE, LYTHAM ST. ANNES. Mr J. Soothill, Willow Trees, 89 Heyhouses Lane, Lytham St. Annes FY8 3RN (01253 727235). Accommodation is quietly situated and centrally heated. Ample parking. Children welcome, reduced rates. Vegetarian diets catered for.

NORFOLK, GREAT YARMOUTH. Mr and Mrs Brian and Diana Kimber, Anglia House, 56 Wellesley Road, Great Yarmouth NR30 1EX (01493 844395). RAC Listed. Warm and friendly atmosphere. Three minutes from beach, pier and town centre. Licensed bar. Tea making facilities. Vegetarian and vegan diets catered for.

NORFOLK, RACKHEATH. Julie Simpson, Barn Court, Back Lane, Rackheath NR13 6NW (01603 782536). Friendly and spacious accommodation in a traditional Norfolk barn conversion built around a courtyard. Vegetarian breakfasts catered for.

NORTHUMBERLAND, ALLENDALE. Mrs E. Finn, Thornley House, Allendale NE47 9NH (01434 683255). ❦❦❦ *HIGHLY COMMENDED.* Beautiful country house. Vegetarian meals available and guests may bring their own wine.

NORTHUMBERLAND, PONTELAND. Mr and Mrs Edward Trevelyan, Dalton House, Dalton, Ponteland NE18 0AA (01661 886225). ❦❦ Bed and Breakfast, optional Evening Meal. Excellent home cooking, using own home and organically grown produce when available. Vegetarian meals on request.

NOTTINGHAMSHIRE, NOTTINGHAM. Mrs J. Buck, Yew Tree Grange, 2 Nethergate, Clifton Village, Nottingham NG11 8NL (0115 9847562). Situated in a quiet, rural setting only ten minutes from the City Centre. Special diets catered for.

OXFORDSHIRE, OXFORD. Diana and Richard Mitchell, Highfield West, 188 Cumnor Hill, Oxford OX2 9PJ (01865 863007). ❦❦ *HIGHLY COMMENDED.* Comfortable home in quiet residential area. Well appointed rooms with colour TV, central heating and refreshment trays. Large outdoor pool. No smoking. Vegetarians welcome.

SHROPSHIRE, CLEOBURY MORTIMER. Robert and Joan Neil, The Old Bake House, 46/7 High Street, Cleobury Mortimer DY14 8DG (01299 270193). ❦❦ *COMMENDED.* Grade II Listed building. Each guest room is fully heated and has its own private bath or shower room and tea and coffee facilities. Evening meals by arrangement. Coeliacs and Vegetarians catered for — full English or continental breakfast of your choice.

SHROPSHIRE, CLUN. Mrs M. Jones, Llanhedric, Clun, Craven Arms SY7 8NG (01588 640203). Attractive old stone house with lawns and garden, spacious accommodation. Open Easter to October. Sorry, no dogs.

SHROPSHIRE, IRONBRIDGE. Len and Daphne Roberts, Woodlands, Park Lane, Madeley, near Ironbridge, Telford TF7 5HJ (01952 580693). ❦❦ *COMMENDED.* Superior quality en suite accommodation in large new detached bungalow. Tea and coffee trays in rooms. Hearty breakfasts and delicious evening meals. Vegetarian food if required. Easy private parking. Open all year.

SHROPSHIRE, IRONBRIDGE. Mrs Rosemary Clegg, Springhill, 2 School Road, Coalbrookdale, Telford TF8 7DY (01952 432210). 🐛🐛 COMMENDED. Three en-suite rooms in an 18th century Iron Master's house. Evening meals can be provided if booked in advance. Vegetarians/Special diets catered for.

SHROPSHIRE, SHREWSBURY. Gwen Frost, Oakfields, Baschurch Road, Myddle, Near Shrewsbury SY4 3RX (01939 290823). 🐛 COMMENDED. Situated in a quiet, idyllic setting in the picturesque village of Myddle. Golf and riding nearby. Pleasant garden for guests to enjoy. Extensive car park. Special diets catered for.

SHROPSHIRE, SHREWSBURY. Anton Guest House, 1 Canon Street, Monkmoor, Shrewsbury SY2 5HG (01743 359275). 🐛 COMMENDED. Tony and Anne Sandford offer a very friendly welcome to guests at their completely non-smoking home. Special diets can be accommodated by arrangement.

SOMERSET, BATH. The Old Malt House Hotel, Radford, Timsbury, Near Bath BA3 1QF (01761 470106). 🐛🐛🐛 COMMENDED. Between Bath and Wells, ideal for touring. Good choice for vegetarians always available, other diets by arrangement.

SOMERSET, BATH. Mrs Chrissie Besley, The Old Red House, 37 Newbridge Road, Bath BA1 3HE (01225 330464). HIGHLY RECOMMENDED. Our romantic Victorian "Gingerbread House" has stained glass windows. The cosy double bedrooms have canopied beds, colour TVs, showers, etc. Breakfast features multi-choice menu with wholesome/vegetarian dishes.

SOMERSET, BATH. Jan and Bryan Wotley, The Albany Guest House, 24 Crescent Gardens, Upper Bristol Road, Bath BA1 2NB (01225 313339). Welcoming accommodation at our Victorian home, just five minutes from city centre. Vegetarians, vegans and special diets happily catered for.

SOMERSET, BRENT KNOLL. Roy and Lorrayne Page, Old Holt Farm, Edingworth Road, Weston-super-Mare BS24 0JA (01934 750245). Listed 17th century buildings and grounds in beautiful rural location. Accommodation in double rooms or self-contained luxury stone cottages. Home cooked evening meals available. Please telephone for more information.

SOMERSET, CHEDDAR near. Winston Manor Hotel, Bristol Road, Churchill, Near Cheddar BS19 5NL (01934 852348). Charming manor house in one and a half acres of secluded gardens overlooking the Mendip Hills. An ideal stop for visits to Bath, Wells, Longleat and Cheddar. All diets catered for; cosy restaurant open every evening.

SOMERSET, CREWKERNE. Mr Gilmore, Manor Arms, North Perrott, Crewkerne TA18 7SG (Tel & Fax: 01460 72901). 🐛🐛 COMMENDED. AA QQQ. Lovely 16th century Grade II Listed inn set in the conservation village of North Perrott. Eight well appointed en suite rooms. Renowned locally for very high standards of home cooking.

SOMERSET, TAUNTON near. Ann and John Bartlett, The Spinney, Curland, Taunton TA3 5SE (01460 234362). 🐛🐛 HIGHLY COMMENDED. Comfortable en-suite accommodation. Special diets, including vegetarian, by arrangement.

SOMERSET, WRINGTON. Joyce King, Bracken Hill, Wrington Hill, Wrington BS40 5PN (Tel: 01934 862261; Fax: 01934 862875). HIGHLY COMMENDED. Peace and tranquillity of a country visit with easy access to many cultural and historical attractions. Pool and croquet garden. Special diets catered for.

STAFFORDSHIRE, ECCLESHALL. Mrs Sue Pimble, Cobblers Cottage, Kerry Lane, Eccleshall ST21 6EJ (01785 850116). 🐛🐛 Eccleshall is ideally situated for the Potteries, Alton Towers and other attractions. Children and pets welcome. Special diets can be accommodated. Non-smoking.

STAFFORDSHIRE, WATERHOUSES. Mr & Mrs J. Little, Lee House Farm, Leek Road, Waterhouses ST10 3HW (01538 308439). 🐛🐛 HIGHLY COMMENDED. Charming 18th century farm house, tastefully furnished. Ample off road parking. All rooms en suite and centrally heated. No smoking in bedrooms.

SURREY, DORKING. Mrs. M. L. Walton, The Waltons, 5 Rose Hill, Dorking RH4 2EG (Tel & Fax: 01306 883127). A listed house of historical interest situated in a conservation area. Evening meals and packed lunches are available if pre-booked, vegetarian diets are no problem.

SUSSEX (EAST), EASTBOURNE. Trevor and Brenda Gomersall, The Alfriston Hotel, 16 Lushington Road, Eastbourne BN21 1LL (01323 725640). 🐛🐛🐛 COMMENDED. Friendly, comfortable, family-run hotel in the centre of Eastbourne. Full English breakfast with free range eggs. Vegetarians welcome. Home cooked evening dinners available if booked. Open March — October.

SUSSEX (EAST), EASTBOURNE. Farrar's Hotel, Wilmington Gardens, Eastbourne BN21 4JN (01323 723737; Fax: 01323 732902). 🐛🐛🐛🐛 AA/RAC Two Star. All 45 bedrooms are centrally heated and have either bathroom or shower en suite, direct dial telephone, radio, colour TV and complimentary tea/coffee facilities. We have three lounges, cocktail bar and fully licensed restaurant. There are two lifts and porters on duty day and night. Private car park. Children welcome, sorry no pets. Brochure.

SUSSEX (EAST), RYE. Mrs Dawn Keay, Aviemore Guest House, 28/30 Fishmarket Road, Rye TN31 7LP (Tel & Fax: 01797 223052). 🐛🐛 APPROVED. Genuinely warm welcome and clean, comfortable accommodation just two minutes' walk from the town centre. Four rooms have private shower and WC, four have shared facilities. Excellent breakfasts, evening meals by prior arrangement.

SUSSEX (EAST), WINCHELSEA. A.N. Roche, The Strand House, Winchelsea, Near Rye TN36 4JT (Tel & Fax: 01797 226276). 🐛🐛 COMMENDED. AA QQQQ Selected, RAC Acclaimed. Full of atmosphere with oak beams and inglenook fireplaces but with the comfort of all modern facilities. Residential licence. Ample parking. Special diets catered for.

WARWICKSHIRE, STRATFORD-UPON-AVON. Mrs Karen Cauvin, Penshurst Guest House, 34 Evesham Place, Stratford-upon-Avon CV37 6HT (01789 205259; Fax: 01789 295322). Prettily refurbished Victorian townhouse. Town centre five minutes' walk. Will cater for any special diet, including vegetarian.

WILTSHIRE, DEVIZES. Mr and Mrs R. Mattingly, The Old Coach House, 21 Church Street, Market Lavington, Devizes SN10 4DU (01380 812879). ✿✿ *COMMENDED.* This completely non-smoking house offers guests the option of a vegetarian breakfast.

WILTSHIRE, SWINDON. County View Guest House, 31/33 County Road, Swindon SN1 2EG (01793 610434/618387). Victorian property situated on main road, five minutes' walk stations and town centre. Bed and Breakfast; Evening Meal available. We cater for vegetarians.

YORKSHIRE (NORTH), HARROGATE. Mrs Allison Harrison, Garden Cottage, Moor Park, Norwood Lane, Beckwithshaw, Harrogate HG3 1QN (01423 530197). ETB Listed. Our two luxury ground floor en suite rooms are non smoking, reasonably disabled friendly and have their own entrance. Vegetarian breakfast if required.

YORKSHIRE (NORTH), SKIPTON. Mr D.W. Oates, Sparth House Hotel, Malham, Skipton BD23 4DA (01729 830315). Country hotel. Delightful Yorkshire Dales village. Imaginative, home-cooked meals. Vegetarian — no problem, by arrangement. For other diets — please ask. Bed and Breakfast reasonable rates.

YORKSHIRE (NORTH), WHITBY. Mrs Pat Beale, Ryedale House, Coach Road, Sleights, Near Whitby YO22 5EQ (01947 810534). Any diet catered for, vegetarian and wholefoods always available. Please state any special needs when booking.

YORKSHIRE (NORTH), WHITBY near. Mrs G. Watson, The Bungalow, 63 Coach Road, Sleights, Whitby YO22 5BT (01947 810464). Large bungalow, ample parking. One double room and one twin, both en suite, TV and tea making facilities. Disabled guests welcome.

YORKSHIRE (NORTH), YORK. Norma and Ted Long, The Green Guest House, 31 Bewlay Street, Bishopthorpe Road, York YO2 1JT (01904 652509). ✿ Choice of vegetarian/wholefood or traditional English breakfast offered at this environmentally-friendly guesthouse.

YORKSHIRE (NORTH), YORK. Mrs Barbara Curtis, Cumbria House, 2 Vyner Street, Haxby Road, York YO3 7HS (01904 636817). ETB Listed *COMMENDED.* AA QQQ. Elegant, tastefully decorated Victorian guest house. Rooms have colour TV, radio alarms and tea/coffee facilities. Most are en suite or have certain private facilities. Central heating. Fire Certificate. Guests' car park. Full English breakfast or vegetarian alternative.

YORKSHIRE (NORTH), YORK. Four Poster Lodge Hotel, 68/70 Heslington Road, off Barbican Road, York YO1 5AU (01904 651170). ✿✿✿ *COMMENDED.* RAC Acclaimed, AA QQQ. Victorian house lovingly restored and furnished. Almost a whisper away from historic York with all its fascinations. En suite four-poster bedrooms. Licensed. Special diets catered for.

YORKSHIRE (NORTH), YORK. Mr and Mrs Whitehead, Holly House, Broad Lane, Appleton Roebuck, York YO5 7DS (01904 744314; Fax: 01904 744546). Approximately seven miles from York centre, conveniently placed for Yorkshire Dales, Moors, Wolds and Coast. Vegetarians catered for.

YORKSHIRE (NORTH), YORK. Ian & Carolyn McNabb, The Hazelwood, 24-25 Portland Street, Gillygate, York YO3 7EH (01904 626548; Fax: 01904 628032). ✿✿ *COMMENDED.* AA QQQQ Selected. Non-smoking, quality accommodation only 400 yards from York Minster, yet in extremely quiet location. Private car park and comfortable en suite bedrooms. Quality breakfast catering for all tastes including vegetarian.

SCOTLAND

ARGYLL & BUTE, LOCHGILPHEAD. Kilmarton Hotel, Kilmartin, Lochgilphead PA31 8RQ (01546 510250; Fax: 01546 606370). Surrounded by the finest examples of standing stones and cairns the Hotel provides the ideal centre from which to explore this area. Excellent quality home cooked food is available throughout the day with comfortable accommodation at very affordable prices for those wishing to extend their visit. CEUD MILE FAILTE — a hundred thousand welcomes.

AYRSHIRE & ARRAN, BEITH. Mrs Jane Gillan, Shotts Farm, Beith KA15 1LB (01505 502273). STB Listed *COMMENDED.* Comfortable friendly accommodation. High standard of cleanliness, first class cooking. Three comfortable bedrooms (double, family and twin), all with tea making facilities, central heating and electric blankets. Children welcome. AA QQ.

AYRSHIRE & ARRAN, KILMARNOCK. Mrs Agnes Hawkshaw, Aulton Farm, Kilmaurs, Kilmarnock KA3 2PQ (01563 538208). Tourist Board Listed *COMMENDED.* AA QQQ. 200 year old farmhouse situated only 10 minutes from Prestwick Airport and 25 minutes from Glasgow. Guests are assured of a good Scottish breakfast and tea on arrival. Special diets can also be catered for.

DUMFRIES & GALLOWAY, MOFFAT. Mr T.J. Hull, Alton House, Moffat DG10 9LB (01683 220903; mobile: 0850 129105). Historic country house situated in secluded grounds. All bedrooms have washbasins, TV, tea making facilities and welcome tray.

DUNDEE & ANGUS, MONTROSE (near). Moyra Braes, Ballochy House, West Ballochy, Near Montrose DD10 9LP (Tel: 01674 810207; Fax: 01674 810739). Victorian House with wonderful views over open countryside. Full central heating and en suite rooms with colour TV, radio alarm and tea/coffee facilities.

EDINBURGH & LOTHIANS, EDINBURGH. Mrs Janet Burke, Patieshill Farm, Carlops, Penicuik EH26 9ND (01968 660551; Fax: 01968 661162). ☕☕ *COMMENDED.* A very warm and friendly welcome is extended to all guests. Special diets catered for by arrangement.

EDINBURGH & LOTHIANS, EDINBURGH. Mrs Maureen Sandilands, Sandilands House, 25 Queensferry Road, Edinburgh EH4 3HB (0131-332 2057). ☕☕☕ Enjoy the friendly welcome and relax in the well furnished and tastefully decorated accommodation near Murrayfield Stadium. Full Scottish breakfast and special diets catered for. Children welcome. Open all season.

EDINBURGH & LOTHIANS, LINLITHGOW. Mr and Mrs R. Inglis, Thornton, Edinburgh Road, Linlithgow EH49 6AA (01506 844216). Family-run Victorian house in peaceful location near town centre. Both our rooms are en suite. Vegetarians and special diet breakfasts are available. Friendly relaxed non-smoking home.

EDINBURGH & LOTHIANS, NORTH BERWICK. "Craigview", 5 Beach Road, North Berwick EH39 4AB (01620 892257). Welcome Host, AA QQ Recommended, RAC Caradon. Situated in the centre of North Berwick with views over the West Bay, the Harbour and the Firth of Forth. Private facilities, four poster beds, central heating, colour TV, tea/coffee and biscuits. Full cooked breakfast with alternative healthy or vegetarian options. Open all year. No smoking. Also self catering flat. Brochure available.

MORAY, FORRES. Verdant Restaurant and Neptune Guest House, 22/24 Tolbooth Street, Forres IV36 0PH (01309 674387). Fully licensed restaurant specialising in Vegetarian and Vegan cuisine which offers a range of meals and snacks throughout the day and into the evening.

PERTH & KINROSS, PITLOCHRY. Mrs Barbara Bright, Craig Dubh Cottage, Manse Road, Moulin PH16 5EP (01796 472058). Family home always providing a wide choice of breakfast. Most diets catered for. Please ask on booking.

ISLE OF ORKNEY, SANDWICK. Mrs Hourie, Flotterston House, Sandwick KW16 3LP (01856 841700). Former manse, built in the 1850s, set in the heart of Orkney's main tourist and fishing attractions. Play area and large family rooms recently refurbished.

WALES

ANGLESEY & GWYNEDD, BALA. Mr T.Glynn Jones, Fronnderw Private Hotel, Stryd-y-Fron, Bala LL23 7YD (01678 520301). ☕☕☕ *COMMENDED.* Bed, Breakfast and Evening Meal available. Special diets can be catered for if advance notice is given. AA QQ, WTB Welcome Host.

ANGLESEY & GWYNEDD, CRICCIETH. Mrs S.A. Reynolds, Glyn-y-Coed Hotel, Porthmadoc Road, Criccieth LL52 0HL (01766 522870; Fax: 01766 523341). ☕☕☕ *HIGHLY COMMENDED.* Lovely Victorian, family-run hotel and self catering accommodation overlooking the sea. Vegetarian, diabetic, low-fat and low-cholesterol diets catered for. Ground floor bedroom suitable for disabled guests, also non smoking room available.

ANGLESEY & GWYNEDD, FAIRBOURNE. John and Ann Waterhouse, Einion House, Friog, Fairbourne LL38 2NX (01341 250644). ☕☕☕ *COMMENDED.* Lovely old house, five minutes' walk from sea; mountain walks start just across the road. Bed and Breakfast; Evening Meal optional. Diabetic diets and vegetarians catered for. En suites available.

ANGLESEY & GWYNEDD, MENAI BRIDGE. Ms Rosemary Abas, Bwthyn, Brynafon, Menai Bridge, Isle of Anglesey LL59 5HA (01248 713119). ☕☕ *HIGHLY COMMENDED.* Welcoming century-old terraced house close to Straits, Bed and Breakfast available. Delicious vegetarian/wholefood breakfast/dinner prepared with pleasure.

CARMARTHENSHIRE, CARMARTHEN. Colin and Jacquie Rouse, Allt-y-golau Uchaf, Felingwm Uchaf, Carmarthen SA32 7BB (01267 290455). ☕☕ *HIGHLY COMMENDED.* Traditional Welsh breakfasts and cosy oak beams in a peaceful rural setting. Georgian stone-walled farmhouse has been furnished and decorated to a very high standard retaining many original features. Open all year.

NORTH WALES, BETWS-Y-COED. Mrs Joyce Melling, Mount Pleasant, Betws-Y-Coed LL24 0BN (01690 710502). WTB ✿ ✿ *HIGHLY COMMENDED.* AA QQQ. A warm Welsh welcome awaits you at our Victorian stone-built house. We welcome children over 12, but regret we are unable to take pets. Totally non-smoking. Diets/vegetarians catered for.

NORTH WALES, TREFRIW. Ann and Arthur Eaton, Crafnant Guest House, Trefriw LL27 0JH (01492 640809). Totally non-smoking Victorian country home in charming village setting. Five en suite double/twin rooms with drinks tray and TV. Traditional/vegetarian menu. Private parking.

PEMBROKESHIRE, TENBY. Mr E. Romeo, Pen Mar Guest House, New Hedges, Tenby SA70 8TL (01834 842435). ✿ ✿ ✿ *HIGHLY COMMENDED.* Table d' hôte, à la carte menus offer a wide choice of English and Continental cuisine; vegetarian, low fat, diabetic diets catered for.

POWYS, HAY-ON-WYE. Peter and Olwen Roberts, York House, Cusop, Hay-on-Wye HR3 5QX (01497 820705). Elegant quiet Victorian guesthouse on the edge of Hay-on-Wye (town of books). Excellent touring and walking centre. Imaginative vegetarian meals available on request.

SOUTH WALES, BLAINA. Mr J.W. Chandler, Lamb House, Westside, Blaina NP3 3DB (01495 290179). ✿ ✿ *COMMENDED.* Set in the Upper Gwent Valleys, close to all major tourist attractions. Full central heating. Children welcome. Special diets catered for.

SOUTH WALES, GOWER PENINSULA. Mrs M. Valerie Evans, The Old Rectory, Reynoldston, Swansea SA3 1AD (01792 390129). A warm welcome awaits visitors to our home in this beautiful peninsula. Special diets catered for happily. Open most of the year. B&B £18, dinner £10.

SOUTH WALES, NEWPORT near. West Usk Lighthouse, St. Brides, Near Newport NP1 9SF (01633 810126/815860 Fax: 01633 815582). ✿ ✿ A real lighthouse with superb accommodation in peaceful and serene surroundings. Great hospitality which is distinctly different and deeply relaxing. Special diets catered for.

SOUTH WALES, ST. BRIDES WENTLOOG. Mr. David W. Bushell, Chapel Guest House, Church Road, St. Brides Wentloog, Near Newport NP1 9SN (01633 681018). ✿ ✿ *COMMENDED.* Comfortable, non smoking accommodation in a converted chapel situated in a village between Newport and Cardiff. Children under three years FREE.

The FHG range of holiday accommodation guides, see overleaf for ordering details

ONE FOR YOUR FRIEND 1998

FHG Publications have a large range of attractive holiday accommodation guides for all kinds of holiday opportunities throughout Britain. They also make useful gifts at any time of year. Our guides are available in most bookshops and larger newsagents but we will be happy to post you a copy direct if you have any difficulty. We will also post abroad but have to charge separately for post or freight. The inclusive cost of posting and packing the guides to you or your friends in the UK is as follows:

Farm Holiday Guide
ENGLAND, WALES and IRELAND
Board, Self-catering, Caravans/Camping, Activity
Holidays. **£5.50**

Farm Holiday Guide SCOTLAND
All kinds of holiday accommodation. **£4.00**

SELF-CATERING HOLIDAYS IN BRITAIN
Over 1000 addresses throughout for
Self-catering and caravans in Britain. **£5.00**

BRITAIN'S BEST HOLIDAYS
A quick-reference general guide for all kinds of
holidays. **£4.00**

The FHG Guide to CARAVAN & CAMPING
HOLIDAYS
Caravans for hire, sites and holiday parks and
centres. **£4.25**

BED AND BREAKFAST STOPS
Over 1000 friendly and comfortable
overnight stops. Non-smoking,
The Disabled and Special Diets
Supplements. **£5.50**

CHILDREN WELCOME! FAMILY HOLIDAY &
ATTRACTIONS GUIDE
Family holidays with details of amenities for
children and babies. **£5.00**

SCOTTISH WELCOME
Introduced by Katie Wood.
A new guide to holiday accommodation
and attractions in Scotland. **£5.00**

Recommended SHORT BREAK
HOLIDAYS IN BRITAIN
'Approved' accommodation for quality bargain
breaks.
Introduced by John Carter. **£5.00**

Recommended COUNTRY HOTELS OF BRITAIN
Including Country Houses,
for the discriminating. **£5.00**

Recommended WAYSIDE AND COUNTRY INNS
OF BRITAIN
Pubs, Inns and small hotels. **£5.00**

PGA GOLF GUIDE
Where to play. Where to stay
Over 2000 golf courses in Britain with convenient
accommodation. Endorsed by the PGA.
Holiday Golf in France, Portugal, Spain
and USA. **£10.50**

PETS WELCOME!
The unique guide for holidays for pet owners and
their pets. **£5.60**

BED AND BREAKFAST IN BRITAIN
Over 1000 choices for touring and holidays
throughout Britain. Airports and Ferries
Supplement. **£4.00**

Tick your choice and send your order and payment to FHG PUBLICATIONS, ABBEY MILL BUSINESS CENTRE, SEEDHILL, PAISLEY PA1 1TJ (TEL: 0141-887 0428; FAX: 0141-889 7204). **Deduct** 10% for 2/3 titles or copies; 20% for 4 or more.

Send to: NAME ....

ADDRESS ....

....

....POST CODE ....

I enclose Cheque/Postal Order for £ ....

SIGNATURE...DATE ....

Please complete the following to help us improve the service we provide. How did you find out about our guides:

❏ Press ❏ Magazines ❏ TV/Radio ❏ Family/Friend ❏ Other.